IN THE SHADOW OF THE ANGEL

*The life of an extraordinary Mexican woman,
Antonieta Rivas Mercado: 1900-1931*

Kathryn S. Blair

San Miguel Historical Press   Mexico City, Mexico

Most of the characters in this book are known historical personages with whom Antonieta–or Albert Blair–interacted. I call this book a novel because I cannot prove all I say is true. I linked Antonieta's life with necessary imagined scenes to create a story.

Copyright © 2011 by Kathryn S. Blair

All rights reserved. No part of this book may be reproduced or transmitted in any form or by any means, electronic or mechanical, including photocopying, recording, or by any information storage and retrieval system, without permission in writing from the author.

This edition was prepared for printing by
Ghost River Images
5350 East Fourth Street
Tucson, Arizona 85711
www.ghostriverimages.com

To contact the author or order more copies of this book
please visit shadowoftheangel.com

ISBN 978-1467932561

Library of Congress Control Number: 2011908390

Printed in the United States of America
November, 2011
10 9 8 7 6 5 4 3 2 1

To my husband,
Donald Antonio Blair Rivas Mercado.
With all my love,
Kathryn

Contents

PROLOGUE - PARIS FEBRUARY 11, 1931 7

CHAPTER I - MEXICO CITY APRIL 28, 1900 11
CHAPTER II - 1903 33
CHAPTER III - 1907 49
CHAPTER IV 69
CHAPTER V 89
CHAPTER VI 101
CHAPTER VII - 1909 113
CHAPTER VIII - 1910 129
CHAPTER IX - MICHIGAN, JUNE, 1910 145
CHAPTER X - APRIL 3, 1911 163
CHAPTER XI - 1911 179
CHAPTER XII - AUGUST 1912 195
CHAPTER XIII - FEBRUARY 1913 215
CHAPTER XIV - APRIL 1913 229
CHAPTER XV - FEBRUARY 1914 241
CHAPTER XVI - APRIL 21, 1914 267
CHAPTER XVII - 1914 271
CHAPTER XVIII 287
CHAPTER XIX - 1915 303
CHAPTER XX - 1917 319
CHAPTER XXI - 1918 337
CHAPTER XXII - 1919 351
CHAPTER XXIII - FEBRUARY 1921 369
CHAPTER XXIV - 1923 393
CHAPTER XXV - DECEMBER 1926 405
CHAPTER XXVI - 1927 421
CHAPTER XXVII - 1928 441
CHAPTER XXVIII 459
CHAPTER XXIX - 1929 473
CHAPTER XXX 493
CHAPTER XXXI 509
CHAPTER XXXII 529
CHAPTER XXXIII - 1929 545
CHAPTER XXXIV - BORDEAUX FEBRUARY 9, 1931 ... 555
EPILOGUE - BORDEAUX FEBRUARY 12, 1931 575

ACKNOWLEDGEMENTS 577
ABOUT THE AUTHOR 579
GLOSSARY 581
FAMILY PHOTOS 589

PROLOGUE
PARIS FEBRUARY 11, 1931

The central portal of Notre Dame let in a gust of wintry air, lifting the black veil of the tall woman who entered the Cathedral and walked toward the sacristy. Adjusting the veil, she stopped in front of the image of the crucified Christ.

A shaft of light from the rose window bathed the central nave in mellow tones of ruby and blue. Behind the open-tracery screen of the chancel, members of the choir began to rise from their stalls as the last notes of the "Te Deum" still trembled in the lofty vaults of the Cathedral. The rehearsal had ended. Chattering in whispers, the choir filed out, confident that tomorrow throngs of the faithful would once more be exalted by the sacred hymn as they celebrated the anniversary of Pope Pius XI.

It was quarter past twelve midday. The nave was almost empty. Only a few scattered worshippers knelt in silent prayer.

A young priest, hurrying on an errand to the sacristy, noticed the tall woman who stood alone, face lifted toward the crucified Christ. Elegantly dressed in black, the simple lines of her dress clung to a slim body, black silk stockings encasing shapely legs. A long widow's veil covered her face. It was a cursory observation, but he sensed something regal in the woman.

The organ came to life again, issuing trills of discordant notes, a prelude to practice. The woman stood motionless, then stepped into a pew and sank to her knees, lifting her right hand to her forehead as she traced the sign of the cross.

Bells chimed the half-hour, reverberating in the hallowed vastness and fading to silence. The woman knelt transfixed, her veiled gaze unwavering upon the suffering Christ. Calmly, she reached for a black purse she had laid on the pew, opened it and drew out a pistol. She pointed it at her heart.

The detonation rent that moment into eternity. Nearby worshippers turned, then screamed as the woman fell to the floor. Magnified by the echoing vaults, the scream spread consternation through the Cathedral.

Emerging from the sacristy, the young priest was shocked by the scene before him. In clipped words, he gave orders:

"Close the doors. No one may enter."

He knelt to examine the victim, cautiously lifting the veil, fearful of what he might see. It was the young woman he had noticed earlier, her delicate face framed by short black hair, the pistol still smoking in her hand. He leaned closer. Her pale lips moved almost imperceptibly in labored signs of life as bloodstains spread across her breast, seeping through the black wool of her dress.

The priest called for the Holy Ointments and began to administer Extreme Unction. He anointed her eyes, her mouth, her ears, intoning the prayers of the Last Rites as he went through the ritual of purification, cleansing her of all past sin, all that she had seen or spoken or heard in her short life. He held a crucifix to her lips and prayed, "Accept her, O Lord, into the Kingdom of Heaven."

A small crowd had gathered, curiosity mixed with compassion on their faces. Someone offered a coat. The priest gently cushioned the woman's head against the cold flagstones. A woolen shawl was produced to cover the thin figure.

"We must ask you to leave," the authoritative voice of the stout Canon rang out as he strode through the circle of onlookers. "And please do not touch anything. We have called the Prefecture of police and a doctor from the Hotel de Dieu."

Privately addressing the priest, he whispered, "Let's have the least possible publicity. The Commissioner is on his way." But he knew that by tomorrow everyone in Paris would know that the Cathedral of Notre Dame had been profaned. "I have advised the Bishop. The re-consecration service will commence as soon as possible. The doors must be closed to the public until we have finished. What a time. What a time." Annoyance tinged the words.

The small group had begun to disperse. The Canon turned to leave, then stopped suddenly and contemplated the prone figure.

"She's young."

"Twenty-eight or nine. Thirty at most," the priest guessed. "Poor desperate soul!"

"Is…was she Catholic?"

"I assume so. She's wearing a medal of the Virgin of Guadalupe."

The Canon nodded, his eyes lingering another moment on the still figure.

"Who is she?" It was a question directed to no one in particular.

CHAPTER I
MEXICO CITY APRIL 28, 1900

Antonio Rivas Mercado sat bolt upright on the seat of the Brougham Coupe, careful not to bruise the bouquet of tulips he had just purchased at the new Japanese greenhouse. Anxiety glazed deep hazel eyes above a full mustache and graying beard. The baby was early. Was Cristina all right? Would the child survive? Beto had dispatched his carriage to the Academy with news of the birth and a message that the doctor was waiting. If anything had gone wrong, Beto would have sent a written message, surely. Bad news was Beto's *metier*. Antonio heaved a deep sigh. If only his irascible bachelor brother and Cristina would keep the peace.

Impatiently, the horse pawed the cobblestones. Feliciano, the coachman, emitted a long whistle, announcing to the gatekeeper that they were home.

Antonio shifted the bouquet and looked out the window. Wrapped in his *sarape*, despite the warm weather, old Demetrio was shuffling up the flagstone entrance. A smile spread across the old man's face as he doffed his straw hat and swung open the heavy wrought iron gates.

I have a new daughter, Antonio thought, born this twenty-eighth day of April, 1900. A child of the twentieth century! The thought pleased him. At forty-seven, Antonio was at the pinnacle of his career as an architect. The new century augured well for him—and for Mexico. He thought of the little velvet box lying in the safe in his bedroom. He had seen the pendant in Cartier's window on his last trip to Paris. Today he would give it to Cristina .

"Congratulations, *patrón*," Demetrio called out.

"Thank you, *viejo*," Antonio replied with a broad smile as the horse started up the circular drive.

The Rivas Mercado mansion projected Antonio's unique style. It was a two-storey house yet its line was horizontal, set back from the street at an angle, high off the ground. It was entered through a long gallery from which a classic portico jutted out flanked by a pair of staircases that descended to the carriage stop and garden level. Breaking the symmetry, the right end of the gallery ended in a secluded arbor filled with plants and birds, and above the high, flat roof, a tower was visible from the street. The brick and stone facade wove a pleasing pattern, and a mosaic frieze across the peaked portico added a Pompeian effect. "Classic Eclectic" Antonio's colleagues had dubbed the style. Pure Rivas Mercado.

The house faced northwest, a mistake Antonio had admitted to Cristina only after they had shivered through their first rainy season. Mexico City may be in the tropics, but Antonio had failed to consider the extreme difference between sun and shade at an altitude of 7,400 feet. His studio on the second floor was the warmest and lightest room, prompting comments that he had built the twenty-room mansion as an artist's atelier.

Today, the scent of orange blossoms perfumed the air and the brilliant magenta and pink potted fuchsias cascaded from the gallery railing. Beto and four-year-old Alicia waited at the top of the landing. His once-erect brother, who topped his own six feet, leaned on his cane, goatee and mustache perfectly groomed, beret askew. Crisply dressed in white, the little girl squirmed loose from her nursemaid and ran to embrace her father.

"Careful, precious. These flowers are for your mother and your baby sister. Did you know you have a baby sister?" He patted the crestfallen child on the cheek and thrust the tulips into the nursemaid's arms.

"Put these in a vase and take them to the Señora," he said. "Tell her I'll be right in." Turning to Beto, he asked, "Is Cristina all right?"

"Yes."

"And the child?"

A scrawny thing, but I counted ten fingers and ten toes. Congratulations." Beto offered a laconic smile. "Are you aware that the women now outnumber the men in this family?"

Antonio chuckled. "I like women." He straightened Beto's beret. "I assume you advised our sisters. They will disinherit you if you didn't."

"I sent the stable boy. Dr. Vasquez Gomez is waiting for you in the anteroom. What took you so long?" Without waiting for an answer, Beto hobbled toward the arbor.

Antonio walked to the left end of the gallery and opened the door to his downstairs office. The anteroom was a small parlor where he received both bill collectors and intimate friends.

Doctor Vasquez Gomez got up from a deep leather chair and greeted Antonio with a firm handshake. A short, rotund, dark-skinned man, he had risen to the top in his field, and was now President Porfirio Diaz' personal physician. Although the doctor shrouded his own political views in discreet, tight-lipped professionalism, Antonio's opinion of the old dictator was well-known to him: "I do not," he had stated firmly, "admire election by self-appointment and self-perpetuation."

"How is Cristina? And the baby?" Antonio began unceremoniously. "Sorry I took so long. Traffic as usual. The birth caught me off guard. She's early. Is she all right? I mean, will the child live?"

The doctor patted Antonio on the arm. "A long time, I would predict. I waited to reassure you. The child is healthy and the birth was normal. I judge she is two to three weeks ahead of term, but when she gains her proper weight you will never know she was an early arrival." The doctor smiled. "Perhaps she was eager to enter this world. Maybe she'll cut her teeth on a new political era for Mexico."

Antonio raised his eyebrows quizzically. "Just what do you mean?"

Dr. Vasquez Gomez wiped his wire-rim glasses and looked up at his friend. "There is unrest, you know. It is rumored that Don Porfirio is looking around for a vice-president. This year he'll be seventy and I think that, at long last, he has faced the fact of his mortality."

Antonio laughed. "Let's have a drink to that, doctor. Anis? Cognac? What is your pleasure?"

The two friends toasted Mexico the new baby, and the good doctor took his leave.

Antonio opened the door to the small chapel that connected his bedroom with Cristina's suite. A heavy-set man, his footsteps left deep impressions on the patterned rug as he tip-toed toward her bed. In the dim light, he saw that his wife was asleep; his prize bouquet had been set on her bedside table. Still tip-toeing, he crossed to the ornate crib, parted the billows of tulle and gazed thoughtfully at the tiny occupant, scarcely three hours old. He returned to the high-canopied bed and stood looking at his wife's beautiful face, framed by creamy folds of a satin pillow. Thick dark hair with glints of chestnut spilled over the edges; his eyes followed one small strand caught in a tiny pearl button that held together the flimsy lace of her peignoir. Carefully, he disentangled it, feeling the warm, smooth skin at the cleft of her bosom. She must be glad it was over, he thought. Cristina abhorred pregnancy. She had already suffered two miscarriages, and thirty-one was not an easy age for child bearing. Well, two children were enough, Antonio decided. He was too busy and too old to attend to a large family. He bent down and caressed his wife's cheek with his fingertips.

Cristina stirred, slowly opening tired, brown eyes. She drew an arm out from under the coverlet and reached for his hand. "Tulips, Antonio. How extravagant." She hesitated, seeking out his eyes. "Have you seen the baby?"

"She's a tiny bundle. Not much hair."

"Are you disappointed she's not a boy?"

Antonio stroked her cheek lovingly. "No, *mi reina*, I am not disappointed. A little sister will teach Alicia to share." He reached in the pocket of his alpaca jacket. "Oh, I have something for you. A small present," he said, placing the velvet box in his wife's hand.

Cristina pressed the catch and gasped with delight. An emerald pendant shone against the black velvet, a cluster of grapes intricately held by a gold stem and delicate tendrils. "It's exquisite!"

Antonio beamed. The pendant was a triumph of craftsmanship and a tribute to his unfailing good taste. Unconcerned with his own wardrobe, it pleased Antonio to see Cristina in the finest fashions, complemented by beautiful jewelry.

"Are you all right?" He leaned down and kissed her cheek. She smiled wanly, her skin pale against the satin sheet, eyes half-lidded under arched dark eyebrows. Reaching again for his hand, Cristina turned and asked softly, "Do you think the baby is a bit brown? I mean, not white and rosy like Alicia. Of course, newborn babies usually are darkish and early babies are wrinkled and, well, skinny."

"It is not the color of the skin but a healthy mind and body that matter. The doctor told me that she fought valiantly to arrive in good health. I think she is quite beautiful."

Cristina sighed. "I've been thinking about names. There're so many fine names in the family."

"We shall call her Antonieta," Antonio said decisively.

"But that's not a Spanish name! Why must you make everything sound Gallic? You are more French than the French! We will call her Antonia, after you. Maria Antonia."

"No. I like Antonieta, a modern Mexican name. Unlike her mother, she may dare to be original," he teased.

"María Antonia," Cristina insisted peevishly.

"María Antonieta," Antonio conceded. "Beautiful!"

"And Valeria for her saint's day," his wife added stubbornly. "The child *is* a Christian." With a sigh of defeat and exhaustion she lay back on the pillow and closed her eyes.

Cristina was like a cameo, Antonio thought, appraising the classic features in profile, a deceptively serene profile, he had long ago discovered. In the dim light, Antonio followed the curve of her cheek, the curve of her neck, the cleft of her breast below the pearl button. In the beginning he had lived with silent jealousy, as he watched his wife provoke flirtations or adroitly cut other women out, until she was the center of an admiring group of men. But he came to understand that flattery and the attentions of men were necessary to assuage some deep-rooted insecurity that lay beneath Cristina's composure. He had come to terms with her "parlor games" long ago. After all, they led nowhere.

Antonio clasped his hands behind his back and surveyed the very feminine bedroom and its occupants. The half-light lent an aura of unreality to the crib. He sank into a familiar armchair and closed his eyes, hoping to nap, but sleep would not come. He was aware of Cristina's even breathing, aware of the tiny presence in the room, but his mind kept wandering back to bachelor days. A slight breeze stirred the curtains, shadow and light taking him back seven years, to a day in '93,

when his attention was riveted by a face in a beaver hat across a dozen carriages in the midst of traffic.

He was returning from a long, dusty drive, sitting beside his coachman as was his custom, his muffler flapping in the chill wind. They turned into the stream of traffic at the beginning of the Alameda Park. As usual, he singled out No.18, his sister Juana's mansion in the middle of the first block. Her carriage was just emerging from the coach entrance. Drawn by two perfectly matched black horses and driven by a liveried English coachman and his impeccable lackey, Juana's carriage was familiar to practically everyone in the city. The crest of the Torres Adalid family was emblazoned in orange and gold on both sides, a hollow ostentation which rankled Antonio, who knew the ignoble roots of his brother-in-law's fortune.

Two ladies occupied the seat opposite his sister, an older woman Antonio could not see very well and a younger one in a beaver hat. Juana's carriage turned at the end of the park on the first round of the traditional afternoon drive, taken solely for the purpose of showing off eligible young ladies. Who, Antonio wondered, was Juana promoting?

"The drive" always ended at the *Café Colón*, a popular restaurant on the western edge of the small city. Antonio's coachman wedged in among the carriages that crowded both sides of an unfinished street and parked.

The *Café* was abuzz with chattering soprano voices. As usual most

In the Shadow of the Angel

tables were occupied by young ladies and their chaperones. Antonio spotted an acquaintance sitting alone near the entrance and asked to join him.

A half-hour later, Juana and her guests arrived. Head held high, long skirt flaring with her graceful, swaying gait, the girl in the beaver hat passed him on her way to the table. She glanced back, a coy smile lingering as she sat down with her profile to him.

He found himself staring at the girl, sipping his vermouth, unable to decide whether or not to approach Juana's table for an introduction.

When the ladies finished their pastry and coffee, Juana made her way to his table and begged for a word in private. Nervously, his short, plump sister fingered a gray curl beneath a puffy, plumed hat. "I need to ask a favor, Antonio. Such a foolish thing to do, I left my money purse at home, never looked in my handbag, and the waiter is about to present the bill. These ladies are my guests." She shrugged her small round shoulders anxiously. "Thank heaven I saw you here!"

Antonio accompanied his sister back to her table.

"May I present Señora María de la Luz de Castellanos." The lovely, older lady extended a shy hand. "And her daughter, Señorita Matilde Cristina Castellanos."

She looked up at him from under the beaver hat, challenge in her eyes, a faint mocking tone in her voice as she acknowledged the introduction.

That night Antonio could not sleep. He saw her pleated sleeve fanning back to reveal the soft white skin of her underarm, the tip of her tongue moving against parted lips, dark eyes accentuated by an unblemished cream complexion.

At noon the next day Antonio presented himself at Juana's house. He was pacing the foyer when his sister came in, surprised and pleased to see her favorite brother.

Without waiting for her kiss, Antonio blurted, "Look here, that Castellanos girl you introduced me to yesterday, is she engaged?"

"Why no, she's not," his sister stammered, caught off guard.

"Does she have a suitor?"

"Why...no."

"Is she in love, interested in anyone?"

"Not to my knowledge," Juana replied, beginning to understand the interrogation.

"What did you tell her about me?"

His sister cocked her head and smiled impishly. "I told her that you were the poor little baby brother of the family who got shipped off to Europe when you were eleven and didn't come back until you were twenty-eight, all covered with architectural medals from the French Government and sporting a fez which some Moroccan vampire—no doubt besotted with admiration—gave you. That you are fickle, that Mexican women bore you and that *Mamá* used to say you had to have time to plant your garden before you plucked a flower. I impressed upon her that your garden is profuse with blooms, that you are a rogue, that mothers chase you, and that I intend to protect you from women like her."

Antonio laughed. "And what are you protecting me from?"

Standing erect, Juana raised her eyes to meet his. "You are almost forty, Antonio," she said solemnly. "I know marriage has occurred to you lately, but I think you should know that Matilde's father is the worst kind of lawyer, a government inspector of cheap theaters. And her two brothers! Both no-account *faranduleros*, gamblers, parasites on society. Now, her mother, Doña Luz, is every bit a good Catholic lady from a politically prominent Oaxaca family. I heard something about her brother saving Don Porfirio's life in the Battle of Puebla. She hates the French, loves the Germans. Doña Luz is half German—her surname is Haaf, a dear, quiet lady, but ambitious for her daughter." Juana paused and squared her shoulders. "The truth is, Matilde Castellanos was recently jilted by a prominent young man whose name I won't mention."

"Why?"

"Because you know him."

"I don't give a hoot about the young man. Why was she jilted?"

"Because his family found out what kind of a lawyer her father is. Mind you, I think the Castellanos are *gente decente*, but I can't entertain them at the house. You know how Ignacio is."

"The devil with Ignacio!" Antonio exclaimed. He could not abide his brother-in-law, a stingy cripple who pinched every penny and kept Juana on a tight leash. He took Juana's hands in his own. "My dear matchmaker," he said, "I appreciate the introduction and would like for you to tell Cristina Castellanos that I want to marry her."

"Antonio!" Juana's mouth fell open. "Her name is Matilde and she's twenty-four, way past the age," she stammered, "and the father…"

"I am not marrying the father," Antonio interrupted. "I have made up my mind. And I shall call her Cristina." Now it was his turn to smile smugly at his flustered sister. "Will you please convey this message to Señorita Cristina and, of course, to Doña Luz, that I am proposing marriage, as soon as possible."

Antonio took his leave with a theatrical bow.

The marriage took place three months later. Cristina was a radiant bride, triumphant as she received the felicitations of the most prominent families of the Capital. Her place in society was firmly established by the presence at her wedding of Don Porfirio, the "Imperial President" of the Republic.

A sensation of motion broke Antonio's reverie. Seeing the chandelier swinging. he sat perfectly still until the movement ceased. A mild earthquake. Nothing unusual. He turned his attention to the crib. This little slip of an infant would surely require Cristina's attention, he mused, hoping that their social pace might slow down. Mexican society bored him, the same people over and over, cloaked in a European mantle that fit very few. Whom one entertained, and by whom, was of paramount importance in Cristina's life. Over the years, with admiration, he had watched her fear of social error give way to the role of Grande Dame. With fluency, Cristina conversed in Spanish, English, or French, presiding over a table at which artists, diplomats, ministers, and prominent businessmen frequently dined. She had even stopped objecting to the fez he wore when they "received" on Sunday afternoons. She had discovered that his eccentricities were a fertile source of stories to be told with wry humor.

Cristina stirred. "Antonio, you are still here. What time is it?"

"Two-thirty, *mi reina*. I'm glad you could rest."

"Heavens, the family will be arriving soon and I must look ghastly. Ask Domitila to bring my comb and brush. And the mirror, please."

"You look beautiful." Antonio kissed her on the cheek, then once more lifted the swaths of tulle and peeked at the little bundle inside. "Antonieta, child of the new century," he whispered. "We shall make you strong." Gently, he rearranged the netting and lit the oil lamps, then kissed his wife again and went to do her bidding.

Cristina reached for the velvet box. She held the pendant in a beam of light and watched green dots dance on the lace coverlet. No one had jewels to match hers. No one! Not even her sister-in-law, Leonor, an overbearing matriarch with a talent for making her feel gauche. With great care, Cristina pinned the emerald cluster on her gown, right at the V of her firm, full breasts. She pressed the hard mounds and grimaced. As soon as the child filled out she would engage a wet nurse. Breast feeding was a function for animals and it ruined the figure. There are ways of making your milk dry up, she thought defiantly, feeling a sudden sharp displeasure for this child she had brought into the world. The tiny features were fine, the nose slightly aquiline, her fingers long and tapered, revealing not a trace of Indian blood. But her color! She was a *morena,* brown, like any ordinary Mexican baby.

From his look-out in the arbor, Beto had watched his brother emerge from the anteroom and escort Dr. Vasquez Gomez to his carriage.

Then Antonio had disappeared into the house. He wondered if he had had lunch. His own lunch had been served in the arbor with only the parrot and canaries for company. Beto settled back in his comfortable old rattan chair. A pile of well-thumbed newspapers lay on the center table. Since arthritis had swollen his joints and made walking painful, Beto's interest in the amorous affairs of high society had been supplanted by a passion for the political affairs of Mexico.

"*Pendejo! Pendejo!*" the parrot squawked.

His faithful old servant, Damiana, had purchased the bird at the market "to keep him company." Cristina had threatened to have the creature exterminated when she heard the vulgar curse; the cagey old bird had learned to keep quiet when she passed through the arbor.

What was Antonio doing fathering a child at his age? Tulips indeed! Beto yanked out a loose piece of bamboo and broke it in small pieces. "Someday I will catch her!" he muttered.

Settling back, he drew out a slim gold case and methodically tapped down a cigarette and fit it into his holder. Thank God he had never married! Beto inhaled deeply, dredging up memories from the moldy crevices of his mind: Late nights at nocturnal establishments where one ate abominable food and danced *habaneras* and gyrated against young breasts and thighs—until the pistols and knives were drawn. His friends had all married well-bred women, but it was at the Blue Angel that they liked to spend their nights, with naughty girls who lied and stole from them, whose robust language added spice to the conversation, who tasted different, even though the taste might poison. Wives were always the same. They tried to subdue a man. They were tiring. Thank God for whores. How could men get through the tedium of marriage without them? How could Antonio? It was a question he had never asked him. Antonio had changed.

An air of the Beau Brummell of yesteryear still clung to the always meticulously groomed Beto, who had once been mistaken for the Prince of Wales at the Paris Opera. Wit, charm, vanity, and a thorough knowledge of the social graces and foibles had been the cornerstones of Beto's life. His handsome profile, the precise fit of his Prince Albert coat, the gold lion's head that adorned his ebony cane—all had distinguished him at every social and cultural event of importance. His unusual height, carried with insolence, cowed the weak-kneed. Alberto Rivas Mercado had never harbored pretensions about the need to work, having achieved at an early age mastery of the art of passing time and letting others handle affairs of the purse. As bachelors, Antonio and Beto had lived together, traveled together, and shared a bohemian life that Antonio gladly supported both in spirit and with his funds. When Antonio took a wife in his fortieth year, it was only natural that his bachelor brother should live with them.

Beto puffed furiously, working himself into annoyance. A baby with a gray-bearded father! How in hell had Antonio allowed himself to be trapped? Vixen! He had caught her in his rooms looking at a book he had left on his table. A lewd book. "How dare you leave such books around for the young maids to see?" she had ranted. "But the maids can't read," he had lashed back. "If you want to read my books, ask me for them! She had not spoken to him for a week.

Kneading the swollen joint, Beto flexed his knee. Even the racy books were dull. He missed the gossip at the cafes and the wonderful verbal fencing matches, arguments which simply surfaced, at another table, in another time. "And now, listen to this," he told the parrot, picking up a paper and punching at a picture. "They are tearing down the Café de la Concordia to put up an American insurance company! Progress, bah!"

"*Cabrón*!" the parrot screeched in protest.

"It's wanton destruction of the last bastion of civilized food! Where will we get live lobsters brought up by runners from Acapulco? And roast venison with purée of chestnuts?"

Beto slumped in his chair. What fate lay in store for the heroes of the Independence, whose portraits hung in crooked grandeur on the back wall of the cafe? Would someone rescue Father Hidalgo with a string of spaghetti hanging from his ear where the paint had flaked off? Now where would Don Porfirio's son-in-law flaunt his ridiculous redingote and his entourage of foppish boys?

Beto thought of his "British" friends, Galvez and Carvajal, tamping down their Dunhills while they discussed the capers of the London stage. Neither of them had ever been to England but ah, how up on it all they had become. Mexico was so bloody backward, one had to light a few sparks of fantasy. He wondered what modern manhole would swallow up old Don Guillermo de Landa y Escandon, who kept in touch with London weather by wireless. If it was cold and rainy in London, he wore his Macintosh and put up his umbrella on the hottest, sunniest day. Wonderful, eccentric people, B.C. Before Cristina. Now the Café de la Concordia was destined to be a pile of rocks. Life was a pile of rocks and la creme de la creme was beginning to sour, along with Don Porfirio.

Hell, he was getting maudlin. And cold.

As though his very thought made her materialize, old Damiana trundled out from the kitchen hallway and draped a shawl around his shoulders. There was an air of superiority in her bearing, no doubt left over from her memories of his bachelor days. Today she was simply the custodian of the larder, the sweeper of the gallery, the mopper of the mosaic floor, the waterer of the plants and the terror of the kitchen, where she was both revered and feared.

"You have had your lunch. You should go to your apartment now," she ordered.

"Who asked you, old woman? The family will be arriving soon to ogle the baby. Have you restored morality in the kitchen?"

Damiana drew herself up to her full four-foot-ten, flouncy cap anchored to her tightly braided gray hair, one ruffle dipping over a wrinkled brown cheek. "We cannot have the young maids corrupted. The rogue and the girl were dismissed."

"You acted well, my dear nosey old woman," Beto said solemnly. "Now, where is my book?"

"Where you left it, under the mattress, Señor." The old Indian smoothed down her apron and took her leave.

Beto chuckled. Morality had been restored in the form of a new houseboy. A succession of houseboy-valets crossed the threshold of the house on Héroes street, No. 45. Their most outstanding talent, it seemed, was making love to the maids. The new houseboy, Beto had noted, was Japanese.

Loud barking now commanded his attention as two Great Danes flew down the driveway. Beto leaned forward and peered through the vines. Leonor's carriage was at the gate. As the Victoria approached the house he saw his sisters, Juana and Elena, riding with Leonor. The family parade had started, his matronly sisters first in line to scrutinize the baby. He met them at the top of the stairs.

Juana was the first, gray false curls dangling beneath a flower-burdened hat. An attractive dowdiness had overtaken her appearance. Having no children of her own, she had always been generous with her nieces and nephews—and Beto. He bent down to receive a kiss from his diminutive second sister.

"Is Cristina all right? And how about the baby?"

"Worry not, dear girl. They will both live." Beto waved her on across the gallery to the front door.

Elena came next. Exuberant by nature, her step was lively as she ascended to the landing. She was the youngest and prettiest of the sisters and, at forty-eight, the grandmother of a child as old as Alicia. Elena's French-Mexican husband owned a perfume store on the most exclusive street in the center of town. Beto permitted her to plant a kiss on his cheek.

"Has Antonio arrived?"

"He has."

"Now be nice to Cristina, Beto, and show some enthusiasm for the baby," Elena said, and followed Juana across the gallery.

Leonor, the oldest, was last. She was a slim, elegant matron of fifty-five who carried her tall figure with an air of distinction. She and Juana had married Spanish-descended brothers whose haciendas, near Mexico City, were a showcase of past Spanish grandeur.

"You are looking pasty, Beto. Is Cristina feeding you properly? We received your note and came immediately. Too bad it's a girl. I assume Cristina is receiving."

"I think you can assume so. Antonio is with her," Beto said drily.

Leonor swept past him into the foyer to be announced.

"Defend thyself, child," Beto muttered and returned to the arbor.

1901

Antonio faced his students in the temporary classroom, feet apart, arms folded, a determined giant challenging his flock.

"Architecture is based on specific Orders. Do you understand that concept?"

There was an uncomfortable silence. In the back of the crowded, high-ceilinged room, cluttered with old archives, someone coughed.

Antonio surveyed the students and waited. He felt restricted, out of his element in this musty old room, and sensed that his mood was shared by his students. It was not only the temporary displacement, more than a year now, that irritated him. It was anger and frustration at the ill-spent attempts to repair San Carlos, the old Academy of Art and Architecture. The work tables were warped, the lighting was unreliable, and the dust of one hundred and forty years of "higher learning" rose, stirred, and resettled with each day's lecture. Impatiently he stroked his beard, then focused on a vacuous brown face in the front row.

"Some things you have to engrave on your mind," he announced. Leaning heavily on the lectern, Antonio thrust out his jaw. "Doric is not just a style, it is one of the very Orders of Architecture!" He pointed a piece of chalk at the abashed brown face. "Engrave it. Engrave it!"

The student nodded and sat up straight.

Antonio not only commanded the attention of his students, he commanded their respect. They liked this *maestro* who believed in discipline, hard work, and professionalism. Quick to note the well-defined lines of good humor imprinted on his affable countenance, they had also discovered that fairness and generosity marked his character. He could generally be counted on to reach into his voluminous pockets for a student in need.

Antonio's architectural work was admired. His mansard roofs, ornamented cornices, balustrades and stately porticos graced the buildings of this growing city. Students stayed late to copy a rich Moorish detail or classical pediment rendered with a master's stroke on the blackboard. Pride in his work and pride in Mexico, which he viewed as a child learning his letters, gave Antonio deep satisfaction. He enjoyed teaching.

Rolling the chalk between his fingers, Antonio looked out at the cramped work tables. "I want all of you to draw the basic Orders of Architecture and their Entablatures. You have until the end of class."

If only education and culture could be injected like a serum! He snapped the chalk in two and leaned over the lectern. "Do you understand the assignment?" he asked the young man in the front row.

The student shook his head, boldly, engaging Antonio's hazel eyes, which always failed to look stern.

With an audible sigh, Antonio turned to the blackboard and wrote: DORIC IONIC CORINTHIAN in even block letters. Then, careful not to press his bulk down on a cracked board in the parquet flooring, he lowered himself into his heavy oak chair. A trickle of fine white dust fell, and a small mound of plaster had collected on his papers. Irritably, he brushed it off. Leaning back, he looked up at the ceiling where loose plaster and water stains were mutilating the Italian ornamentation. The deterioration of the building was reflected in the deterioration of discipline and academic effort. The new Director was a politician, not an administrator! Faculty and student complaints were ignored or met with indifference. Instead of genuflecting to the Minister of Education, the director should be exerting pressure on him to shore up the building and modernize the curriculum in this feeble attempt to emulate Beaux Arts, Antonio's beloved alma mater. Mexico was twenty years behind France. In everything.

Absent-mindedly, Antonio brushed the little pile of plaster into his trash basket. The students remained quiet, working. Year after year, he had devoted two mornings a week to teaching, an endeavor that took up valuable time but which occasionally produced a competent professional. Today he was impatient. He had pressing work to complete in the busy studio in his house.

The bells of the National Cathedral in the Zócalo, only a few blocks west, began to sound the noon angelus. Soon they were joined by the discordant clanging of other church bells and finally the deep tones of the bells of La Merced, the Baroque church surrounded by the produce center nearby. Antonio drew a heavy gold watch out of his vest pocket and, from habit, checked the time. One minute past twelve. The classroom was already astir.

"Class," he announced, pounding his gavel, "is dismissed."

Crude drawings piled up on his desk as the students shoved each other in the usual commotion to clear the work tables and get to the door.

Only one more class, thank heaven. Antonio picked up his agenda. The Pan American Congress would open in a week and his work at the Palace was behind schedule. What with saints' days, national holidays, fiestas—and Mondays, the day of national absenteeism, it was a wonder anything was ever finished!

He raised his two hundred and twenty pounds from the creaky chair and walked over to the open window. The air felt warm and dry. Up the street, the towers of the National Cathedral formed solid silhouettes against a transparent blue sky. From this vantage point he could see the corner of the Zócalo, the great central square, where old cobblestone streets converged and the wind blew up the dust of the drained lake bed of the ancient Aztec city, plowed under by the Conquerors to build their Spanish Capital. Cortes' old palace jutted out at a right angle. It was now the National Palace, firmly occupied by President Porfirio Díaz these past twenty-five years. Antonio was annoyed with the Government. The Minister of Education had turned down his personal appeal for more funds for the Academy. The treasury was spilling its full coffers into construction. Not that he disapproved, but there should be more equitable distribution. Díaz was determined to complete the transformation of the city from a decaying Spanish colonial municipality into a European-style Capital in time for the centennial celebration in 1910. Architects and engineers from France, Italy, England, and the United States were vying for the plum commissions the Department of Public Works continued to hand out. Foreigners were everywhere. Antonio felt a pang of resentment. The old dictator was known to have little confidence in Mexican ability. What did his students have to look forward to? The country was run by old men and foreigners.

The last of the bells clanged in disharmony and faded as Antonio began to contemplate the one Government commission which interested him: the long talked-about Monument to the Independence. Such a monument had been under consideration since 1821, when independence had been won. When Díaz took office in 1876, a design was approved, altered, then plans shelved and only now had the project surfaced as a commission up for assignment. A location had finally been designated, but it remained a closely guarded secret of Public Works.

He checked his watch: ten minutes more. Idly, Antonio watched a blond couple stop to question a guard in front of the National Museum up the street. Then, with a start, he noticed his carriage turning the corner by the Palace, the horse coming at a fast gait down Moneda Street toward the Academy. What the devil? Why was Feliciano turning toward the main entrance? Antonio caught his breath. An emergency? Little Antonieta was already running around everywhere and only last week had tried to climb up the fence and fallen. He had had to fetch Doctor Vasquez Gomez.

Antonio hurried out to the balcony overlooking the interior courtyard of the school and peered down. The Brougham Coupé had pulled up beside a statue of Venus. Huffing, he pushed his way through a stream of students and descended the wide stairway arriving in the open courtyard as Feliciano jumped down from the coachbox to greet him.

"What's happened?" Antonio asked, breathing heavily.

Feliciano stood at attention, holding his top hat respectfully against his chest. "I was dispatched to deliver this communication to you personally. Don Alberto said it was urgent."

Beto hadn't opened it. Antonio took the gold-edged envelope which bore the seal of the office of the President, relieved but vexed.

"I have told you not to park in here. It sets a bad precedent."

He broke the wax seal and read the brief text. It was a summons to be at the Palace at twelve-thirty. Signed by the Secretary of Public Works. Damn! They summoned one urgently, and then kept one waiting an hour. And why hadn't the Secretary sent the message around the corner to the Academy? Had he forgotten that he was still teaching? Who else was there?

"You should have parked in the street. I can walk to the Palace."

"Don Alberto said it was urgent," Feliciano repeated stoically. As a coachman of the privileged class, he enjoyed flaunting his status.

"All right, drive me. Don't unharness the horse. I have to cancel my class."

Antonio closed the door to the Director's office behind him and bumped into Santiago Rebull, a feisty old Catalán and excellent art teacher.

"Antonio! I was looking for you. I want you to talk to Diego Rivera. The boy lets temper overrule talent, and they have suspended him again."

"What has he done this time?"

"Insulted that young priest who is teaching sculpture, accused him of stupidity and barbarism because they are still copying the same plaster casts."

"They should have models, not plaster casts! I'll see what I can do."

"If it were a voting matter, I would put you up for director, Antonio. You would put order in this Institute!" Shaking his head, old Rebull moved down the corridor.

The Brougham Coupé turned the corner of the Palace and wedged into the snarl of traffic in the Zòcalo. Deftly, Feliciano skirted a mule-drawn trolley and a delivery wagon that were disputing the right of way. Shoppers darted across the street and ladies mounted and dismounted carriages at their whim, blocking the flow of traffic. With practiced skill he guided the horse around the square past shaded arcades invaded by makeshift vendors' stands.

They turned the last corner of the square. With a sharp lash Feliciano halted the restive horse in front of the Palace.

"Shall we drive in, *patrón?*"

"No. Wait for me by the flower market."

Feliciano jumped down and opened the door for his master, staring haughtily at the guards while he held up traffic.

An hour later, Antonio emerged from the Palace. He snapped a salute to the guards and set off down the street with a sprightly step. At the corner he tipped his hat to the harassed policeman and crossed over to the Cathedral sidewalk. Entering the courtyard, he stepped around a young Indian woman squatting in the dust, tending small mounds of nuts, garlic, pumpkin seeds and apricots. A pair of skinny legs peeked out from her *rebozo,* and three half-naked children huddled listlessly by her side. He tossed a silver *peso* in her lap and smiled delightedly as she raised stunned eyes and crossed herself.

Minding his feet, Antonio made his way through the usual crowd of worshippers and hawkers occupying the Cathedral courtyard. High button shoes, French heels, military boots, scuffed shoes, spats, Indian *huaraches* and bare feet crossed the threshold in this markedly Mexican Christian parade.

The pungent scent of gardenias filled his nostrils as he walked through the stalls of the open flower market, where nimble fingers were creating funeral wreaths from the delicate blossoms. Grimy little hands reached up to him, lottery vendors pestered, and beggars sidled up as he made his way to the interior stalls. This was an occasion for flowers! Flowers of every color filled tiered shelves: buckets of yellow crysanthemums, pink carnations, red roses, magenta gladioli, blue *agapandas*. The burst of color under white cotton umbrellas seemed painted against the transparent blue sky.

Two little boys with armfuls of fragrant blooms trotted beside him back to the carriage. Antonio placed his lavish bouquet inside the Brougham Coupé and climbed up beside Feliciano, a practice frowned upon by Cristina and his sisters, but a perfect perch from which to survey the city.

"Look, they are going to let us in line. Move!" He was eager to get home. He would announce his good news at the lunch table.

Standing on his traffic box, a white-gloved policeman waved them down Plateros, the main thoroughfare, and most fashionable street in the city. Carriages crawled in both directions, almost scraping as they passed. A stream of tall silk hats and flowered chapeaux passed the stalled carriage as they approached a church where a wedding was in progress.

"Let's get out of this bottleneck," Antonio said impatiently "Turn at the next corner."

"It's worse, Señor," Feliciano declared flatly. "They now have three blocks torn up."

The monstrous machines of Public Works were churning up old cobblestones everywhere, cutting through the narrow streets and alleys that converged on the Zócalo. How soon would they start working on Reforma Boulevard? Maximilian's attempt to match the Champs

Elysée was still a mere path through fields of weeds. Trees needed to be planted, the long boulevard graded - now! Monday he would take his surveyors out. It would be the tallest structure in the city. A coup! Yes, it was a coup. He puckered his lips in a secret smile.

Miraculously, traffic began to move at a steady pace. Out of habit, Antonio looked at the tawdry hotel sign that eclipsed the regal carved stone entrance of an eighteenth century palace. The street name changed as they neared the end of the narrow, congested artery. Ahead on their right was the Jockey Club. As usual, a row of gentlemen sat on camp chairs in front of the entrance to the resplendent house of tiles, sporting the colors of their stables and watching the passing parade. Antonio tipped his hat toward his fellow members.

"Hey Antonio," a dapper observer called out, "I see you have been promoted to lackey."

Antonio laughed good-naturedly and waved as Feliciano broke the horse into a fast gait toward the broad avenue that flanked Alameda Park. They were making good time now, trotting along an extension of tall ashes and laurel trees, flower gardens and colonial fountains. The horse slowed as No. 18 drew near. Antonio had built Juana's house, but rebelled at being called to fix every leaky faucet.

"Don't stop," he told Feliciano. "Let's go on home."

At the north end of the park, Feliciano abruptly reined in; a herd of cattle bumped and lowed, their drivers scrambling to keep them in line as they crossed the street on their way to the slaughterhouse. Antonio put a handkerchief over his nose and sneezed. They turned at the neighborhood market, a succession of stalls which attracted flies, dogs, and little boys who balanced heavy baskets on their heads. They were almost home.

The horse pulled at the reins as they turned north into the new, fashionable neighborhood of Guerrero. The streets cut across an old Franciscan orchard dating back to the early days after the Conquest. It was here that Cortes' soldiers, weighted down with gold, had fled across the Aztec causeway that led to the mainland on the *Noche Triste*, the "sad night" when the Conqueror wept in despair. It was said that Moctezuma's treasure had sunk in the old lakebed when Aztec arrows cut down the fleeing Spanish soldiers massed on the narrow causeway. The captives were led away to be sacrificed. Antonio had not found gold, but he had bought his land for three centavos a meter when people were predicting that the city would not grow north. He still felt delightfully sanguine about his foresight.

They turned down tranquil Héroes Street, a cul-de-sac so named because it was meant to end at an imposing rotunda to Mexico's heroes, still on the drawing boards at Public Works. Now Public Works had a more pressing project: the Monument to the Independence. Don Porfirio himself had given him the commission. Antonio felt a surge of pride, excitement, challenge. There were only three stipulations: that the structure be a column, that it be raised at the fourth circle of Reforma Boulevard, and that it be completed for the Centennial celebration of 1910.

Ornate lampposts, like rows of sentinels, lined the way past mansions with grillwork balconies projecting from high stone facades. The horse pulled up to No. 45. A low stone wall supporting a wrought iron fence screened the circular driveway. Near the fence, an ancient ash towered over flowering mimosas tangled with invading bougainvillea, bright sunshine clothing its old branches in royal raiment. Feliciano whistled for old Demetrio to open the gates.

Antonios felt his whole being filled with joy, the joy of a man in harmony with his work, his wife, his family, his God.

Barking wildly, two Great Danes raced down the Driveway and nearly tripped the old gateman.

Antonio looked up at the house and saw little Antonieta's head poking out from between the flowerpots on the gallery railing. She was wildly waving.

CHAPTER II
1903

Antonieta had been put down for her afternoon nap in the small bedroom she shared with Alicia adjoining her mother's boudoir. A restless, active three-year-old, she resisted naps. Today, through the connecting door, she could hear Domitila clicking the curling irons, a sign that her mother was preparing to go out. Unable to lie still, she got up and knelt at the door, peeking through the keyhole, as she habitually did when she couldn't sleep.

"Go tell the Señor to hurry. We will be late and he is the guest of honor," she heard her mother instruct Domitila.

Feliciano had brought the carriage around, and the horses were neighing impatiently. *Mamá* swirled through the boudoir and into the foyer.

They were leaving.

Hiking up her long nightgown, Antoineta jumped up and flung open the door to her mother's suite. Barefoot, she pattered across the boudoir, the bedroom, the hall, then ran upstairs and squeezed through the narrow space between the swollen doors to the terrace overlooking the side garden. She fell to her knees at the balustrade, and with an energetic thrust, forced her head through the stone pillars.

"*Adiós, Mamá!*" she shouted. "*Adiós, Papá!*"

She was just in time to see the embroidered hem of her mother's cape disappear as the bulky figure of her father handed her into the carriage.

"*Adiós! Adiós!*" she continued to shout, watching the carriage turn down the driveway, catching sight of Demetrio's *sarape* as he swung open the gates to the street.

They were gone.

Antonieta tried to pull her head back in. She wriggled and twisted and pushed with her hands but her head was hopelessly stuck between the stone pillars. The first large drop of a late afternoon thunder shower splashed off her nose. Now tears of frustration and fright spilled from huge brown eyes and a wail of distress rang out. The wail became a series of desperate shrieks as she scraped her knees on the terrazzo floor trying to squirm free, and the rain began to fall in earnest.

Through the claps of thunder and her screams she heard her nursemaid, Sabina, calling out to her as she wrestled with the heavy French doors,

"*Amorcita*, what have you done? Now calm your little self and Sabina will get you out."

The sobs subsided as Sabina's presence reassured the anguished child. A great flash of lightning lit the terrace followed by terrifying thunder, drowning out the now feeble cries.

Sabina's heart was pounding. She kept up a constant stream of chatter as she struggled with the swollen doors. Tonieta was a precocious child, unpredictable, and she, Sabina, was responsible for her. The horses must have awakened her when the carriage drove up for the señores. At times the poor little thing panicked when her parents left the house. She had reason to feel abandoned; her mother rarely kissed the child goodbye or goodnight. Sabina knew it was because she was dark-skinned, a *morena*.

"I'm coming, *amorcito*."

Forcing the door open with a mighty thrust, the stocky Indian nursemaid hurried over to her charge, assessed the situation, and took command at once.

"Now listen to me, Tonieta. If you stuck your head *in* you can get it *out*. Slowly now, calm your little self." She pulled back the long, wet hair. "Let Sabina hold your ears. That's it. Chin down."

She was out! With a joyful sob the sodden child flung herself into her nana's arms and buried her scratched cheek under the edge of a limp lace collar.

Beto sat in the arbor nibbling on a piece of cheese, bored. Life was dull when Antonio was away: Puebla for tile, Querétaro for quarry stone, and now Guanajuato for the opening of his theater. The more successful his brother became, the less he was home. Thank God he had taken Cristina with him on this trip. He would be away more as the Monument progressed, Beto deduced, but he felt a swell of pride as he thought of his brother's architectural coup. The cornerstone had been laid last year and the base was almost completed. A column would rise forty meters to support Winged Victory, flying high above the city. The heroes of the Independence would be exhumed and buried in the crypt. Beto knew every specification of the Monument, since Antonio's conversations always ended on that subject.

Flexing his sore knee, Beto picked up the morning newspaper. "October thirty-first," he read aloud, folding back the front page of *El Imparcial*, which featured a photograph of the stands at the Alameda Park, piled with candy skulls, dancing skeletons, and the usual menagerie of spun sugar goats and sheep confected for the Day of the Dead.

"When is the Day of the Living?" he asked the parrot and thumped the newspaper. "Did you know that that American scoundrel, Doheny, has brought in a gusher in Tampico? Black gold shooting up to the sky and damned little of it splashing into our coffers. Listen to this. Our dear President sold him hundreds of hectares for less than a *peso* each. Fool!"

"*Pendejo!*" the parrot squawked

Beto leaned on the table and gazed out at the garden. He focused on a white hair bow bouncing near a pile of cactus plants and volcanic rocks near the stables, half hidden by a row of orange trees. The hair bow bent over a cactus flower, slipped from sight and reappeared by the fountain.

"Tonieta!" Sabina's voice resounded. "Don't get too close. You'll get wet."

The little girl reached in the fountain to retrieve a capsized sailboat. Beto watched the hair bow limply struggle down her back as sailboat and child were battered by a tempest. She threw the wet ribbon in a flowerpot and disappeared in the direction of the chicken coops.

Alicia had occupied the goat cart for more than an hour. Beto had watched her dust off the seat with a wisp of a lace handkerchief before she sat down. He noticed that when Alicia planted flowers in her garden plot, she wore gloves and a straw hat perched on top of her hair bow. Antonieta's hat, which Cristina ordered worn outside at all times, was usually tossed off and forgotten in a bush somewhere.

How different these children were, even their coloring. From the time she was a tot, the servants called the little one *La Morena* and Alicia *La Bonita*. There could be Moorish blood in their Spanish ancestry, Beto admitted to himself. The Rivas came from Málaga. But it was his bet that it was Cristina's Zapotec Indian blood that had tainted her child! Well, little Antonieta would overcome her dark complexion; she had aristocratic features and a bright, mercurial mind. The child had been seeking refuge in the arbor since she could walk. This little niece had become his companion, attentively listening while he read the news aloud, then "reading" her fairy tales to him, brown eyes growing wide with the drama she invented. Her incessant stream of questions greased the wheels in his rusty brain and her spontaneous affection touched a softness he hadn't known he possessed.

Beto watched the goat prance around the driveway once again, pulling its untiring passenger. He slipped the beret down over his eyes and began to doze. He was still dozing when Antonieta tiptoed up with a baby chick in her pocket and lifted his beret. The chick chirped shrilly. Beto opened one eye and smiled at the little girl in the soiled pinafore, her long curls generously sprinkled with feathers.

"Mamá and Papá get home tomorrow and Sabina is going to take us to the Alameda Park right now to buy some candy skulls. I have to know if you want pink eyes or red eyes."

"Red," Beto said, and pulled the beret back down.

Cristina rested on her chaise longue, exhausted. The journey back from Guanajuato had been endless, the train jerking over narrow, winding roadbeds on the spur line to Querétaro. Then the long wait for the American train from the north. At the station in Mexico City they had been jostled and pushed, fighting their way through the usual exodus for the Day of the Dead. Trains, streetcars, public carriages were jammed with people leaving for their villages, others streaming out to nearby cemeteries and churches, the women with a baby on their backs, a basket of food under their arms and a bunch of bright orange flowers in their hands. She hated these small marigolds which filled the flower markets, the musky odor clinging to fingers long after the flowers had been laid on the graves. She hated graveyards and had forbidden the flowers to be brought into the house. Every year, in spite of this, the unpleasant odor permeated the servants' quarters and weeks later the dried blossoms were fed to the chickens, which in turn produced eggs with bright yellow yolks.

November first and second were always trying days. This year, out of a staff of fifteen, eight servants had asked permission to go to their villages. One could not deny permission and had to put up with the three-day holiday, which always stretched into four or five.

Cristina rang for Domitila, then lay back on the eiderdown pillows.

"I want you to unpack," she told her maid. "Steam the black velvet on my dress form." She removed a false chignon and shook out her hair, running her finger through the curl of an aigrette. "Take these and hand me that program on top of my valise. Thank you."

Caressing the picture on the cover, Cristina pressed out the crease: AIDA - PRESENTED BY THE MILANO OPERA COMPANY. There he was—Georgio Cassini.

It had been a brilliant opening. Antonio had converted the old Juárez Theater in Guanajuato into the Caliph's ruby among the architectural gems of that colonial city. A Doric portico, crowned by eight graceful muses floated in the star-studded sky. Plush red velvet seats complemented the Moorish splendor. When the lights came up, the audience had gasped with admiration.

She and Antonio had occupied the box adjoining the President's. Don Porfirio, all granite and steel, sat ramrod-straight, even when he dozed. At seventy-three, he was still slim and carried himself with military bearing.

Doña Carmelita, the President's wife, sat between her husband and the Governor, turning to comment first to one, then the other to show off her jeweled tiara. Doña Camelita was a handsome woman, thirty-five years younger than her husband. Well-born and well-bred, it was she who had polished that rough soldier to the high gloss of an international figure. If only Antonio were more political, Cristina brooded. "The old man is surrounded by enough people who lick his boots," he had told her more than once. The subject always ended there. Cristina admired the President's refined wife. During intermission they had chatted about their mutual enjoyment of early morning canters in Chapultepec Park, where they often met when the President was in residence in the castle.

Cristina lay back and closed her eyes, remembering how she had felt every eye on her, ruby necklace glowing against white skin, accentuated by the low-cut black velvet gown, knowing she had received easily as much attention as the President's wife. The house lights had dimmed, the curtain rose and Georgio Cassini's glorious tenor filled the theater as he sang the impassioned arias. She had felt hypnotized, floating, reaching out to catch each beautiful note like a firefly. After the last bravos had died down and the lights came up in the packed theater, Cassini had looked up at her—at her!—and bowed one more time, deeply, reverently.

Cristina sank deeper into the pillows, allowing the luxury of fantasy to possess her. At the banquet following the performance, she had extracted a promise from Cassini to sing in the Capital for their guests on Sunday afternoon, when she and Antonio "received" at their traditional late afternoon open house.

Refreshed by a nap, Cristina went to her desk and picked up the stack of letters, messages and invitations that had accumulated in their absence. A note from her brother, José, lay on top. With a sense of foreboding she broke the wax seal: "My dearest sister, this may seem frivolous, but I owe Renata Strozzi a favor. The play closes Sunday. A present or dinner is in order and need I tell you what dinner at Sylvain's costs? Can I count on you? Ever, José?" She ripped the note up in small pieces. Money, money! Her family never had enough. Where could she justify an added expense?

Cristina unlocked the drawer of the French *secretaire* and took out her account ledger. Rapidly she ran down the page of household expenses: last month, three pesos a day for food had been augmented to one hundred ten pesos to pay the Spanish grocer for such whims as escargots imported live in barrels from France and squid from Spain. With servants still away, this week she could save a little on the fifteen *centavos* a day allotted each one for bread. "It's just an excuse to gossip at the local bakery" Cristina had complained to her husband. "I don't care. It's theirs to spend as they please and it might induce them to save," was his insistent reply. Carefully, she went over the staples: corn, beans, rice. There was enough in the barrels to finish the month, but, according to her inventory, she had to order two sacks each of sugar and flour. Antonio paid separately for the shipment of wines he imported from France in barrels. He had already corked the bottles. Only the price of canned goods fluctuated. Sometimes, when Antonio was away, she could save fifty centavos a day on fruit, but this time, while they were in Guanajuato, Beto and the nanas had consumed the usual amount. She knew Beto shared expensive fruit with old Damiana, as he did the cheeses her brothers-in-law sent from the ranches. And what did he contribute to her household budget! She slammed shut the ledger.

Why did she have to render accounts? Economically, a wife was enslaved by her husband. Would her brother José never understand!

Exasperated, she emptied a Chinese jar of its content of coins. Thirty *reales* spilled out - three pesos and seventy-five cents. Not enough!

More calmly, Cristina considered José's request: it was important for her beloved brother to be seen with a prominent actress. Poor José lived on the periphery of the theater, a lifestyle costing more than he earned. A linguist, he translated programs and an occasional play. Recently, he had been hired by Virginia Fabregas, a rising star in the Mexican galaxy, to work in her new theater. The job was a plum, but entailed costly obligations; one could not associate with theater personalities and not reciprocate. Both José and Manuel, her dark-skinned younger brother, lived at home. Neither had married, and each was expected to contribute to the family's economic welfare. Manuel was tight-fisted and a chronic complainer, like her father, who made her poor mother suffer over every penny, including the vulgar toothpicks he used. Accounts be damned! Of course José should take her to Sylvain's! Renata Strozzi was an important Italian actress. Cristina drummed her fingers on the desk. Her only personal income, the rent from a small house she had inherited from an uncle, she passed on to her mother. Poor Mamá. Damn her indolent father! And damn Manuel! He had been fired again, this time from the Public Library. Antonio had managed to secure him a position in the archives; soon after, two valuable books had disappeared. She had wrung a confession from him: he had been bribed by a private collector. She had pleaded with Antonio not to tell Beto. The humiliation would be more than she could bear. How could she solve this latest problem? A visit to a mysterious doctor. That was it! She would complain of female problems.

Cassini was a fat snob, but Antonio knew he would have to endure him. Setting the fez on his head, Antonio walked through his dressing room to the *oratorio*, the shortest way to his wife's bedroom. He called the little domed chapel "Cristina's Caprice." He was still undecided as to whether she had insisted this appendage be added to the house to impress her religious mother or to lengthen the distance between their beds.

Cristina saw him in the mirror. She stood at her chiffonier adjusting a billowing gown of the palest green crepe de chine.

"Good, Antonio, you are dressed. I was thinking of the emeralds." She lifted an exquisite necklace out of a decorated strongbox. "Do you approve?"

"Perfect."

"Clasp it for me, *mi amor*."

"You aren't expecting me to suffer through this whole concert, are you? The house will be full of fainting females. By the way, who is coming besides Cassini?"

Deftly, she squirmed free of his embrace. "I saw Adamo Boari at the Italian Legation yesterday. He's just back from Chicago and said he wanted to see you. So does your engineer friend, Gonzalo Garita. They don't want to hear Cassini sing, they want to hear about your Angel." She laughed.

"I have told you repeatedly, she is not an angel, she is Liberty. Who ever heard of an angel with breasts? They're sexless."

"Anyway, they are all still purple with envy because you got the commission."

Antonio considered Adamo Boari the best foreign architect in Mexico. He was building the huge new opera house. "So Boari and Garita might come. Anyone else I know?" he said teasingly, kissing her shoulder. "I'll go see about the wine and liqueurs."

"Papá!" Two faultlessly brushed and composed little girls stood in the foyer waiting for him. The children were allowed to be seen for the first hour their parents received.

Antonio scooped his daughters up in his arms, exchanged kisses and set them down again. "You both look beautiful."

"Guess what, Papá?" Alicia said. "Tonieta already knows the kingdoms!"

"What kingdoms?"

"The animal kingdom, the mineral kingdom, and the vegetable kingdom."

"Bravo, *preciosa*." Antonio kissed his little daughter again. "Now, ladies, if you will excuse me, I have other matters to attend."

By eight o'clock Cassini had been singing for more than an hour. Antonio tapped Adamo Boari on the arm.

"Had enough? Let's go up to my studio."

"The Italian smiled mischievously. "Obviously the ladies have not had enough. Observe that over-draped Corinthian Column over there;

the old girl looks as though she were having an orgasm. What a curse it is to be Italian and tone deaf."

Beto saw them leave the room. He liked Boari, a robust type with a round but handsome face, dark mustache, dark wavy hair and keen eyes, a man who carried himself with the assurance of a Roman—and knew women. Good breeding rendered him incapable of discourtesy to his friend's wife, but Beto knew Boari had refused to play Cristina's game.

Leaning against the back wall of the music salon, partially hidden by the velvet draperies, Beto focused his eyes on Cristina, looking at some sheet music, whispering to Cassini. She was putting on her "Grande Dame" act. And Cassini, the lascivious devil, was nodding his head while he looked down at the cleft of her breasts. Vixen!

The match flamed and he drew on a cigarette, his eyes fixed on the scene by the piano. When Antonio was courting her, Cristina had tried to play a double game, flirting with him when Antonio's back was turned. He had responded with his finest act, feigned passion, then rejection and ridicule. She would never forget.

Casually leaning one arm on a console near the grand piano, Cristina now posed beside a lavish bouquet of red roses. She knew he was watching her, that he had been watching her, watched her flick off the competition, making a joke in Italian, turning the conversation to subjects that left the other women out. Tempting Cassini. Tempting!

Beto shifted to open space and blew a smoke ring across a fleshy shoulder in front of him. Antonio still loved that she-wolf and closed his eyes to every rotten deceit! There had been other women, B.C., but few had attracted his brother. When Antonio had first returned from Europe, his sisters had pestered and prodded, parading the most beautiful and eligible girls before him; demure Mexicans. Then he had seen a porcelain-skinned, spirited doll, their half-sister from Guadalajara, and made a fool of himself at the Café Colón. Beto took a deep drag on his cigarette and remembered another girl, an American heiress from Chicago, whose father counted his wealth by the hoof. An independent rebel, like most American females, she had wanted to run away with him, elope, but Shin-Bone reined her in. After a dull evening of formal calling, he and Antonio had sought relief in a Spanish gypsy cabaret. Slightly drunk, Antonio had jumped up on a table and danced a wild flamenco. Amid the stomping and clapping and snapping of fingers, he had seen old Shin-Bone enter the establishment with a lady on his arm who was not his wife. Antonio was never allowed in their house again. Beto exhaled a perfect smoke ring. Those were the days. Before Cristina.

Antonio opened the door to the studio and stepped back for Adamo to enter.

The studio occupied one end of the second floor. The large room accommodated five drafting tables, a small roll-top desk for the accountant and Antonio's own massive, flat-top mahogany desk. He had planned the studio to take maximum advantage of the northern light. A skylight eliminated long shadows and galvanized metal roof shingles helped to conserve warmth.

Tacked to a wall was a mass of sketches of columns, platforms, obelisks, allegorical figures, floor patterns, and a row of photographs of commemorative columns throughout Europe.

"I see you have done exhausting homework for your monument. Do you still have time to teach?"

"Of course. I consider myself indispensable," he said with a wry grin.

"And by the way, congratulations. What's it like to be Director of that old relic?"

"I can't say I am displeased." Antonio beamed. "It came on my fiftieth birthday." He produced a bottle of cognac and two snifters and set them down on a drafting table, then pulled up two stools.

"The truth is, I came in on top of a wave of protest. A bunch of hot-headed students stirred up a rebellion, which had repercussions Don Porfirio would rather not face."

"Meaning?" Adamo queried.

"The church. You know how lenient he has been. The clergy pokes its way into government schools all the time. The students accused the priest who teaches sculpture of homosexuality. It became a nasty business between the Church and the Ministry of Education."

"What did Education do?"

"Fired the Director."

"And put you in to restore law and order."

"Rebull and Velasco quit. We've lost our best teachers. They sent me a Sub-director who is a painter of Moors and Buccaneers! I've got a faculty of mediocre pedantic modernists!" He heaved a sigh.

"It must be difficult to be a Mexican with a European perspective." Adamo looked at his hulking Mexican colleague with sympathy and raised his glass. "Here's to San Carlos' new Director, a man of stature. Cheer up, Antonio."

"I didn't invite you up here to talk about the Academy. You know what's keeping me awake nights? This sponge we call our subsoil." Antonio planted his elbows on the table. "What did you learn in Chicago?"

Adamo leaned forward. "I worked with Millikan Brothers. Brought you a bunch of graphs. I think you know Millikan, they have been experimenting, with buildings going up fifteen, twenty stories, on the shores of Lake Michigan."

"Right. They're using that floating foundation concept," Antonio said. "Hydraulic control. Go on."

Soon the two men were engrossed in the subject of the new technology, oblivious to the high tenor notes which floated up from downstairs.

The music still filled the air in the nursery on the second floor, where Sabina had been rocking Antonieta for almost an hour. Would this opera man never stop singing? Her poor *angelita's* stomach was getting worse.

"It hurts, nana, it hurts," the tense little girl whimpered, no longer able to contain the tears.

"I am going to get your mother," Sabina announced, setting her charge down and rising from the rocker.

"No, Nana, please! Mamá says we are not supposed to cry. She pinches us when we cry."

Suddenly, the child vomited. Sabina swooped her up and raced downstairs to the bedroom that the two sisters shared. Nana Victoria was brushing Alicia's hair.

"Get the chamber pot! And the wash bowl!" Sabina commanded.

A white foam bubbled up in Antonieta's mouth as she vomited and gasped for breath.

"And some strong hot coffee. Hurry, Victoria."

Antonieta retched in spasms while Sabina held her head over the wash bowl, a foamy bile rising with each spasm.

This was no ordinary stomach ache. It was acute and convulsive, as though she had been poisoned. Sabina searched her mind. What had the child eaten? Suddenly, she recalled that at about six-thirty they had gone to visit the elderly spinsters who lived up the street. The señoritas always had special treats for little visitors. On the tray with the bonbons had been a vial of medicine; a silver spoon lay beside it. Señorita Gloria had taken a spoonful while they were there. Could it be? A child of endless curiosity, Antoneta tasted everything in sight. *Virgen Santísima*, it could kill her!

Alicia stood wide-eyed, chewing on her hairbrush.

"Go get your father!" Sabina ordered her. "He's in his studio." She grabbed the hairbrush. "Now move! We need a doctor."

Alicia ran out of the room.

Moments later, Antonio burst in. Gently, he laid his limp daughter down on the bed and looked at her pale little face, the eyes closing, rolling back. He set her on her feet.

"Make her walk," Sabina. "Don't stop. I'll tell the Señora and go for the doctor."

Beto had endured the entire concert, bored by the undistinguished repertoire. He drew back against the velvet draperies, a perfect observation post. Over several rows of distinguished heads, he focused on Cristina, posed once again beside the red roses—an arm's length from the piano where Cassini strained to reach a high C.

The door next to Beto burst open and Antonio strode in, shattering the moment. "Cristina!"

Cassini's wide mouth strained but the note was out of reach. He flatted and falteringly continued the aria, as heads turned toward the door and a few people began to rise.

Beto watched Cristina's astonishment turn to outrage.

Antonio marched toward the piano. Cassini stopped in the middle of a phrase, the concert now utterly, irreparably, deliciously ruined.

"Antonieta is having convulsions," he told his wife. I am going to get Vasquez Gomez. Excuse yourself and go to her. Beto can see to our guests." He turned to the astonished assemblage. "I'm sorry," he said and marched out of the salon. It was magnificent!

People began reaching for their wraps, whispering. "What did he say? What happened?"

For a long moment Cristina did not move. Then ashen, hands clutched, she began mumbling apologies and left.

A chesty chortle acknowledged the end of the drama. In his courtly manner, Beto draped two mink skins around the jewel-bedecked neck in front of him and bowed as deeply as his swollen knees would permit.

Antonieta lay gravely ill for days; even the mildest broth brought on spasms and extreme stomach pains. She grew gaunt, with a yellowish pallor. A private nurse had been engaged and the infirmary on the second floor housed its first patient. "I do not intend to contract mumps at my age," Antonio had declared when he included the infirmary in the house plans. It consisted of two rooms, "one for the patient who needs to be alone, and one for the nurse who needs to rest." The space overlooked the downstairs foyer.

Sabina bustled about Antonieta's bed, trying to cast an "evil eye" on the nurse and secretly applying hot onion skins dipped in *aguardiente* to the patient's painful little stomach. Magic chicken feathers to drive out noxious airs were hidden under the mattress; above the bed she tacked a miraculous Virgin, whom she entreated to intercede in the recovery of her beloved charge.

Antonieta discovered the joys of being ill. Everyone in the household pampered her. Her aunts and uncles and cousins came bearing gifts: a stereoscope, paper dolls with pages of chemises, dresses, shoes, hats, muffs. The señoritas gave her a fish bowl with a live fish and Alicia entertained her, recounting the delights of "going calling" with Mamá

One day Alicia shared some pansies she had bought with her Sunday allowance and planted them in her sister's garden next to her own. "A living lesson in botany," Papá had said when he instructed Cástulo, the head gardener, to prepare the ground and lay out the small plots. In the morning, when Mamá and Papá got back from their early morning canter in Chapultepec Park, they came up to visit, leaving a lovely scent of boots and horses which she liked better than Mamá's perfume. Mamá Lucita, her grandmother, walked all the way across the Alameda Park from her house to say the Rosary with her every day, and her grandfather gave her a gold peso, a peso which Papá asked to see before he would believe it.

One night, she was kept awake by laughter and music filling the house. Sitting up in bed, she could see the great chandelier ablaze with a hundred candles, its prisms tinkling and sparkling to the music of the orchestra that filled the second floor balcony. Two large gilded mirrors reflected whirling gowns and sparkling glints from sequins and diadems and diamonds, intermingling and changing like the colors in a giant kaleidoscope, and falling, like confetti on the dancers below. Mamá danced continually, but she only saw Papá dance once. By standing up in bed she could sway back and forth like Mamá, back and forth to the hypnotizing rhythm of the waltz. Finally, she fell exhausted on the bed.

During her long convalescence, school was Antonieta's distraction. A small room at the back of the second floor served as a classroom, presided over by Señorita Chavez, the bespectacled government primary teacher, and Miss Etta, the English tutor who always wore her hat. Her father had ordered a desk to match Alicia's to be made for her in the carpentry shop, and a set of learning aids and materials, required by the government primary program, had been purchased for her exclusively. The best days were when Miss Etta read poetry to them. Beneath her abacus on the desk shelf, Antonieta hid her treasured book of "Grimm's Fairy Tales." Soon, "A Child's Garden of Verses" was added to her hidden library.

When Mamá and Papá went out at night, Nana Victoria would play her guitar and sing, while Alicia sat on her bed brushing her hair. Back in the bedroom downstairs, snuggled in Sabina's arms, she would sing along and shed a few tears for the poor little dolly in her favorite song.

"I had a little dolly all dressed up in blue
Her little shoes were white and her camisole was too.
I took her out one rainy day and dollie caught the flu
I put her to bed when we got home, but my dolly died, 'tis true."

"But I didn't die, did I, Sabina?" Antonieta asked. "Even Mamá was glad, wasn't she?"

CHAPTER III
1907

Alicia was the last one to leave the schoolroom. Neatly, she squared up her class papers and workbook, opened the lid to her desk and slipped them in. Undecided, she looked at the thick "*Historia de México*" sticking out on the shelf below, then picked it up, piled on "Arithmetic" and the "Olendorf Speller" and set off down the corridor toward the new upstairs bedroom she shared with Antonieta. It was Thursday, only one more day of school.

Alicia turned the big brass doorknob to the bedroom, thrust open the door and dropped her school books, suppressing a scream.

Crouched on the windowsill, shutters wide open, nothing but blue sky beyond, her little sister was poised to jump.

"Don't, Tonieta! Please don't!" Alicia screamed.

Antonieta's head disappeared.

Alicia clapped her hand over her mouth and stood rooted with fright. Controlling her wobbly knees, she went over to the window and looked down. Stretched out on her stomach, Antonieta was sliding down over the dome of the *oratorio* which projected out from their parents rooms below. Like a cat she dropped onto the kitchen patio and smiled up, fingers to her lips.

In a flash, her little sister was back in the bedroom, middy blouse and skirt streaked with dirt, a grin spread from ear to ear.

"You see, my *brinco mortal* wasn't fatal, after all." She bowed like a circus entertainer.

"You have no right scaring me like that!" Alicia sniffed in a tear. "This is my bedroom, too, and I don't want you to practice any more death leaps, do you hear? And don't teach your new best friend Chela."

"Chela's almost as good as I am. Oh come on, Licha, you're such a scaredy-cat."

Their eight-year-old cousin, Chela, was a new addition to the schoolroom.

"You and Chela can jump all the times you want from the swing and the trapeze, but not from my window."

"We don't just jump," Antonieta declared, hands on hips. We're acrobatic artists."

Since they had moved upstairs, out from under the eagle eye and sharp ear of their mother, the sisters quarreled freely. A little brother, Mario, now almost three, occupied their bedroom downstairs. Antonieta, just seven, was assertive and independent, no longer subservient to Alicia's senior position. At eleven, Alicia was stretching into beautiful proportions, her head filled with romantic daydreams that left little space for such dreaded subjects as arithmetic and history, both of which Antonieta's quick mind absorbed and retained.

"And what have you done with my book?" Alicia asked accusingly, still shaken by the death leap. She scooped up her schoolbooks and plopped them down on the dresser. "Well, answer me!" Yesterday she had left her favorite Jules Verne adventure story under her night table, marked at the place where a mysterious magnet was pulling out the nails of the ship. When she reached for it at night, the book had vanished.

"All right, all right. I'll get your old book."

Antonieta kicked off her shoes and jumped up backwards on the bed. Long-legged and tall, she was possessed of unusual agility. Landing on her bottom squarely in the middle of the high, ornate brass bed, she reached back and pulled a book out from under the ruffled pillowcase.

Alicia watched the unladylike gyrations and wrinkled her nose.

"You shouldn't be upset. You've read this old book at least six times.

Take it! Tío Beto is going to buy it for me in English."

It was a low blow. Miss Etta, who still wore her hat in class, had been trying for years to drum English into Alicia's head, while Antonieta had been chattering in the difficult language by the time she was four. Alicia died of embarrassment when her mother seated her next to an American or British gentleman in the big dining room. She always pleaded to be seated next to one of Papá's French colleagues. All well-educated Mexicans spoke French; both girls had learned the language along with their native Spanish.

It was better to avoid argument, Alicia had long ago decided. Antonieta always won. She snatched away the proffered book, turned abruptly and, pretending to select a dress in her closet, reached up high on the shelf and shoved her book behind a hat box. An intriguing odor clung to the row of dresses. She buried her face in a swath of soft material to sniff.

The dresses had recently arrived in the inlaid wooden chest from Paris, which traveled across the ocean wrapped in tar paper, in the event the hold of the ship should flood. Once a year, the Paris box brought the girls a new wardrobe, selected from the Bon Marché catalogue.

"It smells like the tobacco in Papá's humidor. Don't you love it?"

"What?"

"This smell. Which dress shall I wear? We're going shopping with Mamá after lunch." She held up one dress after another. They all fit in the modern wall-to-wall closet Papá had had the carpenters build.

Settled on the bed with the pillows plumped up behind her back, Antonieta hoisted up her pleated skirt and crossed her legs. From under the mattress she extracted a notebook and began thumbing through yesterday's notes. A squashed chocolate raisin was stuck to a page; she popped it in her mouth and pulled out a pencil wedged in the base of her new electric lamp. The dog-eared notebook was titled, "Thoughts." Part diary, part poetry, the notebook contained her secret anxieties and experiences. Doodles dribbled down margins and wavy lines sailed through unsatisfactory sentences. While Alicia chatted on about the new dresses, Antonieta bit the pencil and mulled over a poem germinating in her mind.

"I counted a million stars last night
But today they have vanished in the morning light."

She read softly, mouthing the words. Not quite right. She began to copy the poem onto a fresh page.

By the time she was four, Antonieta could read and write simple sentences. She had also learned to play Chopin and Grieg on the piano, and she danced with outstanding grace. The child was talented, everyone agreed, but she would not be beautiful like Alicia. Alicia was the family jewel: wavy brown hair like her father's, milk-white skin like her mother's and a perfect nose, inherited from some unknown ancestor, gave promise of extraordinary beauty, so the family board of judges had predicted. Antonieta's brown skin remained brown in spite of Cristina's iron-clad rules about wearing long sleeves and a hat in the garden. And her nose was a bit sharp, a feature common to Rivas Mercado women, which they all abhorred but tolerated with intelligence and wit. Cleverly, they had learned the trick of hiding their intelligence until after they were married.

Focusing on a rosette on the white plaster ceiling, Antonieta lay back, thinking. Why did grown-ups pretend? They said things they did not really believe or feel. Well, she had learned to pretend—like Mamá. Someday she might be a great actress, since she pretended very well. Her eyes shifted to the little nosegays on the wallpaper and stopped at the one that had a shoe print marked across the flowers. She had kicked her shoe off in anger that day. Did Mamá suspect? She felt a familiar knot in her stomach. It wasn't exactly fear, it was a peculiar feeling of loss. Something was gone. She could no longer trust her mother. Not since she had seen the opera gentleman kiss her in the orchard last month, when Papá was in New York. Her heart cried out in confusion and anger. This was a secret she could not write in her notebook, a secret she did not dare put into words. She folded her arms beneath her head and closed her eyes, remembering:

That day she had been sitting on the bench behind the orange trees looking at a book about Greek gods she had "borrowed" from Papá's library. Often she shared the bench with Tío Beto, who preferred to read certain books in the privacy of the garden. But that day only the birds and the lizards had kept her company.

A Red Cross meeting had been in session in the house all afternoon. The Red Cross ladies had acted silly over the opera gentleman who was going to sing for their spring Benefit. It was his third season, she had heard her mother say. The ladies' noisy chatter had driven poor Tío to his apartment. She was glad when the last carriage had turned down the driveway.

The fading afternoon sun had cast dark shadows on her book, and it had suddenly turned chilly. She was about to leave when she heard her mother's laughter rippling like an arpeggio down the path to the orchard, talking in Italian with him, laughing the way she did when she was excited. They stopped by the big lime tree. Mamá's back was to her. "Cristina, *caro mía*," she heard him whisper. She hunched down behind the bench trying to become invisible.

Her eye caught sight of a white cap approaching. Damiana must have thought Tío Beto was there. Through the slats in the bench, she saw the opera gentleman's big diamond ring sparkle around Mamá's waist. Back, back, Mamá bent and the opera gentleman kissed and kissed her mother's mouth, her throat. In a moment of panic, she had jumped up and run behind the stables, her heart pounding as though it would burst. She was sure Mamá had seen her, had seen Damiana too. But we weren't spying, Mamá, we weren't spying!

Antonieta counted the flowers in each nosegay in an attempt to push the scene from her mind. She tried to pretend it was a dream, that Mamá hadn't fired Damiana, and she was still there to throw a shawl around poor Tío Beto when he stayed in the arbor, shivering. Now he only had the maids to get furious with when he lost things. Poor Tío. A tear welled up and rolled down onto the notebook as her anger dissolved into a curious sense of betrayal. She wiped her eyes and nose with the back of her hand and picked up her notebook. Tears had smudged her poem. She made a wavy line through it, flipped over the page and wrote:

"*I counted a million stars last night*

But today they are gone, erased by the light."
"That's better, anyway," she said to herself.
"What are you mumbling about?" Alicia asked, holding up a white organdy dress and admiring herself in the mirror.
"Is erased spelled e-r-a-s-e-d?"
"You had better put that notebook away and get dressed," Alicia admonished. On Thursdays the Castellanos came over for lunch with them, and Mama Lucita usually arrived early on days when they went shopping.
"I don't want to go downtown. Please, Licha, tell Mamá I have a stomach ache."
"You have too many stomach aches."
"Well, I do have them, you know."
"Better hurry. Mamá will be up to fetch Mario soon."
Their old nursery was just down the corridor from the girls' new bedroom. It was now filled with blocks and a whistling locomotive and soldiers who engaged in noisy battle. Thanks to St. Anthony, whose picture Antonieta had turned upside down for ten days, she and Alicia had been moved upstairs before their baby brother was born. She stretched, paying no heed to Alicia. It was another world here upstairs, a wonderful world. At one end of their corridor and up a few steps was Papá's studio. If you knocked and promised to be very quiet, he allowed you to sit on a high stool at a drafting table and do homework in the afternoon. Sometimes you even got to lick the tax stamps on the rent receipts. Papá collected a lot of rents from apartment buildings and commercial buildings which the government had given him when they couldn't pay for his constructions. He even owned the convent of San Jerónimo, where Sor Juana Inez de la Cruz had written her poetry. Antonieta had knelt in Sor Juana's cell and flung out her arms in supplication and felt inspired to be a poet. Instead of an allowance, she and Alicia each got the rent from one apartment; they kept a ledger of their respective expenses and could save or spend what was left over. Maintenance was very important, Papá had drilled into them. But her renters kept breaking the faucets and the lid to the toilet, the same old expenses over and over.

Way down at the other end of the corridor, past their schoolroom and the back kitchen stairs, was her favorite place of all: the tower. A narrow staircase went up to the tower, where Papá had just installed a shiny brass telescope. Papá said the oratorio was Mamá's appendage and the observation tower was his.

The world of the tower was filled with mysteries and discoveries. There Antoineta became a princess surveying her royal domain, which stretched across flat rooftops to the tall trees in the Alameda Park, and beyond them to the tips of the trees in the Zócalo. The snow tops of Ixtlacihuatl and Popocatepetl rose above the mountains that rimmed the valley. The two majestic volcanoes were guardians of her domain.

Looking through the telescope, she had discovered the entrancing world of rooftops: lots of dogs lived on rooftops, as did pigeons and pigs, and even a cow! A tin shack and an artist's atelier seemed like neighbors, and she felt she knew the naked children who scurried after a rubber ball through a jungle of laundry. In the tower, the whole city lay at her feet, trailing off in scattered tile roofs and splotches of shanties. The view from the tower looked like the landscape painted by *maestro* Velasco that hung over the davenport in the formal salon.

One night she had awakened with moonlight streaming through her bedroom window, bright and alluring, creating a luminous path across the flowered carpet to the corridor door. She had slid out of bed and found herself in total darkness at the steps to the tower. When she opened the door, moonlight flooded the stairs, pulling her up like a magnet.

The snow on the volcanoes glistened in the moonlight and a million sparkling sequins embroidered the black sky. She had confided her midnight adventure to Chela and now the tower was their secret hideaway. Once she had almost told Chela about the opera gentleman.

Like pictures in a stereopticon, the sequel to the scene in the garden loomed in bright clarity in her mind:

She had fretted and worried all night, and woke tired and listless. Feeling sleepy after lunch, she had gone to her old room and flopped on the bed, thumbing through "Ali Baba and the Forty Thieves." Mario was upstairs in the nursery, Mamá was taking her customary siesta, and Alicia was in the front garden trying to keep the visiting cousins from fighting over the goat cart. Mamá had been very irritable at lunch; she was always more irritable when Papá was away. Half-dozing, she heard familiar, uneven footsteps stomping through the foyer. From the sound of his cane on the parquet floor she could tell Tío Beto was angry. He banged on the door to her mother's boudoir.

"Cristina," he thundered, "open this door!"

Tío never came near Mamá's boudoir. His voice trembled with fury as he repeated his command.

"I said open!"

Soon the door opened. Her mother's calm, serene voice answered.

"In what way may I serve you, Alberto? I hope you are not ill."

"You know damned well why I am here. I demand to know why you fired Damiana?" Tío was inside the room now.

Then it was true. Mamá had seen Damiana. Had she seen her, too?

"I didn't fire her." Mamá's tone was restrained. "She chose to leave."

"Why!" The question was a small explosion.

"I had hoped to tell you myself, but I see that listening to kitchen gossip is still one of your favorite pastimes."

Tío Beto was breathing hard.

"In plain language," Mamá went on, "Damiana was caught stealing."

"That's a lie!"

"Because of Damiana's meddling in the kitchen, I was forced to fire the new houseboy. The man was a decent sort. He came back later and told me he had seen Damiana sneaking packages out of the storeroom."

Silence.

Mamá blew her nose, a sign of nervousness. "I checked my inventory and it was true. Two kilos of beans were missing, one kilo of rice and heaven knows how much corn. Then the new maid came to me in tears and swore by the Holy Virgin that she too had seen Damiana steal. I knew you would be upset, so I fired the whole lot."

"You expect me to believe that melodrama? I did not judge you so naive, Cristina."

Tío Beto banged his cane.

Antonieta was tempted to peek through the keyhole but couldn't seem to get up.

"Antonio returns next week. We'll see if he believes you!"

Something rustled like paper.

"Meanwhile, now that the opera season is over you might find this book amusing. It's written by our illustrious and intellectual diplomat, Federico Gamboa. Too daring for the *gente decente*.

Paper ripped.

"Here. It's called "Saint" and describes the trials and tribulations of a whore!"

The boudoir door banged and she heard Tío Beto's footsteps retreating across the foyer.

An anguished sob came from the other side of the door.

She had never heard her mother cry. Trembling, she had gotten up and dropped to her knees at the keyhole.

Loose hair hanging over her white satin dressing gown, her mother looked like little saint Teresa under the bell glass in the oratorio. No, she looked like one of the ghosts in "Don Juan Tenorio", a ghost holding a book. A ghost without a stage on which to perform.

Suddenly her mother burst into tears and cried out, "Spies! You and Damiana both!"

A painful surge of sympathy had welled up and nearly choked Antonieta. She wanted to open the door and comfort her mother, but her knees had turned to stone.

Poor Tío Beto. Damiana was gone and so was Victoria. Alicia's beloved nana had snapped shut the case to her guitar and disappeared on a streetcar. Damiana was Victoria's friend. Poor Alicia. She had cried. Did you see me, Mamá? I wasn't spying.

Antonieta opened her eyes. Maybe she would never know. They would both go on pretending, she and Mamá. She turned her attention to Alicia, still absorbed in the ritual of selecting the right dress. Why was the right dress so hard to find? The determined click-click of high heels in the hall made her jump off the bed. In an instant, before her sister could protest, she had jumped up on the window sill and dropped from sight.

"Why are you standing there with your mouth open? Where is Antonieta? I expect both of you downstairs for lunch in twenty minutes. I asked your father to come home early. He knows I want to go shopping. Why are you staring? For heaven's sake, Alicia, close your mouth."

Relenting, Cristina kissed her daughter on the cheek and riffled through the dresses in the closet. She pulled out the white organdy.

"This is lovely. I am going to buy you girls new white shoes. See that Antonieta wears white too. And has clean gloves. I have told Sabina ten times that gloves and shoes have to be clean, but half the time she doesn't listen. I want you girls to look your prettiest."

Cristina departed trailing a faint aroma of lilac. Two minutes later Antonieta was back. "Oh, Tonieta," Alicia wailed. "Why are you always so—so rash?"

"Because it takes courage to defy death." She grinned. "Did you tell her I have a stomach ache?" The expressive eyes searched her sister's.

"You have to go. She is going to buy us new shoes. Oh, stop moping. You know Papá is always late for lunch on Thursdays. Maybe there won't be time for shopping."

"I don't need new shoes," Antonieta said moodily, jumping back up on the bed. She kicked off her shoes, squirmed out of the blouse and skirt and tossed them on the floor.

Alicia looked sympathetically at her sister. Mamá was hard on her, always scolding and punishing. She didn't understand that Antonieta lived in a separate world, a world of books and strange ideas, a world which Tío Beto shared in part, and Papá when he had time. To lock her in her room as punishment wasn't punishment at all; she liked to be alone. That was why sometimes she provoked punishment. She had admitted as much in her "Thoughts". But there was no clue, even in that book, to her changing moods. Antonieta dramatized everything. She was exasperating, wearing her down. Last week she had found her sister kneeling on the cold tiles of the bathroom floor at two o'clock in the morning with a laundry rope tied around her waist.

"What are you doing?" she had asked .

"I'm suffering."

"Why?"

"Because Mamá Lucita says we must suffer for others the way Jesus suffered for us."

"You'll have a runny nose. You better come to bed."

"But I haven't finished suffering."

"I'll wake up Mamá!"

Antonieta had rocked back on her heels and arisen in a single motion, then followed her back to the bedroom and crawled in next to her, to warm her freezing feet.

Alicia looked at her sister, sitting in her chemise, writing on her knees, oblivious to time. "Better put away that notebook and wash the dirt off your face. Mamá said you are to wear white."

"Is there any other color?"

Although she could not tell time, Sabina always appeared at the precise moment she was needed. The starched little sergeant placed freshly laundered white gloves on the dresser, set down a pair of polished white high button shoes, scooped up the soiled heap on the floor and went straightaway to the closet, where she selected a white dress. Then she hustled the reluctant authoress into the bathroom.

"I didn't tie your rag curlers tight enough last night. Your hair is a mess."

"I am going to cut it off. You watch and see," Antonieta said, resisting the hairbrush. Her brown hair was straight and fine. "I don't want to sleep on any more firecrackers!"

They heard the Great Danes start to yelp, the usual loud barking which heralded their father's arrival. Sabina lit the burner and placed the curling iron on its cradle.

"Go straight to the stables," Antonio instructed Feliciano. "I want to see Cástulo."

The moment Antonio emerged from the stables, the Great Danes bounded around the corner and jumped up on their master, sniffing a package he was carrying.

"Down Kublai, Genghis. Down!" He was in no mood to box with

them today.

Antonio walked around the stable to the rock garden, a cacti collection that had grown with each family excursion to the country. The children called it their "mountain."

He saw his head gardener's battered straw hat bent downward, as he planted a new specimen. "Look, Cástulo, I have something for Antonieta's cave."

When she was quite little, Antonieta had discovered the cave after a rainstorm had washed the dirt away from a large volcanic rock. She had begged her father not to fill it in and placed a rag doll in the miniature grotto "to guard the mountain." Rain and rodents had reduced the little hermit to a graceless clump of cotton.

"What do you think of this new guardian?"

Antonio produced a small stone figure, chunky and ugly. It was an idol he had dug up in a recent inspection tour of the new drainage canals. Antonio knew little of Aztec history; those blood-soaked temples were best left buried. But it seemed there was a frenzy of digging going on these days. The British, especially, were keen on digs. He had kept this idol because it was the right size for Antonieta's cave.

"Look, Cástulo, it just fits."

The gardener stared at the figure, a strange look on his creased brown face. When his patrón walked away, the old man made the sign of the cross and quickly retrieved his trowel, moving out of view of feared Huitzilopochtli, the old God of War who demanded human sacrifice.

Where the hell was his holder! Beto clamped a cigarette between his teeth in disgust, lit it, then mashed it down in the ashtray. Antonio was ascending the front steps, a preoccupied frown on his face.

Grunting, Beto got up and went to the landing. "How about an aperitif before the Castellanos descend? You look terrible. Might perk you up,"

"Sorry, *viejo*, not today. But I will sit a minute."

The rattan chair creaked as Antonio sank into it. He poured himself a glass of fresh juice. "What's new?"

"Nothing much," Beto replied with an exaggerated shrug. "Looks like 1907 will be a banner year. The stock market just crashed in New York and Flores Magón and his anarchists are advocating revolution."

A bemused smile lit tired, hazel eyes. "Anything else?"

"How can one understand Americans? They catch this Flores Magón and put him in jail at Diaz' request, but allow his group of exiled revolutionaries to continue to publish a newspaper ripping apart the very principles the United States defends!" Beto banged his fist on the table. "I told you about that newspaper. It's called *Regeneración*. They print it in St. Louis and pass it over the border clandestinely." He leaned closer to his brother. "I found a stack of them in Villagrande's bookstore." Villagrande was an intellectual and rebel who fomented ardent discussion in his archaic bookstore.

"I suppose you filched a copy," Antonio said. "What are you going to do with all those clippings? Write a treatise? And who will read it?" Antonio cut off a generous slice of cheese. "I was in Villagrande's myself this morning."

"Still looking for maps?" Beto lit another cigarette.

Antonio nodded. "He has blown a ton of dust off ancient archives for me. We're trying to find the exact location of the Aztec causeways. I'm convinced that the Monument is on landfill, part of the old lake."

The Monument again. Beto studied his brother's face: the deep furrows lined his forehead and the white streaks in his beard were new.

"Did Villagrande find anything of use for you?"

"No." Antonio set his glass down on the table.

Beto waited.

"Every calculation proves the column is stable, but with our cursed subsoil the most exact calculations may be meaningless numbers." He sat quietly munching. "I shall confide, Beto, that lately I haven't slept well. One of those hunches. I can't prove it, but I think the column is about to lean. We are up thirteen meters. The next few meters are crucial."

Reading his brother's expression, Beto knew better than to make a flippant remark. Antonio was profoundly disturbed. The Monument had become an obsession.

"Ah, yes, there is another bit of news," Beto said, deliberately cheerful. "Old Vinegar Face will not be gracing our table with his presence today." Cristina's father was a spare, stingy, Spanish type who hated Spaniards, aristocrats, high government officials, and Yankees.

"But am I to assume we will have the pleasure of the company of the rest of the Castellanos?" Antonio asked.

"You assume correctly. Including our illustrious former librarian." In the intimacy of the anteroom, Beto had dubbed Cristina's dark-skinned brother, Manuel, "the constipated Indian," since his most celebrated comments were grunts. Cristina's mother was the only prize in this grab-bag of relatives Antonio had acquired. She was a quiet, long-suffering lady, whose delicate beauty reflected her fervent Catholic faith and serene acceptance of her lot in life. Vinegar Face controlled her with his eyes.

"I am going to eat upstairs in the studio," Antonio announced abruptly. "Make my excuses, Beto, will you?" He got to his feet and buttoned his coat over his protruding stomach.

Beto shook his head. The Monument might be keeping his brother awake, but it had not affected his appetite.

Cristina sat at her vanity, a soft peignoir covering her shoulders. Antonio stood for a moment in the doorway watching her brush back a curl. Young beauty faded so quickly and thick waistlines were the usual price of bearing heirs, but, at thirty-seven, Cristina had ripened into the full beauty which maturity produced in some women.

She saw him in her hand mirror and smiled.

He bent low and kissed the nape of her neck.

"Careful, Antonio," she pleaded, removing the peignoir and rising. Her jewel case lay open on the small dresser. "I was considering the pearl collar. Or do you prefer a simple brooch?"

"How many ladies in your acquaintance have a matched set of gems for each day of the week?"

"Only Cristina Rivas Mercado." She smiled complacently. "Well, decide for me."

"Do I only serve to clasp necklaces?" He picked up the five-strand pearl collar and hooked it around the high neck of her tailored blouse.

"I came to tell you that I would like to have my lunch served in the studio. I am swamped with work."

Cristina's expression was stoical as she faced him. "Whatever you say, *mi amor*."

When Antonio left, Cristina opened the huge carved doors of the armoire in her bedroom and inspected herself in three full-length mirrors. Every Monday she fasted, drinking only milk to cleanse the system. She would never allow rolls of fat to be squeezed into a corset. Trim from every angle, she would never allow herself to get pregnant again! It had been a tedious year, with Antonio away so much. And these weeks since "the incident" had been hell, silently enduring Beto's insinuating glances, mocking, accusing, the cause of her insomnia and headaches. But she was sure, now, that the old woman had not divulged her secret. Right after Antonio returned from New York, he had insisted she accompany him to visit Damiana in her wretched hut on the edge of a dusty lava bed. She lived with her daughter and an abandoned brood of grandchildren. The old woman had been polite and servile, grateful for the generous basket of food and clothes. Antonio had not questioned his wife's right to fire his errant servant, but insisted on giving her a monthly pension. Much too liberal. Antonio had no sense about money. With her eyes, Cristina had conveyed to the old woman that the pension would arrive as long as she never disclosed a certain secret. The bargain was sealed with a glance. Only one small worry remained.

Cristina returned to her dressing room and counted every ring, every brooch and pendant before she locked the strongbox in a secret compartment of her vanity. Looking into the mirror across a forest of perfumes and lotions, she faced her image. How long would Antonieta remember? A child's memory faded quickly, thank God. She would forget, she would forget, Cristina kept telling herself.

Leaning closer to the mirror, Cristina turned her full attention to her coiffure. Meticulous in her personal grooming, she did not like to leave the house unless every hair was in place, every false curl secure. As though she were judging a piece of sculpture, she turned her head from one side to the other. Dressing one's hair was a monotonous affair.

The latest issues of *La Mode Illustré* displayed the flat, wide-brimmed hats now in vogue on a crown of natural hair, discreetly pulled back and simply dressed.

Sunshine streamed through the window revealing a few freckles, outcrops of her German ancestry that also lent a natural blush to her complexion. Only her hair gave evidence of her Indian blood. It was coarse and straight. Not even Antonio knew that the chestnut glints were the result of years of applying chamomile tea.

It was difficult to be a woman, Cristina reasoned, daubing at the freckles with a powder puff. Men could have their affairs, father nameless children for whom they bore no responsibility. A woman had to be subservient to her husband, cater to his whims: "Kill the fly, woman. Hand me my glasses. Do this, do that." The wife's reply was always: "Of course. Of course, mi amor." Hadn't she heard her mother say it a million times? Unmarried women became bitter spinsters, while the married ones were shut in behind their walls. In the meantime, husbands were free to cavort with their mistresses. Men were egotists! A husband thought he and he alone filled all those empty spaces in the heart of a woman, those painful yearnings that cried out to be free! For a woman the struggle never ended. For her, it had always been a struggle: to conceal her Indian heritage, to stay out of the sun, to slowly ascend the social ladder. God alone knew what conniving it had taken to break loose from her father's selfish demands, to get out of Oaxaca, to go to a good school, to learn languages, to be the first in her class, even to be the first white girl to climb to the top of Popo! But, for all that, there were still the empty spaces inside. A woman was born trapped!

With one last pat, Cristina turned to the door. She would dispense with lunch quickly. New hats were on her agenda.

Great clouds of dust veiled the downtown area of the city, rising in puffs into the transparent blue sky. Everywhere, mechanized modern equipment contracted by the Municipal Government seemed to be in motion. People gathered to gawk with admiration at the powerful American steamrollers paving the streets with macadam.

Antonieta sat on the edge of her seat in the open family Victoria, eyes darting in every direction as they rode alongside Alameda Park. "Look, they've put up a new street sign. Patoni has become Avenida Juárez!" she exclaimed, standing up. The loud honking of an automobile forced Feliciano to rein in hard, throwing her back on the seat.

"Can't you learn to be a lady?" Cristina reprimanded. "Try a side street, Feliciano."

They detoured to the right and proceeded along nearly deserted streets, passing a row of small yarn shops, handkerchief shops, notion and millinery stores displaying haphazardly hung "Sale" signs. Centuries of grime clung to sagging walls, soon to be demolished.

"Stop here," Cristina called out. Feliciano halted at the curb, blocking the carriage behind them while his mistress went in to inspect a straw hat which had caught her fancy. The next stop was a dry goods store, where the clerk brought out bolts of cloth for her inspection, rolling out cascades of material on the well-swept sidewalk. Farther along, they pulled up to a pastry shop, its windows filled with delectable confections.

"Please, Mamá, may I buy some Swiss buns?" Alicia begged.

A policeman shooed away several dirty children to clear the way for the elegant lady and her daughters. Antonieta looked back at the cowed assemblage, noses running, bellies protruding, bottoms exposed beneath ill-fitting cotton shirts. On the way out, she reached into Alicia's bag and thrust two, three buns into outstretched hands. Alicia grabbed Antonieta's bag of chocolate raisins and offered them to their disbelieving audience. Timorous at first, then darting up boldly, little fingers reached in the bag and stuffed the coveted treats into watering mouths. Emerging from the pastry shop, Cristina witnessed the end of the little drama. Antonieta grabbed back the torn bag and crushed the paper down over the remaining raisins.

"You can't eat those now!" Cristina told her, slapping Antonieta's wrist. The raisins spilled out, causing a scramble of bare bottoms.

The front seat of the Victoria was piled high with shoe boxes and hat boxes. Feliciano wedged into a parking space on a partially paved street. The perfume shop, last on Cristina's list, was around the corner.

"Wait here."

Flanked by her two little fashion models, Cristina set off toward the perfume shop owned by their relatives, the Labadies.

Clustered on the street corner in their checkered pants, a group of "lizards" watched them approach. Antonieta hated these young men who spent the day in the sun, watching the female parade and making remarks.

"Eh, Señora," one called out, "I will exchange my father for your daughter. He's very handsome and she's going to be a beauty like her mother."

It was a double compliment for a matron of thirty-seven. Alicia tossed her head, but Cristina smiled as they passed the brazen young men. Behind her mother's skirt, Antonieta stuck out her tongue.

When they entered the perfume shop, Alicia's face fell. Cousin Mauricio, who always gave the girls a little sample vial of perfume to take home, was not here.

"Ah, Señora Rivas Mercado, it is an honor and a pleasure to see you and your two beautiful daughters," the clerk gushed.

"You are most kind."

Cristina settled down on a stool in front of the carved mahogany counter, indicating to the girls that they were to wait on a tufted lounge that circled a tall potted palm. Sunlight streamed in through the stained glass dome.

At the end of the counter, a gentleman observed the distinguished lady with practiced interest.

Cristina addressed the clerk with a condescending smile. "You may show me your perfumes. Your latest shipment, of course."

The eager clerk slid open the doors to the showcase and brought out a tray filled with heady samples of essential oils and scents.

The gentleman at the end of the counter strolled over to Cristina and bowed. "I couldn't help overhearing your name. You are Cristina Rivas Mercado?"

Puzzled, Cristina studied the startling blue eyes, quite certain she had never encountered the gentleman before. "Yes, I am."

"I have not had the pleasure of meeting you. A great loss." The gentleman bowed again. "But permit me to introduce myself. I am Antonio's nephew, Fernando Rivas Figueroa."

"Of course. Pedro's son. In fact, my husband's great-nephew. I should have known you by the eyes." Pedro was Antonio's oldest nephew, son of Antonio's oldest brother, twenty years his senior. This man was probably thirty-one, thirty-five at the most, Cristina judged. He had married and gone to live in Spain.

"I hope you will allow me to call on you soon. It has been my intention since I returned from Madrid."

Fernando's manners and stylish clothes belied the ranch where he was born. She had never cared for Pedro, with his churlish pretensions. The breeding and money, what was left of it, belonged to his wife. So did the intense blue eyes.

"We would be honored." Cristina smiled graciously.

Fernando hastened to explain. "My wife was Spanish. I have lived in Madrid these past ten years. But after my dear wife passed away, I slowly disengaged myself from business, and only recently returned to Mexico."

"Please accept our condolences for the loss of your wife. We did not know."

"You are most kind. I would like to stay in Mexico if I can find the right investment possibilities. My father suggested that Uncle Antonio..."

"Of course. I am sure my husband can be of assistance. You must lunch with us. Saturday, perhaps?"

"I accept with great pleasure."

"We shall look forward to seeing you." Cristina stood up and held out her hand, half-gloves revealing her slender fingers. Antonio's nephew was not as tall as most of the Rivas Mercado men, but he was much more handsome and had a worldly air that she found singularly attractive.

Fernando felt the warmth of a responsive nature and bent to kiss the outstretched hand.

CHAPTER IV

It had been a busy week for Antonio. Every day there had been meetings at the Academy and guests to attend: engineers, fellow architects, visitors, students, teachers. His desks at home and at the Academy were stacked with work. Moreover, spring vacation had begun, the time when the faculty judged scholarship candidates for study in Europe. Fund-raising was a distasteful activity, but one that had been forced on him. The Department of Education had cut funds. It had become necessary to find private patrons to help maintain the students abroad.

Antonio turned down Héroes from the streetcar stop. He was irritated, irritated with the government, irritated that he had been obliged to walk all week. His street was still a sticky mess. Mounds of dislodged cobblestones obstructed the sidewalk and shiny black puddles of tar dotted the grass borders. Confound his neighbor! Joaquín Cassasús had simply informed the neighborhood that he was going to pay for the paving of Héroes. Self- interest was at the root of it. Recently recalled as Ambassador to the United States, Cassasús had returned with the latest model Packard, then purchased another automobile in Germany. Maybe it was time to retire Feliciano and the horses.

Antonio picked his way toward No. 45. He was late, and Cristina had invited the whole family to greet their long-absent nephew, Fernando. Pale blue eyes flashed in his memory. An indolent fellow.

What was he qualified to do? Ha! Antonio scraped a sticky glob off his shoe. Damn it, he needed time to himself, time to go over every minute detail of the Monument, to study and rework the complex calculations. He tried to throw off a familiar feeling of apprehension, recognizing that Beto was right. He had allowed the Monument to become an obsession. Last night he was jolted awake by a nightmare, the sheets clammy with cold sweat. In the dream he saw the column leaning, like Pisa. But unlike Pisa, which had managed to sustain its tilt for centuries, he had watched his column slowly topple, the shifting subsoil unable to resist the weight of the platform. He saw the laboriously rounded and fitted stones shaking loose, the white granite steps buckling, his handpicked green Genovese marble and the yellow and red marble from Verona cracking as the mosaic floor of the platform tilted. Horrified, he had watched the heroic bronze Liberty fall forward with a thundering crash, her head rolling down Reforma Boulevard. This morning, his chief mason had confided his own apprehension: he had detected an almost imperceptible fissure in the concrete platform and heard a noise. These people had uncanny perception. My God, they were up at eighteen meters! W. H. Kipp had constructed a reinforced steel mesh tube to which the fitted stones were attached. The column was solid.

His attention riveted on his feet, Antonio proceeded cautiously toward his house. No construction in his long career had caused him such anxiety. There was nothing terribly complicated or original about a column. Columns had commemorated triumphs and heroes throughout history, going back in antiquity to Trajan's column in the city of the Caesars. Alexandria, Rome, London, Paris, and St. Petersburg had similar classical columns. But this one would be an engineering feat, a challenge to resist earthquakes, even lightning. It must be anchored to the old lake bed in such a way that it would never waver. His column must "stand tall," a symbol of pride rising high above the city, a victorious angel of protection and mercy, floating in the sky.

Stand tall yourself, Antonio scolded himself. Everyone knows why you got the commission. Face the truth. It was a gift, a white feather.... Maybe it was time to call in outside engineers.

Eyes alert for black puddles, he allowed his mind to wander back to 1880 when he had returned to Mexico from Europe.

Diaz had inherited an empty treasury when he seized the reins of power in 1876. The shrewd, practical General soon opened the Mexico's doors to foreign investors. By 1880, American and French bankers were financing an era of development and progress. France was the fount of culture; Mexicans were enamored of all things French. With a degree in engineering and another in architecture from Paris, as well as a portfolio of architectural honors bestowed on him by the French government, Antonio had found all his stars in the right position. He had walked right through the waiting room of the Department of Communications and Public Works where young, under-schooled Mexican architects warmed the worn sofas. His first major commission, won in competition, was the gigantic railroad terminal at Santiago de Tlaltelolco.

Railroads were becoming the lifeblood of the nation, uniting north with south, the Gulf with the Pacific, winding through the rugged mountains that for centuries had separated Mexicans from each other, and Mexico into isolated pockets. Antonio's roundhouse, the intricate maze of tracks and the Augustean customs house had brought accolades and prize commissions. Thus began his success and his fortune. But by 1890, Mexicans had to fight for recognition. The foreigners were everywhere, their cultures revered. It was the opinion of Public Works that one had to be a foreigner to be any good. That year, a competition had been held for the Legislative Palace, the most ambitious project undertaken by Díaz to date. All accredited architects could compete.

"I am going to submit two projects," Antonio had confided to a Mexican colleague.

"Why? Only one will win."

"I want to test them. I have already decided. One project will be in the Renaissance style. I'll sign that with an Italian name. The other will be a Neo-Classic dome, signed by a Frenchman."

They had laughed at the conspiracy.

Antonio had learned from a friend on the Board of Judges that his

Neo-Classic project had won first place, but when it was discovered that the mysterious architect was Rivas Mercado he was demoted to third place, after a Frenchman and an Italian!

He had exploded!

"I'll give you the true story," he had declared to reporters from Le Courier du Mexique and The Mexican Herald when they caught wind of the fraud.

His scathing exposé fed a growing anger among young Mexican professionals, who joined the protest against privileged foreigners. Thereafter, the name of Antonio Rivas Mercado had a new resonance. The commission for the Independence Monument was a white feather, offered by Porfirio Díaz to the real winner of the contest for the Legislative Palace.

Wiping his shoes on the mud-rail at the foot of the stairs, Antonio ascended to the gallery. He was hoping to get past the arbor, but Beto was waiting for him and called out:

"You look dejected. Come hear some really bad news."

Antonio chuckled. "Guess I could rest for a minute. What blow has the world suffered now?"

"There's been a strike at a textile mill in Veracruz. A slaughter, a massacre, a nasty affair," Beto said in a lugubrious voice.

"Hmmm." Antonio poured a glass of tamarind water and sat down.

Obviously Antonio was in no mood for discussion. Beto leaned back and crossed his legs. "What's new with you? How are the scholarships going?"

"Diego Rivera got one, thank God. He's been hanging around the shop of a drunken engraver, near the Academy, ever since he got expelled. I've offered amnesty, but he won't come to classes. At least now he can go to Europe. Governor Dehesa of Veracruz is underwriting a year in Spain."

"And how much did you put in the pot?"

Antonio shrugged his shoulders.

"Well, there's one Mexican student who will stand out." Beto snickered, thinking of the fat young man with the bulging eyes whose build equaled Antonio's. "Maybe he won't sink into that damned mire of Mexican inferiority that bogs down your boys over there."

"Has Fernando arrived yet?" Antonio asked abruptly, closing the subject of scholarship money.

"Indeed. He's holding court with his fans."

"Who's here?"

"Leonor and her bevy of beautiful granddaughters. Seems Letty returned from Europe unengaged. Pity. They've been too choosey. Their number one plum is overripe." Beto blew a smoke ring. "And Elena's here."

"What about Juana?"

"Not present. Torres is holding her hostage until you repair the roof of their house."

"I didn't know Juana was that weak-kneed. Is that the roster of guests?"

"No. That eminent theatrical critic, your other brother-in-law, is also here. You are the last arrival."

Antonio served himself a chicken breast and listened in on the feminine babble. The voices of his wife and sisters, of his daughters and nieces rose and fell, orchestrated by Fernando's long dissertations on the habits and habitats of Spanish nobility. A handsome devil. And arrogant. They said his late wife was much older. Dour but rich. Thank God on Saturdays his Torres brothers-in-law played dominos at the Jockey Club. Antonio regarded the sardonic smile on his nephew's lips.

"And how does Mexico look to you, Fernando?" Antonio's voice boomed across the high decibel chatter.

"I was telling your charming wife that it's an adjustment after Europe. When I left, Mexico was a city of peeling walls, foul odors and potholes that could break an axle. Now it's a city of barricades, gaping holes and dust. I haven't seen the volcanoes in a week."

Antonio engaged his nephew's eyes. "I am interested in your observations. Do you think Mexico has progressed in ten years?"

"Of course. There's running water and electricity in my hotel room, and the electric tramways are a welcome change. But I haven't seen many automobiles. Madrid is full of them." Fernando grinned. "I find a sign of maturity in the nude marble statues along the Alameda Park."

A ripple of giggles erupted around the table.

"But my true opinion? Mexico is still pathetically backward." Fernando twirled his wine glass in a beam of cobalt light reflecting off the stained glass peacock.

Why did he feel offended at these remarks, Antonio wondered. He remembered his own shock when he returned to Mexico in '80. It had seemed like a primitive land inhabited by dirty, ignorant people. Naked children defecated in the street, and at every turn the deplorable state of the city had jarred his European-trained sensibilities. But now? Had he become inured?

"The most important change," Fernando was saying, "is that our dear Capital is no longer a fetid Venice. I am happy to note that Don Porfirio has entubed those foul odors in a new sewage system. And Doña Cristina tells me you are working on a drainage system. I got caught in a downpour the other day. Water ankle-deep in a minute. Had to pay an Indian fifty centavos to carry me across the street. When I left, a piggyback ride cost twelve centavos. Galloping inflation, I call it." He laughed.

Sipping his wine slowly, deliberately, holding his audience, Fernando continued. "*Cantinas* seem to have flourished. If it is true that the population of this city is now four hundred thousand, three hundred and ninety thousand are drunken Indians! Yesterday I went looking for you at the Academy, Uncle Antonio, and walked through the Merced market. My God, what a stinking labyrinth. Alleys jammed with carts, mountains of rotting vegetables and donkeys mired in dung. I could hardly get past the merchants and drunks to the old canal dock. There must have been a kilometer of boats crammed every which way. I had to put a handkerchief over my nose. One forgets the stench of dirty, drunk people." Fernando patted his trim mustache with his napkin.

"Ever been to Les Halles in Paris?" René Labadie asked. His blood was French but his loyalty was Mexican.

"Come now, René," Fernando said, "How many drunk Frenchmen do you see there? And if you did they would smell of civilized wine.

The Mexican Indian is a backward and ugly race. Unfortunately, he is eternal and will eternally smell fermented."

Again, a ripple of suppressed snickers and giggles.

Beto had been studying this suave nephew with the sardonic smile. "Your father makes his money from that fermentation," he said. "Were you making a survey of *cantinas*? Your father could use a good administrator on his *pulque* hacienda."

"Extracting cactus juice, even for profit, is not my *forté*, dear uncle."

"What is your forté?" asked Beto.

"Yes, do tell us your plans," Leonor broke in. She wished Leticia would join the conversation, and not act so indifferent. Her two younger granddaughters seemed mesmerized by this handsome, worldly "uncle." "What do you plan to do now that you're back, Fernando?"

"Since we were not blessed with children and I have no home now, I can afford to take a little time to assess Mexico, to see whether I still fit in." Penetrating blue eyes took in everyone at the table. "For the time being, I shall be a dilettante."

Antonieta wondered what "dilettante" meant. She could tell that her mother was annoyed with Tía Leonor, who always talked about Europe. Mamá had never been to Europe. It was a good thing Tía Elena was at the table. She kept peace between them.

"You drive a fine carriage for a dilettante," Beto commented, recognizing a certain talent in this nephew. He speared the last chicken breast as the platter was passed again, smiling maliciously at José in the big baroque mirror.

Across the table, Antonieta caught the gesture and snickered behind her napkin. Once grandfather Castellanos had helped himself to Tío's chicken breast and narrowly avoided having a fork poked in his eye. When she was little, she thought all chickens had three breasts: one for Papá, one for Tío Beto and one for a guest.

Antonieta dropped her book on the night table and closed the curtains. She jumped up on the bed and lay listlessly, not inspired to write, not inspired to do anything. A queasy feeling had possessed her all day. She stretched and wriggled her feet. She didn't like having Tío

Fernando around the house so much. If he didn't come for lunch, he came in the afternoon to go calling with Mamá "to introduce him to the right people." Mamá laughed too much and Alicia was plain silly around Tío Fernando. Only she and Chela didn't like him. He told lies, like telling Mamá he was going to have lunch with an old friend from Spain, when cousin Tita told Alicia he had had lunch at Letty's house. Tita said he was conceited, even if he was handsome. Anyway, Letty could have any husband she wanted; she had even a more perfect nose than Alicia.

Arms rigid at her sides, Antonieta stretched out flat, trying to get rid of a taste of bile which kept coming up. It had started this morning at church. She and Sabina had rushed up to the park where Héroes ended, to hear early morning Mass at San Fernando. Usually, they knelt in the front pew, said a prayer and left. But it was Lent, and this morning she had knelt at the high, gilded altar of "Our Lord of Sorrow" and prayed long for Mamá and Papá, who had not been to church once during the Lenten season. Papá fell asleep in church, which he said was an affront to God, and Mamá had her oratorio, but Sabina said that unless one felt the cold, hard stones under one's knees, God listened to prayers with only one ear.

There was a mystifying aura about San Fernando, a musky odor of incense and wax and a wondrous silence, broken only by the drone of prayers intoned in Latin by the barefoot Franciscan priests. When she had risen to light her candle at the altar of Our Lord of Sorrow, she noticed that the paint had worn off Christ's feet where so many people had kissed them. She looked up at the sad, kneeling Christ and suddenly His eyes met hers, luminous eyes about to spill tears. All day she had remembered those compelling eyes and felt a strange apprehension. Now, her stomach was tied in a tight, familiar knot. Before the bedroom door opened, she heard Sabina's steps in the corridor.

"Are you lying here in the dark again?" Sabina threw open the curtains. "You brood too much. Here, drink this chamomile tea; when you finish, your uncle said to come down to the arbor."

Beto was dozing, *The Mexican Herald* perilously balanced on his knee. Hearing his young niece approach, he sat up with a jerk, sending the paper flying, sheets fanning out on the floor. Quickly, he reached for *El Imparcial*, folded back the pages and cleared his throat with a rasp.

"Blatant cynicism. There is nothing impartial about this paper and not one word about the strike. If you want to know what is happening in Mexico, read the foreign papers! How are you, *princesa*?"

"All right." Antonieta picked up the scattered pages of the English tabloid and began reassembling them. She stopped at a picture of some men being held back by policemen with rifles. "What does 'strike' mean, Tío? she asked, purposely instigating a political dissertation so he could blow off steam.

"It means that certain workers are complainers and they have stopped work to complain."

She read the caption aloud: "Cananea: Strikers demand equal wages with American miners and refuse to work on Sundays." She darted a severe glance at her uncle. "Would you want to work on Sunday?"

Beto noisily turned the pages of his newspaper. "Now here's an item that will interest you," he said, ignoring her question. "It's about your father. Now where was I?" He adjusted his spectacles and read: "Last Tuesday the President of the Republic, Porfirio Díaz, inaugurated the Pacific port of Salina Cruz and the reconstructed railroad that crosses the Isthmus of Tehauntepec to Coatzacoalcos on the Gulf of Mexico. Sugar imported from the islands of Hawaii to the tables of New York, via Mexico, has opened new doors to world trade."

"That doesn't mention Papá."

"I haven't come to the distinguished guests yet." Beto ran his finger down the column. "Guest list, page six. Here it is. 'The renowned architect, Don Antonio Rivas Mercado, the designer of the maze of tracks, the roundhouse and terminal building for the new Tehuantepec railroad...'" He balanced his spectacles on the tip of his nose and looked up at his solemn audience "'accompanied the distinguished President to the serenade and dance that followed, executing a fine tango with the Chief Magistrate.'"

Antonieta laughed at the ludicrous image and danced around the table, lifted her uncle's beret and kissed the bald spot on his head.

"I thought that might cheer you up. You hardly touched your lunch," Beto said.

With a sudden change of mood, Antonieta asked, "Do you think Papá will stay home for awhile? Alicia is in love with Tío Fernando, you know. That's why she acts so silly."

"We were talking about sugar from Hawaii," Beto said. "Stick to the subject." Alicia wasn't the only one in love with him. My God, Antonio should throw that sponging dilettante out! While he was off buying onyx in Puebla and *chiluca* stone in whatever dusty village, Fernando was gorging at his table, ingratiating himself with the children, forming lovely little tableaux with Cristina and the boy.

"I am going to Villagrande's bookstore in a few minutes. Feliciano is going to drive me. Then I will proceed to San Carlos to gather up your father at exactly five o'clock and wait for him at least a half hour. Want to come?"

"Oh yes, Tío!" Villagrande's was her favorite place downtown. "A den of antiquity," Tío Beto called the old bookstore, because they blew the dust off ancient volumes for all kinds of people who gathered there. "I'll tell Sabina."

Feliciano steered the horse into the Zócalo at the National Pawn Shop and drove around by the new French department store at the end of the western arcade. When they reached the corner of the Palace, he waved his whip at two friends leaning against the Cathedral fence, having their boots shined. Recognizing their fellow coachman, the drivers disengaged themselves from the shoeshine boys and made room for the Rivas Mercado Landau.

Antonieta jumped down and stood aside while Feliciano helped her uncle lower his painful legs to the sidewalk.

"Look!" she cried out, pointing across the street. A crowd had gathered and was peering into an excavation where steam shovels had dug a trough for the huge drainage pipes. El Imparcial had carried a picture of some fearsome-looking serpent carvings they had unearthed at the base of an old Aztec temple. "Maybe they found more idols. Let's go see."

"No!" Beto was irritated by the obstructions and detours. He led the way around the flower market, turning behind the Cathedral.

Undulating sidewalks and slanted windows were characteristic of this neighborhood. When he undertook the job of installing the drainage pipes, Antonio had explained to his children that in the days of the Aztecs the heart of Mexico City was an island, always threatened by floods. The Spaniards drained the shallow lakes and filled in the canals to make more land mass. But the spongy subsoil always had its way, pushing up one building and pulling down another.

It was a neighborhood familiar to Antonieta. She often accompanied her father to collect his rents in some of these tumbledown buildings he was constantly repairing. Today, enticing smells dispelled the knot in her stomach. Spicy *tacos* and *gorditas* sizzled on sidewalk braziers, burros loaded with bags of charcoal clattered down the street, young boys stood on corners smoking cigarettes. Youth, here, moved in an exotic world. Villagrande's bookstore, on the ground floor of an old colonial building, was a gathering place for *criollos*, *mestizos*, and literate Indians, many of whom had obtained an education from its venerable volumes. Its interior was dimly lit; high shelves bulged with a hodgepodge of publications, creating a tapestry of abstract design. The clerks slid their ladders back and forth, attending customers of all ages, income, professions, and political ideologies.

Eduardo Villagrande saw them and moved up behind the counter. A short, myopic gentleman who wore his glasses on the top of his bushy, dark brown head, his scruffy appearance deceived. He was a scholarly *mestizo* with a bright intellect and fluid vocabulary who enjoyed baiting his conservative friends with socialist rhetoric. A gentleman in demeanor, Villagrande was nevertheless a rebel at heart, a man certain of his identity, his opinions, and his passion for Mexico.

"Don Alberto!" Villagrande greeted Beto warmly. "What can I do for you, friend? Sorry the children aren't home this afternoon, Antonieta. They went off shopping or someplace with their mother."

Antonieta was glad. She liked the funny house upstairs and she liked the rowdy Villagrande children, but today she was in no mood to play.

"I am here on Antonio's behalf," Beto announced. "Do you suppose you could dig up an old map of Tenochtitlán in that dark hole you call your archives? One that shows the depth of the canals and their exact locations?"

"Short of using a spade, I dug up all I could for Don Antonio," Villagrande quipped, throwing up his hands. "The Spaniards burned the Aztec library and destroyed their records, you know. Few documents remain."

"So I have heard," Beto responded tartly. Villagrande was always giving him lessons on the Aztecs, long ago pigeonholing him as an "invader." The invaded and the invaders. Huitzilipochtli and Aristotle. What the hell was a Mexican! "I thought you might still have something buried back there."

"I found a map showing the Aztec dikes and their aqueducts, but there's no annotation on depths. Did you know that the Aztecs had an aqueduct that brought in water from the springs of Chapultepec? Everyone thinks that aqueducts started with the Spaniards."

"I know that! I'll just browse." He did not know it. He was not interested in the Aztecs, only their canals.

"Look, wait for me in my office. I'll try to find a copy of Cortes' second letter to Charles V. I just remembered, it contains a map of Tenochtilán."

Leaning on Antonieta for support, Beto climbed the narrow stairs to Villagrande's cubbyhole on the mezzanine. His enormous desk was piled high with precariously balanced books, magazines, leaflets, periodicals. Beto's eye caught the title of a handbill held down by a paperweight. EL PARTIDO LIBERAL MEXICANO, printed a year ago, enumerating the anarchists' demands. He took out his spectacles.

Antonieta was playing with the paperweight. Suddenly she blurted, "Look, Tío! There's a huge ant carrying a breadcrumb. Where did it come from? He's weaving from side to side. He's going to fall off the desk!"

"Quiet!" Beto squashed the ant with an inkwell.

Antonieta bit her lip.

"I'm sorry, *princesa*. But I'm trying to read something important." Beto's compassion for his beloved niece was sometimes overcome by exasperation. There was something fragile and hidden in the soul of that child, restlessness tinged with sadness, an impatience to learn. Today she was especially moody. "Why don't you sit down for a minute?"

Villagrande pushed open the door and spilled an armload of books on the overburdened desk. "I found a map in an old Spanish chronicle with a description of the canals."

"You mean there is some order to that disorder downstairs?"

"My bookstore is a thousand times better catalogued than the National Archives," Villagrande boasted.

"But their dust may not be as vermin-riddled as yours." Beto cast a probing look at his rotund friend. "I'll take the map and leave the books to the scholars. Thank you very much."

The halls of San Carlos were quiet by late afternoon. It was a time Antonio treasured. He sat at his desk, reviewing art works and projects, privately rating both students and professors. There was little he considered truly creative produced in the Academy. Students never had enough materials to permit creative experimentation; teachers were underpaid and had to take outside jobs or they lost interest in teaching and didn't show up. He missed Rebull and Velasco, even Felix Parra with his passion for things Aztec.

Methodically, Antonio continued his work, but he couldn't stop thinking about tthe Monument. It was tilting. A proven fact. But would it continue to tilt? Should he request Public Works to send over a team of engineers to assess the situation? He should advise the President first. God, was it beyond the salvage point?

Antonio was startled by a knock at the open door of his office. His caller filled the doorway, a broad-brimmed felt hat in his hand, and an ill-fitting jacket stretched to contain the huge body.

"I thought I would find you here, so I just came on up."

"Diego!" Antonio said, rising to greet the young man, pumping his hand vigorously. "I am so glad to see you. I trust everything is arranged for your departure."

Nineteen years old, Diego Rivera topped six feet and weighed over two hundred pounds. There was an oddly ugly attractiveness in the alert face that Antonio had warmed to from the first time he had met the boy.

Diego pulled out a soiled envelope. "Here is my railroad ticket to Veracruz and my boat ticket to Spain. I came to say good-bye and thank you, maestro, for helping with the scholarship."

"Your talent won it." Antonio patted him on the shoulder then leaned against the desk, plunging his hands deep into his pockets. "You'll now see at first hand some of the great masters you have so adroitly copied: El Greco and Velasquez, Zurbarán, even Goya. Don't miss a single day of this privileged time of life, my boy." The professor looked at his shabby student and smiled. "You know the Conquerors were mestizos themselves, Phoenicians and Visigoths and Romans and Moors, even Jews. Their blood was more mixed than ours. Don't let the Spanish lord it over you. Mexicans are a curiosity over there." His lips curled mirthfully. "And you, my boy, are a Mexican curio."

"I shall capitalize on it, maestro." Diego smiled. "Oh yes, I have a letter." He produced another stained envelope. "It's from Gerardo Murillo and addressed to Chicharro, asking him to accept me in his studio."

Murillo, who signed his paintings "Dr. Atl," had informed Antonio of his own interest in Diego. He had also mentioned some young renegade Spanish painters who were breaking away from the classical and even post-impressionist schools, a certain Picasso and Gris.

"What is your opinion, maestro?" Diego asked.

Antonio's hazel eyes met the wide, bulging eyes on a level with his own. This young man whose passionate nature and wild imagination made him so vulnerable could easily get lost in the Europe of the avant-gardes. He measured his reply.

"Don't be led by the novel, son. Study the techniques of the great masters. Emulate their style. They will be the best teachers until your own style emerges."

Impulsively, master and student pounded each other on the back. The young man placed his hat on his head and lumbered down the corridor. Antonio waved from the doorway of his office as the Cathedral clock rang five times.

Beto clung to the railing as he climbed the wide stairway to the second floor of San Carlos. Antonieta was eager to run ahead, to take the steps two at a time, but dutifully kept pace with her uncle. At the top of the stairs she broke away. The door that read "Director" was always open. With a gleeful greeting, she burst in and embraced her father, who sat behind his big oak desk with the portrait of Don Porfirio looking over his shoulders.

"Hello, angel."

Beto limped up to the desk and victoriously unfolded the map. "Look at this! Villagrande unearthed it."

Antonio studied the stained old print thoughtfully. "Villagrande said he would come up with something. It was good of him to look again." He grinned and regarded his brother with a shade of condescension. "What else did you find there? More seditious literature?"

Beto ignored the sarcasm in his brother's smirk. "Yes. I can tell you with conviction that things are heating up in the north."

Antonio considered his brother's new interest a barometer of the political scene, a sort of game. Instead of social tidbits to chew on, he had found political bones and masticated them with tiger's teeth. Beto's life had been reduced to so little, so pitifully little. He looked at the pinched face of his brother, his proud brother who never complained, who never spoke of his pain.

"Nothing will happen," Antonio replied with assurance. "Díaz is no fool. He will crush the opposition like ants, as he always does."

Antonieta knew her father was right about the ants.

Antonio locked the drawers of his desk and took his hat off the rack. "I have to stop by Boari's for a minute and check Juana's roof before the workmen leave. Shall we go?"

Adamo Boari's studio was a beehive of activity, buzzing with half a dozen foreign tongues. Louis Lamm, an American engineer, was just leaving, but stopped to talk with Antonio in what the gentleman thought was passable Spanish. The American and his partners were filling in the old swampland on the western edge of the city and selling lots for thirteen pesos a square meter! Antonio walked past tables piled with blueprints to where Boari and the sculptor, Alciati, were inspecting a large model of the Opera house. Four bronze Pegasus figures on pedestals had been added around the dome.

"Well hello, Antonio," Boari said. "What do you think?"

"Impressive. But I noticed this morning that one of your bronze beasts is flying, dangling from a pulley. Still worried about weight?" Antonio asked.

Boari shook his shoulders. "Millikan Brothers came down from Chicago to make the calculations. We have pumped enough concrete into the foundation to hold up two opera houses. Where does it go?"

So Adamo was still having trouble. "I am thinking of going to Chicago to see your Millikan Brothers myself. Why don't you come along?"

"And leave this?" Boari threw out his arms.

"You might want to. With this white elephant going up in front of that Venetian Palace you call the Post Office, you just might create a Grand Canal." Antonio chuckled heartily but Adamo was not in the mood for banter. "I came to see Garita."

"He left early," Boari said.

Suddenly serious, Antonio took his friend aside. "I'm worried, Adamo. Damned worried. My calculations show the Monument is leaning two degrees. I want Garita to check it." Antonio had high respect for his Mexican colleague's skill as an engineer. "Would you ask him if he can be at the site Monday morning? Seven o'clock."

Boari nodded with empathy and accompanied Antonio to the door.

Tía Juana's home was too formal and dark, except for the light-filled foyer, Antonieta thought. Tío Beto had remained in the carriage. He didn't like this house either, said it didn't have a single comfortable chair. But Antonieta knew it was because he didn't like crippled old Uncle Ignacio's constant shouting.

She felt uncomfortable in this house, too, but there was a lot to see. Tía Juana collected little boxes and glass animals and especially dolls, which Tío Beto said was because she had no children.

A grand piano partially concealed the doll cabinet in the foyer.

Antonieta ran her fingers across the keys and looked up. Long rays of the waning sun streamed through the stained glass skylight overhead. She could see a shadow on the skylight where Papá had laid a scaffold to fix the leaks. He was up there now and would probably stay until it was too dark to see. She climbed up on the piano bench and peered into the highest shelf of the doll cabinet.

"Tonieta, my dear child. I didn't know you were here. Did I startle you?"

Juana had entered quietly from her sitting room.

Antonieta jumped down and kissed her aunt.

"Sorry, *preciosa*." She returned the kiss affectionately. "I guess your father is up on the roof."

"Yes. He didn't know you were home. You have some new dolls, Tía. I like this one with the dress that wraps around and changes color in the light, the one with the ruby in her nose. Don't tell me; let me guess where she's from. India!"

"Yes!" Juana never ceased to be impressed with the information stored in this child's head. She was much too wise for her seven years. "I have a beautiful new book with pictures of dolls from all over the world. It's in the library. Come, I'll show it to you."

Juana seated Antonieta in a high, straight-backed chair with the heavy book spread open in her lap, then turned to leave.

"Don't go, Tía. Stay and look at the book with me. Please don't go."

"Forgive me, mi amor." Juana smiled apologetically. "I have some things to discuss with your father before it gets dark." She kissed her niece and patted her hand. "I'll be right back."

Antonieta flipped the pages to an illustration of a black doll. Certainly from Africa, but what country? She covered the caption and closed her eyes. Tanganyika, she guessed. Wrong. It was the Belgian Congo.

She had turned a scarce five pages when the house seemed to explode. Glass was crashing, shattering, breaking in the foyer. A high, piercing scream jerked her to her feet. The piano struck a loud, discordant chord. She raced into the foyer and clapped her hands over her ears. Stained glass fell like rain, huge pieces crashing down, breaking, beaming colored rays against white walls. There was a jagged hole above her with Papá's head peering down, his face white, mouth open.

Another piece of glass broke off and crashed.

"Get back, Papá!" she screamed.

Slowly her eyes took in the room: over by the piano she saw a rumpled skirt on the floor. A leg with a high-heeled shoe stuck out. Trancelike, she moved closer. Tía Juana was sprawled on the floor beside the splintered, overturned doll cabinet, surrounded by decapitated little bodies. Blood gushed from her neck and her legs were grotesquely bent, showing the lace on her bloomers.

Antonieta covered her eyes and screamed.

Within minutes, her father was kneeling beside Tía Juana. Workmen, maids, houseboys gathered, gawking.

"Carmen, send for the doctor. You, get me a blanket. And a cot, or an ironing board. Anything flat. You men will help me move her and carry her to her room."

They covered Tía and took her away.

Sickness roiled in Antonieta's belly. She stood paralyzed, her blood pounding. Then her father's arms were around her. He picked her up and she buried her head in his shoulder.

"My God, my God, oh my God," he muttered over and over. "That long skirt. Her heel caught. I couldn't reach her hand."

Antonieta wrapped her arms around her father's neck and sobbed, his own tears disappearing in his daughter's long, singed curls.

The black curtains of the hearse car ruffled out as the streetcar turned into the Zócalo and pulled up to the station. The mourners descended.

Antonio wiped his brow, perspiring under the top hat. The morning coat, with the black armband sewn on the sleeve, was like a hair shirt. The day was hot, hot and oppressive on this "Good" Friday, the day Juana was buried. He could hear *Judas* puppets being exploded with fiery vengeance in the distance, larger-than-life tissue paper effigies rigged with gunpowder, symbolic of Christ's betrayal made in the image of high-hat politicians. Guilt hung on his own soul, a heavy smothering weight.

The family stood on the platform and endured the lengthy condolences.

Antonieta's high-necked black dress itched. Would Papá have to attend the nine Masses? Would Tía Juana care, up there in heaven? That wax face in the casket wasn't Tía's. No one believed her when she said she had seen her aunt's soul rise up right through the hole in the skylight, a little wisp of white that got thinner and thinner then vanished. Life seemed to be a thin thing. Like Tío Beto's canary. Yesterday it was singing and this morning it was a dead, scruffy lump in the bottom of the cage. A tear dropped off the tip of her nose as she sought her father's hand.

A permanent lump seemed stuck in Antonio's throat, though his face was impassive. Juana, Juanita, his beloved, generous sister, covering an unhappy marriage with endless deeds of charity. He squeezed Antonieta's hand. She had insisted on going to the cemetery. They had talked, alone and late the night it happened. Her fascination with death had deeply disturbed him. So many questions, so many answers he could not give. In the end, the child was the comforter and the parent the comforted.

It wasn't fair, Cristina's heart cried out. Six months of mourning! There was a stack of invitations on her desk: two important weddings, a banquet at the castle for Elihu Root, the American Secretary of State, a masquerade ball at the Automobile Club and a select dinner party at the Cassasús' home for that Englishman, Weetman Pearson, now elevated to Lord Cowdray for the excellent oil contract he had just signed She lifted the black veil and daubed at her eyes.

Beto's eyes were focused on Ignacio's retreating back, his crutch digging into newly planted grass as he crossed the plaza to his carriage. He had shunned Antonio, casting a shroud of guilt where no guilt belonged! The old miser was seething, because Juana had left Antonio money in her will, not collectable of course, until the reprobate died. Beto's mind began to weave diabolical schemes as he watched Leonor and her husband catch up to Ignacio, joining him in his censure.

I hate him, Alicia thought. Why had he ignored Papá? And why did Antonieta have to tell her about the blood and the broken neck and the bloomers? She preferred to think of Tía Juana as a proper lady who always did something special for children. Poor Mamá. One lady they knew practically lived in black, so many relatives died.

Alicia felt a comforting arm embrace her shoulder and looked up at Fernando with a wan smile. She was glad Tío Fernando was going to be around while Papá went to Chicago.

CHAPTER V

Provoked by the high-pitched voices of children, Beto parted the vines around the window overlooking the the arbor. Alicia was still holding court in the garden, encircled by friends and cousins, all screeching at once as they argued about how she should decorate her *tonneau*, an odd-looking carriage that had been imported from London for the great Battle of the Flowers. Cristina, Fernando, Leonor and Letty had joined the wranglers. Now Fernando was being pulled by Alicia toward the wicker marvel. The chatter died down.

"I suggest you decorate it with cascades of white ribbon and pink roses," he heard Fernando solemnly pronounce.

"Well, now that that's settled, shall we go?" Leonor said, linking her arms in Fernando's on one side and Letty's on the other. His sister was a striking figure in her tailored navy blue suit and wide-brimmed hat. Beto watched the elegant threesome saunter toward Leonor's new Renault touring car, a custom-made monster the length of the carriage space. Cristina had turned away and run after the boy, Mario, who seemed bent on climbing into the *tonneau*. A keen analyst of human tempests, Beto knew it was a pretext. He had watched the rivalry for Fernando's attention play out. Ha! Cristina had lost her lapdog....and was losing her bloom, Beto thought with sardonic delight. He returned to the rattan chair, and despite the racket, dozed off.

"Oh, let's go, Chela." Antonieta tugged at her cousin's hand. "Let Alicia decorate her old tonneau herself." Graciela had become Antonieta's inseparable companion from the day she first arrived in class. She was a beautiful, willful girl with fair skin, auburn hair and green eyes, attributed to an Irish grandfather. Beto dubbed her dark complexioned sister "the sad Indian.". Chela had quickly surpassed Alicia in arithmetic and shared Antonieta's love of books. In her own home, two tutors had declared her incorrigible and marched off.

"We can go up to the tower," Antonieta whispered in Chela's ear. "Nobody will miss us and we could do it *now.*"

"All right," her cousin whispered back. "Let's go."

They sneaked up the back kitchen stairs, stopping by the hall closet, where Antonieta pulled a small cloth bag and her treasured notebook out of the laundry chute, then quickly scampered up the staircase to the tower.

Free! Here they were free from constraint and prying eyes.

Excited by the task before them, the girls clasped hands and stood quietly for a moment, contemplating the immense panorama before them. The sky was bright cobalt, fading to turquoise as it met the green and purple mountains undulating in the distant ranges. A row of low, flat-topped volcanoes crossed the valley floor, A spiral of cloud puffs hung above the snow cap of the great "Popo," like smoke rising from the long extinct lover who guarded his sleeping lady, a painterly palette in the thin, transparent air.

"Ready", Antonieta whispered.

"You do it," Chela murmured.

The girls settled down on a bench and Antonieta loosened the drawstring on the cloth bag. She produced a packet of needles, and dug out a small vial of alcohol. Selecting a needle, she carefully immersed it in the vial, as Miss Etta had taught them in their hygiene class.

Chela closed her eyes and screwed up her face. Valiantly, she held out her finger. Antonieta pricked it with a quick thrust, then pricked her own. The girls pressed their fingers together, smearing the blood. Gazing steadfast into each other's eyes, they recited: "We, Graciela Eugenia Rivas Mercado Carey and Maria Antonieta Valeria Rivas Mercado

Castellanos are now sisters. We will tell each other all our secrets, and only the truth, and promise to defend each other till the day we die."

"I promise."

"I promise."

"Now make a wish," Antonieta said.

"I wish..." Chela closed her eyes tight. "I wish I had a key to my bedroom so I could lock Mamá *out*. Now you wish."

"I wish..." Antonieta bit her lip. It was difficult to get out. "I wish I had flawless white skin and a perfect nose."

"Why?" Chela asked, surprised.

"So Mamá would like me," Antonieta confessed softly, looking down.

"Oh pooh. You should be glad she doesn't pay so much attention to you. You know how my Mamá hangs around me all the time as though I were going to break or run away or something. The only person she trusts is Tía Cristina. Oh, Tonieta, I'm so glad to be here! Now can I read your notebook?"

"Tomorrow," Antonieta said, holding her very private "Thoughts" against her breast.

"We are blood sisters," Chela reminded her.

"There isn't time now," Antonieta said, lamely. Nobody had ever read her notebook before, although she suspected Alicia had before she hid it in the laundry chute. Her heart cried out to share her secrets! Chela was the only one who would understand.

"Look, I have lots of secrets I have never told anybody, either. We won't tell them all at once. Just one a day, after school." Chela squeezed her new sister's hand. .

With a joyous heart, Antonieta squeezed back.

Firmly holding the hand of her rebellious son, Cristina stalked up the stairs to the house and sought the privacy of the family parlor. She picked up her basket of needlework and smoothed out a half-finished antimacassar. Mechanically, she jabbed the crochet hook in and out, wound the thread around her finger and hooked and pulled, hooked and pulled, trying to control her emotions. Leonor snapped her fingers and everyone jumped—even Fernando. He was weak! An ingrate! Cristina's breast heaved as she hooked and pulled, trained fingers forming a rosette. Little Mario tried to climb up on her lap, but she brushed him aside, her mind in turmoil. She formed another rosette, and another. A dim image began to come into focus: the bandstand in the plaza in Oaxaca. Walking around and around with her cousins, the Mejías. She was only ten, but the boys already looked at her. *Guëra* they had called her. She was fair-complexioned, different. Among their brown faces, she stood out. Round and round, girls in one direction, boys in the other, the bandstand circled by ragged loiterers gaping with open mouths at the gleaming brass blaring out a lively march, or "*Sobre las Olas,*" the familiar old waltz sweeping you round again. The Mejías were a proud family. They had fought for their land, for their rights; had fought against the American invaders in '47 and the French in '62. Her great uncle, Ignacio, was Minister of War under President Benito Juárez. An autographed picture of that most illustrious of pure-blooded Mexican Indians hung on the wall of their parlor, with a captured French bayonet fixed beneath it. Her mother's only brother had been killed saving Porfirio Díaz in the battle of Puebla. For all their pretensions, Leonor and her husband had never been invited to an intimate dinner at the castle. No amount of scheming would obtain them an invitation to occupy a balcony in the Palace on the night of September fifteenth.

Her family counted in Oaxaca!

Mario was trying to crawl up on her lap again. Cristina picked up the little boy and set him down abruptly. She put away her needlework, and with a determined look on her face, left for the kitchen. It was time to herd all the little visitors into the children's dining room. Antonio would be home soon.

"It's a good thing you're late," Beto bellowed from the arbor as Antonio came up the stairs to the gallery. "A pack of young coyotes was just led away to feed. Why must children screech?"

"You are not bad at it yourself," Antonio retorted. "It's a sign of deafness, you know. I am going to buy you a trumpet." Puffing, he walked over and laid a bouquet of roses on the table. "Cástulo just picked them. Beautiful, aren't they?"

"I'm glad to see your mood has improved," Beto said dryly. "Have you finally taken down the last stone?"

"Yes." Antonio popped a juicy fig in his mouth. "Six thousand three hundred and forty-two stones have now been dismantled and numbered. Garita and Beltrán start on the new foundation tomorrow." He wiped his mouth. "They are going to drive a forest of wooden pilings down twenty-three meters below the lake bed."

"My God! Twenty-three meters!"

"The whole city may sink but the Monument to the Independence will never tilt again."

"Are you relieved?"

"I am." Antonio shrugged "Garita and Beltrán are in charge of the new foundation. I miscalculated. The damned subsoil shifted." He picked up a rose and smelled it. "Well, what's new in the world?"

Beto shrugged.

Antonio settled in a chair and unfolded the morning paper, falling silent.

How white his brother's beard had become, Beto reflected. He thought of the day, six years earlier, when he had trekked after Antonio through brush and clumps of wild grass to the site where the fourth circle had been traced. Reforma Boulevard was easily a hundred meters across. "The restricting mass of a tall, slim structure can be lost in such an immense space," Antonio had said. "The column must maintain a monumental aspect from every point of view. Trees, buildings will soon give it another perspective." Beto glanced at his brother. Antonio had achieved his goal. But now his "perfect column" lay in a pile of stones.

"What do you think about the nationalization of the railroads?" he asked, breaking the silence. "Our neighbors to the north are ranting."

"I think Limantour just ruined a good railroad. Two things Mexicans have no use for are timetables and maintenance."

"I say Limantour gave in to the strikers. He's running scared."

"Come off it, Beto, Pepe Limantour is the most astute politician in the Cabinet. It's a conciliatory move. You know Díaz' strategy: 'To keep a growling dog from biting, throw him a bone.'"

"You don't think all that flag-waving means anything? Mexico for the Mexicans! Throw out the foreigners—the Hearsts and Guggenheims and Rockefellers and the rest. I tell you, dissatisfaction runs deep. Just let a leader pop up to open that cesspool. And look at this." Beto picked up a cartoon. "Published in a respected Capital newspaper, eh. Look at Díaz. Look at him! Sitting up in his coffin, refusing to die. And who are those mummies holding candles? There's Limantour and his whole party of untouchable '*Científicos*!'".

Antonio sniffed at the delicate petals....Money was scarce. Limantour and his group were avid advocates of "science" as a panacea. New industries and technology would force progress in the nation in spite of the uneducated, indolent Mexican.

"Stop smelling that damned rose!" Beto blurted. "Tell me, Antonio, do you think I'm a dotty old man who is conjuring up phantoms that are attacking Mexico?"

Antonio laughed. "Not dotty. Just over-read. You need to get out. Go to a bullfight. Take a lady to dinner. I think I'll buy you that ear trumpet. There must still be some lady around who would like to whisper sweet flummeries in your ear." He threw the rose at Beto and got to his feet. "Stay out of Villagrande's bookstore. You'll sleep better".

Beto watched his brother cross the gallery to the front door. Antonio was an ostrich! Well, Antonio had only two interests in life: his work and his family. "How would you like to piss on these mummies before I burn them?" he asked the parrot. He lit a match to the cartoon. "To hell with politics!"

Eyes wide open in the dark bedroom, Antonieta lay awake thinking of all the experiences and thoughts and fears she would share with Chela. First, she would tell her about the opera gentleman, and maybe about the man in the San Cosme market. He had been urinating against a wall and turned and showed his thing to her. It was horrifying, but she couldn't help staring. There was much more to tell: she would tell Chela of her new dream of being an actress. Last week Mamá had left her at the theater with Tío José while she and Tío Fernando went calling. It was the first time she had watched a rehearsal. How much effort it took to be an actress, repeating the same words over and over until you got them just right; remembering when to move, where to stand. When the rehearsal finished, Tío José took her backstage. There she met the famous Virginia Fábregas. Such a beautiful actress! She had kissed her cheek. It was a different world backstage, a jungle of costumes and fake doors and actors strutting around, mumbling to themselves. What appeared to be soft eyes out front were really outlined in heavy black. A stone wall from the audience turned out to be painted cardboard up close. Acting was exciting! Maybe Chela could help her decide whether to be a great actress or a poet or a dancer or maybe a concert pianist. She liked to play the piano when no one was listening; her audience was fat Grandmother Mercado who looked down from her gilded frame on the piano, along with all the other relatives in those faded pictures, who sat among the embroidered roses of the Spanish shawl that spilled its fringes over the sides of the grand piano. Sometimes she played the *Vals Triste* for them, though sometimes they seemed to prefer a mazurka.

Throwing the covers over her face, Antonieta finally fell asleep.

The Battle of the Flowers was a euphoric blur. They cordoned off the Alameda Park. Papá's bowler poked up in the special grandstand amid a sea of flowered dresses and tall silk hats. In the front row, in their striped pants and top hats, sat the solemn judges. Rowdy crowds strained against the barricade as the garlanded carriages lined up. Troubadours played guitars and a hundred violins serenaded them. Then the bugler sounded his call. The Queen of the Fairies paraded in her tonneau, pulled by a white pony. Beside her sat a perfect lady-in-waiting. Around the Alameda Park and back to the Juárez Memorial the contestants paraded. Then the bugler sounded the call for the momentous announcement: "First place, Señorita Catalina Gavaldón Navarro with the cascade of violets! Second place, Señorita Alicia Rivas Mercado with the parasol of peach blossoms and festoons of roses! The musicians serenaded the winners all the way to Chapultepec Park where the "Battle" began:

People in automobiles and carriages bombarded each other with flowers. Alicia had scooped them out of the tonneau and showered the pedestrians who lined the route through the park. Mamá called them her wonderful little winners, and kissed them good night.

"This was a perfect day," Antonieta wrote in her notebook.

But perfect days were few: On her eighth birthday, Antonieta fell from the trapeze and sported a black eye; Alicia was cranky and complained of stomach pains.

Papá was too angry with Uncle Ignacio to take them on their usual spring outing to Ometusco, the Torres Adalid *pulque* hacienda where one rode through immense fields of *maguey* in a little train.

Antonieta found that her little brother was less of a pest when she read stories to him. One afternoon, she was sitting on her stool in the family parlor reading "Grimm´s Fairy Tales" to Mario, Alicia was knitting and Mamá was reading a book by Emile Zola. Mamá had hardly spoken to them and seldom turned the page in her book. Suddenly Mamá flung the book to the floor and ran out of the room. Mario grabbed for Antonieta´s book and she slapped his hand, unleashing screams of protest.

"What's wrong with Mamá?" she asked Alicia.

"I don't know."

Mario screamed.

"You do too know something. Tell me."

Alicia finished her row and put away her knitting.

"Where are you going?"

"To get Nana Pancha. I will not listen to another tantrum."

Antonieta jumped to her feet and grabbed her sister's hand. "Tell me what's wrong with Mamá?"

"She's going to have a baby!"

Cristina hardly ventured from the house nor would she receive on Sundays. A deep depression possessed her. She would be thirty-nine when this child was born and Antonio fifty-five. The hours spent with her young son provided the only inner peace Cristina felt. She became a devoted mother, sewing for hours in the garden and personally supervising the little boy's play.

Huitzilopochtli smiled from his cave in the children's "mountain" where exotic cactus flowers burst into bloom and wilted. Drawn by a rare specimen one morning, Cristina peered into the cave. She stepped back in horror, shocked and repelled. A chicken heart lay in a coagulated pool of black blood at the idol's feet. Beside it was a neat little mound of corn. No one could be accused. No one would ever confess. The next morning it was gone.

Depression gave way to irritability. Cristina became an unrelenting disciplinarian with her two daughters. To eat with Mamá was to hear the Rosary of Manners recited over and over: "Close your mouth. Sit up straight. Don't talk while you are chewing. Don't play with your fork. Keep your hands in your lap."

Antonieta was punished with a sharp caning for committing the same crime almost daily: "Look at your dress!"

Cristina made the girls adhere to a rigid schedule. Life was divided into "before lunch" and "after lunch".

7:00 A.M. - <u>Dress</u>. Sabina brought them each a glass of milk to start the day. Even Alicia was subjected to the yanks of the hairbrush, although she protested that she no longer had need of a nana.

8:00-10:30 - <u>School</u>. Government regulation primary instruction with Señorita Chavez.

10:35 - *Almuerzo*. A mid-morning breakfast whether or not they were hungry: fruit, cheese, hard rolls, dried beef, another glass of milk.

11:00-1:30 - <u>English</u>. Memorize the Olendorf speller, page by page. Read aloud. Identify the oceans and countries of the world on the big globe.

1:30-2:00 - Free time. Chela went home.

2:00-2:30 - Wash up. The hairbrush again.

2:30-3:30 or 4:00 - <u>Lunch</u>. When they ate with Papá they were spared the Rosary of Manners.

4:30-5:30 - Extras. Monday, Wednesday and Friday: piano lessons, Spanish dancing, French lessons.

6:00 - <u>Homework</u>. With Mamá.

Alicia hated homework, hated Mamá pounding arithmetic and

spelling into her. Piano lessons were a torture. She was grateful that she had been allowed to give up folk dancing, where one hopped around like a jumping bean.

Music flowed through Antonieta's slender fingers and lithe body. She kept perfect rhythm to the *fado*, the minuet and the polka. Accompanied by the fiery staccato of castanets, she whirled her long ruffled Spanish skirt with grace and elegance. The piano was a special joy until Cristina brought out the metronome and set it next to her music sheet. The click-click was maddening.

"But I am not practicing scales, Mamá," she argued. "I am playing Chopin."

"Are you telling me how the piano should be studied? Use it!" Cristina commanded, setting the despised instrument back in motion.

In a flare of defiance, Antonieta threw the metronome to the floor. Cristina pinched her arm, hard, twisting the flesh until Antonieta broke away and ran up to her room. She was punished for a week, locked in her bedroom with her meals sent up on a tray.

At the end of June, the schoolroom was closed for the summer. Señorita Chavez kissed her students goodbye, and Miss Etta handed out their summer reading list. The girls accompanied their prim English tutor to the gate, kissed her under her hat and pretended not to notice when the Cassasús' German chauffeur whistled at her as he always did. The next day Chela left for the family hacienda near Querétaro. The house was quiet and lonely.

"Dear God," Antonieta wrote in her "Thoughts, "What can I do to please Mamá? I want to please her, but everything I do is wrong. It was better when Tío Fernando came every day. He doesn't come anymore, only Mamá Lucita still comes every day. She told us a story yesterday about Saint Genevieve, who saved Paris from Attila's Huns with her prayers. Saint Genevieve decided to be a nun when she was seven. Should I be a nun?"

In mid-summer the whole family took a vacation. Don Porfirio loaned them his private railroad car to take them to Lake Chapala. At the station the Presidential guard stood stiffly at attention, ogling Alicia out of the corners of their eyes. The two round mounds of her breasts showed no matter how she tried to hide them. At their cousins' home on the lake, Papá drew funny pictures of dolphins and mermaids, which they tacked up on the veranda wall, and when the family rowboat sank with his weight, he sent their cousin a funeral wreath.

The mimosa trees replenished their blossoms, then scattered yellow flowerets along the crushed red stone paths in the garden. Hailstones battered the gallery one day and an unseasonable freeze bruised the winter roses. By December the cloudless sky was an intense blue and the sun shone with a dazzling light, making mundane objects look as though they had been touched by a fairy's wand.

Two weeks before Christmas Cristina gave birth to a beautiful baby girl whose alabaster skin promised to yield a good crop of freckles. Antonio was adamant in proclaiming Alicia and Antonieta perfectly proper godparents.

"I am not against trying to make Christians of our children. I am against the bundle of money the poor godparents have to lay out for the honor. Damn it, Cristina, a fancy dress, engraved invitations, a gold medal for each guest? It's an unmitigated imposition!"

The baby was named Amelia. The christening dress was unpacked for the fourth time. With only the immediate family gathered around, Antonio and Cristina knelt on their prayer bench in the oratorio. While the priest intoned the ritual of baptism, Antonio prayed: "Oh Lord, please retire this christening dress. It owes us nothing."

CHAPTER VI

The Castellanos' small parlor was rigid and uninviting. Cristina sat down and felt the hard edge of the gilt Louis XVI settee where the padding had worn thin and the cheap gold had worn off. José's message had said it was an urgent matter; he had begged her to come. Where the devil was he?

Claustrophobia constricted her in this room. Anger, fear, old anxieties dwelled here. Cristina's eyes were drawn to a black streak on the faded wallpaper, where a flame flickered in devotion to a perennially young, starched little saint who had always looked down from her gilded pedestal in judgment. Her eyes turned to the opposite wall where her own picture hung above a framed diploma from Madame Pomier's exclusive school for girls. Her gaze lingered. How proud she had felt. First in her class! No thanks to her father. The old anger welled up. Her father with his myopic view of the needs of others. He had never contributed one cent to her education! He said he had no money to educate a daughter. She knew the reason. She had seen it once, when a strange young man came to the house looking for him, claiming to be a relative from Oaxaca, not admitting that the relationship was so close that he was a carbon copy of her father.

She could hear pans clattering in the kitchen. The old servant had let her in. She would wait five more minutes. Involuntarily, she stared at the wedding picture on the marble-top table in the center of the room: father stern, mother so young. Since earliest memory it had resided on the same table, on the same doily. Cristina straightened her soutache-edged waistcoat. *She* had found a way out of Oaxaca! A way to Madame Pomier's school. At ten, she already knew what she had to do. Her savior was a distant uncle, an Englishman who had married a Mejía from Oaxaca. A widower and childless, she became his protégée, his obsession. She and the family moved to the city...and into his house. He bought her a horse and taught her to ride as regally as a queen; he bought her a piano and paid for lessons. She learned English and French and was invited to the homes of people with money and position, accompanied by her dignified "Uncle Robert." When she was sixteen he died, leaving the house to her. Antonio had never intervened in the matter of her house. When they were married, she rented it and passed the rent money on to her mother.

Was that what José wanted to see her about? Had he found out?

The front door was thrust open. José rushed over and grasped his sister's hand. "Cristina! I was detained at the theater. Sorry. Mamá's not home yet?"

"No." Cristina sat erect. "What is so urgent, José, that she cannot hear?"

José pulled up a straight caned-back chair and took both his sister's hands in his. "This is very painful for me to confess." He searched her eyes. "But you are the only one I can turn to."

She felt his fingernails dig into her hands.

"Cristina, I may have to go to jail."

"Holy Mother of God! What have you done?"

"Nothing bad. It's just bad luck. I invested in the stock market, a sure tip. Financial experts were saying the crisis was over."

His sister's eyes revealed no emotion.

"How could I tell that the stock market in New York would take another plunge? I had to sell short."

She pulled her hands free, lips pressed tight. He could feel her anger rise.

"The truth is, I had to borrow money to pay for the stock."

In the Shadow of the Angel

"Who loaned you the money?"

"Wealthy ranchers."

"With what collateral?"

"A friend's recommendation." José got down on his knees. "Cristina, Cristinita, I must have the money by Friday or I go to jail." He buried his head in her lap.

Cristina felt the clammy moisture on her hands and tried to steel herself. Was it really the stock market or his infernal card games? She ran her fingers through the wavy chestnut hair and asked, "How much?"

José sat back, his face pale. "A thousand pesos in round numbers."

"What!"

With trembling fingers José lit a cigarette and waited. He had always been Cristina's confidante. He knew her weaknesses, her insecurities, her mounting frustrations as she felt youth slipping away. He knew her vanities, her self-centeredness, her need to be admired by men, her fear of poverty. And he knew that Fernando was the new occupant of her house.

"This is madness." Cristina stood up.

"I've got to have it!"

"Three hundred. I might be able to get three hundred." Cristina started toward the door.

José grasped her arm and turned her around to face him. "They are demanding it all." He embraced her tightly and whispered, "Don't fail me, Cristina. I beg you."

"Have I ever failed you?" Her voice was controlled but her eyes were blazing.

José helped his sister into the waiting carriage and stood looking after it until it turned the corner.

Night had fallen without his notice. Antonio turned on the lights in the studio and returned to his desk. Absorbed in his work, he did not hear the soft knocking until it became insistent.

"Come in. Come in."

"I'm sorry to disturb you, Antonio, but I must talk to you."

"Of course, reina, what is it?"

Not waiting for him to pull up the side chair, Cristina perched on the edge of a drafting stool and took a deep breath.

"It's Papá's house. Mamá told me it was leaking and I went to inspect it this morning. The beams have rotted. The whole roof has to be replaced in the back area. Thinking of Juana..."

"I'll take a look at it, reina. I can spare some of my boys next week. It won't fall in before then."

"Mamá would be mortified if she knew I had bothered you with repairs to her house. That's Papá's responsibility."

Antonio grunted.

"José got an estimate from the masons who are working on the new dressing rooms at the theater. They would install new beams and tile the roof for three hundred pesos. Does that sound outrageous?"

"No. But, my God, Cristina, before you contract unskilled masons, I want to take a look myself."

"José can handle it. I don't want Mamá to know." Cristina lowered her head and studied her fingers. "I have come to ask you for a loan," she said quietly.

Antonio folded his arms and leaned back in his chair. Then he stood up. "All right. Have it your way." He crossed to the safe and counted out thirty gold coins. "Three hundred pesos is a lot of money, Cristina. This is not a loan to your family. I give this to you for your peace of mind."

Cristina put her arms around her husband's neck. "Thank you, Antonio. You are a generous man. And I am a fortunate woman." She kissed his cheek. "Please don't mention this to ... anybody."

"I shall respect your wish. Now, there is a happy subject I would like to talk to you about. Sit down." Antonio pulled up the side chair. "I have to go to Europe. Soon. I had a letter from the foundry in Florence. They are ready to cast the bronzes for the Monument. Some of them haven't been ordered yet and the column is going up rapidly. I also have work to do in Paris. I am thinking of writing to Jean Joyeaux and asking him to rent a house for us in Paris, near the Luxemburg Gardens." Antonio's eyes lighted as he saw the surprised look in Cristina's. "I am inviting the whole family to keep me company."

Dumbfounded, Cristina stared at her husband. "I am overwhelmed. There's so much to think about, to prepare. The baby is only two months old. I don't know if she should be moved yet ... the trip, the cold winter. I assume you would stay through the winter."

"Eight months at least. Maybe a year. Think it over, reina. I want you with me." Antonio raised her chin and kissed her on the mouth.

Cristina closed the door softly as she left.

Antonio clasped his hands behind his head and tipped the heavy oak chair back as far as it would go. A smile played across his lips. How old was he when he had first seen Paris? Seventeen.

René Labadie had been the bearer of the news that his father could no longer keep him in the English Boarding School. He was to come home at the end of the semester. Thumbing through a folder of sketches he made when school excursions took them to the city, his uncle had commented: "You belong in Paris. Study architecture. You will learn French easily. I have an aunt in Bordeaux. I can ask her about who could put you up." He had written down her address. "I'll speak to your father."

Without bidding the headmaster, or anyone, farewell, Antonio crossed the Channel. Bordeaux was another world: sun, freedom, an open road, the city alive! The Labadies lived in a working-class area where the public school was a forum for fights and introductions to girls. Gone were the stiff English upper lip and the tasteless food. After a year stacking wine cases, he bade the generous relatives goodbye and boarded the train for Paris. The year was 1871. Antonio remembered it well: soldiers marching with Prussian precision, the siege of the city a bitter encounter. It was the beginning of his abhorrence for Germans and love for all things French.

With only enough money to cover the entrance fee, he had enrolled in the School of Architecture in Beaux Arts. Letters from home were few. His father, it seemed, had cut him off completely, forcing him to work.

At eighteen he had assumed Rivas height and Mercado corpulence.

He had not lacked for work: he had stacked cases of wine in Bordeaux, bottled wine in the Loire, became a free wrestler, a carnival barker. He and Jean had hired themselves out as gigolos to see the follies. Jean, now a senator!

Antonio chuckled, remembering a special incident, told and retold until it had become a family legend:

"Hey, you big one, you want to wrestle? One gold *louis* if you throw the bear."

He and his friends had stopped in front of the Cathedral on Saint Germaine Boulevard where street performers passed the hat. A crowd had gathered around an improvised ring, where a gypsy held an enormous brown bear by a chain. He had no takers. The bear stood up, challenging.

"A gold Louis!" The gypsy shouted. "Go on, Antonio, you can do it!" his friends prodded. "We'll eat!"

He had stepped over the rope and looked the huge Siberian creature in the eye. The instant the chain was released, two menacing paws jabbed out toward his neck. He had ducked the blow and locked his foot around a solidly planted hairy leg and yanked. Caught off guard by his bi-ped opponent, the bear fell hard onto his back, all four paws flailing the air. The gypsy had no recourse but to pay.

Rocking in his swivel chair, Antonio laughed aloud. In the annals of bohemia he was thereafter known as *el oso*.

Those first years he had wondered if he belonged in Mexico. He remembered the difficult decision: "Mother is very ill. Her only wish is to see you before she dies," Elena had written. He had taken the first boat home.

A contented smile crossed Antonio's face and he dozed.

It was Mamá Lucita who noticed that the dragon was missing.

"What happened to the little jade dragon, son?" she asked Antonio during a lull at the table. "I noticed this morning that it is missing."

"What do you mean?" Antonio directed his attention to his mother-in-law. The dragon was part of a collection of treasured objects brought over from the Orient on Spanish galleons when his grandfather was

Captain of the port of San Blas, on the Pacific coast of what was then the Province of Tepic, New Spain.

"I was looking in the cabinet while we were waiting. You know how I love your treasures, and I couldn't find the little dragon."

Antonio looked down the table and fixed his attention on Cristina. "Do you know anything about this?"

"It's only a passing remark, son," Mamá Lucita said haltingly. "I may have been mistaken."

"I noticed it was missing, too," Alicia ventured. "Yesterday. When I was showing Miss Chavez our treasures. We're studying about ships."

Beto stared at the pinched face of Cristina's father in the baroque mirror across the table. The old skinflint had been collecting a government stipend for years as an alternate delegate from Oaxaca without, of course, having ever been called to attend a congressional session. Had they cut him off?

"The cabinet is locked, isn't it, Cristina? You have the key." Antonio's voice rose. "Well?"

Cristina contemplated the transparency of her Limoges coffee cup, a flush spreading up her neck. "It was stolen," she said at last. "I did not intend to make a public scene of the issue. It may be in the National Pawn Shop by now." She looked up at stunned faces. "I was dusting the cabinet, as I do periodically, and left it open when I was called out of the room for a moment. I realized when I put all the objects back that the dragon was missing." She bit her lips. "And so was the new housemaid I had just hired."

"I'll have her arrested!" Antonio bellowed.

"Why would a housemaid know it was such a valuable piece?" Beto interjected. "It's worth at least a thousand pesos."

"It's not the price," Antonio said. "I want it back! Who recommended the girl?"

The flush crept up to Cristina's cheeks. "It's useless." She swallowed. "She came to the gate. I felt sorry for her and took her on trial. It was her first day… I have no address for her." Flustered, she drew her handkerchief out from her sleeve and patted her nose. "I am sorry. It was my own negligence." She pushed back her chair and stood up. "If you will excuse me."

Antonio watched his wife leave the room. She knew more than she was willing to admit. He addressed Mamá Lucita. "Why didn't José come today? Where is he?"

"He is out of town, son. Some matter of the theater. He has been gone a week."

Cristina paced up and down the dingy waiting room. The office of the lawyer Manuel had unearthed for her was in a cramped old building in the Merced area. It had been thirty minutes since the man had closed himself in with that clerk from the court, a balding, stringy-haired type with a limp handshake. She hated limp handshakes. Manuel had found this lawyer. He had assured her that if anyone could bribe a judge this man could; he had access to the highest courts and was known to succeed even when the defendant was flagrantly guilty. Her eyes burned, her head was on fire. She wanted to scream!

Cristina stooped and put her eye against a cracked panel in the heavy door. Shiny, pointed shoes scratched a pant leg by his desk. He was saying something to the other man. Could he be making out the *amparo*? That's all she wanted from him, a writ of habeas corpus to get José out of jail. Thank God the press had not gotten hold of the sordid story. She had had nightmares about the headlines: "Fraudulent stock deal. Antonio Rivas Mercado's brother-in-law accused!" Leonor would revel in the scandal.

A chair scraped inside. Cristina whirled back to the waiting room. The door opened and the wiry lawyer approached her, his eyes twitching.

"Please sit down, Señora." He pointed to a sagging leather chair.

"I prefer to stand. Well, what did you arrange?"

"It is no use."

The blood drained from Cristina's face.

"There have been some changes and the judge is not easy to persuade. Your brother's accusers are powerful ranchers. Their only terms for release are that he pay back all the money."

"How much?"

"All of it."

"How much?"

"You do not know, Señora?"

"I wouldn't ask if I did," she snapped, lying, wishing to hear the amount from him. "How much?"

"One thousand two hundred pesos gold. I have the voucher." The lawyer's right eye twitched rapidly. "Plus a small gratification for my services."

Her throat constricted. For a moment she could not breathe. Maybe José had money hidden away. Or he had been afraid to tell her the whole amount. "I can give you eight hundred tomorrow but we need sixty days to pay the balance. Persuade them!"

Cristina slammed the door on her way out, dislodging a large chunk of plaster. To think that she had sold the dragon for five hundred!

Antonio came bounding up the steps, waving an armful of newspapers, which he plopped down on the rattan table in front of Beto. Still huffing, he blurted, "You can stop worrying, viejo. Read this headline. Everybody in town is talking about it!"

Beto grabbed the top sheet and in an incredulous voice read, "DIAZ DECLARES HE WILL RESIGN IN 1910. I don't believe it. WILL WELCOME OPPOSITION PARTIES. It's a joke!"

"It's a bombshell! I brought you three papers and the 'Extra'. Here, this one has a translation of the full interview with Creelman."

"Who's Creelman?"

"An American reporter who came down here to interview Díaz last year. This is a direct translation from the foreign press."

"You mean it has taken a year for the news to reach Mexico!" Beto's eyes scanned the front page. He read at random, quoting Díaz: "'I believe that democracy is the only just principle of government. I received this government from the hands of a victorious army, when the country was divided, and have patiently waited for the day when the Republic of Mexico would be ready for democracy.' Demagoguery. Pure demagoguery!" He picked up another paper. "More about democracy. The Yankees like that word. Listen to this: 'My fear is that the principles of democracy have not been deeply enough implanted in the conscience of our people...The Mexican is concerned over his personal rights but not enough over the rights of others. He cares about his privileges but not his duties.' That's an honest statement!"

"The old man has publicly stated that he is going to resign, Beto. That's the news."

"It sounds to me like words meant for outside consumption. Don't you remember, it was at the beginning of last year that the American press began to question his internal policies. The big investors were worried about the old man dropping dead with no one responsible groomed to fill his shoes."

"You're a hard-headed skeptic, Beto, and getting worse. Look, it's been published all over Mexico now. The old man is committed."

"I tell you," Beto replied, "there's only a thin cover over that cesspool that has been festering for thirty-two years. It may explode before the elections next year. Or the old man will start a brushfire of his own as an excuse to stay in power. You don't understand power, Antonio. Dictators don't 'resign'."

"I have always admired your gift for observation, Beto, but let me tell you why I don't share your concern for that cesspool you always bring up. Because I am a patrón. The Mexican has always obeyed the voice of authority. He expects the patrón to take the responsibility. His patrón will bury a child or buy a cow or pay for the doctor, take him back when he's been off drunk for a week. And the number one patrón is Don Porfirio. If he turns over the reins to a man like Pepe Limantour, another strong, authoritative patrón will swiftly step into his shoes. It's the damned intellectuals and radicals who wave the flag and cry for justice. And the *peon* they defend so vociferously doesn't give a damn about politics! He only cares about filling his stomach."

"Agreed," Beto said. "I agree completely. The *peon* doesn't care about modern plumbing, either," he added with a grin. "I noticed that new carpenter you hired prefers to piss against the back wall. Why waste your money on bathrooms, Antonio?" Beto drew his chair closer to the table. "I shall read every word and ferret out every ambiguous lie the old man has invented. By the way, Sabina advised me that Cristina wishes to be advised as soon as you got home."

Antonio found Cristina in the small family room. She put down her crochet and kissed him. "I am glad you're early," she said. "The baby is asleep."

Antonio sank down in the ample *bergére* and waited. She looked as though she had been crying. She had been nervous lately, complained of headaches. God forbid she was pregnant!

"You wanted to see me?" he ventured.

"I have thought over the trip to Paris, Antonio. I cannot go."

"Why!"

"It's the baby."

"We'll take Sabina or Pancha, and I had planned to hire a governess for the girls and Mario."

"The doctor advised me against it."

"Who? Vasquez Gomez?"

"No. A new doctor who specializes in children. He said that little Memelita has a respiratory condition, which could prove dangerous if she caught a bad cold or influenza in these tender months. Haven't you noticed how her breathing is raspy sometimes?"

"I hadn't." Antonio was silent, disappointment painted across his face. "I can't argue with a doctor." He struggled up from the chair and kissed his wife. "You have made a responsible decision. I can only admire you for it." He turned to leave.

"Wait! I haven't finished. I would like to propose a substitute."

"Who?"

"Alicia."

"I couldn't take the responsibility! I will be spending days in the foundries and traveling…"

"Blanche Joyeaux has no children. And you had mentioned a governess. It would mean so much to her, Antonio. Alicia is thirteen. She'll be coming out in two years; she needs to be exposed to more than these walls."

"Do you think she would like to go, alone."

"She will be thrilled, ecstatic! I am already jealous."

"Wait..."

"Please say it is settled, Antonio. It grieves me to the depths of my soul that I can't go, but with Alicia along I won't worry about losing you to the charms of some French hussy."

Beaming her most enchanting smile, Cristina stood up and embraced her husband. Later, in a few days, she would suggest Antonieta. Antonieta should go as a companion for Alicia. To take the strain off him. There was time to convince him, six weeks. And for her? Perhaps a year of freedom to work out her...problems. Eyes now bright with contentment, she kissed him on the cheek.

Antonio looked at his beautiful wife with sympathy and admiration. Cristina was strong, he told himself.

CHAPTER VII

1909

As the train snaked from the high plateau down to the luxuriant tropics, a salty breeze pricked the girls' nostrils. There it was. The ocean!

"It smells like the tarpaper on our Paris box."

"More like mulch in the garden and a wet horse and ..."

"Oil tankers," Antonio said. "See those boats over there. They carry oil to Europe. And look at that dock." He pointed straight ahead. "That's where I watched them unload Maximilian's golden carriage."

It was true. It was hard to imagine Papá as a little boy of eleven being shipped off by himself to England. 1864 was ancient history. But it was here, that very year, that Maximilian arrived to meet his destiny and Papá left to find his.

Veracruz was hot and humid, the port teeming with activity and the docks crowded with vessels flying exotic flags. Vendors stuck like flies to the arriving city girls, offering little boxes made of seashells and tempting them with watery coconut sherbet.

"There's the ship, *La Navarre*!" Antonieta pointed wildly, knocking off her hat. She shook out limp curls, laughing, letting the sea breeze blow through the long tresses.

A deep sound like a giant frog made them hurry along the wharf to the mooring where the *La Navarre* lay at anchor. The ship was a sparkling white mammoth, rolling slightly with the waves that washed up against the dock. Fascinated, they watched trunks and valises disappear up ramps; huge metal claws swooped down and swung heavy crates up in the air. Brown bodies naked to the waist and sailors in impeccable white moved everywhere. Suddenly, puffs of black smoke spewed from the funnels, and the deep-throated horns brought everyone rushing to the boarding ramp.

As the steamship got under way, the girls stood on each side of their father at the railing, watching the shore dip up and down, growing smaller and smaller. Home already seemed far away. Soon the whole world was ocean, with the land but an image stored in the mind.

On the twenty-first day, they reached St. Nazaire. April 1, 1909, was gray and chilly.

They stood on the Quai d'Orsay, two impeccable young girls dressed in matching white dresses and white dusters, straw hats anchored to their curls. Standing between them, Antonio firmly held their white-gloved hands while he searched over the heads of the crowd for his old bohemian friend. Shivering in their spring attire, the girls peered at strange faces, feeling self-conscious and scrutinized by people clothed in subdued colors and warm scarves who walked in orderly fashion toward the exit signs. No hawkers here, no beggars. Above restrained voices, they heard Papá shout, "Jean! Jean Joyeux, over here. Here we are!"

A dapper gentleman with a handlebar mustache accompanied by a small, skinny lady detached himself from the crowd. Her long navy blue cape swung in martial cadence and a chignon bounced on top of her head as she walked beside the Senator with purposeful strides.

"She must be the governess," Alicia whispered.

"*Tengo mucho gusto en conocerlas*," the lady enunciated in a surprisingly deep voice and kissed each of the girls on the cheek.

"You have not shrunk, Antonio," the Senator said, reaching up to kiss his friend on both cheeks.

"Jean, these poor little *americaines* must be freezing in those flimsy dresses," the lady said in rapid French. "We can talk in the auto. Bring it around, dear. *Vite*."

"I am impressed with your Spanish, my dear Blanche," Antonio said, smiling.

"Ah. I took eight lessons at Berlitz to prepare myself to receive your *petites americaines*." A bright smile lit her plain face. "*Bienvenidas, señoritas.*"

The girls curtsied, speechless.

The Renault turned down the Boulevard St. Michel. Rounding the Luxemburg Gardens they reached the Rue d'Assas.

"There it is! I hope you will find your new home comfortable, my dears."

"Tante Blanche," as the girls were instructed to call this wiry energetic lady, had arranged every detail. Their new home on the left bank was the lower floor of a Romanesque mansion down the street from the Joyeux' own ample house and a block from the Luxemburg Gardens. An extra full bath had been added at Papá's expense and a cramped little room upstairs had been rented to accommodate a maid. A cook had not been engaged because Papá planned to visit every *bistrot* in Paris.

Tante Blanche took vigorous charge of her *petites americaines* and they soon settled into a rigid routine under her pragmatic tutelage.

Out went the hair bows and pretty dresses they had brought from Mexico. Tante Blanche dressed them in severe tailored skirts and jumpers, gray during the week and navy blue on Sundays. Out went the pretty patent leather pumps. They learned to lace clumsy brown boots. "Practical and proper footwear," Tante Blanche unconditionally declared.

"She's too bossy," Alicia grumbled. "The other day I heard her tell a friend she expected her *petites americaines* to be barbarians. Well, I am not a barbarian and I am not petite. I'm thirteen!"

"Pooh. She's fair. I like her," Antonieta countered.

Madame Joyeux was quick to note Antonieta's agility and singular grace. She soon found a nickname for the tall child with the melancholy face and remarkable, expressive eyes who swung around posts and did pirouettes along railings. "*Ma petite singe,* my little monkey, expressed an esteem that Antonieta valued.

Tardiness was an unpardonable offense. The girls rose early to struggle with the ugly boots in order to report on time at Tante Blanche's "Solarium," so-called because it housed two anemic potted plants. Their French history lesson began at exactly eight forty-five under the instruction of Tante Blanche herself.

"In France, we are born with history. It is a rich inheritance to which we owe a debt, and a future for which we are responsible. *Tonton* Jean can trace his immediate family back five hundred years."

"Mexico wasn't even Mexico then!" Antonieta blurted.

"That is why America is the New World, my dear. As for your other classes, *Science Naturelle* you will learn in the botanical gardens, *Literature* will be imparted in a class at the *Bibliotheque*. *Mathematique* I will leave to your father."

At ten o'clock Miss Louise, their English governess, rescued them and was issued the program for the day: museums, exhibits and walking tours completed the schedule. At some point during the day they would stop in at the nearby church of St. Suplice for a fast genuflection, keeping their word to Mamá Lucita. Nearly every day they took their noon meal in a neighborhood restaurant called Le Fleurus, accompanied by Miss Louise, who, like Miss Etta, always wore her hat. The owner of the restaurant functioned as cashier, his wife as the cook and Eugene, the waiter, was a bookmaker who made his books, he told them, at the racetrack.

The river Seine held a special fascination for Antonieta. "The buildings look so solid in the water, until a boat goes by. Then they are all jelly," she explained to Miss Louise.

One day the towers of Notre Dame were reflected in the water; gargoyles stared up at her from the river, shaking apart then coming back together again. "Sometimes I feel like that, solid on the outside but all jelly on the inside," she wrote in her diary. "Even home seems like a reflection. Here in France they don't know where Mexico is."

By the end of May, Antonio had returned from the foundry in Florence where his Winged Victory was being cast. The smaller ornamentation was being cast in Paris. Blazing furnaces turned out oak leaf clusters, acanthus garlands, brass scales, lanterns, railings, urns. Visits to the foundries made the girls feel in touch with home. Wednesday afternoons Antonio set aside for a personally conducted tour of the Louvre, visiting a different gallery each week with his two eager students.

"The primary function of art is to create beauty," he lectured. "You do not ask an ancient Greek statue whether it is moral or virtuous or noble. You contemplate it and let its beauty permeate your soul. There is enough ugliness in the world. Talent should not be wasted imitating it."

As soon as they were installed in Paris, Antonio had begun to look up "his boys." Most had been forced to take menial jobs, living in the most miserable of circumstances, if not frank misery. They frequented cheap cafes instead of classrooms. He found Enrique Freyman clerking in an antique bookstore on the Rue Jacob. Enrique was a bright student, the son of a young Mexican mother and an old German-Jewish father who had migrated to the remote province of Tepic, Mexico, during Benito Juárez' rule. Level-headed, ambitious and possessed of an innate recognition of talent, Enrique had attached himself to an inner circle of artists and intellectuals whose dreams of fame were still shapeless visions.

"And where is Diego hiding?" Antonio asked his scholarship student. Enrique gave him the address.

On a Wednesday afternoon Alicia and Antonieta were settled into a cab and driven with their father to a neighborhood behind the central market where the rancid smell of spoiled produce, piled up on the streets and in open carts, permeated the air. The driver wound through a maze of alleys before he found the address. The stairway was dark and Diego's atelier three flights up.

A birdlike lady greeted them with the gracious manners of someone who did not belong in this neighborhood. Behind her a bulky figure, whose threadbare pants were covered with paint stains, brandished a gaudy carved Mexican cane.

"Maestro! I thought it was a bill collector. Come in!"

The lady's name was Angelina Beloff. She found two stools for the girls to sit on and lit a flame under the kettle.

"I am eager to hear about your progress, Diego. Has Paris been a good teacher?" Antonio quizzed his old student.

"It introduced me to the Impressionists, thank God. My first encounter was with Cezanne."

"You met him?"

"No. I saw a painting in the Galerie Vollard. It was Cezanne's. I stared at that painting for hours, mesmerized, as though the walls of my soul were being scraped of old stucco. The art dealer put up two other Cézannes for my benefit." Diego's eyes were glazed. "Cezanne's impact sent me to bed with a fever for several days."

Antonio withheld a smile.

A lively dissertation on the new art movements flowed in Diego's fluent, expressive French, peppered with idioms to impress his old teacher.

"Is San Carlos teaching these new techniques?" Diego baited its director.

"You know what we teach. Fundamentals. Composition, perspective, balance." Antonio cast a benign glance at his interrogator. "A solid foundation from which an artist can turn in new directions. I notice you took this to heart," he commented, pointing to a wall full of landscapes and portraits. "I see a touch of El Greco and Sorolla and, of course, a strong influence of the Impressionists."

"That's three years ago. Some I painted two years ago, my work in Spain. I hung the collection hoping to find a gallery to take it."

"What about an exhibit?"

"It's impossible for an unknown painter to be sponsored, to ever have an exhibit," Diego declared with some bitterness. "Masters of the Academy of Art bestow their favors on pupils who adhere strictly to the old precepts of classic art. But there is a new, more adventurous generation pushing to the foreground. Have you seen the Cubists, maestro?"

"I have no interest in the Cubists. A fad at best. It is not serious art."

"Angelina, the kettle is boiling. Serve the young ladies some tea and a cognac for the maestro. He may need it." Diego turned to the easel and flung off the cloth covering his painting. "Observe my new style!"

Antonio said nothing.

Antonieta gaped at the painting. It was a horror! There was a nose where an eye should be. She lowered her head and watched a cockroach walk across the floor. Finally her father broke the silence.

Facing his former student, the oracle spoke. "You have talent, Diego. A God-given gift. How is it possible, then, that you are painting such absurdity? Do you call that contrived distortion art? It's trash, my boy. Why do you squander your talent on such idiocy?"

Diego's face darkened. "It provides us with food," he answered. "It's the only painting which is selling today. My friend, Picasso, is doing very well with Cubism."

"But it's an ugly art. Does it fill your spirit? Do you even like it?" Antonio pointed to the wall. "You have some fine paintings here, Diego. They would sell in Mexico, bring a good price." He looked at the young artist whose eyes seemed to protrude even more in a gaunt face. "How would you like to go back to Mexico next summer? I believe San Carlos should sponsor an exhibition by Diego Rivera for the Centennial Celebration."

Diego stuck out his lower lip, still belligerent.

"I think you should accept," Angelina suggested softly.

"Heads of state and important people from around the world will be there," Antonio continued. "You have been in Europe three years. A touch of home will stir up that well of inspiration."

Diego nodded his head. He didn't speak for a long moment. Then: "Thank you for the offer, maestro. I accept."

As Antonio walked past a table, a book fell to the floor. He stooped to pick it up and noted the title, "Das Kapital."

Sunday was theater day: La Gaite Lyrique, where operettas were performed, the Chatelet for light farces, L'Odeon and the Comedie Francaise where they saw Sarah Bernhardt perform in "Camille". The legendary actress seemed like an old lady next to the handsome young duke but she spoke in captivating, modulated tones, a theatrical voice. Antonieta would never forget the experience. The duke made love to the dying old lady with such passion that the play was indeed a tragedy in Alicia's eyes.

One Saturday night they went to the Paris Opera House to see the ballet performance. A new vista—beyond fantasy, beyond dreams—opened before Antonieta's eyes. White tulle billowing, beautiful bodies bending, dipping, arms gracefully moving to the full, symphonic variations of a hidden orchestra. On their toes, the ballerinas danced in perfect unison, then executed great leaps and whirling spins across the stage. With total ease they floated. Oh, how they floated! Could there be anything more beautiful in the world?

That night, possessed by the vision, Antonieta hung onto the bedpost and practiced arching her feet, higher, higher until she could stand on her toes.

"You're shaking the bed," Alicia complained. "Stop it and let me sleep!"

Humming the music, the little ballerina persisted until, at three in the morning, she spun around the room and fell exhausted on the bed.

At Sunday morning breakfast with the Joyeux, Alicia announced in a loud voice: "This child would not let me sleep. She can dance on her toes. Without shoes, she can dance on her toes!"

Straightaway, Tante Blanche asked Antonio's permission to enroll his young dance enthusiast in the ballet school of Monsieur Soria, the ballet master for the Paris Opera.

On a warm June morning, Tante Blance escorted her *petite singe*, dressed in a gray pleated skirt and middy blouse, to the front entrance of the school near the church of La Madeleine.

"I feel all wobbly inside," Antonieta confessed to Tante Blanche, who squeezed her hand and gave her a reassuring hug.

At the end of the foyer, a window looked into the practice salon. Here, a tall wraithlike figure was banging a cane on the floor. Young ballerinas lined up, twirled across the room, bowed, and tripped off.

"We must hurry," Tante Blanche said, marching off down the corridor to the director's office.

"I have an appointment with Monsieur Soria," she announced to the young lady who finally answered her knock. "*Vite, vite*, mademoiselle, don't let him get away!"

Dance master Soria sat behind a simple, mahogany desk, his long hair tousled from the workout. He listened politely to Tante Blanche's laudatory remarks about her protégée, occasionally glancing at the nervous prospective pupil.

"But, Madame, this child has never studied classical dance, and nine is too old," the tall asparagus declared, fluttering his hand to prevent an interruption. "Yes, yes, she plays the castanets and dances *fados,* polkas, Mexican folk dances—all nice little dances. But that is not ballet. The feet must be formed. I cannot take her."

"I think you should see her dance, a little extemporaneous demonstration *n'est ce pas?* We are not asking for a career, only summer school." Tante Blanche rose to her full five feet. "Monsieur the Senator and I are patrons of the Opera. We would be most grateful."

Throwing up his hands in defeat, Monsieur Soria wearily rose and conducted them to the practice salon where the pianist was sorting out sheet music.

"Some practice runs, please Guillaume. Ta-ta-ti ta-ta- ti-ti. The girl will improvise.»

The jelly in Antonieta's stomach stopped shaking. She had never wanted anything so much. Tante Blanche sat in a folding chair with a proud smile on her face while Asparagus stood by the piano, arms folded. The erstwhile ballerina removed her hat, then leaned against the wall, removed her shoes and knee socks and stepped out on the parquet floor. The pianist commenced to play.

Antonieta closed her eyes to shut out everything but the music while she stood in first position through the introductory bars. Then she began to move her body and dance, imitating the ballerinas on that magical stage, improvising, first in a small area and then with full abandon, twirling across the room....

«Enough!» The ballet master banged his cane. «You may start Monday morning at ten.»

In August, Antonio interrupted his ballerina's classes to take her and Alicia on a visit to «cousins» in Provence, a family for whom he had deep affection, and they for him. The girls were hugged and kissed and kissed and hugged, submitting even to the effusive embraces of a mustachioed great-aunt. They rode bicycles and ran barefoot through the fields with the grandchildren and played follow-the-leader through vineyards laden with grapes. Their young hosts tried to outdo each other with stories of brave escapades.

«Once at Lake Chapala a giant octopus caught me by the wrist and I bit and bit until his tentacle broke off and I swam away,» Antonieta chimed in.

«You and Jules Verne,» a twelve-year-old boy teased. «Are you so brave?» He threw her to the ground and kissed her on the mouth.

In mid-September, lines of school children began to form throughout Paris. The summer ballet school closed. Pupils who aspired to continue had to take a rigid exam, in the form of a grueling individual performance before a board composed of master Soria and the *premiere* dancers of the Corps of Ballet.

"Do you think I could pass the exam?" Antonieta appealed to Tante Blanche. "I want to take it!"

"You must do what your heart dictates, my dear."

An exercise bar was installed in the solarium. Pale after two weeks of exhausting practice, Antonieta was the last pupil to appear before the board. Tante Blanche waited in the foyer.

Tears dripping down her face, the young aspirant threw her arms around her unswerving champion, dislodging several hairpins from the tight topknot.

"I am admitted," she sobbed. "I am admitted."

To distract Alicia, Antonio took her with him to the studios of the artists who were still working on ornamental details for the Monument. One afternoon they visited the atelier of the young sculptor who had been commissioned to model the bronze door that led to the crypt. The specifications called for a design that would symbolize "the young nation," but the artist had eliminated a dozen attempts. While Antonio studied the new cartoons and outlines sculpted in clay, the artist stared so fixedly at Alicia that a blush traveled up her neck to her cheeks.

"Please turn your profile toward me and don't move," the sculptor requested. He made a rapid sketch and held it out to Antonio. "I have been looking for a perfect classic profile and your daughter has it! You see, it will be presented like a medallion. May she pose for me, *Monsieur?*"

Alicia lowered her beet-red face. She was mortified and flattered.

"It is up to my daughter. What do you say, *linda*? Would you like to be immortal?"

"Yes, Papá, if you think it is not improper."

The weeks flew by. At Christmastime it snowed and the girls pelted everyone in their path with snowballs. By January only the small bronze pieces were left to be molded, polished and crated. Visiting the foundry for the last time, a feeling of pride swept over the girls. Mexico had a history too! On a table across the room from the blazing furnaces stood a model of the Independence Monument. Next to it laid a huge concave pattern of leaves, part of a discarded broken mold.

"Is that from the crown, Papá?"

"Yes. It's Liberty's wreath. See, she holds it in her hand."

"It's gigantic!" Alicia exclaimed.

"My Lady Liberty measures six meters and seventy centimeters," Antonio pronounced. "Do you know that is more than twice as big as 'Winged Victory' in the Louvre?"

It was time to think about packing. They rushed to Madame Gautier to finish the last garments for Mamá's wardrobe for the grand Centennial celebration. There were presents still to buy, friends to bid farewell, and goodbyes to be said to the puppet show in the Luxemburg Gardens, the ice-skating rink at the Hippodrome, one last movie at the Pantheon. Miss Louise confided to them that she and Eugene, the waiter at Le Fleurus, planned to make books together.

Antonieta felt a lump in her throat so big she could hardly swallow when the realization that they were leaving came over her. She danced with new pathos, such passion and grace that Monsieur Soria was certain some tragedy had happened to this little Mexican who had quite captivated his attention.

"I am going back to Mexico next month," Antonieta said simply when he questioned her sad look.

"Ah. I must speak to your father," her beloved master said.

"I will have nothing to do with 'that type'," was Antonio's reply to the ballet master's petition. Blanche, Alicia, and Antonieta raised such a chorus of supplication that Antonio gave in and agreed to receive the "gentleman" in his house. In his heart he feared the meeting might hurt his daughter more than help her.

Monsieur Soria duly arrived, dressed in a long black coat and tall silk hat. The slim man pumped his host's hand with a firm handshake, and sat down, erect and businesslike:

"You have seen your daughter dance." It was a statement.

Antonio nodded.

"She is exceptional, Monsieur. One in a thousand." The dance master leaned forward. "I shall be brief. If you will leave Antonieta in France for five years, in the custody of an honorable family, of course, she will become the *premiere danseuse* of the Paris Opera. I cannot deny the discipline and hard work required to be the best, but upon my honor, Monsieur Rivas, she will be treated with all the care and appreciation she deserves."

Antonio fell silent. After long deliberation he comprehended the magnitude of the offer and the extent of his daughter's talent. He stood up and faced the ballet master who also rose.

Antonieta felt paralyzed. She looked up at her two giants—the Bear and the Asparagus—and waited for the decision which would decide her future.

"It is a heavy burden to be a father," Antonio began. "Our children are loaned to us for a short while only, Monsieur. I have watched Antonieta grow in Paris, her mind expanding to new horizons, her body expressing sensitive nuances in the dance. I am the custodian of this exceptional talent." Antonio's voice faltered. "Antonieta's size is deceiving. She is still a child, not quite ten, too young to be so far away from home. Too young." He took a deep breath. "I thank you for your offer, for your recognition of my daughter's talent, but what you ask of me I cannot concede. Antonieta will return with me to Mexico."

Tears brimmed in Antonieta's eyes and in the eyes of Blanche Joyeux, who had hoped that she might gain a daughter.

The parting at the railroad station was brisk. Tante Blanche's cheek twitched as she hugged and kissed her *petites americaines*. Antonieta turned away quickly, her heart roiled with emotion.

The voyage home was choppy and windy. Papá spent most of the time in his stateroom, calming his queasy stomach with a liqueur called "Kümel." At Santander a noisy group of gypsies boarded the ship; by night the melancholy strains of guitars drifted up from third class. Excitement came in the heavens: Halley's Comet was clearly visible, dragging a long, fiery tail across the night sky.

With Havana far behind them, Antonieta stood alone on deck, gazing at the ocean. She saw a dark speck way out, bobbing and turning and splashing as though in distress. It looked like a log. Or maybe a person... What would it feel like to float in that immense ocean? Just to float away?

A strange attraction filled her, and Antonieta gripped the railing tightly.

Beto slumped in the old rattan chair, his mind mired in disturbing thoughts. What was Villagrande insinuating when he said that Díaz had not only changed his Indian blood for blue blood, but had forgotten that the jungles were full of hidden idols? Were the anarchists armed? He respected Villagrande, but his diatribes against Díaz had become inflamed: land, oppression, injustice. Now it was workers' rights and the ever-exploited Indian. Cortes and Moctezuma again. The never-ending argument: which was worse, the sword or the obsidian dagger? The bookstore had become a meeting place for young radicals who chewed on Díaz for an appetizer. They never mentioned the thirty years of peace under Díaz. How about good public schools, safe highways and a huge surplus in the treasury? Poor, miserable Mexico, spat upon for one hundred years, was praised and envied today!

"You are going to frizzle your brain with all that heat," he had derided Villagrande. "Don Porfirio may have more medals pinned on his chest than a miracle-making village saint, but they were pinned on him by kings and presidents and a czar! Not to mention that Mexico's credit is good throughout the world."

"Prosperity is a thin veneer. Beneath is a termite-chewed nation."

Villagrande always had the last word. Beto slumped deeper in the chair. Díaz had clamped a lid on the press, but could he keep his boot on the populace? Don Porfirio was a dying man surrounded by vultures.

"Time to go, Don Porfirio," he said aloud to the parrot. "Time to go."

The knowing old bird cocked his head in agreement.

A young maid approached. "I have finished cleaning your apartment, Señor, if you care to go in. It is getting windy," she said softly.

"Thank you, *hija*."

"Shall I bring your shawl?"

"No, don't bother." Beto noticed the smooth brown skin, the sweet face, shy brown eyes. And firm breasts. She was a pretty Indian. Young and pretty. "You may go."

His Spanish ancestors would have been fools if they hadn't lain with girls like that. We are all a little mestizo, some whiter, some browner. When would Mexicans stop judging each other by the color of their skins! Color, he told himself, is the curse of the New World.

Beto sat up and heaved a great sigh. La Navarre was due in Veracruz in two weeks. It was time for someone else to go, too.

Beto rose early. With meticulous care, he tied his cravat in a perfect knot and rubbed the rim of his homburg with a chamois skin. He extracted a small leather pouch from his chiffonier drawer and counted out twelve gold coins, a fitting number for his mission.

Unobserved by Cristina, Beto left by the carriage gate and limped painfully up the street to the corner where he boarded a streetcar. He got off downtown and walked the short distance to a narrow, dead-end alley. A carriage clattered down the cobblestones as he stopped at number 7.

Beto studied the facade of the narrow house, unchanged in fifteen years. Unchanged, like Cristina. He pulled the bell cord hard and heard it clang inside. Fernando himself answered the door, surprise immediately replaced by a sardonic smile.

"To what do I owe the honor of this visit, Uncle Beto? Come in."

"Don't feel so honored. I have come to talk business."

"I am never averse to business," Fernando said, smiling graciously.

Beto came to the point, without menacing accusations, without raising his voice. It was a simple business proposition with high penalties for breach of contract. Fernando listened. There was something cruel in those appealingly soft blue eyes that attracted attention, something cynical that revealed a secret resignation to circumstance, a strange irony which permitted him to rise above emotions and attachments, uninvolved.

"Then you agree?" Beto handed his nephew an envelope. "Your ship leaves Veracruz on Saturday. You will find a ticket for the train and passage booked on the Marseille."

Fernando opened the envelope. "A freighter. You might have been more generous." He shrugged his shoulders as though impervious to fate.

"I am glad to see you are of a reasonable mind. Or have I relieved you of a burden?"

"Come, Uncle, I can't help it if women fawn over me. Like you, sir, I long ago learned the art of letting others pay my bills."

Beto counted out the twelve pieces of gold. "Enough to get you to Spain and meet any contingency. May I remind you that if there is a shred of gossip, if you are inclined to brag, I will see to it that your reputation is ruined in Europe and Mexico. Forever!"

Fernando shrugged again. "And may I remind you that I am not responsible for gossip."

The agreement was sealed.

Saturday was a fitting day for Cristina to receive a bouquet of roses and a note of farewell from her lover. Beto himself had dictated the letter and bought the bouquet. Cristina did not take to her bed. The following day, and the day after that, she followed her routine without a glimmer of emotion, without a hair out of place. Reluctantly, Beto had to admire Cristina's resolute determination to bury Fernando and dismiss his absence.

The following week, Beto again walked to the streetcar stop, boarded a tram to the Zócalo and walked over to Villagrande's bookstore.

"Look here, Eduardo, what do you know about this anti-re-electionist fellow, Madero? I heard at the Jockey Club that he has a formidable following."

"He is the candidate of a legally constituted party. He is a wealthy landowner, an idealist, a defender of the underdog. His little book, "The Presidential Succession" seems to have stripped the veneer off Díaz' tight little cadre of *Científicos*. Limantour and the inner circle are jockeying for position, some actually going over to Madero's side." Villagrande took his glasses off the top of his head and put them on. He looked up at Beto. "You know all that. What do you really want to know?"

"Will Madero fight?"

Villagrande pursed his lips. "Madero stands for free elections and peaceful transference of power. The man is a rich landowner. He doesn't have the stomach for revolution. And if he did, the damned Yankees wouldn't allow it! I have reached the sad conclusion, my friend, that it will be elections as usual in July."

CHAPTER VIII
1910

How is it possible, Antonieta wondered, to be gone from home a year and find everything the same? Even her room was exactly as she had left it. Only little Memela had changed. She was a chubby, gurgly little thing, running all over the nursery and the garden, Pancha fast on her heels.

"Can't anyone see that I am different?" she wanted to shout. "And I am ten years old!"

Antonieta played the last chord of the *Vals Triste*, quietly lowered the lid on the keyboard, and strolled slowly out of the music room to the foyer. Undecided what to do, she swayed back and forth on the big brass knob of the banister, then dragged one foot after the other up the stairs to her bedroom.

It was a gloomy afternoon. Nothing to do in this house. If only Chela were here....but she had been enrolled in a French Nuns' school. Antonieta adjusted the long mirror in the rattan frame and stood staring at her full figure. "You will never be beautiful," she told the girl in the mirror. "But you have beautiful hands and legs, and you can dance." She pulled off her blouse and skirt, tucked her petticoat in her bloomers and kicked off her shoes. "You are Mademoiselle Antoinette, *premiere danseuse*!"

With effortless grace she executed a perfect *arabesque*, dissolving into a deep *plié*. Inspired, she began humming, hands elegantly posed, body flowing in the impromptu dance. Three pirouettes brought her up again to the mirror. Banging an imaginary cane she scolded in French:

"Are you in the Corps de Ballet or are you a corpse? Alive, you must be alive and put springs in your feet!"

Suddenly the door was thrown open.

"Antonieta!"

Cristina banged the door shut. "Stop this ridiculous practicing! You're half-naked," she scolded. "Put your clothes on. I want you to come down. We have a guest who has brought her daughter."

Antonieta faced her mother. "Can I have a practice bar put up in the nursery? Please, Mamá. There's plenty of room."

"And I suppose you propose to teach yourself? Forget ballet. There's not a decent classical dance teacher in Mexico."

"Chela says there's a Russian lady...."

"Hurry, do you hear me. I want you downstairs. Now!"

Cristina slammed the door behind her. She felt like striking this rebel child she had produced! Striking somebody! She knew Beto was at the bottom of Fernando's sudden departure, but he would never know the anguish he had caused her, or the tears she had shed. Never!

Antonieta plopped her poetry book on the table in the arbor and cupped her chin in her hands. Tío Beto was still engrossed in the morning paper. "Have you noticed that Miss Etta is wearing the same old hat?"

"What?"

"Nothing." Tío was not listening. He had that preoccupied look again.

"If I were a dead leaf thou mightest bear
If I were a swift cloud to fly with thee...."

Antonieta recited dramatically. "Do you like Shelley, Tío?"

Beto looked over the top of his paper. "I prefer Ruben Darío. Spanish is the language for poetry."

Tío Beto had changed, Antonieta thought. His face looked pinched and the bald spot was bigger under the beret. Impulsively, she got up and hugged her uncle. "I'd better go in and dress now. Guests will be arriving for lunch at two." She lifted the beret and kissed him on the bald spot.

Beto watched her cross the gallery. Childhood clung precariously to her lithe body, he mused. Europe had changed her, revealed a new reality which would soon be too broad in scope for the confines of this garden. Beto slumped down in the chair. Reality was out there, lurking around the corner.

Antonio found Cristina in the dining room arranging freshly cut iris from the garden. He counted twelve places, the usual number for Saturday lunch.

"I forgot to tell you, reina, that I invited a young American engineer to join us today. He's recommended by my good friend, Professor Walker. You know, the man at the University of Michigan who is working on subsoil problems."

"Where can I put him?" Cristina asked, with some irritation. She looked around at the seating arrangement. "How young is this American?"

"Nineteen or twenty, I would guess. Seems he is a schoolmate of some of the Madero boys from up north."

"Oh?" Cristina looked up at her husband, puzzled. "The Maderos? They're rebels! I hope he fits in. I'll seat him next to Alicia so they can speak English."

"Put Antonieta on the other side. I think she is more apt to understand his English. This Blair fellow is from Kentucky."

The American engineer, Albert Blair, was stocky, blond and loquacious. He was filled with wonder at Mexico, he told his host as the guests filed into the dining room. He did not add that his picture of a Mexican as a brown-skinned fellow with a sombrero sleeping beside a cactus plant had been dissolved on this trip.

Seated at the lavish table, Albert turned to the beautiful young girl on his right and cleared his throat: "Señorita Alicia, I lament I cannot speak Spanish......"

"I speak English," Alicia assured him.

Her luncheon partner launched into a rambling discourse: He had come down on the train with his friends, Raúl and Julio Madero. They were going to write a paper on subsoil problems for graduation, from the Houghton School of Mines, in Michigan, from which they would graduate in June.... Mexico City reminded him of London, where he was born, before his father took over the operation of a family coal mine in Kentucky...

Alicia daintily sipped her flower of squash soup, nodding politely from time to time, unable to follow even the thread of the narrative. Kentucky English was a different language, she concluded.

Feeling the impatient eyes of a servant upon him, the American dipped up a round green thing from his soup bowl and felt steam rise in his throat. Fighting a cough, he reached for the water goblet.

A slim hand laid a hard roll next to his plate. "Bread will put out the fire," Antonieta whispered. "The next course is dry soup, but you eat it with a fork." She giggled.

"Thank you exceedingly," Albert managed to utter. He looked at the young girl with the blue hair bow to his left. Two large, friendly brown eyes met his glance. Her name was something French, he remembered. At a loss to follow the conversations in French and Spanish around him, Albert addressed this younger daughter.

"I am very impressed with the monument your father is building," he commented.

"Papa has confronted many problems," Antonieta remarked in her most formal English, and proceeded to give an astonishing engineering recital.

The girl could not be more than twelve. An impressive family, Albert reflected. Even the name Rivas Mercado was impressive. He wished Mexicans put their last name last instead of second. Raúl said that instead of Señor, his host should be addressed by his professional title, *Arquitecto*.

Observing the young engineer, Cristina concluded that he was gauche, not worth cultivating. She dismissed him from her mind.

At four-thirty, the guests rose from the luncheon table.

"I'll show you our family treasures, if you like." Antonieta offered. "That is, if you don't care to join the gentlemen in the library for brandy and a cigar."

"I would be most interested. I accept your offer." He did not add that he had never been in such a mansion and was curious to see the rest. "With your permission, sir," he addressed his host, "Your daughter has offered to show me around."

Antonio patted him on the shoulder. "I entrust you to a true historian. "If the lesson gets too long, join us in the library."

Alone in the sala, Albert could think of nothing to say. "That's a very pretty bow you are wearing. Reminds me of my sister Dorothy. Look, I believe in being direct. I am intrigued by the fact that you have a French name."

"I don't. My name is Antonieta."

"That's French, isn't it?"

"No, it's a Mexican name."

"But you speak French?"

"Of course!"

Antonieta conducted him to the music room, where a Louis XV showcase displayed a priceless collection of Oriental objects.

"Most of these objects belonged to Papá's family. They came over on Spanish galleons. See that ivory crucifix? The dark halls of the Inquisition were replete with saints and crucifixes carved by the heathen in China," she recited grandly.

"Yes, of course." Albert listened attentively as the history lesson continued. Then he asked, "Who plays the piano?"

"I do." Antonieta lifted the lid off the keyboard and struck a chord. "This is my audience." She pointed to the field of photographs dispersed among the embroidered roses of a Spanish *mantilla*.

"Who is this lady?" her guest inquired, pointing to an ornate picture frame.

"My grandmother, Leonor Mercado. She was born in New Orleans and used to go to the slave auctions when she was little."

"You mean, New Orleans, Louisiana, the United States of America?"

"Of course!"

"Lincoln freed the slaves, you know."

"In 1863."

The girl knew her history!

"My grandmother was born in 1823, two years after our Independence."

The history lesson resumed: her great-grandfather had been sent to New Orleans, like an Ambassador, to establish trade. Seemed the Spanish had never allowed their colonies to have outside trade. You had to be rich to be a diplomat because diplomats had to pay their own expenses. From New Orleans he was sent to Belgium…The recital sounded like something well practiced, but Albert was fascinated, both by the recital and the reciter.

"This is my great-grandfather Rivas." Antonieta said, pointing to a faded daguerreotype of a fierce-looking gentleman with long sideburns. "He was the Captain of the port of San Blas who received the Spanish galleons—the queens of the sea, the prey of pirates and of tempestuous nature." She struck another chord. "He unloaded the cargo, charged the Crown's taxes, and filched what he wanted." She looked up and grinned. "You see, business and contraband went hand in hand."

"And who is this gentleman in the clerical robe?"

"A great-uncle. He was a priest. And a hero. He jumped from a tower of the church in Tepic to protest the incursion of the Royalist troops that were chasing Morelos' band. When I was little I used to confuse him with Father Hidalgo."

"Was he another uncle?".

"Father Hidalgo? He is the Father of our Independence! Would you rather take a walk in the garden?"

"No, no, please go on. I'm vitally interested in Mexico. Tell me about this handsome squire."

"That's my grandfather Rivas, my father's father," the young historian replied, and continued the narrative: "Grandfather Rivas joined an English trading firm after Independence which exported various products, including pearls, from the Sea of Cortés. Princess Eugenie of France was jealous of my grandmother's pearls. It's a five-string collar. I'm going to inherit it when I'm older," she added with a toss of her head.

Albert smiled and leaned his elbows on the piano. "If your grandmother doesn't mind, it would please me greatly to hear you play a piece."

Antonieta blushed, suddenly shy. "What would you like to hear?"

"My sister Dorothy plays Chopin. Do you know any Chopin?"

"Do you like this one?" Antonieta began to play.

Albert watched her hands move across the keyboard, astounded by the shading and ardor she gave to the *Polonaise*. He watched the blue hair bow bob up and down when she struck loud chords, and her eyes soften with long runs of the melody. He wondered if many Mexicans were as remarkable as this young girl.

Before she went to sleep, Antonieta thought about the blond American with the funny accent. He was fired with enthusiasm for Mexico, but had talked incessantly about Mr. Madero, who wanted to help the poor. Maybe there were no poor people in the United States.

Observing the early morning caller from his station in the arbor, Beto was surprised to see Dr. Vasquez Gomez descend from the carriage. The rotund, balding man seemed to bounce up the stairs. Joining Antonio at the gallery landing, the two brothers greeted their unexpected visitor.

"Don Antonio, Don Alberto, it's good to see the both of you. Forgive the early call but I come on an urgent matter."

"Is someone gravely ill?" Antonio asked. "Please come into the anteroom."

"Thank you. To put your mind at rest, this visit is entirely in the interest of the health of the nation." The doctor smiled engagingly and entered the anteroom with his hosts.

"Sit down, please," Antonio invited his friend.

"I shall come to the point. The country stands on the brink of an insurrection. Rebellions are festering all over the nation, there's talk of revolution. Don Porfirio's jails can no longer hold the opposition. I'm sure you agree that revolution would be disastrous for all of us, rich and poor alike. I'm an anti-revolutionist. As you know, I am on the ballot as Vice-President with Madero. Our platform advocates peaceful change of government. We want to avoid revolution at all costs."

"You believe it's that serious, Doctor?" Antonio asked. "It's my impression that Díaz has already defeated the opposition. Ramón Corral has been named Vice-President, and it's only two weeks till elections."

"My very point. Francisco Madero has been arrested in San Luis Potosí and unconstitutionally held in jail."

"I saw that in the paper," Beto said. "The report accused him of defying the authorities and inciting rebellion."

"Propaganda, Beto. Madero is not a rabble-rouser. He's a man of wealth, culture, education; a man, above all, of courage and principle. He's gambling his wealth and his life to restore the power of this country into the hands of a successor called Law and Justice! Our demand is for free elections. Nothing more."

Beto watched his brother playing with his watch chain, assimilating what he was hearing.

"And what would you have us do?" Antonio finally asked.

"Endorse our cause. As patriotic Mexicans, as men respected in our society, as men of intelligence, I come to solicit your support. Just sign this petition demanding that Madero be released from jail".

Antonio stood quietly, contemplating the document. His mind flashed back to the siege of Paris in 1870, a young Antonio, running, running for his life, reviled by a Prussian soldier beating an innocent citizen. With his bare hands he had struck the soldier and run. How many crimes were committed in the name of "Law" and "Justice". He had read that script in Dante, Dickens, Dumas, Dostoevsky, to name but a single letter of the alphabet! The opposition painted Díaz as a booted tyrant, stomping on the masses. The old man was a dictator, yes, but not a bloody tyrant. His government was accused of corruption and greed. Corruption had always existed, a foul fungus planted throughout the social system by the Spanish and the Aztecs before them. As for greed, it was not a class privilege: those at the bottom stole from one another, killed each other over nothing, and filled their nothingness with envy, envy toward a neighbor who had one more chicken or a woman they wanted. Could this Madero pull that poor devil out of his hole? A weak man in power might give rise to revolution. Of course there was injustice. There were *hacendados* who cared more about their burros than their peons! But what about the good *hacendados* like his brother Luis? They worked his large extension of land but Luis provided food, school, doctor and priest for his peons.... Revolution would mean death to the Academy, to his work. He owed his position and wealth to the old man. Signing this petition would declare his ingratitude.

The doctor was waiting. He placed his petition on the table. "I am hoping we can force Díaz to see reason, to resign and call for free elections. The Centennial celebration in September would then be a magnificent tribute, an honorable farewell. Will you sign, Antonio?"

"I cannot. After all is said and done, doctor, I am a *porfirista*. I may not approve of the old man's tactics, but I owe him my career."

"I am also a *porfirista*," Beto declared, pushing himself out of the deep leather chair. "But a good friend suggested that I open the foggy windows of my mind and let in some fresh air." He smiled. "I believe a new government is necessary for the health of the nation. I will sign your petition, doctor."

By August, Centennial fever possessed the land.

"Look at these pictures, Tío Beto," Antonieta exclaimed. "Every village and town has been decorated. They're even having special bullfights."

"A present to his people from our reelected Caesar," Beto remarked with cynicism.

"The fervor of revolution will fade with Don Porfirio's fireworks," Antonio predicted. "The fiesta comes first; to hell with work or causes! Thank God the Monument is finished."

In the capital, barricades came down; detours, which had clogged the main arteries, disappeared and traffic flowed down broad new streets and tree-lined avenues. Green awnings adorned the storefronts.

A new steel-framed dome rose on the skyline, prelude to the projected grand Legislative Palace. A vast garden in full bloom carpeted the front of Adamo Boari's unfinished opera house, now officially called the National Theater. Public schools were scraped and painted, as were the long-closed doors of the University of Mexico, which would reopen with a parade of Caps and Gowns worn by august international figures. The barefoot and booted alike smiled at one another, sharing mutual pride in their city.

The first special envoys arrived in the capital on September fifth. In the grandeur of his office in the Palace, President Díaz received His Excellency Marques Menutolo di Bugnano, representing King Victor Emmanuel of Italy; His Excellency Karl Buenz, representing the Kaiser of Germany; The Honorable Mr. Curtis Guild, Special Ambassador from the United States; His Excellency Chang Tin Fang, representing the Manchu Emperor of China; and the Noble Baron Yasuya Uchida, representing the Emperor of Japan.

On September 6th, the little known *licenciado*, José Manuel Castellanos, was seized by a heart attack while crossing the street. He was dead by the time the Red Cross arrived. The obituary in El Imparcial mentioned that the victim was the father-in-law of the noted architect, Don Antonio Rivas Mercado.

The black dress was hot and scratchy around her high collar. Cristina was stiff with fatigue after standing for hours in the damp chapel, receiving condolences from relatives and friends and endless lines of students and strangers whom she had never seen before. With practiced solemnity, her brother spoke to people in whispers as they filed past to stare at the corpse.

Antonio stood beside his wife. The air was stagnant with the sickly-sweet odor of gardenia wreaths. Toward midnight, Cristina felt suddenly giddy and began to slip.

"I am taking you home, reina. And your mother, too. You need to rest before the funeral tomorrow."

Tucked in the comfort of her bed, Cristina hung between reality and illusion, where the glow of her night lamp became a candle casting a flickering shadow on a waxen figure in a black box. As sleep claimed her, she descended into space, caught in swaths of black veils that floated over mannequins wearing her beautiful Paris gowns and ensembles. She could hear her father's dry laughter as each lifeless garment was pulled down into hollow caverns. Her last conscious thought was that Alicia should attend the Ball in her place.

"Can I help you put up the flag in the tower, Papá?" six-year-old Mario asked. "And can I ride with you to the parade?" The house was full of relatives from the provinces.

Antonio patted his son's head. "Of course. And you shall have a flag to wave at the marchers."

Defying the tradition of mourning, Cristina joined the family to watch the great Centennial parade from the roof of the Majestic Hotel, where they claimed spaces among the other privileged spectators.

With a burst of cymbals, the military bands struck up. Little boys hung on to their precious space in the trees in the Zócalo as wave upon wave of sailors and soldiers in resplendent uniforms from around the world disappeared down Plateros, followed by the Mexican Military cadets, goose-stepping with precision. Cheers and applause were deafening when the *charros* pranced by on their spirited horses, silver trappings and braid-trimmed sombreros glinting in the bright sun, dazzling the visitors. Confetti and serpentines of coiled confetti rained down on the *rurales*, the rural police in their high-crowned felt hats as they turned at the National Pawn Shop and rode down the parade route.

The bandy-legged old Spanish General, the Marqués de Polavieja, wearing the sash of King Carlos III, marched in front of a cannon displaying the personal effects of Morelos, hero of the Independence, captured and executed by the Royalists in 1815, now returned from their long repository in the armory of Madrid. The crowd wept and cheered wildly. The French envoy returned the keys to Mexico City, keys given to Marshall Fauré by a defeated Mexican army in 1863. Fraternal sentiment ran high when the French saluted the Mexican flag.

"Look, here comes Moctezuma!" little Mario screeched. The allegorical parade depicting the history of Mexico had commenced.

As fifty Indians of pure Aztec blood preceded their Emperor across the place where their great temple had stood four hundred years earlier, Beto wondered what dark thoughts stirred behind their stoic expressions. Astride his white horse, Cortés reached the Palace. Moctezuma was lowered from his palanquin and stood erect. The invaded and the invader met.

Antonio imagined the brightly painted temples that once dominated the square. Geometric patterns and human sacrifice had been supplanted by Roman towers and Roman rituals. But it was a thin overlay. The same brown hands that had carved stone idols had carved saints and angels. The overlay had not yet fused. Those brown hands wouldn't know what to do with a ballot. Eighty-five percent of the population couldn't read or write. Ignorance had to be defeated, not Don Porfirio!

True to predictions, Alicia had grown into a beautiful young woman. Almost fifteen, she carried her well-formed body with dignity and breeding. Her demure smile was natural, suggesting innocence rather than inviting flirtation. She stood quite still while her mother's pale lilac gown, embroidered with delicate seed-pearls, was fitted for the Grand Ball.

"The drape of the skirt is perfect. Madame Gautier would approve," Antonieta commented admiringly. She felt no jealousy toward this sister whose profile would soon be unveiled on the bronze door to the crypt of Papá's Monument.

The Zócalo was ablaze with light. Fifty thousand bulbs outlined the historic buildings. Throngs of people pushed to get a glimpse of the line of carriages and automobiles as they discharged their passengers at the gates of the Palace. Alicia's eyes and mind recorded every detail. Mr. Boari handed her out of the Daimler, their elegant new automobile from Germany. Papá offered his arm and they made their way up the grand stairway. Hundreds of musicians played for dancers who whirled and dipped the length and breadth of the balconies above the courtyard. She caught a glimpse of her reflection as they passed through the Salon of Mirrors that Papá had recently redecorated with all the elegance of Versailles.

Just ahead, her diamond tiara crowning this night of national glory, the queenly Dona Carmelita Díaz stood at her husband's side, welcoming their guests. The "Grand Old Man of the Americas" and his patrician wife presented an unforgettable tableau.

Papá found a seat near a banquet table, sumptuous beyond description. Silverware, china, champagne, even the waiters had been brought over from France! Her dance card was filled three times.

One waltz above all left her weak and trembling. Her partner's name was Enrique. Enrique Lozano. In his arms, Alicia was transported to heaven.

On the night of September 15th, holding his daughters by the hand, Antonio again wove through the crowd to hear the *Grito*, Mexico's rallying cry of Independence. Never before had he been in the midst of such a dense mass of humanity; he usually watched such spectacles from a Palace balcony. Tonight the balconies were filled with Don Porfirio's honored guests. Tomorrow, they would also fill the grandstand for the inauguration of the Independence Monument.

At the stroke of midnight, silence fell over the multitude. The sea of humanity raised its eyes to the clock tower. Lights suddenly illuminated the central balcony. Don Porfirio stepped forward, the red, white and green sash of his office a diagonal swath across his chest; white hair and a mustache set off his handsome brown features. His eyes glazed with tears as he beheld the multitude gathered to pay homage to him and to the nation. In a resonant voice, he shouted the first *"Viva!"*

"Viva México!" the crowd roared back. On the Cathedral towers the words *PROGRESO* and *LIBERTAD* blazed. The crowd's response built to a crescendo until the last *"Viva México!"* exploded over the Zócalo. The Cathedral bells went wild and fireworks sprayed the night sky. Another "Viva!" rose: *"Viva Don Porfirio!"* Hundreds of guitars struck up a birthday serenade. Don Porfirio was eighty, at the height of his prestige at home and abroad.

Pushing his way through the crowd, Antonio guided his daughters back to the car. On Plateros, mounted police were breaking up a mob carrying banners which said *VIVA MADERO*.

The first rays of dawn were breaking when Antonieta awakened. At ten o'clock this morning, Papá's Monument would be inaugurated. He had been building it as long as she could remember. She quietly tiptoed downstairs in her robe and slippers. Already the pat-pat of tortillas sounded from the kitchen and pale light veiled the garden. Quickly now, she ran down the front steps and out to the driveway. She raised her face to the cloudless sky and threw up her arms. "Please, God," she beseeched, "let this be a perfect day."

Antonio stood erect between his wife and his eldest daughter. At their side Antonieta held Mario's hand firmly. His other hand was clasped by Tío Beto. Behind them, in the special grandstand, Sabina held little Amelia. The Presidential Guard stood at attention while President Díaz and his attendants took their seats. A fanfare from the military band announced that the ceremony would commence.

Antonio was the first speaker: "Mr. President. Ladies and gentlemen. The Mexican nation had a debt of gratitude to pay to those who made her free and independent. Since earliest times obelisks and columns have commemorated heroes and heroic events. Now, Mexico joins the great cities of the world in erecting a classical column to honor her heroes...." Eulogies to the heroes were delivered by other speakers and an epic poem was read. Then, in his morning coat and tall silk hat, the dignified old President stepped forward and cut the symbolic cord. Applause thundered. The military band struck up the National Anthem, accompanied by the high clear voices of a boys' choir.

Antonieta's eyes followed the stone garlands up, up, up the tall column to the golden angel dancing in the pure, cobalt blue air, a laurel wreath held in her outstretched hand. In her other hand, a broken chain hung limp and useless.

With tears of pride stinging her eyes, Antonieta mouthed the words to the anthem:

"Mexicanos al grito de guerra

El acero aprestad y el bridón,
Y retiembla en sus centros la tierra
Al sonoro rugir del cañon...."

Serene, the golden angel kept dancing.

CHAPTER IX
MICHIGAN, JUNE, 1910

Final exams were over. As the sun began its slow descent over the narrow peninsula of Lake Superior, a wind, still carrying a faint suggestion of winter, swept through the tall northern pines that enclosed the campus of the Houghton School of Mines. In the Sigma Rho fraternity house the sounds of revelry rumbled through the halls. Graduation was three days away.

Albert Blair flopped down on the bed. He pushed back a strand of straight brown hair and methodically flexed his shoulders, stretched muscular legs, and pressed his back flat against the hard mattress. Cramming had become a way of life since his return from Mexico, that unauthorized "research" trip which had so disquieted his family. "You could have been shot by bandits and we would never have known," his father had written when he had informed him of the trip. Well, his father could not berate him for study time lost: He would graduate with honors.

Stuffing a pillow under his head, Albert lay on his back and relaxed, gaze fixed on pink-tinged clouds clustered over the tall pines outside his window. An ephemeral, changing reality, like his future. The future.... Taking over the administration of the family coal mines in dear old Henderson, Kentucky, was the only "future" he had ever considered—until now. A fragment of memory billowed up in the sky: He remembered a boy of ten who stood rooted in admiration as he watched Queen Victoria's carriage pass through the gates of Buckingham Palace. In his childhood fantasies, bugles called her Majesty's brave troops to victorious battles. He dreamed of heroic deeds, transported by G.A. Henty to Pretoria, to Khartoum, the Pampas, to India with Clive! Then a real adventure. He remembered standing on the wet deck of a ship carrying him to America that year he had turned ten, the year the century had begun. In America, his dreams of Empire had suffered a cataclysmic blow: the wild west and cowboys had been superceded by Captains Courageous, and Kim belonged not in Kipling's India but was the name of a black boy who taught him to shoot an agate straight. There came the shocking discovery that Jesus Christ was not an Englishman and that he, Albert, was considered ignorant. Bloody noses after school speeded the metamorphosis that changed his English accent to a southern drawl.

Albert's blue eyes remained fixed on the darkening sky. The trip to Mexico, maneuvered by his roommates, Raúl and Julio Madero, had forced old dreams to surface. His very senses had been jarred awake: in Mexico the sky looked bluer, the stars brighter, cactus grew next to pines , and the poor lived in the shadow of the rich—a country of sharp contrasts. Yet the people were gentle, their courtesy a natural attribute, and time distilled to new essences. He marveled at his roommates' approach to life, to career, to grades, even girls. Raúl and Julio took a casual approach to everything except politics. Mexican passivity was only on the surface, they had assured him; it could explode any minute. Politics had become an obsession since their eldest brother, Francisco, had involved his large and wealthy family in his plans for political reform. In his letters, Francisco, whom the boys affectionately called "Pancho," had heaped fiery criticism on the old dictator, accusing Díaz of making "dead prose" of the Constitution and permitting the poor peon to become mired in near-slavery.

During three years of close college association, listening to tales of growing unrest in Mexico, Albert had come to share the anxieties which plagued his roommates. Sailing across Lake Superior in a small gaff-rigged sloop, they had talked about Pancho's dreams: "Justice for all" carried on the wind, the problems of Mexico fired up over sand-sprinkled frankfurters. He had learned to sing *"Mariquita Linda,"* which Julio plunked on his guitar. Mexico had been part of his curriculum.

In the winter, when the snow piled outside the window, the whole fraternity gathered in the lounge before a roaring fire and listened to Julio and Raúl's ranting discourses on the old dictator's authoritarian rule.

"Why does Díaz bother with elections?" Hank, whose father had lost a heated race for mayor of a Kansas town, had asked.

"So he can stuff the ballot boxes and prove how popular he is," Raúl answered bitterly.

"Can't Congress enforce free elections? They do represent the people, don't they?" Jim, a tall Bostonian and former law student, wanted to know.

"You still don't understand, Jim. Díaz points his finger at a governor or senator and he's 'voted' in. Díaz decides what he wants, then he instructs Congress to change the Constitution!"

Albert's admiration for Francisco had grown—a voice crying in the Mexican wilderness. On the trip to Mexico he had discovered the astonishing extent of the Madero's wealth: They owned vast cattle ranches and cotton plantations in the north, henequen plantations in the Yucatán, a bank, mines, breweries, smelting plants. Yet this man, Francisco Madero, was gambling status and fortune to force free elections, to improve the lot of the wretched peon.

The previous night Julio had opened a new window on Albert's future. "If you want to go back to Mexico, I'll get you an administrative job in one the family's mines. Better than sweating down in that heap of coal." Like a splinter you can feel but can't find, the offer had pricked the edges of Albert's consciousness all day.

The muscles in Albert's jaws contracted when he thought of confronting his father. Ignore a family obligation and go off to that barbaric land! "Idol worshippers," his mother called Catholics. The fundamental Protestant sect to which his parents belonged condemned drinking, smoking, dancing and card-playing. Mexicans were from another planet. Albert sat up. Damn it, he was only twenty years old, too young to wither in the coal mines of Kentucky!

"Hey, Blair, what the hell are you doin' there? Come on, we'll deal you in." Big Red, an ex-lumberjack, filled the doorway. "Five-card stud and draw."

Albert allowed himself to be pulled into the smoke-filled room next door, where a foamy tankard was thrust in his hand. He downed two more beers before the round was over and pocketed four dollars and twenty-five cents.

"Hey, you can't leave now!"

"Says who?" Albert replied with a smirk and ducked out the door.

Back in his room, Albert turned on the table lamp, located his pipe, sucked noisily as he lit it and began sorting his books. A mine in Mexico....Mexico.

The door flew open. Julio yanked off his windbreaker and tossed it on the bed. Brown eyes wide, fair skin sunburned, urgency in his step. He went to the closet and pulled out an empty valise. "We just got a telegram," he announced. "Can one give back a cap and gown?"

Accustomed to Julio's non sequiturs, Albert asked, "What does the telegram have to do with your cap and gown?"

"Where's Raúl? We should leave for Mexico. And where's my guitar?" He began rummaging in the closet.

"Slow down, *mexicano*, Albert said. "You're too damned impetuous."

"You're right, *yanqui*." Julio sat down on a metal foot-locker and clasped his hands between his knees. It wouldn't be fair to my father and grandfather not to bring home a sheepskin, would it?"

Albert sat on the edge of the bed. The brown eyes across from him were serious, worried. Probably one of their twelve brothers or sisters was sick. They were a clannish family. What affected one affected all. "What does the telegram say?"

"Pancho's in jail."

"What! I thought he was campaigning up north."

"Díaz accused him of inciting a rebellion in Monterrey. He's in the penitentiary in San Luis Potosí."

"In jail! It's an outrage!" Shock was supplanted by his own outrage as Albert stared at his roommate. "Look here, with all your family's connections, they can't keep him in jail."

Julio laughed melodramatically. "You still don't understand, Al. We are up against a dictator, a dictator supported by the United States, with all the power in his hands. Unless he chooses to allow opposition, or is forced to, he'll stamp it out."

"Do you think there might be a revolution?"

A muscle flexed in Julio's jaw and he kneaded his knuckles. "You know Pancho's a pacifist. He hates violence. But he hates injustice more."

Albert felt pain in the words. He clapped Julio on the shoulder. "You stay for graduation, you hear? If your brother's in jail, three days more won't make any difference. Come on, let's go next door and beat those thieves. I just drew to an inside straight."

Albert hung his cap and gown in the empty closet and looked around the room one more time. Julio's guitar lay on the bed, and there were a few more books to jam into his own footlocker. He had not brought up the subject of Julio's offer. His father's presence at graduation had made Mexico seem unreal and remote. He loved his father, knew the sincerity and generosity beneath the stiff exterior. The immediate future, Albert had decided, lay in Kentucky.

The room looked suddenly drab, empty. Madero ebullience had filled it. He would miss his Mexican brothers, their good humor and generosity, their emotive outbursts and exaggerations, their loyal friendship, their patriotic fervor, these Mexican who, but for their accent, could pass for Anglo-Saxons. How he had envied the easy manner with which Raúl and Julio treated women. Girls from the University of Michigan practically lined up to polka with "these darling Mexicans."

Julio was three inches shorter than his own five-nine but he gave no thought to asking a tall girl to dance. Raúl was a year older, also short by Yankee standards. Neither seemed inhibited by his height, a feature which sorely bothered Albert, who had hoped to reach his father's six-foot height.

"Still packing?" Julio asked, entering the room. "Your folks are waiting down in the lounge."

"I know." Albert snapped shut the padlock on the footlocker and turned to the window. He swallowed. Goodbyes had to be said. "Look here, Julio, I know you are worried about Francisco and it all seems flat with him in jail. But people will vote for him no matter where he is. What I mean is, I admire your brother immensely and have a great affection for Mexico. And Mexicans." He paused. "Listen, if anything happens, like a revolution, I want to help. I mean it. Send me a wire."

Julio looked at his roommate and grinned. He knew that nothing dissuaded Albert Blair when he made up his mind. He was stubborn and impulsive. "You can bet your bottom dollar we'll let you know if there's a revolution."

"And I want to know what happens," Albert said. "Don't pull one of those Mexican silences. Keep in touch and write, damn it!"

The young mining engineers locked their arms around each other and slapped backs in a demonstrative *abrazo*.

Summer in Henderson was hot and uneventful. In mid-July, the "Chicago Tribune" published six lines about Mexico: "President Porfirio Diaz was elected for his tenth term, now extended to six years, 1910-1916. The orderly election promises six more years of stability in a country fraught with revolution until this fine statesman took the reins." It did not mention the fate of Francisco Madero.

At his request, the Henderson library sent for William Prescott's "Conquest of Mexico"; Albert studied the heavy text in what little free time he had. A letter from Julio was demoralizing: "Pancho is still in jail. Before, my hatred for Díaz was just a bitter taste in my mouth—now it's deep, understand? He has embargoed family businesses and properties."

Once, Albert attempted to discuss the Mexican political situation with his father. The subject was not well taken.

"What do you see in that semi-barbaric country, when we have everything right here?"

His sisters, Grace and Dorothy, went straight to the point: "Mother is sure those Madero boys corrupted you into drinking beer. Did they? Did you get drunk down there in Mexico?"

His father was more reasonable when Albert argued that he wanted to take a freighter and travel before he settled down to a permanent position in the family business. His grandfather had been a tea merchant in London and his father had once remarked that he regretted not shipping out on a freighter before joining his own father's enterprise.

The sober-faced patriarch attributed his older son's restless nature to the "independent spirit of youth." A year on a freighter should suffice to see the world—and return to Henderson. Bushy eyebrows met in serious contemplation. "Of course, such an undertaking must be mostly at your own expense. Grace enters nursing school this fall."

Albert tucked in his chin. "Of course. I do thank you, sir. I am already making inquiries into engineering jobs."

By October, Albert was working on a bridge in Vancouver, British Columbia.

The table in the small restaurant wobbled. Albert lit a cigarette and jammed the wooden match under the unsteady leg. He had spent a solitary, exceedingly wet six weeks in Vancouver, and he already felt the chill of winter. He took a bite of hot cherry pie and began to thumb through the newspaper that lay by his plate. His attention riveted on a headline in an inside page: SLAUGHTER IN MEXICO.

In his haste to fold the paper, he spilled his coffee. He daubed at the brown liquid with his napkin, tearing a hole in the absorbent newsprint.

Somebody named Aquiles Serdan had been killed in a town called Puebla on November eighteenth. The man had planned to assault a Federal barracks in response to Francisco Madero's call to armed revolt.

The revolution was on!

The next few lines were barely discernible, but he deduced that Madero had issued a declaration from his San Luis Potosí jail cell, a declaration inciting the nation to rise against the dictator on November twentieth. The declaration, written October fifth, ended with a statement: "I have done everything possible to reach an agreement.

I was even willing to withdraw my candidacy if General Díaz had permitted the nation to choose, at the very least, a Vice-President to succeed him. But dominated by incomprehensible pride, he turned a deaf ear upon the nation and preferred to precipitate a revolution." A clear call to arms!

It seemed Madero had escaped jail, boarded a northbound train, hiding in the baggage car, crossed the border into Texas, and set up headquarters in exile in San Antonio.

San Antonio! Albert's cheeks grew red with excitement. He had stopped in San Antonio with Julio and Raúl on their way to Mexico City.

Albert stuffed a large piece of cherry pie into his mouth, grabbed his hat off the rack, set out into the drizzle, and walked briskly in the direction of the telegraph office.

"READ ABOUT SERDAN. VIVA MADERO. KEEP ME POSTED RE SITUATION. WILL JOIN YOU IN SAN ANTONIO AS SOON AS YOU SEND UP A FLARE. ALBERT."

On the way back to his boarding house, Albert stopped at a window display in a bookstore. Leaning against a world atlas stood a handsome leather-bound portfolio with the title "Journal" burnished in discreet gold letters. On impulse he went in and spent a week's food allowance on the beautifully tanned and tooled notebook.

March 7, 1911

In this, my first entry in this journal, I write on the Great Northern Railway, about two hours out of Seattle, in a coach car bound for Los Angeles. From there I shall cross the Mojave Desert, then the great southwestern plains, to San Antonio.

I departed Vancouver at 8 a.m. this morning, the day after my twenty-first birthday, a fitting time for a man to act on a decision. As I leave the bitter cold of the north and wind southward, I am cognizant of a change in myself, as though the air I breathe is lighter, as though I have grown three inches taller. I feel I am the captain of my own destiny. I made the decision to join the Mexican Revolution. I telegraphed Julio Madero when I read of his brother's call to arms on November twentieth, but it *seems revolutions get off to a slow start. Madero crossed the border with his rebel troops on February 13th and on the 14th Julio's telegram reached me: "FLARE SET OFF. WIRE ARRIVAL."*

I have in my possession every cent that I own. Happily it is more than $800. Let me confess here that $129.35 constitutes my net winnings at poker while at Houghton. Plus $200 father sent me as a more than generous Christmas present, thinking I was about to embark around the world. The rest I saved from earnings by living in a most frugal manner.

I hereby state that I and I alone have chosen to fight for this just cause and this journal will be a faithful testimony of that experience. Viva México!

A blast of warm air blew up the aisle of the coach car as the conductor stuck his head in and shouted, "San Antonio. San Antonio!"

Albert checked his watch: 7:30 a.m. He cleared a patch of dust from the window and looked down the platform as the train pulled into the station. Julio! Albert grabbed his valise and hat and jumped off before the train had come to a full stop. The old roommates met halfway and pounded each other on the back. Albert felt new, hard muscle in the backslap, and Texas boots made Julio look taller.

"You came. Thanks, Julio. Where's Raúl?"

"Down the line, fighting with Villa."

"Pancho Villa?"

"Of course."

"I bought 'The Examiner' in Los Angeles, and it said Francisco was wounded in a place called Casas Grandes, and that he had shown real leadership and courage in battle, went right on fighting. What have you heard? Is he all right?"

"Almost recovered. We got word by courier last night. Villa's giving them hell now." Julio pointed to the valise. "Is that all you brought?"

"I figured all I'd need is some drawers and a couple of shirts. Why aren't you in uniform?"

"We don't wear them in San Antonio. This is the United States, you know."

"I thought it was a rose plucked from your family's back yard," Albert teased and picked up his valise. Well, do I report to headquarters or go direct to training camp? Look here, Julio, I've got to tell you the truth. I've never fired a gun," he said sheepishly.

Julio laughed. "In this man's army, uniforms and bullets are expensive. If you want a little target practice, you do it on your own, out of town behind some mesquite tree where the police won't hear you. Come on, we can talk at the hotel."

San Antonio might be in the United States, but the Hotel Hutchins seemed to be in Mexico. At breakfast the dining room was a babble of Spanish, and they served hot chili sauce and tortillas with the eggs. Members of the Madero family whom Albert had met on his earlier trip to Mexico greeted him warmly in English, but he had the sensation of being a guest in a foreign country where everyone goes out of their way to be hospitable. He was introduced to aunts, uncles, cousins, in-laws and friends who had allied themselves to the Revolution. They were exiles, Julio confided; their assets had been frozen and confiscation hung over their lands and enterprises.

"We never talk about the Revolution at meals, in the lobby, or public places. Now, get yourself settled and I'll meet you upstairs in your room at nine-thirty," Julio said. "We have to go downtown and buy you some khakis, brother. There's a staff meeting at twelve and you are invited."

Albert examined his face in the tiny mirror which hung over the cracked but clean washbasin in his room. It was an ordinary face, brown hair, blue eyes, nose a bit broad: not an unpleasant face but nothing to distinguish it as that of a *revolucionario*. He looked again, and knew he had to grow a mustache.

He answered the familiar knock at the door and admitted Julio and another man.

"Albert Blair, Sebastián Carranza. Sebastián's on our staff."

Without further ceremony, Julio handed the new recruit a flat-brimmed felt hat and a red, white and green ribbon.

"That ribbon is the insignia of a revolutionary officer. You are hereby commissioned a lieutenant in the Army of the Provisional President of

Mexico, Francisco I. Madero." Julio saluted solemnly. "That's the only army 'issue' you'll get," he added with a grin. "Here's a safety pin to secure the ribbon. It goes around the crown. Now, let's go."

Albert returned from the shopping expedition with two sets each of a khaki jacket and breeches, plus boots and a Colt revolver. He had added a tooled holster and a money belt to his purchases and entered the sum of $80.37 in his account book.

Julio briefed him as they walked toward a small, private parlor in the hotel where the staff meetings were held.

"I recommended you for a staff position, but you have to meet with General Carranza's approval. I told him that a hard-headed southern Yankee might be useful and he said to bring you along. Right now we are three: Sebastián, who's the General's nephew, me and Jesús Hernandez."

"His name is Jesús?" Albert spurted.

"You'll meet a lot of Jesuses in Mexico. But if it makes you feel less blasphemous you can call him '*Chucho.*' OK, some background on the General: He's a northerner, from Coahuila, the same state we're from. He's an old hand at politics, was a Senator under Díaz..."

"You mean one of those Díaz pointed his finger at," Albert interjected.

"Right." Julio explained that Carranza had ambitions of becoming Governor, but broke with Díaz when the old dictator did an about-face on his promise to allow the Vice-President to be elected. "When Francisco issued his call to arms, Carranza came over to our side. He's the senior member of this *Junta.*"

"When do we move down the line?"

"When Carranza gives the order. Says he's holding us in reserve. We all wish to hell he'd move!"

The General, a big, dignified gentleman with a long white beard and tinted spectacles, gave Albert a firm handshake and pointed to a seat. They sat around a table with a map of Mexico spread out in the middle. Albert felt the General's eyes scrutinizing him as Julio quietly translated. Sometimes he caught the gist, but a barrage of Spanish rendered Cortina's "Spanish in Twenty Lessons" as useless as Chinese. The General drew a red dot to identify Villa's encampment near Chihuahua City, and the encampment of a fellow named Pascual Orozco in the vicinity. During the meeting, Albert wrote down a roster of names to learn; rebel leaders who were popping up all over.

After the meeting broke up, Albert headed for the dining room with Chucho and Sebastián.

Julio joined them before the bean soup was served. He thumped Albert on the chest. "You made it. General Carranza sized you up as level-headed. He must have guessed you're a taciturn, stubborn Scotchman under that soft southern skin. My sister Angela's sitting over there. Waving. See? Said to turn you over to her after lunch and she'd give you a Spanish lesson."

Albert sat on the edge of the tub and soaked his feet in hot water. He could hear Angela Madero still playing the piano downstairs, where a group had gathered after dinner to sing. He splashed his aching feet around and tried to sort out the events of the day. Revolutions, he decided, make strange bedfellows. Madero's key "lieutenants" were a mule-driver, that Orozco fellow, a bandit, Pancho Villa, and a desperado named Zapata, who was ravaging the wealthy haciendas in the southern state of Morelos. Where were the educated Mexicans Julio and Raúl talked about on those snowy nights at Houghton? Well, the American Revolution was fought by the rabble. And Madero had the backing of a strong and wealthy clan. The important thing was that the flame Madero had lighted was now a blazing prairie fire. "Madero has loosed the tiger," a senator was quoted as saying.

Before turning in, Albert wrote in his journal: *"I arrived in San Antonio at 7:30 a.m., was commissioned a lieutenant in the Revolutionary Army at 9:30, and was assigned to General Carranza's staff at noon."*

At breakfast, a gentleman whom Albert recognized hurried in from the lobby and whispered something to Mr. Madero Senior. Consternation spread across his patrician face and a rapid discussion followed.

Julio ran over and came back. "Our bank in Monterrey has been closed!" he said, anger lashing at each word. "Diaz is doing everything possible to break us financially. He knows Francisco desperately needs arms and ammunition."

Albert left Julio to intimate family matters and headed for his room. In the lobby he was stopped by a young man whom he had seen the day before.

"You are Bley-eer no? A friend of Julio's?" he asked in a heavy accent. A mustache tried to conceal his youth and light brown eyes met Albert's on the same level.

"Yes. I am on General Carranza's staff," Albert replied, tucking in his chin.

"Juan Andreu Almazán," He stuck out his hand.

"Andrew?' Albert asked.

"No. Andreu. That's Catalán. Where you from, *yanqui*?

"Kentucky," Albert replied

"And why you volunteer?"

"Because freedom is the province of all men and I believe in this cause."

"Whew!" Almazán whistled. "I hope you are as good fighter as Giuseppe Garibaldi. He has three hundred Yankee volunteers, some Italians, who are learning from Pancho Villa what it is to fight. A big cattle rancher refused to let Villa's men wash in his well and Pancho shot him dead just like that."

"Is this Garibaldi related to the Italian patriot?"

"His grandson. He was looking for a fight. And you?"

Albert met the mocking challenge in the handsome young face. "I came to fight. And you?"

"I am a medical student. But I think it is more important to break the yoke of Díaz than to dissect corpses. I join Madero because he is the only one with pants and I have tasted the bullet. I came up here to see Carranza who has lead in his feet so now I think I will join Zapata," the young man said with an ingratiating smile. "You like to go downtown? See San Antonio?"

Julio emerged from the dining room and crossed the lobby. Almazán winked at him. "I invite your friend downtown for a chocolate soda.

Want to come?"

"Why not.?" Julio shrugged.

March 17
Three days ago Pancho Villa stormed the city of Torreón, Coahuila, the most important railroad junction in the north, the center of the cotton plantations. The "Laredo Times" reports that it was a bloodbath. Seems Villa also slaughtered three hundred Chinese in Torreón, senselessly, herding them like cattle to the edge of town. I asked what so many Chinese were doing in Torreón and was told that they are descendants of the coolies brought over from China by the United States to work on the Union-Pacific railroad. Many drifted down to northern Mexico. Poor devils. Villa's a barbarian! But the fact remains: he captured Torreón.

March 21
One week in this hotel. There is little to report. Carranza's static position is exasperating. Furious, bloody battles are erupting like a string of firecrackers in the northern states and we sit in pointless staff meetings marking battle sites on our map.

Julio sat alone in a corner of the lobby, shoulders slumped, a newspaper folded on his lap. Albert caught sight of him and walked over. His friend's depression grew deeper every day. Albert pulled up a chair.

"Listen to me, Julio, I've been thinking. There are enough sympathizers right here in San Antonio to raise the money to buy a carload of ammunition. Suggest it to Carranza. We've got to do something!"

"And how do we get it over the border? Did you see this?" Julio thumped the newspaper. "Taft is amassing more American soldiers along the border, from Brownsville to El Paso. Big American ranchers are yelling at their congressmen for protection. Father is worried sick. Money.... liquidity...cash is the problem. There's not a cent in the family, man. Our best hope is my brother, Gustavo. He's been in New York a week trying to negotiate a loan."

Albert knew that Madero money had bought arms, Madero money had outfitted and paid the troops, every penny of Francisco Madero's personal fortune had gone toward this Revolution, and his brother, Gustavo, had turned everything he owned into liquid assets.

"Any word from Gustavo yet?"

"Nothing. Bankers don't believe in just causes," Julio remarked gloomily.

"Come on, I'll buy you a drink. I'm going down to the Buckhorn Saloon to see what rumors a civilian can pick up."

"No thanks. I told father I would walk with him to the telegraph office."

Albert planted his boot on the brass rail, ordered a whiskey and looked around the popular saloon. He recognized a close-cropped, bull-necked American army officer stationed at Fort Sam Houston.

"Captain Harris, right?"

"Yeah."

"Albert Blair. An engineer from Kentucky, right? Have a seat."

After a few amenities, Albert launched his query. "What do you hear at Fort Sam? I read in the paper that Madero has fifteen thousand men under arms now, nine thousand in the north. Think he's got a chance?"

The Mexican Revolution, that revolt "down there," was the favorite topic in the Buckhorn Saloon.

"He could have twenty-five thousand and it wouldn't make any difference," Harris responded. "Those poor bastards haven't got a Chinaman's chance. I've seen 'em. They take a town, shooting wild, whooping it up, wasting ammunition, getting slaughtered. Now you take the *federales*, those boys are professional soldiers. Their officers are career men, schooled in the best military academies of Europe. Get enough *federales* up here and this "revolution" is over. Just like that." He snapped his fingers.

"I hear a lot of the Federal rank and file have changed their long gray coats for sarapes. This is a war of ideals, Captain." Albert felt a flush crawling up his neck.

March 26

A sinister word hangs in the air: intervention. I had lunch at Fort Sam with Harris today. He would drop in his tracks if he knew I was an officer in Madero's army. But he does know I am their friend. "Tell your friends that if this mess down in Mexico heats up, just one shot across the border and Uncle Sam stops their show! Better tell them." He doesn't know that it might grind to a halt for lack of ammunition.

I am thinking of writing to Grace at her nursing school and telling her where I am. She can tell mother and father. I don't like deception but to worry them is worse. Anyway, this Revolution may be over before they find out where I am.

March 31

Today I got a long letter from Raúl! All smudged and creased but it got here. Should the letter be lost, I quote it in its entirety:

"Dear brother Al: So you gave up your trip around the world to join us. Good man. I am encamped with Villa near the Chief. Saw the Chief yesterday. His arm is nearly healed (tell mother). You wouldn't know me, haven't shaved in weeks and my eyes seem perpetually bloodshot. Every day raw recruits show up ready to lay down their lives for the Revolution. Mostly they're fodder for the Federal cannons. No boot camp this, no time for training, but they keep coming. We lose two or three hundred, then the army swells again with fresh volunteers looking for a way out of the cornfields. Villa's troops have been fighting incessantly since December, with only a bowl of watered down beans in their bellies and a *serape* to keep them from freezing at night. Wouldn't you know that snow, of all things, fell in Chihuahua. It's still bitter cold.

Orozco is at an old hand at guerrilla warfare, learned every trick fighting off bandits while he hauled silver and lead ore from the mines of Chihuahua. You must know about Villa, spent sixteen years outrunning and outwitting *federales* and *rurales*. The Chief has acquitted him of all crimes and he's one hell of a loyal officer, a shrewd tactician and not a yellow bone in his body. We've got the *federales jumping through hoops now.* We chase those blue hats, draw them in, pulling them out of garrisons to defend towns we let them take, then take back. Saves ammunition and keeps them off balance. I've become a sharpshooter and have a magnificent sorrel stallion.

I tell you all this so you'll know this isn't Queen Victoria's Regiments riding in formation. Down here you ride like hell, attack, retreat to the hills, sleep wherever you fall, eat tortillas and beans, get cactus spines in your rump, and seldom have a bath. I want you to know the facts. Carranza should join us soon. Are you sure you want to fight in this Revolution? Bedbugs are not the most desirable bed mates.

Goodbye for now. Raul."

My admiration for Raul soars. I wish to hell we were with him!

April 1

Tonight I met a lawyer named José Vasconcelos who is here to confer with the Junta. He and a doctor named Vasquez Gomez are lobbying in Washington to get recognition for Madero and win support in the United States Congress. The more I study Mexican history the more evident it becomes that the United States has always interfered in Mexican politics. A "behave or I'll pull out the rug" kind of policy. I remember Raúl used to say that when Uncle Sam sneezes Mexico catches pneumonia. Díaz came to power in a barracks uprising and when it looked like he could steer a stable course (favorable to the interests of the U.S., of course) he was officially recognized. Officially, Madero is leading a revolt against a recognized government. But U.S. public opinion is turning in his favor. He's the champion of democracy, which makes him a kind of hero. If only bullets would fall from the sky like manna.

A loud knock interrupted Albert's entry in his journal.

"Al, put your pants on, we're celebrating downstairs." Shouting, Julio flung open the door. "Gustavo got the loan!"

CHAPTER X
APRIL 3, 1911

We are moving out! We are a four-man detail ordered to receive and deliver ammunition to the town of Ojinaga on the Texas-Chihuahua border. Ojinaga is a strategic town, just retaken by the federales *for the third time. This is a clandestine operation with high risk, but I approach our assignment with confident expectations.*

The Revolution got off to a slow start. Detraining at Alpine, in west Texas, the *revolucionarios* rented a four-cylinder Buick, guided it down a winding road and coaxed and cranked it across hot, scrubby terrain to Presidio on the American side, across the river from Ojinaga. Presidio was comprised of fifteen adobe buildings strung out along the muddy Rio Grande. An American border patrol informed them that casualties of the "battle over there" had been four burros killed and one little boy accidentally shot in the belly.

Ojinaga was a piteously poor town, bled of food and provisions by the thousand federales who again jammed the garrison. Impatiently, Carranza's boys held staff meetings on the creaky stoop of their boarding house in Presidio, waiting for their "merchandise." The prodigious, close-knit Madero family was scattered from the border to Washington to New York, spreading pro-Madero propaganda, meeting with confidential agents, negotiating arms sales in Tucson, Phoenix, and Nogales; arranging for delivery up and down the border; keeping a wary eye on the American troops. By the fifth day, the young strategists had unloaded a truckload of ammunition and hidden it in the tall rushes along the river. If the Americans knew, they turned their backs. Support for Madero's cause was openly acknowledged in Presidio, but subterfuge was the game. Disguised in tattered clothes, coming and going over the bridge with the Mexicans who worked on the American side, contacting rebel leaders, delivering arms, the green revolucionarios soon "tasted the bullet." Well-schooled in the art of sniping at "blue hats," rebel leaders started their cat-and-mouse game: hit and run, suck in your belly and move along a wall, keep a corner in sight, cover your men in street skirmishes. Look for well-cut uniforms and gleaming boots. Don't waste ammunition. Shoot straight! The sight of blood became acceptable. Albert was astonished at what his conscience had come to accept in nine days. But it took more courage, he wrote in his journal, to open Grace's letter: "Mother and Father have suspected that you are mixed up in that revolt down in Mexico. They pray for your safety every day. I had to tell them the truth. Now they pray that you will come to your senses and come home. I am in accord. Love, your sister, Grace."

Rumors kept them on their toes: Madero was turning south to the capital. Díaz now had thirty-thousand men under arms. Garibaldi had been killed. Madero was turning north to face General Navarro.

April 12
We have been ordered to El Paso. It has been confirmed by the American press that General Navarro, Commander of the Federal forces, has fortified the town and Madero is marching north. We take the train from Alpine at 2 p.m.

Uncertainty hung in the air in El Paso. A prosperous city in the foothills of the mountains of west Texas, El Paso now swarmed with American soldiers, newspaper reporters, alarmed Mexicans streaming out of Juárez—and American die-hards crossing to the racetrack on the other side. President Taft had mobilized twenty thousand soldiers along the border and blockaded the Gulf and Pacific ports with the U.S. Navy. The eyes of Washington were riveted on Ciudad Juárez, the important northern railroad terminal across the river. The interests of the Anaconda Corporation, the Guggenheims, Hearst, the Rockefellers, Doheny oil interests, and enormous American cattle ranches in northern Mexico were at stake. American investment in Mexico exceeded one billion dollars, more than the capital held by the Mexicans themselves. Colonel Edgar Z. Steever, commander of the United States 4th Cavalry at Fort Bliss, had orders from President Taft to protect American lives and property at all costs. The slightest incident could be an excuse for intervention.

April 18
No need for disguise here. A fair, blue-eyed fellow is as likely to be a Mexican as an American. They come and go at will. There are three bridges that cross the river, each with a guardhouse at the end. The river is about three hundred feet wide, a mere puddle now, but it becomes a raging torrent, they say, after a rainstorm. The Hotel Shelton in El Paso, where we are quartered, is like the Hutchins in San Antonio, filled with Mexicans, supporters of Madero. Madero is expected to march in at any moment. General Carranza, who arrived a few days ago, lends authority to the situation, and people look to him to confirm or deny rumors. But the truth is, he knows no more than they do. We have set up a telescope on the roof of this hotel and take turns keeping Navarro's fortifications in sight, looking for signs of action over there.
The first night I met a Texan named Ed Skidmore in the bar of the Hotel Ormdorf. He's a linotype operator who also writes for a local paper. Skidmore knows Juárez like the back of his hand and we go over there every day to scout around. A Federal encampment is strung out for miles along the railroad tracks at the base of the mountains, and rurales *in their big felt hats ride up and down, patrolling tracks jammed with freight cars. Pancho Villa has blown up track from here to Chihuahua City, so should he try to repair it and use the railroad, he would be stopped dead on the outskirts. Ciudad Juárez makes me think of a frayed beggar who wears a*

suit of armor. We calculate twelve hundred men in hidden barracks over there.

Flowered skirts and parasols, business suits and workers' shirts dotted the rooftops of El Paso as though a show was about to start. Toward noon, April 20th, it did.

The Revolutionary forces began to converge on the outskirts of Ciudad Juárez at midday. A cry went up in the hotel: "*Ya llegaron los revolucionarios!*" In minutes the roof was crowded with the curious. Along the riverbank, the American Army lined up, field glasses trained on the other side of the shallow stream.

Francisco Madero marched in with a battle-weary column of infantrymen. A small escort flanked their chief as they approached the flat plain which borders the Rio Grande River. Enveloped in a plain brown *sarape*, the Provisional President blended into their ranks. Taking his turn at the telescope, Albert focused on the ragtag gathering. Tears stung his eyes. Madero was smaller than he had imagined, but there was no bravado, no strutting in the lead. Training the telescope on the railroad yards, he saw Ed Skidmore standing on top of a freight car. Next to him were Williams of the New York Herald and Elton of the Washington Post, seasoned reporters who had covered the Cuban Revolution in '98. Battle was their meat. Battle!

At four o'clock Julio nudged Albert. "I've counted about two thousand troops now. Navarro's outnumbered!"

Suddenly, General Carranza appeared. Dressed in a khaki uniform, his shock of white hair and long beard commanded attention. "I have just received a message from President Madero," he addressed those assembled. "He is pressuring General Navarro to surrender. I understand they have negotiated a brief truce." Turning to his staff, he added, "Madero has established headquarters on the edge of the camps. I'm going over there now. There's a briefing at 1700 hours. "Change into your uniforms and be ready, *muchachos.*"

Bedlam reigned on the other side. Villa's men kept coming in, leading horses through the scrubby vegetation that hugged the river.

The four conspicuously clean officers ducked through horses, mules and wagons, as soldiers jammed around tents. Soldiers unloaded ammunition and supplies while their women knelt in the dirt, fanning soot-blackened *braseros*. The distinctive pat-pat of tortillas was soon heard in the noisy confusion. Albert followed behind, elbowing his way through soldiers wearing mud-caked *huaraches*, red kerchiefs tied around their necks, cartridge belts strapped across their chests, straw hats flapping on their backs. Small swatches of tricolor ribbon were pinned to their coats, some with a little cardboard virgin attached, others with a religious medal. The smell of animals, human sweat and spicy food filled his nostrils. The buzz of language melded into a string of expletives: *"Anda, huevón, levanta la chingada caja! Hijo de tu puta madre, muévala tu!"* These were Villa's men, ordered to make camp downriver to act as a buffer between the Revolutionary camps and the town.

Julio in the lead, Chucho, Sebastián and Albert made their way through the melee to the edge of the camps. There it was, a small ramshackle adobe building near the river, with a Mexican flag was planted in front and two guards at the door. Adrenalin pumping, Albert followed his companions, identified himself and entered.

The small room was crammed with men in sweat-stained uniforms. Madero sat at a rustic table talking to a group of officers. Albert could see yellow riding boots caked with mud beneath the table that served as a desk. But it was the man's face which held his attention: youthful ebullience and kindness there. Lively brown eyes above a dark mustache and small beard, now concentrated unwaveringly on the officer addressing him. Albert stood only a few feet from this man who had led the Revolution. High morals, discipline, integrity characterized Francisco Madero. His was not a shadowy conspiracy to overthrow the oppressor, but an open battle! Madero had a messianic vision of his role, Julio had once confided. A fervent believer in liberty, he felt his role lay in awakening the soul of this tormented country.

Raúl moved up now. Albert's eyes smarted. His old roommate was a mature man whose very stance reflected strength and self assurance. Tears ran freely as Albert watched Julio step forward and salute his two brothers. Clasped in *abrazos*, the emotional moment filled other eyes—battle-hardened eyes—with tears. A great smile broke across Raúl's face at the sight of his former roommate.

"*Teniente Alberto Blair!*" he cried out. "Dammit, Yankee, you got here!" They pounded each other on the back.

Madero rose and spontaneously extended his hand. "Welcome, lieutenant. Welcome." Then he turned again to the tall, handsome man in a well-tailored tan riding suit and green velour hat, narrow brim turned down, tricolor band wider than the others.

Albert stepped back. Garibaldi. That was Giuseppe Garibaldi, not dead, not dead at all! Albert's eyes scanned the room. He recognized General Benjamin Viljoen, a thin, dark man, veteran of the Boer War and recent New Mexico rancher who had trained rough *campesinos* into his commandos. Chucho nudged him and pointed out Roque Gonzalez Garza, Eduardo Hay wearing a patch over the eye he lost at Casas Blancas, and Abraham Gonzalez, former Governor of the State of Chihuahua, a rock of the Revolution. Albert picked out Oscar Creighton, Villa's dynamite expert, a former New York stock broker.

A blast of cool air swept through the close room and Colonel Pascual Orozco entered. Behind him, a figure filled the doorway and Albert felt something akin to a charge of electricity spark the atmosphere. "Pancho Villa," Chucho whispered.

Orozco planted himself and his 30-30 rifle in front of the Chief. He saluted and tersely declared: "*A sus órdenes, Señor Presidente.* At your service. I have three hundred men encamped downriver, as you ordered, and a hundred horses fed and watered."

Orozco stood with arms folded, his long, dour face expressionless.

Madero directed his remarks to everyone in the room. "Thanks to your brave leadership and brave men, we are here. General Navarro has the city well fortified. I want you to be on the alert every moment for a surprise attack. And under no circumstances provoke one." He looked from Orozco to Villa. "I hold you responsible for the temper of your men. The plan now is to surround Navarro as closely as we can. And wait for his surrender."

Albert had automatically stepped back as Pancho Villa pushed his way forward to stand by Orozco. Mesmerized by the bulk of this near-mythical bandit-turned-hero, Albert had not moved when Villa backed up. Their hands touched. A crude and primitive power seemed to emanate from his very skin.

"Díaz has sent emissaries to El Paso to talk to us. I have appointed Dr. Francisco Vasquez Gomez to head a committee to meet with them. I want you to know that our terms are not negotiable. Díaz, his Cabinet and all his Governors must resign before we lay down our arms!"

A clamor of enthusiastic support went up. Madero held up his hand. "Now get some rest."

April 23
A truce has been arranged, for five days. I don't know how Villa and Orozco will take it. Their men are geared for a fight. While we wait, the fighting goes on in Sinaloa, Guerrero, Morelos, Yucatan, all those rat holes Díaz keeps swiping at, depleting his fighting forces. I wonder how Juan Andreu Almazán is faring with Zapata.

Julio and Albert spent most of their days with Raúl in Villa's camp. A Federal outpost faced the advance rebel guards. As the truce dragged on, insults began to fly:

"Chicken thieves," the federales *yelled. "Yellow-livered, gutless sons of whores, raiders of defenseless ranches, cowards who haven't the balls to shoot a rifle!"*

"Hijos de la chingada! We are under orders like you! Yellow-livered, did you say? Well, look at this, stolen right from under the noses of the gringos."

They rolled up a cannon, an old relic, a short-barrel, short-range wonder, bearing a plaque. A leftover ofof the Mexican-American war, last seen on the lawn in front of the El Paso courthouse.

May 6
Talks of an armistice drag on and on. Five days have become thirteen and now the truce has been extended six days more! Impatience is spreading thorough the camps like fever.

The staccato spit of gunfire brought everyone in the encampment to their feet. Dropping their napkins on the breakfast table, they raced up to the roof in time to see Orozco emerge from a barbershop and Villa racing for a taxi. The rebel leaders disappeared over the bridge.

"I knew they would provoke it. *Cabrones!*" Chucho said. "I heard them plotting."

But the rooftops were full of witnesses to the innocence of the provocateurs.

Fury shook Madero's voice when Villa faced him. "Order your men to cease fire. Stop them, Colonel Villa! Stop them, do you hear? We are negotiating an armistice!" But he knew the fuse was burning. Retreat was impossible.

Hasty staff meetings produced no plan, no accord. Madero summoned Villa once again. As the sun reached its zenith, Pancho Villa studied the map of Ciudad Juárez. By afternoon he had laid out the plan of attack.

The moon cast distorted shadows in the cemetery and a cold wind moved the branches of the willow tree brushing the headstone of a man who had died when he was twenty. Crouched behind the headstone, Albert waited for dawn. He fixed his eyes on Raúl, a ghostly figure leaning on a marble angel several rows ahead. Raúl would lead the pre-dawn attack. Albert's throat felt parched. He licked his lips. Death could be waiting around the corner, across the street, behind a corral gate, on a rooftop, in the schoolyard, behind the iron bars of a shuttered window. Fitfully dozing and praying, Albert's mind projected macabre images: shock on the faces of his mother and father when they received the news; Grace's piano draped with a black mantle. Arquitecto Rivas Mercado recognizing the name "Albert Blair" on a casualty list. A chill shook him, scattering his dreams. What the hell was he doing in this Revolution? He raised his canteen and took a gulp of water. He was leading a platoon. That was reality. He was responsible for Sergeant Saldaña next to him and that group of men who were pretending to sleep.

For the tenth time Albert looked at his watch: 4:30 a.m. He tapped

Saldaña on the shoulder. "Time to move out, *sargento*," he whispered. "You cover me when we get to the warehouse, then wait for my orders."

Up ahead, men were crawling forward, shadows among the tombstones, shadows becoming an elongated stream that threaded its way toward the road. Albert had memorized the chart: Villa would advance from the south, Lucio Blanco from the east, Orozco and Garibaldi from the west. They would converge on the plaza. Target: the Federal garrison.

Crouching, Albert led his platoon out of the cemetery. The only sound was the drip of a faucet. They broke to the relative safety of a wall, caved in where a wagon had struck it, leaving a rusty wheel rim as an obstacle in their path. He swept it aside with his boot and heard it clatter off the sidewalk and echo down the cobblestone road. Holding up his hand to stop his men, he listened. Not a sound. Clinging to walls, they moved up the street, around corners. No sign of life yet. Now other soldiers were creeping up. Orozco's men. He could see the American warehouse ahead, terrain he had scouted with Skidmore.

Catlike, they moved forward. Now the warehouse loomed dead ahead. Like an antenna, Albert's senses picked up movement in the schoolyard, which faced Kettleson's sign over the warehouse door. His gut told him the schoolhouse was fortified with machine guns; probably one on the roof, too. His feet touched the sidewalk in measured steps, moving forward. Forward.

"*¿Quien vive?*" a Federal guard shouted, emerging from behind a barricade. "Who goes there?"

Albert raised his hand and yelled "*Fuego!*" then watched the blood spurt from the soldier's throat as he fell.

In seconds, they were in a raging crossfire. A machine gun in front of the school sprayed the warehouse, forcing the platoon to break ranks. Another wave of soldiers pushed through. Like a crazy man, Albert stood in the street and fired, eyes registering a sandbag to his right. He swiveled and fired again, just as it burst into action with *federales* trying to repel the onslaught. In front of the schoolhouse, a machine gun spat its deadly rounds. Windows crashed. Men fell, screaming with pain and rage. Death was all around him. They were surrounded.

Surrounded, a part of his brain informed him, as his eyes watched a Federal infantryman fly up and hit the ground. Then another, and another. The rapid salvos were deafening. Smoke and dust choked him. Suddenly cavalry hoofs pounded, as horses rounded the corner and disappeared. "Break for the station!" he heard Villa's voice command.

The dust faded and Albert kept firing. Then he ran, retreating, stumbling over bodies, melding with other running feet headed for the railroad station.

For one eternal moment he was pinned against a wall before he could make a dash up the ramp and into the large waiting room in the station. Refugees and troops were pouring in; the wounded sat against the grimy walls with glazed eyes, the stench of humanity dense as they kept coming. Not a familiar face in sight. A dark-skinned colonel with black, frizzy hair jumped up on a counter and started barking orders:

"Villa is leading his men toward the plaza. Only four goddam blocks away. You *cabrones* can make it that far, can't you? Where are your officers?"

A small nucleus began to form by the counter.

"Find your companions. Count off in tens. Orozco's people here. Move in. *Rápido*! Villa's people to the right. Order!" the Colonel yelled above the din.

Albert pushed forward toward this one sane individual and joined the straggling *villistas*, who were forming a group.

"You, *gringo*, what group are you commanding?"

"Whichever you say, *mi_coronel*."

"Take those men and tunnel through the houses that lead to the arcades on the plaza. There's dynamite in that bag. Over there. Use small charges so you don't blow yourselves up, cabrones. Go!"

Zigzagging through deserted streets and alleys, avoiding random bursts of fire, Albert led his platoon to a familiar corner and ducked into a house on a street that led directly to the plaza. Furniture blocked the door but the house was abandoned. Albert had never used dynamite in his life. Before they could break through the first wall, an earsplitting explosion rattled the windows and shook the saplings struggling for existence in the dusty street outside. With total disregard for his life, a young recruit ran up the street and reported back.

"The water tank. We blew it up! Now they'll have no water," the boy announced gleefully.

A loud guffaw burst from Albert's throat. It was old "Whistler," that monstrous cannon built in a machine shop in Chihuahua. The damned thing had fired and hit the bull's eye!

"And the world was without form and void...form and void." The biblical passage repeated in Albert's mind as he rested against the wall of a small dry-goods store, his legs stretched out on the counter. His empty stomach grumbled; his hand was bleeding. Was this May ninth? Tenth? Eleventh? It was all a blur. Attack and retreat, repeat. Gunfire kept blasting through walls like an invasion of rats, until a grenade was lobbed through a hole, throwing up table legs and cushions in the small parlor, blowing the jaw off one of his men. They had scrambled out through thick dust, dispersing, running. Running.

Twice he had seen Raúl with Villa, leading a devastating charge, trying to divert the *federales* from the garrison to the plaza, only to be thrown back from concealed fortifications. Last night he had slept in a clump of weeds down by the river, stumbling up the street with Orozco's men at dawn. This dawn. Today. His hand throbbed where his rifle had been shattered by a bullet. Numb, he had kicked over the body of a *federale*, grabbed his Mauser and a bag of cartridges and ran, jumping over dead bodies laid out like an obstacle course, as volleys of fire whizzed overhead. He had looked up at a formidable Federal column marching toward him: infantry, two mortars and a battery of machine guns. He had jumped and stumbled to the corner, when he heard a voice shout in English: "Run for it, Al! Over here! We'll cover you!" Julio!

Albert turned his head, slowly, and focused on two shadowy figures in the doorway of the store. That was Julio leaning against the peephole in the iron curtain. A soldier stood beside him. He dashed across as Julio blow off the lock and they entered the store.

"Tie up that hand!" Julio ordered. "Grab one of those handkerchiefs."

Albert looked around. It was one of those little stores that seemed to carry everything: cotton stockings, thread, scissors, hammers, nails, bolts of materials stacked on high shelves. Bottles on a low shelf. He picked one up—"Dr. Richard's Pills for Nervous People"—and stared at the label, a ludicrous picture of a man with his hair standing in spikes, wild-eyed. Albert began to laugh. He turned the bottle around: same man, well-groomed, smiling, transformed by Dr. Richard. Low, loud belly laughter convulsed him, until Julio shook him, hard.

"You've got a fever. Tie up that hand, dammit!"

Julio reached up and pulled down a red Mexican kerchief, letting loose a cascade of blue ribbon. Albert watched it dribble off the counter and spiral down into a heap. He remembered another blue ribbon, and how stupid he had felt. Antonieta. He had never forgotten her name.

A piercing bugle call brought him to his feet.

"They're driving Orozco back again," Julio said. "I'm going to push through and get Garibaldi. Get word to Orozco, Al. Tell him we're bringing reinforcements."

In a second, Julio and the soldier had disappeared.

Albert tied up his hand, jumped down and crept outside.

Up ahead, Orozco's sharpshooters were trying to hold their ground against the *federales* at close range. Then Orozco's strident voice ordered retreat. He let himself be propelled by retreating soldiers, scattering to the sidewalks, faltering, swiveling to fire, making their way back to the river, yelling "*Retírense! Levanten los pies, cabrones!*" "Retreat! Pick up your feet, bastards!" Fear gripped Albert's guts and he fell back with the frenzied stream of humanity that broke and ran to the river. He ducked under the edge of the footbridge and crawled his way back, tunneling through the rushes. At the other end of the bridge, sharp against the clear blue sky, the stars and stripes waved, beckoning. An American soldier stood guard in the sentry box. Lined up behind him, like bulldogs ready to pounce, stood American infantrymen, just a stone's throw away on the other side. Albert washed the bloody kerchief in the river, watching the muddy water turn pink. A rainstorm had made the river rise, but he was a good swimmer. A movement in the nearby weeds diverted his thoughts. Out of the corner of his eye he saw a blue visor move and fired the Mauser, stinging his wounded hand. A young soldier stumbled toward him and fell.

"I wanted to swim across," he stammered.

The frightened brown eyes of a boy looked up at him, visored cap gone, the shaved head of a raw recruit bleeding where the bullet had grazed the skull. Federal or rebel, what was the difference? He was just a poor Mexican kid, fourteen at most, pressed to serve in a revolution that was meant to save him. Albert picked the boy up and carried him to the edge of the river.

Ándale, muchacho. You can make it. Swim under the bridge and give yourself up to that American guard over there."

A barrage of fire suddenly exploded behind the *federales* in pursuit. Villa! He had caught the enemy in a crossfire. Frantic voices shouted orders, trying to be heard above rebel yells. In orderly retreat, the *federales* began to fall back toward the plaza.

Rapidly catching up with Villa's men, Albert advanced once again toward the center of town. Street by street, house by house, they moved forward, holding their positions, forcing General Navarro back, forcing him to retreat toward the garrison.

Suddenly the energy of a tiger coursed through Albert's veins. Elation made every nerve tingle as they reached the plaza. He pulled a remnant of his platoon together. Revolucionarios began pouring around the western corner. Albert recognized Garibaldi's green velour hat and saw Julio at his side. A contingent of Orozco's men filed in. He could hear Villa's rebels in the distance, picking off scattered detachments. Lucio Blanco arrived from the east. A sea of Madero's forces now flooded the plaza.

Someone hit Albert on the back. Raúl.

"*Chingado*, you made it!" Albert cried out.

"Get your men ready. We are going to storm the garrison!"

He was gone.

Albert checked his watch: 3:00 p.m. Five hundred revolucionarios stood in the glaring sun, facing Navarro's fortification. They lined up and waited while their commanding officers conferred, eyes fixed on the high, thick wooden doors. Strategy was mapped by circumstance.

Strategy became a matter of quick decisions. The word spread rapidly. In one giant, concerted effort they would storm the garrison.

Sweat dripped off Albert's mustache as he loaded his Mauser, no longer aware of the pain in his hand. He spotted a discarded Federal sword, struck by a bullet but intact in its leather sheath. He stooped down and picked it up. Facing his men, he tore the sword loose from its scabbard, prepared to raise it to signal attention. A roar of laughter was spontaneously emitted as the rusty pieces fell to the ground.

"May the hinges of those doors be as rusty!" Albert exclaimed, breaking the tension. "Stand by. Wait for the order to attack."

Rifle locks clicked. Then silence descended on the plaza.

Albert could feel the muscles of his neck tighten as he studied the high stone wall and invincible-looking doors. Stories of English soldiers scaling fortresses, hot oil pouring down upon them, flashed in his mind.

Eyes glued on Raúl for the signal, Albert stood poised to move. Without warning, the doors of the garrison swung open. Flanked by his officers, General Navarro and his men filed out, hands held above their heads.

They were surrendering!

The gritty, vociferous, tattered horde of revolucionarios was struck dumb. Quickly grasping the situation, Raúl nudged the ranking officer, Garibaldi, forward. Pressing, craning their necks, the rebel forces pushed closer.

"Order in the ranks!" the Italian shouted.

Lieutenant-Colonel Felix Terrazas, a senior officer in Villa's division, quickly stepped forward and received the pistol proffered by Díaz' venerable general.

Standing next to Terrazas, Raúl spoke up. "I'll take your sword, sir."

With dignity, the white-haired general relinquished his cherished armament.

Pushed forward by the surging rebels, Albert found himself standing beside a little office at one side of the main entrance to the garrison. Pointing to him, Garibaldi ordered all Federal officers to surrender their swords to the lieutenant. Reacting immediately, Albert stood at attention as each Federal officer threw down his sword in front of him.

The pile grew. With rare discipline, the troops kept their positions until all the men in the barracks were disarmed.

Apprised of the surrender by one of his cavalrymen, Villa galloped up and took immediate charge.

"Round up these prisoners and escort them to the jail," he ordered. "I shall advise President Madero that General Navarro has surrendered."

He turned his beast around and galloped off.

In the lobby of the Hotel Sheldon, a wild uproar broke out. People shoved their way in and out, out and in. Reporters elbowed their way through the celebrating crowds of Mexicans and American sympathizers to fire questions at the victors of the Battle of Juárez.

"How many *federales* surrendered?"

"We know, now, that their total forces numbered only seven hundred."

"What's the fate of General Navarro? Hear Villa wants to lynch him."

"That will be determined by President Madero."

"Is it true that after it blew up the water tower the old cannon blew itself up on the next shot?"

"Indeed it did. We had no time to give it a proper burial." Oscar Creighton fielded the question.

Albert was almost knocked over by Ed Skidmore's slap on the back. "I want a personal account of the battle, Al. Godammit, I'll scoop Williams and Elton!" he exclaimed, exulted. He pulled Albert aside. "Did you hear that fellow? Those barracks you and I scouted were lightly populated. Navarro only had seven hundred troops! Old Díaz was bluffing when he declared he had thirty thousand field-ready troops - paper soldiers, maybe, like his lists of voters, huh? Anyway, they're falling like tenpins in Yucatán, Morelos and Sinaloa. Tenpins, I tell you! I think this thing is over." Skidmore pushed Albert farther from the crowd. "What's your opinion? With more men could Díaz have won?"

"Tomorrow, Ed. For God's sake, man, tomorrow."

His adrenalin still pumping, Albert elbowed his way to the elevator.

"*Viva Madero!*" rang in his ears. The cry had broken like a wave through the rubble of Juárez, now jammed with madly cheering citizens. He flagged a waiter and ordered a banquet to be served in the room. Once the door was closed, Albert took a swig of whiskey and fell on the bed.

A cartful of mashed potatoes, steaks, biscuits, fresh salad, and ice cream arrived simultaneously with Julio.

"We're bloody heroes!" Julio bellowed, yanking off his boot and throwing it in the air. "What will the Henderson Gazette say to that, cabrón?"

"More respect, please." Albert sat up and grinned. "I have been informed that as of today I am *Capitán* Bla-eer."

"Well, Captain, I bear an invitation from the Provisional President of Mexico. You are invited to join him in his triumphal trip to the Capital."

Albert's boot hit the ceiling.

CHAPTER XI
1911

Antonieta sat in the little park in front of the church of San Fernando waiting for Sabina to fetch her. Her catechism classes were over! Now she would have time to accompany Tío Beto to Mr. Villagrande's bookstore downtown. He said that old den of antiquity had become a den of iniquity, where *maderistas* now gathered to get the honest facts about the Revolution. A big battle was raging in the north and Tío said Don Porfirio should start packing. The thought had sent a wave of fear through the household.

A pigeon alighted on the back of the bench, but flew off when Antonieta tried to touch it. Mamá said Don Porfirio would never resign. She had practically locked herself in since the dread Revolution had started, and refused to receive friends or relatives who spoke Mr. Madero's name. Papá said Mr. Madero was an intelligent, reasonable gentleman who wanted a peaceful transfer of government. Mamá had yelled at him, called him a traitor and slammed the door. "There's a Revolution going on and you can't shut it out behind these walls!" Papá had retorted. Everyone was on edge.

Her new friend, Iwa Horiguchi, came running out of the church. Iwa's father was the Japanese Minister and her mother a Belgian lady, a Catholic.

"Antonieta! I'm so glad you're still here." Iwa sat down on the bench. "Father Xavier stopped me. He wanted to know if my father knew if they've signed a peace accord up there where they're fighting. He's afraid the revolucionarios will attack the church." She squeezed her friend's hand. "I saw a picture of Zapata yesterday. He has piercing eyes. Black."

Mexico frightened Iwa. She had always lived in Europe.

"My father says Mr. Madero is a reasonable man. He will calm everyone." Antonieta patted her friend's hand. "Are you coming to my breakfast? You're all invited, you know."

"That's what I came to tell you. We can't come. Father says President Díaz may resign at any moment and he should not leave the Legation. Oh, I'm so sorry!"

"At least we can walk up the aisle together," Antonieta said ruefully.

The girls had had identical dresses made for their First Communion. A new priest had mistaken them for sisters. They were the same height, brown hair and round brown eyes matched. Iwa's brother had blond hair and slanted eyes.

A hansom carriage with the rising sun painted on the side drew up on the side street. Mrs. Horiguchi blew a kiss to Antonieta and Iwa waved as she ran off.

Strange dreams wove in and out of Antonieta's restless slumber. Sometimes she wasn't sure whether she was asleep or awake. Like a log adrift, she was floating under the Pont Neuf... running through beautiful fields of wildflowers in Provence. She was a naked white statue with firm breasts which a young boy touched every time he passed by. An Indian in white pants shot off her arms. She was immobile and her throat was parched. Toward dawn she awakened with a warm sensation between her legs. An inquisitive hand felt the warm flesh. High. Inside the thighs. She drew out her hand and stared, horrified at the sticky red fingers. Blood! Something inside her had burst. She was dying. Dying.

"Mother of God, forgive me. Blessed Jesus, have mercy on my soul." Warm tears stung her face and turned cold.

At 7:00 Sabina opened the door and looked at the miserable figure on the bed, eyes wide, staring at the ceiling.

"Tonieta, what's wrong." She shook her shoulder. "Answer me!" The girl seemed in a trance. Sabina shook both shoulders hard until tears began to flow out of the rigid eyes.

"I am dying, nana. Look."

Relieved, Sabina daubed at the tears. They talked for a long time, about suffering. Women were born to suffer. God made them that way. All women? Yes, all women, of every color and race. Blood was a sign of suffering and purification. She was a woman now and would someday bear beautiful children. Now they must light a candle to San Antonio de Padua, who found good husbands, when the time came, of course. They should go to the church tomorrow.

Antonieta saw the image of San Antonio in her mind, full of little medals pinned to his tunic in the shape of hearts, his niche full of flickering candles, which leftover ladies lit every day, ladies who smelled like stale powder and perfume.

"I am not going to get married, and I won't light a candle to San Antonio!"

Sabina crossed her arms and looked at her young lady. "What else is there in life for your kind but a good marriage?"

"I shall be a great lady of letters and dance for my devoted public in Paris. I may even give them a concert—Chopin, Grieg, Lizst."

Womanhood, Sabina noted, had released a rebel.

"Why didn't Mamá tell me? And Alicia? That's why she takes so long in the bathroom. Why is it such a secret?"

One did not talk about these things, Sabina told her. It was not a fitting subject, either among her people or the gente decente. She would bring her a hot cup of *manzanilla* tea. Her young lady should rest today.

Sabina had done her duty.

"Look. The roses have opened," Cristina said.

"I told you the garden would be a mass of blooms for Antonieta's First Communion," Mamá Lucita said proudly. They were checking the final details for the garden breakfast. "I wanted it to be a perfect day for you, mi amor." She patted her beloved granddaughter's hand.

Although not one bit of white trim relieved her black attire, Antonieta was glad to see her grandmother in a happy mood.

"Your centerpieces are a work of art, Mamá," Cristina said with sincere admiration. A confection of sugar candy in the shape of a crusader's cross, painstakingly painted silver and dotted with little colored "jewels," was the centerpiece for each table. "I don't know how you have the patience to create such things in these troubled times."

"It is these times that require patience and a deep faith," Mamá Lucita replied resolutely. She looked at Antonieta. Her granddaughter was past the age of the usual communicant. It grieved Mamá Lucita that Catholic traditions were held so lightly in this household.

Antonieta loved her beautiful, quiet grandmother, although she wished they could talk about something other than religion. These days, especially, she was impatient with the drone of "Hail Marys."

Antonieta and her attendants sat at the table of honor: Mamá Lucita, Alicia, Chela, and Mario to her left. To her right, her father, mother, Tío Beto, Tío Luis and Tía Teresa from Querétaro. She helped herself from a tray heaped with fresh fruit, followed next by chicken *vol-au-vents*. Champagne was served to the adults, and a wine glass was half-filled for the children to join in the toast. It seemed like so many other banquets, Antonieta thought, but there was something unreal about this particular feast, as though the guests were actors in a play. People ate with accelerated movements, nervous gestures accompanied whispered conversations. The men left their tables and talked in small groups. The Cassasús' new Irish maid hurried up the path and whispered something in the *licenciado's* ear. He excused himself hastily. Tío Luis, who had come down from his hacienda in Querétaro, was talking with wild gestures to Papá and Tío Beto.

"I tell you, it was an ugly scene," Luis was saying. "I was at the bank on Plateros when that mob came down the street yesterday chanting 'Death to Díaz' and 'Vivas' to Madero. Thousands of them heading for the Zócalo. We heard shots and the mounted police began clubbing their way through the mob. If it hadn't been for a cloudburst, God knows what would have happened. In Querétaro things are very tense. I thought it prudent to transfer some funds to Texas. It was wild in the bank here yesterday. Wild! What do you intend to do, Antonio?"

"Nothing. This is a political revolution, and I am not a political man."

"But that rabble is on a drunken orgy, Antonio!" Cristina's voice rose to a high pitch. "The Gavaldóns are leaving for Paris next week. The Limantours are leaving and the Escandóns too. They say there is not a hotel room in Veracruz. Holy Mother of God, do you think Don Porfirio can still stop it?"

"You don't seem to know what a revolution is, Cristina," Beto interjected loudly. "Let me tell you. A revolution is a violent reaction of the organism to an infection. Don Porfirio should have left while there was still a cure. Now it has invaded the entrails of this country." Beto raised his champagne glass. "The old fool thought he could go on bubbling forever." He laughed. "I would like to propose a toast. Down with those on top and up with those on the bottom!"

"Stop it! Stop it!" Cristina hissed, holding her hands to both ears. Don't you see it's all going. Everything. Everything's going."

"Shut up, Beto," Antonio lashed out. "Not a single person here opposed the old man. Just because you signed a petition! This is no time to damn him." He looked at his brother with exasperation. "They say he makes no sense, plans every military move from his bed in a state of delirium. Added to that he's in excruciating pain from an abscessed tooth. The old man is finished. Please have the decency to let him be."

"I'm angry with him, Antonio. Can't you understand that? He let a cancerous growth develop when he could have prevented it by the simple act of not putting his name on that last ballot. The puffed up old buffoon. Damn him!"

Antonio abruptly walked off to meet licenciado Cassasús, who came striding back through the garden. The two men whispered a moment before walking to the head table. Antonio tapped his glass with a knife, calling the attention of his guests.

Cassasús' voice rang out. "Friends, I have just been informed that

President Porfirio Díaz has sent his resignation to the Senate. He is on the train now, on his way to Veracruz."

The train bearing Madero's entourage left the barren, spiny fields of the north and began to climb steep ranges of mountains to the high central plateau. At every station and water tower crowds greeted Madero, a kaleidoscope of bright pink, blue, orange and red blouses-- draped *rebozos*, gleaming black braids, high-crowned straw hats, a few bowlers and city dresses. Albert was caught up in the shouting and singing, popular serenades competing with discordant brass bands. A small barefoot girl with shy round eyes thrust a bouquet of wildflowers in his hands. He was stared at and smiled at by these Mexicans he had helped to liberate. He shared this great surge of revolutionary fervor.. This strange, beautiful country pulled him. Vague idyllic reams teased his mind.

Ducking the interminable speeches and the banquets offered in every town, Albert found himself in the courtyard of a flower-decked church. Trying to look past the vendors and beggars squatting in the dust, he permitted curiosity to draw him to the heavy, wooden door. He stepped across the threshold and stood rooted, shocked by a figure of Christ hanging over the ornate altar, a gruesome image nailed to the Cross, blood dripping, head hanging, a lace-edged skirt tied around its waist. Did Mexicans think of themselves as Christ crucified? Where was the risen Christ? For Mexicans, suffering was a suffocating value! In the dim, flickering light of candles, he had discerned other images in niches. Images everywhere, bloodied, bowed, weeping.

Albert stumbled out.

The city of Querétaro was the last important stop before the capital. As the last view of the arched colonial aqueduct disappeared, Albert remembered that just beyond this point they would reach an elevation of ten thousand feet before they began to drop into the valley of Mexico City.

Range upon range of undulating mountains grew dim as night bore down on the victory train. A fever of excitement gripped the passengers. It would be difficult to sleep tonight. Madero had planned his triumphal entry into the capital for ten o'clock the next morning, June seventh, exactly one year from the day he had been arrested in Monterrey.

As the first rays of sunlight streaked across the vast sky, Albert felt the train lurch convulsively. And again. They were about to be derailed! He threw open the curtain of his berth and saw that everyone was scrambling out. "Earthquake! somebody cried out. The train swayed and creaked as though it would come uncoupled. Then the wild motion subsided.

Cristina awakened just before dawn. She had slept fitfully, plagued by a premonition of impending disaster. Jose's lawyers were pressing her for money again. The important families had left for Europe, and the revolutionaries were about to take possession of the Capital. She thought of Fernando; it all seemed so long ago. Who was he seeing? She remembered his touch, his lips. His body.

She buried her face in the soft down pillow. Suddenly, a severe jolt made her sit up. The bed shook convulsively. Earthquake! The curtains of the canopy swayed as Cristina watched her perfume bottles slide off the small vanity. The chandelier swung in a menacing pendulum. She lurched to her feet and stumbled toward the door to the oratorio, forcing it open. The bell glass lay broken on the floor; little saint Cecilia looked up, released at last from her prison, a cracked smile marring her porcelain face. Cristina kicked the figure aside and struggled with the handle to her husband's bedroom.

"Antonio!" she cried out. "Antonio!"

The *terremoto* was soon forgotten in the excitement engendered by the arrival of Francisco Madero's train.

"It's a bad omen," Cleotilde, the old washerwoman prophesied. She was believed to have witch's power. Once she had put the evil eye on a young maid, causing her dismissal.

The excitement had spread to the kitchen. In twos and threes, the servants approached the arbor to speak to Antonio. The *patrona* did not wish to speak to anyone. The *patrona* had taken to her bed.

"Señor, we wish your permission to go to the railroad station to welcome Don Francisco Madero."

"We have heard so much about Madero and Democracia that we too want to welcome his wife," a young maid added grandly.

There had been heated discussion in the kitchen. Democracia was the name of Madero's wife. No, it was his mother's name. He was *Madero y Democracia*.

"Aren't you going too, Papá?" Alicia asked.

"No. I think I shall see enough of the gentleman in the future."

"Antonieta and I want to go. We'll be safe with Sabina. Please."

Antonio telephoned his American friends, the Langleys, whose house was near the statue of Carlos IV, right on the parade route. It was arranged for the girls to join the onlookers there.

Sabina ran to keep up with her charges. The iron curtains were pulled down on the neighborhood stores as people streamed up the streets. Close to the station, the crowd swelled, surging forward, forcing the girls to hang onto little Sabina so that she would not be trampled. Caught up in a wave of humanity, they reached the Langley's house just as the first whistle of the train was heard.

Camp chairs had been set up on the flat roof of their house, but their guests had clustered themselves by a low stone colonnade that offered protection and an unencumbered view of the parade route. Saying a dozen or so pleased to-meet-yous, Alicia and Antonieta made their way to a corner of the roof, which offered a view in every direction. A stone cornice served as protection.

"Ohhh! Heights make me dizzy," Alicia complained.

"Well, hang on," Antonieta advised.

The lampposts and trees along the street were draped with dangling legs and a human pyramid was piling on the top of a streetcar. All streets in the area converged on the *caballito*, the imperious equestrian statue which had witnessed every important event since colonial days. Now horse and rider were adorned with a human necklace, one small boy perched on top of Carlos' IV's august head.

"Look at that *mosca*! Over there." Antonieta pointed.

A human fly was climbing up the front of a tall building where he settled on a window ledge. The whistle blew again, closer now. The mass of humanity below them was charged with anticipation. Everyone wanted a glimpse of the man who had overthrown the powerful old dictator.

Looking out the window of the train, Albert and Julio gasped at the scene on the platform. As far as the eye could see, flags were waving, the cheering crowd drowned out by church bells, brass bands, factory whistles shrilly blowing, and the whistle of other locomotives in a nearby station. The train slowed to a stop.

Raúl rushed over to them from the direction of the staff car. "You two are to guard Francisco. Keep an open space around him. Garibaldi and Hay will ride with Francisco and Sarita in the carriage. The rest of us will stick close. You two jump up on the outrider seats to stave off the crowd."

It was an hour before Madero and his wife could enter the waiting carriage. Albert and Julio jumped up behind the radiant couple and waved to the mob to open a path for Díaz' magnificent carriage, driven by coachmen in full dress. The parade route would take them to the Palace, where León de la Barra, sworn in as interim President until elections were traditionally held, would officially greet the hero of the Revolution.

Albert's eyes focused again and again on the crowd nearest the Chief as he tried to take it all in. On either side of the street a solid wall of people cheered, threw flowers, ran alongside. A man with a black box ran ahead, set it on a tripod, cranked a handle and ran ahead again. Again, Albert was struck by the European air in Mexico's Capital as they passed grand buildings, statuary, well-kept parks. When they came out to the equestrian circle, he waved to the people massed on rooftops, whose "Vivas!" rippled along the wide boulevard.

From the Langleys roof, Antonieta shouted, "That's Albert Blair!"

"Who?" Alicia asked.

"That American engineer who came to lunch."

"When?"

"Never mind. Look, I think he saw us. He waved!"

In the wake of victory, Albert remained in the capital. He took rooms at the Hotel Bolivar and was swept along on the tide of celebrations. At dances, mothers eyed him and whispered. He was invited to play golf at the Country Club and got trapped into attending the tea dances that followed.

"You are a mystery, yanquí," Raúl teased. "And a prize."

I have told the girls you are a clod, so you avoid anything but a two-step. But they keep standing around hoping you'll ask them to dance. Better watch out. One is bound to catch you."

"Who would want me without any money or a job," Albert said soberly. "I've got to start thinking about the future."

Dressed in a new suit adorned with a tricolor ribbon in the lapel, he appeared at the Rivas Mercado mansion to pay his respects to the Señor Arquitecto.

"May I have your calling card," the old gatekeeper requested. Chagrined that he did not possess one, Albert scribbled a note and asked that it be presented to the Señora.

Soon the gatekeeper was back. "The Señora is not receiving today," he informed the foreign gentleman.

"When does she receive?" Albert asked.

"Sunday is her day, in the afternoon," the gatekeeper told him.

Sunday afternoon Albert rang the visitor's bell. After a long wait, a maid came to the gate. He handed her his card: *Capitán Alberto Blair*, it read. *Ejército de Liberación*. He watched carriages enter and leave while he waited at the small gate. After a long interval, the maid returned.

"I am sorry, Señor, the Señora cannot receive you today."

Cheeks flushed with anger, Albert marched off, vowing not to bother with the Rivas Mercados again. He would ask Julio about that job in a mine up north.

JUNE 1911 Antonio had new preoccupations.

As was his custom, the door marked "Director" was open. The

students who passed along the corridor scarcely noticed. Few of them had reason to speak to the Director; they were involved with internal affairs. The change in Government had wrought a change in attitude in the classrooms of the Academy. This new gust of neophytes had blown in boldly, stirring up the older students. They had filed a petition demanding changes in curriculum and methods of teaching, as though, Antonio fumed, beneath their thick skulls their uneducated brains were capable of directing their own course of study!

In compliance with a directive from the new Secretary of Education, San Carlos now offered a new degree: Master Builder, a practical course devised to train responsible foremen. Antonio had approved the new career and spent long hours shaping its course of study: a class in higher mathematics with emphasis on how to make calculations, a few engineering principles to limber up the mind, a class in perspective drawing. If a builder can explain with a simple picture, less chance exists for misunderstanding. The new course filled a need: housing in the working districts was a disgrace, a warren of overcrowded, malfunctioning odorous tenements that bred flies and discontent. Adequate housing was a necessity in a growing city. Madero had promised more schools; already an energetic building program was under way, especially in the rural areas where frequently the only literate person was the teacher. A free breakfast was to be provided for every student. Another of Madero's progressive ideas.

Antonio looked up from his papers, his mind charged with the events of the last few months. Looking down behind him was Don Porfirio, resplendent in all his medals, including the Order of the Sun, the Order of the Garter, the Red Collar of the Eagle, all conferred upon him by world leaders: kings, queens, emperors, presidents. Poor devil, he thought he would last forever.

"And now I have an order," Antonio said aloud, turning around and facing the gaudily framed photograph. "I must remove you from that wall."

Another of Madero's ideas: no living political figure should have his portrait or picture hung in a public building.

Antonio got up and took down the heavy picture. Suddenly he felt old. Sixty, after all, was not too far away. Perhaps he should resign, let the new generation take over. As he returned to his papers and put his spectacles back on he sensed someone standing in the doorway.

"*Pase*," he called out, before looking up. "*Pase, pase muchacho*," Antonio repeated with a pleased smile. He came around from behind his desk to greet his visitor. "I am glad to see you are still among us. You disappeared after your centennial exhibition at the Palace," he admonished. "What happened? Tell me about yourself. Come, sit down."

Diego Rivera removed the lopsided felt hat and held it between his knees, contained in paint-stained corduroy pants. He rested two semi-wrapped paintings against the chair.

"I have decided to go back to Europe. There is nothing more to do in Mexico."

"What have you done?"

"Traveled around the country. Sold a few paintings, waiting for something important to happen."

"You don't think anything important happened?"

"Not if you mean the Revolution. It was all over in six months and now the same old mummies are sitting in Congress."

"Not quite, Diego. There are some new deputies and more will be seated as elections take place. Many of the governors are new. There are new ideas...."

"Not for me. Begging your pardon, maestro, it's the same old scene. This Revolution is just a shift of perspective, like when you shift your angle of vision or the light changes and you make a different drawing of the same mountain."

"You are too impatient, Diego."

"There is no life here. I am going back to Paris."

"And the Cubists?"

"Yes." Diego shifted in the narrow chair. "I came to thank you for arranging the exhibition. Doña Carmelita Díaz bought most of my paintings herself. I appreciate the fact that the Academy bought a few. I see one over there." He grinned.

"I like to look at that landscape and I keep it in front of me to remind me that Diego Rivera is a good painter," Antonio said with a fatherly smile. "I cannot agree with you about Cubism or any of these other abstractions. My thesis will always be that the first function of art is to create beauty."

"And beauty, maestro, is in the eyes of the beholder."

"Quite true. But sterile efforts degrade the human spirit. I am a classicist, Diego. I can be nothing else."

"I once looked up the word "classic" It stems from the Latin and means model, excellence, enduring. You, sir, are a classic, and I hope you endure for many years." Diego reached for the paintings, fumbled with the string and rumpled brown paper, freed the paintings and laid them on Antonio's desk. "I would like to present you with two of my drawings from Spain," he said. "You see, they are dedicated."

It was a moment before Antonio spoke. "Thank you, Diego. I shall cherish them. If I am a classic you, my boy, are an abstract who will bend into many forms before you find your own solid substance. I'll see if we can't arrange a little scholarship money. Let me hear from you." He gave Diego an abrazo and saw him to the door.

"Well, it seems Madero is caught in crossfire," Beto commented at supper, opening a subject meant to irritate Cristina. "There are those who consider his reforms too liberal and those who demand extreme liberal changes. He's damned if he does and damned if he doesn't. What do you think Cristina? You went to that reception for educators at the castle."

"His boots were muddy."

"Any other observations?" Beto badgered.

"Yes. They served *tamales* and *atole*." Cristina's forced laugh was disdainful. "Do you know what they call his wife? Her name is Sara Perez de Madero. At the castle they call her *Sarape de Madero*."

Subdued laughter could be heard around the table.

Suddenly the French doors to the gallery were thrown open by a frightened maid followed by two agitated young men. Antonio recognized architectural students. They removed their caps and looked about at the astonished expressions. Without preliminary, they stated their business:

"Señor Director, there is going to be a strike at San Carlos tomorrow. It is best if you don't go. The painters and sculptors want to get you out, force your dismissal."

"And the Señorita," the other said, nodding toward Alicia," should not take her drawing class tomorrow."

Antonio could not believe what he was hearing. "I do not consider a few caricatures drawn on the walls of classrooms and a petition drawn up by a few misguided students as acts of violence," he protested.

"They are threatening to use clubs, if necessary, to keep you out, Señor. We wanted to warn you,"

At eleven o'clock the next morning, Antonio told Ignacio to bring the Victoria around. "If you remember how to drive a carriage," he chided. "I am going to San Carlos."

Alicia pleaded with her father not to go. Antonieta pleaded to go with him.

"Antonio, *por Dios*, in an open carriage. They will kill you," Cristina argued.

"I am too big and nasty." Antonio dismissed the remark.

"Then I am going with you. Wait."

Cristina was back in record time with her hat on and a cape flung around her shoulders. Her face had that determined look that Antonio had long ago learned rendered any argument useless.

As they turned the corner of the Palace toward the Academy, a group of students tried to stop the carriage. Ignacio plowed on. As they neared the school. a barrage of tomatoes and eggs spattered the sides of the Victoria.

Antonio became infuriated. He stepped down from the carriage and confronted his assailants

"Rebels!" Cristina yelled. "*Desgraciados*! You wretched curs. Don't you dare strike a defenseless old man!"

Her eyes followed Antonio, who stood a head above the mob. Aghast, she watched him grab two of the most aggressive agitators and, holding one under each arm, begin to knock their heads together, immobilizing his struggling victims.

"Antonio, *por Diós*!" Cristina shouted, standing up in the carriage. "Don't kill them!"

A brigade of architectural students ran out of the courtyard brandishing sticks to defend their Director. In short order, the Fire Department arrived and diluted the strikers' ardor with a good watering down.

The newspapers carried a full account of the strike and a splendid picture of Antonio with his two victims, one under each arm. Antonieta cut out the picture and pinned it up on her closet door. The following week Alicia attended her drawing class as usual.

CHAPTER XII
AUGUST 1912

Alicia sat cross-legged on the bed with her head bent down, running her hairbrush through cascading waves of shining brown hair. "Did I tell you that I sneaked out right past Mamá and met Enrique at San Hipólito this afternoon?"

"What did you say?" Antonieta was plumped on her pillows writing in her notebook.

"That I met Enrique at San Hipólito."

"Again? You just saw him yesterday."

Alicia sat up straight and threw back her hair. "Oh, Tonieta, I just have to tell you. It's so wonderful to be in love! Nobody was in that musty old church and we sat in a side pew. He kissed me."

Antonieta put down her notebook and squirmed around to face her sister. She looked like one of those paintings in the gallery at San Carlos in her ruffled white nightgown and her long hair let loose. Alicia was sixteen, all soft and agreeable since she was in love. It was their secret. Antonieta acted as messenger and courier when it was necessary. Mamá had refused to allow Enrique to call for more than a half hour once a week. For once, Alicia had had the courage to defy Mamá.

"He was so pleased that I went to that reception with Mamá at the castle. You know how much he admires President Madero. I lied a little bit. I didn't tell him that the ladies' waists were a bit too pinched and they wore a bit too much lace on their cuffs. I only told him that President Madero made a wonderful speech about the importance of education." Alicia gave a deep sigh. "I wish the Lozanos weren't such outspoken *maderistas*. People call them 'liberals'.'"

"You should be glad he's a liberal. They want to help people."

"Isn't it wonderful that he likes poetry? You know what he said to me at the Ortega's tea dance? 'I would rather listen to you recite poetry than listen to senseless political arguments.' Everybody wants to talk to him. He's so intelligent. And you know what he said when I spoke to Mrs. Ortega in French? 'Teach me to speak French. Everything you say sounds so beautiful'." Alicia lay back and put her arms under her head. "I thanked the Virgin again that *Mamá*'s terrible predictions about the Revolution haven't come true. Enrique says Madero is trustworthy and sincere. I only wish he weren't so short."

Cristina turned over on her side and put her arm across Antonio's chest. He had fallen into the peaceful sleep that follows satisfied desire.

"Are you asleep?"

"Umm."

"I must talk to you."

As Antonio awakened completely, Cristina laid a laprobe on his favorite chair. "This is important. I want your full attention." She sat on the edge of the bed in a gossamer thin white negligee and smiled at her husband.

Antonio settled into the deep bergère. "What's molesting you, reina."

"That young man Alicia is seeing."

"Which of all the swains that come around here?"

"Enrique Lozano. They are meeting in the church and arranging little trysts at friends' houses."

"Is that so unusual? I thought all girls liked secret meetings."

"You don't understand. She thinks she's in love and well, he's just not suitable."

"What do you mean? The Lozanos are fine people, well-educated, honest, hard-working. What's wrong with the boy?"

"He's all caught up in these new liberal ideas. He will never amount to anything. Look, Antonio, I am trying to tell you that this Lozano will ask for our daughter's hand, and soon. And she will capitulate. She will weep and sulk until we allow the engagement. Alicia needs to be distracted. Taken away for awhile."

"For God's sake, Cristina, you can't send her off to a nunnery!"

Cristina's smile was beguiling. "I have something far more attractive in mind. Europe."

Antonio sat quietly, pensive. Alicia had blossomed into an extraordinary beauty. A romantic child. That romantic fervor could lead her into an early marriage she might regret. His daughter married? Not yet, not yet. And Cristina had never been to Europe. He knew that smile. Her scheme served two purposes.

"When were you thinking of going?"

"Perhaps October."

"That soon?"

"It's a perfect month for touring. So many of our friends are over there and Alicia will be invited everywhere." Cristina's eyes lit up. "Perhaps you could join us for Christmas. We could finish our Grand Tour together."

"Not so fast."

"But you do agree? Is it settled then?" Cristina put her arms around her husband and kissed the back of his neck. "Please say yes."

"I guess so. Yes."

The small restaurant Cristina had chosen was dim. She removed an earthen pot of flowers to see José better. For the first time she noticed how gray his sideburns were.

"I paid the lawyer yesterday. Thank God, that's over." She looked at her brother long and hard. "But you will have to give Mamá money this month."

"What about your rent?"

Cristina took a sip of tamarind juice. "I had to sell the house."

"You sold your house!" José's look was as piercing as his sister's.

"For Fernando. Damn it, Cristina, that leech is bleeding you. Even I got a letter. He's looking for money everywhere."

"I sent him a small loan. When his assets are recovered I'll get it all back."

"*Inocente!*" José exclaimed with a cynical smirk. "In affairs of the heart you are a damned fool, my dear sister. Do you believe all that poppycock about his 'assets'?"

"I believe your stories," Cristina snapped, stopping further comment. "I asked you to meet me because I want to tell you that I am going to Europe."

"You are mad, Cristina. If you meet Fernando over there it will be your ruination."

"I am taking Alicia, to take her mind off an unsuitable young man."

"And Antonio is in accord?"

"Of course." Cristina interlocked her fingers and leaned toward José. "I wanted to see you alone for another reason. There is something very important you must know." She took a deep breath. "I forged Antonio's signature and mortgaged two of his properties."

"What? What are you saying...."

"If I hadn't, you would be rotting in prison!" Tears welled up.

Contrite, assimilating the confession, José took both his sister's hands and kissed them. "What pain I have caused you."

"We are proud people, José. I won't have you abused."

"Cristina, Cristinita." José released her hands and ran his fingers through his hair. "Antonio is certain to find out."

"He won't as long as the mortgage payments are made. There's a little money left from my house."

"You have committed a felony against your husband. He will never forgive you," José muttered.

"I want you to make the payments while I am gone. I can pay through January, but you will have to pay February if I stay that long."

"My God, Cristina, that's four months!"

"I am being pulled apart, don't you understand? But when I come back I will still be Señora Rivas Mercado and I'll live behind the walls of Héroes 45 for the rest of my life!" She squeezed her brother's hands in a tight fist. "For once in my life I have to rely on you. The payment is two hundred pesos. Promise? By all that is holy, so help you God, promise!"

"I promise, Cristina." José kissed her hand again. "I promise."

There was something amiss. Beto could actually feel it. Cristina was up to something and Antonio, as usual, was burying his head elsewhere. Beto had sensed a plot, and now it had come to fruition. Cristina and Alicia were going to Europe. She would see him, of course. Let it be. Life was a chore. The sheer act of getting up and getting dressed was a chore. Often Beto writhed in pain in the privacy of his apartment. He missed Damiana. When Antonio sent the next monthly stipend, he would go and visit the old woman in that miserable hovel out in the lava bed. Yes, he would visit her once more while he could still walk. Damned legs. Even his good leg was swollen. He dared not see a doctor. Doctor would cut it off. Only the parrot knew his secret suffering. That ignoble creature had pulled out most of its tail feathers and was molting. Just like me, Beto thought.

The political news no longer fascinated him. The press was so free that even El Imparcial had the audacity to publish a cartoon depicting Madero as a midget, a buffoon. Ha! He had that bureaucratic hive of bumblebees angrily buzzing. Madero was plugging up the honeycomb through which they customarily drained out bagsful of treasury money and he was making each agency account for every centavo it spent! The hacienda owners and foreigners were bristling over disputed land reforms. Pancho Villa, thank God, was harvesting corn up north and Zapata was still trying to plant it in the south. But Madero had better keep an eye on the Generals. Old General Reyes was locked up in a drafty cell in the military prison for an attempted insurrection, but it had been noted by Gustavo Madero, he of the glass eye which saw everything so clearly. Ha! Military luminaries: traitors, plotters. Don Porfirio would have applied the *ley de fuga* to Reyes, simply opened the prison door, shoved his enemy out and shot him in the back while he tried to "escape." Not Madero. He believed in constitutional law!

"I hate her!" Alicia cried out. "*She* wants to go to Europe. You think she loves me. Well, she doesn't. She just likes to show me off. The only person she loves is herself!"

"But you loved Europe and you will see Tante Blanche." Antonieta tried to console her weeping sister. "If he really loves you, Enrique will wait three months. Oh, Licha, I envy you this trip."

"Then you go," Alicia sobbed.

"Mamá would never take me." Antonieta put her arms around her miserable, distraught sister and patted her comfortingly.

Beto refrained from goading Cristina or making sly allusions to Fernando. He felt tired. Nothing was clear anymore. Mexico was in the grip of contradictory forces, like little earthquakes which only dogs could hear. Let Cristina go for the sake of Alicia, but he should at least talk to his beautiful, innocent niece. He asked Sabina to convey a message to Señorita Alicia that he wished to see her in his apartment.

Alicia sat erect in Beto's straight chair, her feet demurely crossed, hands folded in her lap while she listened to her uncle. He sought the right words to prepare her for the Europe she would see with her mother.

"Listen, my beloved niece, Europe is full of fortune hunters who roam the salons and lobbies of the great hotels, using their tarnished titles to impress the mamas and chaperones."

"Leticia didn't find one. And don't worry about me, *tio querido*, I am not interested in meeting men."

"But they will be interested in you. And your mother is susceptible to titles. These fortune hunters are suave, with generations of tainted history behind them. Their noble lines sprang from brutal old adventurers who killed and conquered. These diluted descendants are adventurers, too, who use their titles as a gilt-edged introduction. Don't let your mother fall prey to their flattery, hear? Be sure you check a man's real credentials before you permit him to court you. Tante Blanche will be a wise ally."

"I shall not be courted by *anybody*, Tio."

"Are you planning to enter a convent?"

"No, sir."

"I am trying to impress upon you the need to keep your eyes open. I do not want some tarnished title to carry you off."

Alicia giggled.

"It might suit your mother, but it is you who will suffer the consequences."

"Thank you, Tio, for advising me, and for thinking that I shall be the prey of nobility, even though tarnished."

"And beware of young swains who have been educated under the protection of their mother's skirts. They will invite you to the symphony and exude long flowery phrases to describe the trill of the flute and the tremble of the violin."

"I don't care for symphonies. One can never tell when they end. I start to applaud and everyone says 'Shh'."

"I wasn't talking about symphonies. I was warning you about effeminate men."

Alicia was not exactly sure what "effeminate" meant.

"Remember, the only nobility that counts is personal integrity and valor. I have known a host of scoundrels in my life; they bring nothing but suffering. Be forewarned, my precious niece, and remember that your old uncle only wants you to be happy."

Beto felt it was a weak ending.

Alicia thanked him and kissed him affectionately on the cheek. She had a puzzled expression on her face as she took her leave.

The baggage was piled on the landing. Memela was crying. Mario stood with his feet planted apart and arms clasped behind his back. He would not move and turned his cheek when Cristina kissed him.

"Take care of the children," Cristina whispered softly in Antonieta's ear. "And of yourself, *querida*." Tears brimmed her eyes as she bent to kiss her.

Beto permitted a peck in the air close to the cheek.

"Write every day," Alicia said, clinging to her sister. She slipped a note in the pocket of her skirt. "San Hipólito at six. Tell me everything."

Ignacio brought the Daimler around and suitcases were soon placed in the trunk. Antonio handed his wife and daughter into the back seat before taking his usual place beside his chauffeur.

Antonieta watched the long, black automobile go through the gates, turn left, and disappear. Somehow she knew that the house on Héroes Street would never be the same again.

DECEMBER 1912

The cry of the fruit vendor brought Antonieta and the cook to the carriage gate. From a sunny bench along the driveway, Beto watched the play of bargaining and selecting. The status of Señorita had effected a change in his niece. Childlike naturalness was being replaced with studied little mannerisms, modulated tones, a haughty toss of the head when she was displeased, and a condescending approach to her brother and sister. Antonio had turned over the keys to the storeroom to her, the sign of maximum authority. In three months Antonieta had changed. Indeed, Héroes Street had changed, Beto noted with misgivings. Pressed for funds, Public Works had abandoned the project of building a rotunda to Mexico's heroes on the Plaza of San Fernando. The cul-de-sac had been opened to traffic.

With the air of a grande dame, Antonieta walked back up the driveway ahead of the burdened cook. She was all haughty grace.

"Can you spare an apple for an old beggar," Beto called, holding out his beret.

Mario suddenly charged through the gate, up the driveway and ducked under the basket. He danced in front of his sister.

"We baptized five," he said. "Five on Saturday morning!" He had recently seen two little blond boys bicycling on his sidewalk and discovered they belonged to the Baptist church down the street. A fast friendship had developed. "And Bobby invited me to a track meet at the Tivoli right now. Can I go?"

"Did the Reverend Day invite you too?" Antonieta asked.

"Of course. He's the coach."

"I don't know, Mario."

"I'll hide this if you say no." The eight-year-old imp dangled the key to the storeroom in front of his sister.

"Where did you get that!"

He was off to the stables, Antonieta swift on his trail, picking up her long skirt and running like a gazelle. The Great Danes ran wildly back and forth in the kennels, excited spectators of the race. Antonieta caught him at the door to the carpentry shed and wrested the key from his tight fist.

Defeated, Mario planted his feet apart and clasped his hands behind his back. "Well, can I go?"

Tender compassion flooded Antonieta and she embraced her defiant little brother.

"Yes. I'll tell Papá when he comes home for lunch. Sabina can walk you up to the church and deliver you properly. Now go wash up."

The little Baptist church in the neighborhood had long intrigued the children, but in all the years they had walked past it, the nanas had never permitted a peek past the doorway. Loud singing was known to take place there, along with heretical baptismal dunkings. Recognizing the benefits the new friendship had brought his son, Antonio had called on the American preacher and his wife, affable people who believed in a strict God and healthful activities. With parental approval, Mario was initiated into the joys of camping and had become an avid sports fan and participant. Criticism rained down on Antonio's head from his sisters. To appease them, he had agreed to send his "wild" son to the Jesuit Boys' School in the fall. A little discipline wouldn't hurt. Cristina had spoiled the boy.

Antonio grew accustomed to a household without Cristina and life without the Academy, from which he had resigned at the end of the term. Undefined burdens seemed to be slipping from his shoulders. He sang loud, tremulous opera in his bath, a long leisurely affair from which he emerged wrapped in a huge sheet, like a Roman Senator.

Wooing his brother out to a bench in the garden, Antonio watched little Amelia sail a boat. The sky was cloudless and the garden was graced with the colors and aromas of winter blooms.

"Luis has invited us all to spend Christmas at the hacienda. What do you say, old boy, are you up to it? I told him I wouldn't accept until I consulted you."

Beto shrugged his shoulders. "We might as well, while we still have a Government."

"For God's sake, Beto, loosen up. Smell the flowers, stretch your legs, look up at the sky." Antonio directed a side glance at his brother slumped beside him. The only thing that kept him going was engaging in political battles with Villagrande. "What's Villagrande telling you now?"

"Nothing you don't know. The free press is making an ass out of our President. Twelve months in office and he has had to put down three rebellions. Don't you think that's significant! He was an ass to put Huerta in charge of the Army."

"Huerta's a professional, not a paper general. Trained in Europe. What's wrong with Huerta?"

"He's a dangerous man, a shifty bastard and a drunk. The generals will have their day."

Ignacio was approaching with the morning mail.

"Look, I'm going to wire Luis that we accept." He patted Beto on the knee. "The country air will do you good."

Ignacio handed Antonio several postcards and a letter. Postcards were piling up on the hall tray, from France, Italy, Austria, now Germany. Antonio passed them to Beto and opened Cristina's letter: "We witnessed a military parade in Berlin. The Kaiser's Army is magnificent! Wave upon wave of soldiers marched by, not one out of step, their spiked helmets and polished boots a gleaming display of perfect precision. One cannot help but admire the quality of goods, the cleanliness and discipline of this nation. I plan to spend more time in Germany than scheduled. Alicia prefers to take a side-trip to Switzerland with her friends. We will meet in Paris on December 15th. We are crushed you cannot join us for Christmas but appreciate your permission to stay through January...."

Antonio replaced the letter in its envelope and sat quietly, hands folded in his lap.

"Bad news?"

"No. She's enamored of Germany. Will stay on for two weeks, by herself."

Trying to keep his balance on the swaying train, Antonio put his weight against the heavy door and held it open while the family squeezed past him to the dining car.

"I want the window," Mario piped up and slid in, Amelia right beside him and Sabina next. Antonio, Beto and Antonieta sat with their backs to the moving landscape.

Seated at a table in the rear of the car, Albert Blair immediately recognized the big man and his lame brother. He kept his eyes averted while they sat down. Could that tall girl be Antonieta? Or was she the older sister? It had been two and a half years since that luncheon. He raised his eyes. The Señora wasn't with them. Slowly, he sipped coffee grown cold and bitter. They were ordering. It would take awhile for the food to arrive. This would be a good time to approach them. Should he introduce himself again? With sudden decision, Albert walked over to their table.

"Señor Arquitecto, I am Albert Blair, a student of Professor Walker from the University of Michigan. I had the pleasure of dining in your home in May of 1910," he said," holding out his hand.

"Of course, of course." Antonio extended his own hand. "I see you returned to Mexico, and sympathize with Madero." He pointed to the tricolor ribbon in Albert's lapel.

"I fought with him, sir. In the battle of Juarez," Albert said, trying to stand erect in the swaying car. It was Antonieta, he decided.

"I saw you in Madero's carriage." Antonieta spoke up. "You waved. Did you see us on the roof?"

"Afraid not. There were masses of people. I see you still have a preference for blue hair bows. Very becoming, if I may say."

"I assume you are going back up north," Antonio said.

"Only as far as Zacatecas. I am the manager of a silver mine up there. Do you know Zacatecas, sir?"

"Indeed. One of our colonial jewels."

The conversation turned to the Revolution and continued until the food was brought.

Back in their compartment, Antonio quipped to Beto, "A migrant bird come to defend Mexican liberty, that young Blair."

"Sounded more like an immigrant bird," Beto retorted. "Such loquacious admiration for Mexico. Strikes me as one of those types who admires everything Mexican and at the same time would like to change it all."

"Albert Blair had remembered her! Antonieta had been in the company of adults most of her life: young men rarely interested her. He was quite handsome and he had fought in the Revolution! She longed to hear more. On a pretext, she left the compartment several times, but he was not in their car.

"Settle down and change into your jodhpurs," Sabina ordered. "Here are your riding boots." She had anticipated her own ride over a primitive trail in a hard buckboard and packed a little tin of lard to rub on her sore buttocks at night.

Soon after lunch the train whistled three times and slowed down at a water tower, a signal from the engineer that he intended to stop.

"There's Tío Luis," Mario announced, pressing his nose against the window of the compartment. Sabina hustled her brood along the narrow passageway to the vestibule. Antonieta looked around for Albert Blair but did not see him.

Through his window, one car behind, Albert watched the family greet each other with the affectionate kisses and hugs so ingrained in Mexicans. Yet they were guarded and reserved with strangers. True aristocrats these. The Revolution had not affected them, or their way of life.

Two of the cousins were waiting astride their horses; extra horses were tethered to a post, saddled and ready. Everyone crowded on the small strip of cement, baggage piling up around them. A ranch hand reached up and handed the engineer a jug of pulque, his reward for stopping the train. It whistled and chugged off.

"How are you Antonio? Well fed, I see," Luis teased. "Teresa will straighten up that stoop, Beto. What do you say, Antonio, would you like to ride that mare or get bruised in the buck board?"

Luis was the tallest in the family, clean-shaven except for a bushy mustache, at ease in tight riding clothes and a broad-brimmed hat. Manuel, his oldest son, sported a thin mustache waxed and curled up at the ends, emulating the *charros*, Antonio marked.

"I'll ride if she's strong and tame," he answered.

Antonieta patted a big gelding. "May I take this one?"

"Listen, city flower, that beast can be mean. This one's tamer," Paco, her youngest cousin, advised.

He still had that mischievous look, Antonieta was glad to see. Although Paco was three years older, he had teased and challenged her since she could remember.

"I like him," Antonieta said haughtily. She fixed her boot firmly in the stirrup, swung her leg over and mounted astride, at ease with the huge animal, her lithe body easily controlling her mount as she wheeled around and faced the boys.

Paco whistled admiringly and remounted. "May we go ahead, father? I think Antonieta can keep up."

The Hacienda de San Felipe was five kilometers from the station through country thick with cactus and mesquite trees. In sudden contrast to the arid terrain, the entrance to the estate was through a forest, planted by earlier generations. By the entrance gate hung hunks of dried beef and covered vats of water for wayfarers en route to the village. Ahead lay the long, straight road leading to massive walls in the distance. A river had been damned to form a shallow lake along one side of the road. Ancient *sabino* and *alamo* trees watched over graceful willows, and a few white swans played follow-the-leader, completing the bucolic scene. Tall trees lined the road on either side, delineating pastures where cows, sheep and goats grazed, protected by a long wooden fence. In the midst of wild, arid country, here was nature's response to a plan for beauty.

They slowed to a trot. Antonieta drank in the surroundings, exhilarated and flushed from the unrestrained gallop. The giant wooden gates to the lower courtyard stood open. They rode through and dismounted, handing their horses to waiting grooms.

"How beautiful!" Antonieta caught her breath, spinning around to take in the bright red poinsettias against the old adobe walls, and clusters of flower pots spilling over with geraniums which had overcome the attempt to contain them.

"The one who is beautiful is you! How did you get that way?" Paco asked with straightforward admiration. Paco was sixteen, muscular and solid like a bull.

Antonieta hurried ahead to conceal the flush which burned her cheeks.

The day at San Felipe began with the braying of burros and the infernal crowing of roosters. By sunup, the house dogs were barking and the bells of the village church began to ring. House servants were required to attend morning Mass and evening prayers; houseguests were expected to follow the example. Antonio managed to disappear and Beto pleaded total weakness by sundown, hobbling in the direction of the library as the priest hurried in the direction of the chapel. Politics left behind, Beto enjoyed the placid peace of the country, acquiring healthy color in his lined face. A straw hat replaced the beret. Mario spent hours hanging on the gate in the corral, watching the charros work the horses; little Amelia discovered the joys of playing in the mud and, when clean, rode with the young children in a bright red carriage pulled by a spotted pony. News of importance was the birth of a new bull, breaking a spirited horse, a christening in the village.

Paco took personal charge of Antonieta, his ranch-bred character teasing, but his knowledge of nature and the business of the hacienda as limitless as were his city cousin's questions. They walked and climbed and rode and watched the charro work out. With the young bulls, Paco was brave and impulsive.

Breeding fine bulls was the ardent interest of the men in the family, and the bullfight their passion. Antonieta had never seen a bullfight, "That barbarous pageant of the masses" TíoBeto called it, though he admitted to having been a fan in his younger days.

"When we come to the city, I'll take you," Paco promised. "You would look elegant in a Spanish comb and *mantilla*."

Antonieta bent over to pick a wildflower to conceal her blush. "I blush every time he comes near," she wrote in her diary. "I wish I could control it, but all he has to do is look at me and I feel a flame burning my face."

One morning, when the sun was at its zenith, Paco drew rein abruptly at the edge of a ravine.

"There's a little waterfall down there," he said. "Let's cool off."

Jumping off the saddle, Antonieta secured her horse and followed the shouting Paco down to the arroyo, nimbly hopping to avoid cactus spines. Thickets tore at her jodhpurs; she paused on a large boulder to admire the symmetrical pyramid of flowers majestically crowning the tall stalk of a maguey. She climbed up the rocky ledge to an even level with the giant cluster. Throwing out her arms she cried to the sky:

"Oh, noble plant, in this moment of glory you rise to lofty heights, to bloom but once, and die!"

The wind whipped at her hair, loosening the bow which held it back. Far below, Paco scrambled after the undulating wisp.

"You look like a goddess?" he called up, triumphantly displaying the ribbon. "Was that a poem? Who wrote it?"

"I did," Antonieta answered, climbing down to where Paco waited. "I just made it up."

They sat in the shade of a giant pepper tree, its luxuriant leaves arching down like cascades of soft feathers. Lacy shadows played across Antonieta's face, creating changing patterns, like her mood.

They rested awhile, pensive, not daring to touch.

That evening the family gathered in the jasmine-scented courtyard. Through the entrance arch, the sun began to wash the secluded valley with a mystic light, softening the mountains. To one side a squat tower provided a solid foreground. Antonieta had only been up in the tower once. Now Paco asked permission to invite his cousin to see the sunset from the parapet.

They climbed up the narrow, winding stairs.

"I've been sneaking up here since I was about five," Paco said. "Come over here. Look at these slits. Know what they're for?"

"Of course. Guns," Antonieta said, keeping her distance. She could feel the flush begin to climb up her neck.

"And these are old powder burns," he went on, absorbed now in the view from the tower. "We have shot a lot of bandits from up here"

"What do you mean 'we'?" Antonieta goaded.

"The family, *tonta*. In grandfather's time, bandits swooped down on the mule trains loaded with silver from the mines up there in Guanajuato." He pointed to the distant mountains. "Our men were on the alert to defend the military escort and wagon drivers. We put them up overnight and fed them."

It was like one of her own well-rehearsed stories. She peered through a slit. It looked like a painted landscape.

"Have you ever been afraid?" she asked suddenly.

"Of what?"

"I'm afraid sometimes when I look out from our tower. Almost every day smoke rises in the pass to Cuernavaca and I've seen the sky turn red at night from the fields he's burning."

"Who?"

"Zapata. They say he cuts the soles off people's feet and hangs everybody he catches. Sometimes I have nightmares about him." Antonieta shivered. "I see him riding into the city with soldiers spilling all over."

"Never! Madero won't let him. He would have to fight the whole Federal Army."

"They say he won't stop until Madero gives the land to the peones."

"That will never be. The *desgraciados* would ruin the land. They wouldn't know what to do without a patrón. They would be drunk all the time and fighting each other."

"Most of Papá 's friends think President Madero is weak."

"Ha! You're interested in politics." Paco exploded with laughter. "A girl! You had better stick to poetry, even if it doesn't rhyme." His smile was condescending. "Leave politics and defense to us men."

Antonieta bristled. "Do your peones get drunk a lot?"

"Of course. All peones get drunk. They rob your noble plant of its milk before your flower does. Have you ever tasted pulque?"

"Ugh. It smells horrible." Antonieta held her nose.

"Everybody drinks pulque, even babies."

"Before it ferments," Antonieta added, flaunting her knowledge. Abruptly, she turned and leaned against the wall. "Papá says pulque is the elixir of the gods for peones. It makes them forget their misery."

"It makes them drunk."

"Then they must be miserable."

"Peones are born miserable."

"Let's go down," Antonieta said impetuously. She had meant to talk about poetry, not pulque.

Paco shook his head. "I don't understand you," he said, following on her heels as the last rays of the sun streaked the sky with gold and orange.

The three brothers argued and reminisced over the long, late *meriendas* in the dining room, where twelve out of twenty chairs were occupied. Beto told colorful stories of the Spanish galleons that had filled the Rivas Mercado house with treasures. He viewed his sister-in-law's taste with secret horror. A plaster Victory of Samothrace spread her wings under the dour face of a peeling Bishop, a long-vanished relative of her Spanish family.

The young people at the table hung onto every word, savoring family folklore, drinking in the new stories, and wondering how these heirlooms would be divided among them.

The days augmented into a week, two weeks, nearly three. Tantalizing odors emanated from the kitchen; guests began to arrive. Then it was Christmas Eve. Four generations lived at San Felipe. All participated in the traditional *posadas,* enacting the holy story; innkeepers turned wayfarers away in song; a nativity scene spread the length of the living room wall, large frogs and small elephants sharing the same habitat in the extensive menagerie. Memela was selected to lay the baby Jesus in his crib in the manger at midnight. The exchange of presents and midnight feast of smoked codfish went on and on. One by one the children were carried off to bed.

Antonieta felt a deep content, a oneness with nature and an appreciation for strong family ties. And a new feeling possessed her, a sense of an intoxicating feminine power.

Her tender adolescent breasts throbbed as Antonieta prepared for bed the last night of the vacation. She had sat around the fire with the boys. Tonight the guitars had sounded sad and melancholy. They had sung romantic songs, ballads of love, voices blending in perfect harmony. Then Paco made up a *corrido*. The impromptu verses had made her blush again.

"What does my pretty cousin hide behind eyes that beguile?
Why does she look sad when her mouth smiles..."

When they said goodnight she felt a little dizzy.

Submitting to the infernal rag curlers which Sabina still rolled up at night, Antonieta asked her beloved nana a question she had never asked before.

"Were you ever in love?"

"That's a ridiculous question." Sabina tied and yanked.

"Please answer me."

"Yes. Once."

"What was it like?"

"He was a liar who whispered pretty words."

"Ouch! Tell me, oh tell me, Sabina."

"We lived on a little ranch where I saw nobody but my brothers, my birds and my chickens. My mother feared all strangers and trusted no man."

"Not even your father?"

"He was killed by the rurales."

"Why?"

"For no reason."

Sabina's attention turned inward, to remote, sad memories, as she separated each lock and rolled it in the cloth square.

"And your love?. How did you meet him?"

"My brothers took me to the fiesta of our village. I was fourteen. I hadn't been to a fiesta since my father died."

"And you met your love."

"He had on a military cap pushed way back to show off his eyes. Light gray they were. He started talking to me."

"Did he kiss you?"

"He was one of those *machos* who must conquer every girl who strikes his fancy. A *canalla*!"

Sabina twisted the last curl and stood up.

Antonieta waited expectantly. "What did he do to you?" she finally asked, but Sabina was spreading out the crocheted coverlet. The conversation had terminated.

The bells of the village church announced the dawn. The dogs barked and performed their capers on the patio, frisking about with the old housedog, who escaped to rest under a luxuriant elephant-plant leaf. Antonieta stretched slowly under the warm covers. Then she pulled up her nightgown and raised her leg to watch the sun paint its shape on the high white walls. She had pretty legs. The sense of power sent chills through her body.

Antonieta's last view of San Felipe was of the high adobe wall which protected the store, the bakery, the school and the little church of the village. Behind it a cluster of shacks were separated by muddy streets, their red-tile roofs forming an uneven pattern in the late afternoon sun.

Chapter XIII

FEBRUARY 1913

Light had filtered through the curtain by the time Antonio awoke, before dawn, to bursts of firecrackers. Why were they shooting off fireworks today? Had he dreamed the horses, parading in regimental cadence? February ninth wasn't a feast day. Too early for any civilized human being to be awakened on a Sunday morning. He rolled over and tucked the comforter around his shoulders.

Antonieta lay in bed listening to the distant burst of fireworks. Curious, she went to the window to see if they were coming from the *feria* mounted by the railroad station. The lights from the Ferris wheel were still flickering past midnight when she had finally put down her book and fallen asleep. At eight, careful not to awaken Memela, who had begged to sleep with her, she got up and dressed. Today was special. She and Iwa were meeting at San Fernando for eight-thirty Mass, and she was invited to spend the day and night at the Legation. A famous Japanese dancer was going to perform.

Antonieta pulled a velveteen dress over her head and tied the sash, fluffing out the taffeta bow. Hastily, she packed an overnight case, rummaged for her gloves and hat. Remembering the mirrors, she tucked them in on top.

Sabina was waiting in the children's' dining room.

"I am not going to eat anything, Sabina. I promised Mamá Lucita I would take communion this morning."

"I am sure the good Lord will not object to a glass of water with a little lemon juice." Lemon water before breakfast washed the intestines. "Here, drink this down. What time are you coming home tomorrow?"

"Early, I guess. I bought fresh fruit for Papá's breakfast tray and there's some English tea in the canister. And oh, Sabina, try to get Tío Beto to eat."

"Humm." Sabina did not approve of her senorita spending the night out.

Two elegant young ladies settled back in the carriage with the Rising Sun emblazoned on each side. They wore matching wide-brimmed velvet hats, selected by secret accord.

"I brought the code book," Antonieta told Iwa. "And some mirrors. We can practice up on your roof. S.O.S. is easy."

The girls had experimented and found that through the telescope they could see from Antonieta's tower across treetops and low buildings to the gabled roof of the Japanese Legation. With her father's strong binoculars, Iwa could see the Rivas Mercado tower. They had practiced signaling with flags. If the dreaded *zapatistas* rode into the city they could warn each other and save their families.

The carriage was held up crossing south on Reforma Boulevard by a stream of mounted military cadets who galloped by carrying the Mexican flag. The bursts of firecrackers had grown louder, and now they could see yellow smoke billowing up from the direction of the Zócalo. Traffic stalled.

"What are they celebrating?" Iwa asked."

"I don't know. The firecrackers woke me up at dawn."

"Me, too."

People were running along the street heading for downtown.

It was an hour before the coach pulled up at a French-style mansion on the little Río de Janeiro Park. Mrs. Horiguchi herself, her blonde hair in disarray, threw open the door. She embraced the girls tightly.

"My darlings, thank God you are safe!"

"What's happened, Mamá?" Iwa asked anxiously.

"There has been a terrible battle in the Zócalo. Your father was informed that General Reyes was let out of prison and led an attack on the Palace. He was killed. Thank heaven the situation is under control now. Father was just advised that President Madero has arrived at the Palace."

The chandelier in the hall tinkled as a barrage of fire sounded nearby. Frightened, the girls looked for assurance to Mrs. Horiguchi.

"We think the shooting is coming from the Citadel, but there has been no confirmation. It may get worse." Mrs. Horiguchi believed in telling her children the truth. "Your father is distraught, Antonieta. We hoped you had turned back to *Héroes*. I talked to him not ten minutes ago. Go and telephone, my dear."

"Shouldn't I try to get home?" Antonieta asked.

"My dear, dear child, the situation is too unsettled. My husband is trying to find out exactly what has happened so that we may know what to do. He has cancelled the performance and has forbidden anyone to leave the house."

Guns had been going off at the Citadel, some two kilometers away, for more than an hour. Mr. Horiguchi privately confessed to his wife that the situation was dangerous. A rumor had been circulating that the store of ammunition in the old fortress might be blown up and the garrison taken by the rebels.

"I know you are safe there, preciosa," Antonio assured his troubled daughter. "We are safe too." It was a tearful conversation. "I'll find out what information Mr. Boari has gotten from the Italian Legation and we'll talk again tonight."

During lunch, the Minister's secretary appeared bearing an urgent message: The American Ambassador, Henry Lane Wilson, was calling an emergency meeting of all ministers and representatives of foreign nations to a meeting at the American Embassy at four in the afternoon. Mr. Wilson was dean of the diplomatic corps, and the only one with status of Ambassador. Further conversation at the table ceased with the unmistakable boom of cannon fire, which set the prisms in the chandelier spinning wildly, clanging with each successive explosion. Mr. Horiguchi ran up to the roof.

"It's coming from the Citadel," he reported. "No one is to go up on the roof. Nor outside. You must instruct the servants," he told his wife. "I shall try to arrange for an armed guard."

Promptly at three-forty-five, dressed in a frock coat, striped trousers, spats and a tall silk hat, Mr. Horiguchi took leave of his wife. Machine-gun fire sounded ominously close as the stern-faced Minister stepped into the warm afternoon sunshine.

That night, in the privacy of their bedroom, Mr. Horiguchi paced as he talked with his wife.

"What was finally decided at the meeting?"

"According to Wilson, the Madero Government is finished. Only the Palace remains loyal. He said that he had informed his Government to that effect."

"Is it true?"

"No. The man was irate. In the most deprecating terms, he insulted the President, called him a crazy fool who consulted spirits. 'He wouldn't take my advice,'" Wilson said.

. "We have encountered his arrogance before. What do the others think?"

"Marquez-Sterling, the new Cuban Minister—you haven't met him yet—pointed out that we are all accredited to the Madero Government. He suggested we offer all possible assistance to the beleaguered President. I concurred. This is a garrison uprising, not the people against Madero. We elected a committee to personally speak to the President at the Palace tomorrow."

Later, Mr. Horiguchi telephoned Antonio.

"I regret to inform you that your daughter must stay in the Legation until we can guarantee her safety in crossing the city. Already, barricades are preventing the movement of citizens as you, sir, must know."

"I do. And how do you assess the situation, Señor Ministro?"

"The diplomatic corps seems to be divided between those who believe the Government has fallen and those of us who believe the revolt has failed. I have sent a personal note to the President offering all possible assistance."

In the late evening, an aide reported back to the Legation. The girls sat in the parlor with the family, tense and frightened, yet an edge of excitement riveted their attention.

"Soldiers are posted everywhere. The Zócalo is bristling with armament. There are machine guns mounted in the towers of the Cathedral and cannons placed in plain sight in the courtyard. Soldiers line the arcades. Barricades have been erected at all the strategic crossings and rural soldiers are pouring in from the provinces. They say President Madero has refused to negotiate with the rebels and that General Huerta should have the rebellion put down by tomorrow."

Monday morning an eerie silence hung over the city. Peering through drawn curtains, the girls noted that there were no children playing in the park, the doors of the neighborhood church were closed, and iron curtains remained pulled down on the stores.

Streetcars were nowhere to be seen. Only blaring horns lingered in the silence, improvised ambulances, Mrs. Horiguchi told them, picking up the wounded and the dead. Antonieta's acute ears heard the boom of cannon in the distance and occasionally a heavy barrage from the Citadel. Her stomach was in knots; she telephoned the house on Héroes Street several times a day.

February 11th, 12th and 13th, the battle continued to rage, creating panic in the city. The stench of rotting bodies permeated the air, followed by the stench of black smoke, as pyres of dead bodies were burned with petroleum, to protect the city from epidemic. The constant staccato of machine guns coming from the Citadel sent chills through the Japanese Legation.

In the middle of the night, Antonieta suddenly sat upright in bed and nudged her sleeping companion.

"Iwa, suppose they cut the telephone wires? We are both here, so we can't signal!"

"Huh?" Her friend opened and closed her eyes.

Antonieta lay awake. How would she know how the family was doing? If Tío Beto was eating as he should? Poor Memelita was frightened of the dark and had been having nightmares lately. Over the telephone, would try to comfort her little sister. A plan formulated in her mind.

After breakfast, Antonieta telephoned her house. Her father answered, optimistic, as usual. Mamá Lucita was staying with the children, praying for peace; she exhorted her granddaughter to do the same. Memela was crying, Tío Beto was not up yet, and Mario regaled her with stories of the refugees at the Baptist church, which Reverend Day had turned into a shelter.

Antonieta let her excited brother talk, then asked: "Is anyone around?"

"No."

"Then listen carefully. This is a secret between us. I want you to take a white pillow case and stretch it on a stick. Tie it to the ledge on the outside wall of the tower that faces the volcanoes. There's some rope in the gardener's shed. If anything goes wrong at home, if anyone is sick or in danger, change it for a red flag. There are some red flannel dust cloths in the upstairs cupboard. I'll call you tomorrow to tell you if we can see the flag."

"I want you home, Antonieta," her brother said fiercely. "Is the shooting bad over there? They put a big cannon by the railroad station and we heard it go off this morning."

"Don't worry, love. The American Ambassador has asked Mr. Madero to confine the shooting to downtown, so we are both safe. Now remember, this is our secret code. I love you. Goodbye."

Antonio felt like a prisoner in his own house. Many of the servants had left, slipping out at night, with the complicity of Demetrio, preferring to be shot than not know how their families fared. They weighed on Antonio's conscience. And what of his tenants in the old convent of San Jerónimo near the Zócalo? Were their bodies being burned in those ghastly human pyres? It was only a week ago that his family had dined here. He remembered Rene's remark: "Every shopkeeper and beggar knows that the generals are plotting. Madero is a good man, but my God, a good man is not what we need. We need a tough leader!" Elena had proposed a toast to Felix Díaz, a general and a gentleman. "May he soon be released from prison," she had said. Prophetic words. Author of another insurrection, Diaz, Don Porfirio's handsome nephew, had the sympathy of the ladies.

"There is no sense to this bombardment!" Antonio exclaimed, knocking over his coffee cup with a wild gesture.

The cannonade at the railroad station had struck terror into the residents of Colonia Guerrero; wild shots had shattered windows in the seemingly impenetrable mansions.

"How in the hell can Huerta order an attack on the Citadel from such a useless position!"

Beto refrained from reminding his brother of his predictions back in December. The pain in his leg was excruciating; he missed Antonieta. This morning her reassuring voice had made him laugh. "I am learning to be a butterfly, Tío. "Don't tell me you are planning to fly away," he had teased. "In a dance, Tío. I wear a beautiful kimono." She had gone on to describe seaweed soup that the cook had prepared for the Japanese refugees who were sleeping on cots in the office, and told him which diplomats came and went every day. At least the girl was distracted and safe.

Antonio's mind was preoccupied with another thought: Cristina and Alicia were booked to sail on February 20th. It might be wise to cancel. The fighting was more intense every day. No telling how long it would go on.

That afternoon an "Extra" was shouted in the neighborhood. "AMERICAN INTERVENTION THREATENED." "If peace and order are not restored, if any American citizen or property is touched by gunfire, my government is ready to intervene. Madero must resign to avoid such an action," Ambassador Henry Lane Wilson was quoted.

Veracruz could be a city under siege! This was no time to return to Mexico. It was imperative to send a telegram, Antonio decided. How? To attempt to cross the barricades was to invite suicide. Only diplomats were allowed direct access to the telegraph office. Horiguchi! He would dictate a telegram to Antonieta on the telephone and that honorable gentleman could be counted on to send it. Antonio wrote it out: "Cancel February sailing. Stop. Capital in chaos. Stop. Remain in Paris until further notice. Stop. All family well and safe. Antonio."

Dawn of the seventh day was announced by a deafening cannonade that brought Antonio to his feet. Stumbling into his slippers, he ran from his bedroom to the oratorio. Had he dreamed it or was it glass he had heard, glass shattering. He opened the door to the little chapel and was assaulted by the odor of burning wool. A small flame crept across the carpet, whipped by the wind blowing in from the broken stained glass window. Quickly, he smothered the fire with his robe. Sabina. Of course. She always lit a candle to Saint Cecilia.

The little image lay smoldering on the floor under the altar, her new bell glass smashed and her scarred face broken. A victim of Madero's earthquake and Madero's rebellion, he thought with irony.

Antonio peered into Cristina's empty bedroom, expecting to see a gaping hole. Intact. That explosion was nearby. He was sure the house had been hit. His heart pounding, Antonio approached the jagged stained glass window of the *oratorio* and looked out. Crumbling debris was still falling down on the kitchen patio. The tower! They had fired on the tower! Misjudgment by the Federal Battery or harassment by the rebels? No matter, the tower had been hit.

Belting his robe tight, Antonio made his way up the narrow stairway. Thank God the damage was minimal. Outside a broken window he found a stick on which dangled the remnants of a white cloth. Halfway down he met an ashen-faced little boy.

"Come down to my bedroom, Mario!"

His son was small for nine, small and wiry. Antonio hoisted the culprit under his arm and continued down the stairs.

"Now…Who hung out that flag?"

Mario idolized his father. The formidable beard and mustache framed a generous face, but his hazel eyes were angry now.

"I did, Papá. It was a signal that we are all well and safe."

"And who were you signaling?"

The boy swallowed. "It's a secret."

"And what will you signal now that the tower is blown half away?"

Apprehension clouded the boy's steady gaze. "She'll worry when she sees the tower with a big hole in it!"

"Antonieta." Antonio had guessed the initiator of the scheme. "Now the telephone wires are dangling down in the garden and the electric wires as well."

A sob escaped the tight mouth and tears rolled down trembling cheeks. The penitent boy spilled out the whole story. "Why did they shoot a cannonball at our house, Papá? We're not against President Madero."

"Have you seen any of our neighbors flying a white flag? The rebels probably think we are harboring maderistas and the Federal soldiers no doubt think we are harboring rebels. Now go get another pillow case. We'll tie this flag farther back where it can't be seen by the soldiers. Antonieta will understand the message."

The nearest access to a telephone was across the street at the Cassasús' house. The house had been locked by the owners when they left for Europe and abandoned by the servants when the cannonade started. Only the old caretaker from the ranch was left. He was reported to be drunk and hiding.

At Antonio's insistent banging, the dazed Indian opened the kitchen door a crack. Antonio forced his way in. Scolding and blustering, he prodded the frightened man into locating the key to the butler's pantry. The kitchen was littered with empty wine bottles. Antonio picked one up, a vintage Bordeaux.

"There is no food." The old Indian shrugged trying to keep his balance. "*Uste disculpe.* It is better to be drunk than hungry."

After an interminable wait, Antonieta's voice came over the wire.

"It's so tragic, Papá!"

"What? For heaven sake, what?"

"The house is full of Maderos. When they went home last night their house was on fire and all their clothes heaped on the sidewalk. As soon as Mr. Horiguchi heard, he rushed over to get them and brought them here. Iwa and I slept on tatami mats in the sewing room and...."

Her voice fading and coming through, Antonieta embellished the events of the night. The President's wife, mother and father and two sisters had been given asylum by the Japanese Minister.

All day, friends and sympathizers of the Maderos rang the bell at the Japanese Legation. Camp chairs were set up in the ample reception room.

"My darlings, I need your help," Mrs. Horiguchi said to the girls. "You can usher the Maderos' guests into the *sala* and pass sandwiches and refreshments. These are seaweed crackers, Antonieta. Keep the dish filled. Here's another tin when this one is finished. Now, go dress up a bit."

Making the rounds of the room, Antonieta suddenly found herself looking at Albert Blair. She hobbled over on stilt shoes, hidden by a long kimono, and nearly tripped. She bowed as she offered her crackers.

"Have we not met, sir?" she asked in a sing-song voice.

"I think not," he replied, looking a bit confused. "I have only just arrived to offer the Madero family my assistance and I have not yet had the pleasure of meeting your fine family." The eyes did not look oriental, Albert noted.

Antonieta bowed again and moved on trying to suppress a giggle.

In the late afternoon, Marquez-Sterling, the Cuban Minister, was ushered into the office of the Legation in a great state of agitation. He requested an urgent private conference with his colleague. Horiguchi left his guests immediately.

"Madero has been taken prisoner," the Cuban informed his colleague.

"When?"

"About an hour ago. I was held back by a bayonet at the Palace. The sentry informed me that, on orders of the Commander of the Palace Guard, no one could enter. I fear the President's life may be in danger. We have to take action, Horiguchi, use all the influence we can muster to insure his safety."

On February 19th, headlines carried the news of the Palace Coup. Conservative newspapers applauded General Huerta for siding with the rebels and bringing hostilities to an end. The President and the

Vice-President were being held prisoners in a small office on the ground floor of the Palace. Congress called an emergency meeting and demanded Madero's resignation.

Out of touch with his defenders, coerced by his Congress, fearful for the fate of his family, the imprisoned President drafted his resignation.

Ignacio zigzagged through rubble as he crossed the battle-scarred city to the Japanese Legation. The midday sun highlighted the destruction. Invisible dogs barked on roofs, human scavengers picked through piles of debris. He made his way down Reforma to the new intersecting Avenue Insurgentes, recently opened to traffic. Deep ruts marked the paths where artillery had been dragged.

Antonieta threw her arms around her father, all reserve falling away. He clasped the kimono-clad figure in a bear hug, then held her at arms' length.

"Antonieta, preciosa, you've grown taller!"

Her tear-streaked face broke into a smile and the Japanese miss opened her kimono to reveal stilt shoes.

"I can walk on them perfectly, Papá. Oh, Papá," she hugged him again. "It's so tragic. Mrs. Madero is in the *sala*, weeping"

"Go get your things, angel. I'll pay my respects to the Horiguchis while I wait."

"Papá," Antonieta detained her father. "Remember Albert Blair, the American engineer we met on the train? He's in the sala." She snickered. "He thinks I am Iwa's sister. Don't give me away."

The large reception room was crowded. A young contingent had gathered around the Madero family Blari was among them, standing in a corner with a group of Antonio´s acquaintances and his friend and colleague, Gonzalo Garita. Antonio joined them.

"Doña Sara has just returned from a meeting with the American Ambassador," Garita told him.

"The arrogant bastard was rude and would not commit himself to intercede on behalf of the prisoners."

"Wouldn't she do better to contact President Taft directly?"

"It has been done. A few minutes ago Doña Mercedes dispatched

225

a telegram to Washington through this Legation. It's a mad situation! How do you like the circus Congress put on, dissolving and reconvening to 'legally' install Huerta as interim President? Good God, Antonio, the country has gone berserk! We finally have a constitutionally elected President and he is overthrown in fifteen months! Look, here comes Marquez-Sterling, let's hear what he has to say."

The Cuban Minister's face was ashen as a solemn-faced group of men gathered around.

"Gustavo Madero was assassinated last night," the Minister announced in a hushed voice.

Shock rooted the group.

"The President does not know yet. Nor does the family."

The Cuban was besieged with whispered questions. "Has it been verified? Who told you?"

"I have just spoken to an American doctor who was at the Citadel when they brought him in last night. It was brutal." Marquez-Sterling sucked in his breath. "He was spat upon, hit, tormented and mutilated beyond recognition. His good eye was gouged out with the tip of a bayonet and they say his glass eye is still passing from hand to hand among the 'victorious' rebels."

Shocked into silence, the listeners bowed their heads. The shame of a nation suddenly weighed down on Antonio. He understood the degree of madness produced by lust for power. A small minority had again fired their guns to get to the top. We are victims who allow ourselves to be victims, he thought. Anger, guilt and recrimination choked him. I should have served in the Congress when they asked me! It was evident that all the men in the group, patriots who loved their country, felt the same shame.

"They shall be brought to justice!" a young lawyer, José Vasconcelos, spoke out passionately.

"I share your grief, Señores," Marquez-Sterling said. "Now, our task is to see that President Madero is released immediately. Huerta has assured us there is no threat to his life."

The Cuban's face showed his profound pain and indignation. He could not bring himself to elaborate on the story told him by the witness; it was too shocking to put into words. Tricked by Huerta to attend a luncheon, Gustavo Madero was yanked from the table, locked up in a closet, then taken to the Citadel after midnight and handed over to the rebel commandant. When Gustavo tried to invoke his immunity as a member of the Chamber of Deputies, he was slapped by the man. Drunken, jeering soldiers pushed him along a corridor leading to a courtyard, striking him in the face, piercing him with their bayonets. Exasperated, he pleaded; incited to anger, he struck back. Pinning him against the wall, one infamous rebel flicked out his good eye with the tip of his rifle bayonet. Blinded, the terrorized man screamed in pain. "Crybaby! Coward! Stone-eye!" they yelled, spitting out insults and manhandling the helpless man. From then on, Gustavo did not utter another sound. He turned toward the wall, his face bathed in blood. With loud guffaws they jabbed, pushed, and tore his clothes as he groped his way along the wall. Then he was led stumbling out to the courtyard, where a fusillade of bullets pelted his body and his jaw was blown off. The frenzied rebels slashed his body, vying for the ultimate trophy: his glass eye.

Albert Blair attended the celebration at the American Embassy on February 22nd for one purpose. His messages unheeded by the Ambassador, he seized the opportunity to try talk to Wilson personally and propose that he join the diplomatic plan to escort Madero out of the Palace.

Champagne flowed at the lavish reception, but as close as Albert got to the Ambassador was to hear him toast "the savior of the Mexican nation, President Victoriano Huerta."

As glasses clicked in the brightly lit Embassy, Madero and his Vice-President were removed from the dark Palace in separate automobiles and driven to the federal penitentiary, where they were forced to get out in an unlighted courtyard and were peppered with a rapid barrage of gunfire. The next day, their bullet-riddled bodies were returned to their families for burial. The official version was that the automobiles were assaulted in an attempt to rescue the prisoners and that they were accidentally shot in the ensuing fight.

Albert wrote in his journal: "These ten tragic days have written their black history. The Revolution is dead and I am ashamed, ashamed of the Stars and Stripes that fly over the Embassy of the United States."

CHAPTER XIV
APRIL 1913

Confined to his apartment for a week with a nasty cough, the notion of spring lured Beto out to his favorite sanctum, the arbor, where the scent of orange blossoms made the stench of burning human pyres seem like a bad dream. Shivering, he wrapped his muffler around his neck and pulled the beret down closer to his ears. He could hear Antonieta talking to her grandmother in the children's dining room adjoining the arbor. Antonieta was his only solace in these useless, empty days; he hoped she would come out. She had been quiet and withdrawn since Madero's assassination, playing the piano as though she would drown in the music, then letting the notes die into silence. The girl took everything to heart, suffering each blow suffered by another. Beto coughed to let her know he was there.

"Now, Tío, don't catch more cold," Antonieta admonished as she joined him. She tucked his lap robe around his knees, then sat down at the table and rested her chin on her hands, observing her uncle with a sweet, contemplative expression. "You still miss Damiana, don't you?"

"I do. And what do you miss, Princess?" Beto cocked his head and smiled wanly. "Here's a new poem by Ruben Darío." He recited:

"The Princess is sad,"
What does she repress

That lets sighs escape
From lips still so fresh?
She has lost her laughter
She has lost her glow...."

He paused. "Why are you sad? I would like to hear you laugh."

A thin smile turned up the corners of Antonieta's mouth. "It makes me sad to see you suffer, Tío darling. I wish you would let Papá call a doctor."

"What can a doctor tell me?" Beto shrugged. "Only what I already know, that I have an incurable disease called old age." He began to cough.

Antonieta stood up and gently rubbed her uncle's back until the cough subsided. "I am going to bring you some hot broth." She turned toward the kitchen.

"In my old age," Beto told the parrot, "I appreciate what it is to be loved." Uncontrollable tears brimmed his eyes. They came frequently these days, called up by sentiments he was loathe to admit. His thoughts turned more and more to his childhood; little incidents long buried were resurfacing.

Beto's reverie was broken by an insistent clanging at the visitor's gate. Two men were walking up the drive. He met them at the head of the landing and was presented with their cards.

"We wish to see Arquitecto Antonio Rivas Mercado on urgent private business," the spokesman stated. "We understand he is home."

"Yes," Beto said, vexed with the new maid for allowing them to enter. He studied the cards, looked again at the intruders. Lawyers? They looked more like bill collectors. What did Antonio owe that made it "urgent" business? He instructed the maid to take the cards up to his brother and told the strangers to wait on the gallery, then hobbled back to the arbor.

Antonieta had returned with the broth by the time her father came down from his studio and addressed the strangers on the front gallery.

"Good day, Señores. To what do I owe this visit?

"We represent the Intercapital Mortgage and Loan Company," the spokesman said. "It concerns your properties." The man hesitated and glanced toward the arbor.

"Continue," Antonio said.

The man named the properties. "We hold the mortgages, and as it has been two months since our office reopened—after the uprising," he amended, dismissing the rebellion and coup as a temporary halt in business, "we are serving notice of impending foreclosure, Señor."

"Those properties are not mortgaged," Antonio stated indignantly. "I have no mortgages outstanding. There is some mistake."

The second man opened a portfolio and drew out a sheaf of papers. He handed them to Antonio. A look of incredulity shrouded his eyes; he stared at the papers in silence, a deep flush spreading upward from his neck. He unhooked wire frame glasses from a misshapen buttonhole and studied the signature closely. Cristina's. There was no mistake.

"Step into my office, please."

Beto finished the broth and read Ruben Dario to Antonieta. An uneasy feeling made him glance repeatedly toward the door of the anteroom. After twenty minutes, the men were escorted to the gate by the maid. It was another twenty minutes before Antonio stalked out to the arbor. Two bright red spots flushed his cheeks. Back turned, he stood gazing at the garden, feet spread, hands clasped behind his back.

"Would you like some juice, Papá?" Antonieta asked timidly.

"Leave us, Antonieta. Go! Go!"

The bewildered girl looked over her shoulder as she walked back toward the children's dining room, where Mamá Lucita still sat embroidering.

Antonio wheeled around and banged his fist on the table. "She forged a power of attorney and mortgaged my properties!" he roared.

Beto did not have to ask who.

"Why did she need to take so much money to Europe?" Antonio stormed. "Tell me, Beto. You know."

With painful eyes, Beto looked at his brother.

"For Fernando. Of course, Fernando. Always hanging around. Needing money. To pay for all those marvelous little out-of-the-way places she's been discovering. By God!" He took a breath. "I am a cuckold, a damned stupid cuckhold!" He overturned the juice as he banged on the table.

Antonio strode off in the direction of the foyer.

Mamá Lucita's fingers trembled. She had long suspected her daughter. Such useless guile. Men always found out. That was why Cristina had postponed her trip home again. The outburst in the arbor had left a numb ache in Mamá Lucita's heart. In the depth of her Catholic soul, she could not forgive her daughter. Infidelity condemned a woman to hell and gossip would condemn her to a life as a social outcast.

"I shall be returning home today, querida," she told Antonieta, patting her quiet granddaughter's hand reassuringly. "I should have gone weeks ago. I packed this morning," she lied. "Will you tell Ignacio?" She would never feel comfortable in this house again.

What did "cuckold" mean? Antonieta stared at the wall, bewildered by her father's rage. It was about Mamá.

Beto wiped at the sticky juice. The lid is off Pandora's box, he thought wearily. Cristina has lost the game. With sudden anger, he turned to the parrot and shook his finger. "She is more than a virago, more than a wanton woman, she's a thief!" he told the poor, rumpled bird.

Spring had erupted like a mighty volcano.

"What have I done, Tío?" Antonieta asked, her tone hurt and confused. "Papá hardly speaks to me."

"He won't speak to me, either," Beto answered, patting his dejected niece. "There are times when a man cannot share what gnaws at his heart. He must purge it alone. We live in difficult times and your father has many decisions to make."

"Does it concern Mamá?"

Beto shrugged his shoulders.

Settled in the lotus position with her eyes closed, Antonieta broke their meditation and spoke to Chela.

"I have something to tell you."

"Speak."

"My father is a cuckold."

Chela opened her eyes and looked at her cousin, "Just what is a cuckold?" she asked.

"It's a man whose wife is unfaithful. Tío Fernando is Mamá's lover. I hate her!" Antonieta jumped to her feet and faced Chela. "I hate her, do you hear? She will never live in this house again!"

The afternoon sun still filtered into the arbor and the parrot was chattering gaily when Antonio joined his brother and decided to breach the barrier that Cristina's name always erected between them.

"Yesterday I went downtown and cornered José. I found out that Cristina sold her house. It was her patrimony, her pride. It made her feel that she was landed gentry, not a pauper. I realized it must have been an act of desperation. My God, Beto, he told me the most tangled story of a stock fraud and bribes to keep him out of jail. Gave me the lawyer's name. Blamed himself for the whole affair." Antonio paused, his voice rasping. "He acted like a simpering idiot, begged me to forgive Cristina. She has cancelled two bookings, you know, something about Alicia and a suitor. Well, I wired her not to come home. Told her to embark Alicia. I would meet her in Veracruz..." Antonio heaved a great sigh. "Do you think I am wrong about Fernando?"

Antonio forced Beto's eyes to meet his. Beto only shrugged.

"I paid off the mortgages in gold. They wouldn't take Huerta's paper money."

"Don't get yourself pinched for hard cash. We may all have to run yet," Beto commented. "Carranza's 'Constitutionalist Army' is growing by the day. They say he has a thousand men under arms ready to avenge Madero's death."

The noisy backfiring of an automobile commanded the attention of the brothers as they watched a Lancia turn up the driveway and stop at the foot of the stairway. Leonor was handed out by her chauffeur. She was attired in a stunning white spring ensemble with a black trimmed hat and the slim ebony walking stick she fancied. She waved to her brothers and ascended the stairs.

"Hello, dears," she greeted them, giving each a kiss on the cheek.

"Beto, you look like a scarecrow. If Antonio can't set a decent table without a wife, I'll take you home and fatten you up. And you shouldn't be smoking. You're wheezing like an old locomotive."

"Now that the amenities are over, have a seat," Beto said.

Leonor removed her gloves and took an envelope out of her purse before she sat down. "Have you received your mail today, Antonio?"

"I only dispatched Ignacio to the post office a few minutes ago. Why?"

"Look what arrived in mine." Leonor waved the envelope coyly and handed it to Beto.

"Umm. From Madrid." Beto smelled it. "With a coat of arms and a regal aroma. Don't tell me you are invited to have *tapas* with the King?"

"That envelope you are sniffing is a wedding announcement."

Leonor laughed. "Here, give it to me." She drew out an elegant engraved card and read grandly: "Fernando Rivas Mercado y Figueroa and Condesa María de la Gracia Miranda y Escobar were joined in the holy bonds of matrimony on February twenty-fifth, 1913. The nuptials were performed by the Archbishop of Spain, etcetera, etcetera. We introduced Fernando to the old Countess," Leonor announced with peals of laughter.

"And why does this particular news merit a special visit?" Antonio asked.

"I thought a bit of gossip would cheer up poor Beto. He's always buried in newsprint. Well, aren't you going to ask me about the Condesa?"

"What about the Condesa," Beto complied.

"She must be sixty-five, dyes her hair black, sometimes blue, and orders special bust supports from Paris. She demands absolute attention. Poor Fernando will be her slave." Leonor paused and looked from one solemn face to the other. "My news doesn't seem to amuse you. I must be intruding."

Leonor began to put her gloves back on. "When is Cristina coming home, Antonio? I wonder if she was invited to the wedding."

"Why would she not be invited?" Antonio asked with a searching look.

"Well, she might not approve of such an old bedmate for Fernando."

Antonio walked around the table and faced his sister. "Why would she not approve of his bedmate?"

Leonor stretched the gloves over each finger as a slight flush began to rise. "Good heavens, Antonio, Fernando practically lived at this house. Don't you think Cristina would be interested in his choice for a wife?"

"Why don't you speak the truth?" Antonio's voice rose angrily. "What are people saying behind my back? What are you saying?"

Leonor stood up and picked up her walking stick. "This conversation is getting out of hand. I had best leave."

"No!" Antonio detained her. "I want an answer to my question. An answer!" he badgered.

Beto shot a warning look at his sister.

"You, too, Beto?" Antonio's eyes were blazing. "Now answer my question, Leonor. What are you saying behind my back? That I am a slow-witted cuckold?"

"Yes!" his sister snapped. "Yes. It's common gossip all over Mexico and all over Paris!" Leonor poked him with her walking stick. "Take hold of yourself, Antonio. Goodbye."

Antonio watched the Lancia disappear and sank down in a chair.

"You knew it, Antonio." Beto said with quiet affirmation. "You just didn't want to face the truth."

Slumped over, Antonio was silent. Finally, he pulled two letters out from his vest and threw them on the table.

"Alicia wants to get married." His chest rose in a great sigh and he blew out the breath. "His name is José Gargollo. A Mexican. Cristina had mentioned his name and so I had the man investigated.

"Is that the Gargollo who owns all the stagecoach lines?"

"The same. The business is in the hands of administrators since, to quote, his passion is to travel. He's a devout Catholic and a conservative and a damned lecherous *canalla*!" Antonio flung the letter toward Beto. "Here, read it yourself."

The handwriting was cramped and precise. Beto's eyes scanned the impressive list of references. All expenses for the wedding would be paid by the groom, since they would like to be married in Paris as soon as possible and travel to Egypt on their honeymoon, where he hoped to acquire some very important archeological pieces. It was their plan to return to the house in Paris and remain through the winter season. Afterward, if the situation permitted, they would like to take up residence in his house in Mexico City, which, Beto had heard, housed one of the most important collections of *objets d'art* in the country. Gargollo finished by praising Alicia, whom he considered quite the most beautiful and amiable girl he had ever met, a perfect lady. He prayed the Arquitecto would accept his offer of matrimony in the knowledge that his daughter would receive only the finest of care and affection. Señora Rivas Mercado had already expressed her approval."

"You should drag her home by the hair of her pretty head. When that man says she is 'amiable,' he means malleable like putty. The poor girl will live under his thumb all her life!"

"You haven't read Alicia's letter. They arrived together. Antonio tossed a pink envelope to Beto.

"My beloved Papá," he read. "I am honored to have Señor José Gargollo ask for my hand in marriage. He is a wonderful, kind gentleman and plans to show me the world! With your blessing, I would like to accept. Mamá has already given her consent and is in accord with Señor Gargollo (José) that we be married here. Is it really so terrifying at home? I love you all and pray for your safety every day. How I long to feel your kiss on my cheek, Papá. The apartment in Paris is very large and very nice. I shall change the draperies because they are too dreary. My eyes fill with tears when I think of home. How I wish you could all be at my wedding. Tell Antonieta that Madame Gautier will make my wedding dress and tell Tío not to worry. Señor Gargollo is kind and generous and I shall be very happy. He is sixteen years older than I, the same difference in age as with you and Mamá. I stretch my arms across the ocean and give you many hugs and kisses and wait for your blessing. I miss you and love you. Your daughter,

Alicia. P.S. I hope Mamá will be able to go home soon. It would distress me very much if she could not."

Beto was silent.

Antonio stuffed the pink sheets back in the envelope. She was only seventeen. Too young! How could he give his precious daughter to this man? He propped his elbows on the table and held his head. It was out of his control. She had made up her mind. Did Gargollo know about Cristina's lover? It was evident Alicia did. Antonio felt like a drowning man whose whole world was being sucked into the maelstrom with him.

Alicia's hairbrush used to lie on the chiffonier. A beautiful, porcelain-faced doll used to sit on her bed. Antonieta looked around the room and felt the emptiness. She threw open the closet and buried her face in her sister's clothes. Alicia would be somebody's wife when she came home. With a thirteen-year-old's sentimentality, Antonieta sank down on the floor and contemplated this new fact of life. The family would be half a family now. She put her head on the bed and wept.

The bright light of a crisp November morning caught the brass door handle to the little library and brought the dark Persian rug to life as Antonieta and Chela entered. The room had become Antonieta's island, where she could read and write in her notebook, think and let her imagination wind through labyrinths of fantasy, caught up in Buddhism, William Blake, Homer, spiritualism. The girls practiced telepathy, sometimes transmitting thoughts as if by magic.

Antonieta was the only person who was not impressed with Chela's beauty. "Titiana," Antonio had nicknamed his niece, her reddish hair and green eyes suggesting a Renaissance painting. Her pupils grew large when she got excited, accentuating the color of her eyes. Friends and competitors since childhood, there was no jealousy between the two cousins.

The girls sank down on Moroccan pillows and closed their eyes.
"I have something to tell you," Chela said, breaking the silence.
"Speak."
"Mamá is getting panicky about the revolution up north. Yesterday, Papá mentioned taking the family to the United States, to New York. He has business there."
"I don't want you to leave!"
"Oh, Tonieta, I don't either. I mean, I don't want to leave, but I

don't want to get killed in a revolution either. That murderer, Pancho Villa, has killed most everybody in Torreón and they say it won't be long before he gets here."

Chela pulled her cousin up by the hand. "I want you to come with us. Will you?"

"No. I would never leave Papá and the family!" The girls put their arms around each other, the peace of the meditation broken.

Tension ran down the long bar of the Jockey Club and a few humorless jokes forced reticent laughter from dry throats. Antonio felt as though he were attending a wake. The old influential clique that had spiced discussions with inside information had left for the United States or Europe. They said that a daily rush of foreigners crowded the railroad station, trying to squeeze onto the train to Veracruz, people heading for Havana, Europe, New Orleans.

Pancho Villa, with a formidable force, had joined General Carranza, who refused to recognize Huerta, and was moving south, engaging Federal strongholds. Panic had begun to infect the populace; hundreds were fleeing the country.

Someone was talking about the banks.

"I took all my gold out in February, but anyone who doesn't take his silver out now is a fool."

"I did just that yesterday. The scene at the Banco de Londres looked like a mass holdup, people staggering out with canvas bags full of silver, exchanging Huerta's paper money before he decides to close the banks."

"They say Carranza's printing millions in paper money in his home state, Coahuila, to supply his army. If other states follow suit we will be up to our asses in paper."

"Which reminds me of a story."

Antonio sat at his desk, got up and paced, then sat down again. In his gut he knew the situation was more critical than people wished to admit. Villa's *División del Norte* was bearing down on the Federal Army in the north, while Zapata was on a rampage in Morelos, never having lowered his banner demanding "Land and Liberty." Soon they would spill over the mountain for whatever food, guns, money, and necessities the Capital could provide. Could Huerta contain them? Damn Woodrow Wilson for imposing an arms embargo. He was a professor, not a politician! Huerta could stamp out this rebellion if he had arms. There was fighting near Querétaro, only two hundred kilometers away, perilously close to Luis' hacienda, Antonio reflected with a stab of fear. Grisly tales of the atrocities committed against the haciendas were too hideous to contemplate.

Antonio paced again. He had to think clearly, to squarely face his situation. If the rebels took the country, he, personally, could not be accused of being a politician or a military sympathizer. His only official connection with the government had been through education, with the Academy. Whether Huerta held out or the Capital fell, there should be no cause for personal persecution. This was a fight for power, not to avenge Madero's death! With Carranza at the helm, the country would be no worse off. He had declared himself the First Chief of the Constitutionalist Army. That implied that once he occupied the presidential chair, he would have to convoke a constitutional assembly, Antonio reasoned. With law and order reestablished, the country would get back on its feet. The nagging question was, could Carranza keep Zapata and Villa in line? How much blood would be spilled?

Cold sweat ran down Antonio's brow as he paced. Huerta was the best option. Anger at the United States welled up within him. Woodrow Wilson was a meddlesome idealist, bent on avenging the death of another idealist, Madero. Wilson looked the other way when Villa bought arms across the border. His goal was to force Huerta out no matter what it cost Mexico! If Wilson invaded, every revolutionary faction and every Mexican citizen would rise against the Americans, unleashing a worse bloodbath. But the painful truth was that no Mexican president had ever been able to stay in office without American backing. There were those who said that only under American surveillance could free elections and peace be enforced. Peace at what price! Antonio's mind reeled with doubt, fear, guilt. Was it a mad obsession he entertained, to stay and protect his properties, his home? Was it too much of a risk for the children? Rumors. So many rumors. He looked around at the once active studio. There was an emptiness in this room, in his life--a vacuum, he had to admit—that made this home incomplete. He missd Cristina. But he would never take her back! He missed someone to embrace, an anchor in his home. Antonio felt suddenly old and lonely. In a rare moment of religious sentiment, he prayed for strength and protection.

Rather than believe the headlines, Antonio began to frequent the Jockey Club, where nuggets of inside information could sometimes be found.

"Well, how do you tally the score at the Jockey Club this morning?" Beto asked, dipping his toast in his coffee.

"Even the maderistas are praying that Huerta holds out. Thank God he is getting arms from the Germans. France and England have recognized him, Why the hell can't Wilson!"

"Because he doesn't have a practical, European mentality. He wants Huerta to grovel on his knees." Beto folded back the American tabloid he was reading. "Read this speech by that Churchill fellow, First Lord of the Admiralty. Eloquent! He has convinced Parliament to convert the British fleet from coal to oil. He knows the importance of their Mexican oil fields. Huerta might get British help."

"Boari doesn't think Huerta can hold out. He sees the cesspool spilling out slime all over the country."

"Listen, Antonio, how many insurrections and coups have you and I already lived through? It doesn't matter which general sits in the presidential chair. We'll just put up another triumphal arch, shout another "Viva!" and go right on breaking the rules." Beto grimaced. "It doesn't matter who is in."

"Yes, it matters!" Antonio replied with sudden passion. "We have to bring Mexico out of this ignorant morass! The land of eternal revolution, they call us. Mexico has to join the twentieth century, damn it!"

"It's too late for causes, Antonio. You have done your share. We will live through this, and so will the children."

CHAPTER XV
FEBRUARY 1914

Albert spurred his horse up the last rise to the highest peak overlooking the city of Zacatecas. Dismounting, he dropped the reins and scaled a large boulder from which he could see in every direction. Wave upon wave of mountains undulated in the distance. He lifted the binoculars around his neck. Below, the soft glow of late afternoon bathed the old colonial city in a rose-tinted aura of breathtaking beauty. Zacatecas was squeezed into a narrow canyon running north and south. On the southern outskirts, wagons were clustered around an abandoned mine. Nearby, Albert watched men haul up buckets of water from a well and fill the horsehide bags in which the precious liquid was delivered to the residents of the city.

No unusual movement. He scanned the tranquil countryside again. Bandit raids had become a constant irritant as disorganized rebel groups sprouted in the area. The small Federal garrison was insufficient to deter the dreaded forays. A rich mining town halfway between the northern cities and the Capital, Zacatecas would be in the path of this new revolt Carranza and Villa had stirred up in the north.

Albert stood up, hands on hips, and planted his boots firmly on the smooth rock, reveling in the majesty of his surroundings. He felt a swell of joy in a job well done. These had been two years of hard work and discipline. He knew he had won the respect of his miners; his Spanish vocabulary astounded the Americans and the few British in the town. Hats were tipped by the Mexican elite of Zacatecas, descendants of the owners of the Spanish and Cornish gold and silver mines.

Life was good. He liked Mexico. He liked the Mexican people. Shy, gentle, hospitable, they asked little of life. The sky was immense in Mexico and so were opportunities to make money. He stretched. Ah, he would found schools and orphanages and old people's homes. Then an old guilt pricked his conscience. In his last letter his father had said: "When you decide to return home, your job here in Henderson will be open." Albert had seldom given himself license to explore his feelings and emotions, an indulgence superseded by "duty" at an early age. He had carefully considered his reply: "I do not know when I will return to the United States," he had written his father, "as these are difficult times in Mexico, especially for the Madero family, and I want to lend my knowledge and support in every way I can. As you know, I owe this job to them. The experience is invaluable."

Raising his arms high, Albert breathed in the pure mountain air, a balm after a day in the poorly ventilated mine tunnels, supervising operations during the endless digging and carting of silver. He took another deep breath, flexed his arms and settled down on the boulder. He lit a cigarette, reached in his pocket and drew out Raúl's letter. An idea had been germinating in his mind since he had received it three days ago. Raúl had joined Villa's forces in the north. He was a colonel now. The *Division del Norte* had grown into a powerful army, he reported, and soon they would swoop down on the *federales* and crush the assassin, Huerta.

Albert unfolded the sheet for the tenth time and read: "For me, holding a rifle and riding in the wind is preferable to sweating down in a hole, but if you are still a passionate civilian, at least get out of the way of the federales. I don't want gringo blood on my conscience. Villa is Carranza's right arm and his left arm is a general in the northwest who has balls and knows how to fight. Alvaro Obregón. Keep your eye on him. Carranza has tried to get the *zapatistas* to acknowledge him as First Chief, but Zapata is an independent cur, doesn't trust any politician. Villa calls Carranza a *perfumado*, says he combs his whiskers all the time and smells of jasmine instead of sweat. No matter what kind of ogre they paint Pancho, he is still loyal to Madero, says he's going to make Huerta dance out of the presidential chair to the tune of lead pellets.

"Emilio is a general now and I am a colonel but most of the family is in exile, spread out in San Antonio and New York. Father is in New York, trying to borrow money to salvage our crops. As long as Villa controls the north our haciendas will continue to work. We had a bumper crop of cotton and there it sits in the warehouse costing money, with nobody from the family able to take charge.

"Pancho is big news. Our headquarters is always swarming with reporters. One Washington newshound asked him if he spoke English. 'Si,' Pancho answered, 'American Smelting and Refining y Sonofabitch.'

"Now don't sit on your ass, Yankee. *Move,* before it gets too hot down there."

Albert thought about the tremendous tracts of Madero cotton he had seen near Torreón, and an idea churned in his mind as he guided his horse down the precipitous path to town. Stern wrought-iron balconies hung over cobblestone streets, softened now by the last pink rays of sunset. He turned down the dirt road that took him to a stone, walled-in house. His house. The silent Chinaman would have his dinner ready and MacGlashan would be waiting in the *sala* for his Wednesday night whiskey and cribbage game. The thought of a stiff drink made him spur the horse.

"Well, have you decided to leave or stay?" MacGlashan asked him. The Scotsman poured another generous whiskey from a crystal decanter and settled his long, lean frame into a comfortable chintz chair left by the wife of the former manager. MacGlashan was the company assayer, a graduate of the University of Glasgow and well-connected; his father was an intimate friend of Andrew Bonar Law, Prime Minister of England. A bachelor, MacGlashan had his own house in town, but preferred to drink Albert's whiskey. Albert tolerated the Scot because he was a competent chemist and a good cribbage player. MacGlashan was also a drunkard and, according to his boastful tales, a superior cocksman.

"I am going to give the company thirty days' notice, then go up north to see what I can do to help the Maderos."

Albert measured out two jiggers of whiskey, hesitated a moment before cutting his own with water.

"Your Madero is becoming a saint to the peasants. He's more persuasive dead than alive. But his name isn't doing you much good around here. Everyone knows you're a maderista. If the federales liven up the garrison here, they just might string you up. Where up north are you going?"

"Probably to Torreón," Albert answered.

"An evil place," MacGlashan said, striking a match on the sole of his boot and lighting a bent cigarette. "Did you know I was in Torreón when your friend Pancho Villa took the town last year? He slaughtered the prisoners like damned cattle. Bodies of chinks kept piling up. He flushed 'em out of their laundries, drove 'em out of their orchards and cafes. They ran like rats through the streets with their pigtails flyin'. You never heard such screaming in that gibberish of theirs. Machine guns ripped 'em at every corner. Villa marched a bunch up the stairs of the Bank of China and pushed 'em right out the windows. The streets were spattered with chinks. 'Bout two hundred, I heard." MacGlashan shook his head. "Wonder what Villa has against Chinks?"

"Well, Torreón is where I'm going," Albert said, a tight expression on his face. "Villa is loyal to Madero and that's important for the cotton business. That's what I'm going into."

"What do you know about cotton?"

"Nothing."

"Better stick to mining," MacGlashan advised. "I heard there's an opening at a mine in Naica. Pays a bundle."

"Where's that?"

"Naica? It's a one-tree town out in the desert. They provide you with a wooden house and a watchman. Know what makes it attractive? The watchman's daughter. The last manager told me he got her in return for a few privileges. Probably fat by now; she's past sixteen.

Good pay at Naica."

Albert did not comment. MacGlashan got up and emptied the decanter. That was the end of any show of decorum. Mac would now take the bottle out of the cupboard and bang it down on the silver tea tray. Albert started to pour himself another drink then stopped, the usual prick of guilt restraining his hand. MacGlashan picked up a fresh pack of cigarettes and sauntered back to his chair. Now he would settle in and begin his crude stories before he shuffled the cards.

The joke was abruptly interrupted by the Chinese cook who scurried into the room wildly waving a knife. "They come," he cried out. "They come!"

"Who?" Albert asked.

"Federales!" He ducked back into the kitchen.

The whinny of horses erupted outside. Albert felt his Colt revolver in his hip pocket and bolted the door. He had been forced to give food and money to irregulars who roamed the countryside before. The last manager had been killed in cold blood resisting a bandit raid. The man's frantic wife had fled, leaving everything behind. But these were Federal soldiers, the cook said. What did they want?

Albert stood tensely waiting. MacGlashan made no move to get up from the chair.

"Open!" The loud order was unmistakable, "or we will shoot out the lock!"

With rapid stride, Albert threw back the bolt. Soldiers pushed their way into the parlor, rifles firmly grasped.

"Who's in charge here?" the officer barked.

"I am," Albert replied.

"I am Capitán Garza of the Federal Army. We have come to borrow money." The Captain's black eyes swept the room.

"On whose orders, Capitán," Albert asked boldly.

"General Juan Andreu Almazán," the Captain snapped.

A glow lit Albert's eyes. "The General is a friend. Where is he quartered?" He had last seen Almazán in San Antonio, before he left to join Zapata. What the devil was he doing in Huerta's forces?

"What does it matter to you?"

"I request that you take me to him, Capitán. He is a good friend and I am glad he has come to Zacatecas to establish order and stop these infernal rebel raids which keep us from our work. I know the General to be a man of honor and...."

"He is also impatient," the Captain broke in, studying Albert with obsidian eyes. "Your friend is in need of money. Where is it?"

The menacing impact of the black eyes suddenly struck primeval fear.

"The money's in my office."

The Captain jerked his head toward a sergeant who stepped up and frisked Albert. He examined the outdated Colt .32 and tossed it on the table. Then he pulled out his own .45, spun Albert around and stuck it in his back.

"*Vámonos!*" the Captain ordered.

He was cold and surly. Albert knew the type. There was no point in stalling for time; empty the safe and pray they would leave quickly. With the gun at his back, he started across the room, noticing that a soldier had approached the silent MacGlashan and was smelling his glass. The fellow yanked the Scotsman to his feet, frisked him, pushed him back in the chair. God, don't let Mac get belligerent, Albert prayed.

The Captain turned and ordered his men to search the house. The sergeant prodded Albert up the hallway, kicking open the door to his office. Ledgers lay on the cumbersome old desk where he had left them the night before. The Captain's eyes swept the large room, checking off every item, and came to rest on the new Mosler in the corner. He turned to Albert.

"Open it!"

"It belongs to my company," Albert said impulsively. "My company is English. You know they want to help General Huerta establish peace." He planted his feet firmly.

"Open the safe!" the Captain commanded, pushing him.

Turning his back on the deadly trio, Albert crouched down on one knee and fumbled with the dial. He could feel the hair rising on his neck. ALBERT BLAIR KILLED IN THE REVOLUTION IN MEXICO, a headline in the Henderson Gazette crazily flashed in his mind. Nervous, he mis-dialed the combination.

"Hurry! Your friend the General does not like to be kept waiting."

A pistol ground into Albert's shoulder blades. Numbly he worked the combination again, his brain making him a mere observer of his actions. As the handle clicked open, he waited for the explosion that would end his life. But the pistol was withdrawn. He reached in and dragged out a heavy canvas bag. Then balancing unsteadily, Albert stood up and faced the Captain. With both hands he handed over the bulging bag.

"*Plata*," the Captain said flashing white teeth. He dumped the contents on the desk and began to stack the silver coins.

Albert watched silently, allowing himself to accept the reprive the Lord had granted him.

A scuffle in the hall diverted the Captain's attention. An excited, shrill voice was jabbering unintelligible words. A soldier dragged the Chinese cook through the door of the office, wrestling to remove a cleaver which the struggling man held on high.

"I found this cabrón in the pantry", the soldier informed the Captain, pulling his victim into the room across the bare tile floor.

The single blast of a gun made the cleaver crash on tile as the soldier let go and doubled over, his body slumping in a heap. MacGlashan stood in the doorway, weaving, the Colt .32 smoking in his hand. Enraged, the Captain whipped out his gun and fired, hitting the Scotsman in the thigh. The wounded man sank to the floor and dragged himself over to the desk as soldiers crowded into the office.

"Leave him," the Captain ordered, keeping his pistol pointed at MacGlashan, who had propped himself up against the desk, eyes closed, his breathing heavy, a dark stain spreading through his pants. "We'll deal with him outside."

"Capitán Garza," Albert spoke up, his mind searching for words, "this man is an *inglés* and unfortunately drunk. He is well-known in Zacatecas, a trusted mining engineer with my company. You see he cannot escape. It's an international case. General Almazán should settle this affair."

"Your *inglés* is a murderer. He killed in cold blood." The Captain picked up the hand of the dead soldier and dropped it back with disgust.

"But he is drunk, Capitán. You know a man acts without thinking when he is drunk. He's an Englishman! With very important connections. If you kill him you will have to answer to General Almazán. General Huerta has the support of the English."

Stone eyes stared at Albert, who returned the look with unflinching gaze. With sudden decision, Captain Garza replaced his pistol in its holster and dismissed his soldiers, ordering the sergeant to guard the wounded inglés.

The Captain turned his attention again to counting the money. Albert's chest heaved as he knelt beside MacGlashan and felt his pulse. "Are you all right, Mac?" he whispered.

"Only scratched m'leg," came a weak reply. He winked. "Did you notice that the Chink escaped? Get me a drink, will ya?"

The Captain poured the silver back into the canvas bag and jerked Albert by the arm. "*Vámonos*! Let us see what a good friend General Almazán is."

"I'll come back for you," Albert called over his shoulder.

Their hostage in tow, the federales rode through a dark labyrinth of streets. Where the streets narrowed, the horses clattered single file up stone steps, then spread out onto a broad esplanade in front of an ornately carved stone mansion. Albert recognized the house of one of Zacatecas' aristocrats, an arch-conservative. The Captain dismounted and ordered his men to wait, indicating to the sergeant that he should guard Albert as the trio walked up to the great wooden doors.

A dignified old gentleman in a velvet jacket and cravat received the group in the spacious entrance hall. "*Buenas noches, Capitán*," he greeted the officer. "To what do I owe the pleasure of the presence of this foreign gentleman?"

"*Buenas noches, caballero*," Albert interceded. "I have come to see General Almazán. Is he here?" he asked politely in well-pronounced

Spanish.

"Of course. He is my guest," the old man said, looking uncomfortably from the foreigner to the armed soldier to the canvas bag in the Captain's hand. "The General is in my office. You know where it is, Capitán." He dismissed them with a polite nod of the head.

He's frightened, Albert thought. They walked down a hall hung with tapestries and lugubrious paintings. The door to the office was partially open. The captain knocked and stepped in.

"I have a gringo sonofabitch here, *mi general*, who insisted on seeing you. Claims you are a friend," Albert heard him say.

"You know I have no time to see anyone!" Almazán's familiar voice was angry.

"Juan Andreu Almazán," Albert called out, "it's Alberto Blair. We stayed at the Hotel Hutchins in San Antonio and went to the Buckhorn Saloon with Raúl," he said in Spanish. "Remember?" He did not dare to mention Madero's name in the Captain's hearing. "I must talk to you. It is urgent, sir," he pleaded. "It's Capitán Alberto speaking."

The name and voice stirred the General's memory. "Pase," he called out.

The soldier shoved Albert through the door.

With recognition and surprise, Almazán rose and greeted the hostage. The Captain snapped to attention.

"Albert Bla-eer, what are you doing here?" Almazán asked in heavily accented English.

Albert grinned at the young General with relief. "I would like to ask the same of you," he answered in English.

"Yes, I know him, Capitán. Put away your arms." Almazán extended his hand to Albert across the desk. "Sit down, please. Now, in what way may I serve you?"

They sat across from each other at the elaborate Spanish baroque desk while Albert recounted the events of the night in Spanish, complimenting the Captain on his cool head, calling him a man of reason who had considered it wisest to bring the case before the General.

"You acted sensibly, Capitán Garza." the General commended his officer. "This is no time to create an international incident over an unfortunate drunken affair. The English are our friends. If it were known that the *inglés* was defending the life of a Chinese, the Federal Army would be accused of the same inhumane crimes as the villistas. Did the Chinaman get away?"

"The cabrón escaped," Garza replied scornfully.

"Señor Bla-eer, will you see that the inglés receives medical attention and leaves the country as soon as he is able to travel. That is an order," Almazán admonished in an authoritative voice. "That is all, Capitán. Arrange to bury our soldier. And, Capitán, you can leave the money here," he finished with a wave of dismissal. "I shall write out a receipt for this loan," he said turning to Albert.

The Captain looked at Albert with passionless eyes as he deposited the bag on the desk. He and the sergeant saluted and left the room.

Almazán got up and closed the door. He was an unusually handsome man, no more than twenty-six, Albert guessed, but a seasoned soldier. He remembered that he had left medical school to join Madero.

"Now, friend, how about a *copita*?" Almazan asked. A full jet-black mustache enhanced his good looks and made him appear older. He reached in a drawer and pulled out a bottle of brandy. "Martell?"

"Of course!" Albert grinned, feeling the tension drain out as he sank down in the big leather chair. "Do you always live like this?"

"Only when I can." Almazán smiled. "This house was relinquished with good grace. The wealthy are on our side, you know. But it is only for tonight. We leave at dawn to join my division up the line. I suspect we will encounter Obregón before Villa."

They talked of mining and Albert's career. After the second drink Albert asked the question which had been scratching at his mind.

"Why did you join Huerta?"

"I saw Madero was a weak President."

"Yet you knew Huerta had him assassinated."

"Of course! What does one do after the fact? You take your best option."

"What about Carranza?"

"He's motivated by personal ambition."

Albert's lips drew together in an unconcealed snicker.

"So the same motive moves Huerta," Almazan continued. "Yes. But get this straight, my Yankee friend, Huerta may look like an ass in a cutaway and a tall silk hat, but he's a tough professional. He does what has to be done and pacification of the country is the only thing worth fighting for now. Villa's *Division del Norte* is nothing but a bunch of *campesinos*. Huerta has political control, for now. We have the men, the arms and the influence, for now. I'll let you in on a secret. This is the beginning of a grand offensive." He raised his glass. "To victory!"

"May you live to be an old man," Albert said, and clicked glasses with his friend.

The first rays of dawn streaked the sky as Albert arrived at the railroad station. He had left the keys to the house with the nuns at the hospital and a note for MacGlashan: "Remember what I told you. You have been ordered to go, so get the hell out of here as soon as you can. I shall wire my resignation to the company and ask them to pay the men. You are a good man, Mac. Stay away from the bottle."

The sleepy clerk at the telegraph office punched out the long message to the company. Albert sent a telegram to Gabriel Madero in San Antonio, advising him that he was on his way.

"It is wise, Señor, to return to your country," the telegraph clerk said. "It will soon not be safe here." He did not add that as Villa took over the railroads he also assumed control of the telegraph offices, and that it would soon not be safe for him either.

Albert hoisted two heavy valises onto a slatted wooden bench and rested his back against them. The train was not due for an hour. I'm only twenty-three, he thought, and I have to start all over again. Frustration soon gave way to sleep.

In San Antonio, Evaristo and Gabriel Madero welcomed Albert in a tidy, two-story house set back from a tree-shaded street by an expanse of lawn. The house had become a center for exiles attempting to transport their cotton and cattle through Federal territory to the United States' market. Cotton and cattle dominated Madero thoughts and conversation; they provided the principle livelihood of this large, dispersed clan in exile.

"It's not just the cotton in the warehouses we're worried about. The ranches keep producing and there's another crop ready to pick and bale. We need cash. So right now we're trying to drive a herd of cattle up here to San Enrique on the border. Let the feds see our brand—and it's goodbye."

"There's no brand on a cotton pod. I'll get your cotton baled and sold," Albert announced.

Evaristo whistled. "You're a groundhog, Al. What do you know about cotton?"

"Nothing yet," Albert replied, with a haughty grin. "But I followed that Benton affair carefully."

There was a diplomatic outcry against Villa in the States over the killing of a Scotsman who complained to Villa that his rebels were stealing his cattle in Chihuahua. The outrage in the American press had labeled Villa an assassin and a bandit.

"I do know that neither Villa nor Huerta want to get entangled in foreign interests. I'll ship your cotton in my name. I'm a foreigner. Villa will protect Madero cotton and I have a safe-conduct letter from Almazán."

With wide-eyed admiration, young Evaristo noted the determined set of their friend's jaw. "When we go back to Mexico, I would like to be your partner," he said.

Gabriel rubbed his chin. "There are a hell of a lot of risks involved."

"I'm used to risks."

"You'll have to talk to father. Julio's with him in New York. Why don't you take a vacation and go up there?"

The following week, Albert boarded the Spirit of St. Louis. In New York, he was received in the modest hotel which served as the Maderos' headquarters in mid-Manhattan. Francisco Madero senior listened attentively, impressed with the young man's concern and astuteness.

"My proposal, sir, is based on a percentage of sales. Gabriel and I can open a joint bank account so that you can have a cash flow coming into the United States." Albert tucked in his chin. "What do you say, sir?"

"I say you have a lot of courage, son," the old patriarch declared, smiling. "What we need is someone to be in overall charge. Would you be willing to take that much responsibility?"

"I would be honored, sir. And you have my word that your trust will not be broken."

"Then I say, God bless you."

A contract was drafted, in which Albert would administer the eight cotton-producing haciendas. It also put him in charge of the cattle ranches, and cutting *guayule* rubber on other haciendas. His power of attorney included the collection of all dividends from mines and other properties. Señor Madero marked the haciendas on a map, pointing out that most were within a days' journey of San Pedro de las Colonias, where the head office of the House of Madero was located. San Pedro was sixty five miles from Torreón, the main junction on the central railroad. He would have a house at his disposal with trusted servants to look after him.

It was late afternoon when Albert guided the buggy into San Pedro de las Colonias, exhausted from the long trip west from Monterrey, a route dotted with bodies hanging from trees. The dirt streets were flat and rutted. Like so many Mexican towns, a central plaza formed the core. At one end stood the Municipal Palace and jail. Across the square stood the high-domed church and bell tower. Stores and the homes of the well-to-do occupied the arcades on either side of the plaza. A water-wagon circulated around in the dusk, filling the tanks of the houses through a cracked rubber hose.

Few people loitered on the streets. One could feel the Revolution here hanging like a silent shroud over SanPedro. Albert set to work, immersing himself in the study of planting, picking, baling and transporting cotton. He applied his engineering mind to the complicated machinery of the huge gins, laboring long hours to learn the processes through which a little cotton ball passed in preparation for sale to traders and brokers. He liked the efficiency and unadorned language of the north, quickly establishing a good relationship with his staff. Money was the constant worry, essential cash for the payrolls. Both rebel and Federal forces blew up railroad bridges and cut telegraph lines, until the only communication with the banks in Torreón was through armed couriers. Huerta's money and Villa's money; he had to keep a supply of each, and when that ran out he issued his own cardboard money: "By power-of-attorney for Francisco Madero; (signed) Albert E. Blair." The most negotiable currency was the U.S. dollar, clandestinely circulating all over Mexico. It was essential to have a dollar reserve. In March Ablert decided to make the hazardous trip to El Paso. He would set up banking arrangements for the cotton he had shipped and bring back dollars

The weather in El Paso was unseasonably warm. A breeze slid down from the Franklin Mountains and stirred the leaves of the trees along the riverbank. Almazán had wrenched Torreón from Villa's hands, and Villa had again wrenched Juárez from the Federal forces. Juárez was a beehive of rebel activity. Villa was shipping carloads of confiscated cattle and cotton across the border to be sold on the American market. His freight cars came back packed with coal for his locomotives, ammunition, dynamite and supplies. It was rumored that Villa was about to start a big push out of Chihuahua. The "Atila of the North" was at the peak of his power, and his *Division del Norte*, Albert sensed, was about to move south.

No time for a leisurely lunch. Albert dropped his fork on the limp salad. It was time to face Jimenez, the customs agent on the other side of the border.

The sun felt good on Albert's back as he made his way to the customs house in Juárez. Across the plaza, the forbidding looking garrison jarred his memory: he thought of the day General Navarro had laid down his sword. Three years ago. Three years that seemed like ten. Francisco Madero's fragile dream had been chipped and hacked at until it shattered. The nation's energy was being expended in destruction, brutalizing men, making killers out of simple, peaceful people. The Revolution had become a way of life.

Pushcarts crossed the plaza, horns blared, and a mule-drawn tram pulled up as Albert proceeded at a rapid pace to the customs' house.

He had proof that Villa had shipped cotton stolen from northern ranchers in the Madero name, to make it look legitimate, of course. Yesterday he had confronted Jimenez, the customs' agent, threatening to expose the truth to the American press. It had been a nasty scene. His mission now was to insure his own shipment. Once his cotton crossed the border and he got paid, he would proceed to Torreón and embark a shipment from San Pedro to Mexico City as soon as possible, while the railroad going south out of Torreón was in Federal hands. The textile mills in Mexico City were paying premium prices for high-grade cotton.

Angry with Jimenez for not recanting his collusion with Villa, Albert stomped up the steps to the customs' house office. Every chair in the stuffy waiting room was taken. Overhead, the fan only stirred up the flies. People stood outside on the wooden porch, shoving to get inside each time the flimsy door banged and a seat was vacated. He would wait outside, Albert decided. He swung his legs over the porch railing and observed the busy flow of pedestrians. A large, familiar figure with a rolling, pigeon-toed gait caught his attention. The man was walking directly toward them, eating an ice-cream cone, the brim of his Texas hat tipped back. Others on the porch had also noticed him and were moving away. His body stiffened as he recognized Pancho Villa. A cold sweat broke out. Had Jimenez told Villa of his confrontation and threat?

The bow-legged Villa started up the wooden steps where Albert sat riveted to the railing. Two hundred pounds of muscle, Villa stopped in his tracks, staring at Albert, his eyes scrutinizing every feature. He took out a large red handkerchief and wiped his mouth, then deftly twirled it and tied the roll around his neck.

"Capitán Alberto," Villa said in a flat voice, lips smiling but his eyes hard. "What are you doing here?"

Albert slid off the railing and faced the granite figure. "I am waiting to see Jimenez," he replied, trying to control his voice.

"Then why do you not see him?" Bright flecks of topaz lighted Pancho Villa's eyes as he pulled at the curly end of his long mustache. "Come with me," he said, taking Albert by the arm and pushing open the screen door.

All chatter ceased in the waiting room. Villa took absolute possession of the place with his eyes. People twisted out of their chairs and disappeared until only the seat nearest the office door was occupied. Its occupant was a middle-aged man who wore a tie.

"Get up!" Villa commanded.

A sullen stare regarded the menacing figure. Villa stared back, then whipped out his pistol. A single blast exploded in the silent room. Slowly, the body toppled over in a slump, sliding sideways off the wooden chair to the floor. Overhead the blades of the ceiling fan stirred and scratched. Stepping forward, Villa shoved the corpse to one side with his boot and motioned to Albert.

"Have a seat," he said. "You're next, after me."

With the heel of his boot, Villa kicked open the door to Jimenez' office, momentarily dislodging the flies. Then the door slammed shut behind him.

Out! Albert pushed the screen door, tearing the mesh, leaving the splintered frame dangling from a single hinge as he ran out.

Back at the hotel, he pulled down his valise and packed, throwing in typewriter ribbons, light bulbs, a few canned goods and cartridges for his pistol. He fastened his money belt, padded with dollar bills, and snapped shut the lock of the valise.

Shaking, Albert crossed over the bridge to Juárez once more and waited for the midnight train heading south.

The train lurched and pitched over the mutilated roadbed, started and stopped at isolated towers and crowded stations. Albert watched booted legs dangling outside his window. Inside, men swilled mescal and belched all night. The car was rank with the stench of urine and unwashed bodies. Through the endless night, Pancho Villa filled every crevice of his mind. Fear, revulsion, blind hatred, or total capitulation to his magnetism held Villa's men together. His passions, people said, were war, women and ice-cream. He had his own morals: every woman he coveted was escorted to the altar, in full bridal regalia, the priest performing the ceremony with a pistol to his head. He neither drank nor smoked. Raúl said he wept for widows and orphans. The man was mad, a maniac to stay away from. Torreón! Thank God, Albert thought, trying to turn his mind in a positive channel. He would leave for Torreón immediately, and get there while Almazán was still in control...and he still had his skin.

It was late afternoon. The last four carloads of cotton had arrived from San Pedro for shipment to Mexico City. The sour stench of the sugarcane pulp that fueled the cotton gins in Torreón hung heavy in the air as Albert headed for town for dinner with an American acquaintance. He felt elated at a job accomplished and the prospect of a growing bank account. Although he had no respect for Huerta, the Federal forces were more civilized, decent fellows who permitted one to transact business without putting a dozen obstacles in one's path. The timing was perfect, with the railroads in Federal hands. A letter from Gabriel Madero introducing him to their administrator in Mexico City lay in his portfolio and a hiatus from Villa's *dorados* and their ilk would be a welcome change.

Savoring the thought of a leisurely dinner, Albert did not at first pay attention to a resounding boom in the distance. As he approached the center of town he became aware that people were scurrying about, locking up.

"It is cannon fire, Señor. The cannons of Pancho Villa!" a shopkeeper informed him, slamming down his iron curtain.

It was quickly confirmed that hordes of villistas were coming over the hills to the north of town. The battle was on!

His portfolio! It lay in the strongbox of the Hotel Francia down by the railroad station. As terror gripped the populace of Torreón, Albert dodged the fleeing crowds and arrived at the hotel. He shoved his way up to the desk.

A loud explosion shattered the glass window in the café next to the lobby. People were running down the stairs, some half-dressed, clutching their valises. The desk clerks were flailing their arms in vain attempts to stop guests from fleeing without paying, and trying to make change for those who stopped to pay.

The barrage of gunfire was constant. A harassed clerk finally handed Albert his portfolio and dashed out into the street.

Upstairs in his room, Albert opened the portfolio and extracted the letter from Gabriel Madero. He stuffed it in his pocket. It would serve to identify him if necessary. He shoved the portfolio under the bed and made his way up to the roof. Four men lay on their bellies on the flat rooftop trying to make out what was happening. Crawling catlike, he joined them. In the darkening twilight, they could see the flash of guns in the distance. The fighting was fierce now, the flashes intensified against the dark sky.

"Should we stay here?" a young man asked. Three of the men were from Mexico City, cotton buyers and a machinery salesman, the fourth, a gray-haired rancher from the area come to buy supplies.

"Where else can we go?" the salesman replied.

"The Federal garrisons are their objectives," Albert ventured. "The hotel should be relatively safe."

By dawn the hotel was surrounded by federales, making it impossible to leave, and by nightfall the Federal troops were in retreat, preparing to abandon the city. Within plain view, Federal officers were trying to drive back the rebels with whips and pistols, losing ground against their enemies, who yelled like Comanches and kept coming. The whine of bullets sounded like angry hornets swarming in the streets below. Villa's fierce *dorados* galloped over the tracks, hooves grinding the bodies of fallen men into the dirt. The survivors broke and ran. With horrified fascination, the five lone hotel guests lay on their bellies and watched the *federales* abandon the area where the hotel was located and saw Villa's forces pour down through the Canyon of Fernandez. Sweaty, excited, fired-up, rebel foot soldiers began to spill into the street below them.

"Get those *hijos de putas* in the hotel! They've been shooting at us!" someone shouted.

Fear tightened like a vise around Albert's chest. He knew that when you attack a city, you, can get the impression that people are shooting at you from the surrounding buildings, although the buildings may be empty. Soldiers would be searching at any minute. They were trapped. His four companions began backing away toward the stairs. Crouching, monkeylike, Albert stopped them.

"Meet in my room," he whispered hoarsely. Number 58. We should stay together."

The five men stumbled down the iron stairs from the roof and gathered in Albert's room in the center of the hotel; it opened onto an inside courtyard, safe from the firing on the street.

"Hand me your guns," Albert commanded. Hesitating at first, the rancher pulled a long revolver out of his waistband and handed it over. The racket downstairs was a raucous din. Albert yanked his Colt out from his belt, stepped out to the corridor, took careful aim and threw the guns over the railing where he watched them land in a large potted palm. Back in his room he faced ashen countenances, taut with fear.

"I fought in Madero's Revolution. I know these bastards," Albert explained quickly. "We can't afford to be found with weapons. Now listen. When the soldiers get here, hold your hands above your heads and say, 'We are pacific civilians.' Since they'll find us unarmed, we may get away with it."

The trapped men nodded assent, feeling a kinship, as though they were prisoners awaiting execution.

A crash of glass below announced that the etched doors to the bar had been shattered. Above the swearing and shouting they heard a second crash of glass: the cigarette stand in the lobby. Over the din, a voice rang out in the courtyard.

"Vacate your rooms, *chingados*, or we'll flush you out like rats!"

In a stupor, they waited. A hand grenade exploded down the corridor. Mustering courage, Albert peered around the door. He knew the effectiveness of these homemade bombs, dynamite stuffed in a tin can, a short fuse attached, lighted by a cigarette and—bang! A wall was blown out, a stairway disappeared. Smoke billowed at the far end of the corridor. Soldiers emerged through the smoke, flinging open doors, stomping down toward them. Albert backed into the room behind the half-closed door.

"They're coming," he whispered, bracing himself.

The barrels of three Mauser rifles were jammed through the doorway, cartridges slammed in as the soldiers entered. Albert stared down a long barrel, his hands above his head.

"*Somos gente pácifica*," he recited, robotlike. "We are peaceful men."

The rancher found his voice. "*Somos gente pácifica*," he echoed. Stammering, the others mouthed the phrase, hands held high above their heads.

Sweaty hands frisked them. Brown eyes looked at the foreigner. With a nod of silent agreement they ordered their captives downstairs, prodding the group with their rifles around the undamaged part of the corridor.

Lead seemed to weight Albert's shoes. He stumbled. Piss on them! Contempt, anger, indignation regenerated his strength. He felt the letter from Gabriel Madero in his coat pocket, addressed to one Carlos Vasquez, identifying the bearer as an American in charge of the Madero ranches. If he could just get to an officer. These were villistas. He thought of the guns lying in the flower pots.

"Move!" The butt of a rifle prodded him down the wide, tiled stairway. In the lobby, their captors lined the five men up with their backs against the wall, hands on high. Soldiers butted other prisoners along, brushing against them.

Albert spotted an officer coming toward them. "*Coronel*!" he spurted, stepping in his path.

The man stopped, facing Albert.

"We are peaceful citizens only passing through Torreón." The words raced at a high pitch. "I have a letter..."

The man's blood-shot eyes stared blankly. He stepped up close, diverted for a moment from watching some Federal prisoners being yanked into the courtyard.

Albert groped for the letter, one hand held high. Don't go, don't go, he prayed, probing. He pulled the letter out of his pants' pocket and shoved it in the officer's hand.

Dumbly, the Coronel looked at the envelope, turned it over, removed the sheet and stared at it. Then he stuffed the sheet of paper back in the envelope and handed it to Albert.

God, he couldn't read!

"Firing squad form!" the Coronel yelled. "Squad form."

The volley of fire was deafening. More prisoners were yanked past them. One of the cotton buyers turned toward the wall and vomited. Albert knew they were about to be herded into the courtyard and executed. From habit, he looked at his watch. 9:20 p.m. Dash for it! That's all he could do. Taking a deep breath, he prepared to run across the lobby, when a rider on horseback ducked through the entrance, overturning furniture as he guided the huge animal to the reception desk and fired a pistol at the ceiling. Big silver spurs gleamed. The rider was a general.

"What *chingadera* is going on here? Who's in charge?" he roared.

A volley of fire drowned out the questions.

"Who's in charge!" the General yelled.

The Coronel and two other officers emerged from the courtyard and saluted. A space had cleared around the nervous horse.

Albert made a dash toward the General, waving his letter. "General," he shouted, "we are peaceful citizens and they are about to shoot us. I have a letter." He stuck his hand up and waved it frantically.

The General looked down at the foreigner and Albert stared into the hardest eyes he had ever seen. Recognition froze his breath. It was Rodolfo Fierro, the most bloodthirsty general the Revolution had produced. Villas's butcher.

The envelope waved in Albert's outstretched hand.

General Fierro snatched it.

"P-p-please .. p-peaceful citizens," Albert stammered, his tongue making vain attempts to produce a speck of saliva.

"Are you Carlos Vasquez?" the General snapped.

He could read!

"No. I .. I am the American who is mentioned down below. We are five civilians." Blood was pounding in his ears.

The General read the letter and handed it back. "*Coronel, atención!*" he shouted. "Leave this man alone. And the other civilians."

"Could you assign guards...?" Albert heard himself asking in someone else's voice.

"You won't need them." The General fired his pistol in rapid succession. The racket subsided. Coronel, these men are not to be molested," he ordered, getting the full attention of his officer. "I hold you responsible, you hear? This simpering *pinche chingado* gringo is close to the Maderos. There are more prisoners down by the railroad station. Get your ass over there and take care of them!"

The horse wheeled around, knocking over the newspaper stand. Papers flew up from the desk like a flock of pigeons. He was gone.

Albert backed up to the wall and put a clammy hand on the rancher next to him. "*Gracias a Diós, gracias a Diós*," the man murmured over and over and sank to his knees. He was yanked to his feet. In single file the group was led across the room to the reception desk, out of the way of the prisoners who were still being herded into the open courtyard.

Throughout the night, the five men huddled behind the big oak counter in the lobby, not daring to sit down, or fall asleep. Every muscle, every nerve ached. They kept coming. Irregular troops burst in, straw hats clamped down on their heads, some hatless, some with hats tossed over the back of their necks, secured with the familiar red cord. A piece of red rag was tucked into their hatband or sewn on their sleeve, labeling them Villa's men.

They came in thirsty, demanding water from the hotel's jugs. To make sure it wasn't poisoned, they made the civilians take a swallow first. The same test held for liquor. Rum, tequila, mescal numbed Albert's brain and swelled his bladder. Streams of urine ran down his pant legs. Spikes pierced his head. All night they jabbed. Trying to light a cigarette, he dropped it and fell on all fours attempting to pick it up. His hands slipped on something slimy. A pair of arms pulled him to his feet. He heard a gasp of repugnance. Albert held up his hands. Blood dripped between his fingers. He looked down and traced the pool of blood to a stream seeping out from the courtyard. Frantically wiping his hands on his wet pants, for the fourth or fifth or tenth time, Albert vomited, a dry retching that came in spasms, again and again.

At about three in the morning the troops stopped coming in. The lobby emptied. On unsteady legs, the trapped civilians helped each other up the tile stairway to their beds. Someone shoved a hard roll into Albert's hand. He ate it and it stayed down.

Somewhere a dog barked. Albert opened one eye. Light flooded the room. His mouth tasted of cobwebs, his head was splitting and someone was shaking his shoulder. Four men came into focus, bags in hand.

"We should go down together," the rancher said. "There may be guards posted."

The smell of gunpowder and human flesh was choking. The hotel lay in ruins, smashed, vandalized, destroyed. A humming sound emanated from the courtyard, the hum of thousands of flies. The grotesque scene they beheld shocked every brain cell, every nerve. Death was tangled in death, corpses fallen on each other, wearing the macabre masks of a violent end. The courtyard reeked of death, reeked with the excrement of fear, reeked with every foul protest of the body. Numb, Albert stepped over corpses sprawled among the flowerpots and retrieved their guns from the potted palm.

The street was testimony to the villistas triumph. Locks were blasted, windows shattered, doors kicked down. Sacking, pillaging, they had destroyed homes, small stores and businesses, a lifetime of work gone in a drunken rampage. The gray-haired rancher began to weep uncontrollably.

"*Ay Diós*," he cried, crossing himself over and over. "*Ay Diós. Ay Diós!*"

Albert turned to the man. "You are alive," he said. "Go home, amigo, while you have life. And pray you have a home to go to."

The group dispersed.

Albert walked along deserted sidewalks, alive among the dead. A bloated horse lay in his path, legs sticking up like pokers, a Federal cap hung on its hoof. Aimlessly he walked toward town, toward God knew what. He could hear guns in the distance. They were still chasing the remnant federales. Contempt for the Revolution welled up. He would shoot anything or anyone who got in the way of his tenuous survival! He lit a cigarette and walked on.

On the outskirts of town a few intrepid citizens opened their windows a crack, but no one seemed to stir behind the curtains.

A boarding house located down from the railroad station by the tracks offered refuge. He bathed. He lay naked on the bed while his clothes were washed. Then he just laid there, sick to his stomach and soul.

Villa pursued the retreating cavalry to San Pedro; a slaughter, they said. Then he took the scattered Federal garrisons left in the north. Now his train was rolling south.

For three days Albert had not stirred from his bed. Now the screeching whistle of the locomotive cut through his brain like a sharp knife. The screams of a young girl in Zacatecas echoed again. San Pedro, San Pedro. Had they raped the spinster typist too?

Soot settled on the sill as Albert stood before his open bedroom window watching Pancho Villa's train roll by. Powerful locomotives belching smoke. Coal cars, steaming baggage cars, checkered boxcars where soldiers squatted, packed in. Crowded on top, troops held tight to their women under a fiery sun, women who wedged a piece of rickety tin under their skirts to be laid over a charcoal fire in some desolate field. Pullmans crammed with the fortunate; the full sleeve of a woman's dress billowed out from a window. Soldiers legs dangled from the top of the car. A blur of brown faces rolled by. Horsemen churned up dust along the tracks, Villa's elite dorados rode guard in their yellow shirts and Texas hats, more feared than Satan himself. Flatcars bristling with cannon, the screech of wheel on rail as they jerked slowly by. Freight cars with munitions: Howitzer, Louis and Maxim, Winchester, Albert knew them all. Hospital cars wafting up iodine, staffed with inexperienced practitioners swabbing down the wounded day and night. A chicken feather flew up from a slatted boxcar and settled on the window sill. Cattle cars packed with live cattle rolled by. Freight cars and more freight cars filled with cotton. Five thousand bales of booty bound for Mexico City. He watched the dining car and the club car roll slowly past, swarthy officers drinking and playing cards. Last, the caboose, with little flowered curtains fluttering at the windows, the housekeeping efforts of Villa's latest "wife."

He was there, in the caboose, rolling south. Albert's hand sought the grip of his pistol. He pulled it out and his hand trembled as he put down a wild desire to shoot. The caboose passed from sight. He shuddered to think what he would find when he got back to San Pedro.

CHAPTER XVI
APRIL 21, 1914

Antonio unfolded the newspaper on his breakfast tray and stared at the bold, black banner across the front page: AMERICAN MARINES OCCUPY VERACRUZ. A crisis had been building for more than a year, but the reality of invasion came as a shock. Anger followed, anger that his rational mind tried to quell. He pushed the tray aside, the platter of fruit untouched, and rang for the maid, his valet long gone, pressed into Huerta's forces.

"Tell Ignacio to bring the car around. I am going downtown." Life didn't stop because Veracruz was invaded.

Antonieta heard the Dodge touring car turn on the gravel drive and ran out to the gallery. "Where are you going, Papá?"

"Downtown for lunch."

"Why did American marines kill our naval cadets?' she asked, anxiety in her voice.

No point in lying: she would ask a hundred questions. "The Americans have done a great wrong. They landed in Veracruz without warning and killed people who tried to resist. I want you to understand that it is an illegal act, unwarranted, a vicious display of power on the part of the United States, but there's been no declaration of war. I don't think there will be any more aggression." He lifted her chin. "Let your father worry, if worry need be. Agreed?"

"What does 'martial law' mean, Papá?"

"It means an American admiral is in command in Veracruz. They have blockaded the port to stop German ships from delivering more arms to Huerta."

"Will they invade the capital? Will we be a city under seige like Paris when you were there?" Antonieta flung her arms out dramatically.

Antonio smiled and patted her on the head. "In a crisis it's important to stay calm." To put her mind at ease, he reeled off his itinerary: he was going to the bank, to the post office, then to look in on Mamá Lucita. After that he was having lunch at Gabrinus' restaurant with an American engineer. Antonio paused, suddenly struck by the irony. "See that Mario does his lessons, will you? And maybe you can keep Memela from hiding in the trees when Miss Ortiz comes." He kissed his willowy daughter on the cheek and began to descend the stairs. He had heaped responsibility on this child. He would make it up to her. "If you need me, for any reason, angel," he called up, "you have Grambrinus' telephone number."

Antonieta waved and turned back toward the house. She would take the newspaper to Tío Beto. Perhaps news of the invasion would put a bit of life in his aching bones and tired voice. He hardly ever left his apartment.

The buzz of conversation was loud and agitated when Antonio and Fred Gaston entered Gambrinus. Well-dressed businessmen and bureaucrats occupied the tables, and a few stylish ladies' hats bobbed among the palms. With deft maneuvering, the maitre d'hôtel ecorted the two men to a small table near the bar.

Antonio's dining companion and friend was a sandy-haired American consultant for a prestigious engineering firm. Fred Gaston looked about uncomfortably. He had always been cordially received and treated by his Mexican associates, but today only belligerent stares greeted him as they were seated. Excited voices argued back and forth across the large room. To their left, a stout man pounded the table. Behind them, loud denouncements of the United States became vehement.

"Look here, Antonio," Fred Gaston said in a low voice, "I don't think we chose a good day for lunch. You know I don't agree with Wilson's policy, but today is not the time to debate it." He finished his scotch and soda. "Think I'll bow out and get back to the hotel."

"As you wish," Antonio said, feeling ill at ease himself. Powerful emotions churned his own sentiments, and although reason told him his anger was not personally directed toward his friend, resentment threatened to spill over the edge of every word. Why couldn't Wilson let Huerta be! Antonio motioned to the waiter to bring the bill for the drinks they had ordered.

Suddenly the stout man stood up and confronted Gaston. "Huerta won't salute that cabrón Wilson's flag even if he sends his whole goddam army and navy!" he shouted into Gaston's face. "I say declare war on the gringo bastards!"

"*Cálmate,*" the man next to him hissed, trying to pull him down by the sleeve. Their companions raised their voices, outdoing one another.

"Huerta is through! Whether he fights the Americans or Carranza, he is finished."

"I say let's support the villistas and zapatistas and turn *those* bastards loose on the gringos in Veracruz."

"*Que mueran los gringos!*" the stout man shouted again. "Death to the gringos!" He raised his glass and flung its contents into Fred Gaston's face.

Shocked, Gaston stumbled to his feet and started toward the door, ducking to ward off a pelting of hard rolls that a well-groomed hand was tossing from a bread basket. The beveled glass doors swung shut behind him.

Antonio sat numbly silent. He had not lifted a finger to defend his friend. Friend? We are all savages under this thin veneer of culture and respectability, he thought. Months later, he would call Fred Gaston.

Antonio sat idly in his studio. All attempts to work on his book, "The Art of Teaching Architecture," failed, all creativity, all inspiration amounting to nothing as he faced the consequences of his decision to stay in his house and try to make life as normal as possible for the children. He missed Adamo Boari, gone to Italy, taking with him a bride. At least he won't be alone, Antonio thought jealously, fingering the paper on his desk. Tonight he would go out, shake off this gloom, find a woman. He knew an attractive widow.

The door to the studio burst open. Mario strode to the desk and stood in front of his father.

"May I go to the Fourth of July celebration tomorrow at the Tivoli?" the boy asked in a single breath.

"What?"

"Reverend Day says that there is going to be a sack race and track competitions and a football game, which is much more exciting than that old rugby, and I know I can win at track and get a prize. Please?" Mario had learned long ago that when he interrupted his father it was best to state his business quickly.

Antonio stared at his son. The boy was a sinewy bundle of energy. I've spent too little time with him, he thought, with some guilt. He's small, but has the build of an athlete, and Cristina's features. He will make a lean, handsome man.

"Well, may I go?"

"No, you may not go," Antonio answered resolutely.

"Please, Papá. The Fourth of July only comes once a year."

"I will not have a son of mine celebrate the American Independence with American marines occupying our territory!"

Silenced for a moment by the outburst, Mario added in a subdued voice. "May I play with Bobby and George?"

Antonio turned his chair to face the chastened boy. "Yes, but here on our grounds. I will take you to the Bastille Day celebration on July fourteenth."

The subject was closed.

CHAPTER XVII

1914

A summer storm loosed its wrath as Antonio picked his way under the awnings of the opulent stores on Avenue San Francisco toward the Jockey Club. Shaking the rain from his homburg, he handed it to an attendant and crossed the restaurant to a booth under a large mural in which a peacock spread its magnificent tail.

The man he had come to meet was seated, waiting. He was an acquaintance, a dealer in clandestine arms. Huerta had requisitioned all the arms in the city, confiscating private arsenals where he knew they existed. Now Huerta was gone. Quietly, he had abandoned the city, disenchanted by an American Ambassador named Wilson, persecuted by an American President with the same name, his army defeated by the rebels. He had submitted a brief resignation to Congress. To cushion the blow, he took with him a sizable pot of gold from the Treasury and boarded a German boat at a secluded port. The confiscated private arsenals were beginning to trickle back into circulation.

"I shall expect delivery on Saturday," Antonio said, draining his coffee."

"Payment in gold," the man mouthed softly."

"Understood." Antonio got to his feet. "Thank you."

Saturday afternoon, Antonio escorted Ignacio, Demetrio and Cástulo into the back orchard and handed each a rifle. The Fifth Police Precinct adjoined the side wall of his property, but the police did not question the shooting. They were accustomed to hearing pistols being fired in the big house on Héroes, where competitions among the Arquitecto's friends were a regular weekend sport. Peppered with holes, the old target still hung in the orchard. Today, hardly a bullet touched it. Only the cows that grazed in the primitive little dairy next door were aware that the "contestants" were poor marksmen whose bullets ricocheted off distant trees in their pasture.

On Sunday, Antonio took the children to Chapultepec Park. They rowed on the lake, watched the Indian *voladores* "fly" around the high maypole, gracefully unwinding headfirst to the sound of the drum and the conch shell, an ancient ritual for which their training began at an early age. Sabina spread a picnic lunch under a centuries-old *ahuehuete* tree while Antonio kicked a soccer ball around with Mario. The following Sunday, they took a balloon ride. An intrepid entrepreneur loaded his gondola at the railroad station and drifted off in the direction of the mountains in the southern end of the city. A cross-current of air, a sudden gust could send the balloon off-course. It was exhilarating; nothing existed but the sky. From their lofty position they could see the smoke from zapatista entrenchments in the mountains. Even as he reassured the children that the fighting would not spread, Antonio knew that Pancho Villa was rolling south. First Torreón. Then Zacatecas. The blood of twelve thousand Federal soldiers had run through the streets of Zacatecas, bodies clogging the ravine of that beautiful colonial city, bodies dumped into mine shafts, bodies everywhere. He thought of young Blair and wondered whether he had been caught in the holocaust.

As he listened to the laughter of his children, panic stabbed at Antonio's groin like a knife.

On a cloudless morning in mid-August, the household was awakened by the insistent clanging of church bells, echoed discordantly by the neighborhood bells of San Fernando and the old church of San

Hipólito.

Interrupting the family at breakfast, Ignacio announced: "General Obregón is on his way through the Toluca mountain pass!"

"Is Pancho Villa with him?" a young maid asked, apprehension and excitement lighting her eyes.

"No. General Obregón is a *carrancista*."

The maid quickly cleared the table and hurried off to the kitchen.

"Sooner or later they had to arrive." Antonio spoke matter of factly. "Anyone who wishes to watch the troops come in may do so. Advise the staff, Ignacio. Thank you." All these people had been affected by the Revolution. They had a right to see and judge this "victorious" army for themselves.

"Well, Boari was right, the lid blew off the cesspool and the slime is spilling over the mountain," Beto intoned drolly.

"I read an interview with thec *carrancistas*," Antonieta was quick to interpose. "They sound like simple people, simple people who are seeking a better life." She wanted desperately to believe it. Behind her placid countenance, ugly images lay waiting to disturb her sleep. Last night she had awakened choking, trying to let out a scream. He was so real, the rough soldier who walked right through her door with a gun. In her dream she had screamed for Chela, Chela who was now so far away. She had screamed for Iwa, but Iwa and her family had been recalled to Japan. Even in her waking hours, fear tore at her. She had seen Federal soldiers snatch men off the streets, yank them out from behind their stalls at the market and tie them up in the transport wagons. Even the poor boy that milked the cows in the vacant lot next door had disappeared, perhaps never to see his loved ones again.

"My dear, hatred and revenge are the passions that drive those men," Beto began and stopped abruptly. He knew fear lurked beneath his beloved niece's pretense at equanimity. Was she only fourteen? This Revolution had robbed her of the slow flowering of her youth, that fragile world of adolescence. All at once he saw her, very clearly, catapulted into adulthood by this Revolution, to forever be influenced by the guns, the deaths, the hopes, the meaninglessness of...of... He didn't complete his thought. "I exaggerate, as usual," he remarked.

"We should be glad they have arrived. Perhaps we will have peace."

"Well, since they have arrived," Antonio offered, "let us hear what they have to say."

Cold, skeptical eyes greeted the Constitutionalist forces. No firecrackers were exploded, no "Vivas!" shouted as the hordes filed down from the western mountains and paraded the length of Reforma Boulevard to the Palace. Rabble, Antonio thought, the country is in the hands of illiterate, ignorant rabble! Clutching the hands of Antonieta and Mario, he forced his way to the front of the crowd. A steady beating of drums grew louder and louder, approaching the junction where they stood. Columns of Yaqui Indians paraded past, Obregón's fierce, crack troops. Antonieta stared at their stone faces. A group in blue overalls ran alongside the ragged soldiers, waving a banner, words rippling down the street: HAIL GREAT LEADER, SYMBOL OF JUSTICE AND LIBERTY, VENUSTIANO CARRANZA. LONG LIVE THE REVOLUTION!

Swept along with the crowd, they arrived at the Zócalo, where a robust, one-armed general appeared on the central balcony and began addressing the multitude.

"Citizens, the assassin has fled and the Revolution has triumphed!" General Obregón shouted. "General Carranza will soon assume command. We assure you that we will take over with peace and order. Let it be heard that the sale of liquor is prohibited and looters will be punished. Anyone who damages private property will also be punished. You may go about your business and your daily affairs as usual."

Beto punched the newspaper and adressed the parrot: "Peace and order." *Mierda!*"

"*Mierda!*" The parrott screeched.

On the heels of Obregón's announcement, Carranza had occupied the city at the end of August, but was unable or unwilling to control his troops. Looting, stealing, destroying at will was the order of the day. Frightened citizens locked themselves in.

The insistent ringing of the upstairs telephone made Antonio hurry as he emerged from the tower, where he had trained the telescope on a band of soldiers who were overturning the stalls in the market three blocks away. He picked up the receiver.

"Antonio, lock your gates and stay in!" a neighbor's voice warned, a voice charged with anxiety. "There's a general heading in your direction, followed by a stream of soldiers. He's looking for a house to set up headquarters."

The insolent generals—and God! there were enough of them—were quartered all over the city, requisitioning whatever took their fancy. Obregón had taken over Tomás Braniff's house, one of the most luxurious mansions in the city. Who might want his?

"You know that they kidnapped Nacho de los Monteros' children when he resisted?" the excited voice continued. Last night a bunch of these drunken monkeys beat up two policemen, and then killed them in cold blood right in front of my house! Law and order, bah! They're rapists and murderers! Listen, they have just turned the corner by the streetcar stop. I have 12:10. It won't take them more than twenty minutes to get to Héroes. Lock yourself in!"

Grabbing the bell in the children's schoolroom and clanging it forcefully, Antonio rushed down the stairway to the foyer.

"Sabina, Ignacio, María!" he shouted, clanging and clanging. In a moment the alarmed servants had gathered in the gallery.

"Go fetch Don Alberto, Sabina. Drag him here, if necessary. Ignacio, bring the men. I want everybody here in two minutes! Antonieta, find Conchita. And Mario, hold your little sister's hand and stay right here. Don't turn her loose."

Antonio unlocked a closet in the hall and removed three rifles while the staff gathered in a tight, frightened group. Antonio held up his hand.

"Revolucionarios have just turned down our street. They are taking over the big houses to quarter their troops and may choose ours. I want all of the women and children to get down in the basement until we know if there is any danger. You men wait here with me."

Conchita, the frail thirteen-year-old cook's helper, cowered behind the big woman, trembling, twisting a rag in her hand, chewing one end. Antonieta put her arm around the frightened girl, her own heart hammering.

"Where is Don Alberto?" Antonio barked.

"I could not persuade him to leave his bed, Señor. He is ill."

"Antonieta, get the key to the storeroom. Run!"

Conchita grabbed the cook's apron and threw it over her face, wailing in muffled sounds.

"Hush!" María scolded, yanking at her apron.

Antonieta took the steps two at a time. When she came down, Sabina was herding the women toward the storeroom door. Suddenly, no one spoke. Outside the gates, they heard the clatter of hooves on pavement, the scuffle of boots, voices yelling obsceneties, laughter. Antonio unlocked the storeroom.

"*Virgencita sálvanos*" Conchita wailed. "Holy Virgin, save us!"

The cook grabbed the hysterical girl by the arm and pushed her toward the wine cases Antonio was struggling to move. Hinges squeaked as he lifted the trap door. Narrow iron steps led down to an ample basement. They trooped down: Sabina and the children, the little helper, the cook, the washwoman, two maids. Antonieta was last.

Antonio kissed his daughter. "Keep them quiet, angel." He spoke in near whispers. "I'll come and report as soon as we find out what these fellows are up to." He slammed the trap door shut and returned to the gallery.

"Demetrio, go back to the gatehouse and watch them. Raise your broom if they try to force their way in," Antonio said. "Under no circumstances open the gates, even if they shoot. And for God sake don't expose your head in the window. Cástulo, keep watch in the kitchen patio. You have a clear view through the fence from there. Ignacio and I will be upstairs on the studio terrace above the arbor. If they demand to see me, I'll go to the gate. Cover me with your rifle while Ignacio goes over the wall to bring the police. Understood? Now you, Juanito." The stable boy was a thin, agile lad, excited and eager to be part of the team. "Bolt the doors to the garage, the carpentry shed and the stables, and keep a vigil on the back wall. If you see anything, you can signal us from the orchard."

Antonio handed out the rifles, belted his pistol and hung binoculars around his neck.

The men parted as loud guffaws and whinnying horses told them the soldiers were in front of the house.

Crouched behind the stone balustrade above the arbor, Antonio watched a lean, handsome officer dismount in front of the carriage gate. A small contingent of uniformed horsemen reined in behind him. Dirty soldiers and barefoot, ragged women gathered in the street. Hands on hips, the lean officer stood back and studied Antonio's gate. He looked through the gate at the house for a long time, so long that Antonio believed the officer had seen him. Then abruptly he turned and walked across the street to the Cassasús mansion. He stooped to pull up a weed. Unattended, the stretch of grass in front of their neighbor's high, stone wall had grown long and brown. The fine brass lock on the gate was lusterless in the midday sun. Nimbly, the officer climbed over the gate and walked up to the imposing double doors to the entrance. He tried to force the handle, then tested a shuttered window. Antonio wondered where the old, drunken caretaker was hiding.

In the street, restless soldiers dismounted, crowding around.

"*Oiga, mi general*, I'll open the lock for you," a soldier shouted. He took out his pistol.

"No, Plasencio," the General called back, holding up his hand to stop him. "You might blow off the door and we could catch cold."

Laughter rippled down the street.

"I'll see if the back door is open. You two come with me," the General said, indicating two of the horsemen.

Rifles and packs began to fill the sidewalk as soldiers unburdened themselves, urinated, and squatted on their haunches in the shade of the wall. The women set down heavy market baskets. A few chickens tied by one leg tried to escape.

"Hey, *Tuerto*, throw me a cigarette. One of the good ones," a young soldier yelled. "We are in the Capital!" He stood up and emptied his pockets, scattering what appeared to be corn husks on the sidewalk.

The soldier's woman jumped up and caught the cigarette, eliciting a whack on the bottom. "Give it to me, *chingona*," the soldier commanded. He lit it, gave her a puff and put his arm around her.

The front door opened and a smiling General displayed a ringful of keys to his men. "Welcome to headquarters, muchachos," he announced exultantly. "I'll assign rooms later. There are ample stables in the back."

Bundles collected, the women began to crowd through the door of the Casasús house. A distant roll of thunder sped up activity as saddles were removed from tethered horses, blankets sticking like large scabs to the complaining beasts. Bed rolls, provisions, cartridge cases were pulled down from mules, and heavy loads of hay and charcoal from burdened donkeys. The animals were led through the carriage gate, fanning out across the gardens to the stables in the rear of the house. Antonio had been observing the General closely. In his thirties, fair-skinned, a long black mustache accentuating fine features. Who the devil was he? Which of the five hundred generals this cursed Revolution had produced? The face looked intelligent and the manner not too aggressive, thank God.

"Do you recognize him?" Antonio nudged Ignacio and handed over the binoculars.

"No, patrón. But I don't think they're going to bother us."

Antonio left his post and went down to open the trap door. "It's safe now," he called down, lowering his huge bulk through the small opening. "A General and his soldiers have taken the Cassasús house. We don't know which general he is." The frightened women looked up at him from the foot of the stairs. "Tonight, I want you to bolt your doors. Padlock them on the inside. Use the path behind the stables to get to your rooms. Tomorrow, go about your work in the house as usual. But stay out of sight! Ignacio will do the marketing. Now, María, see what you can stir up in the kitchen. We are all hungry."

It was past midnight when Antonio climbed into bed. Satisfied that Beto had taken his medicine, he had left his brother sleeping. Sabina slept with the children. Ignacio was bedded down outside their door, rifle within reach. Antonio tucked his pistol under his pillow and tried to sleep, listening to the water that splashed down from the drainpipes, subsiding as the night wore on. At five o'clock, he awakened again, drawn to the gallery by some unfathomable instinct.

Antonio tightened his grip on the pistol and looked out at the garden through the vines of the arbor. Was that a shadow or a figure he saw? He tried to still his labored breathing. Etched in the beam of a street light, a figure darted behind a tree, then moved with catlike certainty toward the orchard. A second figure followed. Antonio's chest heaved as though he had been running. He heard the creak of the gate that separated the orchard from the kennels. Then an explosion of wild barking rent the silence. Chickens cackled, the rooster crowed. Again, all was silence, chilled to the bone, Antonio waited in the arbor. At last he returned to bed. They must have come over the side wall from the cow pasture. How many were there? Had they only intended to steal a chicken or did they intend to break into the house? These men knew no fear. They took what they wanted.

He lay awake feeling danger all around him. Thoughts of Europe plagued his troubled mind. The dreaded war was a reality. The Germans had marched into Belgium, and now France and England had declared war. He had a sudden vision of the whole world in flames. Alicia's face loomed like a lantern in his mind. Was she in danger? And Cristina? He pushed her name down as he felt anger rising. Antonieta, Mario, little Amelia, they were his concern now. Before dawn broke, Antonio had made a decision: During the day the children would remain in the basement, out of sight.

From outside what appeared to be air ducts were in fact windows in the basement. They were long slits in the stone foundation, covered with iron gratings. Confined to the basement, Antonieta had shoved an old steamer trunk against the wall under a small barbed window that looked across the driveway and through the fence to the house across the street. With Mario and Sabina's help, she had hoisted an empty wine barrel on top of the trunk. Arms propped on the ledge of the window, she spent hours watching the rebel soldiers as they came and went.

Curious soldiers stared through the gates of Héroes 45 and rubbed grimy hands over the French grillwork. Horrified, she watched a soldier climb the visitors' gate. He attempted to break off the crown, pulled at the brass initials and finally gave up. They broke branches off the trees and in a drunken spree, trimmed a tall ash in the kitchen patio with a spray of bullets. A nest fell to the ground and protesting sparrows rose in twittering panic.

The general had shown up at the carriage gate unexpectedly, demanding that Demetrio summon the owner of the house. He seemed a decent sort, Antonio had reported, Lucio Blanco by name, known for his victories in the northeast. Antonio did not report that it was known he had no use for the rich. Moreover, the General made no effort to discipline his foul-mouthed, brazen soldiers. Their officers were little better. Soldiers had soon stolen most of the chickens and stripped the fruit trees at night, but the pigeons eluded them and the Great Danes protected the goat. María kept the surviving chicks in the kitchen.

When Antonieta grew tired of keeping the vigil, Mario clambered up on the barrel and took over the post of lookout. With Conchita's help Antonieta cleaned up some heavy chairs and found a footlocker to serve as a table for her books. Sabina retrieved an old bed with creaky springs from behind a stack of packing cases. Memela uncovered a trunkful of old toys and, dipping into her treasure, discovered a wigless, one-legged creature that she cradled and dressed and undressed, and sang to in a loving monotone. When the soldiers streamed out of the house across the street, Antonio allowed the children to play upstairs in the nursery. At night they slept together in the infirmary, while Ignacio rolled up in a blanket on a folding cot outside the door.

It was Conchita's task to bring their food down to the basement. As the days dragged by, Antonieta patiently encouraged the timid, silent girl to linger and listen while she read a story to Memela, illustrated with dramatic tones and gestures.

Huddled close to a packing case, trying to become invisible, an occasional giggle would be heard when Antonieta's drama became clownish. In brief moments, Conchita permitted herself to be lured closer. Antonieta soon broke through the girl's silence and timidity and began to teach Conchita her letters. Under Antonieta's apt tutelage, the empty tray was forgotten at the foot of the iron stairs.

"Today I scored a great triumph!" Antonieta wrote in her notebook. "Conchita can write the whole alphabet. This is the tenth day in this dungeon. The only ray of light is that we may be confined long enough for me to teach Conchita to read."

Sabina observed these antics in stoic silence, sitting stiff-backed on her bed, crocheting.

"You are filling her head with nonsense," she scolded Antonieta when the "scullery mouse" had disappeared up the basement stairs after a lengthy lesson, a notebook tucked under her arm. "What good is it to teach her letters?"

"She's intelligent!" Antonieta retorted. "Just because she's a girl doesn't mean she shouldn't learn."

"She was brought here to work," Sabina replied with self righteous dignity. The girl was an orphan, the fatherless child of the washwoman's sister, brought up under a cement washing trough, mud her main nourishment, tin cans and rocks her toys. Her mother had died bearing fatherless twins, who also died. The child must have been born under auspicious signs to have stumbled into the position of cook's helper in a good household. But Sabina knew fate should not be pushed.

To Sabina's chagrin, one day Antonieta presented Conchita with a pleated skirt and middy blouse unearthed from a bundle of undelivered clothes for the poor.

"Try them on, Conchita. They're your prize for being a good student."

The girl darted behind a crate and bashfully emerged. She fluffed out the accordion pleats and watched them fall back in place. Over and over she fluffed out the pleats. Pushing back lusterless dark brown hair, she made a timid whirl.

"Well?" Antonieta waited for a comment.

"It's beautiful, Señorita," Conchita stammered at last.

Sabina sat unsmiling.

"I'll get you a mirror when you have taken a bath and washed and brushed your hair. Then you can see how pretty you look," the pleased teacher told her pupil.

Conchita put her uniform and soiled white apron back on and scampered up the steps, carefully balancing the empty tray.

Days became weeks. It was dark in the basement. Only the mornings squeezed sunlight through the window gratings. Lengthening shadows cast weird patterns on the walls, distorting outlines of old furniture and trunks, empty boxes and candelabras spotted with wax.

One day, rummaging among the empty boxes, Antonieta smelled tar paper, and a scent like Dunhill tobacco that took her back into the long-ago. It was their Paris box, hers and Alicia's, the box which had caused such breathless joy and anticipation when Mamá removed the layers of tissue paper and held up each ensemble that had crossed the ocean. She blew the dust off and removed the long lid. Tucked inside was a tiny organdy dress with musical notes embroidered on the skirt. She shook out the delicate material, tears welling up as dim memories spilled over the dam of blocked remembrance. It was her birthday dress. The birthday of that three-year-old who was poisoned and almost died. Mamá had rocked her and kissed her. Why had Mamá saved this dress? *Mamá*! A sense of longing, of something incomplete overtook her. Caressing the soft folds, Antonieta sat on the cold cement and wept.

Morning sun bent its rays through the high basement windows. Perched on top of the barrel, Mario manned his post. Suddenly, the trap door opened, bringing the children and their guardian to the foot of the iron stairs.

"Sabina!" Ignacio's crouched body and head appeared. "I am going to round up the women. The soldiers are coming over. All of them!"

The cook, the washwoman and the two maids soon stumbled down the iron stairs.

"Where is Conchita?" Antonieta demanded to know.

"I couldn't find her, Señorita," María said. "I looked everywhere but lately she has been going off with her pad and pencil and disappears." With a foot planted on the bottom step, the cook looked down at Antonieta accusingly.

Mario was back at his post. "They're coming in!" he said in a hoarse whisper. "Lots of soldiers with their rifles are coming through our gate."

"*Virgen santísima*! Sobs and whimpers rose in unison. The women fell to their knees and began to pray, "Holy Mary, mother of God, save us!" All but Cleotilde, the washwoman, who made strange signs in the air with her hands.

The crunch of stomping boots over gravel began, growing nearer.

"Hail Mary full of grace," Antonieta began to recite, kneeling on the cold pavement and clasping her hands. She thought of all the rosaries she had said with Mamá Lucita and asked God to accept them in a bundle right now. Was this the end? The taste of bitter gall rose in her throat.

The stomping faded, grew louder and faded again. Somebody shouted shrill words, like a command.

Amelia began to cry. "Shh," Antonieta cautioned, embracing her trembling little sister and holding her close.

Mario balanced precariously on the barrel, trying to see the man who was shouting. The soldiers were around by the front of the house now. Out of sight.

A shot rang out.

Amelia screamed; Antonieta clapped her hand over the the child's mouth.

The vision of her father dead or Beto lying in a pool of blood constricted her own outcry. Antonieta rubbed her cheek against Memela's soft face, seeking refuge in the arms of the child who clung to her.

The sharp crack of rifle fire filled the basement again.

Then the stomping ceased.

Laughter... voices... cabrones, chingados, obscene words which the children were beginning to recognize rang clear.

The lookout squirmed, twisting his head as far as he could, "They're leaving!" Mario cried out, "marching back across the street to the Cassasús house!"

The women huddled together on the bed. There was nothing to say. Sabina took Amelia from Antonieta's arms and walked her up and down, rocking the heavy child and cooing words of comfort. She removed her rebozo and put it around Antionieta's trembling shoulders.

The trap door was thrown open and Antonio's voice boomed. "You can come out now." His frame filled the narrow stairway as he descended.

'Papá!" Antonieta ran to her father and clasped him around the neck, kissing his cheeks, his nose, his eyes. "We heard shots and..." She could no longer hold back the tears.

Antonio kissed her wet cheeks. "We are all unharmed," he said, looking over her shoulders at the servants. "We had a visit from General Blanco and his soldiers, lined up in files behind him. I sent Ignacio to warn you. What do you think the General wanted?"

"Our goat!" Mario blurted.

Antonio laughed. Deep, comforting laughter warmed the cold basement. "No. Permission to practice marching in our driveway. They are going to parade on the sixteenth of September and those fellows have never done an about-face." Antonio demonstrated, turning his large body sharply, barking out the garbled command, bringing smiles to the tense faces, giggles behind covered mouths.

"They will practice here half an hour every day," Antonio continued, addressing the women. "You will stay in the basement while they are here. They still don't know how many we are in this household. I want you to stay out of sight."

When the soldiers had flooded through the front gate, Conchita had run behind the stables, down the side drive to the room she shared with her aunt. Antonio did not see her. But other eyes saw the slim, fleeing figure. She had been seen before, hiding under a bush near the back wall, writing something on a pad. She had been stalked by two soldiers, waiting for the moment when the dogs were in the front garden, when she was alone.

Following the parade practice, that moment came. She emerged and returned to her bush. The two soldiers jumped over the wall, landing noiselessly a few yards behind her. A rough hand was clamped over her mouth, smothering the screams. The girl was gagged and handed over the wall to other hands, many hands.

When they had finished, they dumped the limp, childlike body over the wall near the place where they had caught her. A gust of wind rustled the leaves of the trees and the sun hid its warmth from her bruised, battered body.

It was María who found her little helper. The stern woman's heart melted as she looked at the splotched, swollen face of the girl, her apron in shreds, twisted above her naked body, now bloody where they had used her. One shoe was missing, the big toe stuck through the hole in her sock. The child was breathing but unconscious.

"Mother of God!" the cook moaned. Shock gave way to the full impact of the deed. They had left her alive, but had they left her with child? Would the patrón dismiss her?

The big woman bent down and lifted Conchita in her arms, warm tears falling on the cold face. She carried her into the kitchen and laid her near the glowing brazier, cushioning her head with a sack of flour and covering her body with an apron. Wringing out a dishtowel in warm water, she began to wash the disfigured face, the bloodied thighs.

Conchita opened her eyes and screamed, a long piercing scream which brought Sabina running. Antonieta raced down from the infirmary and Antonio crossed the gallery from his office.

They stood stupefied, staring at the figure on the kitchen floor.

"I found her by the back wall. She must have tried to climb over... and fell," the cook said lamely, avoiding Antonieta's questioning eyes.

The eyes that stared up at them spoke a language Antonio understood. "My God!" he said. "Take her up to the infirmary, Sabina, and take care of her. "My God," he repeated in a choked voice and turned away.

Slowly Conchita recovered. But she would not talk, not even to Antonieta. The maids talked of little else but Conchita's "dishonor," whispering, speculating: How many were there? How did they do it to her to make so many bruises? Was she with child? This "shame" would ruin her for life. Horror and morbid curiosity colored their whispers. Conchita said nothing.

Antonieta spent hours reading to the girl, holding her hand, silently trying to imagine her horror as though it were her own. Conchita was only a year younger than she, just past thirteen. Sitting beside her silent protege, Antonieta waited for a miracle to bring her back to life. She wrote in her notebook: "Conchita has reverted to a pitiful creature. She is back in the kitchen now, doing her tasks, but the joy is gone."

The reality of the Revolution plunged Antonieta into a deep depression. Love for her father and ailing Tío Beto were the only healing balm.

"September days are traitors," she wrote. "The mornings promise eternal sunshine, which quickly fades as the clouds gather, casting damp shadows in the basement. This is the home of fading memories and faded people. Sometimes I feel them, like my Grandmother Leonor. I thought she was only a fat lady in a picture, but I have read the yellowed pages of her diary and I know now what she suffered when she was my age. We are so alike."

CHAPTER XVIII

Life was cheap in this Revolution, Antonio reflected. They said the restaurants and bars were filled with generals who ate with their fingers, and bodyguards who flaunted pistols with silver stocks. They brawled in cafes and killed each other for sport, careening around the city in commandeered automobiles: Daimlers, Italas, Cadillacs, Mercedes, Renaults, Hudsons. Ignacio could identify every one; he flinched at the smashed fenders and crude occupants. The Dodge touring car was under canvas in the garage, guarded by Juanito and the Great Danes.

Food was Antonio's concern. Food became his obsession. He had bought out the Spanish grocer's supply of canned goods. Twice a week he dispatched Ignacio, dressed in overalls and carrying a tool box filled with food, to Mama Lucita's. Angry citizens rioted and railed against a government that could not control its troops. How long would it be before Carranza could establish order in the city? How long before his horde of soldiers would be properly billeted? How long?

One morning, the unmistakable sound of shellfire aroused the household. Bullets whizzed across the garden, over walls toward the fifth Precinct. The shooting came from the roof of the Cassasús house and the roof of the police station. Rebel soldiers and Federal police shouted insults between rounds. Then, just as quickly as it had begun, it was over.

Antonio sat in the dark sala that night, anxiety gnawing at every nerve. Brutish peasant soldiers now surrounded the neighborhood police station. They had been curt, uncivil when he went to inquire about the shooting. Antonio stood and walked to the window. Parting the draperies slightly, he gazed again at the house across the street. A huge bonfire shot up flames in what had been the rose garden. They were roasting hunks of meat. The women who tended the fire flaunted new skirts, which shimmered as they hiked the garments up over bare feet. Where had they gotten the fancy skirts? Antonio focused his binoculars. Of course! Damask and fine French cut velvet, ripped off curtain rings was wrapped around their waists, secured with a rope. Beasts! That's what they were, primitive beasts consumed with greed and an urge to destroy whatever suggested order, authority, wealth! Wrath and indignation festered as he observed the antics around the bonfire.

"God help us!" Antonio muttered to the darkened room as he let the draperies fall closed. The city belonged to the rabble now. The whole country belonged to the rabble. No one could offer guarantees; there was no one to invoke constitutional law. Defeated, Huerta had fled, and his successor followed soon after. No one sat in the Presidential chair.

Antonio flopped into an armchair and dozed off.
"Patrón," the stableboy whispered, shaking his arm.
"What is it, Juanito?" Antonio asked, fully awake.
"There are some policemen in the stables who wish to see you."
"Policemen?"
Antonio hurried through the dark house and crossed the garden to the stable. Four uniformed figures emerged from the empty stalls and faced their neighbor.

"We tried to prevent them from stealing a calf from Anastasio's dairy, Señor," the spokesman said. "It is our duty to protect this neighborhood. But, begging your pardon, the cabrones began to insult us. Well, what can one do? We are sorry for the disturbance. They chased us across the roofs. We hid. Now we seek shelter, Señor."

"That's a long jump from the roof next door. Was anyone hurt?"

In the Shadow of the Angel

"No, Señor. But they will be searching the houses soon. Is there someplace we can hide?" The man's eyes pleaded.

"Yes, there is. I will get you the carpenters' shirts and pants. You can change in the basement, where you will be safe. Juanito will lead you the back way to the kitchen. Tomorrow we will plan how to get you out of the house. You are welcome, Señores," Antonio said with a broad smile.

Smoke from the bonfire still rose high in the sky. They will be so busy drinking and feasting on the fatted calf that the policemen will be safe tonight, Antonio reassured himself, feeling a sudden exaltation.

"General Blanco is waiting to see you," Ignacio announced the next morning while the family was at breakfast. "I showed him to your anteroom."

Blanco was idolized by his men. He would defend them against all reason. Antonio braced himself. He had never been a good liar.

"I am sorry, angel, you will have to go down to the basement. Mario and Memela, you go with her. Now scoot. Wait, I forgot to tell you that you will find some visitors there."

"Who, Papá?" Antonieta asked, eyes wide with curiosity.

"Four policemen we are trying to help escape back to their homes. Now go."

Antonieta picked up the basket of sweet rolls. "They may be hungry." Sometimes the Revolution was exciting.

General Blanco stood waiting with his arms folded when Antonio entered the anteroom.

"I will make this brief, Señor," the General said. "Are you harboring any policemen?"

"No."

"My soldiers have orders to shoot fugitive Federal policemen wherever they are found. And to apprehend anyone who aids them. Good day, Señor."

The next day, the policemen escaped undetected.

The basement soon had another visitor: A ragged beggar appeared at the gate and convinced Demetrio to call his patrón. The man, according to Demetrio, claimed to be a priest from the Hacienda of San Felipe, which belonged to Antonio's brother, Don Luis.

Antonio received the beggar in his office, vaguely remembering a young Indian priest who assisted old Father Sebastián. One look at the man's face confirmed the nightmare which had plagued Antonio day and night since his last communication with his brother two months earlier. But nothing could have prepared him for the story the priest related:

"It was during morning Mass," he began. "That day, all the family attended. I was officiating. One of the charros came to warn us. Suddenly, there they were in the courtyard, about thirty rebel soldiers astride horses, shouting and shooting their guns in the air. We all ran out. Don Luis stepped forward and approached the leader, said he would give them anything they wanted: food, ammunition, horses.

"I saw the man's hand pull hard on the reins. He was sweaty and excited and just laughed, pushing his hat back and laughing at Don Luis. All of them were riled up, a wild bunch. Then the leader dismounted and strode up to where Don Luis was standing. He took out his pistol and twirled it in the air. 'You say you have food, horses and ammunition?' His laugh was mocking, nasty and there was a deathly silence. 'We have enough ammunition,' he said, 'for you and your *puta madre*!' and he lurched forward and spat in Don Luis' face. I saw the man's eyes, like flint. It happened so fast. He aimed the pistol and the shot exploded in Don Luis' face."

The priest's voice faltered.

"Did he die instantly?" Antonio asked in a barely audible voice.

"Thank God he did. Doña Teresa screamed when he fell, so they gagged her and tied her up. The other women, too. The old one was blindfolded, made to stagger around the patio, then shot."

"And Paco?" An image of his nephew floated across Antonio's vision.

"They tied the boy's hands and bound him to one of the pillars of the arcade."

"Manuel?"

"Away. Gone to escort Father Sebastián to Querétaro. Don Manuel, his wife and the child saved." The priest took out a wadded up red handkerchief and blew his nose. "They caught the charro. They tied his leg and dragged him round and round the patio. 'See if you are as brave as a steer?' they taunted."

The man broke down, unable to continue.

Antonio held his head in his hands and watched the tears splash on the desk in glistening spheres. At last he looked up. "Go on. I must know."

"They found axes and hacked at the doors, hacked at the furniture. Then they piled it all up in the patio, heaps of broken furniture, paintings, carpets. They separated the silver, carted it out in bundles and tied it on the mules. Books, bedspreads, some huge vases. All dumped on the heap. Then the leader dragged Doña Teresa out and handed her a torch. A bonfire flared and in its light, I saw Paco's eyes. Suddenly he burst his bindings and flung himself at the leader, scratching his face like an animal, trying to gouge out the man's eyes. Oh senor...."

The priest stopped. His chest was heaving, shoulders moving up and down.

"Paco..." he began again.

"Tell me," Antonio whispered.

"Paco...they..." He caught his breath trying to control his heaving chest. "In the end they hung him from a tree, down by the fence where the salted beef is hung for passersby. His pants curled around his boots, his genitals dangling, penis slashed."

The young priest laid his head on Antonio's desk and sobbed, Antonio put his hand on the man's shoulder.

After a long interval, Antonio asked gently, "Doña Teresa? What happened to her and the women?"

"They made them crawl down the driveway, their hands and feet tied."

The priest fell silent, his eyes confirming the missing part of the story. Then, in a halting voice, he continued. "The hacienda was torched, the village set on fire. The peones who protested or refused to join them, hanged; their women abused, the young ones stolen. Animals rounded up and herded off. All in a few hours, Señor, a few hours. Miraculously, they overlooked me, so preoccupied were they with other matters. I found Doña Teresa still alive, untied her, the other women too. We made our way to Querétaro, by the grace of God alone. I left them there, hidden, with Don Manuel and the daughter in-law and the grandchild. The city was in ruins. A hideous battle there..." He scraped the air in front of him as if to erase a vision.

The priest didn't speak for a long minute,. He said he had been traveling, moving about constantly, hiding, being hidden by good people in the villages, begging for food, once escaping in a woman's clothes. Near San Juan del Río he had run across a band of nuns who had escaped from the hills in peasant's clothing, some of them pregnant, embittered, innocent victims dragged from their convent and used as whores. The churches, he said, were sacked, each worse than the other. The Capital was his goal, the only sane island left, or so he thought. He had hoped to find refuge in this very diocese which Don Luis had so often spoken of with affection. But he had found only disorder, the priests of San Fernando and San Hipólito themselves afraid, hiding, removing treasures of the church to old crypts and secret cells.

"Is there anyone left who will listen to the word of God?" the anguished man asked.

Tears again stung Antonio's eyes. "We will, padre," he said softly. "Would you please say Mass for this household? Tomorrow morning, down in the basement. Let it be a silent Mass for my brother, Luis, and his son, Paco. I do not want my daughter, Antonieta, to know what has happened. She must not know."

"I understand."

"Now, Padre, a hot bath, clean clothes. Food."

Before breakfast Antonio assembled everyone in the basement, including Demetrio, their key lookout.

"A weary beggar has found his way to our gate," Antonio announced, "who is in truth a priest, escaped from a sacked and ravaged parish up north. I have asked him to celebrate Mass, so that this household may give thanks to God for our safety." His voice broke.

Antonieta recognized the Indian priest. She watched the tears well up in her father's eyes. She knew.

Mario was at the lookout post in the basement, doubled up like a monkey on the window ledge. It was a chilly day in November.

"There's an awful lot going on over there," he told Antonieta, who had come down bearing extra blankets for the bed and cots. "They are bringing out a lot of stuff from the house and saddling the horses. Loading the mules, too. Hey! I think they're going to leave!"

"Let me look, Mario. Please." Antonieta hoisted herself onto the barrel beside her brother, who would not relinquish his post. The soldiers were packing their animals, the women swishing in and out with bedrolls and cooking pots. One soldier was strutting up and down in front of a huge mirror; she recognized it, the Florentine mirror from the foyer. The soldier stuck his tongue out, got close and kissed himself, snickering like a child. He examined the ornate frame and tried to shake the mirror out. He strutted again, then raising his foot and cocking his eye at his image, he kicked hard with his huarache. Antonieta gasped, clamping her hand over her mouth. He kicked again and again until the venerable glass shattered. Seizing the gilded crownpiece, he finally broke of a section of the delicate carving and stuffed it in his saddlebag.

"All you know how to do is destroy!" Antonieta shouted, shaking the window bars. Then she saw some officers mount their horses and start up the street. "They're leaving!" she cried out, jumping down and grabbing Sabina and Memela by the hand. "They're leaving!" She danced them around and around in a circle.

When the last soldier had turned the corner, neighbors began to gather in the street. Up and down Héroes gates were thrust open and people walked out of their houses, greeting each other with unaccustomed warmth and joy. They stayed in the street, talking, laughing, until the sun tinted the distant volcanoes in pastel shades, ending with a deep purple. Finally, only their outline was visible against a pale sky.

Beto, looking tired and pale, hobbled to the children's dining room for the first time in a month. "It's nice to breathe," he said.

Antonio patted his brother's hand. "I hope you have an appetite. I saved some dried fish for this breakfast and we have some fresh cheese."

"Too rich for my old entrails," Beto said. "But Antonieta and Mario look hungry. Even you, Memela." He smiled wanly.

"I have one nasty chore left," Antonio remarked. "I am going to inspect Cassasus' house."

"I am going with you, Papá." Antonieta declared.

"No!" Antonio said. "You have seen enough destruction."

"Let her go," Beto said. "She has lived with the drama outside that house for three months. Of course she wants to see what they have done to the inside. Take her with you."

After breakfast they crossed the street. Antonio found the old caretaker unharmed and reeking of pulque.

"They did not treat me bad, Señor. Plenty to eat, plenty to drink. But the house? He shrugged his shoulders and led the way.

The parquet floors were pock-marked with holes, "to keep the boots from slipping," the caretaker explained. The white marble floor of the dining room was cracked, blackened with the soot of charcoal braziers, and the adjoining mosaic terrace reeked of rotted food and defecation. The stench was overpowering in the billiard room, where contests had been held to see who could urinate in the corner holes of the billiard table. The French wallpaper was ripped, the chandeliers broken and disfigured by target practice. Heaps of garbage were piled in the ballroom, the concert grand piano smashed. One cherub on the ceiling mural was outlined in bullet holes. Remnants of draperies hung like rags from sagging rods. Only the bedrooms had escaped the vandals. "Officers' rooms," the old Indian said.

Outside the garages were empty, automobiles and carriages gone. In the stables, they found two huge Persian rugs trampled with manure. A pile of broken furniture filled one stall, smashed crystal and china interspersed. Antonio picked up a fragment of a plate: Limoge, the Cassasus' gold initials still visible. Everything that could be carried, or ripped off the wall had been taken. A few paintings, too large to roll up and strap to a saddle, were discarded on the rubbish heap.

Silently, father and daughter stood in the sala and surveyed the wreckage of what had once been a gracious reception room.

The caretaker looked at them sidewise and shrugged.

"What you are seeing, my daughter, are the ravages of victory," Antonio said in French. He turned to the old man. "As soon as I can, I will send carpenters over to board up the doors and windows." The house had suffered indignities too painful to be stared out. "In the meantime, lock up what you can. I will advise your patrón."

Antonio took a last look around. "It could have been our house," he said quietly to Antonieta.

As they left, he patted the old caretaker's shoulder. "It's not your fault," he said.

In November, the Carrancistas left, headed for Veracruz to regroup. The last soldier had no sooner left when the Capital near midnight, wrecking the water pumps at Xochimilco as they marched in. The carrancistas had sacked the city so badly that the zapatistas seemed less extreme, carrying their standard of the Virgin of Guadalupe and amulets to ward off the evil eye. But they proved equally destructive, looting, killing, even stealing the works of the Cathedral clock and mopping up every morsel of food in their wake. One isolated band pushed through the doors of the Jockey Club and meekly sat at the counter and ordered breakfast.

On December 6th, the villistas paraded thirty thousand men down Reforma Boulevard. To show his utter contempt for culture, Pancho Villa had stabled his horses in Adamo Boari's unfinished white marble opera house. Villa and Zapata would not accept Carranza as First Chief of the Revolution, much less Interim President, since he had been appointed by his own Convention. They had driven him out of the Capital to Veracruz and established their own "Conventionist" government. In all its history, such a formidable display of power had never been seen in the Capital. Between the zapatisitas and villistas, 50,000 men had to be quartered. Even the timid could not contain their curiosity. Antonio had cut out a newspaper picture of Villa and Zapata sitting in the President's office in the Palace. Pancho Villa filled the vacated Presidential chair, leering like a jackass; Zapata was slumped in the seat next to him, fierce black eyes staring straight ahead, holding his enormous black hat, swirling with silver braid, in his lap. A gesture of respect for his surroundings, one hoped. The Revolution had split into three factions and degenerated into a battle of personalities. The generals, Antonio concluded, were eating each other up.

"Here they come," Antonio said, training the telescope on a band of women who were marching up Juárez Street toward the Zócalo.

"Who are they?" Antonieta asked. Hearing the beat of drums, she had rushed up to the tower to join her father. The telescope was their daily communication with the world outside Héroes Street. The telephone lines had been cut, the telegraph office closed to civilians, and no newspapers had been printed for weeks.

The sun slanted across the low buildings, highlighting the ugly water tanks strung out across the rooftops. Water tanks that had been empty for months.

"Well, what do you see, Papá?" Antonieta asked, trying to restrain her impatience. "What do those banners say?"

"Can't tell, a line of grayish laundry is obstructing my view, but there are zapatistas in the vacant lot next door, feeding their horses on the weeds María has been throwing into the beanpot. Leave us the weeds!" Antonio shouted, his eye pressed to the telescope and his fist punching the air. "I will not feed another hungry soldier who presses his nose against my gate, do you hear? Not one more wretched soul!"

"Try to read the banners, Papá."

"Look at them. Now they are stuffing the weeds into their own mouths, wretched devils. Carrancistas, zapatistas, villistas, they are all alike. Who the hell is running this country!"

"Let me look, Papá. You will miss them!"

"There, they have moved into the clear. There's a mob following."

"Who are they?"

"Women wearing black skirts and white blouses and wide-brimmed straw hats. Here comes a banner. It says SOCIALIST BRIGADE OF MEXICO. Here, you look."

Antonieta focused on a banner that stretched across the avenue, held up by marching women. WOMEN, JOIN AN ORGANIZED MILITARY GROUP TO KEEP ORDER IN OUR PILLAGED CITY. IF THE GOVERNMENT WON"T DO IT, WE WILL! OUR CHILDREN ARE HUNGRY! she read aloud and swung the telescope away. "I want to join them!" she burst out. "Let me join them, Papá, please!"

Surprised at the outburst, Antonio looked at the young, pleading eyes. "You are helping more at home than you would marching with a bunch of militant women." He spoke gruffly.

"I admire them!"

Antonio turned his daughter's defiant face around and lifted her chin. "Listen, my dearest daughter, we are living black days, like a storm, a terrible storm. The most important thing for a boat in a storm is to keep afloat, not to be swallowed up by the waves. The storm will blow over and then the boat will sail on."

He looked at her closely.

She sighed. "On what course will the boat sail, Papá? Nothing will ever be the same," she said, frustration enlarging the pupils of her eyes. "I feel so helpless! Helpless, do you hear? I'm always shut up in this house. It would be better to join those women and do something."

"Don't ever get caught up in causes, Antonieta," her father said solemnly. "They only destroy you. Think of this house as a boat becalmed. Once these rebels stop warring with each other we will have peace again. The city will be rebuilt. It has been rebuilt before," he said with an optimism he did not feel.

"We are prisoners, Papá. I can't write. I can't play the piano. I can't even concentrate on a book," Antonieta exclaimed. "I just want this Revolution to end!"

At night she could hear the eerie, shrill whistles of the *máquinas locas*, locomotive engines sent careening down the tracks, turned loose to crash into an oncoming train of the opposition. Weathered brown faces pressed against the gates, looking out from under high-crowned straw hats, ragged white shirts crossed with cartridge belts hung on thin shoulders, muddy huaraches sticking out from under cotton pants tied with a drawstring. Hungry zapatistas humbly asking for a morsel of food, villistas demanding food. Demetrio's rifle trained on the villistas, murderous thieves every one. Was he a villista, that soldier in the dirty khaki uniform who had seen her in the back patio when she was pulling up some hidden onions planted under the hedge? He had climbed up on the fence and startled her. When she looked up he stuck his penis through the bars of the fence and motioned to her, moving the thing up and down, a swollen thing with veins standing out. She had stifled the screams and run, stumbling into the kitchen with the onions in her hand. "Why aren't you here with me, Chela?" she had asked the dark window. "And why aren't you here with your children, Mamá! Come stand in line at the bakery or at the mill when there is a bit of corn to grind. Try to get a few pieces of charcoal! Three years you have been gone!" Anger at her mother had exploded and at night she beat her pillow with fury. "Don't judge her too harshly," Alicia had written. "She has lost everything. José gives me money for her but won't receive her in the house. We meet in a little cafe when we can. I want to go home! I want my baby to see Mexico. If this dreadful war with Germany would only end!" Alicia has her war and I have my Revolution, she had reasoned dispassionately.

Giving in to Antonieta's coaxing to get him out of his cold apartment, Beto hobbled to the arbor and sat in his worn rattan chair. He removed his glasses and began to clean them with a monogrammed silk handkerchief.

"I made you some hot tea, Tío dear. It's orange leaves with cinnamon and cloves." Antonieta watched him, remembering when pride prevented him from wearing his glasses. Now his face looked naked without them. His eyes were too small, nose too long, goatee grown sparse. Even the hand-rolled hem of his handkerchief was raveled.

Beto replaced his glasses and smiled at his niece. "Well, tell me who is in charge of the city today?"

"I don't know, Tío, they say 'Carranza.' He has dispatched General Obregón to chase Pancho Villa up north. Then he will retake the city. But let's not talk about the Revolution. I brought Browning and Ruben Dario," Antonieta said. She reached out and took her uncle's hand. "I love you, Tío, and it makes me sad to see you looking so frail.

Please feel better."

"If I but could, I would, for you," Beto said. "You see, I, too, am a poet."

A fit of coughing overtook him, hoarse, deep coughing. Beto spat into his handkerchief; Antonieta saw the blood. Stumbling along, she led him to his apartment and helped him to bed, tucking a down comforter all around his trembling body.

"Papá!" Antonieta flung open the door to her father's studio. "We must get a doctor. Tío is dying!"

That night, Antonio brought a doctor from the market area, where he had seen the man's shingle hanging in a doorway.

"Pneumonia," the doctor pronounced. "I regret there is no medicine in the hospitals, nor in the drugstores, Señor. If you know a military doctor..." He shrugged. "Let's pray the fever breaks."

Day and night they kept vigil. Sabina was in constant attendance, changing the mustard plasters, bringing hot herbal teas, cold compresses for his brow. Antonieta sat at his bedside reading Browning and Baudelaire and Ruben Darío. At night, Antonio slept in Beto's big club chair, plagued by troubled dreams, awake at the slightest change in his brother's breathing.

The lucid moments became fewer as Beto sank into delirium. Caravans of vagabond bohemians crossed the threshold of his memory. Sometimes he talked to old friends and chuckled aloud. Then dim recollections of a musty, ancient city of peeling colonial palaces took shape. Once, he held his nose to ward off the smell of malodorous, open drainage canals. A lantern swaying on a lamp post cast a pale light on a carved stone saint, who looked down from her cloistered corner on a building at a little boy hurrying along a rain-soaked street. The boy entered a courtyard through huge doors studded with nails and bumped into the water carrier who was trotting across the courtyard of the hotel, his cans slung front and back, balanced on a long pole across his leather-capped head...a cascade of water spilled over a lady in a long red dress...his mother...chasing him and scolding, shouting with concern and anger... He could smell the garlic through the wooden screen of the confessional. A priest tweaked his ear so hard it hurt for days.... He reached up on the dresser and stole a gold coin from his father's purse. His father thrashed him with a belt, raising welts on his bottom....

"Tío, you must drink this."

"Señor Beto" Sabina shook him vigorously, bracing his back with her strong arm. "Drink this, then you may sleep again."

"Has Don Porfirio died?" Beto suddenly asked. "Light a candle for him, princess. I hold no rancor." He heard bugle calls echoing through the forests of Chapultepec, his carriage joining the parade of magnificent liveries. Castle guards pranced on noble steeds, the plumes of their helmets waving in the wind. With a sudden jerk, he tried to climb up, up and out of the deep well he was in. He sat up.

"Where is Villagrande?" he demanded in a raspy voice.

Antonio took his brother's hand. "Nobody knows. His bookstore was boarded up, remember? Nobody knows where he went."

A sly smile parted Beto's thin lips. "He went to Baja California with Flores Magón. Remember? To establish a socialist colony. They'll catch him, poor damned bastard." Beto sank back.

As the sun sent its final rays through the beveled windowpanes of his bedroom, Beto weakly beckoned to his brother.

"Toño," he whispered, reverting to a childhood name. "Promise to put up his statue."

"Whose statue, Beto? Whose statue do you want me to put up?"

"At the third circle."

"Whose statue, Beto?"

"Cortés." Beto's lips parted in a roguish grin. "In proper historical order. Columbus, Cuahtemoc and Cortés before Independence. They will lynch you, of course." He chuckled dryly.

Antonio smiled. The third circle on Reforma Boulevard had a palm tree. No president had ever dared to erect a statue to the Conqueror, father of the mestizo race.

"You hated our father, didn't you? I hated him too. But his blood is our blood. We can't deny it...."

"Don't talk, Beto." Antonio's voice faltered as he reached for his brother's hand. He did not feel the life go out of the limp hand—not until it grew stone cold, and slipped from his grasp.

The casket was made in the carpentry shed and lined with the white velvet draperies that had once adorned the window of Cristina's boudoir. Four tall tapers in magnificent brass candlesticks lit the music salon where Beto lay in state. No one was advised. There was no one to advise, no one close. The servants kept a twenty-four hour *velorio* and prayed for the soul of the departed, and wept, and helped Antonio honor his dead brother. Even Memela was lifted up to gaze at the wasted face. She whispered to Sabina: "He looks so little, doesn't he?" In a rented cart, Antonio transported the casket to a public cemetery where Cástulo dug a pit. When it was lowered, he helped shovel the dirt back into the grave until the simple box was buried.

Antonieta could not cry. Her eyes were dry as she helped her father go through Beto's possessions. An envelope with a few gold coins was left to Damiana, his silver hairbrushes to Mario. Tío Beto had left her a note, tucked in an early volume of Ruben Darío: "I have seen so many people pass by and so few souls. You, princess, are a beautiful soul. You have been the brushstroke of happiness on the bleak landscape of my old age. I leave you my gratitude and my love and this medal of the Virgin of Guadalupe which was my mother's. May she always protect you. Devotedly, Tío Beto."

Tears filled Antonieta's eyes as she clasped the gold medal around her neck and read the poem:

Oh the poor princess with the rosebud lips
Wouldst a swallow or butterfly be
With light wings that dip, that fly 'neath the sky
Or lose herself in the wind
That stirs the waves of the sea.

CHAPTER XIX

1915

A hurricane wind tore through the valley of Mexico, uprooting trees and destroying shacks in its wake. Cleotilde, the washwoman, interpreted this omen as a sign that famine lay ahead for the beleaguered Capital.

Exasperated, Antonio examined his larder. He pulled the lids off one bin after the other and rattled the empty containers: beans, rice, flour, sugar, dried corn. Empty. Every one empty. A fury boiled up, rage at the warring revolutionaries who had halted the city's wagons and trucks, confiscating their provisions, while they fought their bloody battles just beyond the periphery of the Capital. The Zapatistas had returned, cutting the repaired electrical lines in order to oblige Carranza to leave in the dark. The whole city had been plunged into darkness, exposing the terrified citizens to bloody attacks and robberies. Hungry, angry people lashed out in vain at the ever-changing revolutionary forces that rode into the Capital, taking possession, imposing their rules and their money, annulling the authority of the previous faction. Throughout the city iron curtains had been slammed down by furious grocers who refused to accept worthless paper currency. Hunger, like a vise, had tightened its hold on rich and poor alike.

Antonio tightened his belt another notch. With dogged determination, he resolved to find food. Gold talked. Gold would pry open the larder of some avaricious grocer. He called Ignacio into his office.

"I am going downtown," he said, "to find out what the zapatista's "convention" has to say. Don't let Demetrio take his eyes off the gates and tell Juanito to guard the orchard. Shoot anyone who tries to steal one single lemon! Should you need them, God forbid, there are more cartridges here in this drawer. The zapatistas are swarming the city. Sabina must keep the children in the nursery while I am out of the house."

Adjusting the brim of his felt hat, Antonio buttoned his old alpaca jacket to conceal the stock of his pistol and marched out the gate. On the sidewalk, he paused to peer through the high iron fence to see whether a telltale carrot or onion top could be detected in the unattended flowerbeds. They had let the grass grow high and watched it turn yellow. Precious water from the old artesian well had kept the orange and lemon trees alive during the dry season and now June rains had encouraged new shoots and weeds. The Great Danes were sniffing woefully at the gate, living on peelings and bean cakes while they lasted. Sabina had informed him that the spinsters down the street were mixing sawdust with cornmeal to stretch every grain.

The streetcar clanged to a stop and Antonio boarded the near-empty car and rode toward the Zócalo. Food dominated his thoughts and his pampered stomach protested its emptiness. The stalls at the neighborhood market were nailed shut. Rats attacked heaps of decomposing garbage, raising a stench that could be smelled for blocks. Screaming, a woman held a corn cob on high, trying to ward off a pack of starving dogs. Human wolf packs roamed the neighborhoods, fighting over scraps in garbage cans.

He didn't notice her until she sat beside him. A gloved hand began to stroke his thigh and a shoulder rubbed against him. He turned and looked at her, a middle-aged woman, attractive, a decent sort.

"Anything you want," she whispered, holding his gaze with anguished brown eyes. "Pay in silver, understand. For my children...."

Antonio pushed her hand away. "Sorry. Sorry..."

She stood up and with an air of dignity got off at the next stop.

At the Zócalo, Antonio walked across the huge plaza, where a crowd had gathered around the entrance to the Palace. Necks craned to peer at the bulletins posted on the Palace wall. He pushed his way in and read a manifesto printed in bold type: CITIZENS, YOU NO LONGER NEED TO SUPPORT THE CRIMES OF VILLA AND ZAPATA. THE REVOLUTION HAS TRIUMPHED! THE CONSTITUTIONALIST GOVERNMENT OF THE PEOPLE WILL ESTABLISH LAW AND ORDER.

"Cowards, they have left!" someone boomed out and began to rip off the graffiti-defiled bulletin. "Who wants these re-fried promises?" he asked, holding up the shreds.

The crowd thinned out as embittered citizens digested the fact that no accord had been reached by Carranza and Zapata. With some gratefulness, Antonio heard the news that General Obregón was chasing Villa farther and farther north.

In hand-blocked letters, an extemporaneous sentiment declared:
THIS REVOLUTION ISN'T WORTH A DAMN
THEY SELL MILK BY THE OUNCE AND COAL BY THE GRAM.

A young man leapt out in front of the group and, waving his arms like a choir master, began to improvise a verse to "*La Cucaracha*":

The poor, sad cockroach, the poor sad cockroach
Cannot party anymore.
He has no money, no marijuana
Nor to dance upon, a floor.

The floors of public buildings had been ripped up for fuel. Even the trees on Reforma Boulevard had been chopped down.

Abruptly Antonio moved away, all humor dissolved. Across the park, a spontaneous orator was ranting at a small audience, God only knew what about. The man's hair and beard had grown to lion's proportions and glazed eyes sent out sparks of fury. Another orator jumped up beside him and the lion began to roar and snarl at the dissenter, both soon losing their disenchanted audience.

There must be a warehouse at the Merced market which could be pried open, Antonio reasoned, automatically turning the corner of the Palace toward San Carlos as though that venerable building could put order in his life. A notice tacked to the heavy baroque doors read: "Closed. Classes suspended until further notice."

Like a man in a trance, he began to wander down narrow streets looking for a grocery store. The stench of clogged drains assailed his nostrils. The jarring screech of a streetcar ahead stopped him. A dead man lay across the tracks. The conductor got out and tugged at the inert body. It didn't budge. The stalled streetcar clanged its bell frantically, until two ragged pedestrians helped pull the dead citizen onto the sidewalk, allowing the streetcar to pass.

A ragged cadre with sunken eyes telegraphed danger as Antonio brushed past the pedestrians. He caught sight of them in the jagged remains of a store window and began to run. They tripped him in the middle of the block. In an instant, pistol, watch, gold, gave themselves up to probing fingers. In another instant they were gone. Antonio pushed up on bruised hands, rubbed a bleeding knee and staggered to his feet, shaking with humiliation and anger. What good was a pistol if you didn't use it? He pulled up his pant leg and tied his handkerchief around the throbbing knee. Still dazed, he retrieved his hat. It had happened in an instant. Life can end in instant, he thought. Limping, he began to retrace his steps toward the Zócalo.

Out of the corner of his eye, he noticed a man in a business suit walking fast behind him. The man blocked him at the corner of San Carlos.

"Maestro," he said, puffing, "you were always so kind. I will sell my carrancista money at fifty percent of face value. You know they will be back. I need gold. Please."

"I have none," Antonio said irritably, breaking the man's hold and walking rapidly on.

"Then silver," the man insisted, clinging to Antonio's sleeve. "I have to buy food. For my wife, do you understand? You must have silver...."

Antonio stopped and jerked his arm free. He reached deep in his pocket and took out some copper coins. "I have no gold or silver," he said. "If these will serve you, take them."

The man stared at Antonio's open hand. Suddenly, he struck the outstretched palm with the flat of his hand, scattering the coins, and with a sharp cry furiously pounded Antonio in the belly. Then he wheeled about and ran toward the plaza.

Antonio stood on the sidewalk, dumbfounded, staring after his assailant. He shook his fist at the vanishing figure, still yelling at the man as he turned the corner. "I have not insulted you, Señor. I have no silver and I have fifteen mouths to feed. The body of my brother, Luis, lies rotted, unburied, as does the body of his son! I feel what you feel, Señor. I am hungry. My children are hungry. Do you know *my* desperation?" he ranted at the air.

Curious eyes momentarily stared at the big man, gone mad, shouting at no one and fighting the empty space in front of him.

Rioters swarmed into the market near the house. Screaming housewives, brandishing sticks, chased a storekeeper down Héroes. With Antonieta at his side, Antonio watched from the tower, aghast, as the man was knocked down and viciously beaten.

"My God, it's Don Manuel!"

"What have they done to him?" Antonieta asked anxiously.

Antonio did not answer. He watched the Spaniard who was their grocer stagger to his feet, stumbling, retreating down the street.

"Let me look, Papá."

"Not yet." His daughter had seen enough.

Antonio swung the telescope around to the market where the mob was smashing locks on warehouses and ripping market stalls apart. With iron bars, they tore doors off their hinges, pulled up floor planks and in their frenzy nearly killed the few merchants who tried to protect their goods.

"Hurry down and tell María and Ignacio to run to the market. Tell them to steal anything they can! Hurry!"

Carranza's soldiers stood by, making no attempt to stop the mad forays. Carranza had returned in August, threatened by a general strike and faced with a populace that was furious and starving. Now, like brushfire, word had spread that Carranza had retreated, moving his headquarters out to the Shrine of Guadalupe, leaving the city to the mercy of the mobs.

Antonio spent the night taking turns at the watch with his servants and his shadow, Mario. Feelings of guilt obsessed him. Antonieta had witnessed hideous scenes of human behavior. Her senses, every one of them, had been battered by this damnable Revolution. He wondered if it would ever be erased from her mind. He should have left this insane country when the sane people left. His stomach growled with hunger and each night he feared facing the next day.

Dawn broke without the crowing of a single rooster. Not a feather of a single fowl remained. Long ago he had turned the horses loose to fend for themselves. Now, carefully, Antonio opened the chamber of his shotgun and loaded it with two bullets. Resolutely, he walked through dark, quiet rooms to the gallery. The pale glow of dawn lighted his way to the orchard. He unlatched the gate and proceeded to the back garden, to the kennels.

The Great Danes stood up against the wire fence and howled in greeting. Antonio could see their ribcages sticking out under loose, flabby skin. His sleek dogs, noble animals.

"Genghis. Kublai," he called softly.

The dogs whimpered and pawed the chain wire fence.

Taking careful aim, Antonio fired. Twice. Then he walked away.

Cástulo met him in the driveway. "I heard shots." He looked at the face of his patrón and bowed his head.

"Take them to the kitchen," Antonio said, turning his eyes away from his gaunt gardener.

Death claimed its toll during the black summer of 1915. Famine swept across the city. Starving, people dropped dead in the streets. Then, smallpox and typhus began their killer course. Mamá Lupita died quietly in her sleep, her emaciated body a final denial of self, her face still beautiful with the serenity that comes of accepting the vicissitudes of life. A lady with a rare gift of silence, silenced now forever. Antonio and José buried her in a crude coffin and found a priest to say Mass. The children were not allowed to see their grandmother in her casket.

"The parrot died today." Antonieta wrote. "Memela cried and cried, but I have no tears left to shed. I had the same nightmare again: I am crawling toward a pit where wild beasts are kept. Their roar is deafening as I come closer, unable to conquer my fear or stop my advance. I get to the edge, then Mario and Memela grab my legs and pull me back. What drives me toward the pit? Is it because my stomach is empty? William James says that we are the architects of our own fate, but how can I build on this emptiness which sucks me down?"

The bell on the visitor's gate clanged loudly one afternoon in late August. Demetrio shuffled across the lawn to admit Ramón Betanzo, an old friend from the days of receiving lines and costume balls. "Señor Dramón," Antonio had long ago nicknamed his friend whose dramatic exaggerations were well known. It was with true joy that Antonio received his elegant guest.

"Antonio, I bring important news. They would shoot me if they knew I knew. It's been such a well-guarded secret."

Ramón pounded his friend in a warm abrazo, his ebullience a balm in the bleak day.

"What news, Ramón?" Antonio asked eagerly.

"Nobody was to breathe a word. Under penalty of death."

"What? For God's sake, man, speak."

"Do you know where Pancho Villa is?" Ramón asked in a mysterious voice.

"Haven't heard anything about Villa since he locked a French woman in the bedroom of his borrowed mansion and the French Government brought charges against him. What has he done now?"

"Pancho Villa was defeated at Celaya in April. Then Obregón finished him off at Aguascalientes and his leaders began defecting like rats from a sinking ship. He's bankrupt, bled and finished!" Ramón made a sweeping gesture, his eyes bulging with the importance of his message.

"Who told you?" Antonio asked skeptically.

"A soldier who was there. A defector. My cook's brother."

"Well, we shall drink to that, Ramón," Antonio said, a lilt in his voice. Leading his friend into the anteroom he speculated on how many people he had told his "secret" to. From the smell of him, quite a few. "There's nothing to eat in this house but I have saved some brandy for just this moment. Will you join me?"

"I accept," Ramón said with an impish grin. With relish, he recounted details of the battles. "My hat's off to Obregón, a real strategist. And he obviously has kept up with the war in Europe. Listen to these tactics: Villa's horses were entangled in barbed wire, tearing, ripping those poor beasts. Villa's troops rode into machine-gun nests, his elite dorados slaughtered. Obregón even acquired a couple of American airplanes and dropped bombs on the bastards! The blood of ten thousand villistas flowed through the streets of Celaya and Aguascaliente." Lowering his voice, Dramón continued: "Mark my word, now the zapatistas will slink back to Morelos and Carranza will stay. Entrenched! It's over, my friend. It's over!"

"Here's to food," Antonio said, elated, and poured his friend another tumbler of brandy.

"You don't happen to have a good Havana cigar left, do you old friend?"

In October, the Cathedral bells rang wildly, joined by all the bells in the city. Carranza was firmly established in the Capital, assuming the office of President of the Republic. The legality of his office had been recognized by the United States, which clamped a tight arms embargo on Villa, who continued to fight sporadically up north. 1916 brought a sense of calm to the battered Capital.

"Look, Cástulo, it has bloomed," Antonio said. In an old smock and straw hat, the pátron had worked side by side with Cástulo and Juanito to replant the garden. The cactus had looked dead, dried up, and now, with a light spring rain, these orange phenomena had blossomed.

Antonio caressed the flower with the tips of his fingers. This rough, spiny plant knows how to survive, he reflected, marveling at its resilience. He nodded his head. We, too, have survived. And so will Mexico.

Her white skirt billowed as Antonieta whirled, revealing shapely ankles.

"I love you, garden. I love you old trees. I love you house. I love you, and you, and you!" She buried her nose in the petals of a magnificent red rose. Spring had burst upon the world and all her senses were alive with the joy of being.

Amelia hugged an ancient elm tree with one arm as she waved to her brother, running down the driveway, school books strapped to his back. Mario had not complained once about punishment meted out by the Jesuit priests at his new school.

They all felt it. Freedom!

The stench of human misery and uncollected garbage still clung to the city and the market stalls were only partially filled, but Carranza's soldiers were now quartered in barracks, while brigades were slowly cleaning and patching the streets and buildings. Happily, Antonieta had watched her father become his old, cheerful self once again. He was up in the studio, engrossed in work, as usual.

Antonieta followed the path to Tío Beto's favorite bench and plopped down, folding her arms behind her head as she gazed at the sky. Pure, crystalline blue, not a wisp of a cloud. What made some days perfect from the moment you opened your eyes? Even Conchita had smiled at breakfast. The girl had set the table, perfect in every detail, and served as though she had been born knowing her right from her left. Next year I will make her my personal maid or secretary, Antonieta thought munificently. But today, today was special. Chela was coming! Bright, beautiful, Chela. Papá had engaged a philosophy teacher for them and this afternoon they were scheduled for their first discussion.

"As long as you girls have read everything within reach," Papá had said, "you might as well learn the art of discussion and be properly exposed to Plato and St. Augustine."

Privately, Chela had mentioned Nietzche and Freud. Americans were up on everything, she recounted. Three years in New York had filled her head with new ideas and made her, in the process, fiercely independent.

"In the United States, girls go to universities and are allowed to go out alone with a man. Here, I am practically under lock and key. For

God's sake, I'm seventeen!"

And Chela had confided that she was in love. In one month, she had fallen in love! Her father was acting horridly, she had reported. Not because Alfonso was beneath them socially; he was very rich! But he was twice her age and had had scandalous affairs. Her parents wanted her to marry one of those "proper" young men who sniffed around her all the time and bored her to death. Stupid, Chela called them. She didn't know that she intimidated young men. Her beauty overwhelmed them, made them act sillier than they actually were. "When you meet Alfonso, you will see how handsome, how wonderful, how intelligent he is," Chela claimed. She was taking wild chances, she boasted, meeting him secretly in out-of-the-way restaurants. Last week he had kissed her as though he would swallow her; his tongue had burned her throat and his hand had touched her thigh under her skirt, shooting fire through her body. She said she knew what ecstasy meant and wanted to lie naked with him, to be possessed! Antonieta closed her eyes and tried to imagine what it would be like to be possessed by a man. She couldn't fit this imaginary man into any picture. What kind of a man would he be? A cloud crossed her reverie as she gazed at the sky. Chela was thinking more about marriage than philosophy. Antonieta sighed. She was sixteen and hadn't even met a man!

The Dodge was turning up the driveway. Antonieta jumped up and followed the automobile to the entrance.

"I'll be right down, Ignacio," she called out. Today, Mr. Grieg, she said to herself, hurrying up the stairs to the gallery, I am going to expose every shading, every feeling, every secret you have. Maestro Manuel Ponce had said that Grieg came to life with her touch, that her fingers struck notes he had seldom had the privilege to hear. He said she was the most talented student he had had in the conservatory. His very words!

Antonio stood on the balcony of his studio and waved as Ignacio held open the door of the shiny, impeccable touring car and Antonieta settled into the back seat. She looked up and blew him a kiss. She is so alive, Antonio thought. Thank God, alive and enjoying new interests, making new friends, arranging her own social engagements, and being his delightful hostess. Antonieta had wit and a gift with words. She attracted people. His sensitive angel had emerged a full-blown señorita with a mind of her own. Recently returned from war-ravaged Europe, Leonor had criticized him for allowing her so much freedom, but how could he deny her freedom when she had been imprisoned so long? Her life is full and busy. Happiness thrives best in a crowded life, he told himself.

A sense of well-being settled over Antonio as he returned to his desk. He too had a new interest. A smile broke across his face as he thought of her, this new interest. Her name was Maruca, a friend of his sister Elena's, a young widow whose only child was married. She was intelligent and charming, unencumbered, past menopause, and a provocative lover. Antonio moved the tassel on his fez and leaned over the desk. He planned to make time for his new interest. A lot of time, he promised himself.

1917

"You had better come down from that tree," Antonieta called to Amelia from the arbor.

"How can you see me? I'm hidden," a small voice replied.

"If you are not careful, you will turn green and nobody will ever see you again," Antonieta admonished. "Come down, do you hear. It's rude to keep Miss Ortiz waiting."

Reluctantly the little girl climbed down and disappeared into the house.

Enjoying a fig he had plucked from a tree in the orchard, Antonio oberserved the scene with a smile. Antonieta had indeed taken charge of the children. She turned to her father. "Don't you think it's time to send her to a regular school, Papá? Memela is eight and poor Señorita Ortiz can't handle her anymore."

"Hmm, I guess you are right." Antonio sighed. "I'll look into schools."

"I already know of one," Antonieta said, picking up a juicy fig. "A fine parochial school run by American nuns in San Angel. You needn't concern yourself, Papá. We can enroll her for fall."

"San Angel is a long way out," Antonio began.

"Sabina can take her on the streetcar. You yourself have said that the city is perfectly safe now. It'll be a nice outing for Sabina, don't you agree?" Antonieta kissed her father on the cheek and picked up a section of the newspaper. "May I?"

The matter was settled. Antonio excused himself and walked off toward his office.

Antonieta let the paper slip to the floor and dreamily began planning the weeks ahead. She had been preparing a concert at the Conservatory of Music and had been asked to dance for a charity affair. Well, not exactly a charity, the French Colony was sponsoring a benefit to raise funds for the war effort. Now that things were stabilizing, it seemed everyone was sewing for the Red Cross or planning benefits. She had decided to dance a fado and the *Jota Aragonesa*. When she arched her back and stamped out the toe-heel rhythm of a Spanish dance, a passion possessed her she had never felt before. The castanets trilled wildly or talked softly in the palms of her hands. Señorita Petra Lopez said she suspected that gypsy blood flowed through her veins. She liked to pretend she was a gypsy when she danced, her steps now lively, now softly beating to the haunting strains of a flamenco guitar. She pretended that she was suddenly caught and passionately kissed, then quietly wooed to the wail of a high falsetto. It was a lovely fantasy. During those black days in the basement, she had found a Spanish shawl which had belonged to her grandmother, Leonor. With practice she had learned to make the fringes swing in rhythm to the intricate toe-heel movement and whirling turns of the dance. Antonieta closed her eyes and envisioned herself on stage.

The jangle of the visitors' bell broke her spell. She peered out to see who had rung. Demetrio had admitted a lady. He doffed his hat and bowed as he let her pass. Then he hurried on ahead, looking neither to right nor left, and disappeared toward the kitchen.

The lady was elegantly dressed, wearing a straw hat which she held down against sudden spring gusts which blew up the driveway. She paused at the edge of the rose garden and bent down to smell a bloom. The pose was somehow familiar. Then the lady turned abruptly and with a swaying stride began walking up the curved driveway toward the house.

Antonieta sank way back into the shadows of the arbor, her body shaking, lips trembling. Antonio had peered out the window of his office, and now stepped out into the gallery. Arms folded, he stared at the woman who was ascending a few yards away. Two red splotches inflamed his full cheeks.

"Antonio!" Cristina cried out. She ran up the last steps, arms outstretched.

Firmly, Antonio clasped her arms and lowered them to her sides.

"I didn't cable because..." Cristina's voice faltered. "You don't know how difficult it was to get here. Until the German submarines were no longer a threat...."

Antonio said nothing.

"Won't you invite me in, Antonio?" his wife asked in a tremulous voice.

"You may come in," Antonio replied dispassionately. He walked ahead and held open the door to the anteroom of his office.

Anger choked Antonieta as the reality of her mother's presence sank in. How many times had she dreamed...how many times had she hoped...and now she was here, a stranger, a slim woman in a straw hat who thought she could just ring the bell and move back into her old quarters. Four years, Mamá! Her chest heaved and anger turned to tears, and the tears to a heavy heart, because her mother, who had never liked her, never loved her, was home. A sense of her own worthlessness washed over her like vinegar. Then a familiar brown arm encircled her and Antonieta laid her head on Sabina's shoulder.

"It is between them, Tonieta," Sabina said. "It is between your mother and your father. Nothing is your fault."

Word spread rapidly. The old servants knew the Señora, and the new servants looked out of windows hoping to get a glimpse of the mysterious lady of the house. Señorita Ortiz descended from the schoolroom, Amelia hopping down the stairs in her wake. The tutor was ushered out by Sabina, and Amelia flung herself against Antonieta, hugging her waist.

"They say Mamá has come back. Is it true, Tonieta?"

"Yes, it's true. She and Papá are talking in his office. You can't see her yet."

"I never want to see her. I don't like her!"

"Don't say that, Memela." Antonieta tried to control her voice. "It's not her fault she was caught by the war. Now tell Conchita to serve your lunch. Mamá and Papá have a lot to talk about."

Amelia wiped her sister's eyes with the edge of her pinafore. "She doesn't make me cry," she said, and departed.

Antonieta sat down in Beto's old rattan chair and waited.

Angry voices rose to a high pitch, then subsided. And rose again. She sank deep into the chair, her mind shooting out questions. What would it be like with Mamá at home again? Would Papá take her back? Never! She had left Papá for a lover. Now she must pay! As though God himself were passing judgment, a clap of thunder roared across the sky.

Suddenly the office door was flung open.

"Sabina!" Antonio called.

Sabina emerged from the foyer and hurried down the gallery. "Si, Señor."

"Ask Antonieta to come. Tell her"... he hesitated..."that her mother is here."

"Si. Señor." The obedient servant crossed quickly to the arbor. "You heard," she whispered. "Go up to your room and wash your face and brush your hair before you go in."

Antonieta knocked at the door to her father's anteroom, her heart beating wildly beneath the poised facade. Antonio ushered her in. Tear-streaked, her mother's face looked up at her, pleading, seeming to say, "I need your support, forgive me, please, please." Antonieta kissed her mother's cheek.

"How are you, Mamá? How did you get home with the war still going on?"

"I took an American boat from Le Havre. It was sheer luck," she replied, fighting for composure. "You are a young lady, Antonieta. A pretty young lady," she added.

"I am sure I am not as pretty as Alicia," Antonieta heard herself reply sharply, then, ashamed, she asked softly, "How is Alicia? And the new baby?"

"Beautiful, both of them. He's hardly a baby anymore."

An awkward silence pressed down in the small room. Antonieta looked at her father, her stomach queasy with uncertainty.

Antonio cleared his throat. "Your mother is no longer going to live with us," he announced evenly. "I have agreed to furnish an apartment for her. We will live apart."

"I understand, Papá," Antonieta said, not daring to look at the thin figure engulfed in the big leather chair.

"And I want to tell you, in her presence, that your mother does not have visiting privileges in this house. You and Mario and Amelia will live with me, as you always have, unless..." Antonio studied his tall, erect daughter's eyes. "Unless you are not happy here."

"What do you mean, Papá?"

"Would you rather live with your mother?" Antonio asked, averting his eyes.

"No!" She stared at her father, unbelieving.

"She suggested you might like to keep her company."

Antonieta's gaze froze. Mamá wanted her? Of course Mamá wanted her. She would serve as a pawn between her and Papá and a buffer against a society which would spurn her.

"My place is at your side, Papá. It always has been and always will be. May I go now?"

"Yes." Antonio held the door for her.

Amelia was hiding in the arbor. "Does Mamá look like her picture?" she asked, hazel eyes round and wide.

"She looks older, that's all, but she is very beautiful."

"Why doesn't she come out?"

"They're still talking. You don't have to hide."

What can they be discussing, Antonieta wondered. Tío Fernando? What can two people talk about when there is no longer love, or respect?

The door to the office opened again. Cristina emerged, followed by Antonio.

"Memela!" she cried out, running across the gallery.

The confused little girl rushed over to her father and clasped his hand.

"I am your mother," Cristina said softly.

Amelia backed away.

Antonieta stood in the open arch of the arbor, unable to say anything as she watched her mother look from one daughter to the other. Back and forth.

Anchoring her hat, Cristina smiled at them. "Goodbye," she said sweetly. Then she turned abruptly toward the front stairs and descended, her smile fading, her back as erect as a wall.

CHAPTER XX
1917

The Hotel Genève, owned by Thomas Gore, an American, was a meeting place for the international set. The wicker tables in the long palm court were filled with foreigners and Mexicans sipping aperitifs when Antonieta hurried through. Tennis players headed for the courts in the rear and children brushed past her, chasing each other in and out of the lush fronds.

Impatiently, Antonieta punched the elevator button and rode up to the third floor, where Mrs. Gore's suite was already crowded with young people, American, French, British, and Mexicans, all waiting for instructions from the organizing committee. The United States had entered the war in Europe and a new bond united the foreign colonies. Mrs. Gore, a heavy-set former opera singer, had given up her career when she married and moved to Mexico. Now, the enterprising lady had wasted no time in planning a big, amateur benefit for the American doughboys. The show was to be a mélange of skits, recitations, music and dance numbers, accompanied by an orchestra. The Grand Finale was daring and dramatic: A chorus line of young girls dressed in red, white and blue tights would form the American flag, unfurled and waving as the girls turned and undulated. Most important, the renovated Virginia Fabregas Theater had been engaged; they would perform for the largest audience ever gathered for a benefit.

"Antonieta!" Mrs. Gore called out, sticking a hairpin in her perpetually disheveled blond topknot. "Come over here, dear. We are ready to select the dancers."

Antonieta's star position in the program was accepted by the lesser performers, whose lavish praises, she knew, were meant to influence her vote in the auditions. Today, she stayed on to hear the final auditions of Mrs. Gore's own voice students, who would sing a selection of operatic arias.

"You were wonderful, Susana," Antonieta said enthusiastically, congratulating her new friend who had won the leading role. "Come home with me to supper and help me sell a stack of tickets to Papá and his friends. They're easy marks."

"I wish I could, but I don't have permission."

"You can telephone."

"Mamá's not home."

"Then what's your rush? You can telephone from my house and my chauffeur can take you home later. Come on. Papá's friends are interesting old artists and teachers who always have wonderful arguments. This is their domino night and they'll all buy tickets."

"I really can't, Antonieta," Susana said with a sigh. "My family is not spontaneous like yours."

"Well, come Wednesday afternoon, then. On Wednesdays I have a little literary salon. Not that you can sell many tickets there. Nearly everybody who comes is poor. They are students of my philosophy teacher and I lend them books from father's library. I think you will enjoy it and a little musical education might stick to them." Antonieta's smile was beguiling. "It would please me very much if you would sing."

"Thanks. I would really like to," Susana said. "I'll ask permission." She might be allowed to go, Susana thought. Her mother was curious to know what went on in "that Rivas Mercado girl's so-called 'salons'." Antonieta's unorthodox comportment was a topic of gossip among the mothers of her peers.

Quietly, Antonieta slipped through the beaded curtain and took off her shoes. Chela was seated yoga-fashion on the thick Persian rug. As though touched by a magi's hand, Antonieta had transformed the children's old bedroom into an Arabian den. She had scoured the thieves' market and the National Pawn Shop in search of treasures. A Chinese table that served as a desk was dominated by an enormous Mohammedan marriage throne, but Señorita Elena Lambarri, the philosophy teacher, preferred to sit on the pile of Moroccan pillows, placing teacher and students on the same level.

"You disturbed my meditation," Chela complained.

"Sorry." Antonieta sat down, assuming the lotus position.

They were silent, attempting to dwell on planes of mysticism they could only glimpse. Daily, they practiced yoga, trying to keep their bodies in perfect condition by "diversion of the senses from the external world and concentrating on thought within". When Antonieta had tried to introduce yoga culinary practices into the kitchen, her father had raised a vociferous complaint. "Yoga is not a serious philosophy and I have fasted enough in the last few years!"

"But you are getting fat again, Papá. Our bodies are a result of what we eat."

"And what our ancestors ate," her father retorted. "I come from a line of good eaters, not yoga mystics."

Antonieta persisted in experimenting with different "foods for the mind." Antonio had watched her swallow a single raw egg for breakfast for a week, the length of time most of her dietary adventures lasted.

Chela broke the meditation.

"I have decided," she pronounced solemnly, rising from her pillow.

"Decided what?"

"To marry Alfonso."

Antonieta sprang to her feet and hugged her cousin. "Oh, Chela, Chelita! When will you tell him?"

"Now. He's parked around the corner, waiting. He told me I had to decide today. We will be married on my eighteenth birthday. I saw it clearly in my meditation."

"But that's only two months away!"

"I know. Mamá will have to do some fast planning." She giggled.

"Everyone will think I am pregnant."

"What do you think of Rabelais, Papá?" Antonieta asked, accosting her father in his studio.

"I am surprised you're interested in such an obscure rascal. Sixteenth century, I think, A priest or a doctor. Wasn't he one of those Renaissance writers who were accused of indecency?"

"Right you are," Antonieta said admiringly. "Señorita Lambarri says that the Mexican mind is too closed to understand him."

"I don't think the Mexican mind cares a hoot about Rabelais. Is this what I am paying for?" Antonio asked with mock severity. "For you to dig up a minor, moldy philosopher?"

"I admire him," Antonieta rejoined. "He was a free thinker." She put her arms around her father's neck and kissed his cheek. "Now, Papá, that kiss is shameless guile, the prelude to an assault on your pocketbook." She held up a block of tickets. "These are to the matinee on Saturday. Memela and Mario and Conchita and Sabina want to see me dance, so that's four. Any more?"

"Three for the evening performance," Antonio said.

"Who are you taking?"

"Your aunt Elena and a friend of hers."

"Oh." Antonieta cast a curious glance at her father. "Do bring them backstage. I would like to meet Aunt Elena's friend. And Papá, remember there's a dance after the performance. When you finish with Ignacio, can he wait for me?"

"It would be more proper for me to pick you up," Antonio said.

"I would rather not, Papá. I may get bored and want to leave early."

"Hmm," Antonio mumbled.

Albert Blair and Evaristo Madero were escorted to their seats in the crowded theater by a young Mexican volunteer who wore a small American flag pinned to her blouse. Evaristo was the youngest Madero, taller than most of the clan, and with a wit that attracted women and men. Having witnessed Albert's success in the cotton business, he had asked to become his partner, an alliance which had made for a solid friendship.

"Are you the star of the show? You are pretty enough to be," Evaristo teased the young girl who escorted them up the aisle. Flustered, the girl stumbled.

Albert pushed his partner ahead and they settled into their seats. "She looks about fifteen," he whispered. "Have pity on the poor child. God knows why I let you talk me into this. Amateurs are not my dish. Did you get a program?"

"She was out of them. But I finagled these." Evaristo waved two tickets. "They're for the dance at the hotel after the benefit."

"Oh God," Albert held his head.

"Well, I can introduce you to the chaperones. Come on, Al, loosen up. Don't be so goddamned stiff. Women won't bite you. Circulate tonight. Have a little fun."

"I circulate plenty on the ranches," Albert said testily.

"You can't spend your life selling cotton and you're not old enough for the celibate life. Come on, relax."

Albert looked about at the fashionably dressed people who filled the theater. The couple to his right was speaking French. Red Cross uniforms dotted the audience. He was acutely aware of American flags pinned to lapels. He would be shot simply for wearing one by the renegade villistas up north. In his fury at the United States, Villa had crossed the border and shot up the town of Columbus, New Mexico, eluding capture by General Pershing, whose "punitive expedition" failed to find him. Scattered bands still raided the ranches and towns. But now citizens had formed defense brigades and had no compunction about shooting. He had bought some new rifles on this trip. And he must see the American Consul. The war in Europe weighed heavily on his conscience. Perhaps he should volunteer... Albert's mind was far away when the house lights dimmed and the orchestra came to life. The curtain opened on a Parisian street scene where a band of troubadours was playing.

As the troubadours faded into the background, Susana Porrás came on stage and began to sing her aria in a soft but pure coloratura, bringing her fans to their feet when the aria ended. Evaristo stood up and boomed out "bravo" through cupped hands.

"Isn't she beautiful? That girl I intend to monopolize," he confided to Albert. "Watch me get rid of the competition!"

The scenery on the stage changed to an enchanted forest where a rather stout enchantress lept and thudded to the strains of "Swan Lake." A group of *estudiantinas* followed, ribbons streaming from their guitars and mandolins.

Albert began to yawn; the amateur antics were lengthy. He had just decided to return to the Madero's house, where he was staying, when the curtain rose again. A guitarist walked onto a bare stage and sat on a chair near the wings. Nimble fingers began to weave an intricate flamenco overture and a Spanish dancer appeared. Slowly, she began to blend into the music, arching, hands gyrating, torso twisting and dipping, her feet tapping a perfect rhythm. The softest trill of the castanets marked the gypsy rhythm, beating faster as the guitarist's voice rose in a wailing falsetto. Her body melded with the music creating sensuous patterns, exposing her ankles, calves, knees, the fringes of her shawl swaying in erotic movements. Graceful arms flowed with every mercurial spin and twist as her supple body arched and her feet stomped to the ever faster tempo of the castanets.

Albert watched, mesmerized. Never had he seen a dance performed with such passion. She was the essence of grace and he felt his heart beat to the sensuous rhythm. The pitch became electric and then ended abruptly to wild acclaim. He nudged Evaristo. "Who is she?" he asked.

"I borrowed a program. Here."

As the encore began, Albert made out the name: Antonieta Rivas Mercado.

The palm court of the Hotel Genève was crowded with couples milling about during the orchestra's first intermission. Albert had managed to hold a small table alone as he waited for Evaristo, who soon emerged from the dance floor with the singer on his arm.

"I would like to introduce you to Susana Porrás," he said. My friend and partner, Albert Blair."

Albert stood up and acknowledged the introduction, congratulating the young lady on her beautiful voice.

"I can now assure you that she dances as well as she sings," Evaristo said. "I have threatened to spend the next ten days warming the sofa in her sala if my slave-driving partner will permit it," he said grinning. "By the way, Al, Susana is a good friend of that Spanish dancer you admired. Her name is Antonieta. Would you like to meet her?"

The direct approach of the north did not escape Susana. "Do you always call people by their first names even before you are introduced?" she asked, mildly reprimanding. "You're very forthright."

"He's worse than I am," Evaristo said, nodding toward Albert. "Too many years on the ranches, and horses are not known for their brilliant conversation. But he's an intelligent fellow."

"I should like to meet your friend," Albert said, feeling sudden apprehension. Would she remember him? He was much older than these young swains who clamored for her attention.

Out of the corner of her eye, Antonieta watched the trio approach across the empty dance floor. She was surrounded by a group of admirers, young people whose compliments soon wore thin. Watching Albert Blair approaching, she wondered if he would recognize her. She waited until Susana called out to her before she turned away from the group, noting that his brown hair looked sun bleached.

"This is Evaristo Madero and his partner, Albert Blair. They are here on business from the north and saw our performance."

Antonieta held out her hand. "We have met," she said, addressing Albert. "Have you learned to eat *chiles*?" Her smile was engaging.

"Yes, I even like them," Albert replied, staring at the poised lady who faced him.

The orchestra began to play again and Evaristo put his arm around Susana's waist, whirling her off with the dancers who had quickly gathered. Albert's feet felt like lead and he could think of nothing to say.

Antonieta waited.

"Do you mind if I smoke," he finally uttered.

"No. But I think we should move off the dance floor before we are trampled," she suggested, amused at his discomfort.

"Of course." Off the floor, Albert gave an inordinate amount of attention first to lighting a cigarette and then to blowing perfect smoke rings.

"You blow lovely smoke rings," Antonieta said in English.

"I had forgotten how well you speak English," Albert said, regaining his voice.

"And your accent has changed. What changed it?" Antonieta asked.

"It's a long story. I thought I was an American, but it seems I am a British subject and a southern accent would hardly do, would it? Look, I wasn't thinking. I hope smoke doesn't offend you. I don't dance very well, but if you are willing to have your toes trod upon, I'll try." Albert put out the cigarette and offered his hand.

It was a waltz. Albert's arm circled Antonieta's waist. She was not made of ephemeral fairy dust. She was made of lips, and breasts and a perfectly formed body, and eyes that held deep mysteries. She moved close to him and he hoped his awkward steps managed to conceal the desire rising in his trousers. He had possessed few women, always loose women who left little impression once the sexual drive was spent. Now he wanted to take this young woman in his arms. He thrust himself away from her and guided her to the edge of the dance floor.

"Shall we have a refreshment?" he asked.

"Yes," she answered quickly. She had felt the hard male organ pushing against her thigh and knew a blush was burning her cheeks. It was quite the most exciting sensation she had ever felt.

They sat at the small table in the palm court and smiled at each other. Soon the conversation flowed:

"I thought of you in Zacatecas when that terrible battle took place. Were you there? What made you decide to fight in the Revolution? Did you really know Pancho Villa? What kind of person is he?"

"Let's not talk about the Revolution."

"Well, what do you do on your ranch? Isn't it terribly provincial up north?"

"Yes. The girls still hide behind their fans at dances."

Antonieta laughed. "Are all northern ladies so closely guarded?"

"In the provinces, yes. And it's all province up there."

"I'm glad I'm from the Capital," she declared. It was not said with haughtiness, it was self-assurance she projected.

While they chatted, Albert studied the captivating young woman across from him. The delicate features called attention more for their expression than their beauty; remarkable eyes challenged, softened, questioned, dominating her countenance. Aquiline nose a bit too long perhaps, lips a bit thin, skin a shade dark. Never mind, everything about this girl suggested breeding: her hands, her feet, the way she walked, the timbre of her voice. People turned to look at her. He had never looked at a woman in such a way before. And, yes, she was a woman now. Now he knew why the blue hair bow had always held a place in his memory.

He was staring again.

"Do you know Rabelais?" Antonieta asked, breaking the brief silence.

"No, should I?"

"Well, do you?"

"Who is he?"

"Never mind. You don't know him."

"Tell me, who is he? I insist," Albert said puffing on a cigarette. "If he is important to you, I want to know who he is."

"He was a free-thinker, a philosopher in the times of the Renaissance," Antonieta answered with a shrug. "Are you interested in philosophy?"

"'Fraid not. When bullets are whizzing over your head you don't have time to think of philosophy."

"Or poetry?"

"I have never cared for poetry. Had to study Chaucer in school and that put me off. I like history and biographies of men like Admiral Lord Nelson and Luther and Thomas Edison. Those inspire me. What do you like to read?"

"Everything. I am studying philosophy now."

"What philosophers? I like Aristotle and St. Thomas Aquinas."

"I'm studying Nietzche." Antonieta said.

"What does he believe?"

"I won't tell you. It's too depressing."

"Then why do you study him?"

"Because life can be depressing and it's important to understand ourselves," Antonieta answered quietly. A melancholy reflection glazed her eyes.

"Well, I believe that God created us in His image and we are free to direct our actions and our thoughts. The world is made up of good and evil and we have the power to choose." Sympathetically, he covered Antonieta's hand. The Revolution had obviously affected her. Albert smiled. "Don't dwell on depressing thoughts. Shall we take a stroll?"

Her arm linked with the hard muscle of this attractive, older foreigner whose blue eyes transmitted unabashed interest. Other eyes, feminine eyes, flashed jealous looks as they walked down the palm court, even as she reaped accolades from admiring fans.

When they returned to claim their table, parents had begun to appear looking for their children. Susana and Evaristo emerged from the dance floor.

"I have been granted permission to deliver this nightingale into the hands of her parents," the smitten young man said. "They might as well take a look at me. Then I'll go on to the house. See you there, Al." He leaned toward Antonieta and in a feigned whisper said, "He's very stubborn, but he has a good heart. I trust we will meet again."

Susana held out a gloved hand. "Good night, Mr. Blair." She looked at her locket watch, then at Antonieta. "It's one o'clock," she said. "Well, good night, Antonieta."

At two o'clock in the morning, the strident notes of "The Star Spangled Banner" ended abruptly. Mrs. Gore approached the last couple left in the palm court.

"The dance is over, my dear. Is your father coming for you?"

"No," Antonieta answered. "Heavens, I had no idea it was so late."

"Who's seeing you home?" Mrs. Gore inquired, shocked.

"Allow me," Albert said. "May I?"

"No, thank you." Antonieta arose and draped the Spanish shawl over her shoulders. "My chauffeur is waiting. Good night, Mrs. Gore. It was a wonderful dance." She held her hand out to Albert. "Good night, Mr. Blair."

Albert's eyes held hers, unwilling to break the enchantment. "May I call on you? Tomorrow?" he asked impetuously.

"Look here, sir," Mrs. Gore interrupted, "I suggest that you telephone so that Señorita Rivas Mercado can get permission for you to visit."

"Yes, please telephone," Antonieta said. "Our number is 22."

"He's going away, Chela, to join the American army!" Antonieta's grief was acute. "We have only had ten days, ten days in a whole lifetime!"

"Love is painful. Now you know," Chela sat on the bed and gently stroked her cousin's cheek. "Why does he have to join the army?"

He says he could never live with his conscience if he didn't. His brother volunteered."

"Has he asked you to wait for him?"

"No. But I know he loves me. He doesn't take his eyes off me."

"Has he...well, tried anything?"

"No. I think he's afraid to touch me. We have walked all over the city, and talked, and talked. I plan something new for him to see every day. I think he's afraid to be alone with me." Antonieta sniffled and grinned. "He insisted on climbing up the spiral staircase of Papá's Angel. When we got to the top and came out on the platform, he nearly fell over the railing trying to retrieve my hat. It blew off and landed on Father Hidalgo's head."

The girls giggled.

"Did you get it back?"

"Yes. The fire department rescued it." Antonieta's eyes turned serious. "He hasn't even kissed me. Maybe it's because he still thinks of me as a little girl. I confessed my charade at the Japanese Legation. He couldn't believe I managed to fool him so completely. How can I make him kiss me? Oh, Chela, he leaves tomorrow!"

The last day they hardly talked. Antonieta took Albert through the Academy of San Carlos, breaking the silence with a dissertation on classical art. Albert had nothing to say. Walking down the street they stopped at the National Museum, stalling, talking trivia, trying not to think the day would end. Inside the palatial colonial building, fearful carnal demons, uprooted from rain-drenched forests, stared at them while squat stone giants, inhabitants of Tenochtitlan, bared their teeth.

"Do you like these things?" Albert asked.

"They do look evil, don't they? But they're part of the history of Mexico," Antonieta replied defensively. Then she drew close and looked up at his face. "Let me show you the courtyard." Oh God, he must kiss me, she thought. She walked on ahead into the bright light of the gracious courtyard and sat on the edge of the fountain.

"Let's go," Albert said

They said goodbye in the garden, standing , of the children's mountain. Huitzilipochtli peered out from his cave. Carefully, Antonieta pulled him out and showed him to Albert.

"He's not sinister," she said. "He's an old friend."

Confusing thoughts crowded Albert's orderly mind: imposing cathedrals and pagan rituals, poetic monuments and carnal demons. Every time he thought he understood Mexico the coin flipped over. Antonieta was just as confusing; so close and then so remote, her moods unpredictable. How would she like the ranch? Her luster of culture and intellect and manners made him aware of his own lack of polish, a defect he would remedy, he determined. Shrimp forks and strawberry spoons would be high on his list of priorities—if he survived the war. His nostrils were bombarded with the fragrances that surrounded them and his breath came in short spurts. He knew only one thing. He wanted this woman for his wife. He wanted to possess her! Albert walked away, then suddenly turned back.

"I shall miss you dreadfully, Antonieta." The words gushed out at last. He stepped close and Antonieta leaned her head on his shoulder.

"And I shall miss you," she said in a trembling voice.

Albert crushed her in his arms and pressed his lips down on hers, kissing frantically until she was breathless. Then he straightened up quickly and let her go. His voice sounded formal, unnatural: "Sorry. Please forgive me. I had better go and say goodbye to your father."

"The days dawn clear and bright but soon fade into monotony," Antonieta wrote, "and night descends suddenly, like a widow's veil and I wonder where Albert is, what he is thinking, if he thinks of me. In this solitary silence I ask my soul, what would fill this emptiness? Am I to be denied love?"

Conchita knocked briskly at Antonieta's door. It was three weeks since the foreign gentleman's departure and now a message had arrived.

"What is it, Conchita?" Antonieta asked impatiently.

She held out the telegram. "It's from him," the girl said.

With trembling fingers, Antonieta opened the envelope.

WAS NOT ACCEPTED BY THE ARMY STOP THEY CONSIDER GROWING GUAYULE RUBBER MORE IMPORTANT THAN BEING A DOUGHBOY. STOP. EXPECT TO BE IN THE CAPITAL IN OCTOBER. STOP. WILL CALL. STOP. ALBERT

On impulse, Antonieta decided to walk over to San Fernando. The barefoot Franciscans were back, wearing their brown robes once again. She felt a need to sit quietly and offer her thanks. On the way home, she walked by the old insane asylum. She paused and contemplated the crumbling walls. The sun cloaked the naked patches in soft shadows and bent a golden beam on a rusty drainpipe. A sense of enchantment carried her back to childhood. The child in her lurked in the shadows and the woman tried to see her, knowing that she would soon live in another time of life, an adulthood leading her on an unchartered course.

The air was fresh with the scent of wildflowers and new grass and flowering cacti as Albert's train climbed to the high plateau. After a steaming summer in Washington, Chicago and the northern ranches, Mexico City seemed like paradise. Albert patted the engagement ring in his vest pocket as though the large diamond had already wrought the miracle of pledging Antonieta to him as wife. He had thought of nothing else since the army had turned him down, nothing else since he had left her, nothing else when he undressed at night and awoke in the morning and went about his business during the day. She would be his wife. She must be. Yes. Yes.

Antonieta watched Albert walk up the driveway with the quick step she had come to recognize as characteristic of his impatient nature. He carried a bouquet, probably not characteristic, she thought drolly, but he looked the part of a proper suitor. She ran to greet him.

Antonieta found her father in the arbor. She knelt at his side and looked up at his face.

"We would like to be married right away, Papá. Please say you will allow it. Albert's parents just moved to Chicago and he told them all about me and they want to meet me. He loves me very much, Papá, and I love him. Why should we wait?"

Antonio looked at the pleading eyes and winced. He had put Albert through a grueling interrogation when he had formally asked for his daughter's hand. Antonio did not object to Albert as a suitor; he seemed a sensible, practical foil for his volatile daughter. Here was a foreigner who went in and out of the Palace at will, whose destiny seemed to be tied to Mexico. He would not take Antonieta away from Mexico. He was ten years older, a mature man who would protect her. This American or Britisher, or whatever he was, obviously espoused the ethic of "work hard, keep your word, and stay out of debt." No doubt "be faithful" also formed part of his basic ethic. Why, then, did he have this reserve? There was something rigid about Blair, unbending. The two cultures, he felt, would clash and so would temperaments. But was there ever a guarantee in marriage? He sighed. Preparing for this moment, Antonio had decided that he would only consent to an engagement. They must wait a year to be married.

"I am seventeen, Papá," Antonieta argued. "Alicia was married when she was seventeen. Please don't make us wait a year!"

"I will not be pressured, Antonieta," Antonio replied firmly. "If you are really in love, your love will be stronger in a year."

"Six months, Papá. Let us be married on my eighteenth birthday. Chela was married on her eighteenth birthday. She has even offered me her wedding dress." Antonieta pressed her cheek against her father's hand. "Six months is a fair compromise. Please."

Antonio lifted his daughter's chin and looked into her eyes, eyes filled with dreams and a longing he recognized. Could this man's love fill the void within her?

"You are so young," he said ruefully. "If there weren't a war going on I would send you to Europe to mature, to a good university. You would be a new kind of Mexcan woman."

"I am a woman," Antonieta said emotionally. "You wouldn't want an old maid on your hands, would you? "Six months, Papá."

Antonio patted her hand. "All right. You can get up now," he said lightly, berating himself for his weakness. She had been forged for other things. "I don't know what I will do without you."

"You won't have to," Antonieta quickly assured him. "I have been thinking about converting Mamá's suite into an apartment for us. We can divide our time between the Capital and the ranch."

"Your future husband is proud and stubborn, my precious daughter. Have you convinced him of such a plan? And where will you be married? Will he become a Catholic?"

"I haven't pressed it. Albert feels very strongly about his religion and, after all, we are both Christians."

"I thought you were a yogi."

Two white bouquets and tall tapers flanked a lace-draped altar in the recessed window of the salon in the house on Héroes. A string quartet played softly in the background. A priest intoned the vows of the mixed marriage, justifying the dispensation on the grounds that the marriage was not consecrated in the church itself.

There was something too somber about the occasion, Elena reflected as she stood with the family to witness the marriage. She felt Cristina's absence. Antonio had been adamant: Cristina would never enter this house again. None of the groom's family was present, not even his great Madero friends. Was it because he was ashamed he had submitted to a Catholic wedding that he hadn't invited them? One could tell he was anti-Catholic. At least this English-American was a good match. Antonio had had the family investigated. The parents were well situated, it seemed, in a nice suburb of Chicago and the sister was married to a physician. Elena squeezed Rene's hand as she listened to the wedding vows. Too bad Antonieta had not found a European. She looked at the solemn faces around her and wrinkled her nose—Antonieta should have opened the heavy draperies and let the light in.

The most severe critic of the simple ceremony was Amelia, who confessed to her schoolmates that it was the dullest wedding she had ever attended.

A huge bouquet graced the console in their suite at the Hotel Genève, a gift from Mrs. Gore. A telegram from Susana and Evaristo, just married themselves, lay on top of the stack of cards and notes of congratulations. Self-consciously, the newlyweds read their messages and sipped champagne, not daring to voice the thoughts which filled every crevice of their minds.

"Antonieta held out her champagne glass. "Fill it again, please."

"You like champagne, don't you," Albert said.

"Good champagne, yes." She spilled a bit as she sipped. Would she actually see his penis before it entered her? Chela had told her that a woman reached a sexual peak, something called a climax, which was the most euphoric, indefinable, complete feeling a woman could have. Her breasts felt hard and she was breathing too fast.

Albert ground out his cigarette. Suddenly he stood up and pulled Antonieta to her feet. He kissed her again and again, pressed her slim body to him and whispered "You are my wife, my wife and my sweetheart." Antonieta felt his hard male organ and closed her eyes and tried to imagine it inside her. Would it hurt like his kisses?

"Will you let me see you naked?" he whispered, and led her to the bedroom.

Carefully hanging each garment in the closet, Antonieta undressed, uncomfortable with her nudity, not daring to look at her nakedness in the mirror which reflected an exquisite body: long, beautifully shaped legs, hands narrow, with tapering fingers, slim torso perfectly proportioned and small firm breasts displaying pink nipples against bronze skin. She unpinned her chignon and shook her head, loosening long black hair, waved by the twists she wore to look older. Her naked body trembled. Chela said that sexual love was something that built and built until you floated over the top of a huge wave and crashed. Antonieta crawled under the covers and circumspectly pulled the sheet up to her neck.

Albert emerged from the bathroom in a silk dressing gown that he removed as he pulled back the covers. Antonieta stifled a gasp. Then Albert's heavy, muscular body pressed down on top of her and he sought her lips. "I won't hurt you," he whispered. "You are my sweetheart, my wife."

When it was over, a warm trickle ran down her thigh and made a wet spot beneath her buttocks. Albert pulled her toward him and she folded her body into the warm circle of his arms.

"Did you like it?" he whispered.

"Yes," she lied.

"You are so beautiful, mi querida." He kissed her cheek. "I love you with all my soul."

Antonieta lay quietly in his arms, listening to Albert's even breathing as he slept. All thoughts were blocked out by one overpowering realization: this man who lay beside her was her husband. In a single day, her life had changed.

CHAPTER XXI
1918

Gazing out the window of their compartment, Antonieta watched the landscape change to dense cacti and yucca trees, bleak terrain strewn with broken box cars, pieces of track rails, wheels, rusted engines: the debris of the Revolution.

"At any moment I expect to see Villa and his dorados riding out of the bush." She shuddered.

Albert laughed and took her hand. "There are three cars of armed Federal soldiers traveling with us and Pancho Villa is occupied with his hacienda in Durango."

Antonieta did not turn from the window. The Revolution felt near. Slowly she began to comprehend that Albert had *lived* the experiences he recounted. They were real.

They crossed the border at Laredo, Texas. Squalid shacks with tenacious geraniums growing in tin cans, mangy dogs running loose, burros burdened with gunny sacks and half-naked children hovering in dilapidated doorways disappeared as the train crossed the bridge. Neat houses with white picket fences lined paved streets leading to the station. Antonieta would ever remember her shock at crossing the border for the first time. An indentation in the earth where a murky, shallow river ran seemed to divide two worlds: chaos and order, poverty and prosperity. She wondered what Mexico would be like if the English had been the *conquistadores*. She smiled at Albert.

At the station in San Antonio, efficient redcaps pushed their carts up to the steps of the Pullman. Nearby, a neat row of taxicabs waited. She and Albert remained in their compartment while their sleeper was switched to a faster train, which would carry them to St. Louis and New York.

As the train headed north, green replaced the burnt brown earth of Mexico. Fields of wheat and barley and alfalfa and potatoes sped by. A new thought crossed Antonieta's mind: she was Mrs. Blair, now a part of this vast United States unfolding before her eyes. Her new name held promise of a new and exciting life. At night she lay awake in the narrow berth they had decided to share, feeling the weight of her husband's muscular body and wondering when she would experience the sensations Chela had described. Sleep always eluded her after his desire was spent and he fell into deep slumber. But she put the thought aside as she pondered the many facets of being a wife. Would his family like her? They would have a week in New York first to be alone, to tour, to talk to make love in a spacious suite.

Antonieta was captivated by New York, a modern, dynamic hive of languages and ethnic cultures that one encountered on every corner. New York seemed to keep in rhythm with her restless nature, and Albert permitted himself to be dragged to museums and art exhibits and concerts and the theater. On the last day he took his indefatigable wife to the planetarium, where the whole universe seemed to sing to her heart.

The train to Chicago was sleek and fast. Long after Albert had fallen asleep, Antonieta lay awake, the old fear rising as she thought of meeting his family. They were conservative, Albert had said, so conservative that he had never had a drink or danced or taken a puff of a cigarette until he left for prep school. In the dining car tonight she had ordered a Chateau Lafitte 1903 to celebrate their last night on the train. Albert had covered her hand with his and looked at her earnestly.

"This will be our last drink for awhile. My parents don't serve anything alcoholic in their house, so please don't talk about wines, querida."

"They never drink anything at all? I mean, even at Christmas or weddings?"

"Never."

"What about communion? You said you do take communion in your church."

"It's grape juice," he murmured defensively.

In Chicago they boarded a commuter train to a suburb on the North Shore where the Blairs lived.

Antonieta's heart was pounding as Albert waved to a nicely dressed, middle-aged couple, who waved back. Mother Blair was less austere-looking than she had pictured her, a small lady standing beside a stately gentleman with a trim beard.

Antonieta kissed her new relatives on the cheek when Albert introduced her.

"Welcome, my dear," Mother Blair said, breeding overcoming any misgivings she might have felt. "You will meet the rest of the family at dinner." Her blue eyes looked gentle behind the pince-nez.

The houses in Highland Park were set back on expanses of lawn, with neither high fences nor walls to provide protection and privacy. There was an openness in the attractive neighborhood, an openness which appealed to Antonieta.

The Blair house was a spacious white wood structure set among laurel trees and lilac bushes in full bloom. It was attended by a black couple who did the "yard work" and "heavy work," according to Mother Blair. The servants left after dinner. The house was comfortably, if conservatively, appointed, devoid of superfluous ornaments. A silver tea tray reposed on a fine English sideboard in the dining room and a few Persian rugs were scattered on polished, planked wooden floors. The library, easily the most inviting room in the house, had a bay window and a fireplace. Mother and Father Blair had come to Chicago to be near their married daughter, Grace, and two young grandchildren. A younger daughter, Dorothy, Antonieta's age, lived at home. Albert's brother, Alexander, had recently joined the United States Army and embarked for the front.

Upstairs, Albert's old bedroom served as the "spare room," quiet, striped wallpaper and organdy curtains adding a feminine touch to an otherwise plain chamber. An adjoining bathroom was shared with his sister Dorothy.

Antonieta dressed carefully for dinner, selecting a pale blue silk ensemble, adorned only with her mother's long string of pearls. She pulled her black hair back in a becoming chignon and took a last look in the high mirror above Albert's chiffonier

"Do I look all right?" she asked nervously.

"Quite beautiful," Albert replied, inwardly apprehensive about the questions his parents might ask his Mexican wife.

"Albert says your father has been to Chicago," Grace commented, her plainness offset by a beautiful smile.

"Oh yes," Antonieta responded. "He has been here many times." She sat with her legs gracefully crossed, the silk falling in soft folds, her back comfortably settled against a cushion.

"And that he speaks English very well," Grace added.

"He went to school in England as a boy," Antonieta said, "then he did his professional studies in France."

"And what about your mother, dear?" Mrs. Blair asked. "We haven't heard much about your mother."

"My parents are separated," Antonieta said simply.

"Oh I am sorry," Mother Blair replied, a flush covering her face.

"Our religion doesn't recognize divorce," Antonieta explained. "My brother and sister and I live with my father."

An awkward silence was broken by Grace. "And now you and Albert will have your own ranch, not far from your father, I hope."

"It's pretty far, Grace," Albert interjected. "More than five hundred miles. Twice as far as Henderson is from Chicago."

"My!" Mother Blair exclaimed. "And you are taking this child up there, Albert? Is it quite safe?"

"Quite, Mother. The Revolution is over."

"Now, are you just saying that to reassure us?" Father Blair's voice was deep and resonant. "That bandit, Pancho Villa, is still alive, is he not?"

Everyone in the United States seemed to have heard of Pancho Villa, Antonieta thought. It was as if Mexico and Pancho Villa were synonymous.

The conversation was interrupted by the arrival of Grace's husband, a successful doctor who commuted to Chicago. He strode into the room with a pile of newspapers tucked under his arm and deposited them on the long coffee table in front of the newlyweds.

"So you are Antonieta." He looked at her appraisingly. "You are quite as lovely as Albert claimed. Welcome to the Blair clan. Lee Gatewood." He put out his hand.

"Thank you," Antonieta said, rising. She returned the warm greeting with a kiss on the cheek.

"I brought the afternoon papers," Lee said, "with news of real interest to this family. Alex's division has landed in France."

"Oh." Mother Blair's intake of air was audible.

"Does it say where they will be sent?" Father Blair asked, anxiety tingeing his deep baritone. The British lion had been badly mauled, and his American son had gone to its rescue.

"No, sir. Only that a dozen American divisions landed in France yesterday and General Pershing has put them at Marshall Foch's disposal."

Talk of the war dominated the conversation. Then Pancho Villa again.

"Didn't General Pershing chase Pancho Villa all over Mexico?" Dorothy asked.

"And never caught him," Albert added with a pompous grin.

"Chasing bandits who only know the bush cannot compare with commanding disciplined troops," his father countered sternly. "Tell me, Albert, do you think this President Carranza is reliable? Wasn't he conspiring with the Germans to draw us into a war with Mexico?"

"Despite all the conjecture, Father, the fact remains that it didn't happen. I think the Germans pushed that situation as a tactic to ensnare the Americans, and Carranza used it as a foil against Wilson."

"God wants us to live in peace with our brothers," Mother Blair spoke up. "We must all pray that these conflicts will be over soon." The clock in the hall chimed six. The dignified lady stood up. "Shall we go in to dinner?"

"Why didn't you defend Mexico?" Antonieta derided her husband. When your father was asking about the poor, and whether we have homes for beggars and old people, why didn't you tell him that our beggars don't like to be put in institutions! They escape and are back on the same corner in a day or so. And we don't need a Mutual Aid Society! We don't need it because old people and widows and leftover ladies are taken in by their families. Why didn't you explain that?"

Albert pushed up on one elbow and looked at his irate bride. "They wouldn't understand," he said lamely. "Mexico is like China to them."

"Do you think they like me?"

"Of course, querida. They just don't understand you yet."

At dinnertime Antonieta heard a new rosary of manners recited to the grandchildren by Mother Blair: "Did you scrub up, dears? Let me see your face and hands. Now, leave your plate clean. Lee, remember the world is full of starving children. Help Henrietta pick up, Gracie, she only has two hands." Another rosary was time: time to get up, enough time in the bathroom, time to catch the train. Don't waste time. And watch out if you weren't on time. Americans, it seemed, were directed by the clock. It kept Antonieta on edge.

On Sunday, the service in the white wooden church was an experience beyond her imagination. She was handed a program when the family was ushered to their pew. There was no cushioned rail for kneeling and the brass cross on the altar was the only indication that this was a Christian church. The minister faced the congregation and preached a simple but uplifting sermon on Christian values, speaking in English, not Latin, preaching from a low lectern, not a high pulpit. In unison they recited the Lord's Prayer. She shared a hymnal with Dorothy, and followed passages in the Bible, passages she had only heard chanted by priests. Mother Blair sat at one end of the pew and

Father Blair at the other, stalwart guardians of their family. They were good people, good people who were trying to include her in their alien ways. A part of her cried out in protest; but a stronger part wished desperately to be accepted.

During their last night in Highland Park, Albert and his sisters accompanied their parents to a church meeting. Antonieta remained at the house, suffering from an acute case of diarrhea, probably caused by the drinking water which contained minerals and chlorine she was not used to, Lee had said. She was glad to be alone. Cautiously treading in someone else's home, speaking English all day, swallowing her ire when unintentional remarks showed their ignorance of Mexico; all of it was wearing. A sudden desire to feel the solace of music took her downstairs to the piano.

Antonieta adjusted her satin dressing gown and sat down at the upright. A trill proved the fidelity of tone and her fingers began to explore familiar patterns. Pathos and joy and grandeur filled her being as she played her beloved classical music. She did not hear the front door open.

Lee put down his satchel and quietly stood in the doorway, caught up in admiration at the unexpected concert. When the last strains of Chopin's Nocturne faded, he applauded vigorously.

"Bravo!" he exclaimed. Why didn't you tell us you play the piano? I mean, you are a pianist! To think you have put up with Dorothy's little schooled recitals."

Antonieta swung around and smiled. "I play for myself mostly. I don't practice enough to play for others anymore." She stood up.

"I am glad you stayed home," Lee said. "We haven't had much chance to talk. If the concert is over, please come into the library. I noticed Robert laid a fire."

Lee took off his coat, loosened his tie and sank into a deep wing chair. Antonieta curled up in the window seat of the bay window and plumped up the cushions around her. She felt comfortable with Lee. His manner was warm, understanding, interested. And he was handsome; his sandy hair went with his soft blue eyes. He must be a good doctor, she thought.

"What's your specialty, Lee? I mean, what kind of a doctor are you?"

"A good doctor," was his smiling reply. "I have patients of every size, age, and color. How are you feeling?"

"I think I am over it. Thanks."

"Oh, almost forgot. I brought a special prescription for you. Wait here." He went out to the hall and brought in his medical satchel. He opened it and removed something that looked like a flask. Then he poured a liquid into two little glasses. "Here," he said with a grin. "Martell. Hope it's your brand."

"Martell cognac!" Antonieta exclaimed, horrified. "Albert will smell it on my breath. And what will Grace think?"

"She doesn't mind," Lee said. "You mustn't judge everyone by the old folks. My wife is a Christian to her core, but in her own habitat she is quite lenient. And I think Albert has become a good tippler since he opted for revolutions. Sorry we couldn't have you two at our house alone for an evening."

"I'm sorry too," Antonieta said, sipping daintily.

"I know it has been rough for you," Lee said, settling back. "The Puritan Reformation hates Catholic Spain. They are still fighting the Armada under Good Queen Bess. Looks like Albert has reverted to English roots himself. They used to call him "Kentuck" in school. What happened?"

"His accent became more understandable, thank God." Antonieta laughed. "Seems nationality depends on where you were born and where you were on your twenty-first birthday. You know the answers to that. London and Vancouver. Although they aren't required, Albert decided to obtain a passport as an identification and safeguard during the Revolution. He was shocked when they told him he is British. Now I am a British subject too."

"Long live the King, my dear! Have another shot."

Antonieta held out her glass.

"Cheers."

They talked about Mexico, her likes and dislikes, her impression of the States. They talked about marriage.

"The Blairs were born in Scotland and Scottish blood is thick stuff," Lee said. "Albert is like steel. He will be hard to bend, but I don't see how anyone could help bending in your direction. You're an extraordinary young woman, Antonieta. If I weren't married, I'd court you myself. Another shot?"

"Better not. I might get drunk." Antonieta giggled, curled up against the chintz pillows, relaxed and warm.

Then: "Don't let Albert wear you down," Lee advised. "Scottish blood has a propensity to save souls and gobble up character." Lee looked at his watch. "Guess I'll go in the kitchen and see what's left from dinner. Join me?"

"No, thank you."

"Then get some rest." Lee picked up his coat and hung it on the rack in the hallway. "You can count on Grace and me to be your friends."

Before they returned to Chicago, Antonieta walked alone to the end of the quiet, suburban street and stood on the bluff overlooking Lake Michigan. The endless body of water mirrored her disquiet and she meditated long upon this new course her life had taken. "Oh God, make me a good wife," she prayed.

Before the wedding, Antonieta had transformed Cristina's suite into a charming apartment. The *ortario* had become a small office for Albert and the beaded curtains and Moroccan trappings had given way to the comfort of a sitting room.

The first weeks back in Mexico, Antonieta found herself making comparisons with the United States. At every opportunity she tried to shake up the young Mexican matrons whose conversation seemed limited to new fashions, babies and servants. Most of the girls she knew had been reared to be demure, accomplished in household matters and account ledgers, but subservient to their father and brothers from an early age, thus trained to be subservient to a future husband. At parties, the women were seated in a row together, like magpies on a line, gossiping in whispers, excluded from male conversation. Their education was limited and the only book that interested them was their engagement book.

Sitting on a drafting stool next to his desk, Antonieta shared her impressions of American life with her father.

"Everything is so orderly," she said. "Americans are disciplined and engaged. Everyone in the community seems involved in some cause or project. People are open and informal, even the garage man calls Lee, a doctor, by his first name! I was shocked when Father Blair helped to clean up the kitchen. Of course, we made our own beds. And women have so much liberty, Papá. They work. I mean, they have respectable jobs in offices. And housewives get out: they attend meetings, take classes, go to lectures." Antonieta paused. "I bought a typewriter..."

Antonio let her ramble on.

"Why are Mexican women so...so submissive!" she asked at last.

"Who encouraged them, or encourages them, to think independently?"

"You encouraged me!"

"I'm an exception," Antonio said with feigned solemnity. "These contrasts in culture have a basis, Antonieta. Let me give you a little history lesson: The Spaniards came as conquerors in quest of gold, and the English came to settle the new land and for religious freedom. For three hundred years, we had no voice in self-government. From the beginning, the English settlers ran their own colonies. Men and women tilled hard soil together. The Spaniards mixed with the Indians. The English killed them. Are we different? Now," Antonio pointed a finger at his daughter, "take my advice: Learn from the foreigners, but don't demean your own culture." He finished the lecture with a benign smile.

"I am glad you are my father," Antonieta said kissing him.

Household duties were always time-consuming, but now there were many more details to attend. Albert liked to entertain in the impressive mansion, invitations which were reciprocated by their expanding circle of English and American friends. Embassy receptions and luncheons at the American and British Clubs filled their agenda. They became members of the Country Club, but Antonieta preferred horses to golf. She sorely missed her philosophy lessons with Chela and seldom had time for the piano.

Prowling the thieves market with Chela one day, Antonieta bought an exquisite Chinese urn that she filled with feathery dry flowers and placed in an empty corner of their small sitting room. It filled the corner just as she knew it would. When Albert came home she showed it to him with pride.

"This probably came up from Acapulco on the back of an Indian runner maybe two hundred years ago," Antonieta boasted. "Isn't it a find!"

"You should have consulted me," Albert said, tucking in his chin, a characteristic gesture which Antonieta had come to recognize as denoting displeasure. "You can't just give in to every whim, querida. We do have a budget, you know."

Since Albert had joined the household, there had been a change in Papá. He and Albert spent hours discussing politics, engineering matters, technical advances, the state of the world, the war, and the interminable subject of the Revolution, verbal jousting that went on as though she were not there. A sort of male fraternity existed between them that excluded her. Antonieta recognized it as jealousy and dismissed it, but it added to the small frustrations she was beginning to feel.

"How can people defend their rights when they can't even read them?" Antonio argued at lunch, refuting Albert's argument. "This Constitution of Carranza's you defend so eloquently, do you think it can govern fifteen million Mexicans who speak 165 different languages and have one thousand idiosyncracies? I appreciate your association with Carranza, but he is letting corrupt local bosses run the country. The Constitution isn't regulating that!"

"But it does guarantee rights," Albert repeated stoically. "Rights which can be defended in a court of law."

"Ignorance is the tragedy of Mexico," Antonio declared, pounding the table. "Get notions of democracy out of your head, Albert. We have had constitutions before. They are amendable, bendable. Carranza may talk rights, but what rights does he defend?"

"Let Carranza be. Both of you! Let us be grateful for peace." Antonieta stood up. "Coffee is being served in the arbor."

The war in Europe had created an economic boom in Mexico. Albert's crop of castor beans, a vital lubricant for aircraft, brought a preferential price in the United States. Evaristo had planted a thousand additional hectares of *guayule*, a rubber-producing desert shrub that had become another prime commodity. Mexican oil was fueling the British and American fleets. Every day now, Albert was out calling on business acquaintances and soon rented an office downtown.

"Albert's no fun," Memela complained, and stayed out of his way.

News that Alex Blair had been wounded arrived two days before the Armistice. Albert bore his grief in silence, turning away from Antonieta's attempts to comfort him. She longed to penetrate his reserve, to get through that barricade that cut her off from his deepest self. At night, she would put her arms around her husband and try to share his pain. Rejected, she huddled on her own side of the bed and wept silently. For him, pain was to be suppressed; one suffered alone. Was she spilling tears for Albert or herself? If she expressed her own spiritual thirst, her own longings, he changed the subject. Antonieta's rich imagination created dialogues that never took place.

With the cessation of war in Europe, passenger ships began to cross the ocean again, bringing back the flood of expatriates who were caught by the war and a wave of Europeans who sought a new life in America. The Mexicans who had fled from the Revolution, seeking safety in the select suburbs of New York, Paris, and Madrid, now jammed the port of Veracruz. Every day the railroad station in Mexico City was the scene of joyous reunions.

In January, Alicia, her husband, two little boys, a French governess and thirty-five pieces of baggage were handed off the train at the station near the house on Héroes street. Cristina was not advised. It was an emotional reunion. Antonieta looked at the tall, elegant lady who was her beloved sister and her heart overflowed.

Early in February, Chela bore a still-born son in a difficult birth.

Chela's grief affected Antonieta deeply. Her emotional reserve was thin when Albert announced that they had to pack and move north without delay. There were problems at the ranch, problems that demanded his personal attention.

"We have to make the break," he insisted. "Look, my dearest, I am not spiriting you off to an alien land. My wife is leaving her father's house, not her country. Besides, Susana is in San Pedro."

CHAPTER XXII
1919

San Pedro was a crude station. An empty railroad car served to store freight and a stone building housed the maintenance crew. A few passengers waited to board the train. A line of scrawny chickens being chased by a disheveled woman raced across the platform, nearly tripping Antonieta.

"We will only be here overnight," Albert said. "Miguel will take you to the house while I check in at the office." He kissed her reassuringly. "I think you'll find the house very comfortable."

Antonieta hung her fur coat in the closet and explored the "town house" where Albert stayed. It was full of mail order frippery as well as monogrammed napkins, French crystal, Limoge dessert plates, down quilts and linen sheets. Neatly stacked on the narrow shelf of the nightstand were the catalogues from the Bon Marché in Paris, chock-full of items with a guarantee of three months' delivery to America. Practical items were marked in the thick Sears Roebuck catalogues from Chicago. Fascinated, she studied the catalogues and wondered what she would find at the ranch. Tucked under a warm quilt next to Albert that night, Antonieta listened to an old, familiar sound from her childhood, the cry of the night watchman as he swung his lantern down the street.

In the morning they loaded the buggy and left the dust of San Pedro as they traveled out through flat, green fields rimmed by distant mountains. Antonieta pulled her fur coat around her, listening to Albert's commentary on the idiosyncrasies of the north.

"You'll like these people up here. They're open and frank and the ranch parties are fine affairs, lively." He looked at his wife with anticipation in his eyes. "As you know, I don't own any of this land, only the ranch house and twenty hectares, but Evaristo and I own a batch of crops spread out as far as Torreón," he went on, chattering. "Might as well tell you, querida, I have a surprise for you. It's a thoroughbred, a fine mare. We'll ride out to the ranches and you will see what northern hospitality is like."

"Is it safe?" Antonieta asked. The "dregs of the Revolution," as Albert called them, were still raiding the towns and ranches.

"We will always ride with one or two armed boys. Don't worry."

Antonieta placed a kiss on Albert's cheek with the tip of her finger. Listening with one ear to his commentaries, she wondered whether the primitive road they were following could be made fit for an automobile.

The ranch was nearly two hours' drive from town. Her first view of Santa Cruz was of high, blind outer walls, a grim fortress set in a flat, open space. The gracious tree-lined entrance to Tío Luis' hacienda flashed in her mind and she rebelled at her austere-looking home.

"A bit forbidding," Albert admitted, patting her hand. "Those outer walls were built for protection against Indian raids. These people have been fighting Apaches and Comanches for generations, but they know how to defend themselves! This area was settled by Spaniards, you know. No Aztecs up here."

"You mean my Huitzilopochtli statue wouldn't fit in this house," Antonieta said facetiously.

The buggy drew up to high wooden doors and was admitted into a small courtyard and stables. The residence nestled within the high adobe walls was built around a square, sunny patio, the plants now shriveled by the cold winter. Antonieta tried to conceal her disappointment at the meager furnishings and the

Spartan kitchen. It would take time, and a generous budget, to furnish this place properly. She consoled herself that Albert had efficient servants and that he had installed an *excusado* inglés, a noisy marvel which hissed and gurgled when it was flushed.

As the weeks passed, Antonieta's principal distractions were visits to Susana Madero, who lived on a ranch about ten kilometers away. When Albert left in the morning for a day's trip, she would saddle her thoroughbred and ride out with the guards to Susana's comfortable retreat.

"Don't you feel your life is ebbing away out here? How can you be so placid?" Antonieta finally asked her friend.

"I just believe that you have to put down roots of your best self wherever you are," Susana replied. "I love Evaristo very much and I want to share the life he's chosen."

Antonieta pondered Susana's words; they posed a question ever present in her mind. Why do I resist this place? Resist Albert?

"How I wish I could be like you, Susana," Antonieta exclaimed. "I feel so apart from Albert here. It's as though he fits in and I am an intruder. I thought we would be closer at the ranch, but Albert is hardly ever there." She turned troubled eyes to her friend. "I am so lonely." Now she hugged herself. "Riding over here I saw a skeleton hanging from a tree, and there are so many bugs and critters."

Susana laughed. "You'll get used to them."

"I don't even have my books to study. Albert wouldn't let me bring them."

"Find other things to do," her friend advised. "I am giving singing lessons in San Pedro."

"And pruning your own voice before it comes to full flower." Susana has surrendered even her talent, Antonieta thought.

"You miss the stage, Antonieta, and your salons," Susana said with an understanding smile. "There are one or two stimulating people in town. I'll introduce you."

Letters from Chela were filled with unhappy news: her dead baby hung heavy on her heart and, although he denied it, Alfonso was seeing other women. "I don't want him to touch me anymore," Chela wrote. "That which I used to enjoy repulses me now, because I have lost my trust." Antonieta burned Chela's letters for fear Albert would ask to read them. Letters from the family in Mexico and the family in Chicago were read aloud. Even Mario wrote. Next week he would be leaving for Worcester Academy in Massachusetts, grateful that Albert had convinced Papá that he should go away to school. It was boring at home, Mario had written.

Later, Marios' first letter from school evoked welcome laughter. "Dear Antonieta and Albert: I really like Worcester, all covered with green ivy and good masters. The boys wouldn't believe that I am Mexican—no sombrero, no guitar. They wouldn't believe we have twelve servants, either, so I didn't tell them fifteen. Don't they get mixed up, one guy asked? How do you call them? I said Papá wore a big hat and sat in the patio and fired a pistol at a gong: one shot for his valet, two shots for the chauffeur and three for the housekeeper who runs the rest of the bunch. They believed that."

With pregnancy came a deep, satisfying joy. The child in her womb seemed to reciprocate her love, and Albert became more thoughtful, letting small reproaches pass. The thought of fatherhood pleased him. For Antonieta, the prospect of a baby gave her new hope for this marriage. She and Albert talked of the future, of buying a house of their own in the Capital and spending summers there to escape the northern heat. They talked of schools for the baby, if it was a boy. Also if it is a girl, the future mother added adamantly.

The heat began in April, an insidious sultry oppression which increased with every day. Cold nights. Hot winds at midday, swirling across the spiny land. June was unbearable. "Black clouds gather," Antonieta wrote, "blown by a strong wind that squeezes out a dozen rain drops on the parched earth. I watched a child torture a lizard and rained my own drops down dry cheeks. Why is it that tears are always so close to the surface these days? The heat has made me lethargic. Even baby is complaining, moving and jumping when I least expect. This colorless place drains me. Nature is stingy here, her palette bereft of the jewel tones of the high plateau, those brilliant colors that linger in my mind's eye. Drab, dull, hot, the days drag by. Only teaching in the little schoolroom we built distracts me. There was a snake coiled at the entrance to our bedroom today. I couldn't breathe until it slithered away. I must convince Albert that I have to go home to have my baby... my consolation...my squirmy beloved."

"You are not having problems with your pregnancy, querida," Albert said stoutly. "Women have babies right here in San Pedro. They need you at the ranch school. You're a fine teacher, and the baby isn't due until September." Antonieta could hear the reproach in his words.

"I need a respite from this heat," Antonieta responded with an edge of desperation. "It saps my energy. Please understand."

Albert drove her to San Pedro and put her on the train. In the steamy compartment, Antonieta clung to her husband, this man who retreated to silences and turned his cheek when she tried to kiss him. "Oh, Albert, I shall miss you!" she said. "I will come back as soon as the baby can travel."

"I'll be in the city first," Albert said, softening. He embraced her. "You can't have our child alone."

The scandal which greeted Antonieta in Mexico City centered on Chela and was the topic of gossip in the highest social strata. Chela had left her husband to become the mistress of a prominent, married doctor. Antonio made no attempt to hide his disapproval. With considerable reluctance, he admitted his niece to the house. The young matrons threw their arms around each other and locked the door to Antonieta's bedroom.

"Tonieta! You hardly look pregnant and you're six months along. I looked like a barrel," Chela said.

"Well, you look radiant now!" Antonieta took Chela by the hand and turned her around. "More beautiful than ever." But there was a new look in her cousin's eyes, a mature look tinged with suffering. "If you are happy, my dearest Chela, I am happy for you."

The story soon unfolded:

"It was after the baby was born dead. I knew something was wrong,

wrong with me. It began with a burning sensation when I did pee-pee. A few months after I lost the baby I started to have sudden high fevers and terrible abdominal pains."

Antonieta's eyes reflected indignation, then anger, as she began to suspect the cause. She and Chela had looked up the dread word when they were fourteen. "What did your doctor say?"

"I went from one to another, for weeks, and they all said I had a urinary infection. No medicine worked. Finally I got to Carlos. He told me the truth."

"Oh my poor Chelita," Antonieta said, putting her arms around her cousin.

"When I knew the truth, I hated Alfonso. I wanted to gouge his eyes out! He had infected me and infected our baby! I am glad it was born dead and not blind."

Intimate details spilled out. The long, painful treatment, the complicated operation.

"I'm sterile now," Chela said bitterly. "No more babies."

Silence cloaked her wound.

"Carlos was so kind, so understanding, and such a good doctor. Visits to his consulting room became my only solace. You weren't here, and I didn't want to burden you; you had enough problems in that desolate place. We began to talk, to have coffee together."

"And what did Alfonso say?" Antonieta asked gently.

"I refused to speak to him, much less share a bed with him. It was like living with a stranger. He pleaded, he begged but I was dead inside." Chela turned toward the window and bent her head.

Antonieta stroked the red-gold glints in the beautiful hair. A man could destroy a woman's life, she thought, go to confession and be forgiven his sins, then sin all over again. But the church would not recognize divorce and give a woman another chance. She was condemned to hell!

"And now you share a real home with Carlos," Antonieta said comfortingly.

"You know I feel guilty. Mamá and Papá can't hold their heads up. I must admit I've behaved in a barefaced manner."

The sun highlighted tortoise shell combs in the Titian hair. Head still bent, Chela went on.

"Carlos has separated from his wife. Now he sees only the children. He loves me," she said simply. "He bought a beautiful house for me and lives with me all the time." She raised her head and turned around. "Did you ever think I would be somebody's mistress in a *casa chica*?" Chela asked with a giggle.

"No," Antonieta responded, giggling too. "I am sure you are the most beautiful mistress in Mexico. And the most talked about."

Chela's face sobered. "This is real love, Tonieta. I swear it. Let all the tongues in the world wag. We love each other."

"I am going to tell Papá the truth," Antonieta said. "Do you mind?"

"I want him to know. I want him to accept me," Chela said with a tremor in her voice.

"Donald Antonio Blair Rivas Mercado. Born September 9, 1919," the little card stated. Propped up in her bed in the American Hospital, Antonieta tied a litle blue bow in the corner of each dainty card as she addressed the envelopes. Albert had ordered the announcements from the best engraver in the city. And he had refurbished their little sitting room as a nursery. Antonieta pulled out a monogrammed sheet of stationery and wrote to her sister-in-law Grace and her husband Lee:

"Dearest Ones,

Thank you so much for your kind loving letter and your telegram. We are simply crazy about our darling. Dear Albert is delighted with his son, and I find no words to express my joy. Baby looks like both of us, his blond hair and forehead are Albert's, but I think his eyes are mine and I believe he will be a not too ugly little boy. My first two weeks here in the hospital, the nurses did everything for him. Now that we are leaving, however, they let me take care of him. I have plenty of milk, but only have to nurse him once at night. He is very good-natured and only makes queer little noises during the night then goes back to sleep so that Mother can sleep, too.

Thank you for your prayers, thanks to all the family. God was kind and the delivery not as complicated as the doctor anticipated. He has advised against another child, but that, too, I leave in God's hands. Thanks to your wise advice, Lee, I knew what to expect, and my sister Alicia was at my side. From the moment the baby was born, the worry and pain were forgotten, as though he had dropped straight down from heaven without my intervention. Not even in my wildest dreams and longings did I expect life to be so wonderful.

I pinch myself to believe he is mine. My cup runneth over.

Deepest love to you both from your sister

Antonieta.

Little Donald was received at the house on Héroes street as though he were the Crown Prince. Sabina fluttered over the child, Conchita was all coos and smiles, and the aunts and cousins and second cousins flocked to give him their stamp of approval. But José forbade Alicia to attend his Protestant baptism, held in the arms of his outcast Catholic godmother, Chela.

A profound metamorphosis was taking place in Antonieta as she watched her son change from day to day. "I, Antonieta," was like a skin peeling off, while "Antonieta, Mother" was a new skin that grew. Fatherhood softened Albert and he showed his affection in public with noisy kisses and loud blowing on the baby's soft tummy. Only the baby's name was a problem: Albert insisted on calling his son Donald and Antonieta called her son Toñito. Sabina found yet another name:

"Da-no What kind of a name is that? Dano Bla-eer. Ha! I shall call him Chacho. He's a fine Mexican muchacho who knows how to direct a stream of pee-pee right toward his old Sabina's eye."

Happiness flooded Antonieta's days. She took dozens of photographs: Chacho's big bear of a grandfather holding his tiny grandson, fez askew when the baby suddenly pulled the long tassel. Chacho in his bath. Chacho sunning. Painstakingly, she recorded his miraculous progress in a baby book.

In an intimate moment, while he watched Antonieta nurse the baby, Albert studied his wife's delicate face bent over the child's. His Madonna. He walked over and kissed her tenderly on the cheek. "How beautiful you are. You are still my sweetheart," he said, "and it's time for me to take you home. "We're a family."

Long after Albert had left the bedroom, Antonieta thought about that word, sweetheart. A woman should not stop being a sweetheart at the altar. A sweetheart was capable of guiding love through the tempest of marriage. She would make every effort, every sacrifice, bend in every direction to stabilize the course of her marriage. She would endure the north. Of course, she would take Conchita with her. And her books.

1920

In July the temperature at the ranch had risen to a burning 105 degrees. Chacho broke out with a rash and the poor, miserable child complained bitterly day andnight. He was an alert ten-month-old, crawling everywhere, standing up in his crib and displaying numerous teeth to anyone who would play with him. Conchita kept wet towels around the crib. They had no electricity at the ranch,, so the nursery turned into an oven without even a fan to offer relief. Antonieta sat with the baby by the hour, reading her beloved French authors: Remy de Gourmont, Baudelaire, France, Verlaine. When morbid meditations threatened to possess her, she would pick up Marcel Proust, the latest Parisian sensation, and read his provocative, minutely embellished stories of Paris salons,. To the baby's utter delight, she read to him in French and sang French nursery rhymes as though through this language she could escape to a private world. To a world apart from Albert.

"On our honeymoon there were a few times times when my body melded with his, when my passion rose to that sublime realm where I was lost in him and he in me. He wanted so much to please me. Then I would awaken serene, rested, emerging from a deep sleep with him beside me," Antonieta wrote in a new, locked diary. "Now I am an object of coitus. He neither cares nor can tell the difference in me. He has asked me not to speak French to Chachito. Because he does not speak French, he feels I am trying to woo his son away from him. 'It's those damned French books which are putting bizarre ideas in your mind, romantic pretensions that have nothing to do with real life and only leave you melancholy.' His ways, his interests, his ethics alone are reasonable and right. 'You are spoiled,' he once shouted at me. 'You think life is to be lived one way: your way.' There is a heaviness in Albert that badgers and batters until he wears people down. And another trait has revealed itself: jealousy! When I mention activities that will take me away from the ranch, his temper flares. He is even jealous of my books! I have hidden my philosophers—villains, he says—that are poisoning my mind. We discuss his books, the heroic deeds of Wellington and the success of Henry Ford and Andrew Carnegie, but we never touch upon our feelings, this acid burning inside, tormenting me when I lay by his side. If I am tormented, what must he feel? Some nights I want to reach out to him. Poor Albert, so correct, so honest, so hard-working—so rigid."

No water had come down the Nazas River to irrigate the cotton lands, so no crop had been planted in the spring. Albert came home from a trip to Torreón, where he saw his bankers, in a dark, pensive mood, and avoided her. He closed himself in his office in the mornings and rode out to inspect the ranch in the afternoons. At lunch, he was remote and moody. Antonieta noticed he was not smoking and, after a few days, commented on the fact. They were sitting in the formal salon, a stiff, bare little room which she had not yet refurbished.

"You haven't smoked in days, Albert. Have you made another wager with Evaristo?"

"No. I've given it up."

"If you were Catholic, I would guess you had made a pact with the saints to bring down some rain," Antonieta commented lightly.

"Evaristo and I can sustain the loss. Our guayule crop doesn't need much water."

"Are you ill, then?" Antonieta pursued.

"No. I am perfectly well."

Antonieta toyed with her coffee cup. "What made you give up smoking?" she asked, her curiosity unappeased. Albert had been a heavy smoker.

He raised his eyes and looked questioningly at his wife, as though wondering whether she merited the truth. "I bumped into an old mining engineer in Torreón, a fellow I knew a few years back, a heavy drinker. I hardly recognized him, drunk at ten o'clock in the morning. He begged me for a loan, so I gave him some money and watched him stagger down the street. A thought I've been unwilling to face struck me full force: If we have the choice, a healthy body is the best shell for a healthy soul, and tobacco isn't good for anyone. Neither is alcohol."

"Does that mean you have given up your whiskey, too? Reverting to childhood mores to please your parents?" Antonieta asked with an edge of sarcasm.

Albert reached across the coffee table and clamped his hand on top of hers. "Listen, I battled with my will power for two days in Torreón. On the train coming home, I reached in my pocket for a cigarette and the pack was empty, a little assistance from God, my dearest. Then and there I swore off. When I got home, I threw out all the cigars." His eyes held hers for a long moment. "My clothes won't smell of tobacco now. You might at least find my clothes less offensive." " He squeezed her hand hard, tightening his grip.

Antonieta looked into the intense eyes of her husband and felt something constrict the nerves in the back of her neck. It isn't the tobacco I find offensive, she cried out in silence, and withdrew her hand.

At night, Albert attempted to read while Antonieta slept, or pretended to sleep, on her side of the bed. With every fiber of his being he was trying to conquer his physical desire for this woman who rejected him, this wife he did not understand. Subtle refinements in Antonieta rebelled against this environment, against the ranch life he loved and accepted. But did not he, too, have a right to rebel against her refusal to adapt! The origin of her melancholy was the pernicious influence of those books. Those books were threatening their marriage. Albert put down his own book and glanced at the sleeping figure. Well, for better or for worse, they were bound to each other. She was his wife!

Antonieta withdrew deeper into her books, and gave in to the lethargy the heat produced in her. She made little attempt at conversation.

Breaking a lapse of silence at lunch, Albert introduced a new subject. "I read a new concept last night, a metaphysical key to harmony in life."

"Really?" Antonieta replied with interest. "What is it called?"

"Christian Science. Its thesis is that everything that God created is good, therefore evil cannot exist. Its wrong thinking. If we acknowledge and fear evil, we give it power. If we deny it, it has no power, do you see?"

"You mean, we can think evil out of existence?" Antonieta asked, incredulous. "The terrible injustice we see every day—a child abused, a maimed soldier, a starving dog, killing, disease, the infirm and deformed. We can think these out of existence! How can you entertain the thought that evil doesn't exist. It exists in us!"

"A manisfestation of error in our thinking. We can overcome error," Albert replied emphatically.

"If you have become interested in the metaphysical, I suggest you read a primer first—by a Frenchman, Rene Descartes' "Discourse on Method and Metaphysics."

"Are you attempting to educate me, Antonieta? I read that in Prep School." Albert's voice rose. "I am only trying to explain a simple concept to you. One that interests me!"

"I disagree that it's simple. We are the most complex of all God's creations, body and mind and soul in constant conflict."

"We can control the body and the mind. The only real life is the life of the spirit, nourished by faith in God. That, my dearest, is the truth. The absolute truth!"

Shaken by his fervor, Antonieta thought long before speaking: "I don't believe in absolutes, Albert. I only believe in quests."

"Wrong quests!" he flared in anger. "Your damned Nietzche has put you on the wrong quest. Wrong! He's the anti-Christ, I tell you. Why do you fill your head with such trash?"

"It is not trash! I am trying to understand myself. I would like to understand you. I want to know why I am here. Why God put me on this planet."

"What about us," Albert asked, coming around to her side of the table and pulling her to her feet. He mashed his mouth down on hers and held her waist in a vise.

"You're hurting me," Antonieta gasped. "Stop!"

Albert released her and walked into the parlor, where a servant was setting down the coffee tray. In a few moments Antonieta followed, taking her place in front of the silver service. Albert watched her sink into the chair with that singular graceful movement and reach, with trembling hand, for the coffee pot.

Antonieta threw open the door to Albert's office. "Where is my Nietzche?" she demanded. "And Verlaine, Baudelaire, Proust?"

An intense, intimidating stare met her unflinching gaze. "I burned them."

Shocked, Antonieta stared at her inquisitor. "You beast! Beast!"

"I will destroy all your books before I will let them destroy you!"

Still shaking, she controlled her voice. "You have taken leave of your senses, Albert," Antonieta said stonily, and slammed the door.

Ashamed of his rage, ashamed of his lack of control, Albert begged for forgiveness. And when Antonieta offered it to him, the inquisitor's fire forged a truce. Peace was restored in Santa Cruz and Antonieta resumed her teaching. But something had happened. In Antonieta, fear of this man who was her husband had taken root.

The wail of a child awakened Antonieta. Toñito! She had decided Chacho was not an appropriate name; his name was Antonio and she would call him Toñito. The baby had screamed tonight when she touched his stomach. Not bothering to inspect her slippers for scorpions, she slipped her feet into the satin mules and hastily crossed the narrow corridor to the nursery.

Conchita was walking the baby, holding the limp little body in her arms, soothing, comforting, to no avail. Toñito cried louder when Antonieta took him.

"He vomited," Conchita said. "I was about to awaken you and the Señor. I think he has a fever."

"You think? My God, Conchita, he's burning up!" Antonieta held the baby against her shoulder. "Go get the aspirin." Constant wailing was muffled against her neck.

Albert appeared in the doorway. "What's the matter?"

"Toñito is violently sick and we are miles away from civilization,"

Antonieta moaned. "Go into San Pedro, Albert, and bring Dr. García. Please!"

"At one o'clock in the morning? Be reasonable, Antonieta. A baby's temperature flares up and comes down just as quickly. Here, I'll give him the aspirin."

"What if it's the Spanish influenza?" Antonieta's eyes were wide with fear. The terrible disease had come over in the ships from Europe striking all over Mexico, killing young and old alike.

"There've been no cases reported in San Pedro," Albert said. "Let's see how he is in the morning."

Conchita poured water into a little silver cup, dissolved the aspirin and tried to make the fussy baby drink it, but he refused. Finally, by forcing tiny spoonfuls, they succeeded. Albert returned to the bedroom and Antonieta dozed in the rocker. An hour later the fever had not abated.

"Albert." Antonieta shook her husband. "Go and get Dr. García, I beg you. Toñito's fever is worse and I am at my wits' end. I don't know what to do!"

"My mother used to plunge us in cold water to bring down a fever."

"How cruel. Sadistic!" Antonieta exclaimed. "I want Dr. García."

Albert looked at his distraught wife and got up. He dressed and hitched the horse to the buggy.

The dim light of dawn appeared in the nursery and the sun was rising through the sultry haze, a red ball framed in the far arch of the patio, when Albert returned with the doctor.

The slow-moving, provincial doctor took the baby's temperature, pressed a stethoscope to his chest, ponderously recited a list of possible causes, left some medicine, and departed.

The next day Toñito was no better and the doctor was sent for again. He applied hot compresses, left more medicine, and offered lengthy advice on the need to remain calm.

"I would just as soon have a witch doctor as that imbecile García!" Antonieta ranted. "I tell you, Toñito is dying, Albert, dying out in this godforsaken place."

"Calm down!" Albert commanded. "Don't you think Dr. García

has seen sick babies before?" He put his arm around her and she broke away. "Have faith, Antonieta. The medicine has hardly had time to take effect and the baby is not crying anymore."

"He's not crying because he no longer has the strength." Tears streaked Antonieta's cheeks.

"I have faith in God's love and mercy but not in Dr. García's medicine. I want a competent doctor!"

Albert held her arms. "Now stop! I tell you Donald will be all right. God has no intention of letting him die or letting him suffer."

"How do you know what God intends?" Antonieta lashed out, accusingly. Hysteria possessed her. Albert's grip grew stronger. "Let me go!"

Albert loosened his grip and held her against his chest. "Calm down, *querida*, please. We have both been living under a strain. I promise if Donald is no better tomorrow we will take the train to Torreón." He kissed her gently. "Now come to bed and get some rest. Conchita will watch him."

"No," Antonieta said. "I'll stay here. You go to bed."

The word "train" rang in her mind as Antonieta sat beside the crib holding the hand of her small son. She listened to his weak moans and sang softly.

"He is no worse," Conchita said comfortingly. "But he is no better."

"Oh Father, God in heaven, please make him well." Antonieta bent over the crib. "I am trapped, Father. Trapped and helpless."

The train.... The train. She had often heard the whistle of a train as it crossed the road to the ranch, not more than a kilometer away. About five in the morning, it was, a freight train most likely. A reckless, desperate plan began to formulate. Antonieta looked at her watch. Four o'clock.

"Conchita," she whispered, touching her loyal companion who dozed in a straight chair. The exhausted girl was wide awake in a moment. "We're leaving. Pack a small bag for Toñito, bottles with manzanilla tea, a warm blanket, and plenty of diapers. Then get the kerosene lamp that hangs by the kitchen door. Hurry." Antonieta tiptoed into the bedroom where Albert was sleeping and got her money, her boots, and a rebozo.

With Toñito securely wrapped in her rebozo, Indian fashion, Antonieta set off down the dark road with Conchita, away from the ranch. The lantern cast a small circle of light on rocks protruding from the ruts. Exhausted, at the railroad crossing they leaned against a *huizache* tree and waited.

The beam of the locomotive broke through the dark haze as it rounded the water tower. Antonieta's heart pounded against her rib cage. Conchita stepped up to the tracks and frantically waved the lantern, up and down, back and forth, as the powerful headlight grew brighter.

The train screeched to a halt and the engineer poked his head out of the window and looked down through the steam at the two women.

"I must get to Mexico City," Antonieta shouted. "My child is dying. For the love of God take us! I will pay you."

The engineer had stopped for emergencies before. "Come aboard," he called down. A man in sooty overalls jumped down and helped them climb into the locomotive.

Antonio and Amelia had just closed the shutters in the salon as they prepared to go to bed. Since Mario had gone off to the United States, they were the only members of the family left in the large mansion. It was a crystal clear night and a bright moon lighted the gallery as they crossed to the anteroom and continued the routine of checking the doors. The servants still talked of the infamous burglar called *El Tigre de Santa Julia,* who could remove your socks without taking off your shoes. Moreover, everyone was talking of the new wave of kidnappings and assassinations sweeping across the city. The assassination of President Carranza in May had again brought the leader of an insurrection to the Presidency, and a shaky peace kept citizens in a state of nervous tension.

"It's locked," Antonio told his ten-year old companion, testing the anteroom door.

The little house dog who followed them around began barking incessantly.

"Let's go in, preciosa," Antonio said, trying to hush the dog.

Amelia picked up the dog as they returned to the foyer. Suddenly, growling and barking, he jumped out of her arms. The front door burst open and an apparition appeared on the threshold which brought a scream from Amelia.

"My God!" Antonio gasped, recognizing the soot-streaked face and the child in her arms.

"Papá!" Antonieta cried out, "Toñito is dying and I have come home!"

The melodrama of the moment, her entrance and outcry, stunned Antonio, who could only say, "Come in. Come in."

Two days later, Albert appeared at the visitor's gate. Antonio greeted him as he came up the stairs to the gallery. With purposeful formality, Antonio held out his hand.

"I have come for my wife and my son, sir," Albert declared, standing stiffly on the landing.

Antonio looked at his son-in-law with steady eyes. "You are speaking of my daughter and my grandson," he said, "who sought refuge in my home." His tone was calm, even. "You are welcome here, Albert, as long as you conduct yourself with reason and Antonieta wishes to see you. The baby had a bad bout of stomach poisoning. Dr. Garnett attended him."

"I am sorry. I have caused so much trouble," Albert offered, suddenly dropping his shoulders. "May I see Toñito?" he asked humbly.

"I suppose there is no harm. He is your son," Antonio replied. "Come in, my boy. I'll tell Antonieta you're here."

As he followed his father-in-law into the Blair's private apartment, Albert knew he had lost the battle. Antonieta would never live at the ranch again.

CHAPTER XXIII

FEBRUARY 1921

Carranza's assassination had shocked the world. Now Obregón sat in the presidential chair. There was a new, progressive spirit in government and the shaky peace was beginning to stabilize.

At the house on Héroes, old Demetrio shuffled back and forth to the gates all day as people came and went. Workmen were back on the job, painting, repairing the walls, and installing a new bathroom in the servants' quarters. Once more, draftsmen occupied the studio upstairs as Public Works began to allocate funds to repair the damages of the Revolution.

Antonio took a blueprint out to the terrace to dry, and breathed in the fragrance of his beloved garden. Below, he could hear bursts of laughter. The warmth of family permeated his house once again.

"Come on, mi amor, come on. You can do it." Antonieta sat in the arbor engrossed in her little son's attempts to catch a large rubber ball. She offered a steadying hand to the blond, curly-haired toddler as he lurched forward and held out his arms to his devoted pitcher, Amelia, now a robust eleven-year-old. Sabina clapped and praised the little prince of the household each time he caught the ball. Babbling happily, the untiring boy chased the ball over and over.

A clanging at the carriage gate interrupted the game. Antonieta spread the honeysuckle vines and looked out.

"Sabina, you go to the gate. It looks like another homeless girl. If she has a hungry baby, take her to the kitchen."

"The city is flooded with fatherless children. You can't run a nursery! And we don't need any more mouths to feed."

"It's only temporary shelter. Just do as I said," Antonieta retorted serenely.

Grumbling, Sabina descended the stairs to the driveway.

"Come here you precious thing." Antonieta swept up her little athlete and kissed him under his soft baby chin. "He's really filled out, don't you think?" she asked Amelia, Toñito's beloved playmate. "I used to dream of this garden. I knew it would heal him."

"Did a snake really crawl into your bedroom at the ranch?" Her little sister was still filled with admiration at Antonieta's audacious flight.

"Yes, it did. Here, love, take Toñito up for a nap. I have to see about lunch." Albert arrived for lunch punctually at two o'clock.

In the year since they had taken up residence at her father's house, Albert had sold his interest in the ranches up north and dissolved the firm of Blair & Madero. Touched by his willingness to dispose of the ranch and return to the Capital to live, Antonieta made an effort to break the impasse their marriage had reached; a *modus vivendi* of tolerance began to replace hostility, and Toñito provided a keen concern and interest they could share. She discovered she was pregnant, but early on miscarried, an experience which left her depressed and weak. Albert respected the doctor's suggestion that he occupy a separate bedroom.

A colored beam from the stained glass peacock played across Albert's plate. He waited until the soup was served to break his news.

"Well, I got it," he said with a broad smile.

"You saw Obregón!" Antonieta guessed.

"And got the permit. I sent in my business card attached to my safe-conduct signed by Madero and avoided two or three hours of warming a chair in his anteroom. It was packed. The President knew who I was," he added with a self-satisfied grin.

"How did he impress you?" Antonio asked.

"A genial sort, straightforward. I spread out the plans and explained our proposition. The main road leading from the city would be built at our expense, a continuation of Reforma Boulevard, subject to the approval of the city council, of course. I told him my partners and I would sink the wells and pay for the installation of all services for the subdivision."

"Did he like the plans?" Antonio asked.

"Obregón's a shrewd judge. I could see he was very interested but cautious. He looked over the topographical study carefully and asked me whether I thought people would buy up on the hill. 'The Park,' he said, 'is a large obstacle to have in your front yard.' 'We are turning it into an asset, Señor Presidente,' I told him. 'Our slogan is 'Buy in Chapultepec Heights and the park will be your garden.' He liked that. He's in favor of more housing and only insisted that the Park be protected."

"I see you have changed your mind about Obregón," Antonio remarked. His son-in-law's headstrong convictions rarely allowed him to change his opinion.

"I can't condone the assassination of Carranza... a plot, obviously. But he's a practical businessman," Albert said defensively. "And I think Mexico is ready for business."

After two years in office, Obregón's efforts to reconstruct the nation were bearing fruit. Confidence was slowly building. His budget allocated as much to schools as to barracks. Luncheons at the Rivas Mercado table were now sparked by new controversial discussions: Reds in the preparatory schools, Isadora Duncan's marriage to a Russian, Mahatma Ghandi, a composer named Stravinsky. But the most talked about person in Mexico in 1922 was the outrageous Diego Rivera.

Diego's gigantic, voluptuous nude figures were overpowering the auditorium of the National Preparatory School, almost a thousand square feet of wall and ceiling being painted with twelve-foot allegorical figures. Diego's "ugly monkeys" were creating an uproar. The unfinished work rained criticism down on the head of José Vasconcelos, the new Minister of Education, even as it also attracted foreign painters, who flocked around Rivera, spellbound by the dynamic new fresco. Pro or con, its impact became too powerful to ignore. The press pounced on a new victim for caricature, the *gente decente*. The mural gave café devotees a new topic for heated dispute. Antonio Caso, President of the University of Mexico, called the mural "stupendous". A French critic referred to Diego's work as "new revolutionary Mexican art". Most felt he should be dragged down from his scaffold. Antonio had stayed outside the arena, so was thus relieved of having to comment.

"Papá, you haven't seen Diego since he got back from Europe," Antonieta chided. "Don't you think you should at least acknowledge his presence?" They were sitting on a bench in the garden watching little Toñito attempt to run over Amelia in his new push-pedal car.

Antonio got up and began trotting around a tree. "Come on, son, run me down." He had recognized the plea in Antonieta's voice. Attending household affairs was wearing thin. She needed a diversion from guests and children's parties. Huffing, he settled his huge frame back on the bench.

"I was talking about Diego, Papá. Aren't you interested in what visions he has of Mexico after fourteen years in Europe? You haven't poked your nose in his studio or the school."

"You're right. I should go." Antonio patted his daughter on the knee. "You will accompany me, of course. Tomorrow morning."

Ignacio parked the Packard behind the Cathedral in an area crammed with hole-in-the-wall shops, bookstores, cafes, and run-down dwellings. A rehabilitated colonial palace was now occupied by the newly created Secretariat of Education. The medical school, law school, and other faculties of the University of Mexico were scattered around the colonial center. Students with books tucked under their arms pushed past other pedestrians on the narrow sidewalks. As they approached the Preparatory School, Antonieta noticed a cafe filled with boisterous young students. Here the city was alive!

Curious onlookers milled around the courtyard of the old *prepa*, which had once served as a convent and later as a Jesuit school. Standing a head above the group gathered in the auditorium, Antonio made his way to where a bulky figure was planted on a sagging scaffold. From time to time, Diego Rivera looked down at the spectators, responding jovially to insults and compliments:

"So you wouldn't want to be married to that naked woman, eh? Well, you wouldn't want to be married to a pyramid either and a pyramid is also art." He pointed his long paint brush at his critic and saw Antonio. "Maestro!" he called out. "Five more minutes and I'll be with you. There's a sketch on that chair under me which explains all of this."

Antonio backed away from the scaffold and tried to take in the whole composition, a gigantic work called "Creation." Ugly, distorted "Man" rose out of the Tree of Life, green-fleshed "Knowledge" instructing him. Above, brown, thick-lipped, tormented "Tradition" stared at nothing; above the arch, her pallid green-eyed blond friend, "Erotic Poetry," poked her head up. Who could have posed for that one! Antonio cocked his head, moved away, squinted at the sketch of "Charity," clad only in her hair, and "Woman," a gargantuan Neanderthal who occupied the left-hand corner. He raised his eyes to where Diego was working on "Wisdom" and shuddered.

"If that symbolizes wisdom," he said to Antonieta, "may the ignorant inherit the earth! Diego has taken leave of his senses. Let's go. I don't think I can even be polite."

"I had better tell him, Papá," Antonieta said.

"Wait till I see Antonio Caso," Antonio mumbled, walking away. "Stupendous? Bah!"

"You can't just leave," Antonieta argued. "Wait. I'll be right back."

She returned to the scaffold and waited until the artist finished painting a patch of wall.

"Señor Rivera!" She caught his attention. "My father has an appointment, unfortunately, and we see you are busy. He will come another day."

Diego waved his brush and continued to work.

Antonieta looked once more at the mural encompassing her. Severe, elegant lines traced a forceful composition, and pure, strong colors seemed to radiate from a golden center. Primal Energy. She could feel it.

A reporter recognized Antonio and stopped him at the door of the school. "Diego Rivera was a student at San Carlos when you were director, was he not? If memory serves me, you got him his first scholarship to study in Europe."

"I only helped," Antonio said trying to brush off the man.

"What opinion do you hold of this controversial work?" The reporter persisted.

Loathe to condemn an artist whose work he had once admired, Antonio was careful with his reply. "The spell of Italy is evidently still upon Diego. But the fresco painters of the Renaissance created beauty and Diego has only created shock waves. I trust this experimental stage will pass and the true talent of this fine artist will show again." He marched off, taking his daughter by the arm.

As though it were a part of some unexplored self within her, the dynamic work she had seen drew Antonieta back to the Preparatory School. She stood in the auditorium again the next day. Only a few spectators circled about. Again, she felt the impact of the powerful mural as she approached the scaffold and studied the foreshortened figures that adorned the vault. Diego, it appeared, had not moved: he wore the same paint-stained overalls and plaster-spattered shoes, the same misshapen Stetson. He was holding the same graniteware plate he uses as a palette. Only the mural had moved. "Wisdom," alive with color now, was to the right of him.

A bell rang and students began to pour out of classrooms. A few stopped to watch Diego's assistant grind colors and spread wet plaster, while the big man swirled his brush. They watched idly, as though he were a steam shovel, Antonieta thought.

A young girl came running around the corner and bumped into her. "Do you know why he paints so ugly? Because he's so ugly." She planted herself under the scaffold and shouted. "Hey, you big frog, do you want a sweet roll? I told this woman that you paint so ugly because you're so ugly. Isn't that right? I brought you something. Why don't you come down?"

"Go away," Diego shouted, looking down. He saw Antonieta. "Well,

In the Shadow of the Angel

hello. Did your father come with you?"

"No. I came alone."

Hands on hips, the hoyden stood firm at the foot of the scaffold. Two black eyebrows seemed to grow together above her taunting eyes.

Diego climbed down, wiping his hands on his overalls. "Go away, kid. Come on, go to your class or the bathroom or whatever you have to do."

"I said I brought you something, fatty." She held out a sweet roll.

Diego snatched it from her hand and swatted her on the behind. "Scat."

The girl made a face at the elegant lady who obviously had Diego's attention and reluctantly moved away.

"That's Frida," Diego said with a deep chuckle. "A pesky kid who insults me to get my attention. She wants to be an artist." He looked at Antonieta appraisingly. "Didn't I see you in Paris when you were about Frida's age?"

"That was Alicia. I'm Antonieta, the younger daughter. She removed a calfskin glove and held out her hand.

"A lady should never shake hands with a painter," Diego said. "Why did you come back here? What did your father think? Hey, Máximo," he called up to a boy assistant, "stop spreading plaster. I'm going to take a break. What did your father really say?"

Antonieta smiled at the genial, disheveled man next to her. "If you will buy me a cup of coffee, Señor Rivera, I will tell you. I saw a cafe around the corner."

"Call me Diego."

The Cafe Esperanza was full of students. A young couple vacated their table with a nod to Diego and squeezed in with friends. A waiter smeared the fly-specked oilcloth with a wet rag and took their order. Seated opposite Diego, Antonieta put her elbows on the table and rested her chin in folded hands. Diego took note of the long, tapering fingers and expressive eyes.

"Well, what were his comments?"

"My father said that if he had the authority he would order the walls whitewashed," Antonieta replied with mock seriousness.

375

Diego chuckled.

"He said that you have taken leave of your senses and he is glad it's not contagious."

"I thought so," Diego said, laughing aloud. "That old classic, your father, is impermeable. I can't break through that Greco-Roman crust."

Antonieta sat back. "He did say you had learned the theory of the Golden Section and applied it with dynamic symmetry. Now that's a compliment, don't you think?" She smiled.

"You made that up. What's your opinion?"

"I think it's awesome. Dynamic! Your mural is a very important work. And it has certainly focused attention on Mexico." She leaned forward. "To tell you the truth, Father was surprised you left Europe."

"I came back because the Revolution promised something," Diego said, "even if it's only walls. For now that's enough. But my walls shall speak and I shall get more walls, for all of us, for Clemente Orozco and Xavier Guerrero and David Siqueiros and Fermin Revueltas and Jean Charlot and a whole bunch more you have never heard of. We have formed a syndicate. Tell your father that we ask no more than a laborer's wage because we work with our hands. Eight pesos a meter, including plaster."

Diego planted his elbows on the table and leaned his chin on paint-stained hands in imitation of Antonieta.

"Are you a revolutionary?" His eyes bulged even more as he looked directly at her.

Her gaze unwavering, Antonieta paused. "I have some revolutionary ideas."

"Could those include posing in the nude?" Diego asked.

She knew he was trying to shock her. "From the looks of your mural you have plenty of models," she answered obliquely.

Diego sat back in the chair and studied her. "I would like to paint you," he said.

"Why?" Antonieta asked, taken by surprise.

"For the money," Diego said. "You are a rich girl and we laborers still have to be supported by the rich." He grinned. "Why don't you come to my house on Sunday and I'll make a sketch. I'm not working

Sunday afternoon. Come along, you'll meet a lot of painters."

"Do you mean that?" Antonieta asked, "or are you just being polite?"

"I am never polite," Diego said. He tossed some coins on the table for the coffee. "You can pay next time." He stood up, gallantly offering his arm as they left the café.

All week Antonieta debated whether to accept Diego's invitation. Did one telephone? Did one just show up? He had scribbled an address on a scrap of paper, but had not indicated a time. There was something seductive about him, an earthy element that was frightening, vulgar. Not quite vulgar, but unclothed, everything stripped of veneer. That was it. Nudity, after all, was natural to an artist. Yet a keen intellect gleamed from those frog eyes. Did he really intend to paint her, or did he have other intentions? What excuse could she give Albert? What would her father say? Well, she was twenty-two years old and would make her own decisions!

Sunday morning, Antonieta dressed in an old skirt and a sweater. She was sitting at her dressing table twisting her long hair into a chignon when Albert came into the bedroom. He kissed her on the cheek, then walked over to the armoire and began knotting the loose tie around his neck.

"Aren't you going to church?" he asked casually.

"Not today," Antonieta replied.

"I'm disappointed." He attended an English-language Protestant church and Antonieta had voluntarily accompanied him the past months. He watched her putting up her hair and stifled a painful desire to pull her to her feet and crush his lips on hers. Albert worked at the knot and waited for his wife to offer an excuse.

"It's no reflection on your church, Albert. It's just that I have an appointment this afternoon and there are some things I must do."

"May I ask what kind of an appointment?"

"Diego Rivera is going to paint my portrait," she said nonchalantly.

Albert yanked at his tie. "Have you taken leave of your senses? Rivera's 'monkeys' are the laughingstock of Mexico! Is that what you want to be? Have you told your father?"

"Yes I have," Antonieta replied sharply. Her father had recommended that she stay away from Diego, who consorted with Bolsheviks, not fitting company for a lady.

"Then you certainly will not listen to me," Albert said. He turned on his heel and stalked out of the bedroom.

Ignacio pulled up beside a warped wooden door in a rundown building not far from the Preparatory School. Antonieta checked the number. There was not another automobile on the narrow street.

I'll be at least an hour," she told her chauffeur. "You can walk around, if you like, but don't disappear for long."

"I'll wait in the car," Ignacio said, not concealing his disdain for the neighborhood.

Antonieta pulled at a cord which was strung through the door and heard a bell clang inside. She waited a minute, then pulled it again. The door was flung open by a dark young woman with wild curly black hair. She stood insolently in the doorway, sea-green eyes looking her up and down, challenging her very presence.

"Who are you?" the woman asked.

"Antonieta Rivas Mercado. Does Diego Rivera live here?"

The young woman craned her neck out and noticed the Packard. "Diego invite you?"

"Yes," Antonieta replied, wondering whether she should leave.

"What's your name again?"

"Antonieta".

Like a cat ready to reach out and claw, the woman touched her arm. "Come in."

Inside, Antonieta's heel caught in a woven rush mat and she nearly tripped. A gigantic red-green-purple papier maché devil leered in a corner of the small entrance, a leaning post for a stack of canvases. Printed declarations of the Syndicate decorated the walls and a small sign declared, "We paint only on walls and toilet paper." Just ahead, a heated discussion was going on in a small room filled with smoke and humanity.

"*Oye*, Diego!" the cat called out, "you have a guest."

Diego extricated himself from a heap of pillows on a low wooden bench and came over to greet her.

"You came," he said, extending his hand. "I won't try to introduce you. Just find a seat. Here, Lupe, take the señorita's jacket."

Lupe tossed the proffered coat defiantly on a painted wooden chair.

"Come on, Lupe, behave. The señorita came to have her picture done." Diego put his arm around the voluptuous dark woman whose lips seemed to be perpetually parted waiting to be kissed. "She's jealous of all women," Diego explained, "but since she *is* all women, there is no need."

"You posed for 'Woman'?" Antonieta asked with overstated admiration.

"I did." A haughty smile revealed beautiful teeth against the olive skin. She was a truly striking woman. "Go on, fatty, get back to your discussion. I'll find this girl a chair."

The claws receded and the cat began to purr.

"They never stop talking," Lupe said. "The painters are worse than the poets. That's Jean Charlot in the chair, from Paris; and that one is Carlos Merida from Guatemala. That gringo over there is Paul O'Higgins from California. And Noguchi from someplace." She shrugged. "That one they call 'The Parrot' because he never talks." She pointed to a stocky Indian with high cheek bones and straight, coarse black hair.

A woman dressed in an exotic white robe adorned with bunches of beads and a painted face floated in from someplace and sat on the floor.

"That's Nahui Olin, a little too full of mescal. Real name's Carmen Mondragón. Thinks she's so smart. One of Diego's camp followers."

Antonieta recognized "Erotic Poetry" and remembered rumors. She was the daughter of General Mondragón, one of the conspirators in Madero's overthrow, a well-educated woman of the "decent class." They said she was a bit deranged.

""Nahui is *loca*," Lupe confided in a whisper. "She was married to a homosexual painter. Handsome brute. Smothered her own child. Now excuse me." Lupe left.

The group on the floor moved to make way for the stranger as

Antonieta edged forward and squeezed into a corner on a make-shift couch. They were talking about the Revolution, this time the Russian Revolution. That is, Diego was talking about it. The others seemed bent on talking about the future of mural painting in Mexico.

"All right," Diego said, "we want walls. Well, I think I have convinced Vasconcelos to let us paint the Secretariat of Education. My argument was that the old relic needs a good coat of plaster and paint anyhow. Have any of you really looked at that building? It's two blocks long and three stories high, enough walls to shake Mexico when we finish!"

A hubbub of approval arose. A few people got up and moved around. The man named Jean Charlot squeezed in next to Antonieta.

"You obviously have a theme in mind, Diego. What is it?" Charlot asked.

"I worked on some sketches last night. They're symbols, bold symbols for a new age, something to penetrate the popular mind. Hey, Lupe, bring me my pad." Lupe threw it to him. "Look. Symbols, rhythms. I want to paint the brutal rhythm of workers cutting cane and the exhausting work of miners. Like metaphors in poetry," he added. Rivera was wound up, said he intended to paint bold yet, harmonious plastic analogies that pointed up the disharmonies between man and man, the worker versus the industrialist, the agrarian versus the hacendado, the Aztec versus the Conqueror, all the injustices and inequalities Mexico suffered, each line and gesture and panel calculated to merge into a whole: the land, the people, the fiestas, Mexico's history and dreams and broken promises. "The new class struggle," he vehemently declared.

"Slow down, Diego," someone named Fermin said. "You might bring our walls down with reactionary objections."

"To stir up controversy is our objective! Our walls will educate the illiterate. They will be our school. Can't you see it? The courtyard will come alive with color. It will be the monastery where our new religion will be proclaimed!"

"I would use more abstract symbols," Carlos Mérida broke in. "The age of pictorial art is past."

"Mexicans don't understand abstraction," Diego said, brushing the comment aside. "And I intend to exalt human sacrifice, show it for what it was, the highest good for which a mortal can reach, liberating him from the slow, miserable rotting away of life."

The sharp, wood rim of a board was pressing into Antonieta's thighs, but she made no effort to move. Diego talked as he painted, in splashes of colorful imagery, a rich flow of words sprayed out to keep up with his thoughts.

"I want to show the popular arts as they are, the magnificent, barbaric shapes and colors."

"I agree with that!" O'Higgins interrupted.

"The basis of iconography..." Diego was off on another theme.

After an hour and a half, her cramped position was demanding attention. People began to move about and Antonieta stood up. She would slip out as she had slipped in. Diego saw her stand up and called out.

"Antonieta! Sit in that painted chair over there. I want to sketch you." He picked up his pad and took a pencil out of his shirt pocket.

"You really don't have to do this," Antonieta told him, feeling embarrassed.

"I said sit down."

She walked over to the painted chair. "How shall I pose?" she asked. A few people turned to see who the model was.

"The way you are," Diego answered, commencing to draw and initiating another discussion.

A barefoot girl came in and passed a plate of hot *buñuelos*, sugar spilling off the crisp cakes as people broke off pieces and began munching.

So he has a servant, Antonieta thought. I must chide him about equal rights for all the workers of the world.

In fifteen minutes Diego got up. He ripped the sheet off the sketch pad and came over to his model.

"The middle class has no taste," he said. "Their idea of elegance is a copy of a bad European bibelot, and their idea of a portrait is something vapid and pretty, something the artist is to produce if he is to be paid. I am glad you do not belong to the middle class." He handed her the drawing.

Bold, black lines traced a familiar face, huge eyes dominating a wistful countenance. Not a pretty face, she thought, but her face. "It will take me awhile to see myself like this," Antonieta said, "but I shall treasure this sketch, Diego. Thank you."

"A gift," Diego said and returned to his place among the pillows.

As though she had been waiting, Lupe appeared with Antonieta's jacket. The full lips were parted and the sea-green eyes assessed the visitor once again. She took the sketch from Antonieta, looked at it and handed it back.

"That will be fifteen pesos," Lupe said.

José Vasconcelos was cutting paths through the cornfields, building rural schools, declaring war on illiteracy. Eighty five percent of Mexicans could not read. Despite his critics, he awarded thousands of feet of walls to the painters. Diego Rivera became one of the "sights" of the city, sitting on his sagging beam, painting twelve to fifteen hours a day. The walls of the interior courtyard of the Education building glowed with patterns of exuberant nature, peopled with rhythmic groups of figures guiding the eye where the master led it. Clemente Orozco, Jean Charlot, David Siqueiros and other painters straddled their scaffolds to create bold murals along corridors, above stairways, in dark corners. Masters, masons, apprentices, plasterers, and gawking spectators gave the aspect of a Renaissance engraving to the seventeenth-century Spanish palace.

Antonieta waited until the sun was almost down and the fading light would oblige Diego to come down from the scaffold. She had not dared come for weeks, not wishing to provoke more of Albert's bombastic ranting. But she was drawn to this place, and had come again in spite of Albert's accusations and the raised eyebrows of the family. Only Chela understood its attraction. This was the real Mexico, tinted with savagery but full of life. A Mexico on whose periphery she stood, an observer of the action, but more alive through the mere contact. She stood in the shadows and waited, so as not to distract the master.

In the Shadow of the Angel

Diego climbed down from his beam, squinted at his work, moving his cumbersome body back and forth, here and there, appraising, his critical eye observing every detail. Then he clambered up again and made a correction. Tomorrow would be too late; the plaster would be dry. When the fading rays of the sun abandoned the wall, he descended again.

Antonieta stepped forward and greeted Diego with a kiss on the cheek.

"I was beginning to think you had been swayed by your father's opinion," Diego said jovially. "Do you see progress?"

His arm swung in a half circle toward the wall. "How does it look?"

"It's too much to encompass." Antonieta took it in slowly. "It's magnificent. Art supersedes content," she added with a smile.

"You're wrong," Diego declared, wiping wet stains off with a big red handkerchief. "It's the content that matters. This is deliberate propaganda."

"I don't agree with all your 'symbols,' but I would like to discuss them," Antonieta said. "How about some coffee? It's my turn to buy."

"Can't," Diego said. I have a meeting."

"I'm disappointed."

His friends approached. Antonieta greeted Nahui Olin, dressed today in a black peasant dress and gray rebozo. An attractive dark-haired woman she had never seen spoke to Diego. An Italian, her accent suggested.

"Diego has joined the Communist Party," Nahui announced to Antonieta. "So has she." She pointed to the stranger whom no one had bothered to introduce.

Antonieta fell into step with Diego as they crossed the courtyard. "You must miss Frida. Who brings you sweet rolls?" she asked in a light vein.

"Do you know what happened to that kid? She was expelled from the *prepa* just before I finished over there. So she gets all dressed up in baby blues and hair bows and personally complains to Vasconcelos. Vasconcelos made Lombardo Toledano reinstate her, saying that if he couldn't handle a little girl like that, Toledano had no business being

Director of the Preparatory School. Ha!" Diego's laughter rang out.

They walked along ahead of the others. "How's Lupe?" Antonieta asked.

"She got married."

"Oh, Diego, I'm sorry."

"To me," Diego added. "And I'm sorry, too. She slashed one of my canvases for a wedding present."

"Why?"

"Jealousy."

"Who made her jealous?" Antonieta asked pointedly.

"That girl back there. Beautiful, isn't she? She's a photographer and a Communist. Want to come to the meeting? I think you're old enough."

"No. I told you I think collective societies are dehumanizing. Here, I am returning your Karl Marx and lending you my Prometheus. I'll be back next week."

"Well, goodbye," Diego said. He turned away, then wheeled around. "Say, Antonieta, I only just found out that you're married."

Troubled by Albert's mounting jealousy and continual badgering, Antonieta turned again to Chela, with whom she could discuss the new ideas that whirled in her head. Ostracized by her own class, Chela mingled with a group of pseudo- intellectuals whose favorite topics were Communism and the Radicals, and the dissection of Diego Rivera. Carlos was away from the house a lot these days, giving classes at the medical school and the University, where a new attitude of liberty prevailed. After ten years of intellectual isolation, educated young Mexicans were hungry to be part of world society. Neither the Rector of the University, Antonio Caso, nor José Vasconcelos, Minister of Education, favored Communism, but they defended the right to discuss, to debate, to think for oneself. Modern French works were augmented by Humanist Russian writers such as Tolstoy, Dostoevsky, Chekov and Andreiev, all of whom found fertile soil in young Mexican minds. A passion for all things Russian surged: Stravinsky, vodka, icons, ragtail fur hats.

The girls were sitting in the garden of Chela's pleasant house, enjoying the sunshine before the puffy white clouds turned gray and loosed their afternoon downpour. The garden was bursting with color and the intoxicating scents of summer. Auburn hair caught up in a bow, Chela looked like an illustration by

Charles Dana Gibson, Antonieta thought, admiring her beautiful cousin.

"Carlos says that the Communist International has passed its peak, that their Red Star is falling," Chela said.

"Not with Diego," Antonieta told her. "His Red Star is rising. I have furious arguments with him. Sometimes his vision of the future frightens me. What does Carlos think about the Communists in Mexico?"

"Obregón is playing a game, don't you see? After all the hell Mexico has gone through, he's finally established a strong central government. Dictatorial, of course." She shrugged. "Carlos says any other form of government is out, unpatriotic, anti-national. Anyway, the Obregón Government controls the labor unions, so who's going to join the Communists?"

"Diego just joined the party. I admire his being faithful to his ideals," Antonieta confessed.

"Diego has converted himself into a Red icon," Chela berated. "Do you think he believes in real equality, like letting his peons tramp through his house, breaking the plumbing and forcing him back to using an outhouse? She laughed and lit a cigarette, taking a long, deep drag. "How I would like to discuss Marx with Diego! My 'intellectuals' don't understand half the things I say and are shocked by the other half." Chela sighed deeply. "It's hell having to wait for Carlos. He's getting deeper into politics and I have nothing to do but read."

She puffed again, and then mashed the cigarette down in the ash tray. "Are you a little bit in love with Diego?"

"No, I am not," Antonieta quickly answered. "The truth is, I'm flattered that he bothers with me at all. Diego and Toñito are the only bright spots in my life. And you, Chelita," she added softly. "I hate to see you so unhappy." She pressed down the smoldering cigarette.

"I thought the subdivision would keep Albert's time and mind occupied."

"It does. He's away all day. But when he comes home, I have to account for every minute. What I did, where I went, who I saw, who called. I have to tick off the events of the day like a clock. It's maddening. And if I stay home and read, it's just as bad. He has even threatened to take away my books. He burned them once, remember? Albert still thinks they separate us. Oh, Chela, how can a man once so charming become such a tormentor? I tell him the truth and he doesn't believe me. I'm becoming a sarcastic shrew." Antonieta lowered her eyes. "What can I do?"

Chela patted her cousin's hand. "We're a great pair. I left my husband for love and I am trapped. You married for what you thought was love and you're trapped. At least you have Toñito."

Both girls were lost for a moment in private thoughts.

"Sex for him has become a mechanical release. I try to get to bed before he does and pretend to be asleep. Last night Albert woke me up in the middle of the night to accuse me of having a lover."

Chela exploded. "Of course, like me!"

The Chapultepec Heights Company had now purchased land exceeding eleven million square meters. Sales had gone well at seven pesos a square meter, with ten percent down and sixty months to pay without interest. Albert had increased his shares in the form of ploughs and scrapers and mules and wagons left from the ranches. He worked from dawn to dusk with the graders, marking streets, planting hundreds of trees on the bald hills. Antonio agreed that the city would grow west, up in the hills, and grow it must; the Capital now exceeded four hundred thousand inhabitants.

Antonieta had taken a keen interest in the sprawling subdivision. She had been assigned the task of naming streets, engaging in a project that pleased Albert. Now the project was nearly finished. With a stab of pain, she thought of the day he had invited her to choose a site for the house he planned to build. In her imagination, she had turned the bald hills into shaded boulevards and gardens. The whole valley of Mexico lay at their feet, the outlines of the two volcanoes chiseled in the crisp, transparent air. From their hilltop, she could see the golden angel stretching skyward atop her monument. Albert had put his arm around her and said, "I want you to supervise every detail. This is going to be our house, where we will entertain the most important people in Mexico."

She tried to shut out the future as she sat at the desk in Cristina's old oratorio, now converted to her workroom. A large atlas lay open before her, and a random collection of geography books, notepads, and reference books were piled beside it. For a week now, she had been researching the names of mountains and mountain ranges, names she had chosen for the high hills in the Chapultepec subdivision. The section from which the castle was visible she had named for the Viceroys. She turned the pages of the atlas, wrestling with her private hell. Her marriage had become a torment. When she invited him to her bed, it was punishment he inflicted, not love. If he would just talk! He had ignored every attempt she had made to talk about their marriage, or even to discuss their different views of raising Toñito. She could never question his beliefs or confront him on a deep, personal level. They had argued about religion again. "I don't need to go to church to feel God's presence," she would tell him again and again. She had tried to talk about her own belief in salvation through a love which transforms, a love which pacifies and reconciles, not salvation as a reward for good deeds. He had ignored her words and let loose a tirade against the Catholic Church for stealing from the poor, for accepting alms for those "idols and bleeding Jesuses that fill every church."

"Those 'idols' teach us about suffering," she had retorted fiercely. "My Christ is not a judgmental savior who leads you along a black-and-white path that says Should and Should Not. Christ forgives. He suffered. And His love implies serving all those who suffer. We accept suffering and pain and death and share it with our loved ones because we feel it, not because we should! Albert had glared at her stoically. His truth was the only truth. Her attempts to make him understand met with oppressive silence.

Antonieta was immersed in a geography book when she heard Albert enter their bedroom. Every nerve tensed. He was home early.

"Hello," Albert called out jubilantly. He walked into the little office and kissed his wife on the cheek. "Still buried in the atlas? We had a good break today on that well we are drilling, struck an underground river at seventy meters and in no time the water level rose only a few meters from street level. It may be the only well we have to drill."

"I am so glad, Albert," Antonieta said, without looking up.

"And your father was right. That deep strata of *tepetate* runs right through the whole subdivision, an effective shock absorber for earthquakes." He paused and looked expectantly at Antonieta. "How would you like to go to the club for dinner?"

"I am in the midst of this," she replied, continuing to run her finger down the page of cross-references.

"I see." Albert stiffened. He turned back to the bedroom and picked up his hat, hesitated, then returned to the workroom. "Why didn't you tell me you had been to see your damned Diego on Wednesday?"

"You didn't ask me," Antonieta replied calmly.

Albert pulled her to her feet. "I am asking you now. Who are you meeting? Where? One of Diego's Reds or a friend of Chela's? Answer me!"

"I have no lover!" Antonieta cried out, pulling her arm free.

"You lie. You are away from this house more than you are in it. Where do you go? Who do you see? Diego Rivera? Is he the one?"

"You are talking like an idiot, Albert. Diego's only love is his art." She threw back her head and laughed. "Ask his wife. She would scratch your eyes out if you suggested he had a lover."

"People have seen you with him, in that cafe. Where is your sense of propriety, your decorum, for God's sake? People are talking about you. You're making a fool of yourself and a fool of me." Albert lowered his voice suddenly. "Antonieta, you are my wife. I won't have you behaving like a tramp."

"You don't own me!"

"Are you a tramp? Beneath that intellectual crust and inside that pure, untouchable body, are you a tramp?" Albert burned her with his sarcasm.

Antonieta faced him. "Why did you marry me?" she asked, her eyes blazing. "You seem to think that women are like a string of paper dolls, all cut with one whack of the scissors. Did you think you were marrying a servile, demure Mexican girl who would say 'yes' to everything you think and want, someone who would stay home all day and embroider! You need a different wife, Albert."

"You are my wife," Albert said, defeated. For better or for worse." He paced up and down and finally faced her. "What have I done wrong?" There was desperation in the question.

He looked so pitiful, so proud and pitiful standing there, desperate, flinging words at the air like darts.

"It isn't a matter of right and wrong. We are very different, that's all," she said quietly.

"It's those books. You think too much, so much that you don't really know what you believe in."

"Yes, I do. I believe that women have rights too."

"Do I restrict you? Is that what you feel? You want to be free to sleep with anyone you please!" Albert picked up his hat and left, slamming the door to the boudoir.

The waiters began to talk among themselves in the dining room of the American Club, hoping the few stragglers would finish their long dinner. The rattle of dice had ceased in the nearby bar, and a few lights began to go off in the elegant Porfirian mansion where Albert and his associate, Samuel Rider, were finishing their dinner. Albert was purposely dawdling, postponing the time he must return to the house on Héroes.

"Too bad the Mexican papers gave Obregón such bad press. That luncheon in the castle really impressed the American trade delegation," Samuel was saying.

"Obregón's no fool. He has to court the United States and have his Government recognized," Albert said tersely, "no matter what they say. Mexicans may resent us, but they need us."

A waiter approached with the dessert and Samuel set about eating the rich cake.

"I laid out the site for the public school today," Albert said, "right on the main thoroughfare in the middle of the hill. And I am going to sell two of my lots to start that orphanage I've been talking about."

"That's damned generous," Samuel said. "We'll give you some help."

"I am not tooting my own horn, Sam. I owe a lot to Mexico and I am tired of seeing poor, shivering children sleeping in doorways. So damned much poverty, filth, and corruption in this country!"

Samuel looked surprised at the outburst. "It's not like you to be cynical. What's the problem, friend?"

Albert shrugged his shoulders. "Funny, how what once seemed charming can irritate. I wanted to give the benefit of my American training to Mexico. Not just technically, but morally as well. Pay a decent wage, pay on time, set an example of discipline and responsibility. You know, give a boost to a poor devil along the way."

"Nothing wrong with that," Samuel said.

"They don't really care. That's what irritates. You may have observed that Mexicans are filled with good intentions, but resist being structured. The truth is that they don't give a damn about sanitation and more efficient methods. They'll do it their own way every time." Albert toyed with his cake. "When we finish this project, I think I'll go back to the States."

Samuel Rider looked at his friend. "Listen, you're the largest shareholder in this company. We can't let you go. Whatever disillusionment you're suffering will pass. How many foreigners can walk in to see the President?"

"I'm tired of being a foreigner. I tell you, the foreigner will never be understood." Albert paused and broke off a piece of his cake. "Corruption bothers me. Forget civil corruption, they are so damned casual in their morals. Sin and get dirty, confess and be cleansed. They don't believe in divorce, but the acceptability of *casas chicas* has made illegitimacy a part of this society. It's rotten, I tell you." Albert punched little holes in the cake with his fork. "My wife says I am a typical Yankee do-gooder. She also calls me an inflexible Yankee conformist."

"Albert, would you like a drink?" Samuel asked abruptly.

The question brought Albert up with a start. "But you don't drink, Sam."

"I wasn't asking for myself," Samuel replied with a grin.

"I admire you for your abstinence. I have meaning to tell you that." Albert sat up straight. "I gave up smoking. I should give up drinking, too. That's a fight I can wage against myself." He looked at Samuel. "Did you ever drink?"

"A lot."

"Mind telling me why you gave it up?"

"My wife and I joined the Christian Science Church."

"I've been wanting to study Christian Science," Albert said thoughtfully.

"Say, would you like to go to church with us on Sunday?" Samuel asked. "We're a small group, but growing."

"I would," Albert said. "Yes, I would."

Antonieta took refuge in silence. Her heart filled with pain and her mind in turmoil, she wrote in her diary: "The impasse has gone on for over a week. He wants to catch me in a deceit that does not exist, to force me to confess to a lover to expiate his own failings, to cast sin upon me. If I am sinful, he might show his largesse by forgiveness. At times I am so tired that I am tempted to invent a lover, to give him the first name that comes into my head. Anything to stop his hammering. Surely, this is hell. The hollow physical contact left is repugnant, even a kiss on the cheek which I force myself to give him in the presence of Papá and Toñito. Daily I watch the fragile structure of our marriage collapsing. I look at Toñito and weep."

CHAPTER XXIV
1923

Elena brought the news. Juana's husband, crippled old Ignacio Torres, was dead. It had been sixteen years since that dreadful day Juana had fallen through the skylight, sixteen years before this devil's twisted frame had, at last, given up the ghost.

Standing in the hot sun, drained by the long-winded eulogies, Antonio whispered to his sister, "Why is vanity so often confused with charity? This one was a balloon. Pulque made him rich! He fed beggars and orphans for the Sunday Rotogravure and squeezed every last penny out of his tenants, the cantinas."

"Such sacrilege, Antonio." Elena poked him in the rib.

"I'm neither sacrilegious nor a pretender to virtue and piety," Antonio continued in a whisper. "I came to get my inheritance. See those nephews over there? They're vultures."

"Shh."

"The old miser was irascible and violent. Poor Juana's every little expenditure irritated the hell out of him. I am going to demand my inheritance in gold."

The relentless sun beat down upon the mourners, who were beginning to file by, throwing little handfuls of dirt on the coffin.

The nephews disclaimed any knowledge of Antonio's inheritance.

But tucked in his safe, Antonio had a copy of Juana's will. The nephews produced lawyers who claimed that Ignacio Torres' will nullified his dead wife's. Antonio's lawyer claimed that the husband was merely the custodian of his wife's estate during his lifetime, enjoying the interest derived thereof. The battle heated up.

"Well," Antonio exclaimed a month or so later, tossing his hat on the table in the arbor where Antonieta was coloring with Toñito. "I got it!" His eyes sparkled with deviltry.

"What did you do to them, Papá?" Antonieta jumped up and kissed her father.

"You know how long a civil suit can drag out. Well, I threatened to slap an embargo on the ranch until the will was settled. Those young punks want their money now. So we settled. Ha! In gold!"

"Bravo!"

"Bravo," Toñito echoed. He was drawing a picture and making funny faces.

Antonieta turned back to observe her son's prowess. "And what is King Midas going to do with his gold?" she asked.

"I am going to spend it," Antonio said.

"I hope your plans include a trip. It's time you breathed different air, renewed your youth, Papá." She wondered whether she should bring Maruca's name into the open. "Travel with a companion who makes you happy, a good friend, preferably a female." She didn't lift her eyes from the drawing book. "You have such a friend, do you not?"

Toñito suddenly jumped up and presented his anatomically impossible animals to his grandfather. Draw me an elephant, *grandpère*, please."

Antonio accepted the purple crayon and sat the boy on his knee. "My friend is going to be married," he answered Antonieta's question. "It is only fitting for a lady like my friend." He looked up with an impish grin. "But a trip is what I had in mind. I plan to invite the whole family to Europe!"

"Me, too?" Toñito asked. "You too, son. And your mother and your father and your uncle and your aunt."

Antonieta suddenly saw the broad horizon of Europe, of her beloved

Paris. "When can I start packing?"

"After I order my custom-built automobile. I am not going to ride in cramped quarters, squashed down by grandchildren, on this trip!" Playfully he tweaked Toñito's ear.

The little boy ran to his school box and took out a pad and more crayons. "Please draw me a whale. Will I see a whale, *grandpère*?" He had chosen the French word for grandfather like his Gargollo cousins.

"Many."

"When will you speak to Albert?" Antonieta asked, suddenly serious.

Antonio invited Albert into his anteroom and poured a glass of plain soda and an aperitif.

"You are still not drinking, Albert?"

"No, sir. Soda is fine."

Antonio broached the subject of the projected trip.

"I have been wanting to return to Europe for years, before I am too old to enjoy Paris and too feeble to travel. I'll be seventy this year and I would like to share this milestone with my family. Antonieta hasn't been to Europe since she was ten and Mario and Amelia have never been there. Alicia and her family plan to accompany us on the boat. I am sure you can appreciate this desire, this dream of mine, Albert. You haven't been to Europe since you left London as a boy, have you? Well, I invite you as a friend and a son." Antonio paused and sipped his vermouth. "I think the trip will be a healthy change, my boy. "

Antonio was still a commanding figure, though the buttonhole on his jacket was stretched to the limit and his copious hair and beard almost pure white. Albert admired his father-in-law.

"I appreciate that, sir. I appreciate the invitation very much."

"Mind you this is an all-expense-paid invitation."

"You are very generous, sir. How long do you plan to be gone?"

"Possibly a year."

"A year!" Albert exclaimed. "This is a wretched time for me to take any time off at all. I have responsibilities and partners."

"I thought this would be a good time for you to take some time off," Antonio said. "The project is going well, isn't it?"

"Yes, but I'm the only one who can deal with certain people." He went into a long monologue about the difficulties of marking the road, of continuing Reforma Boulevard up into the hills of their subdivision. Last week he had discovered that the Military planned to put a polo field and casino right across their projected road, and he had spent the night with ploughs and scrapers marking the extension so that they would agree to move the polo field to one side of the road. "How can I leave?" he concluded.

"I see your point," Antonio said.

"And we're having a rough time trying to sell shares in the Golf Club, even at one hundred pesos a share. People think it's the end of the world out there at the top of the hill. Everyone loves your design, sir. Your clubhouse captures the American country feeling exactly." Albert went on and on.

"Relax, Albert," Antonio interrupted. "I didn't expect you to stay in Europe the whole time. I have an alternative suggestion: Mario is coming over when Princeton is out in June. Why don't you come with him, travel with us in the summer, and bring Antonieta and the boy back with you? That is, if they have your permission to leave. You know how important their company is to me. Think it over, please."

Albert was silent for a time, whirling a piece of ice around in his glass. "That's not necessary," he replied at last. "Of course they may accompany you. I'll be lonely, but this offers a perfect opportunity for me to build a proper house for my family to occupy when they return." His eyes clouded. "The change will be good for Antonieta."

Diego wrote a handful of letters of introduction, scrawled notes bearing thumb prints of paint which he handed to Antonieta over a farewell cup of coffee in a little cafe near the Cathedral owned by a Chinese.

"Do you ever miss Paris, Diego?" Antonieta asked. "You lived there so long."

"I hate Paris," Diego said, toying with his coffee. "Water frozen in the pipes, my fingers so cold I could hardly hold a paint brush. Guillaume Appolinaire pierced by schrapnel, leaving a scrap of poetry on a cannon. Modigliani starving, freezing and staggering around the Quartier drunk, dead at thirty-six." He spoke with bitterness. "No, I do not miss Paris."

Antonieta cupped her hands around her thick, white mug

"Paris died with the war," he went on. "Five hundred and thirty-six artists swept away in the storm. Madness. A society that produces and tolerates such madness must fall." He pointed his finger at her. "Understand that." Diego sipped his coffee. "Anyway, I was a citizen of Montparnasse. They tell me it is in Paris." He grinned. "But Paris will be good for you. Open up that keen intellect and let it all in. There are a few old friends left. Elie Fauré is one." Then a frown crossed his face like a shadow. "Listen, if you run across Angelina, tell her I am fine."

Antonieta looked into the painter's bulging eyes and remembered Angelina, Diego's diminutive Russian wife. The tragic tale of their little son who died of cold and starvation in 1917 had touched them all.

"Thank you, Diego," she said, rising. "The very first postcard I'll write will be to you from Montparnasse."

Ignacio brought the Packard around and began to load the bags. Impatiently, Amelia made the round of kisses and seated herself in the front seat.

Albert stood with the servants at the foot of the gallery steps. It was spring and the perfume of damp earth and flowers assailed Antonieta's nostrils as she hugged first Sabina and then Conchita. Finally, she turned to Albert. He embraced her stiffly before they kissed.

Toñito, dressed in short pants, knee socks, and a beret, manfully held his hand out to his father.

Albert swept the little boy up in his arms and hugged him tight to his breast. "Goodbye, son," he said. "Goodbye."

For a fleeting moment Antonieta wanted to fling her arms around her husband. He looked so forlorn standing beside the servants. She turned and waved, but by the time the car had rounded the corner her feeling of guilt was overpowered by an intoxicating feeling of freedom. An odd thought flashed in her mind. Had her mother felt such freedom when she left? Goodbye, she shouted inwardly. Goodbye. Goodbye.

1926

Adjusting the combs in her long hair, Chela sat at the desk in the small library of her house and made another attempt to write. In front of her, Antonieta's typewriter awaited her touch, to break the dreadful indecision which locked her emotions. She inserted a sheet of paper and typed "Dearest Tonieta." Then she looked at the words and yanked the paper out of the roller. She had been struggling with the old dilemma since Antonieta's last letter had arrived. Now summer was over and Antonieta's course at the University of Madrid was finished. In every letter Antonieta had pleaded with her to join them in Europe, and as the "trip" was extended—two, now three years—she had postponed the fateful decision.

"What is there for you in Mexico now that Carlos has moved back with his wife?" Antonieta had asked. The words burned in Chela's brain. She picked up the letter on top of the stack and read again: "Relationships end, sometimes through circumstances, as yours has ended. Why hang on when there is no future? You have no legal tie. Fate has been good to me. Albert has made excuse after excuse not to join us here. I would have returned if he had insisted, for Toñito'sake, to live with him, a dead love occupying my heart and house. Any life together we might try to make would be a sham. I am sure, now, that he is as relieved as I, and knows that the marriage is over. When I return home it will be a new beginning for me. I want to be flexible, open to new ideas. I'm a different person. You will see. All that I have soaked up in these three years I am ready to rain down on Mexico, and I shall not be afraid to expose my heart. I needed Europe and so do you. You must remake your life, my beloved Chela. You have known love, cherish it and move on. I can't bear to think of you vegetating in that house, alone. You mustn't waste your life waiting for Carlos. Join me here at the university in Spain, and follow the road wherever it takes you."

Chela bit her lip. For a week now, she had not gotten beyond the salutation. One moment she was ready to leave for Europe and the next she was incapable of taking even a step. Antonieta did not understand that love could also bind; it spun an invisible net and pulled the drawstring tight. There was no escape.

She must convince Antonieta that it was an involuntary move Carlos had made. He had not moved back with his wife, he had moved back in their house. His new political position demanded it. "Don't you see, he really loves me," she typed at last. "His private life ceased when President Calles named him Secretary of Education. He felt honored and challenged by the appointment. How could I do less than to encourage him to accept it? My Carlos!" Chela's throat felt tight. "Mexico needs him and I had to take second place." She did not say that she felt like a prisoner in this house, waiting for Carlos to insert his key in the lock. She knew, too, that her own pride had pulled the drawstring on the net.

Chela finished the short letter to Antonieta, explaining her agony, her vacillation, her reasons for not writing. Bluntly, she stated her unequivocal decision. She could not elaborate; every word drove another spike in her heart.

Finally, it was done. Chela folded the sheet of paper and sealed the envelope. How she wished she could set off on a pilgrimage to some distant shrine, drop her burden there, as the Indians did, or light a candle and leave it all in the hands of God and the saints. But her prayers were blocked by an unfathomable resentment against life.

Depression overcame her. She rang for a strong cup of coffee. The morning sun was still high. She picked up Antonieta's letters and went out to a bench in the garden, sat back and let the warm sun caress her cheeks. Antonieta was close to her today. With her gift for words, she had painted a vivid canvas of her life in Europe. The letters had sustained her, permitted her to travel in fantasy as a voyeur, sometimes even filling that emptiness which grew deeper every day. She felt the changes in Antonieta and envied her experiences. From the moment they had sailed, Antonieta had dropped the name Blair. As though she could go back in time and be single again. Single.

Chela picked up a recent snapshot of her beloved "Tonette." Short hair became her, and her bronze skin glowed, free of the white powder that was the mode. Her hemline was mid-calf, showing off beautiful legs. "A Coco Chanel design," Antonieta had written on the back. "Chanel overlooks the architecture of the body. Breasts, waist and hips disappear in her simple lines. Alicia haunts the couturier salons with Mamá. Yes, she is here. Papá agreed to pay her way over, on condition she stay completely out of his sight. Although he avoids her, Papá is generous with Mamá's allowance. I must also comment that Pepe tolerates my presence, but it's obvious Alicia's husband does not approve of me. Thank heavens, we're on the Left Bank and they live on the other side of the river. Since the birth of her twins, Alicia's posture has become absolutely terrible. The other day I put a broomstick through her corset and we walked for miles until she begged for clemency. Poor Memela suffered at my hands, too. This winter I enrolled her in a studio of "esthetic dance" owned by Raymond Duncan, Isadora's brother. All his students went leaping about in sheer Greek robes and sandals, while Memela huddled around a miserable little heater and begged me to save her from pneumonia. Tante Blanche's topknot barely comes to my shoulder these days. The darling has shrunk to a shred of a lady, but her spirit is intact. Did I tell you that I commissioned Angelina Beloff to do a portrait of me with Toñito? The poor woman barely ekes out a living. She has not heard a word from Diego since he left (four years ago!); she tried so hard to be discreet with her questions."

Methodically, Chela sorted Antonieta's letters again, by number. The trip had started out well. On the boat she had met the owners of a bookstore-gallery near Notre Dame. Antonieta had described the paintings and the artists who gathered there, names that at first meant nothing to her: Picasso, Gris, María Blanchard, Leopold Gottlieb, Adam Fischer, Lipshitz, and a pair of Japanese "Greeks" who laced sandals to their feet and wore robes they had woven themselves. Chela smiled. Carlos had been a bit shocked at some of Antonieta's acquaintances, and even more at her descriptions of sensuous black dancers, the gyrations of Spanish Apache dancers, Josephine Baker smothered in feathers, the gatherings in the night clubs where she drank Pernod with the Cubists. Diego had quarreled with the Cubists, but they were enormously curious about his murals in Mexico, which were making news in Paris... I must see Diego, Chela thought.

In the Shadow of the Angel

He would cheer these dull days, relieve the frustration.

"The mediocre is so evident when you have seen the masters," Antonieta had written. Vicariously, in the seven-passenger touring car, Chela had been taken along to the great museums and galleries of Europe. "In Florence," one letter said, "we saw a portrait by Titian that took my breath away. You are a reincarnation of his model. His special ochre tones give a soft glow to the face, like your skin. You belong in Europe, Chela." The words went around in her head.

She had shared Antonieta's attraction to the new, modern symphonies and the avant-garde theater that held her spellbound. "Simple sets, dialogue that flows, that rings true, that seduces. I saw Andre Gide's 'School for Women,' which tells the truth about sex." Most of all, Chela envied Antonieta's attendance at the new literary salons of Paris. Doctor Elie Fauré, Diego's good friend, had taken her under his wing and introduced her to minds that counted. "Last week Jean Cocteau read a piece by Marcel Proust reflecting on 'time lost.' When I used to read his narratives at the ranch, I could only glean the character of this sensitive novelist. He died three years ago. Proust was a neurotic and a homosexual and, like so many here, addicted to cocaine. The external life and the internal fire feed upon each other, although we are loathe to admit it. Oh, Chela, I want to dedicate my life to things that count. I never expected to be in Europe so long, and I thank God Albert has almost forgotten I exist. His letters have become brief inquiries after Toñito's well-being and Papá's health. Perhaps he understands that Papá counts on me to make all the arrangements. Although I know it's over, my marriage constricts, like hand-cuffs on a prisoner. Somehow, it must be resolved. When I get home, that will be my first priority." The letter ended: "It is important to get out, Chela. Please don't lock yourself into that house."

Now Antonieta was studying Spanish literature at the university in Madrid. A student with a seven-year-old son. "Yesterday we had coffee with Ramón Franco, who told Toñito all about his flight in the 'Plus Ultra.' Aviation is the talk over here. Today, Toñito was baptized (again). Mamá and Memela returned from their trip to Egypt and the Holyland and brought back a jar of water from the River Jordan. My 'heathen' child apparently weighed on Mamá's conscience (the ghost of Mamá Lucita must haunt her). I agreed to the baptism in order to avoid another squabble. Toñito says you are still his godmother, but he thoroughly enjoyed the lofty ritual and it did serve a purpose. I dropped the name 'Donald' from his baptismal certificate."

Besides enjoying student life, the University provided another diversion. Chela smiled, thinking of Antonieta's description of her first affair. He was a professor, an erudite, arrogant Don Juan. "He courted me with his questions and eyes that undressed. I let him take me to bed and discovered the sheer pleasure of sex, not the sex of obligation which most women endure. Why should only men enjoy sex without commitment? Through the university, I published an article on women in Mexico, exposing our poor, suffering martyrs. Now I am working on another article about women."

A line from Antonieta's last letter clung to Chela's mind: "Follow the road wherever it takes you." She mashed her lips together. Three years and umpteen opportunities had passed and she still sat in her garden. She stood up now and restlessly began to wander, inspecting plants, snipping off dried leaves, breaking little hidden growths at the joint and sticking them in the damp soil. She looked at her muddy hands and began to walk toward the house. Her chauffeur met her on the path.

"I have brought the mail, Señora," he said.

It was another letter from Antonieta. Eagerly Chela tore off an end and sat down at a wrought iron table on the terrace.

"November 1, 1926

My dearest Chela: I packed and returned to Paris immediately when I received Memela's telegram saying that Papá wasn't well. They had returned to Paris in August, Papá looking pale but in high spirits. I was shocked to see him. As though a spring had snapped in my beloved bear, he was shaky and wasted. In two weeks! I had a private conference with his doctor and, oh Chela! He confided that Papá's illness is incurable. My mind can hardly bear the weight of this confession. I know Papá is dying. I think he knows it too. He wants to start home as soon as we can pack and close the apartment, to die in Mexico, I am sure.

We hear nothing but alarming reports. Is it true that President Calles has closed the churches and a war has broken out between the Catholics and the Government? Oh my God, will we have another period of upheaval in Mexico?

Life here is such a rich tapestry; it makes Mexico seem threadbare, uncivilized. But is it true that Mexico is now permitting divorce? If the law has been passed, I shall file for divorce immediately. I am told that three years separation is enough to legally terminate a marriage.

I can hardly wait to see you. We will be back at the house on Héroes for Christmas.

My love,
Tonieta

Afternoon descended quietly as Chela attempted to concentrate on "War and Peace." Suddenly she rose and flung the book to the floor of the terrace. I would like to be in Montparnasse, she thought, where life moves from party to party. A wild thought took form and locked in her mind. She would call Raúl, one of her "bohemian intellectuals" and get out of the house tonight. She had to get out!

A snapshot of Antonieta was stuck in the mirror on her vanity. A chic woman wearing a camel's hair coat with a red fox collar smiled out at her. "Oh, Tonette, will I seem like a backward provincial cousin?" Chela asked aloud. She stared in the mirror and tried to imagine how Titian would paint her. Cautiously, she applied a little rouge. A bit of lampblack would enhance the eyes and a bare touch of crème-rose on the lips. She was pale. She forced a smile at her image, a somber face would not do. Nor a demure dress. She fingered the dresses in her armoire and selected a green silk with a flowered sash. It was short and saucy. She twisted her hair into a loose bun and added long gold earrings. Raúl was pedestrian and a boob, but he was, at least, an escort. Maybe they would go slumming. Carlos would understand when she explained how closed in she felt. It had been three weeks. And now he was on a tour with the President!

Smoke was thick in El Imperio. Weary dancers hung onto each other, arms wrapped around necks as the violins scratched out another fox trot and the brasses blared. The trumpet wailed off key and finally synchronized with the rhythm, repeating the same monotonous beat. One-two-three, one-two-three. Chela puffed on a cigarette and watched.

"Have a *mota*," Raúl insisted. Voice raspy, eyes bleary, he offered the stump of a marijuana cigarette to his bored companion.

Chela took a deep drag, spilling the last ashes. The music changed to a *corrido* and the vocalist bleated out the words to a popular tune:

I am not married.
My love is free.
If someone be married
My wife that would be.

"Dance?" Raul asked, trying to rise.

"Not now," Chela said. She felt numb. They should go. Maybe she could sleep now. An argument at the next table was grating. Two men were teetering on their feet, shouting slurred accusations at each other, egged on by the boisterous support of their friends. Someone backed into her chair then lunged forward with his fist. The men slapped an arsenal of arms down on the table.

"Let's go," Chela said. She stood up and reached for her jacket. The sharp crack of pistol fire split her eardrums as the man facing Chela shot from his hip. She fell to the floor, her head hitting the rough wooden leg of the table. She knew that life was flowing out in the sticky substance that gushed from her chest. She knew—and she didn't care.

CHAPTER XXV
DECEMBER 1926

The glow of sunset along the shoreline of Veracruz sharply divided land from sea. As the ship approached the port, a green streak rippled across the blue surface, a dark shadow moving below, breaking into a sinister dorsal spine that attacked floating garbage as they neared the wharf.

Antonieta and Toñito stood at the rail, waiting for Antonio and Amelia to join them.

"There they are." Antonieta pulled Toñito toward the gangplank, joining the crush of passengers who crowded the narrow ramp. Antonieta took her father's arm as he cautiously made his way down. His beard was stark white against a pale face.

"We are here," Antonio said. "We are here."

The scene on the wharf was the same. As though time had stood still, brown stevedores, like those portrayed in Diego's murals, moved along the pier, bodies straining under loads supported by leather bands around their foreheads. Weaving in and out among natives and tourists, vendors hawked their wares, and mangy dogs scavenged whatever dropped to the ground. All contributed to the smells and sights of this Mexico they loved.

"I've booked Pullman seats on tomorrow's train. There were no compartments left," Antonieta said, returning from the depot in a taxi that wheezed.

"Did you telegraph your sister to meet us?" Antonio asked.

"No, I telegraphed Ignacio," Antonieta replied.

She was angry with Alicia. Mario had written that Albert was a frequent visitor at the Gargollo's mansion. Pursuing a beautiful young Mexican heiress he had met in Europe, Mario had returned with Alicia and José at the end of summer, staying in their home until the house on Héroes could be opened. He had reported that Alicia was against the divorce, and José openly voiced his disapproval of Antonieta's position. What right had they to judge! The heat exacerbated her irritation as they drove to the arcades in the Spanish colonial heart of Veracruz.

The old Hotel Diligencias was a horror of flies. Damp, clammy sheets stuck to her perspiring body as Antonieta lay awake, the joy of being home mixed with a churning anxiety. The ceiling fan hung immobile, tilted by the dislodged metal plate that held it to the high ceiling. She looked at Toñito, lying almost naked on the bed next to her, rivulets of perspiration streaming down from his short, brown hair. He had lost his blond curls and had stretched into a lean little boy. She looked at him tenderly and remembered his fright at a performance of Jules Verne's "Michael Strogoff" the first year they were in Paris. When the cannon went off on the stage, Toñito dove under his seat. She found him three aisles back. Her baby. Would he remember his father?

She got up and flicked the fan switch up and down. It didn't work. Mexico hasn't changed, Antonieta thought, with amusement and annoyance. She went back to bed.

As the train snaked up from the tropics, the symmetrical cone of Orizaba loomed high, capped with snow, dominating the entire panorama as they climbed to the high central plateau. The transparency of the early morning sky made the mountains stand out in bold relief.

"There is no climate in Europe to match this, no landscape more beautiful," Antonio said, drinking in the scenery. He looked at his watch. "We should be in Mexico City by six o'clock."

Antonieta saw Alicia and José standing on the platform before the

In the Shadow of the Angel

train had come to a full stop.

"Papá, Papá!" Alicia shouted, running toward them as the family descended. She embraced her father, then bent down and kissed Toñito. Amelia met her kiss halfway, but Antonieta stepped back. Mario strode up to the group and gave his father an affectionate abrazo, then kissed his sisters on the cheek. Both Alicia and Mario looked at their father with shocked expressions.

"How are you feeling, Papá," Alicia asked anxiously.

"Fine, fine, reina," Antonio replied. "It was a good crossing. Let me help Pepe sort the baggage."

Antonio took Mario by the arm, following his son-in-law to the pile of luggage at the end of the ramp. Toñito trailed behind the men.

"Why didn't you wire?" Alicia asked her sister accusingly. "We wouldn't have known you were coming if Carmen Fonseca hadn't called to say her mother was coming up on the same train."

"I didn't want to bother you," Antonieta answered coldly. "Ignacio should be here somewhere."

"I told him not to come," Alicia said. "We have prepared supper at the house. You can all stay with us a night or two until the Héroes house is ready. You didn't give the servants much warning."

"We're going directly home," Antonieta said. "Papá is tired. I am sure the lights are working and the beds are made. We will take a taxi."

Alicia's face fell. "No," she said. "I have arranged everything. Besides, I want to talk to Papá. I want to know exactly what the doctor had to say."

"Papá won't tell you anything. You can see him tomorrow. He wants to go home and I must get him to bed. Amelia, ask Mario to help you look for a taxi. Two taxis."

"Antonieta," Alicia said, hurt and bewilderment in her voice, "Why are you being so hateful?"

"I, hateful?" Antonieta responded, her eyes suddenly blazing. "It is you who have shown your true colors, encouraging Albert to block our divorce. You have known all along I was going to get a divorce."

"He's Toñito's father," Alicia began.

"And I am your sister."

"The Church won't recognize your divorce. It's wrong, don't you see?"

"I don't care about the Church!"

"That's blasphemy!"

"In whose judgment is divorce wrong? In God's or José's'?" She refused to call her brother-in-law by his nick-name, Pepe. "My private life is none of your husband's affair, and if Albert is your friend, then I am not your friend." Antonieta turned and walked down the platform to where the men were counting the bags.

Two taxis pulled up and Amelia broke the tense silence. "We're going home," she said. "Come on!"

Antonieta opened her eyes. For a moment she assumed she was in the apartment in Paris, until she saw the familiar objects in her old bedroom, bathed in the bright Mexican sun. Hurriedly, she dressed. It was important to set the household routine in motion early. The sooner the house was rehabilitated, the faster Papá would improve.

The familiar pat-pat of tortillas grew louder as she walked through the arbor toward the kitchen. Sabina's rebuking voice rose above the chit-chat, giggles, and laughter subsiding as they heard the patrona approach.

"*Buenos días*," Antonieta greeted them effusively. "It's wonderful to be home again."

She gave instructions to María and Conchita and one of her "temporaries," whom she only vaguely remembered. A small staff had remained on the premises in their absence, under Sabina's eagle eye. Sabina herself had a broom in hand.

"Conchita, set an extra place. Señora Graciela may come to lunch."

Chela's phone must be out of order. There had been no answer, but surely the telegram she had sent from Veracruz would bring her rushing over, Antonieta reasoned. She started across the gallery just as her father approached the stairs to the garden.

"I see we are of one mind, Papá. I want to inspect every plant."

Together they descended the broad stairway. The caress of the air was fresh, but neglect hung over the garden. Dead leaves cluttered the flowerbeds and uninvited parasites had curled the young leaves of the tangerine trees struggling for space in their cracked clay pots.

Antonieta took her father's arm. "Cástulo retired to his village last year and that young punk over there is a relative of Demetrio's."

"I think the only plants he has ever cultivated are tall and grow ears," Antonio chortled. "Here, let's sit down. I'm not used to the altitude." He was breathing with difficulty.

"Look at the fountain. If I had but the strength of one blade of grass," he said, pointing to a crack in the stone base where a green tuft emerged.

"Things deteriorate without love and care," Antonieta said softly. "And that is why we came home, Papá. To make you well again."

Antonio nodded. "Have you noticed how Demetrio has shriveled? Just like a prune. "Do I look like that?"

Antonieta laughed. "Indeed not, but you do look like a poor relative in a hand-me-down jacket. We will have to stuff you with *tortillas* and *frijoles* and put some weight back on. It smells so good in the kitchen. I didn't know how much I missed Mexican food."

Antonio reached over and covered his daughter's hand with his own. "I called Rafael Lara this morning. He's the best lawyer in town. He is coming over tomorrow to talk to you about the divorce, and to both of us about my will. I want everything in order."

"Oh Papá, you'll get well. I'll make a pact with all the saints," Antonieta said.

"If he dies, it's the doctor's fault and if he lives, it's by the grace of the Holy Virgin." Antonio replied, quoting the old Mexican proverb. "Save your heavenly pacts, angel. I'm not afraid of dying. I'm afraid of living too long."

The subject of death was uppermost in Antonio's mind. He had known about Chela before they left Paris. The Government had muzzled the press, but the scandalous story was still being aired in high and low circles. Alicia had warned him that he could no longer put off informing Antonieta.

At last, holding his daughter's hand tightly, Antonio cleared his throat and recounted Chela's tragic, senseless death.

Enclosed behind the walls of her grief, Antonieta hardly spoke or stirred from the house. She refused to answer the telephone when Albert called, delegating that dreaded confrontation to her lawyer. Chela's death made her rail against God, then fall on her knees at her bedside and pray for the soul of her dearest friend. For the first time in years she felt a need to seek consolation at the baroque altar of San Fernando, so filled with childhood memories of innocent faith. She would implore the Virgin Mother and Jesus Christ to hold Graciela, Chela, Chelita, in their love.

Then she remembered: the doors of San Fernando had been shut, the bells silenced. The Government was in open conflict with the Church. President Calles had expelled thousands of priests and nuns. The churches throughout the nation were closed, as were the convents and the parochial schools and religious asylums and institutions. Another barbarous civil war was raging in the provinces: Catholic *cristeros* crying "*Viva Cristo Rey!*" were warring against Government troops. Simple peasants deprived of their churches, their sacraments and religious freedom had again taken up arms. Antonieta prayed for them, for Chela, for herself and her need to be consoled in a congregation of the faithful, denied by a dictatorial President bent upon controlling the country with an iron fist. She ranted at Mexico, suddenly angry with them all—Chela, Mexico, and death itself. She wept.

In Sabina's room, a votive candle always burned beneath the picture of the Virgin of Guadalupe. Quietly sitting on the edge of Sabina's bed, they prayed together. Antonieta fingered the gold medal of the Virgin she always wore as the little flame flickered in the glass and finally sputtered out. Finished. It is finished. Dust to dust. My beloved Chela.

Rafael Lara reported to her in a week.

"The divorce will be easy to obtain, Señora, if your husband will agree to mutual consent. You will have to appear in court together."

"Are there no other grounds?" Antonieta asked, remembering the time he had burned her books, when his insane rage became evident. "We were separated for three and a half years. Is that not valid?"

"Only if you can prove non-support, which constitutes a rupture of the marriage contract."

"He did not support me or my son," she asserted with a ring of victory in her voice.

She didn't want a court confrontation. She didn't want to see Albert. She had permitted him to have Toñito for a day and the little boy had returned ill-tempered and moody. Her absolute custody would have to be spelled out before she could establish visitation rights. Before any other order of business, this divorce must be put behind her.

Within fifteen days, Antonieta was advised by the lawyer's office that the divorce had been approved by the court. Lara's influence had been used to obtain a rapid decision. In the lawyer's office, a clerk read every line of the decree to her to make certain that the statements were correct, then handed her the lengthy, ribbon-bedecked document. Albert would receive a duplicate document. She was free!

In a contemplative mood, Antonieta dismissed Ignacio and walked up the driveway. She removed her hat and sat down on a bench, feeling an unexpected emptiness, as well as the sense of failure that accompanied divorce. Like relics of another age put away in little boxes, scenes from her childhood glided across her memory. She had had this feeling before, in this very place. Why had she felt lonely then? Why now? She had Papá and Toñito to take care of, and a career to define. She must work. Doing what? After Europe, Mexico seemed dead. Tomorrow she would go out to Chapingo to see Diego. They said he had covered the roof of the chapel with his monolithic Indian figures, the chapel which Papá had restored in such caring detail. Old President Gonzalez' hacienda had been taken over by the Government for its new agricultural school.

Raindrops splashed on Antonieta's face before she noticed that the afternoon had grown dark and threatening. A blaze of lightning rent the sky and a loud thunderclap announced the unseasonal storm. The heavens hurled down sharp crystals of water as Antonieta ran up to the gallery, hailstones shattering like marbles on the mosaic floor. She thrust open the front door and entered. Papá would be in his studio.

Upstairs, the hail bombarding the mansard roof was deafening.

The studio was cold and dark. She could see her father napping in his chair, but he did not hear her greeting. Antonieta removed her wet coat, shook it out, and hung it on the rack. In minutes, the clatter of hail ceased and rain began to pound down in a relentless din.

"My God, Papá, how can you sleep? Anyway, you're working too late and the light is terrible. I got the divorce!"

Antonieta turned on the light and saw that Antonio had not moved. His mouth was open and his eyes closed.

Exhaustion numbed her as Antonieta sat by her father's bed. He had had only moments of lucidity in the last two days. She could hear the Victrola playing in the little room where Mario was teaching Amelia the Charleston. They had exchanged jokes with Papá during his lucid moments and seemed satisfied that he was improving. All day they went in and out of the house in their respective directions, returning to fill the room with friends who practiced the Turkey-trot, the two-step, and the tango, with the unconcerned attitude of the young, to whom death was not even a specter. Guilt rimmed the persistent thought that she should advise Alicia. But Papá would pull through. The doctor said he would recover from the stroke.

Antonieta was reading at her father's bedside when she looked up and saw Alicia standing in the bedroom door. The two sisters faced each other across his bed.

"Mario told me Papá had been taken ill. Why didn't you call me?"

"He's better. The doctor said he needs rest," Antonieta answered.

"Then why don't you send that noisy bunch home?"

"We don't have to live in a morgue. Mario and Amelia would only sit around and mope. Besides, I'm telling you that Papá is better."

Alicia bent down and shook her father's shoulder. "Papá, it's Alicia." Antonio's eyes were closed and he did not stir.

"He's sleeping." Antonieta's said lamely.

"I'm going home to pack my bag. I'm moving in until Papá recovers," Alicia was resolute.

"No, Alicia," Antonieta pleaded. "Please don't. We will only quarrel and that won't help Papá. I promise I will keep you informed of his condition."

"I don't trust you," Alicia said. "I'm moving in."

During the succeeding tense days, Antonieta divided her time between her father and Toñito. Routinely, she ate alone with her son when he returned from school, a time she spent going over his "important papers." Second-grade projects were filling a large scrapbook.

"I almost forgot to bring them home today, Mamita," Toñito said, "because Father was there when the bell rang and said he had come to fetch me. But Ignacio got there and said he had no instructions from you, so Father got mad and left and I came home."

"Oh my God," Antonieta said. She took a bite to calm down. "That's right, mi amor. You are only supposed to go with your father when you have written permission." She took another bite. "Let's look at your papers."

Sabina interrupted and handed Antonieta a letter. "It was delivered by hand. The man said it was important."

The letter was addressed to "Señora Antonieta Rivas Mercado de Blair." The return address was a law firm. With a dry throat Antonieta opened the envelope.

"My client, Mr. Albert Edward Blair, contests the legality of a divorce decree recently issued by the court. An appeal has been filed and your presence is requested in court on February 5, 1927. If you wish preliminary clarification, we are at your service." Antonieta recognized the signature of her brother-in-law's attorney.

Just as he seemed to be improving, another stroke paralyzed Antonio. He prayed for a quick death as his heavy body was lifted and bathed and fed and changed. He could feel the warm urine run down his legs, and was unable to stop the flow. Between lucid moments, his thoughts drifted back to another time when urine had run down the pant-leg of a fat, eleven-year-old boy. He had crossed his legs, to no avail, and it had made a puddle on the floor of the grand hotel, as his father stood right there watching. It was fright that had let loose the urine. Unannounced, his father had entered the parlor where his mother was entertaining and, without explanation, said he had come for his son. He could still see his mother's shocked expression. She had just passed some English tarts to Doña Catalina Escandón and Doña Margarita O'Gorman, her English-speaking friends, who extolled the virtues of England and Ireland respectively. He had been listening attentively. "If you cannot learn languages, I will dedicate you to the Church," his mother had said so many times. "I don't want you to grow up to be a *ranchero* whose career is chasing women and bulls. Better to be a priest than a donkey." He had been sitting on a stool by his mother's side, listening to the conversation, trying to avoid the priesthood, when his father—his father who rarely left his mistress in Guadalajara, his father who had turned his mother into a fat, bitter woman—strode into the room and took him away.

At the Hotel Diligencias, his father announced, "You've been around skirts too long. In the morning you are leaving for England to be educated. This is a ticket for the stagecoach, and this one is for the ship. My associate, Mr. William Forbes, will meet you in Southampton." His father had seen the puddle on the floor, but his eyes were unflinching. "Someday you will thank me," he had said. How many years ago? How many years?

He tried to turn over but couldn't seem to move. With slurred words, he indicated that he wanted no more visitors. The effort took all his strength and he fell back, immobile. He could see Antonieta sitting by his side and tried to speak her name. But no sound came. He wished he could leave her in the hands of someone who loved her. He was grateful to his father, he thought with irony. Money. He had made a fortune. The bulk would go to Antonieta. Thank God he had gone over every provision of the will before he slumped into this imbecility. How long had he been lying here? Cobwebs blurred his mind. Yes, Alicia got the house. They would quarrel, but this would force Antonieta to start anew. And Alicia didn't need anything more. Pepe might dissect every nuance of a joke trying to find its humor, but he was an excellent provider. Amelia was well provided for, her inheritance left in Antonieta's care until she was twenty-one. Mario was a man. He should work like a man. There were properties for Mario.

But the bulk, the fortune he had amassed, much greater than anyone suspected, that was Antonieta's. Much of it was safely invested with a stockbroker in New York.

A smile hovered on crooked lips and Antonio tried to touch the long tapered fingers clasped by his bed. Suddenly Antonieta took his hand, her brown eyes brimming with...what had Beto called it? "The deep, suffered memory that glistens in Mexican eyes." He had seen it in so many eyes, an inward gaze that transcended reality, creating its own landscape of fantasy. In her own fantasy, what did she see? In his fantasy, this woman he had procreated, this most Mexican of his children, would help to plant the cultural desert in this land they both loved. Suddenly, the vision of a golden angel filled his mind. That Victory he had raised on a high column would inspire and give courage to Mexicans. How many times had Mexico fallen, only to rise again? How many times... His eyes closed. Life was running down, like that Victrola when they didn't wind it.... A door closed. He sensed that Antonieta had left the room. Someone called her. Was that Alicia bent over, kissing his face? And who else was there? A priest? Other presences crowded about as shadowy figures gathered in his mind.

Always chic, with every hair in place, Cristina waited in the salon. She stood when she heard the familiar quick steps across the foyer.

"Hello, Mamá." Antonieta greeted her mother with a peck on the cheek. She had not seen her since the last visit to her mother's favorite couturier in Paris. "I suppose Alicia called you."

"Yes. I must see him, Antonieta."

"He does not want to see you."

"Let me make you understand." Cristinas's voice was sharp. "By law, and by the Church, he is my husband. I have a right to see him."

"You gave up that right long ago, Mamá. Just as you gave up the right to your children. Papá didn't need you to raise us. He doesn't need you to die."

"I want my jewelry!"

"You will have to wait until the will is read. After he dies," Antonieta said with deliberate coldness.

"That's not the reason I came." Tears quivered in her eyes. "I beg you, Antonieta, let me see him. I must see him before he dies." Now, tears were streaming down Cristina's cheeks. "I need his forgiveness…"

Antonieta touched her mother on the shoulder, a momentary caress of compassion. "It's too late." She said gently. "He's in a coma."

The new maid showed Cristina to the visitor's gate.

They came from far and near. A constant flow of people filed past the casket in the formal drawing room of the house on Héroes street, pausing to pray, to speak to the family: students, bricklayers, carpenters, government officials, artists, people who arrived in limousines and people who had walked across the city. Antonieta watched their faces and began to appreciate the fullness of his life, the far-reaching influence of the man who had been her father.

Cristina stood beside the bier, a long widow's veil covering her face, a chic black dress accentuating her slim figure. Solemn, grim, Albert joined the mourners. Antonieta saw him enter and faced him with dread, but the encounter took place with polite indifference; he was only another of Papá's admirer's come to pay his respects, neither ogre nor friend.

"Tell me how he died and I will tell you how he lived," Sabina whispered. Antonieta squeezed her hand. The old Mexican proverb said it all.

Among the mementos Antonieta found was a scrap of paper tucked in his wallet. In childish print on lined paper it declared:

"*El pa-ja-ri-to can-tó y el ga-ti-to brin-có.* Antonieta 1903"

The scent of gardenias from the funeral wreaths still lingered in the house when the aunts came to call on the mistress of Héroes 45, mistress by permission of her sister.

"Your father was very generous, I suppose because you don't have a husband. A woman with a husband is respected; he's a shield no matter what goes on behind the scenes. I wouldn't get that divorce if I were you," Leonor admonished. At eighty, she still stood as erect as royalty.

"My dear," Elena began in a gentle tone, noting Antonieta's blue dress. "I do think it would be more fitting if you wore black."

"Papá never liked me in black. Mourning is in your heart, not in what encases your body, Tía dear."

"Aren't you acting rather high-handed?" Leonor suggested.

"We spend too much time living lives others think we should live. I plan to live my own life, Tía."

"Then you must accept your own consequences," Leonor said hotly.

The second confrontation was with Alicia.

"You influenced him, Antonieta. That will was written after you returned from Europe. Papá knew I yearned for the convent of San Jerónimo. It's historic, it's where Sor Juana Inez de la Cruz wrote her immortal poetry."

The venerated convent in question had been deeded to Antonio as part payment for the railroad terminal he built before his daughters were born. It covered two square city blocks. "How can you let renters live there? It's the house of God," Cristina had once chided him. Antonio's answer had become family folklore: "It may be the house of God, but I am the one who has the deed."

"It's so run-down," Alicia went on. It has dreadful little stores on the grounds and laundry hanging out in the convent courtyard and squatters living everywhere. Pepe has the money to restore it as it should be restored. You knew I wanted that property!"

"Why are you complaining? Papá left you the church. He did not discuss the will with me, Alicia. Only his lawyer and the notary knew the full terms. Why didn't you speak to Papá about the convent when he got back?"

"It was inappropriate. And I didn't know what was in the will. But you did!"

"Stop accusing me, Alicia."

"You could always influence Papá, worm him around to have things your way. I saw so little of him after Mamá took me to Europe. It isn't fair."

"You could have come home," Antonieta said.

"You seem to forget I got married," Alica retorted.

"You were sold into marriage, Alicia. You let Mamá sell you and put you in a damned gilded cage."

"You are hateful!" Alicia cried out. "Hateful!" She straightened her back and faced her sister. "I respect and love Pepe. And I would rather live in my gilded cage than be in your shoes without a husband to stand behind me!"

"You let Mamá choose a husband for you and I chose unwisely," Antonieta said dispassionately. "But I have the courage to admit my mistake. I shall get a divorce."

"Listen to me, Tonieta," Alicia said, touching her sister's arm," can't you see the scandal you will stir up? It will drag Amelia and Mario down along with you. Albert is not a bad person."

"I don't love him. Alicia. That is the simple fact. To give love, love must be free, and love has been shut up in an ignored corner of my soul. Don't you understand?"

Alicia looked at her sister and nodded. Yes, she understood.

Antonieta faced Albert in the courtroom. A hard, imperious expression had congealed on his face. The lawyers argued. Albert's lawyer produced letters proving that his client's wife and their son had been invited to Europe by her father and had departed with Señor Blair's permission. A trump letter in his possession contained proof that a check, sent in good faith for the maintenance of his wife and son, had been returned by his father-in-law, who insisted that it was his wish to pay all expenses for the trip. More letters were produced in which offers of money had been turned down by his wife. Antonieta's lawyer advised her to try to come to terms with her husband out of court.

Steel blue eyes met Antonieta's in the plush office of her attorney. Folding her hands on crossed knees and leaning toward him across the low table, Antonieta refused to capitulate to his humiliating stare, steadfastly holding his gaze under the brim of her tailored hat.

"I plead with you to be reasonable, Albert. If you will not accept the grounds of non-support on which I obtained my divorce, will you agree to mutual consent? I believe I speak for you, too, when I say that our marriage has ended." She leaned forward, searching his eyes.

"We can divorce each other," Albert said icily, "but Donald cannot change his parents. I agree to the divorce, but I want custody of my son."

The blow struck with full force. Her illusions shattered. Antonieta knew the man sitting across from her would fight her forever, if necessary.

CHAPTER XXVI
1927

To Ignacio's delight, a shining blue seven-passenger Cadillac touring car replaced the aging Packard, larger and more powerful than any automobile he had driven, and a new chauffeur's uniform matched its elegance. Wherever it was parked, Antonieta's automobile attracted admiration. She located her old philosophy teacher, and soon the house on Héroes began serving as a center for loosely organized salons, a few cultural seeds planted in shallow soil. The old carpentry shed was converted into a schoolroom for the children of the "temporaries" and of the vendors in the market.

"The poor little devils live like animals. They must at least learn to read and write," Antonieta told Mario and Amelia.

"And who will remove the lice from their heads?" Sabina asked, her lips compressed in disapproval.

"You will," Antonieta replied, smiling. "You and Conchita can bathe them every day.

The Cadillac wound down narrow streets in once decent working-class areas, searching for the addresses of some of Antonieta's lesser properties. The deterioration of the neighborhoods was appalling. Old buildings, weighted with heavy balconies, had buckled sidewalks that left holes big enough to break a leg. Flapping laundry obstructed courtyards heavy with the odor of urine. In four years, not a single tenant had made a move to maintain his abode, and some owed four years' rent. Should she sell or repair? An assessment of these properties would have to be made by an administrator.

"Sabina," she announced one day, "I want to find Damiana's grandaughter, Ofelia. I dreamed about Damiana last night."

She remembered why her mother fired Damiana and how Tío Beto grieved at the loss. On Antonieta's last trip with her father to search for Damiana's family out in the old lava bed in the south of the city, they had found Ofelia alone, living in the nearly destroyed shack with an "uncle." Her grandmother was long dead, her mother and brothers killed in the Revolution. To survive, a girl had to have a man or a family to live with. Papá had offered Ofelia a job at the house, but the girl had never shown up.

"You said she came by while we were gone. She may have children by now who need to be educated. Get the address, Sabina. Let's find her."

Filled with altruistic intentions, Antonieta summoned Ignacio.

It was necessary to park the Cadillac on a side street; it would not go down the alley. Antonieta and Sabina picked their way around potholes in the sidewalk as they penetrated deeper into the unfamiliar neighborhood. The acrid smell of clogged drains and the putrid odors of human filth and garbage permeated the air. Solemn, silent women, burdened with heavy buckets and babies, stared as they crowded around a water spout that had once been a fountain. Half-naked children played in the dirty gutter, screeching with delight.

"This is it." Sabina jerked Antonieta's arm. She pushed a high wooden door that scraped the cement, leaving just enough space to get by. It led to a stark, filthy courtyard, worse than anything Antonieta had ever seen. They brushed aside damp laundry and found No. 4 near the entrance on the ground floor. Antonieta stepped back with repugnance. What was she doing here? She should have sent a servant with Sabina. They knocked on the iron door and a little boy cautiously opened it halfway. Two other sets of curious eyes stared out behind him.

A man, naked to the waist, staggered forward, buttoning his pants. Behind him, a woman lay on the bed. Antonieta moved out of sight.

"Who are you looking for?" the man demanded, knocking back the children who had crowded around. A baby began to cry.

"Ofelia Lopez," Sabina said boldly.

"She don't live here," the man said and closed the door.

Sabina put her fingers to her lips and met Antonieta's eyes. They conveyed the message: if it was Ofelia, she was beyond redemption, another of the disgraced of this world, without father or family, washed down the drain in the aftermath of the Revolution.

The search for Ofelia haunted Antonieta for weeks. The realities of Mexico jarred her. Did she have the stomach for such poverty? Should she give up the idea of a school for the poor and concentrate her energies on young intellectuals emerging from university? Hold real salons, like the ones in Paris, where mind-stirring discussions would flush out talent? She would consult Diego. He had friends in literary circles. She would go out to Chapingo again.

The Cadillac turned up the dirt road to the old hacienda and parked. The stately entrance hall and stairway, decorated by Diego's strong hand, served students now. Over the stairway, Diego had painted, "Here it is taught to exploit the land, not man." The beautiful Spanish baroque chapel that her father had so painstakingly restored had been converted into an auditorium for the new agricultural college. The ceiling, a complicated structure of arches and pendentives, had challenged Diego's ingenuity. Stripped of its altars and everything religious, the chapel now spoke its own fiery catechism of nature and man. Fecund "Earth," a gigantic figure with Lupe's unmistakable, provocative mouth, held in her hands the germ of life, surrounded by the fierce figures of "Water," "Wind," and "Fire." A French critic had called Diego's murals at Chapingo "the Sainte-Chapelle of the Revolution, the Sistine Chapel of the new age."

Antonieta stood in the doorway and looked around. As always, the scale of the work irresistibly seduced the viewer. Her eyes followed the line of an arch to a flying nude who had a snake running between her knees, moving toward phallus-shaped plants which sprouted nearby. "How can you deny the role of sex in life?" Diego had declared when she had first seen the mural. He had talked her into posing for one of the faces. That was weeks ago. Now he was adding finishing touches; the work would soon be inaugurated.

Diego sat at the wooden work table opposite a young woman in a cloche hat. Nearby, Tina Modotti was focusing her Graflex, preparing to take their picture. Tina had come to Mexico from Hollywood with a photographer named Edward Weston, as his model, lover, and student. Antonieta recognized her well-formed body in the flying nude. Tina had long left Weston, and become Diego's favorite model, inciting Lupe to fits of violence. Antonieta had first met her at the Secretariat of Education. There was a mystery about the attractive Italian photographer, an air of innocence, of refinement and something introverted, in spite of her reputation as a femme fatale. A reserve stood between them, yet there was respect. Tina was a dedicated Communist.

Antonieta waited until the photograph had been taken, then walked up to the group and deposited the picnic basket. "Anybody hungry?"

"Of course," Diego said, a smile breaking across his face. "Will it feed the multitude?" He pulled an apple out of the basket and crunched down on it. "Antonieta Rivas Mercado, Miss Mary Carty. You know Tina. I'm starved."

"Mildred McCarthy," the young blonde corrected.

"Miss McCarty has been interviewing me for a magazine put out by the Art Student's League in New York. Isn't that right?"

"Miss McCarthy. Yes." The young lady beamed. "May I read back this quote? 'From the Byzantines to Michelangelo, frescoes told a story that moved the masses and reformed their taste. That is my purpose here.' Do you mind if I ask you a few personal questions? Is it true you are a vegetarian, Mr. Rivera?"

Diego laughed. "Who gave you that idea? I am a voracious meat eater." He folded his arms, opened bulging eyes wide and explored the naive face in front of him. "Miss McCarty, I am going to divulge something which has never been divulged before. It may shock you."

His interviewer leaned forward, pencil poised. Fascinated, Antonieta and Tina listened.

"Only last week I visited a small island off the Yucatan coast," Diego began. "I won't tell you where it is, because it belongs to an exclusive association, pledged to secrecy."

"And you belong to that association," Miss McCarthy said.

"Yes. I am a founding member. We are pledged to protect the natives so they can carry on their ancient Mayan rituals, including sacrifice." Diego paused.

"What do they sacrifice…I mean, like rare birds?" the eager reporter asked.

"No. They practice human sacrifice," Diego answered.

"Like… like who?" the startled young lady asked.

"Unsuspecting people they capture in the jungle , like butterflies, and fatten up in cages."

Miss McCarthy was breathing hard. "Are you implying that you eat human meat?"

"Not human. Divine. A rip of flesh eaten in the company of mystical priests is sheer ecstasy."

The girl turned pale.

"Miss McCarty," Diego said, crunching on the apple, "there is no ecstasy like the ecstasy in communion with the divine. One is eating flesh made godly by sacrifice." He elaborated with vivid descriptions.

Antonieta noticed that the young reporter was swallowing hard, her chest heaving, and led her to the bathroom. When she emerged, Diego escorted Miss McCarthy to her waiting taxi and waved as she drove off. He returned to the chapel.

"I don't know which is more fantastic, your imagination or your paintings, Diego," Antonieta said, engulfed in laughter. "Poor girl."

"What makes you think it is not true?" Diego challenged, heavy lids at half-mast. "Let's eat under the trees today. Maybe Tina will take our picture."

Diego's eyes met the annoyed glance of the young woman with whom he was reported to be having an affair.

"I am not staying for lunch," Tina said. "I have work to do in the studio."

Antonieta and Diego found an empty bench. It was useless to spread a tablecloth under the trees and try to serve Diego. He would not sit still long enough.

They made small talk: Nahui was living with Dr. Atl, the affair lasting longer than his usual. Atl had prepared some mushrooms in a green sauce the other night. For a painter, he was a marvelous cook... Diego stuffed a handful of pitted olives into his mouth. Still chewing, he said: "I'm going to Russia."

"You haven't told me," Antonieta said.

"In a couple of months. I just got invited to celebrate the tenth anniversary of the October Revolution. You know my only regret? I won't meet Trotsky." He leaned toward Antonieta and whispered solemnly. "He's my secret hero."

"Still in exile, isn't he? Look, Diego, I came to seek advice. Will you bear with me awhile?"

Driving home, Antonieta mulled over the names Diego had given her, some poets, some writers she had never heard of. Then there was the group called *Los Contemporaneos*. Should she stop the carpenters from adding onto the school and go ahead with formal salons?

Alicia solved her dilemma. Unannounced, as usual, Alicia interrupted Antonieta's lunch with Toñito.

"Have you decided to run a boarding house?" she asked without preamble. "Mario spent the night at my house last night because someone was in his bed when he came home."

"That was Eulalia. I forgot to leave Mario a note telling him to use father's room. It was late after the lecture and it was raining."

"What right has that woman to Mario's room?"

"Eulalia Guzmán recently discovered Cuahtemoc's bones!" Antonieta replied haughtily. "She is a distinguished person."

"I don't care who she is, Mario is entitled to his room. If you want to offer lodging, offer to harbor priests! I have come to tell you, Antonieta, that I am selling this house to a private school. You'll have to move."

Shocked, Antonieta stammered. "Move from my house?"

"My house," Alicia corrected."

"I'll pay you any rent you want."

"Sorry. I've already signed the contact."

Antonieta stared wide-eyed at her sister. It was a moment before she spoke. "All right. I will begin packing every stick, down to the last bibelot. The house may be yours, but everything in it is mine. Nothing stays with the house, you hear. Not even a light bulb!"

The word "evicted" was only whispered. A solution came from an unexpected source: Manuela Boari was in Mexico visiting relatives. She and Antonieta had become good friends in Rome. The Boaris owned a spacious house in a quiet, new suburb. Her sympathetic friend called on Antonieta and offered to rent her the house if it suited her needs.

"It's lovely," Antonieta said to Manuela, admiring the features that especially pleased her as they walked around the premises. The Boari house occupied a large triangular block enclosed by a wall and fence and a handsome wrought-iron gate. A sunny garden was dotted with shade trees. Modern style, it had four bedrooms and quarters for four servants.

"You don't think it's too small?" Manuela queried.

"I want to reduce my life to a manageable level," Antonieta replied. "It's perfect." She kissed her friend on the cheek. "But what about the furniture? You have some lovely antiques and I have enough for a warehouse. I like the eclectic look.

"Why don't you store yours, Antonieta. It will save me the trouble of storing mine. We won't need this house for a year or two. Adamo has plenty of work in Rome. Consider this house your transition to a new life."

No contract was drawn up but the Boari administrator insisted upon an inventory, which Antonieta duly signed.

By April, the house on Héroes was cleared out. Antonieta chose the nuns' dining room at the convent of San Jerónimo as the safest warehouse and supervised the careful packing of a lifetime's accumulation of Rivas Mercado treasures. The paintings alone took up a long wall. Tapestries, oriental rugs, French and Chinese carpets were all sprinkled with mothballs and piled up. Furniture was stacked. Barrels filled with priceless oriental artifacts and ornaments that had arrived with the

Spanish galleons were stored. More barrels with crystal, china and silver were hoisted into place. Antique furniture was protected with sheets, and chandeliers were hung from the ceiling. When the last load was accommodated, Antonieta had to squeeze through a narrow passageway to get out of the storeroom. She hired an extra watchman to guard the old convent and cautioned Mario and Amelia to keep the storage place a secret. Only the Grand Piano was moved to the new house.

The small family moved into their new home in the suburbs where Toñito immediately staked out his private corners. Ignacio occupied the chauffeur's quarters, Sabina and Conchita shared a room and a new cook and houseboy completed the staff which lived on the premises.

Every day Antonieta awakened with a sense of expectancy, the joyous feeling that comes with a busy, full life. Her calendar was filled. In six months, her salons at the house on Monterrey Street were the talk of the town. She was ferreting out young, fertile minds, finding them at the university, among Diego's friends, among the aristocracy, even a few among politicians she had met through Carlos. His Cabinet position as Secretary of Education opened important doors, and he had pledged to help her wherever and however he could. Chela's death was a strong bond between them. The international and diplomatic sets had yielded a crop of invitations, marketplaces where Antonieta scouted for those with knowledge to impart in the form of lectures. Between sips and bites, she extolled her special projects. She sponsored concerts, literary forums, poetry readings, charity affairs to raise money for the projects of others. Her most singular talent, it seemed, was as a catalyst: things happened around Antonieta Rivas Mercado.

Alone at night, Antonieta dwelled on the new turn her life had taken. Close to the surface of her consciousness was the family: Mario's growing moodiness was a reflection of his ardent love for Lucha and frustration with chaperones. They needed time alone to talk, to explore each other's mind and heart, to taste each other's lips. As the only daughter in a strict Catholic family, Lucha would be closely guarded until her marriage. Amelia was occupied with flirtations and sports. She spent most of her time at the Country Club, out of harm's way. It was Toñito who weighed on her heart. She was tormented by Albert's threat of abduction and had transmitted her fear to her son. One morning she had found two empty magnums of champagne flanking the head of his bed. Not knowing whether to laugh or scold, she had questioned the little boy. "In case a robber comes, Mami, I can crack him over the head with the bottles," Toñito had replied solemnly. He was alone too much, too confined to the house.

Below the conscious level, Antonieta battled her own contradictory nature. She yearned for close relationships, even as she cut people off. Men were attracted to her, she knew, but they kept their distance. Diego had once accused her of social bigotry and the shame speared her conscience. In fantasy, Antonieta appraised the acceptable men she had met, a few attractive bachelors in the diplomatic corps, a professor, a doctor. Why did they step back from her, withdraw? She did not understand that her intelligence got in her way. Men did not like to feel small in the presence of a woman.

Without knocking, Amelia came into the library and sat down in front of her sister's desk.

Antonieta looked up. "Pull your skirt down, Memela. They seem to be getting shorter all the time."

"Pooh," Amelia commented. She sat up straight. "I have to talk to you."

"About the car?"

"How did you know?"

Antonieta had given Mario the money to buy a long, green LaSalle that was the focus of admiration of the young set.

"Mario needs a car," Antonieta went on. "He's looking for work and can't go about on streetcars."

"Work?" Amelia twisted in her seat. "Mario has two obsessions, Lucha and airplanes, at extreme ends of the city, I might add. I never get to go where I want to go anymore. I need a car of my own."

"Under no circumstances," Antonieta said. "It's one thing to drive around with your brother, but quite another to drive a car by yourself. No."

"For heaven's sake, Antonieta, I'm eighteen! You were married at eighteen."

"God forbid you follow in my footsteps. If age is a factor, I am twenty-seven and still in charge. Why don't you take those art classes at the Department of Education I told you about last week? You could be a good painter if you weren't so lazy. Wouldn't that be better than being a bad tennis player?"

"A good tennis player," Amelia corrected. "And a fair golfer, and I'm becoming a whiz at bridge."

Antonieta folded her hands on the desk and leaned forward. "You spend your mornings at the club or poking through the same old stores over and over with your friends. Your afternoons you spend at the movies or those gossip sessions you girls call 'teas.' Aren't you bored?"

"No. I like my life," Amelia was unruffled. "I don't share your enthusiasm for half-starved literary *locos*. The cook says they are stealing the silverware."

"Don't be insolent," Antonieta retorted. "Listen, mi amor, I only stopped in here to file these papers and make some notes for tonight's lecture. Can we consider the car a dead issue?"

Antonieta's hat and gloves lay on the desk next to a leather portfolio. Amelia looked at her sister with sympathetic eyes. "You lost again, didn't you?"

"Yes," Antonieta answered.

"Damn Albert. Mierda!"

"Memela!"

"You should learn to swear. Albert has more political influence that you do. Why don't you ask Carlos to help?"

"I thought I had it won." Antonieta sighed. "We have filed an appeal. But they are moving the case to the jurisdiction of Albert's court now, out of our district. It may drag on for months. Rafael Lara says there is nothing we can do about it."

"We could shoot him," Amelia suggested.

"Thanks, mi amor." A smile alleviated the strained look. "Until custody is awarded, there can be no divorce. I still have no court order to prevent him from taking Toñito. He could walk right into this house and kidnap him."

"Never!" Amelia came around and put her arms around her sister's shoulders. "We'll guard him. Nobody's going to take Toñito from us."

Bright December sunlight streamed into Antonieta's study as she reviewed her notes on Maxim Gorki. Tonight was her last lecture in her series on contemporary writers. Gorki would appeal to her young students. Her "boys" had become more verbal, more articulate in these six weeks, as their intellects were stirred, overcoming an innate reticence to speak. Few bookstores in the Capital carried the new works. Antonieta sent to New York for most of their material. With difficulty she had obtained ten copies of Gorki's latest work, "Fragments from my Diary," to be shared among fifteen students. No one had money for books. Antonieta made a note on her pad: serve a buffet supper and wine tonight instead of *tamales* and coffee.

Conchita's knock at the door interrupted her. Antonieta pushed aside the papers on her desk to make room for the tray, knocking a carafe of water off the edge and breaking a fingernail in the attempt to catch it.

"Damn! First, mop up the water, then get my manicure case, Conchita," Antonieta instructed. "I want you to trim this nail and file the others while I eat with the other hand. You know where my manicure case is."

The flustered girl looked at her patroness in disbelief. One could always expect the unexpected with the Señora. "Do you trust me with the scissors?" she asked.

"If you cut me, you are fired. If you don't, my suspicion will be confirmed that you have been practicing with my manicure things." Antonieta smiled at the blushing girl. "Now hurry. I have a lot of work to do."

Conchita deftly groomed her mistress' nails while Antonieta read her notes and picked at the cheese and grapes on her breakfast tray. When both hands were finished, Conchita sat back nervously and waited for the verdict. Antonieta popped the last grape into her mouth and inspected her hands, tapered fingernails buffed to a high sheen, a pale crème rose outlining the cuticle as effectively as her regular manicurist could have done it.

"You have a professional touch, Conchita," Antonieta said, admiring her nails. "It occurs to me that you're wasting your time as a maid. There's a new French salon on Avenida Juárez. I'll find out who owns it and ask them to take you on as an apprentice."

Conchita's mouth fell open.

"Don't worry. You can live here. But you'll have a career!"

At lunch, Amelia announced casually, "I have invited Profesor Manuel Rodriguez Lozano to your lecture tonight."

"It's a closed group, Memela. Who is this professor?" Irritation clipped the question.

"My drawing teacher."

"But you have only taken two classes. What do you know about him?" Antonieta protested.

"What do you know about your starving *literarios*? Professor Rodriguez Lozano is the handsomest man I have ever seen, with the bluest eyes."

"Is he a good teacher?"

"Of course. He's the Director of the Manuel Arts Department at the *prepa* and an important modern painter. He says I have talent and has offered to give me private lessons."

Even a Director was paid a pittance, Antonieta knew. This "professor" needed money. Don't scold, she told herself. If he could hold Amelia's interest, she would pay for private lessons.

"He wants to meet you," Amelia added.

"All right, I will put in an extra chair for your *profesor*, but don't ever again invite anyone without consulting me."

Three rows of folding chair had been set up in the salon. Conversation ceased when Antonieta entered. Tonight she wore a white silk dress with an embroiderd Spanish shawl draped over one shoulder, a touch of drama accented by long gold earrings that swung free below her short, dark hair.

Antonieta greeted her students, set her papers on the polished top of the piano and took her place on the cushioned bench. She was immediately aware of blue eyes surveying her from the back row, next to Amelia. Quite a few of her students had greeted the man before taking their places. Evidently he was well-known. Not one you would forget, she assessed quickly. Indeed handsome, after the manner of an actor. No, a Spanish bullfighter, with the insolent look of one who thinks highly of himself. With a little nod of recognition, she commenced the lecture.

Without referring to her notes, Antonieta traced the biography of Gorki, words and intonation holding her audience as she talked. "He was a vagabond and novelist. His works have been translated into nine languages. Yet at fifteen he could hardly spell. Not erudite, not a molder of phrases, Gorki writes what he knows, what he has seen and experienced." Antonieta crossed her legs and let the fringes of the shawl spill over her lap. "His characters are thieves," she continued, "prostitutes, cheaters, people who sleep in the street...."

After the lecture, the students filed awkwardly into the dining room. Amelia served a plate for the professor and disappeared with it into the salon where she had left him comfortably seated. Antonieta felt sudden anger with her young sister's guest. He should have had the good manners to make more of a comment than "very interesting." The man was an arrogant, pseudo intellectual.

Second servings left wine bottles empty and the buffet table bare. Then Antonieta invited her students back to the salon to listen to a modern symphony. They sat stiff, like statues, throughout Honegger's harmonic audacities. When the music stopped, they stumbled to their feet and began to bid Antonieta goodbye. Amelia and her teacher remained seated on the divan.

"Andrés," Antonieta said, holding back a young man who spoke with a heavy Zapotec accent. "And you, Moreno Sanchez." She indicated his companion. "I want you to come back. I will be happy to receive you any time." They were worth cultivating, these two bright ones.

The professor stood up and extended his hand when she returned to the salon. He was the same height as she.

"I must be going, too. It was a privilege, Señora. You live up to your reputation. You are a muse." The blue eyes were admiring now.

"I think I turned my audience to stone with Honegger." Antonieta could not suppress a smile.

The professor laughed. "They would have been more at home if you had served tequila and played a *corrido*," he said. "Even I have difficulty with Honegger. I heard him personally in Paris."

"Oh," Antonieta said, intrigued. "Won't you stay awhile, professor? Amelia says you paint. Perhaps I can induce you to lecture to our group?'

"Only if you retract your invitation to the 'Professor'. I am Manuel Rodriguez Lozano and I flatter myself that I am a very good painter. I only teach from necessity."

Amelia quietly left the salon.

A week passed before he telephoned. Antonieta's calm voice belied her internal fluster. Manuel had been uppermost in her thoughts since the night of her Gorki lecture. They had talked until three in the morning. He was a devotee of the theater, knew the works of Gide and Cocteau and André Salmon. He had lived abroad for eight years; they shared an admiration for Marcel Proust. Not married. But there was a mystery about him; he was almost too elegant and cosmopolitan to be the bohemian he claimed to be. If she could see his paintings she could better judge the real man.

"Lunch tomorrow, Manuel? Let me see. Yes, I would be delighted."

Antonieta hung up the receiver and looked at her calendar. She would cancel the luncheon she had. The following evening there was a reception for Charles Lindbergh at the American Embassy residence. She was already on a first-name basis with the wife of the new Ambassador, Dwight Morrow, who had been sent down to placate Calles. In view of her relationship with the Ambassador, she had obtained an invitation for Mario and Lucha. Did she dare take Manuel as her escort? Lindbergh's nonstop "goodwill" flight from Washington to Mexico City had made him a national hero. Everyone in Mexico was clamoring to shake the aviator's hand. It was a form of bribery, she admitted, but it might pave the way to inviting Manuel to escort her to other holiday affairs. Christmas was around the corner.

The old Porfirian mansion which housed the Centro Austuriano restaurant was crowded. Manuel rose at once when he saw his guest enter and led her to a table by a window. Antonieta's expression changed abruptly. There was another man at the table.

"This is Lorenzo," Manuel said, without adding a last name. "He is my model. I have been painting all morning, and even he gets hungry." He held out a chair for Antonieta next to his own.

They talked animatedly during the meal, Lorenzo fading into the background as though he were not present. After dwelling long on the subjects of art and Europe, Manuel suddenly asked, "Do you like the bullfight?"

"The only time I have been in the bullring is when Pavlova performed there in 1919. The whole place went wild when she danced the *Jarabe* on her toes and bent down to scoop up the hat. Can a matador promise a more dramatic act than that?"

"One has to be taught to appreciate the bullfight," Manuel said. "Is there anything you can be taught?" His eyes mocked.

"I have been a student all my life," Antonieta replied defensively. Then she smiled. "I would consider it a privilege if you would allow me to visit your studio."

Manuel studied the intense eyes. "I am proud of my work. I shall be proud to show it to you."

"When?" Antonieta pursued.

"Tomorrow afternoon," Manuel answered. "Does four o'clock suit you?"

"I shall be there." She did not mention the reception for Lindbergh.

The house was downtown, tucked away in a neighborhood which bordered on the working-class area, not far from the Academy of San Carlos. It was a narrow house; the front wall had recently been painted an earth brown. She surmised that his studio was on the roof where a few potted geraniums hung down, grazing the small windows on the second floor. At exactly the appointed hour, Antonieta rang the doorbell. A sandal-shod servant girl answered. To her surprise, Andrés came in to greet her, the young Zapotec student whom she had invited to return after her last lecture on contemporary writers.

"Señora, welcome," Andrés said, extending his hand, his tongue still coating his words with an Indian accent.

"What are you doing here?" Antonieta asked, pleased to see her young student who wanted to be a writer and was struggling to dominate the Spanish language.

"You brought me luck," the young man informed her. "The next day in school, the professor said, 'Look, you and your books will fit in the servant's room on the roof next to my studio. I will lend it to you.' The servant girl is going home," he added. "I call him Manuel; he is waiting for you in his studio."

From the second floor they walked up a winding iron spiral to the roof. An ample, white-washed room took up most of the space. Andrés knocked and disappeared.

Manuel opened the door. "You came," he said.

"Of course." Antonieta handed him a bouquet of fresh violets. "I wanted to share the aroma of my garden with you."

"Thank you." Manuel removed some paint brushes from a cracked Chinese vase, and placed the violets in it. The easels were covered with cloth and the paintings which hung on the wall were turned around.

For a painter to show a stranger his work is like exposing his soul, Antonieta knew. She sat on a stool and folded her hands. "Well?"

"I want to show them to you one by one," Manuel explained, "so that each painting stands on its own merit."

Slowly, he began to reveal his work.

The collection was a striking chronicle of Mexican life. The style was stark, devoid of useless objects or ornamentation: a humble man seated on a park bench, silent, white-robed women wringing their hands in lamentation, a prostitute in a desert setting, children of the street turning sad faces to the spectator. His compositions were precise, his figures grim, stylized, even ugly, not the idealized indigenous race portrayed by Diego. Antonieta could see traces of academic conventions, but his style was his own, colors dominated by gray, brown, and black tonalities, coming from the soul of a man haunted by human misery but not truly able to capture its essence. Certain affectations and elegance kept his realism from ringing true.

With the keen eye of a trained observer, Antonieta took it in, wondering what tormented him.

"It is too much of an impact on my poor brain to encompass it all," she commented. "I can't compare you to anybody else. It is the style of Manuel Rodriguez Lozano." She turned and faced him where he leaned against the wall, arms folded, watching her. "I feel your struggle, Manuel, and I admire your work. It is not easy to be oneself. When did you paint the self portrait? You don't do yourself justice."

"In 1924," Manuel replied flatly.

"And whose portrait is that?" she asked, pointing to an intense male face which she recognized as the model in several nude drawings.

"His name was Abraham."

"Was he a friend?" she asked gently.

"He died in this studio," Manuel replied in the same flat tone. "Shall I tell you about his death?" The question had a belligerent tone.

Antonieta folded her hands in her lap and looked up at the artist. "If you will trust me with your feelings, Manuel, I would like to be your friend."

Manuel picked up a pack of cigarettes, lit one and walked over to the Victrola. The music of Mahler began to fill the stark studio; tinted with a strange nostalgia, it calmed him. He drew up a stool opposite Antonieta and blew smoke toward the skylight. At last he began to talk.

"Cocaine is a palliative for the misery of the world, a transitory relief, a putting off of things that suffocate. Abraham was obsessed with death, but he thought youth was indestructible." The smoke from his cigarette rose in ribbons to the ceiling. "I am more like Dorian Gray. In my hallucinations, beauty and youth are always present. Death is the pinch of salt in the sweet. It makes life more intense. If we knew when we were going to die there would be no urgency in living. Abraham never understood. He didn't mean to take an overdose."

Mahler, in a profound lyric movement, touched the human chord. "He was very dear to you," Antonieta said softly.

"Yes."

Manuel crushed the cigarette in a paint-stained ashtray and began to turn his paintings back to the wall. "I know you are a friend of Diego Rivera and so I must tell you that I consider his work commercial, pretty, without substance. Folkloric stuff. I also have no admiration for David Siqueiro's sensationalism or Orozco's crude figures. I'm a severe critic. And I am a better painter than any of them! I don't spend my life living a conception of how I think I should live or how others think I should live. I live my life as I feel it. Totally. Have you the fortitude to be my friend, Antonieta?"

The blue eyes held hers in their grip. Antonieta felt vulnerable; she was attracted to this man. Finally she said with a trace of amusement: "I would like to know you better." It was a statement without commitment.

The reception for Charles Lindbergh sparkled with the elegance and bright chatter of the international set. Antonieta greeted friends, moving about the gracious mansion, but Manuel's tense face lingered in her mind. She had left him alone in the studio, before he wished her to go, silently demanding that he be more important than this reception. It had been necessary to break away abruptly.

She made small talk. She pretended to listen. She watched Mario engage the tall, lanky aviator in conversation during a moment when Lindbergh was miraculously free. Carlos waved to her, and across the room she saw Albert turn and walk toward the dining room. Sidestepping a waiter balancing a tray of hors d'oeuvres, she moved onto the veranda, smiling, joining fragments of conversation. She had played this scene before; suddenly it was all a stage. Manuel's stark studio was reality.

"Antonieta!"

Her attention was claimed by the Ambassador from Colombia, who led her to a circle of Latin American colleagues discussing José Vasconcelos' scorching criticism of Calles in his latest article published in "El Universal".

"How long do you think 'El Universal' will continue to publish

Vasconcelos?" a South American asked.

"Vasconcelos has a wide following in Mexico. It may not be wise to silence him," the Colombian remarked.

Antonieta moved on.

A group had formed around Anne Morrow, the Ambassador's attractive young daughter, who was on vacation from college. They were talking about Mexican Christmas traditions.

"There you are!"

Mrs. Dean, an American acquaintance, accosted Antonieta. "President Calles has asked Mrs. Morrow to help with a puppet program they are preparing for the schools. It's a way to teach children some of the basic rules of hygiene and good nutrition through entertainment." Mrs. Dean whispered. "Frankly I think it was Betty Morrow's idea. Calles listens to her, you know. Have you heard about it?" Mrs. Dean touched Antonieta's arm to focus her attention. "Betty is forming a committee of volunteers. We need your help, Antonieta. You will help, won't you?"

"Of course," Antonieta replied mechanically. "Have you the fortitude to be my friend?" rang in her head.

CHAPTER XXVII
1928

Life took on a new hue, a new accelerated pace. Antonieta moved from her crowded salons to popular cafes to Manuel's studio to the sawdust-covered floors of dance halls, a life that moved to the sensuous rhythm of rumbas and tangos, fast-stepping *danzones* and the paso doble. She became a devotee of the bullfight and mixed with threadbare intellectuals and women with florid vocabularies. Manuel lived on another plane of city life.

"Mexico is composed in counterpoint" Antonieta wrote in her diary, "two highly charged extremes: stagnation and forward movement. Like the artist he is, Manuel sees everything in sharp contrast. He has become my mentor, teaching me to see this Mexico I did not know. We still address each other as *usted*. I think the familiar *tu* is hidden behind fear of intimacy. I long to tear down the veil of formality that hangs between us, but I patiently wait for a sign from him."

Mario came storming into the breakfast room one morning holding a shirt in his hand.

"I found this in my closet," he said. "Whose is it?"

"Sorry, dear," Antonieta said. "The new maid's mistake."

"It's Manuel's, isn't it? Now you are doing the cabrón's laundry!"

"Don't be vulgar! His maid is on vacation, so I offered. Is that a crime?"

"Well I want to make my position clear. I can't stand him! He's an arrogant bastard, thinks he's the king of the world, but the truth is he's just a poor, lousy bureaucrat. And a worse artist. To think you paid him for that portrait he did of you!"

Mario draped the offensive shirt on the back of a chair and sat down. "What do you see in him?"

"A brilliant mind and a sensitive human being who has more talent in his little finger than your whole bunch of dilettante friends put together," she retorted sharply.

"He's a poor, damned homosexual, Antonieta." There, it had been said. "So are those *Contemporaneos* you hang around with," Mario added.

Antonieta looked over at her brother. "Where can I be safer than among homosexuals? Let me explain something. They're the most intelligent and stimulating people in Mexico, and they are creating something new, exposing the soul of Mexico in poetry, essays, books, painting!" Antonieta stopped abruptly. "You don't understand, do you?"

"No. Look at you, you're exhausted. You stay up half the night translating their works. And now you're paying to have their works published, aren't you?"

"You've been snooping in my office!" Antonieta accused her brother angrily.

He jumped up. "The bills were lying in plain sight on your desk." Wadding up the shirt, he threw it at her. "They're using you, Antonieta. Why don't you find yourself a man!" Mario slammed the door behind him.

Her brother's tirade pierced Antonieta's calm exterior. She leaned on the table and held her head in her hands. She knew that Manuel was beyond her reach. Yet, for awhile, she had hoped. He had been married once, to Carmen Mondragón, that half-crazed woman who was Dr. Atl's lover. They said she was young and beautiful then, the daughter of General Mondragón, who had conspired with Huerta to assassinate Madero. She was a good catch for a military cadet of meager means. Antonieta could not picture Manuel in a military uniform, but she knew it was true. The General was given a diplomatic post and took his daughter and son-in-law with him to Europe. It was in Paris that Manuel started to paint. When they returned to Mexico six or seven years later, he found the official artistic doors closed and took up with the fringe artists. Carmen divorced him and became the eccentric outcast called Nahui Olin. With some doubt, Antonieta contemplated the story that she had suffocated their child in Europe. Only a deranged mind could commit such an act. Or had she become deranged because her husband was a homosexual? No matter, Carmen had destroyed herself. Manuel was not responsible, this Manuel who had opened up a world of new values to her, this irrational Manuel who lived on the periphery of the great new Mexican art movement, launching his malevolence at the muralists. I don't care what you are, she thought. You're my teacher, my alter ego. You understand me. And I am your friend.

In theater, cheap vaudeville, mediocre comedies and operettas seemed to satisfy the society they served. Mario did not understand that they did not satisfy her new friends, the Contemporaneos. Remembering the freakish clothes and shocking language of Montparnasse, Antonieta was amused by these literary novices who had bestowed upon her the title of "Muse."

Antonieta stretched and let the spring breeze blow across her scantily clad body. Then she put on her robe and rang for the maid. "We will be eleven for dinner tonight, possibly twelve. If you have any questions, ask Sabina how to set the table. I won't be home until late."

She had a date with her lawyer this morning. Albert was on a protracted trip to the United States and her lawyer wanted to take advantage of his absence to advance her case if at all possible. He was trying to move it to the Supreme Court. Now she could at least breathe freely.

Tonight she had invited the elite cadre of the *Contemporaneos* to discuss a new project. They would start the meeting with a reading of O'Neill's "The Great God Brown." O'Neill slashed romantic sentimentality; his was the drama of realism. O'Neill would set the mood for her new project.

Promptly at eight o'clock that night the doorbell began to ring. Xavier Villaurrutia was the first to arrive, a pile of folders under his arm. Xavier was handsome, aristocratic and malicious. Brooding Gilberto Owen brought his translation of Paul Valery's "Unedited Prose." Bernardo Ortiz de Montellano had completed two translations, of T.S. Eliot and Joyce. They continued to arrive: Jorge Cuesta's good looks were spoiled by a drooping eye. A chemist, Jorge could fix wine so it wouldn't make you drunk and could also de-toxify cigarettes. Elias Nandino, a young doctor, showed rare sensitivity in his attempts at poetry. Carlos Pellicer far overshadowed the other poets. Dubbed "the longhair" because of his aversion to barber shops, Carlos was a published poet, sometimes compared to Pablo Neruda, the young Chilean who had broken into the international literary set at age twenty-four. Arriving late, Salvador Novo apologized to Antonieta.

"Mr. Ford is forming a new caste. My taxi got caught in the most god-awful traffic jam. Sorry, Antonieta."

Last to arrive were Manuel and Malu Cabrera, daughter of the lawyer who had spearheaded the Constitution of 1917. Malu's mother was the granddaughter of a Belgian lady-in-waiting to the Empress Carlota. An avant-garde young woman, Malu had spent most of her life in Europe and New York. She was among the few women Antonieta had cultivated and liked. Antonieta was thirsty for intellectual stimulation.

At two in the morning, they still lingered at the table making tentative calculations. Could this group finance an experimental theater?

"In order to move fast, and before some of you begin to back out, I will fund

the theater until the productions themselves can pay me back," Antonieta offered. "And I have a property I think is suitable. If the Washington Square Players started in a warehouse on the docks of New York, our Teatro Ulises can start in a converted warehouse, too."

Salvador tapped his glass for attention: "I propose a toast to El

Teatro Ulises and its patroness, Antonieta Rivas Mercado.
More toasts were made. Wine flowed.

Theater fever affected everyone, creating a cooperative mood, where no one was reluctant to do the most menial task. At the play readings, acting talent was soon revealed. The most promising actress among the neophytes was Antonieta herself. "Orpheus," by Jean Cocteau, was selected to open the theater. Tickets were by invitation, the program hand-typed.

One reporter mentioned the performance in his column: "Members of this experimental theater declare that the Mexican stage is backward, mediocre, shoddy. What virtues do these amateurs bring to the theater? The play, itself, did not entertain, which everyone knows is the purpose of theater." Contradicting the critic, the next day a French theatrical "expert" wrote that the Cocteau play was well understood by the director, and the young Mexican actors showed promise. The professionals laughed, predicting that *Ulises* would soon be dashed on the rocks. But a core of fans continued to fill the seats. Only a select audience understood the wedge these dedicated young people were driving into the world of dramatic art.

In her diary Antonieta noted: "I cringe to think what Cocteau himself would think of our production, but it is a beginning." Soon the theater totally absorbed her. Antonieta translated plays by Gide, Shaw, and Lord Dunsany.

A rehearsal of Gide's "School for Women" was in full sway when Manuel entered the theater. Under his talented direction, the simple set had magically transformed the small stage. On cue, Antonieta moved to center front.

"All right, take a break," Julio, the director, called out. "I'm glad you came, Manuel. I want some changes made on the set. That window's too high and this black wall is distracting. Can you tone it down?"

"If you stand at the back you will see that the window is the right height and as for the black wall, I created it for stark contrast," Manuel answered hotly.

"Look, I am the director and I think I have the right to make alterations."

Antonieta stood still. Tempers flared when Manuel did not get his way. That periphery he lives on, she thought. If only he would allow himself to be accepted. He was an asset to the theater. Again, she played arbiter in the argument.

After the final performance Antonieta's long Cadillac pulled up to El Pirata,

the dance hall she had recently opened on the premises of the convent of San Jerónimo. Waiters scurried around to clean off a table. The presence of the elegant owner and her entourage always caused a stir.

"Why didn't you tell me you owned El Pirata?" Mario demanded to know, accosting Antonieta at breakfast. "Lucha's mother just found out, and you know how that sets!"

"I inherited a wreck of a building and decided to remodel it into a dance hall. I like to dance and a dance hall is good business."

"You mean you like to dance with Manuel!"

"Yes, he's a superb dancer." Calmy, Antonieta continued. "You may tell Mrs. Rule that to enter my dance hall all men must wear ties." She shrugged.

"Ties? And sawdust on the floor! You're crazy, Antonieta. Besides, a dance hall on the grounds of a convent is sacrilegious."

"You sound like Lucha's mother." Antonieta hugged her brother. "Sneak off and take Lucha. Dance all night. I'll give you a card, carte blanche."

Poor Mario was smoldering in a private hell. Mrs. Rule would not permit her daughter to be married until the churches in Mexico reopened their doors. Mario and Lucha needed time alone. Antonieta thought of the professor in Spain. Physical passion was only a memory, a dead realm in her life. There was no one.

Quite by accident, Antonieta recognized Tina Modotti through the smoky haze. She and Manuel and their usual entourage had followed avid fans of the bullfight downtown to a cafe where *aficionados* gathered. She slid around the crowded booth to the outside seat. The bar was filled with boisterous men and women who moved from one partner to another. Tina saw her and waved. Antonieta motioned her to come over and stood up to greet Diego's sultry Italian model.

"Tina! It's good to see you."

She introduced her friend, Julio Mella. "I saw your play. I would like to come by and take some photographs. You look wonderful on stage."

"I accept. We need some good publicity shots." Antonieta turned to Tina's friend. "She has rare talent with the camera."

"She has rare talent in everything," Mella replied. They kissed.

"What news of Diego?" Antonieta asked. "I haven't seen him since he returned from Moscow."

"Lupe left him. Got a divorce and married someone else."

"Oh. Where is he living?"

"I'll give you his address." Tina scribbled it on a paper napkin.

Antonieta entered the dingy building and walked up to the first floor. Diego himself answered the doorbell.

"Well, hello!" he greeted her with obvious pleasure. "Come in."

The apartment was much larger than the little house he had shared with Lupe. In the ample studio, life-size papier-mâché devils hung from the ceiling, Aztec figures crammed shelves and stacks of canvases leaned against the walls. Diego led her to a table where a tin coffee pot perked.

Antonieta ducked under a devil's spear and took off her hat.

"I wondered when you would show up," Diego said. "Hear you have been cavorting with that Rasputin, Manuel Rodriguez Lozano. He is a real devil, you know, carries people off to his paranoiac hell and burns them at the altar of his ego."

"I hope that means you're jealous."

"Of Rodriguez Lozano? He can't even paint. Here, have a seat. You're looking very beautiful." He pulled up a painted wooden chair.

"I like your place. It has the bachelor touch." Antonieta grinned, looking around at the disarray. She emptied a rancid ashtray into a small trash can by the table.

Diego sat down beside her, his eyes roving over her face, the V-neck of her dress. "I like the smell of rancid tobacco. It's a human scent like the smell of sweat in a wool shirt and the musky odors of passionate love. Can I assume that it is my masculine magnetism that has brought you here?"

"Yes and no. I just like to talk to you, Diego."

"It can get pretty sterile up here."

"You miss Lupe, don't you."

"Lupe who?"

"The lady who slashed your canvases. The one you were married to."

"Did I tell you we were married? I exaggerate, you know." Diego reached out and turned Antonieta's face to a profile view. "I should paint a good portrait of you. How about a tequila? I'm tired of coffee."

"Tell me about Russia. I hear you did a portrait of Stalin." Antonieta looked at the disheveled painter with a beguiling smile. "I have missed you, Diego. What's the status of art in paradise?"

"Paralyzed," Diego said. "We'll talk about that at another time."

In his baggy best, Diego began to be seen around town with a variety of ladies; soon, the most talked about was Antonieta. The sight of Diego and Antonieta driving down Reforma in the long Cadillac with the top down, a black fur lap robe thrown over their legs, Diego leaning grandly on his painted wooden cane, became an item for the gossip columns: "What do the the chairman of the Russian Anti-Imperialist League and the Muse of the "Contemporaries" have in common? Could it be romance?" a tabloid writer asked.

"What do you see in him?" Amelia asked at supper.

"Diego's amusing. He makes me laugh. The other day he said he wanted to show me the best murals in Mexico. You know where he took me? Into a cantina in that tangle of the Merced market. The caricatures were abominable—and fantastic! Now Diego claims he's going to paint murals all over the walls of the Palace. Can you imagine?" Antonieta laughed.

"Albert's back," Amelia said quietly.

"How do you know?"

"Rafael Lara called. He's been trying to get hold of you. But since you're never home, I took the message. And did you know that Toñito had a fever yesterday!" she finished accusingly.

It was Alicia who was the harbinger of news that robbed Antonieta of all peace. While Toñito and his cousins were scrambling under a broken *piñata* at a birthday party in the garden of Alicia's mansion on Reforma, she took her sister aside.

"Come upstairs, I must talk to you," Alicia said.

Antonieta followed her sister up the sweeping stairway to a private sitting room, where a tray of refreshments awaited. Her heart was pounding for some inexplicable reason. Alicia sipped a glass of tamarind water and swallowed several times.

"First, I want you to know that although I don't approve of the company you keep, what I am going to tell you is not a rebuke." She bit her lip. "Please try to understand. Whatever you may think of Pepe and me, you are my sister and your well-being will always concern me."

A knot tightened in Antonieta's throat as she observed the beautiful, poised lady who sat in front of her. She waited.

"Josefina Godoy was here for lunch on Monday. She is the wife of Ruben Godoy, one of Pepe's attorneys, from the north somewhere, a bit crude, but a good Catholic. Anyway, she is a first cousin of Calles' private secretary and brags that she has inside information. Calles' doesn't know that she's a member of The League."

"What League?"

"The Catholic League of Defenders of Religious Freedom. All of us at the table belong to it." There was pride in Alicia's voice. "Of course, we were eager to hear any new rumors about reprisals against The League. So many houses have been raided lately, and we are all harboring priests and nuns." She took another sip. "I left the table to attend to one of the children …" She paused, deliberating, looking for words. "When I came back I heard a snatch of gossip, about you, of course. Josefina had her back to me and I heard her say, "Antonieta's husband is preparing to declare her an unfit mother. Maybe that will bring her to her senses.""

Antonieta's face was ashen.

"Ruben is also Albert's attorney." Alicia reached out and placed her hand over her sister's. "Be careful. He plans to have you followed."

"You offer asylum to priests, you said yourself that you hide them in this house." Antonieta squeezed her sister's hand. "Please hide Toñito."

"Albert's purpose is not to kidnap him," Alicia said reassuringly. "He wants legal custody, to send him away to school in the United States. Away from you."

"Hide him, Alicia, please. I can't take that risk."

"You must, to prove to Albert you have nothing to hide."

Antonieta stared at her sister, her brain numbed by Alicia's disclosure.

"I take risks every day," Alicia said matter-of-factly. You get used to it. People die, children have to be baptized, couples have to be married, Mass must be celebrated. Because Calles has declared war on the Church, the laws of God don't cease to exist." Alicia's voice was calm as she talked. "I am so grateful that Pepe built a private chapel in this house. Priests perform their pastoral duties here every day."

"My God, Alicia, aren't you afraid they will be recognized?"

Alicia's eyes had a glint of mischief. "They rotate, and we send them out on the street in workers' clothes, a chauffeur's uniform, even disguised as women." She laughed. "You should see Father Agustín. He looks pregnant. Of course, if a priest were caught he would be shot, like Padre Pro, and Pepe and I would go to jail. But who is to tell on us when every family in the block is a member of the League? We work in cells to raise funds for the *Cristeros*. You are not living this war, Antonieta, you don't know how easy it is to take risks."

Antonieta felt humbled by Alicia's speech. "I didn't know how involved you were," she said. "And you are right. I have nothing to hide."

The sisters kissed, a new respect established between them.

As Antonieta drove home, the irony of the Cristero war struck full force. The Constitution that divided the Church and State had closed the Catholic churches, but Albert's beloved Christian Science church was open, as were all Protestant churches. And the Masonic Order was flagrantly displayed in the Palace. That same sacred Constitution that the Calles' Government so loudly defended had just been changed to allow Obregón to run again for President. Photographs of the President-elect were plastered all over the city, even on the walls of her dance hall. The Sacred Constitution! Hypocrites, she thought angrily.

Wherever she went, Antonieta imagined eyes following her. She stopped visiting Manuel and Diego altogether. At the theater, she gave notice that she was taking a vacation, and pleaded with her lawyers to use every foul means to obtain her divorce. At night, she fought dark shadows and by day poured her energy into translations of plays, essays, and poetry. She pondered long over William Blake and James Joyce. She met Carlos in the Secretariat of Education Building to set up the new Cultural Department she had suggested. She couldn't be criticized for promoting cultural events in the schools. Walking past Diego's magnificent murals evoked nostalgic pangs. Eyes seemed to follow even there. Her lawyer advised her not to give Albert the smallest reason to accuse her. She fought to put down anger and a desire for revenge at this calumny, this affront to her self-esteem. More than the failure of a marriage, which mattered little to her now, was confronting her own huge error in handling her divorce. She should never have charged him with failure to support her in Europe. Albert's pride could not bear the slightest accusation of impropriety. She would rather throw a bomb, create a scandal, cause a storm which cleared the air, than live with the ever-tightening screw of fear of losing her son. After a month Antonieta's nerves were stretched like a tightrope wire.

"Mamá, Mamá!" Toñito ran toward the car, waving to his mother when he got out of school. "Can I invite Jaime and Lalo to come over this afternoon?"

The Cadillac filled up with Toñito's playmates. She invented games to amuse them and took them to the see Charlie Chaplin and "Our Gang" movies. Memela and Mario organized a trip to Xochimilco, where the little boys "helped" to pole the flat-bottomed boat through the canals and dragged their fingers through the water collecting lily pods, which they popped with gleeful vengeance. Antonieta enrolled her son in an equestrian school so that he could ride with her on Sundays. She organized family picnics. After a few weeks, the big bottles disappeared from the head of Toñito's bed. Contentment filled the little boy's heart, but he sensed the tension in his mother.

"Why haven't you been working at the theater, Mamá?" Toñito asked. "It's been more than a month."

"I'm on vacation," Antonieta replied, stooping to kiss him. Guilt pierced her when she realized how much she had neglected her son. "Don't you like to have me on vacation?"

"Of course. But you are happier when you work."

Coming into her office without warning, Amelia unleashed a tempest of tears and wrath: "How could he! He's been flirting with me for a year, kissing me, mauling me, and now he announces his engagement to Margarita! The snake, the worm, the bastard!" she ranted and refused to leave her room.

"I am thinking of starting a small airline with some friends," Mario told her. Out of Acapulco. There are some economics to work out...."

"In early July, Antonieta received a note from Salvador Novo: "Last night I dreamed you invited me for lunch. The ravioli was heavenly. Could my dream be prophetic?"

Ignacio delivered her reply. "If you and Xavier will come Thursday at 2:00, I will interpret your dream."

At lunch, Salvador turned his saucer-like eyes toward his hostess and said, "Now, dear friend, tell us why you have abandoned us. Teatro Ulises is foundering without you."

"The truth is, Ulises has reached the shore," Antonieta said. "All of you are ready to go on to a bigger theater, bigger productions. It's time to close Ulises."

After Toñito was in bed, Antonieta sat in her office. She tried to review a translation of T.S. Eliot, but depression pulled at every attempt at concentration. I shall bury Ulises, she told herself, in a plain pine box, without mourners. And then, what would fill her hours? She reached up on the bookshelf and pulled down Xavier's book, "Reflections." A note fell out. She read it again: "Antonieta, I travel around in my bedroom in a tedious ocean, trying to write. This work did get published, and I value your opinion. Xavier." She opened the book at random and read: "I am more my own reflection, my echo, my shadow than I am this 'I' I have invented." From deep inside her a question welled up: "Have I invented this Self that inhabits an empty shell? This Self that is never satisfied?" She looked at the picture of her father on her desk. And Tío Beto. In her turbulent ocean, they were a receding shore. A nostalgia seemed to rise from that deep well and seep through her skin.

The German Shepherd barked outside her window. Antonieta closed her diary and locked it in a drawer. There were decisions to be made: She would send Memela to Europe with Mamá. The trip would distract her, and she got along with Mamá. Mario needed to become rooted in something, perhaps the airline. Air travel was defintely the way of the future.

Manuel called and insisted they meet.

Every eye turned to look as Antonieta entered Monotes, *a* popular cafe frequented by artists and the young bohemian crowd. The owner was the brother of the painter, Clemente Orozco, and tacked on the walls were dozens of his brutally satirical drawings and caricatures from the world of drunkards and prostitutes. Clemente depicted the Revolution as it really was, Antonieta thought, not the fantasy which Diego saw. For a pittance, one could remove the tack and carry off his pictures.

The proprietor greeted her effusively.

"How is Clemente?" she asked, extending her hand.

"Still painting gigantic murals in Guadalajara, Señora."

Orozco had left for Guadalajara at the invitation of Governor Zuno, a socialist who sheltered the Red artists' syndicate. "Please ask him to call me when he comes to the city. I miss him," Antonieta said.

The pleased proprietor escorted her to Manuel's table.

"Manuel," Antonieta greeted him warmly, "How I've missed you."

Manuel kissed her hand. "I thought it was time to get you out of seclusion."

"It's my divorce, you know."

Manuel lit a cigarette and blew the smoke in the air as though to dismiss the subject. He always recoiled from personal discussions. Soon, their conversation began to flow: They talked of Novo's new theatrical venture, of Heifitz' concert, of Antonieta's newly formed Cultural Department.

"I want to introduce dance, art, poetry contests, theater at the grammar school level, stir a child's creativity at an early age. But I can already see that bureaucracy moves with agonizing slowness. Maybe if I had a desk. What do you think?"

"Demand one while your friend Carlos is still Secretary of Education. And be prepared for your beautiful plans to gather dust with the change of administration." Manuel's voice was astringent. "With Obregón coming in again, God knows if I'll have a job."

A portfolio lay on a chair. Antonieta knew that her opinions about his work had always been important to Manuel. "Are these drawings for your new mural Manuel? May I see them?"

With that peculiar reserve which he still exhibited when it came to his creations, Manuel opened the portfolio. Antonieta went through them one by one. Hard, stark lines portrayed a crueler Mexico than Clemente's bawdy gallery. Emotions here were studied.

"I want the truth," Manuel said.

She had to tell him. "I find them too severe." She reached out and put her hand over his. "You speak more fully with your colors."

Manuel retreated again behind his wall of reserve. "I had another reason for inviting you here. Carlos Chavez wants to meet you. He wants to form a symphony orchestra. I don't know if you should meet him."

"Salvador mentioned him. In fact, I made a date to meet him next week. Why are you opposed?"

"He's a self-centered bastard who wants to use you. Why didn't you consult me first?"

Manuel's reaction stunned her. "Chavez sounds like a capable musician," Antonieta answered.

"He approached me for an introduction to you and I refused. He wants your money." Manuel's voice rose, strident, caustic. "So now

Novo is your adviser," he continued. Every eye was on their table.

"Oh, Manuel, for heaven's sake. If you want to be an adviser in my life, I must at least form an opinion before I can be advised," Antonieta replied with quiet ire. "This man seems well versed in modern works and Mexico needs to face a few realities...."

"There's the reality of Mexico!" Manuel cut in, pointing to a dirty child who was begging at the tables. "It seems you only throw your gold coins out to those who can satisfy your whims!"

Shocked at the public tirade, Antonieta abruptly stood up, went over and took the little beggar by the hand. She marched with him to the front door and stalked out. Curious patrons got up and went to the door, watched her cross the street to a small bakery and emerge clutching two huge paper sacks. She handed them to the mother of the small beggar, huddled in her filth on the corner. Then she walked back to the cafe and addressed the proprietor.

"Señor Orozco, please take down every drawing on the wall. I want to buy them all."

Prostitutes, burdened workers, wild-eyed revolutionaries, murderous drunkards piled up as the tacks were removed.

"Thank you. Tell Clemente that I shall treasure these drawings. They're vibrant examples of the real Mexico."

Antonieta gathered up the pictures and swept out to applause.

On the way home, she began to feel contrite. Then she thought about her relationship with Manuel: handsome, brilliant, witty Manuel was another illusion, a reflection she had invented.

As the truth dawned, she began to laugh. Manuel was as arrogant and unyielding as Albert. His need to stand stage center had provoked the scene.

On July seventeenth, 1928, at a victory luncheon for President-elect Obregón, an artist made his way to the head table and took out a drawing pad. He deftly sketched an excellent portrait of Obregón and walked around behind the long table, receiving the approval of high officials as he made his way to the guest of honor. In that instant, the artist took out a pistol and blasted Obregón in the back of the head.

The newspaper extra exploded on the streets as Antonieta was driving to her appointment with Carlos Chavez. The assassin, the headlines screamed, was a member of the Catholic League.

"Ignacio," Antonieta called out, "turn around and go back to Reforma. I must see my sister."

Cold fear gripped her. There would be a crackdown. They would begin to search every house, round up every member of the League and arrest them. It was rumored that the basement of police headquarters was worse than the Inquisition. Alicia and Pepe and the children must leave Mexico!

The mansion on Reforma looked as serene as usual. A starched maid opened the door and led Antonieta up the stairway to her sister's sitting room. Soon Alicia appeared, unruffled.

"Leave?" Alicia scoffed. "They can prove nothing! But I will tell you that the maid who opened the door is Sister Dolores and the parlor maid is Sister Cecilia from Puebla. They are on their way to Guanajuato to serve as nurses. The fighting there has been fierce."

"I didn't know you had such strength, Alicia. It's dangerous. How will you get them to Guanajuato?"

"It's all arranged," Alicia said. "We have done it many times. Thank heaven we have only one priest as a guest at the moment. Father Agustín Alvarez."

"But he's too well known to hide!" Antonieta exclaimed, shock and concern in her voice. Chela's wedding flashed in her mind. Father Augustín had officiated at society weddings since she could remember. His round, florid face and balding head peering out from the Sunday Rotogravure was pinned up in the homes of poor and rich alike. Sabina revered him next to the Virgin and Jesus. "I thought he had been expelled from the country long ago. "He's back?"

"Yes." Alicia stated simply. "Mexico needs him. Father Augustin's pen is as powerful as his oratory. He writes letters to the Cristeros all the time, providing spiritual support so needed by our poor Cristero fighters. When he is not writing, he spends his time going from house to house, praying for the sick, comforting the grieved, and counseling the needy." A sly smile spread across her lovely face. "Of course the authorities know he is back, but they can't find him. Come, I'll show you why. He has a special room in our house," Alicia said.

She led the way down the stairway to the paneled English library on the ground floor where the men gathered after dinner. The heavy brass andirons glowed in the ample fireplace, already laid with wood for a rainy July evening. Alicia ran her hand over the polished wood paneling and touched a small square to the right of the mantle. A crack appeared and she swung open a door, revealing a room large enough for a bed, a straight chair, and a nightstand. Antonieta peered in, fascinated, and saw that the room was vented by a window-grate which opened onto the front garden, hidden by a hedge. Scenes of the basement at Héroes came to mind. Alicia turned on a small electric light and closed the door. No vestige of light or of the secret door could be detected in the symmetrical paneling.

"There's a trap door under the nightstand which leads to the the wine cellar and out through the back of the house. Pepe added that touch last year." Alicia's voice brimmed with pride. "Pepe built this room to store his most valuable treasures when he travelled," she explained. "Four priests have hidden here."

"Where is Father Agustín now?"

Alicia looked at her watch. "He should be driving back in a gray wig and cook's uniform pretty soon," she said. "A poor woman arrived all the way from Jalisco today to have a Mass said for her dead husband. Only Father Agustin could comfort her."

Tossing from side to side, fighting insomnia, fear began its insidious invasion of Antonieta's mind. In addition to the fear of being followed, fear for her sister's safety battered her conscience. She remembered a sleepy little girl in rag curlers trailing a tall angel, who was sleep-walking with a candle in her hand. Mamá had removed all candles and lamps from their room and they had slept in the dark after that. Would turmoil be Mexico's course forever? Old fears gnawed at her stomach. In her mind, she saw Father Pro put before a firing squad in the patio of Police Headquarters just a few days ago. Reporters were invited to witness the execution. Calles had made an example of the popular priest. There wasn't a glimmer of mercy in Calles. Ironically, Obregón, during his presidency, had closed one eye to the rigid religious reforms set forth in the Constitution. Antonieta had always taken pride in her religious liberalism. God did not belong locked up in boxes. Against Catholic dogma, she read the Bible. But now something alarming had happened in Mexico. Wherever one turned there was discontent.

At night, depression pulled her down; awake, she felt rudderless, adrift in a world turned suddenly sinister.

CHAPTER XXVIII

Sabina knocked briskly at Antonieta's door.

"Can you receive Conchita?" she asked, setting down a steaming cup of manzanilla tea laced with other potions that she hoped would fix her beloved

Señora's aches and sniffles. The poor girl had gotten wet and caught a bad cold. In truth, she was run down from going around with the wrong people. For months, ever since that arrogant painter had entered her mistress' life, Sabina had kept a candle burning beneath a picture of San Antonio de Padua, who straightened out affairs of the heart.

"Didn't Conchita go to work? I hope you didn't tell her I was ill. I'll be up in awhile."

"You'll be up when you stop coughing," Sabina said stoutly. "Well, what shall I tell her? She's waiting in the hall."

"Of course I will receive her," Antonieta said. She plumped up her pillows and sat up.

Antonieta noticed Conchita's fashionable dress and new high heels. She was a good-looking young woman. With a nervous grin on her face, the former maid approached the bed.

"Sorry you are not feeling well. I brought you some chocolate raisins," Conchita said, "maybe not so good for a cold, but good for the spirit."

"How thoughtful." Antonieta opened the cellophane bag, noting the sticker of an expensive sweet shop, and popped a raisin into her mouth. "Now, what's all this about?"

Conchita licked her lips.

"Go ahead and tell her," Sabina prodded.

"I have met a man. He wants to marry me, and he wants to know what day he can come to call on you," Conchita stammered.

"I told her that the only man who would not deceive her is her guardian angel," Sabina pronounced pontifically.

"Have you met him?" Antonieta challenged her old nana.

"I don't have to." Sabina's answer was uncompromising.

"Then let's both reserve judgment. Come here, Conchita," Antonieta beckoned. She hugged the girl. "How happy I am for you. I want to hear all about it."

The blush on Conchita's face came and went as she talked. His name was Celestino Garza and he owned a barbershop where she had gone to give manicures on her day off, recommended by a customer in the beauty salon. He was twenty years older, a widower and a gentleman whose three children were grown. She had only known him a few months but he was so kind and...and he wanted to marry her! Since she had no family, he insisted that he he should ask the Señora for her hand. When could the Señora receive him? Conchita's face was radiant as she looked expectantly at her patroness.

A date was set for the following Saturday evening.

Antonieta received Don Celestino and Conchita in the vestibule. After proper introductions were made, she graciously escorted them to the salon. Conchita sat stiffly, not daring to lean back in the hand-carved chair. Don Celestino selected a straight chair next to her, his hat on his lap.

"Señora," he addressed Antonieta, "I know the regard in which you hold Conchita, and I have heard from her own lips the kindness and generosity and affection you have always shown her. You are her family," the very proper gentleman said. Surely a porfirista, Antonieta thought, listening intently. "I, too, esteem Conchita and have the deepest respect for her intelligence and her comportment. She would honor my name and my home if I could call her my wife. I own my business and I also own a small house—your house also, Señora." Don Celestino sat up ramrod straight. "Señora, I have come to ask for Conchita's hand. Will you concede me the privilege of marrying your protgee?"

Moved by the speech, Antonieta looked at Conchita and saw love and respect for this man in her eyes. He would be father, husband, and lover all in one. She was almost envious of the little waif who used to scamper down the basement steps to listen to her read.

"Conchita has spoken very highly of you, Don Celestino. And I do not doubt that you will provide for her well. If you allow her to work in your barbershop, your business will grow. I see a bright future for you both, as long as there is respect and love. I grant permission for my protégée to marry you, if that is her wish."

Conchita was overcome with emotion and did not trust herself to speak. She nodded her head.

"I only regret that the churches are not open," Don Celestino said, shaking his head. "I should like to buy the most beautiful bridal gown in Mexico for Conchita." He shrugged. "But it would not look well at a civil wedding."

The florid face of Father Agustín Alvarez flashed in Antonieta's mind. He would do it for Alicia. "You shall buy the bridal gown and Conchita will wear it!" she said grandly. "I know a priest who will take every risk to marry you."

Antonieta invited the engaged couple to the breakfast room, where hot chocolate and tamales awaited them.

Conchita and Don Celestino were married in the little chapel in Alicia's house, with full sacraments and High Mass celebrated. A lavish luncheon in the garden of the house on Monterrey Street followed, attended by elegant attired guests, the employees and customers of the beauty salon and barbershop, Don Celestino's children and the Rivas Mercado family. Sabina wore a flowered dress and long, gold filigree earrings. The guests were soon joined by a stout, florid-faced business man in a flaming cravat, his balding head covered by a derby. With

Antonieta's influence, a small picture of the bride and groom appeared beside an ad for cough medicine in the Sunday Rotogravure.

Antonieta began to spend mornings in the Conservatory of Music, where she had been given space to compose drafts of projects she hoped to introduce in her "Folklore Department," as Amelia referred to it. Antonieta considered the projects she presented important, and well-structured, but the bureaucrats in charge, it seemed, shunned making decisions. Papá was right: bureaucracy would ever consider cultural needs with indifference.

The political arena was shaky. Politicians who had backed Obregón were reshuffling their alliances, trying to find safe slots in an unstable situation. Calles could not succeed himself. Obregon's assassin was executed. On September 1st, in a surprise announcement, President Calles declared in his State of the Union address that an interim President would be appointed by Congress until free elections could again be held.

Antonieta followed José Vasconcelos' scathing rhetoric in "El Universal" newspaper with interest. If anyone would hold Calles to his promise of free elections, Vasconcelos would. The man's pen knew no fear.

Interim President Portes Gil was duly installed on a Friday. On Monday Antonieta arrived at the Conservatory, burdened with copies of a grammar school play she had written, which included native dances. She had seen the eager faces of the children when she had held tryouts at a nearby public school. They all wanted to be actors and dancers.

With her free hand, she pushed open the door to her office. A man was sitting at her desk.

"Who are you?" Antonieta asked imperiously.

"Gerardo Moreno, Señora." Without apology, without standing up, but directing his eyes to some papers on the desk he said, "I am the new director of this department."

Stunned, Antonieta turned on her heels and stalked down the hall, fury mounting. She swept into the director's office and confronted her friend, Moisés Saenz, Sub-Secretary of Education, who had granted her space in the Conservatory. "Who sent that man to occupy my desk?"

Moisés rose. "It all happened fast," he replied to her question. He was obviously uncomfortable. "I'm sorry about this, Antonieta. Orders received this morning. Politics....." He shrugged.

"You know I founded this Department and have served it with devotion and enthusiasm," Antonieta said passionately. "Now you tell me that politics sifts down to the lowest level of education. Am I just to pack up and leave or can I expect some period of training a new person? There are projects in process, only half accomplished..."

"I can't answer your question," Moises said lamely. "Aside from the secretaries, I think everyone in Education is new. I expect to be replaced any minute myself."

"Down with those on top and up with those on the bottom, my uncle Beto used to say. I know you are not to blame, Moisés, and I'm grateful you're been here. At least someone recognized the cultural vacuum in this country."

Antonieta had a sudden desire to escape from the city. Yes, a change of scenery would give her a new perspective. She would take the family to Michoacán. Toñito would relish a trip and Mario and Lucha would have that private time together. She would tell Mario to invite a friend and she would invite her friend, Malu, to provide proper chaperonage. Mrs. Rule could not object.

Their first glimpse of crystal clear Lake Zirahuen was breathtaking. It was late September, wildflower season, a time of freshness and renewal, the true spring of the high plateau after the summer rains.

The scent of wet pine perfumed the air as Antonieta walked down to the edge of the lake, luminous water reflecting a perfect cerulean sky. A chorus of blessings was provided by the soft hymn of insects and birds and rustling leaves in the forest. She let the pain float to the top and escape through her eyes. Why do my efforts always abort? My divorce, the theater, the Cultural Department? And now Manuel. Their hard-achieved friendship, the trust they had vested in each other…it would never be the same. He was committed to his sexual games and she must free herself of that mystical commitment to love she always seemed to make. "Follow the road wherever it takes you," she had once written to Chela. What road was she to follow?

The valley was splashed in pinks and yellows, the wild cosmos displaying their delicate beauty as they bent in the breeze. Antonieta threw a pebble in the water and watched the circles grow ever wider, unto obliteration.

That night, in the cabin, she took out the Bible which Mother Blair had given her and read from Psalms. The Bible always brought peace. In her diary she noted: "I pull these petals from David, Psalm 91.

He that dwelleth in the secret place of the most High
Shall abide under the shadow of the Almighty.
I will say of the Lord, He is my refuge and my fortress;
In Him will I trust."

The turmoil in her mind calmed. Antonieta took out a sheet of paper and wrote: "Memela, my beloved baby sister: I follow you in my mind's eye as you laugh and chat and flirt in the interesting corners of this world you are exploring. Don't commit yourself to anything or anyone. Just have fun. I have never known how. It seems my motto is 'search, but do not find.' How I envy your light heart. Mine seems always weighted with some unfathomable burden. You know how to be happy. Be happy, my darling. Enjoy the good things that life offers." Antonieta reread her words. Decisively she tore the letter in shreds. Why burden Memela with her elusive anxieties? Toñito stirred. She stood beside his cot and looked at the tousled head of her sleeping son. How could Albert accuse her of being an unfit mother when her heart overflowed with love for this child they had begat? She pushed a lock of brown hair away from his cheek. He looked healthy and tan. They had ridden through forests and eroded valleys, urging horses along muddy lanes which led to colorful villages where the people made beautiful handicrafts.

On the little pine table beside his bed, Toñito had placed a clay figure which had caught his fancy that she had allowed him to buy

In the Shadow of the Angel

from a Tarascan Indian. It was the fearsome god *Tlaloc,* the rain god. Antonieta picked it up and ran her finger along the rough stone, remembering her own beloved Huitzilipochtli. As a child, she had scarcely been aware of Mexico's indigenous past. She knew only that the Spaniards had brought Christ to a pagan land. She wanted Toñito to understand that religion was not locked in a church built by the Spaniards. Religion had always guided Mexico: sun, moon, wind, and sky were all moved by the gods. Rain and crops depended upon them, even life itself. To the Spaniards, Tlaloc was just a hunk of carved rock. To the Aztecs he was a symbol of survival they had to appease.

At heart I am a teacher, Antonieta, reflected, just as Papá was. My God, how I have neglected the education of my son!

The last night they built a bonfire by the lake. The mystical play of light upon forms and faces, the special light in Lucha's eyes, the open and starry heaven glimpsed through the flickering patterns of the pines.... Antonieta drank it all in, peace washing over her like the soft lap of the waves.

Toñito flopped down beside his mother. "Is it true that the woods are full of witches?" he asked.

"Maybe."

"A witch gave Tomás the evil eye last week and made him sick. His gardner's a witch."

"Forest witches don't bother children. You are quite safe."

Toñito ran back to the bonfire.

Mexico is full of witches, but not witch hunters; Antonieta's thoughts rambled in meditation. "Let him be a witch," was the Mexican attitude, "or, for that matter, a homosexual. After he dies, Satan will carry his soul down to hell or Jesus will take his soul to heaven. Meanwhile, it's none of my concern."

Malu walked over to where Antonieta was leaning against a tree. Sparks from the bonfire rose like fireflies in the night.

"Do I dare bring up Manuel's name?" Malu asked.

"Oh course. It can always be spoken," Antonieta answered. Malu was a good friend, one she occasionally confided in.

They cleared some pine cones and sat on a grassy knoll.

"I just want to say that I feel your association with Manuel is dragging you down. I know what a loyal friend you are, but you'll never win your divorce case if you continue to let Manuel in your life. In court, he would appear as an undesirable influence on Toñito."

"Toñito hardly sees him!" Antonieta exclaimed. "Does homosexuality bother you, Malu?"

"You know it doesn't. We were surrounded by homosexuals in the theater. I admire their talent."

Antonieta turned her face toward the lake and said in an almost inaudible voice, "I knew from the beginning it was an impossible love. But there's a sensual connection between Manuel and me. I see myself more clearly in his anxieties, his dreams. He's my mirror. Can you understand?"

"I understand. But Albert comes from Puritan stock. I am sure he labels all homosexuals 'evil people'." Malu chewed on a blade of grass. "Listen, come talk to my father, he has friends on the Supreme Court."

Someone threw a stone in the water. They heard it plunk.

"Thank you so much, Malu." Antonieta touched her hand. "You're a good friend."

The volcanoes stood out in all their majesty as the group returned home. Antonieta went directly to her study and consulted her calendar. Then she picked up the telephone and called Salvador.

"Salvador? Her voice rang with vitality. "Tell Carlos Chavez I shall be enchanted to meet him, Thursday, this week, at the Broadway restaurant. Shall we say two o'clock sharp?"

Carlos Chavez was younger than Antonieta had anticipated, thirty to be exact, muscular for a musician, with strong features. From the moment they were introduced, she recognized a driving edge to his character. He belonged to the rebel class, which always stirred her interest. According to Salvador, he had left Mexico, weary of being paid a pittance for playing the organ between movies, unable to perform as the professional musician he wished to be.

The amenities were brief and the chatter of the luncheon crowd did not distract Chavez as his voice projected in a clear, resonant tone.

"There is no money for a symphony orchestra in the Department of Education, Señora. Anyway, my dream is to form a Mexican symphony orchestra, free of government subsidy. I want my musicians to be well paid by patrons and a public that appreciates professionals. I want to form a disciplined, modern philharmonic group."

Chavez took a bite and continued.

"What about the existing symphony?" Antonieta interrupted.

"You mean that unionized group of men who can read music? They're paid by the hour. Did you know that singers who pay musicians for a rehearsal have no guarantee that the same ones will show up for the performance!" He laughed cynically. "I want no unions, nothing official. I shall ferret out the best musicians through the Conservatory of Music."

"Would you include Stravinsky, De Falla, maybe Copeland in your repertoire?" Antonieta asked.

"Of course. And I would like to perform Honegger's 'King David,' if we can get the music and full orchestral arrangement." It's been acclaimed all over Europe. I heard it in London in '22'."

"Well, be prepared to have tomatoes thrown at you in Mexico," Antonieta said to Chavez with a wry smile.

The lunch dragged on as Chavez talked and talked of his musical experiences, his friendship with musicians, running down the roster of modern composers, of decadent Europe and dynamic New York, of his plans and his preferences.

Salvador ate while they talked.

"I understand you compose, Señor Chavez," Antonieta broke in again. "I would like to hear some of your compositions."

"I wish I could play the piano as well as you."

Antonieta raised her brows, puzzled.

"You don't remember me, but we were students at the Conservatory at the same time. I envied your touch on the keys. I think we all agreed with maestro Ponce that you were an outstanding pianist. Do you still play?"

"Very little."

Chavez studied this unusual lady before he continued. "I'm not sure you will like my compositions. They weave indigenous roots into tight, geometric constructions. But if you insist, I shall give you a private concert."

"Then I have something to look forward to," Antonieta said reaching for her purse and gloves.

Salvador stood up only to be pulled down by Chavez. "Señora Rivas Mercado," Chavez said insistently, "before you leave, I must know whether you'll help me."

"What are you proposing?" Antonieta asked, laying aside her gloves.

"The formation of a symphony orchestra modeled after those in the United States and other countries." Chavez spoke quickly. "Its monies will be derived from ticket sales, private donations and subscriptions bought by people interested in becoming patrons. Look, this will be a professional orchestra that will have continuity. I understand you are interested in raising the cultural level in Mexico. That's my desire too." Chavez looked hard at Antonieta. "I am told that you,

Señora, are the person in this Capital who can form such a patronage. I am asking you outright if you will be the patroness of the new Mexican Symphony Orchestra?"

Antonieta stood up and with maddening deliberation stretched the kid glove over each finger. A waiter began to clear the table, nosily stacking dishes. Salvador snatched Chavez' dessert.

"Señor Chavez," Antonieta said at last, "you have a patroness."

The only thing that started on time in Mexico was the bullfight. Before Carlos Chavez, that is. And once a rehearsal began, not even the President of Mexico could get in.

Antonieta waited until the last strains of the violins had died out, then rose from her seat in the back of the theater and walked toward the stage.

"Maestro," she called out, "may I have a word with you?"

Carlos Chavez jumped down and joined her on the front row.

"I have arranged a patrons' luncheon for Sunday week and I want you to be there. Do you think you can impress the President of Mexico?" she asked with a coy smile.

"You got Portes Gil!" Chavez exclaimed. "How?"

"I went to call on him. He received me most cordially. I suggested to him that it would be a public show of his support for modern artistic endeavors. I reminded him that Mexicans had laid down their guns and should now engage in a cultural revolution."

"Incredible," Chavez uttered, grinning.

"I think you will agree that we live in a nationalistic and, I might add, xenophobic country. I felt an international committee of patrons would set the right tone for a modern symphony orchestra. So I got the American Ambassador, Dwight Morrow, two prominent American businessmen, the Secretary of the Treasury, the Sub-Secretary of Education, a French intellectual, and a few social lights to form the nucleus."

Chavez whistled.

"I expect about forty people at my garden luncheon," Antonieta finished smugly.

Chavez looked at his patroness with obvious admiration. "William Blake said, 'Great things will happen when men and mountains meet.' I am a man and you are obviously a mountain, Señora."

The first concert of the Mexican Symphony Orchestra was scheduled for 8:30 p.m. on December twenty-eighth. At 8:15, members of the orchestra began to cross the stage to their seats and started tuning their instruments.

Her eyes riveted on the stage, Antonieta suddenly gasped.

"What's the matter?" Lucha and Amelia asked in one voice.

"Look at them!" She clamped her hand over her mouth.

The members of the Mexican Symphony Orchestra were dressed in every manner of garb: white shirts, blue shirts, wide ties, bow ties, brown trousers, navy blue. Why hadn't Chavez told her? She resolved to send each and every musician to Emilio Perez, the finest tailor in Mexico City, to have a proper "smoking" made to order and a *frac* for Chavez.

Exactly at eight-thirty, Carlos Chavez strode onto the stage. He faced the noisy audience and held high his baton. The house lights did not dim. No one paid attention. Antonieta saw Chavez' determined expression and hunched down. She knew it would be a half hour before the President arrived and people quieted down.

At eight thirty-five a voice rang out, "*tercera llamada, tercera llamada!*" Chavez stepped up on the podium. The house lights went out and Stravinsky's "Firebird" commenced.

The audience continued to file in, amidst catcalls and whistling, but the "Firebird", under the menacing baton of Carlos Chavez, proceeded to its crashing conclusion. Half the audience applauded frenetically, while the other half whistled and stomped and shouted insults as though they were at a boxing match. Antonieta noticed that the President and his family had been seated.

Chavez turned to the audience and raised his arms. Oh God, he will release his fury and walk out, Antonieta thought dismally. Without anger or reprobation, the conductor shouted, "If you are ready to take your seats, we would like to get on with the concert."

Quiet was finally achieved and the concert continued to its conclusion in relative tranquility.

Most critics were virulent. In his column, Salvador Novo addressed the gum-chewers: "Greta Garbo, Valentino, Gandhi and Chavez must be discussed if you are to be considered civilized."

The Mexican Symphony Orchestra was launched.

Sabina knocked loudly on the study door and poked her head in. "You have an urgent call on the Ericsson and a visitor in the vestibule."

Annoyed, Antonieta got up from her desk, where she was going over a pile of bills with her administrator. Mexico City had two telephone systems: one Swedish and one American. The Ericsson was across the vestibule in a hall. She saw that Andrés, her young Zapotec student, was the visitor, and motioned to him to wait in her study. In minutes she was back, elation in her step and voice. The call was from licenciado Luis Cabrera, Malu's father, who informed her that her divorce case had been accepted by the Supreme Court.

"Forgive me, Don Esteban, I am not in the mood for this today," Antonieta said. "Will you come back tomorrow?"

Andrés sat awkwardly in the big chair in front of her desk. "Señora

Antonieta," he said,"I have come to ask a favor. May I store my books at your house until I find another place to live?" A Zapotec accent was still discernible in this serious, hard-working young man.

"Why are you leaving Manuel's?" Antonieta asked, surprised.

"He needs a fulltime servant now. There's no room."

"I see. And where do you plan to go?"

Andrés shrugged. "Maybe a park bench tonight."

Antonieta looked in the earnest eyes and flashed a dazzling smile at her pupil. "This house is nearly empty, Andrés. My sister is in Europe and my brother spends most of his time in Acapulco. You can move in here, share Toñito's bedroom and take your meals with us." Andrés started to protest and Antonieta raised her hand. "My poor son lives in dread of robbers and will welcome you warmly. Please accept."

With wide eyes, Andrés nodded agreement.

That night Antonieta slept soundly. The next day she felt more alive and composed than she had in weeks. It was Andrés who felt awkward. At lunch, he eyed the assortment of knives and forks and spoons with great apprehension. "I don't know how to use all these tools," he said simply. "Can't I just have some *tacos* in the kitchen?"

"I am going to teach you to use these tools," Antonieta replied firmly. "Then you will feel at ease when you attend great literary banquets and dine with senators and ministers. You are going to be a fine writer, Andrés."

At night, Antonieta read the classics to Andrés, translating from English, French or German as she read. Only his tongue could not keep up with his quick mind.

Using his fish knife, Andrés was trying to filet a red snapper when Mario joined them in the dining room for a late lunch one afternoon. Mario tossed a newspaper "Extra" on the table. "Your friend Tina's in jail. Her lover was shot last night while they were taking an evening stroll. Name's Julio Mella. A Cuban. Seems he's a well-known Communist."

Antonieta seized the paper. Calles' men had cracked down. Tina was held without bail, without trial, without justice. Voices rose in her defense. Men like Diego accused Calles of collaborating with the Cuban dictator, Machado, and accused Machado of the murder of the young Communist. Behind the scenes, Calles' was still running the country with his henchmen. Everyone knew that the interim president, Portes Gil, was merely a rubber stamp. Under Rivera's vociferous protest, Tina had been released.

Fledgling political parties were being formed; the Communist Party proposed a candidate. Andrés' enthusiasm grew daily as it became apparent that José Vasconcelos would return from the United States and run as an independent candidate for the presidency.

A rap on the door made Antonieta lay down her pencil. She closed the heavy accounting ledger and called out, "Come in."

It was Andrés. "I've come to say goodbye, Señora Antonieta. We only decided this morning and there was no time to tell you before." The words tumbled over each other.

Antonieta could not conceal her surprise. "Where are you going?"

"To Guadalajara, to offer our support to José Vasconcelos. He's campaigning there now. There are ten of us taking the train tonight."

"I didn't know you were so interested in politics," Antonieta said.

"I'm interested in José Vasconcelos. He made it possible for me to come to the Capital to study. No one else ever bothered with provincials. Now that he is a candidate for President, I shall devote all my energy to helping him get elected."

"I admire your attitude, Andrés, and I admire licenciado Vasconcelos. If women could vote, I would vote for him. Will you tell him that?"

"Of course!"

Antonieta got up and patted her protegé on the shoulder. "Remember, I'm here if you need me."

CHAPTER XXIX
1929

The name Vasconcelos was a wind stirring up her literary students, Antonieta reflected, as she stepped out of the tub. They had not forgotten the Minister of Education who had sent out his "missionaries" through the corn fields to build rural schools, train teachers and distribute books. She dried her hair and began to dress, her mind filled with the new turn in politics. A quote from one of Vasconcelos' speeches had hit the mark: "Governments should serve the interests of the people, not the people the interest of those who govern." She went into the bedroom, looking for the morning paper. It wasn't there. Mario must have filched it.

The newspaper was spread in front of Mario when Antonieta joined him for breakfast. He dished some hot sauce onto his omelette and looked up.

"Can I tempt you? Or are you still on that awful diet? How can you stand a raw egg and milk?"

"Yoghurt," Antonieta corrected placidly.

"Come off it, Antonieta," Mario taunted, "Memela, Toñito and I live here too. Now that's she's home, put Memela in charge of the kitchen. She hasn't anything else to do." He made a face. "Brains and liver and raw oysters. We haven't had a decent meal since Andrés left.

Say, I wonder if he was caught in the riot."

"What riot?"

"In Guadalajara. Seems they tried to assassinate Vasconcelos at the station, but a cordon of students surrounded him and thwarted the attempt."

"Let me see the paper."

Mario handed it over, pulling out the sports section.

Rapidly, Antonieta scanned the report. "Thank God nothing happened. Just look at this sea of people who turned out to hear him!"

Her brother was absorbed in sports.

"From Guadalajara," Antonieta read aloud, "the candidate proceeded to Michoacán, where he addressed the Cristeros, declaring that the Government and the Church can live in harmony, even under the Constitution. He promised land reforms that would place modern farm implements in the hands of the campesinos and declared that the first land to be divided would be the haciendas of Obregón and Calles. 'We did not fight the Revolution for the land to fall into the hands of generals,' he was quoted."

Antonieta thumped the newspaper. "Those, should anyone ask, are fiery words! What do your friends have to say?"

"What?" Mario looked up. "Oh, before I forget, I am going to Guadalajara to play in a golf tournament tomorrow. We are going to fly over."

"Mario, is that safe?"

"For God's sake, Antonieta, what do you think I do in Acapulco?" Mario had organized a small coastal airline with an American pilot and a Mexican partner. "We're not living in the dark ages," he went on. "Guadalajara has a civil airport and hangars and mechanics and they're constructing a hotel out there. You ought to take more interest in what's going on in Mexico."

"How long will you be gone?"

"Three or four days." Mario lit a cigarette and finished his coffee. "When will Andrés be back?"

"When Vasconcelos arrives in Mexico City, I would assume," Antonieta answered.

Daily, Antonieta followed Vasconcelos' campaign in the newspapers and in the jerky silent newsreels. The candidate had an air of gravity and confidence. Next to Nandino Sandino, the Nicaraguan rebel who opposed American occupation and had been given refuge in Mexico, Vanconcelos was the most applauded. Women in the theater always applauded the loudest. He had declared that if he won he would give women the right to vote. Even the *Contemporaneos* were talking about him. José Vasconcelos was clearly Mexico's most distinguished man of letters. His books on philosophy, metaphysics, political analysis and history had earned him international respect. In South America, they had conferred the title of *Maestro de las Americas* on him, and in the United States he had taught at the most prestigious universities. Could a culturally oriented, civilian president be possible?

Reading the newspaper on her breakfast tray in bed one morning, Antonieta noted that the candidate had arrived in Toluca and would enter the Capital on Sunday. Vasconcelos' campaign headquarters had been predicting that thousands would line the route. She remembered Madero's triumphant entry into the Capital and resolved to take Toñito to see the popular candidate.

Lazily, she got up, did a few exercises and ran a tub bath. So many had come again last night, the literary readings had gone on and on. Over the running water she heard Sabina's voice at the bathroom door.

"Andrés and some friends are waiting for you in the salon and he says it's very important. Something about a licenciado. What shall I tell him?"

"That I'll be right down," Antonieta shouted. Andrés was back! What lawyer was he talking about? He knew no lawyers connected with her divorce case. Vasconcelos, of course! He was usually referred to in the press simply as the licenciado. What could have happened?

She dried off hastily, selected a simple ensemble, and surveyed herself in the mirror. She added a little color to her lips and cheeks, struggled with the clasp of her pearls, got it fastened as she descended the stairs, heels clicking rapidly.

"Andrés, are you all right?" Antonieta greeted him with a worried look, nodding to the three young men who accompanied him.

"I'm fine. You remember Chano and Mauricio and Alfonso," Andrés said. "We are here as a committee, Señora Antonieta."

"To do what?"

Andrés cleared his throat. "To ask permission to borrow your automobile."

Relieved, Antonieta laughed. "My automobile? Whatever for?"

"To conduct the next President of Mexico into this city," Andrés announced.

Please sit down," Antonieta said. "Now tell me what this is all about."

Mauricio took the floor. "Licenciado Vasconcelos has been traveling by train and borrowed automobiles. This campaign has had little money, but a powerful following, and now he is scheduled to enter the Capital tomorrow with only an aged Ford to conduct him."

"He suggested that he might ride in a carriage like Madero," Alfonso said grinning, "or a donkey like Christ. It's Palm Sunday, you know."

"I offered him your Cadillac," Andrés concluded sheepishly.

Antonieta addressed the young men with mock drama. "My automobile will be honored to conduct such an august personage into the Capital," she said. "Shall Ignacio drive it?"

"With you in it," Andrés hurried to say. "The licenciado wants to meet you. I gave him your message, and anyway he knows all about you." The words were tumbling again.

"Are you sure?" Suddenly the absurdity of the situation struck Antonieta. A presidential candidate riding in her car!

"He said exactly that, that he would like to meet you," Mauricio confirmed.

"And will one of you drive me back in the aged Ford?"

"Tomorrow. If you wish."

Antonieta looked from one to the other. They were very serious. "All right. When do we leave?"

"Now."

The winding, mountainous highway snaked up to ten thousand feet, over grades that a less powerful vehicle could scarcely make. The young men talked incessantly of their adventures on the campaign trail, of the burgeoning headquarters in Mexico City, already bursting out of the small, rented office, of the men of substance around Vasconcelos, of the coming convention at which he would officially be nominated the candidate for Madero's old party, the *Partido Anti-Reeleccionista*, and of the multitude expected to turn out to greet him in the Capital tomorrow.

The air was electric with excitement as they neared Toluca. A civilian president, a lawyer and such a learned, erudite man of high ideals would change Mexico!

As the Cadillac pulled up to the hotel which served as temporary campaign headquarters, Antonieta suddenly felt uncomfortable. It was presumptuous to offer her automobile to a presidential candidate, presumptuous of her to be here at all. How had she allowed herself to get into this preposterous situation? With cautious reserve, she entered the lobby.

Standing by the desk talking with Chano and Mauricio, Antonieta saw the elevator door open and Andrés step out with the candidate at his side. Vasconcelos was not quite as tall as he appeared in the newsreels, but he was certainly more handsome. She took in the whole person quickly: high forehead, dark hair, mustache, light skin, quick step, a disregard for clothes and a friendly smile.

"Señora Rivas Mercado," José Vasconcelos addressed her without waiting to be introduced. "What a pleasure to meet you. How deeply I appreciate your coming all this way. Welcome." He extended his hand and held hers for a moment, taking in the lines of her body, the air of breeding which seemed free of affectation. "I understand from the boys that you have offered me your automobile."

Earnest brown eyes on a par with hers met Antonieta's.

"If I can serve you in any way, licenciado, it will be my pleasure. I have followed your campaign and join my friends in their admiration for the goals you have set for Mexico."

Her voice had cadence, a well-modulated voice. "Thank you," he replied. Their eyes appraised each other. She was an attractive woman, not what one would call pretty; rather, she had a magnetic quality that beguiled.

"The Señora's car is outside, licenciado," Andrés interrupted. "Do you want to see it?"

"I saw it from my window. I must discuss this situation with you, Señora." Vasconcelos looked at his watch. "Have you had lunch?"

"It's not important." Antonieta said quickly. "I know you must have a full agenda."

"Seldom is anything more important to me than food. Vasconcelos smile was engaging. He turned to the young men, still smiling. "We have a committee meeting in my room at four o'clock. I'll see you then." He cuffed Andrés on the shoulder and turned him toward the elevator.

This man was married, but known to have had numerous affairs, if one could trust the scandal sheets. She waited.

"Shall we go, Señora? There is a passable little restaurant in the arcades if you like *chiles rellenos*." He touched Antonieta's elbow and guided her toward the door.

The popular restaurant was crowded when the candidate and Antoineta entered. He was recognized at once, and people came over to shake his hand. Cordial and buoyant, he encouraged them to turn out for the rally in the plaza at seven. Antonieta sat patiently at the table, observing his natural way with people, the sincerity he projected, the ease with which he answered questions. It was a small, family place; soon two young daughters showed up to take their orders, red ribbons woven through thick black braids. Sent to rescue him, they moved people aside.

José Vasconcelos pulled up his chair and faced the lady across from him. He had not felt so attracted to a woman in many years. She had those rare qualities of grace and intelligence, humor and an imponderable mystery in her eyes, beautiful brown eyes which observed him closely.

"You must forgive me. This whole campaign has been a Rabelaisian experience." he said, "I have been relishing Mexico, her food, her provinces, her people, her exuberance. I have been away for four years." He paused. She was looking at him strangely.

"Did you say Rabelaisian? Then you know Rabelais?"

"The more I study him, the more perplexed and intrigued I am by that old philosopher. And you? Does Rabelais intrigue you?"

"Totally. Since I was very young," Antonieta replied with a warm smile. "I have read your books on philosophy, licenciado. I hope we can discuss them sometime."

"I shall make the time, Señora." His eyes conveyed intense interest. "Before we talk about the matter of your automobile, let me give you some background."

The tortilla soup was piping hot and the stuffed pepper superb. Antonieta ate with appetite while she listened to Vasconcelos, asking an occasional question and finding herself swept up in his ideas and ideals.

"Why did you leave Mexico at the peak of your career?" she asked.

"An altercation with Calles, over education, of course. His bought labor union preached the dogma of the proletariat and denounced the curriculum I had established in the school system as a monopoly of the 'enemy class.' I had already given Diego Rivera his walls. I could see that Calles intended education to be used to fan a class struggle." Vasconcelos spoke straight to the point. "I had to get out of government, or stay in as one more bureaucrat without power or personality. So I left and traveled in Europe and the United States."

"I kept up with you through your articles in 'El Universal.'"

Vasconcelos grinned. "That's where I read about you, when you started the theater, Mexico's illustrious lady who didn't permit a few critics, or shall we say vipers, to deter her from a project she believed in." He folded his arms. "Shall I accept your offer to ride into the Capital in your imposing Cadillac or should I not?" His eyes searched hers. "If it were rented, or belonged to a member of the committee, I would not hesitate. But it is your automobile, Señora, and from what Andrés tells me, it would be recognized by just about everyone in the city as belonging to you." He covered her hand with his own. "It would compromise. both of us."

Antonieta nodded, feeling the warmth of his hand.

"I'll be truthful. This campaign has been conducted with no pretenses. We have had very limited funds. To raise money, I have charged for my talks—in theaters, auditoriums, bullrings, anywhere a crowd could gather. Each of my men has had to pay his own expenses. It's been a campaign of honesty and hard work. My greatest asset is words, words that need to be spoken, words that have no threat of arms behind them, a nonviolent campaign which will sweep us to victory because we need a change in government, and because people believe in us. I can do nothing false." He paused.

"I understand."

"One of my promises is to introduce the vote for women, equal suffrage."

"I know." Antonieta's eyes were suddenly wide.

He studied her as he sipped sweet aromatic coffee from a little earthenware jug. "Would you be willing to support the women's movement? Your personal endorsement would be of the greatest value."

Her heart raced. "Do I interpret you correctly, licenciado? Are you asking me to collaborate in your campaign?"

"Yes. I am asking you to stand up for women's suffrage."

"You've just touched on a subject of real interest to me. In fact, an article I wrote on the Mexican woman was published in Madrid last summer."

"So, you write. I would like to hear your views. Would you mind telling me?" Vasconcelos leaned forward attentively.

"Well, I think it's generally accepted in Mexico that women are 'good' and men are scoundrels. I believe that 'goodness' is really passivity. The Mexican woman allows herself to be used as a floorboard for masculine license, because basically she's afraid of men. Look at it from her perspective: She's trained to be submissive from the moment she's born. Submissive to her father, submissive to her brothers and all the males around her. As wives, Mexican women tolerate and suffer. As mothers, they suffer and tolerate. I'm convinced that only through education will the Mexican woman be exorcised of the passivity that has chained her for generations and generations." Antonieta smiled. "Amen."

Vasconcelos raised his brows. It was quite a speech. "Then you believe education is the answer?"

"Absolutely. In Mexico, men spend more time and money educating their dogs and horses than they do their daughters."

She was a classic beauty lit by a modern torch, Vasconcelos decided. He leaned forward and said earnestly: "With such a thesis, I beg you to support the women's issue." Again he covered her hand with his. "Will you?"

Antonieta hesitated only a moment. "You have my wholehearted support, licenciado," she replied.

"Good!"

Politics was for men, to be discussed over brandy, to be loudly debated with other males, but not for women to be involved in. Only Papá had broken the rules, Antonieta thought, encouraging her interest in politics, but she was not prepared for the emotion aroused by the rally that night in Toluca.

String of lights illuminated the bandstand and were draped across the trees, festooned with red, white and green tissue paper streamers. A crude wooden speaker's platform had been erected across from the church. The band played Souza marches and the stirring martial clashes of "Zacatecas" rang out as the candidate approached. It was much like a fiesta in any small town, except that the boys and the girls were not promenading around the square. A mob had gathered. Antonieta observed them from where she stood with Andrés' group at the foot of the platform. Indian women bundled babies in rebozos against the chill night air; men in straw hats stood silently beside them. A few men in business suits and housewives with glittering diamonds in their ears pushed through soldiers holding rifles and leather-jacketed men sporting showy pistols. Calling out their wares, vendors circulated with baskets of sweet cakes, hard candy, crystallized fruit, pumpkin seeds, toys. An occasional young girl in a short dress leaned on the arm of her beau, but straw hats and overalls dominated the crowd.

Vasconcelos was mounting the platform. She watched men hoist children onto their shoulders as the crowd pressed in tighter, Indian dialects and Spanish interspersed. These were the Mexicans, the people, Antonieta thought, a cross-section of sixteen million more.

A young orator held up his hand. "The moment we have all been waiting for has arrived," he said, "this moment, tonight, when you will know that your dream of a government free of corruption and self-interest, a government pledged to serve the people, can come true. I introduce to you the candidate for President of this Republic who will change Mexico: José Vasconcelos!"

Cheers and whistles and "Vivas!" made the leaves tremble. Then there was silence.

Vasconcelos raised his arms. "The last time I was in Toluca, the nation was celebrating four hundred years of the apparition of the Virgin of Guadalupe. You, the citizens of this city, contributed generously to the new crown of diamonds and rubies for Our Lady. There was celebrating in the streets, faith and pride in your eyes. Today your beautiful churches and parochial schools are closed because of absurd regulations imposed by President Calles, based on arbitrary law. Did you vote for this man? Is this a reflection of your will? Are you satisfied with Portes Gil, a servile, inept puppet of Calles, a follower of Huerta, who served that infamous general who assassinated the leader of the real Revolution, Francisco Madero?"

He had their full attention. Only the leaves stirred.

"You have lived through the confusion of 1928, like blind mules made to turn the grinding wheel in a vicious circle. Are you willing to accept this yoke in 1929? Or is this turbulent, impoverished nation ready to throw off the yoke in defense of its rights and liberty?"

Young faces and old faces tensed as the candidate continued.

"Our Congress is packed with deputies who are nothing but trash picked up by the wind and blown skyward. People of good faith have been deceived!"

People crushed closer to hear this man, a different kind of man, who was not just mouthing old chewed, demagogic phrases. They heard something sincere and honest.

"For the vote to be effective, each one of you must break out of your apathy and express your will, stand behind your convictions!"

A vision was moistening eyes.

Antonieta listened.

In the Shadow of the Angel

"Take the destiny of your country into your own hands! The destiny of Mexico is up to you!"

The applause was thunderous. What force moved José Vasconcelos, Antonieta wondered. Without money or military backing, he had arrived within reach of the Palace.

In the hotel that night, the wild cheering still echoed in her ears as she fell asleep.

Palm Sunday dawned bright and clear. There was snow on Toluca's volcano. Nested in a valley, the town slowly disappeared as the Cadillac started for Mexico City. Two committee members rode beside Ignacio in the front seat; Andrés and the three boys flanked Antonieta in the back. It had been decided that the blue seven-passenger Cadillac would be in the middle of the five car entourage. Ahead, in the not-so-old Ford convertible, they could see the candidate standing and waving to people as they began the climb through the thick pine forest.

The two-hour trip was prolonged as they passed through small mountain pueblos, where the villagers awaited him in fiesta dress.

Winding, hairpin curves gradually brought them down to the pass that opened out into the valley of Anahuac and the approach to Mexico City. Antonieta talked little, her mind filled with poetic images. Mexico City, an indifferent Capital for more than a hundred years, had tolerated the comings and goings of rebellions, their winners and their losers. How would the city receive this man? They reached the turn-off that bordered Chapultepec Heights; new construction and greenery dotted the hills as far as she could see. For a moment, Antonieta remembered the bare hills, planting trees, naming streets, but the old, painful thoughts of Albert were mere wisps now, blown away like dried thistles as she began to feel a part of this momentous cavalcade led by José Vasconcelos.

The small stream of people who waved flags and shouted their welcome became a river flowing down the long stretch of Reforma Boulevard. Bareheaded, the candidate stood up in the Ford, waving, smiling, radiating enthusiasm. At the Angel Monument, the entourage was forced to stop while a welcoming speech was made, cheered by

"Vivas!" and more "Vivas!" Women thronged around his car, waving palm branches and reaching for his hand. It took two hours to travel the four kilometers to the little plaza of Santo Domingo. Palm branches were everywhere. A divine madness gripped the crowd; mothers lifted up small children to see the Messiah of Hope.

Vasconcelos stood on a balcony above the arcades overlooking the beautiful little colonial plaza and began to speak. The mass of humanity listened, ignoring fatigue, sun, hunger. He recalled the ancient myth of the plumed serpent, Quetzalcoatl, protector of the arts, of peace, the founder of civilization and adversary of the blood-thirsty god of the Aztecs, Huitzilopochtli, who was appeased only by human sacrifice.

"The human Quetzalcoatl, the white priest who mysteriously appeared among the Toltecs, was not punished by the gods, but destroyed by his own mortal friends, those betrayers who today still dispute this land of the eagle and the serpent!"

The silence of the multitude testified to their understanding of Vasconcelos' message in recounting the legend.

The candidate drove home his points: hard work, honest government, constitutional rights, education: "Education is inspired by Quetzalcoatl. For him to succeed, we must destroy Huitzilopochtli!"

He called upon a new generation to embrace the ideals of the older generation, Madero's ideals. When his ardent appeal to vote reached its crescendo, the crowd exploded with "Vivas!" and applause.

"Vasconcelos for President!"

José Vasconcelos was radiant as he crossed the plaza, where his committee waited. Antonieta was invited to attend the banquet that the organizing committee had prepared. Close to midnight, the festivities finally broke up. They had all been up since five in the morning and were numb with fatigue.

"What did you think of him, Toñito? I want your opinion. Did you see me?" Too excited to sleep, Antonieta had risen early to have breakfast with her son.

"It was like the sixteenth of September, Mamá," Toñito said. "I waved a flag, did you see me? Will I be able to go to the castle if he's

President? None of my friends have ever been inside the castle. Mamita, can I tell everybody that you are his friend?"

"I think at least a hundred thousand people know that," Antonieta said, kissing his cheek. "You can tell them I am going to work on his campaign. Specifically, for the right of women to vote."

Dressed in a gray suit with a white tailored blouse and a wide-brimmed gray felt hat, Antonieta left the house on Monterrey Street. She and Vasconcelos had agreed that she would come down to the headquarters of the organizing committee at about ten o'clock.

With difficulty, Ignacio found the building, not far from the old Ulises Theater. The neighborhood had deteriorated drastically, Antonieta noted, as she approached the grim entrance to his headquarters. A textile company occupied the ground floor. She climbed rickety stairs to the organizing committee's office.

The large room buzzed with activity. Two young girls sat at typewriters set on simple wooden desks; bare lightbulbs hung down from an electrical wire above them. At a larger desk, an older man cradled a telephone on his shoulder and motioned to a young man who was pasting up lettering on a large cardboard poster. Nobody said hello. There was no one there she knew. Antonieta sensed their indifference, or was it antagonism? Surely they had seen her yesterday. They knew who she was. She walked over to one of the typists, trying not to show her surprise and disappointment at the appalling condition of the office.

"Is he in charge?" she asked, pointing to the older man. "I would like to talk to the man in charge."

"Yes, that's the one," the girl answered without looking up from her work.

Antonieta walked over and waited until he put down the telephone. "I am Antonieta Rivas Mercado," she said, smiling, offering her hand.

"Yes, I know." The man stood up and shook her hand.

"I have come to offer my services to the licenciado. I must say, I am a bit surprised to find his campaign headquarters in such cramped circumstances."

"Money, Señora. We are hoping to move to an appropriate address on Avenida Juárez as soon as donations come in. After yesterday's rallies, we are expecting strong financial support."

"I see." Antonieta wondered how long that would be. She surveyed the office carefully, then turned back to the man. "I am sorry, I don't know your name, Señor." He had not had the courtesy to introduce himself.

"Lopez."

"Señor Lopez, would it expedite matters if the rent of the new locale were guaranteed?"

"Yes." Lopez' unfriendly eyes showed sudden interest.

"Then I will guarantee the rent through November. Please tell me how much it is and I will bring you a draft tomorrow. And, Señor Lopez, tell the licenciado it came out of donations, which is true. Just don't tell him whose." She smiled and held out her hand. "I want to contribute to this campaign; I believe in it."

Lopez recognized sincerity in her eyes.

As she was leaving, Vasconcelos came through the door with a retinue of young followers. He stopped and apologized to Antonieta for his tardiness.

"They detained me at the hotel. These young men all want to work on my campaign committee. What shall I do?" He threw up his hands and indicated the cramped space.

"Licenciado," Lopez said, rising from his desk, "tomorrow I sign the contract for the new offices on Avenida Juárez. You are welcome, boys, if you bring your own desks."

Everyone began gathering around the candidate. It was clear to Antonieta that she was in the way.

"I'll report when you've moved and are settled," she said, moving toward the door. Then, she turned back and faced him. "Licenciado, I will never forget Palm Sunday, March 10, 1929."

"Nor will I," Vasconcelos replied, looking at her with a warmth that seemed to eliminate everyone else in the room.

Antonieta dedicated the next day to structuring committees, outlining their work, writing down the number of volunteers she needed for the myriad jobs she planned. To head the committees, she would chose women who had served her the most effectively on other organizational committees. They would work in cells, like the Catholic League, raising funds and converting voters.

The following day she started her personal telephone campaign. By the end of the week, Antonieta sat at her desk, chastened by the experience. None had accepted. The replies had sounded studied, like parrots that are taught the same song: "I know nothing about politics. It's not a woman's concern. Speak to my husband. A political campaign, my dear? Is somebody running?" The more involved women declared: "It's a lost cause. He can't defeat Calles." These same women had worked hard to promote art exhibitions, to organize festivals for poor children, sell tickets for the symphony. But politics? It was a disease. It was Conchita who set her on the right track.

"Of course I will help, Señora. So will all the girls in the beauty salon and their sisters and their mothers. We want Vasconcelos to win!"

These were the women who had swarmed around him, the shopkeepers, clerks, teachers, factory workers, people who were rising to the blessed middle class. She thought of Conchita's beginnings.

It was a week before Antonieta appeared at the new headquarters. Now she had something to report. Two women's clubs had been established. She walked up the wide, marble stairs to the second floor of the office building on Avenida Juárez. A few doors down the street she had noticed the headquarters of the PNR, the government party. Calles had institutionalized his Government calling his party the *Partido Nacional Revolucionario*, cannonizing that brutal insurrection as though it were the will of the people! Well, we are on equal footing now, she thought smugly as she reached the landing. Vasconcelos will fight to the end!

She saw him as soon as she opened the office door, working at an old desk with his glasses down over the bridge of his nose. Typewriters were clicking, a phone rang, people milled about, but the office did not look crowded.

"Good morning," she said appearing at the candidate's desk. Vasconcelos looked up; a pleased smile displayed even white teeth.

"I'm reporting for work."

He was on his feet in an instant and pulled up a chair with a hole in the caning. "I didn't call because I wanted to give you time to get organized."

"I have good news," she said.

Antonieta sat down and opened a portfolio. She told him about the disappointing reaction of her friends, then enthusiastically described the women who had offered their services. He looked at her plans with interest and made intelligent suggestions. But his eyes reflected something more.

"Look, I have been working on this speech since eight this morning. I'm stuck. I think I need to get up and stretch, brain and body. How about walking down to Sanborn's with me for a cup of coffee?"

"I accept. Why don't you bring the speech." She wanted to know this man, to help him.

He took her by the arm and walked her to the door. Although no one looked up, Antonieta sensed disapproval in the air.

They sat in a booth in the former Jockey Club and analyzed his speech. It was addressed to campesinos in a small town in the arid State of Mexico. He would be introduced by a fine young orator from the state, Adolfo Lopez Mateos. Antonieta remembered him as a student, a bit younger than Andrés and his group.

"Educated youth makes an impact on Mexicans," Vasconcelos said, "but I must hold the baton in my own hand."

At his request, she made notes on the margin of his outline, took his salient points, and rearranged their order. Vasconcelos was impressed, open in his appreciation.

"That's a big improvement. You have a way with words. Better than me," he conceded. "I think I should take you along with me to Cuernavaca next week, then Cuautla and Puebla in May. We could practice on the way." The tone was half-facetious, half-serious.

"I don't think your staff would approve. Anyway, I can't leave my son."

Vasconcelos looked into the serious brown eyes. "Bring him along. At least to Cuernavaca. I would like for you to sharpen my speech, hear it, then be my critic. There's no one who can do that."

"Licenciado, are you serious?"

"Dead serious, Señora. How old is your son?"

"Nine. I really would like to take him. I want him to remember this campaign as an important event in the history of Mexico."

A softness had come into Vasconcelos eyes. Antonieta wanted to ask him what he was thinking about, but a wall of formality separated them.

His popularity established in Cuernavaca and Cuautla, it became imperative that a convention be held by the Anti-Reelectionists to proclaim Vasconcelos their official candidate. Obstinate differences separated the old veterans from the young vanguard. Vasconcelos' independent platform, which was anti-American and in favor of certain quasi-socialist reforms, irritated the men who had fought beside Madero, but whose party was stagnant. Antonieta took it upon herself to lobby fervently at campaign headquarters for an accord. Her interference was as welcome as the arrival of the bubonic plague. She cornered Andrés in her study and wrung the truth out of him.

"You are the only woman who speaks up at headquarters, Señora. The men resent you," Andrés admitted. "I know you're sincere, and I know you are putting money into this campaign, but I can't convince those hardheads that you are anything more than a rich heiress who wants to be his 'muse' and will drop him when you are bored. They think you are amusing yourself with politics."

"Thank you, Andrés." She reached across the desk and took his hand. "I will only work in the office when the committee has gone home."

Andrés picked up a sheaf of papers and left. Suddenly Antonieta felt alone. She could hear Toñito laughing with Ignacio and Sabina in the kitchen, and the dogs barking at the gate. Still, she was alone. And lonely.

The rally in Puebla was scheduled for April twenty-eighth. Antonieta and Toñito rode in the Cadillac behind the candidate and his staff. Toñito liked the licenciado, who made no effort to impress or amuse him, as so many of his mother's male friends did, but simply accepted him like anybody else.

"Do you have any children?" Toñito had asked his new friend.

"Yes. Two."

"Why aren't they here?"

"Because they are studying in the United States," Vasconcelos had replied, ruffling Toñito's hair. "They're much older than you."

"If I were your son, I would want to hear you make every speech. The cheering is so loud; it's exciting."

"It is, isn't it? Now we have to make those loud people vote."

The Cadillac climbed around to the base of Ixtlacihuatl. The volcano was streaked with snow on the eastern slope. Soon they entered Puebla, colonial gem, city of churches and cloisters, a Catholic bastion.

As usual, a young orator seduced the audience to prepare it for the candidate, with words of optimism, demonstrating pride in his generation., as well as their candidate, his words pouring out in clear, well-stated phrases.

Vasconcelos was obviously moved by the introduction and picked up his cue on a high note.

"In this beautiful, aristocratic city of Puebla, where the first martyr of Madero's Revolution fell, I feel privileged to stand before you. Let us talk about that Revolution."

The old maderistas in the crowd interrupted with cheers. At the end, he referred again to the Church. "I have met with Cristeros, and although they offered me armed assistance, I assured them that not arms, but the will of the people, must win this election. They took up arms only because Calles declared war on the Church."

Suddenly the loud voice of a heckler rang out: "Calles did not close the churches. It was the Catholic Episcopate."

The crowd closed in on the man and began to push him back. Vasconcelos shouted, "I do not want to cause violence in any form. Let him go."

"He is Calles' paid agitator," someone informed him.

"He spoke the truth," Vasconcelos replied. "We all know the Episcopate closed the churches to protest Calles' decree, which was to go into effect that same day. Who is to blame? Calles or the Church?"

The speech continued without disturbance.

At the banquet, the candidate was besieged by supporters. The steaming chicken *mole* burned Antonieta's unaccustomed palate, the fire caused by chiles combined with every kind of ground nut, spices and bitter chocolate, the specialty of Puebla. Extemporaneous speeches competed with *mariachis*. Toñito was restless, glad when Andrés came to take him on a tour of the arcades. When they returned, the little boy ran up to the table with a box of sugared sweet-potato candy for his mother, announcing that it was her birthday. Vasconcelos immediately sent for a cake and asked the *mariachis* to play *Las Mañanitas*.

"If I had known it was your birthday, Antonieta, I would have practiced my singing. Then again, maybe not. It would have driven you away." He laughed. "I have a terrible voice."

"Then we can sing off-key together," Antonieta said, laughing with him.

CHAPTER XXX

As the campaign of 1929 gathered momentum, telephones rang incessantly at the house on Monterrey Street. Daily, committee heads reported the work of their teams. Housewives talked to vendors in the public markets, teachers circulated their candidate's name in the public schools, clerks talked to customers in department stores, typists chattereded in small offices, handbills were distributed in theaters. Women were inspired, both by the thought that they might vote in a future election, and attracted by a man who took time to listen to them. Antonieta cleared the garage to accommodate long tables for the women, who lettered posters, licked stamps, and chattered enthusiastically.

A tray of cold food sat on Antonita's desk, untouched. The sun had gone down and she had not stopped. The telephone rang again.

"Bueno." Her tone was clipped, businesslike.

"Antonieta?"

"Manuel!" Her voice softened.

"I tried to get you on your birthday, but you were out all day."

"We were campaigning in Puebla. I am sorry."

"We?" The sarcasm came through. "Are we still friends?"

"Forever, Manuel."

"Then let me unburden my conscience. Politics is not for you, Antonieta. You are too sensitive, too artistic. Your role in life is to foment culture. We need you back with us."

"I am sorry, Manuel, if I seem to have deserted you...."

"Let me finish," he broke in. "I know you. You are also too generous. Vasconcelos hasn't a chance in Hades. He's a dreamer, thinks he's Madero and Quetzalcoatl and Jesus Christ! You're throwing away your money."

"What do you mean?" she asked.

"Andrés has told me you are paying for the boys' campaign trips and God knows what more. This political campaign will bring only disillusionment. Please listen. I speak to you as a friend."

"I'm committed, Manuel, and he will win. Mexico needs José Vasconcelos!"

"Mexico will always be Mexico," Manuel replied. "Call me when you have time. Goodbye."

The Ericsson was ringing in the hall. It was her realtor.

"The best properties to sell are the ones in Chapultepec Heights. Prime lots are bringing good prices. Cash. Shall I sell them?"

"Yes," Antonieta said. "Sell them." A new word had entered her vocabulary: Liquidity.

She riffled through a stack of mail. She had to wire her stockbroker in New York to give Amelia money. She and Mamá seemed to run out of money at every stop in the United States. And call Malu's father. What the devil was the delay now? Antonieta glanced at her watch. Her appointment with José at headquarters was at seven-thirty. She flew upstairs and grabbed her coat and a knit hat. They had cleared this Monday night to work together on his speeches.

Headquarters was nearly deserted. José stood by his desk, instructing the last of his student aides, the "advance battalion" that spread out through the streets every evening, posting handbills and handing out leaflets.

Antonieta waved in greeting and crossed over to the small desk she called her own in the evenings and took the typewriter out of its case. A pile of papers to be edited was already there. Within minutes, the boys left.

José pulled up a chair beside her desk. "Thanks for coming." He took a deep breath. "This has been quite a day. But I feel a new surge in the campaign. That keeps me going." He cocked his head and looked at her. "I like you in white; it sets off your Mexican heritage. Are you sure you want to work on speeches?"

"We have to. There's Xochimilco, Jalapa, and Veracruz on your immediate agenda." Antonieta pushed her chair back and crossed her legs, facing him. "What do you think of this idea, José? You talk and I will take notes. I mean, just talk; let the thoughts tumble. Describe your aspirations, your feelings, your dreams for Mexico, the dangers you see, the ills you want to correct. Then I'll organize those thoughts into outlines you can follow for your speeches, emphasizing special points according to the audience you're addressing." She smiled at him. "Agreed?"

José grinned. "How is it that you can organize my thoughts and I cannot? Another thing...."

"Yes."

"Why do you always make me feel as though I am the only man in the room?"

Antonieta laughed. "Because you are."

"I mean, every person you talk to feels they have your undivided attention."

"I only talk to one person at a time."

"You are remarkable, Antonieta. A special lady." José got to his feet and stretched his arms high. "I like your idea, but let's make this true confession short because I'm starved and I plan to take you to dinner. Agreed?"

"Agreed."

"All right, where do I start?"

"How about just telling me where you think Mexico stands and where you would like it to be?"

"That's all!"

"Just talk." Antonieta turned back to the desk and picked up a pencil.

"Very well." Vasconcelos stood up and plunged his hands into his pockets. "Write this: I believe that Mexico is a dynamic country, pushing ever forward, progressing in spite of herself. What we need now is a dynamic social conscience."

"Explain."

"We have so many extremes here. The rich do not have the social conscience of the Carnegies or Rockefellers, and the poor just wish to survive. Mexicans accept inequality, but they do very little to help each other because, at bottom, the social castes don't trust each other. The great division between those who side with *Cuauhtemoc* and those who side with *Cortés* pulls at us. The mestizo is the one who pushes. And for Mexico to become a truly independent nation, everybody has to pull together. I'm lecturing, am I not? Sounds stilted."

"No matter. Develop the thought."

"Let me explain what I mean by a dynamic social conscience. We have to change our attitudes about ourselves and about our country. The rich have to be more concerned with the general good, and the poor have to be stirred from their apathy. We have to learn to believe in ourselves, otherwise stagnation and corruption will never be defeated." He paused. "Is that clear?"

"Perfectly. Continue."

"We are a rich nation, yet our people are poor." He came over and sat on the edge of her desk. "Here's a story. Not long ago, I spent a weekend in Taxco with an Egyptian friend. It poured cats and dogs. You know what he said? 'Look at all that wealth gushing down the street.' We are rich but we don't know how to take advantage of our riches." He threw up his hands. "We have two long coastlines with abundant fish and our people eat *frijoles*. My God, silver, gold, minerals, great pools of oil are in the belly of our soil and the veins of our mountains, yet our people live in poverty. They have to be trained, educated, given incentives. Of course it takes money. That's why we have to stop the drain of corruption and make the foreigners pay! They are taking our natural resources and paying a pittance in return. We stumble along and allow our livelihood to depend on the United States. As someone said, they sneeze up there and we catch pneumonia."

Warming up to his theme, Vasconcelos paced. "Underline this. Our most urgent matter is to attack the political structure. Long ago, when Chinese warriors won power, they found it would not function without the scholar-bureaucrats, the mandarins. The transfer of power from arms to government was necessary. Obregón understood it, but he became greedy. Had our generals gone back to the barracks, it would be a different story. The purpose of this campaign—my campaign—is to make the people see that our political structure is wrong, that our political problem is the basis of our economic problem. We have to hit Calles' thieves below the belt, because we are insisting that until we can change the political structure, we can't stop the drain of wealth in the rotten bureaucratic system!" He paused. "Am I going too fast?"

"No."

"In my government, the President would be responsible before a court of law, and I would do away with congressional immunity."

"You would have no congress left," his scribe commented, swinging her chair around.

José threw his hands in the air again. "You asked me to describe my Mexican utopia..." He looked at her. "Did you know that you have beautiful legs?"

"You have digressed, licenciado," Antonieta said with a trace of a blush, tucking her legs under the chair. "Talk about the changes you would make."

"The first thing I would do is wage a campaign to make corruption unpatriotic. Start at the bottom, with education, and at the top with honest officials." José wheeled around. "All we can do is plant seeds. But we have to plant more seeds than they can pull up."

His eyes were on a distant horizon now.

"Apathy and inferiority are our greatest enemies. Americans look south of the border and see a mass of brown people down here whose destiny it is their sacred duty to guide." He paced again. "Did you know that the highest culture of Egypt belongs to a mixture of white and black which took eight hundred years to mature? Do you think in another four hundred years Mexico will be there, a highly cultured race?" He spoke with some cynicism.

"You're digressing again. Talk about education."

Education was his mania. José began a long discourse on his plans for education.

"Every Podunk town in the United States has a library, but we don't have one decent library in the whole Republic! Every American school child knows who Shakespeare is, but Mexican school children have never heard of Cervantes. They called it my aristocratic fantasy when I translated the classics, but I gave the people something to read! It's worse to read stupid things than not to read at all."

He talked about cultural programs at the primary level: choral groups, native dancing, painting contests, spelling competitions at the village level.

My programs, Antonieta thought, taking notes. He digressed. She brought him back to the labor problem and the ever-festering land reforms. His ideas were still murky, but it helped him to try to put them in words.

He got off on a tangent of ethics.

"For me the Christian ethic is the best. According to Christ, man is worth more than what he possesses. The value of material goods depends on man's cultural image. I think of Ghandi. Look at the power in his saintly austerity. And India has retained its cultural essence."

Suddenly José stopped and sat down by Antonieta. You know how I see Mexico? Like a mass of dough which was baked too fast, so it formed a hard crust of corruption, envy, inferiority, suspicion, laziness, apathy—all those ills that hold us back. We have to break off that crust and get down to the basic ingredients, our infinite abilities and talents. They'll rise if we let them. The Mexican destroys himself because he doesn't believe he can succeed. I want to open broad horizons for young minds, make people think, not simply accept. That's where I want to spend my energy. I want to teach by example, help mold and lift the spirit of Mexico! I believe in the people, Antonieta."

José pulled the chair with the hole in the caning closer and took her hand. His brown eyes conveyed something mystical, a nebulous destiny forming. "They call me an idealist, a dreamer, and I probably

In the Shadow of the Angel

am. But tell me that you believe a man would perish without a dream. Tell me you believe in me."

Tears brimmed in Antonieta's eyes. She took José's hand and placed it on her wet cheek. Then he kissed her fingertips, kissed the smooth brown skin of her wrist.

"Let's go to dinner," José said gently.

It was after ten o'clock. The crowd in Gambrino's had settled down for the long discussions and conversations which follow good food, lingering over cognac and picking at the few bread rolls left. Shaking hands along the way, José guided Antonieta toward a central table. She, however, continued on to an empty table near the bar where she sat facing the heavily carved mahogany behemoth, hiding her face from the public. Fear of being followed still plagued her.

José reached for a roll and began breaking off little pieces that he dunked in the chile sauce. "I want a big fillet of beef and a bottle of full-bodied Chianti." He reached for her hand. "I am sorry. What caprice directs your appetite? Don't look at the menu."

Inadvertently, Antonieta's eyes were directed to the mirror above the bar. Suddenly the color drained from her face. Two cold blue eyes met hers from a table behind them, where some men had just settled. Albert. She took a sip of water, hardly able to control her trembling hand.

"What's the matter?" José asked, alarmed. "Are you ill?"

"Please...just take me out of here. Now."

As they walked along the street, Antonieta relaxed. José respected her silence.

"Is there somewhere we can talk?" she asked. "I want to tell you something important."

"My hotel is only a few blocks away. That's private. Do you want to go there?"

"Yes," Antonieta answered, quickening her pace.

José occupied a small suite in a modest hotel. Neat stacks of folders lay on the coffee table in the sitting room. Antonieta sat down in a cheaply upholstered armchair and studied the floral pattern in the worn carpet before she spoke.

"My husband came and sat behind us at Gambrino's. I saw him in the mirror. I have been trying to divorce him for nearly three years; he has made my life hell. I'm tired of fighting him, that's why it upset me so." She accepted the glass of port wine he offered.

José sat on the sofa and let her talk. He remembered Albert Blair, a man close to the Maderos. He could understand Antonieta's attraction, and the clash of temperaments. He listened while she poured out the story of her battle with Albert for custody of Toñito. Antonieta felt this man's empathy.

"I have a wife," José told her. "We've gone our own ways for years. I support her financially, of course, but there's no marriage. In recent years I've recognized the hypocrisy of the Church." He sighed deeply. "In spite of our domestic problems, I have maintained a close relationship with my children. I can appreciate the pain at the thought that you might lose your son."

"Albert is a strong adversary. Sometimes, José, I feel as though I am going to fall apart, just be swallowed up by some black pit that's inside me." Tears spilled down Antonieta's cheeks freely now.

José pulled her to her feet and embraced her, cradling her in his arms, just holding her. Then he kissed her eyes, her cheeks, her lips.

She felt his warmth and his strength flow through her, holding her up, nourishing her. The passion that began to possess her took hold gently, building until it made her want to crawl inside him, to possess and be possessed by this man who now demanded her.

He led her to the bedroom. He undressed her, one stocking at a time, kissing her ankles, her knees, her thighs. An expression of ecstasy washed over her face, and he knew her desire was as great as his. An almost unbearable delirium overtook her, like a far-off sound suspended in space, the tone suddenly loud, acute, splitting into a million vibrating atoms.

An hour passed, two hours, three....

José held her in his arms and Antonieta drew close. Supreme contentment filled her as she lay in the narrow hotel bed protected by his embrace. It was as though her whole life had been lived for this moment.

Streaming through the open curtains, the sun beamed its warmth in her face to awaken Antonieta. She rubbed a hand across her eyes and looked at her watch, then quietly tried to extricate herself. Sabina would be frantic. José pulled her down again and kissed her.

"I am not going to let you go," he whispered. "I don't think I will ever let you go. Agreed?"

"Agreed." Antonieta laid her head in the arc of his arm.

"Let's sleep another hour before my neglected stomach demands my full attention."

Every thought was now directed to José, José her lover and José Vasoncelos, the presidential candidate. This was the love that Chela had talked about. Love, however, was a word she would not burden him with. She must in no way compromise José. His kindness and thoughtfulness in the midst of a punishing work schedule, his affection and response to her, were enough proof of his feelings.

Their desire in fact became a sword that hung over them both. They invented acts of subterfuge to conceal their feelings in public. He called her "Antonieta," but she continued to address him as "*licenciado.*" Because she knew eyes were watching them at campaign headquarters, she learned when to stay away. But the speeches she helped him write were inspired, and her gift for words became imprinted in slogans, weekly handbills, radio publicity, and political articles. Even the suspicious and the skeptical recognized her contribution.

They stole moments for coffee, an occasional lunch, a night together when a secret meeting could be arranged, passion and exhaustion accelerating the dawn, the fear of discovery ever present in their minds.

The busy, tense weeks of spring gave way to the rainy season. Calles' men began to harass the young orators more openly. The official candidate of the PNR, Ortiz Rubio, began to pound home the myth that the nation had called him and the people were with him.

Women handed out handbills as a crowd filled the theater where Vasconcelos was to speak.

"Aaron Saenz was Obregón's choice, touted to the four winds by Calles as the PNR candidate, and in a second dropped like a clay doll." Vasconcelos clear diction rang out. "Then Calles brought up out of Brazil a man who has been absent from his country for seven years, another rubber stamp named Ortiz Rubio. In a poetic fiction, the National Revolutionary Party clapped Ortiz Rubio on the shoulder and said to him, 'This free and soverign nation has called you.' Their candidate repeated, 'The people have called me.' And the people said, 'Who is he?'"

The roar of laughter which swept the jammed theater echoed in the markets, the cantina

s, the high-priced restaurants and homes where the joke was repeated. Since Portes Gil's lusterless inauguration as interim president, taxi drivers had been pointing out the castle to tourists and reciting a satirical epigram: "That is where the President lives. But his boss, *el jefe máximo,* lives across the street."

"Our only weapon against Calles is words," Vasconcelos told his new followers. "Spread out and talk. Talk!"

Like arrows shot into the wind, their words rang out:

"We must break the continuity of the Revolutionary Family, which passes the mandate from one to the other!"

"The provisional government is a smokescreen to pacify the United States. Calles has no intention of letting go!"

"Citizens, vote!"

Far to the south, little flower-decked boats jammed the banks of the old Aztec canals, and people carrying flags and banners crowded into the restaurant on the main landing where Vasconcelos faced the white-clad Indians of Xochimilco. Mingling in the crowd, Antonieta listened.

"Are you with the false revolutionaries?" the candidate's voice boomed out.

"No. May they die!"

"How much money has the agricultural bank loaned you to improve your parcels?"

"None!"

"Your Yaqui brothers in the north and your Maya brothers in the south haven't seen a cent, either. Because it is going into Obregón and Calles' great haciendas! Are you being paid a fair price for your produce?"

"No!"

"Why? Because the intermediaries are putting your profits in their pockets. If I am elected, I give you my solemn word that you will benefit from the work of your hands. I have heard it said that our Indians are not ready for democracy. I ask, are you ready to determine your own destiny?"

"Yes!"

"Vivas!" rang out across the canals as the white-clad populace acclaimed him.

Breaking away from the surging crowd, Antonieta followed a path through a wooded area to a predetermined meeting place, where José would pick her up in his hired automobile. She could smell the barbecue and spicy food offered at the generous banquet, and ate a few apricots she had bought to quell her own appetite. At last she saw the Dodge turn into the lane through the weeping willow trees. He stopped and she got in.

"Did the committee believe you?" she asked.

"Of course. Even a presidential candidate has to rest now and then. I told them I was going to Cuernavaca for the week-end and would see them at headquarters Monday morning. Your valise is in the trunk."

They laughed like truant children. Long, gradual curves took them high above the city. José put his arm around her and she helped him steer.

"You were marvelous," she told him. "You have become a first-class speaker."

"With Antonieta's coaching. I like those short questions and answers. They drive the message home."

"Did you see their eyes? Skeptical at first. Indians don't believe in promises. Why should they? But you won them over, José. They believe in you!" Antonieta kissed him on the neck. "Where are we going?"

"To a friend's house. Did you pack your bathing suit?"
"Yes."

The sprawling pink house was set in a blaze of garden colors. Purple mixed with red, pink and orange in the shadow of huge laurel trees and lush grass. The servants were waiting; a tray of ice, fresh limes, a bottle of rum, cheeses and fresh fruit soon appeared. Its bearer discreetly vanished, retreating to the rear of the house.

They placed their lounge chairs close to one another on the open terrace and held hands, watching the glow of sunset wash over the garden, not needing to talk, each feeling the other's nearness, the contentment of shared companionship.

José mixed two tall drinks, rum and soda, squeezed in lime juice and broke off chunks of pineapple and plopped them into the glasses. The warm, semi-tropical air filled their nostrils with sensual fragrances. They talked in whispers.

When the afterglow of sunset faded, moonbeams filtered through the trees in the garden. The constellations converged in the patterns which foretell events and destinies. The moment wove its magic.

"I want to kiss you. All over." José squeezed her hand. "Come." He pulled Antonieta to her feet and put his arm around her.

The world stopped as she reached out to him, rousing a feeling that flowed from the top of her head to the tip of her toes, through her and around her. She touched it again. Love. José led her into the spacious, high-ceilinged bedroom with its faint aroma of night-blooming jasmine and closed the door.

In the morning they swam in the tiled pool, playing, splashing. José pulled her down through the cold water and kissed her neck, her mouth, her wet hair as they surfaced. They swam and raced, then lay exhausted on their towels on the cushioned grass. Lazily, Antonieta stretched her long legs, listening to the strains of a *paso doble* on the Victrola. She got up in an easy, flowing motion and began to dance, her swimsuit outlining a perfectly shaped body.

José watched her, bronze skin gleaming, each movement a sweep of infinite grace.

"If I had a veil, I would be Isadora Duncan," she said, dipping close to him.

"I think you are more like Pavlova," he said, catching his nymph and pulling her down beside him. "There's expression in your smallest finger."

"I'm a dancer. Let me go."

"I don't think I will ever let you go."

Their lips met, long, lingering, reluctantly parting.

"Now talk to me," José said. "Where did you learn to dance? Tell me about your childhood."

Antonieta smiled. "When I was a child, my Mexico was contained in a gilded frame."

"Carved in Europe."

"Of course."

"Sometimes I think of my childhood like scenes played in the settings of Proust. Mother was beautiful, elegant and distinguished. She has milk-white skin like my sister Alicia. She hated me, I think because I'm the dark one. Mother had a Zapotec grandmother and a German grandfather. He left for his coffee plantation in Oaxaca one morning and never came back. My beautiful grandmother, Mamá Lucita, never stopped mourning him." She paused. "Father loved to show my mother off. He adored her and could deny her nothing. She threw it all away."

Antonieta shrugged. "Saturday callers preferred to ignore whatever disturbed their way of life. Don Porfirio was the status quo, forever amen y gracias a Dios. We had a houseful of servants who took charge of us, but Mamá was the one who scolded and punished. My beloved Tío Beto taught me to cheat at cards." She laughed. "You would have liked him." Folding her arms under her head, she continued. "Oh, I took all the lessons: dancing, piano, art, English, French. How I wish you'd known Papa. Papa's laughter healed all wounds. He was all goodness...and far more. That's the way it was."

"When Don Porfirio was the Alpha and the Omega," José agreed. "I must admit I owe a good education to him. He had the wisdom to keep qualified men in his cabinet. When I came to the Capital, Justo

Sierra was his Secretary of Education, a brilliant man. Now we have sacrificed quality. Mediocre teachers are turning out worse than mediocre students. When I was in the university we were made to work and think. Justo Sierra said, 'Read Plato, Homer, Virgil and Dante. And when you have finished, read Dante, Virgil, Homer and Plato.'"

Antonieta rolled over on her stomach and propped her chin up on her hands. "Tell me about that little town on the border where you lived."

"It's called Piedras Negras now, across from Eagle Pass, Texas. It's still one of those small, arid towns—greenery centered around the plaza, fiestas centered in the church. We were very proud of our beautiful church and elegant bandstand, donated by Don Porfirio. There was a big locomotive repair center in town; it gave the place an important aspect. I suppose you would call it a plain, insignificant town, but I never thought of it that way. We had a fine house, with two rocking chairs on the porch, and a French settee and caned chairs around a carved center table in the *sala*."

"Did it have a crystal vase with French silk flowers in it?"

"Yes, how did you know?"

"My grandmother's house was like that. Tell me more."

"Let's see. The house had spic-and-span tile floors. We were seven, plus two servants. We weren't poor." José sat up. "You have an exquisite body, you know."

"We were talking about your childhood. What was your mother like?"

"She was pretty and young looking, believed only in the Roman Catholic Apostolic Church, and was very wary of those Protestants across the river. I went to school over there."

"What did they teach you?"

"Everything. The American teachers were fine women and very fair. It didn't matter which side of the river you lived on. Of course I got plenty of bloody noses trying to prove that a 'greaser' could fight. Then I discovered the library over there...."

Antonieta punched him in the stomach. "Go on."

"You're really interested?"

"Vitally."

"Let's see. There were two maps of North America in our school room. The teacher would point to one map with a long stick and say, 'This is when Mexico was the largest nation of the continent.' Then she would point to the other, the one of 'present' Mexico. You know, I've never forgotten those maps."

They lay quietly on the grass, each absorbed in their own thoughts for a moment. Suddenly José jumped up, scooped her up in his arms and headed for the house.

Every fiber of her being responded to this man. He kissed her breasts, her back, her throat...She felt as though she had left her body, rising high into an ethereal realm. Then she lay on the bed, limp. Now it was peace that welled up from deep inside her, a contentment she had never known. She reached over and kissed José once again.

After lunch, they sat in the plaza in town, under a huge laurel tree in view of Cortés' Palace, and licked lemon ices.

"I have spent a few week-ends here with the Morrows," Antonieta confessed. The American Ambassador was often the brunt of Jose's attacks on Calles. She took a lick of ice cream then asked, "Why do you hate Americans?"

"I don't hate Americans. I hate their attitude toward Mexicans. I worked for an American law firm before I joined Madero. They paid a decent wage, but I was treated more like an office boy. In American eyes, a Mexican could never be an equal."

Driving home, they sat close, in a contemplative mood.

"I wish we could hear Carlos Chavez tonight. He's playing Copeland's 'Salón México,'" Antonieta commented wistfully. "Never mind, we have work to do."

The peak of Popo rose above the pines, as one hairpin curve after another brought them out of the valley of Cuernavaca to the crest of the mountain; the volcano disappeared as they began to drop again. Soon the city spread out below them. It would be night when they got home and there were still speeches to polish. José was leaving for Veracruz Monday night.

A nervous committee woman was waiting for Antonieta when she arrived at the house. A young man sat beside her on the little bench in the vestibule, his face streaked with dried blood.

"Señora," the woman moaned, "he's a nephew from out of town, a staunch *vasconcelista*. He shouted a few insults at the police, who were trying to prevent a street meeting this afternoon. Look at him! Brutally beaten! He escaped and they chased him to my house. We got out the back door and came here. Señora, will you hide him?"

"Did you provoke the fight?" Antonieta asked the young militant.

He nodded. "They're pigs!" Hatred blazed in young eyes.

"Of course I will hide him. He can work with your group until the incident blows over."

Antonieta doctored the young man, fed him, and installed him in Ignacio's room.

She was weary, not in the mood for Mario's midnight harangue when she returned late from headquarters the next day. Her brother was waiting for her downstairs.

"Have you lost your mind, harboring a criminal?"

"He's not a criminal, Mario. The police are harassing Vasconcelos' boys, that's all."

"If the police are after him, it's a dangerous situation."

"Flying is dangerous, but you do it."

"Antonieta, I wish you would give up this campaign. You're getting in over your head. Go back to your literary salons. Please."

"I can't." Antonieta kissed her brother. "Goodnight, mi amor."

CHAPTER XXXI

On a clear June morning, the sound that awakened Sabina made her jump out of bed. The church bells were ringing! There was shouting in the streets as the clanging persisted and neighbors rushed past the gate on their way to the church a few blocks away.

Throwing open the door to Antonieta's bedroom, Sabina shook her mistress' shoulder. "We're going to church!" she announced. "Listen to the bells!" She placed the morning newspaper on the bed and disappeared in a blur.

Groggy after days and nights of ceaseless work, Antonieta sat up and listened to the bells ringing out the morning Angelus. She picked up the paper and saw the banner headline announcing the end to the Cristero war. "Mr. Morrow, the American Ambassador, was instrumental in bringing about the agreement between the Bishops and the Government," she read. "Officials of the Catholic hierarchy in the United States acted as intermediaries in getting both sides to lay down their arms."

Fully awake now, Antonieta reached for the telephone. It was seven a.m. José's train had arrived at midnight; he should be up by now. She had to talk to him before he was swallowed up by meetings. An idea had been germinating in her mind since Cuernavaca.

"José! Wait breakfast for me," she pleaded. "I'll be down by the time you dress."

"Who said I am going to dress?"

"I did. We've got to talk. Can you hear the church bells? Isn't it wonderful!"

"I am not in favor of the agreement," José told her. "The poor, damned Cristeros were betrayed. But there is good news. I'll wait. Hurry."

A waiter wheeled in a cart with a platter of fresh fruit and piping hot omelets. Antonieta listened while, between mouthfuls, José recounted the excitement of the successful campaign tour.

"Veracruz is with me. Even the Governor of the state, a Calles man. I wish you could have been there. Our rallies in Jalapa, Cordoba, Orizaba were tremendous! Of course, the militant Communists turned out, well-organized and widely dispersed, but they helped to put down the hecklers. Waldo Frank accused me of being a bourgeois candidate." He laughed heartily. "I was too keyed up to sleep last night. Kept thinking about the barriers I have to tear down. November is only five months away."

He pushed his plate aside and stood up, flinging his arms in the air in that characteristic gesture that Antonieta had come to recognize as an expression of inner battle.

"No matter how many votes we win in the province, the election will be decided right here in this city. We have to step up our war of words." He paced, eyes vivacious now. "People are tired of violence. But we are beginning to feel Calles' aggression in the provinces, a sign he is worried. The local authorities turn off the lights in the plazas at night, turn off the water in our hotels, shove and push and harass the crowds when I am speaking, and there are armed soldiers at every meeting."

Antonieta listened.

"Calles has the military, he has the United States and he has throttled the press." José threw up his arms again. "What can we do? Can you suggest a new strategy?"

"Sit down, José. Please," Antonieta said. "I've been thinking too. And I would like to make a proposal." She spooned a speck of hot sauce on her cold omelet. "I know how you feel, but hear me out before you say anything." She took a bite and engaged his eyes across the low table. "I believe a personal meeting between you and Morrow, where you can lay out your political and social programs, would help immensely."

"*Estás loca!* Morrow is Calles' mentor! He's a Wall Street man! What does he care for political ideals? Forget your idea."

"But I know Morrow, José. He's a reasonable human being. And a humanitarian. Didn't he get Calles to halt this dreadful Cristero fratricide?"

"I told you I am not in favor of the agreement. Damn the bishops and the bankers! The Cristeros could have won if they had just hung on."

"Won what? More bodies piling up!"

"You don't understand. With the help of Morrow's airplanes and guns, Calles put down the Escobar rebellion, and now he's forced the Cristeros to put down their arms. He's consolidated his power. The only one left he has to fight is me."

"José, listen a moment. Morrow sincerely wants to help Mexico. He is enamored of Mexico. So is his wife. The problem is that he doesn't understand Mexico. You can make him understand."

"Morrow is enamored of Mexico's oil. He has just signed an agreement with Portes Gil for subsoil rights, for which the American oil companies will pay us fifteen percent per barrel. A pauper's pittance! Be realistic, Antonieta. He's a partner of J.P. Morgan."

Antonieta did not push him. She picked at her food while José piled sausage and eggs onto a tortilla and drank his coffee. Finally he stood up and ran his fingers through his hair.

"Americans haven't the vaguest idea of what we are all about. We mean nothing to them. They think Mexico City is in some remote jungle." He laughed. "After a lecture I gave in Washington, a man came up to me and said, 'That was very interesting. The State Department is transferring me to South America.' 'Where in South America?' I asked politely. 'Costa Rica,' the fellow replied."

Antonieta laughed with him. When the waiter had removed the

cart, she tried again. "José, I think you underestimate Morrow. He knows all about you and admires you."

"I met him, Antonieta, when I first arrived."

"But since then things have changed. You can win this election if you convince him he is backing the wrong man."

José looked out the window. He was silent for a long time. Finally he turned and said, "Tell me about this plan of yours. What do you have in mind?"

"A private meeting."

"Where?"

"At my house. I will call his wife, Betty, and invite them to lunch. I'll tell her you are my guest too. They will come," she said simply.

José ran his fingers through his hair again, and sank down on the sagging sofa beside her. "I trust your instinct, *querida*," he said softly, seriously. "All right, we will meet, but I want it understood that I am not yielding to Yankee imperialism. This must be strictly a private affair, you and I and the Morrows."

"No one will know." Antonieta kissed her finger and placed it against Jose's lips.

The luncheon was arranged within a few days. A social affair, nothing official, nothing in the press.

With a certain reluctance, José arrived a few minutes early.

"You're looking very handsome and impressive," Antonieta said, greeting him at the door. "I see you even got your shoes shined."

"I am not trying to impress him," José said, grinning, "I am trying to impress you."

A small table had been set on a terrace adjoining the garden. The atmosphere was informal, cordial as the foursome took their seats.

"You speak extraordinarily good English, Señor Vasconcelos," Morrow said. "And I understand a number of your books have been translated into English. I admire learned men."

"Thank you," José said. "Not everyone agrees with my philosophy. If it's difficult for individuals to understand each other, how much more difficult it must be for nations.".

"Isn't that what diplomacy is all about? Trying to bring about understanding and reconcile differences between nations? Delicious bisque, Antonieta," Morrow said, pausing. "I have been following your campaign, Señor Vasconcelos. You are a very popular man."

"I hope so." José looked Morrow square in the eyes. "You see, Mr. Ambassador, I intend to win this election. I know you side with General Calles and his candidate. It's natural for Americans to admire dam projects and road building and a national banking system. That spells progress. But whose properties do the dams favor? And what portion of those bank deposits will be available to those who really need money? How much will be spent on education?"

"I should think a good deal. I'm told the government has an active rural school program."

"Have you read the text books, Mr. Ambassador? They are pointing the youth of this country on the solid road to socialism. Will a generation of young socialists be welcomed by the United States?"

Morrow was silent.

"Can one admire a President who was elected without opposition?" José struck his fist on the table. "Can one admire a president supported by a bought labor union, to which he now pays lip service while he amasses a fortune?"

"Here, here, Señor Vasconcelos," Morrow admonished. "Even if those accusations are true, our government must deal with the government in power, however it came to power. The 'de facto' principal, sir. My government is aware that Mexico is beset by problems."

"Then may I suggest that it let Mexico find its own solution to those problems."

"And what do you suggest those solutions are?" Morrow asked tartly.

"First, we must be free from military tyrants who place the destiny of the people under their thumb. We are a nation of extremes; to function as an integrated country we must have true representation in Congress. Our structure should be education at the bottom and honesty at the top."

"A commendable platform, sir."

José leaned toward Morrow. "Mr. Ambassador, does the United

States respect Mexico's sovereignty."

"Of course!"

"Will it exercise its influence to that end?"

"We are not responsible for the outcome of Mexico's election," Morrow stated, bristling.

"Then I ask a favor of you, sir. Will you tell General Calles that all I want is a guaranteed free election. I will win if he keeps his guns in their holsters."

Morrow faced José coolly and wiped his glasses. "Politics can be a nasty game, Señor Vasconcelos, and I wonder if a scholar like yourself fully understands its implications? Would it not be best to collaborate in the area of education for which you are so well qualified?"

Jose's face grew red, but he controlled his temper.

Antonieta laid down her napkin and stood up. "Shall we have coffee in the salon?"

The leave-taking was as cordial as the salutations. Comments were made about Aaron Copland's plaudits for Chavez' composition "New Fire," recently introduced at a superb concert.

"You are to be commended again for your splendid work for the Symphony, Antonieta," Mrs. Morrow said warmly. "I am hoping maestro Chavez will agree to a charity performance. May I call you, my dear?"

"Of course."

José accompanied Antonieta and her guests to the gate and shook hands again.

On the way back to the house he squeezed her hand. "You tried. The only new thing I learned is that the eminent Mr. Morrow is shorter than I am. Short and myopic."

That evening Amelia greeted her with shocking news: Albert had called.

"What did he want?" Antonieta asked.

"To speak to you, naturally. He wants you to call him."

In the morning she called her lawyer. "Should I speak to him?" she asked.

"If your husband has requested that you call him, I advise you to comply," was the lawyer's answer. "It would be ill-advised to ignore him."

Albert's familiar voice took her back six years. Her heart was beating fast as she listened.

"I'll be brief, Antonieta," he said. "I want to see my son. I am asking you in the most civilized fashion I know."

"No! It isn't convenient. He's in school, and has lessons in the afternoons. I...he..."

"Then I shall get a court order."

"But custody hasn't been decided!"

Albert had hung up.

"Can he get a court order?" She asked her lawyer.

"He doesn't need one," the man replied. "Until custody is awarded, there is no restriction on visitation rights. He's the boy's father. I understand your anxiety, Señora. We're doing everything we can to expedite your case."

New energy began to power the staff at campaign headquarters. Strategy meetings, budget meetings, meetings to establish the route of the important northern campaign occupied the thoughts and time of every committee member of the Anti-Reelection Party. Generous donations had come in from well-to-do backers, but there was never enough, not enough to send Andrés and a group of hard working young supporters on the campaign trail. News swiftly reached Antonieta, who made a private offer to pay the expenses of the group. These young organizers and orators were his best asset. They had to go!

Cash. Always cash.

Battling only briefly with her conscience, Antonieta sold a property in Chapultepec Heights that belonged to Mario. She also instructed her realtor to accept a sacrifice offer for one of her large buildings, and to sell El Pirata. She remembered the last time she had been there, with Manuel and his coterie. They had danced and danced, and then sat hunched around a small table, watching the *cañas* of mezcal collect, the mezcal paralyzing the brain, invading good judgment, provoking loud argument. A man at the next table staggered to his feet and demanded that she dance with him. Manuel stood up to protest and the man slapped a pistol on the table. She watched it spin crazily, until Xavier stopped it. The man stuck it in his belt and had staggered off, laughing. All she could think of was Chela as she ran out of the dance hall. Antonieta pushed her hair back. Yes, *El Pirata* must go.

The office was at last quiet. Everyone had left. Antonieta stayed on alone, studying the statistics in her card file, making outlines for speeches. The northern campaign would be a four-week trip, covering eighteen towns and cities by train and automobile. Close to midnight, she heard a key turn in the lock.

"José, you frightened me!"

"I knew I would see a light under the door."

"You should have gone back to the hotel after the dinner. You need the rest," Antonieta admonished gently.

"And you?" He kissed her and wearily sat down in the chair with the hole in the caning. "I should go over these outlines with you."

Antonieta stroked his cheek. "You're working so hard, José. Let me take some of the burden. Take me with you. I can be useful on this campaign. Listen to me." She turned his head and searched his eyes. "I'll be your secretary, your chronicler, your messenger girl. Amelia is home now. She will guard Toñito with tooth and nail. I want to go with you."

José pressed her hand. "If you want to come, how can I refuse you, *querida*," he said, sighing. "You have become my foundation."

Torrential summer rains turned provincial streets into rivers: San Juan del Rio, Querétaro, Celaya, San Miguel de Allende, Dolores Hidalgo, Guanajuato. In the heart of colonial Mexico, where the conspirators of the War of Independence against Spain plotted and fought, Vasconcelos drove home the need to change government, to forge a new Mexico.

"Intellectuals gathered here," the candidate's voice rang out in historic plazas, "patriots who forged this nation. But their sacrifice was betrayed. Our country is again dominated by tyranny. Only the servile are rewarded. Are you going to stand by and let it continue on this path?"

The sun beat down on the crowds in the morning, and in the afternoon a sea of umbrellas faced him, the weather ignored as they continued to fill the beautiful colonial plazas.

The train moved on. Antonieta learned to sponge off with a pitcher of water in the small inns; she learned to wait patiently at primitive railway stations for the next train.

On a hot July day, the locomotive broke down and they were stuck in a small town. Perhaps all day, they were told. It was Sunday. Antonieta raised her umbrella for relief from the sun as the group crossed the tracks and made their way to the shade of trees in a small, dusty plaza.

"Wait here," José said. "We are going to scout around, find out what goes on in this town."

Antonieta seated herself on a rusty bench. Small, half-clothed children stared at the lady with the umbrella, and a mangy dog rubbed against her leg. Soon, José and his entourage returned, followed by a group of *campesinos*. She watched, with certain amusement, when his spokesman, Ibarra, jumped up on a bench.

"Amigos," he called out, "I would like to introduce licenciado José Vasconcelos, your candidate for President of Mexico!"

A campesino stepped up. "We've heard of you. Welcome to Santa María de Palo Solo, Señor. We would be honored to hear what you have to say."

José stood up on the bench and began to speak, his voice carrying across the plaza, soon attracting artisans, shopkeepers, women with bloated bellies carrying baskets and babies. His audience grew. Suddenly an old man on a ragged burro was nearly knocked off by a band of boisterous men wearing pistols, who followed their chief across the plaza. A gun went off.

"Who wants to listen to this haranguer when there is a good cockfight! Break it up."

No one moved.

"I said, break it up!"

A solid wall of vasconcelistas faced the armed men.

"All right, pendejos, waste your time!" Weaving slightly they followed their chief.

Antonieta took out her pad: "While Vasconcelos was speaking to the campesinos, men with pistols followed their *cacique* across the plaza like goats. The campesinos did not budge; many may have been Cristeros who were forced to put down their arms. Beyond the candidate, on the edge of town, a lone campesino plows his field with oxen. This hard, parched soil is his *tierra*, a tie to which he is rooted for life." Antonieta sat back examining the scene. "A young woman offered the candidate flowers," she wrote. "Her face spoke of suffering, and her belly of her role as a woman. She told me this was her seventh child. 'Are you happy'? I asked. Evidently the question was one she had never pondered. After long deliberation she replied: "I guess so. My husband doesn't beat me "

Long boards and trestles suddenly appeared in the plaza, followed by women carrying heavy clay pots filled with *nopales*, rice, stuffed peppers, frijoles and steaming stacks of tortillas. They had prepared a banquet for the candidate and his party.

An orange line across the horizon was all that remained of the setting sun when the train's whistle blew, loud and insistently.

Gray-green cactus became a blur. Kilometers of stone walls wound up and down the parched hills, a barrier for animals and evidence of the toil of these rugged farmers. Antonieta sat next to Andrés.

"They're like the walls in Oaxaca," he said slowly, controlling his tongue. "But up here the best workers go north across the border between the planting and the harvest. They say half a million left after the Revolution." Andrés shook his head. "I think people are worse off up here in the north."

Antonieta took notes, went over José's speeches, reminded him to get a shoeshine, to eat. They learned more of each others' history in private moments, moments snatched from the consuming, ever-moving campaign.

"Has there been a town where you were not well received?" she asked José, marveling at the crowds that lined the stations.

"Yes. Morelia, on my way down from the border. That was the worst."

"In colonial Mexico? I thought it was a city of well-mannered people."

"Ruled by gunmen. I could feel the repression and fear there. On the surface, polite, tolerant words of welcome. Hypocritical words. General Lázaro Cárdenas is beholden to Calles. Calles put him in as governor, but I can tell you that Cardenas rules with absolute power in Michoacán. Only a sprinkling of brave souls turned out to hear us. It may happen again. Morelos is only a sampling of Calles' stronghold."

José was indefatigable. He breathed life into people, opened hearts to faith in the destiny of the nation. In his young staff, Antonieta saw rising patriots, future leaders. It was José's dreams and ideals that upheld them.

They moved north, founding clubs manned by volunteers pledged to turn out the vote. Meals were sporadic. Overcome by the tantalizing scents that emanated from smoking braziers in small towns, they ate roast corn, devoured roast goat, succulent chunks torn off and wrapped in a tortilla, bending way over to avoid the drippings. The boys explored local stores and returned to the train with jars of pigs feet immersed in oil and vinegar, marinating in herbs.

León, Zacatecas, Durango. The train groaned as it climbed to towns in the mountains, then dropped down into flat, hot country.

At last, Torreón.

As the familiar landscape came into view, a chill ran through Antonieta's body. Railroad junction of the northeast, the immense roundhouse, the complicated criss-crossing of tracks, the station platform dug up scenes she preferred to leave buried. She had bought *quesadillas* here, that night she had flagged down the locomotive with Toñito lying limp in her arms. Painful thoughts were blown away by the bedlam on the platform.

"Viva Vasconcelos!"

Abrazos, handshakes, short speeches. Finally, the delegate of the

Women's Organization led her to the Hotel Francia. In her room, Antonieta remembered Albert's description of the battle of Torreón and shuddered. This was a new era they were campaigning for! The Revolution was dead, and so were its leaders. Madero, Zapata, Carranza, Pancho Villa, Obregón: all assassinated. She dismissed the disturbing thought and quickly washed up in preparation for tonight's rally at the meeting hall.

"Citizens, this is the decisive hour! Who placed in power the officials who regulate your lives, who make you grovel for favors and pay bribes when you demand your rights? You have heard Ortiz Rubio mouthing revolutionary ideals like a puppet. Are you going to let Calles dictate your future?"

The candidate's voice was powerful and positive as he faced the crowd.

A burly man stood up and shouted, "Who is Calles? He's just a citizen, a private citizen with no public office."

"Does anyone here know who Calles is?" Vasconcelos asked.

A single roar of laughter from a giant throat was his answer.

Victory with Vasconcelos!

The unmistakable burst of gunfire split the air. Surrounded by a tight cordon of his young guard and a multitude of followers, the candidate was led out of the meeting hall.

It was past midnight before Antonieta could have a word alone with José. Raw fear scratched at her voice. "Do you think they were trying to assassinate you?"

"No. I think they were trying to frighten me. No one was hurt. Get some sleep, querida, tomorrow is another day."

San Pedro de las Colonias had not changed. In the stifling heat and the dust, the water truck with the patched hose was rounding the plaza when they entered the town. Antonieta walked ahead with the young staff, talking, planning, and dispelling unhappy memories.

Six thousand inhabitants had swelled to ten thousand. Ranchers and farmers had converged from every direction to see and hear the candidate, waiting two hours in the hot sun. Sharp tacks scattered in the road had delayed the candidate's caravan while tires were patched.

Darkness fell before the new club leaders left the plaza, assigning committee heads, writing by the light of oil lamps placed on park benches when city officials cut off the lights.

Antonieta glanced back at the house where she and Albert used to stay, as Vasconcelos' rented Dodge again raised the dust of San Pedro.

Monclova. A few intrepid youths climbed on the running boards and honked the horns, opening the way to the plaza. The candidate and his staff stepped out of their grimy automobiles into the crowd that waited in the oppressive heat. Someone offered refreshments. Food was laid out on a long table near the speaker's stand.

Writing in her own special shorthand, Antonieta kept notes: "In the confusion, Ibarra, who was to introduce the candidate, was grabbed by the police, taken to the station and accused of drunkenness. He was criminally lashed, then released, his shirt soaked with blood beneath his jacket. Ibarra returned in time to give an impassioned oration to introduce the candidate."

When the cheering died down, a man jumped up on the platform and addressed the candidate.

"We have all seen the election circus. They brought in truckloads of *campesinos* last week, had a forced parade of storekeepers and teachers and workmen, threatened people. We want you to know that we are here of our own free will and we will vote with guns in our hands!"

Victory with Vasconcelos!

Now there were armed soldiers on the station platforms. Vasconcelos' advance battalion pushed through the cheering crowds, chanting his name and waving banners, opening the way, protecting the candidate with a human cordon.

Like a kaleidoscope with its endless variety of forms, Antonieta's pen captured images, caught the mood of the people, quickly sized up their problems and their hopes. José's voice began to crack and she rubbed his throat with eucalyptus oil.

The worst critics of the Government were in the industrial north.

In Monterrey, Vasconcelos hit hard at the powerful labor union headed by a corrupt leader, Morones. Coddled by Calles, he told the crowd, the labor leader had discarded his overalls and become addicted to tailored suits.

"I will convert the palaces of Morones, built with the funds of the laborers he leads, into schools for your children. Rich labor leaders and rich officials are bleeding the country, putting their money in the United States, out of sight."

The latent social unrest troubled the men of Monterrey. Individuals and groups came to see the candidate, offering economic assistance and even arms.

"Power emanates from the mouth of guns not words," a spokesman said. "Your men should be armed, licenciado, and you should be prepared to rise in arms if the election is a fraud."

"Ghandi is not armed. The secret of words is to turn them into action, gentlemen."

The men studied him, this presidential candidate who refused to carry a gun. "Very few raise their voices in Mexico," Vasconcelos continued. "but the silence of the Mexican is not a sign of conformity. It is fear of power. You must vote. Abstention is the voice of a coward. The way you can help me best, gentlemen, is to guard the ballot boxes on election day. Get the people out to vote!"

In a moment alone, José whispered to Antonieta, "In Victoria, I'll ask them to go on to Tampico to prepare the way. I'll tell them I need a night to rest. In Victoria, *querida*."

But the city of Victoria was in turmoil, a local election in progress. Guns blocked those opposed to the official slate when they tried to vote. People were mauled and kicked. Open ballots were filled out on a wooden table, folded and dropped in a cardboard box. Would it be like that on November seventeenth? His young guard kept a tight cordon around the candidate as the throngs pushed through soldiers to hear him in the plaza. Later at the hotel his supporters posted guards in the lobby and outside his door.

In the morning a correspondent from "El Universal" stopped the candidate in the lobby. "We have run your column for years, licenciado, but I am now restricted from reporting the truth. The paper is in danger of being shut down, accused by the government of being reactionary. I have been ordered to limit my reports to short telegrams. I wanted you to know that."

"Revolutionary, reactionary," José said angrily, "What's the difference? They are words which have lost their meaning."

Antonieta ripped a piece of paper off her pad and handed it to the correspondent. "I think this will fit in a telegram." He read, "Thousands upon thousands have heard the licenciado say, 'Only fear or indifference can keep you from going to the polls. If you want a change in government, vote!'"

José shook the reporter's hand. "I hope we will see you in Tampico."

Antonieta fell on her bed, exhausted. Tomorrow they moved on to Tampico, the oil center of Mexico. The crucial test. She tossed, unable to sleep, images winding in her mind like a movie film. Her eyes had been opened to a Mexico that had never existed for her before. She had seen grinding poverty, the gentle kindness of provincial people, the fear of political power. Guns spoke louder than the will to vote. José carried a gun in his valise. His committee had insisted he do so, but he had sworn never to fire it unless it was a matter of life and death. Would the moment come? Fearless, confident, José was a target at every meeting. Would he be killed like the rest? She tried to push away the fear scraping at her insides.

Antonieta was as tense as an archer's bow as the train neared a station on the outskirts of Tampico. The disagreeable odor of petroleum filled the muggy air. She peered out the window as Mauricio outlined the route into the city. Automobiles would conduct them along the eight kilometers to the plaza. Local club leaders had made elaborate plans.

José slid in beside her and put his hand over her pad. "You have circles under your eyes. Are you all right?"

"Yes." Their eyes met, speaking a private language. "It's just excitement."

"You don't know how desperately I wanted you last night. I almost got up and went to your room, but the boys are light sleepers."

"They're guarding you all night, aren't they? They gave you that pistol hidden down among your books and papers in that Gladstone bag, didn't they?"

"Yes. Forget about that pistol. I told them I would only use it in a life or death situation. Calles isn't bold enough to shoot me in the open. Listen," he whispered, "I told Ahumada and Pacheco that after the rally in Tampico I was going to spend two days at a *finca*, as a guest of an old friend."

"And where did you tell them I was going?"

"Home by airplane, after the rally."

"Do you think they believe you?"

"I don't care. But for your sake I have arranged for a private plane to fly you back to the city."

Her eyes held his, questioning.

"I do have a friend with a *finca*, a beautiful place with a private beach and a runway for his airplane. Pack tonight." The train was slowing down. "Looks like we're almost there," José said, standing up. He bent down and whispered, "Tomorrow."

"José!" Antonieta stopped him. "Give me your suitcase and I'll go on ahead to the hotel in a taxi. Your suit should be pressed."

"No, querida, you're my showcase for the women here. Today you will ride with me on the parade route."

It was noon. Black clouds hung over the Gulf of Mexico, but only a light tropical shower rained down, cooling the suffocating air. Vasconcelos and his staff were guided through the crowd to assigned cars by well-organized local volunteers. The route to Tampico was lined with thousands of followers, the streets flooded with placards, banners, and Mexican flags. Doting mothers held up children to see the candidate. Waves of tropical rain came and went, refreshing the human wave. People tore at the wet remnants of Ortiz Rubio's picture, which had been plastered on the walls only a few days before.

A stream of taxis joined them, horns blaring as the procession approached the central plaza. Heads poked out of trees, and balconies bulged with onlookers. The smell of petroleum, drifting in from the tankers crowding the port, seemed more bearable now. There were signs in English everywhere. Antonieta pointed out a "Piggly-Wiggly" grocery in the arcade.

Local club members surrounded their automobile when it stopped, eager to shake hands with the candidate and bring him up to date on activities in Tampico. The pressing news was that gangs of the PNR, known assassins, had arrived. The leaders of the Club turned out masses of vasconcelistas to protect the candidate during his stay. Six men would stand behind him on the platform, guns ready. The lady would stand to one side with the leaders of the Women's Committee.

Applause and cheers broke out as the candidate climbed the platform and was introduced.

José held his hand up for silence. He faced five thousand people.

"Citizens, I have come here to make a contract with you. A democracy elects its government and that government has a contract with the people, a contract which provides for social justice, education, equality under the law. It promises to protect the welfare of the people and share the wealth of the nation. When that contract is broken, the people have an obligation to ask for an accounting, to demand their rights. Democracy is the free expression of the people."

The air was electric. Antonieta's eyes glistened as wild enthusiasm acclaimed his statements. José's words injected trust and confidence, fortifying the cheering crowd.

"We are free!" they yelled. "We want you to know that we are here of our own free will. No one has trucked us here and paid us a few pesos and plied us with drink. We will vote as we please!"

Vasconcelos for President! Cheers for an Honest Candidate!"

A man in blue overalls pushed his way to the front and stood up on a bench. Waving his dark calloused hands, he spoke out:

"I don't know how to talk, and I have never talked before, but in a book with a green cover which this man made, I read that an orator is someone who has something to say. And something comes up to my mouth now, that is why I have stood up, to say that this is our man because he is not a thief and because with him our children will have books and schools."

Cheers greeted the worker as he retreated through the crowd.

Someone else spoke out.

"Will your contract protect our rights as workers? Will you make the Yankee oil companies pay us equal wages?"

"That's right," another voice shouted. "We work harder than the gringos, but we don't get their pay or their houses."

"Fair treatment! Fair treatment!"

"A vote for Vasconcelos is a vote against the Yankees!"

Victory with Vasconcelos!

Nervous, Antonieta's eyes roamed through the crowd. No soldiers here. Maybe because of the Americans. The irony struck her. No soldiers, but Calles' gangsters were out there.

José descended the platform to thundering applause and whistling. He took Antonieta by the arm and guided her through the crowd to the waiting automobile. Driving at the pace of the escort, which walked on each side of the car, they crossed town to a small hotel.

"The big hotels all claimed to be booked," José explained. "They belong to Americans," he added bitterly "who have been instructed to close their doors to us."

"Oh José, what does it matter? The whole city is for you. We're riding in your victory parade!"

At the hotel, a band was playing. A banquet had been set in a garden festooned with *papel picada*, small cut-out tissue paper flags. Glasses were raised, speeches given. The sun set and the lights came on. The mariachi trumpets blared. It went on and on.

The leader of the local club, a dynamic worker and organizer, leaned toward José and said, "Last week, when Ortiz Rubio was here, in addition to truckloads of workers, they brought in whole railroad cars full of soldiers in civilian clothes and civil servants from all the surrounding towns. This circus paraded to empty streets, and when Ortiz Rubio spoke in the plaza, so many insults were hurled at him that the soldiers had to draw their pistols and fire into the sparse gathering."

"Was anyone hurt?" José asked.

"Several were killed. But you will never hear about it. Even the rich families are incensed. They boycotted the dance at the casino." The man raised his glass and clicked it against the candidate's. "May God protect you. The armed repression has commenced, and there are still ten weeks to the election. You can expect worse from now on."

José clapped the man on the shoulder. "It's men like you who give me strength."

Antonieta stood with José and his staff in the lobby, saying goodbye to the last of the celebrants, whose conversation was rivaled by crackles from the infernal radio on the night clerk's desk. At three in the morning, she excused herself and shook hands with José.

"Goodnight, licenciado. I will be leaving in the morning before breakfast." She turned to the club leaders. "Señores, you can be certain that we shall work in Mexico City until we claim victory! Goodnight."

She closed the door to her room and broke out in a crazy dance, laughing like a maniac. He was going to win! She packed her suitcase, ready to be spirited off in a taxi to the finca. In just three hours!

Waves washed over them gently as José and Antonieta lay in the moist sand, reviewing the events in Tampico, talking about the coming weeks, dreaming of the future. The joy of desire fulfilled, the joy of love shared, the joy of success filled each with an ecstasy they had never known.

"You must create a new Cabinet position, Señor Presidente. Secretary of the Department of Culture. I shall be that Secretary. Agreed? The first woman in government," Antonieta said, packing wet sand around him as he lay still, unresisting.

He sat up, shaking off the sand. "I have greater plans for you. You will be much more than that. Much more." He pulled her to her feet. "Come on, I'll race you down to the water."

They swam and made love, talked and walked, and fell on the beach and rolled in the sand, wrapped in each other. There was neither yesterday nor tomorrow, only this moment.

"My unique Antonieta," José said over and over. "I knew one day I would find you. Did you know there's a power down deep where the soul dwells which guides fate? I feel it, and I know you feel it, too."

Two stolen days. Golden days of 1929.

"I know now that you have won, José," Antonieta said. The mist in her eyes blurred the stars overhead, the most luminous night she had ever seen. "Mexico is in the palm of your hand."

They lay side by side on the warm sand. José drew her into the arc of his arm.

"When I was a boy, I used to gaze up at the stars and let my mind wander through the universe. It overwhelmed me and I felt like a tiny grain of sand. Tonight," he said, "I feel like a giant."

CHAPTER XXXII

Toñito saw the suitcases in the hall, dumped his school books and threw open the door to the study. Antonieta was standing by her desk sorting her mail. She caught him in her arms.

"You're home!" he cried out, kissing and hugging his mother.

A wave of guilt swept over Antonieta as she put her son down, as recognition that her "little boy" was now this tall ten-year-old sank in. "How could you grow so much in a month?" she asked. "I can hardly lift you."

"A lot of things happen in a month," Toñito said reproachfully. "You were gone a long time."

"What things happened while I was gone? Tell me," she said, kissing him again.

"The police came looking for Ranulfo. You remember, the bloody one who stayed here. Memela told them we didn't know any such person."

The police at her house? They had never made any inquiries before. "Have they been back?" she asked, feeling a stab of panic.

"No, but I see them looking in through the gate sometimes. The dogs scare them off. You are sunburned. Is licenciado Vasconcelos going to be President?"

"I think so, Toñito." She sat down and drew him close. "There were huge crowds everywhere we went. I am going to whisper a secret. How would you like to be the son of the President of Mexico?"

"Do you mean it, Mamá!"

"Sh." She put her finger on his lips. "Keep that idea tucked way back under your *coco*," she said, tapping on his head. Now," she stood up. "I brought you lots of presents. Want to see some?"

"Later, Mamá. "I have to wash up. Memela is taking me and Luis and Guillermo to see a movie that talks!" He rushed out then stuck his head back in the door. "I have to pick her up at Malu's. Tell Ignacio I'll be right down."

"Of course," Antonieta said. "Do you mind if he comes back for me?"

She heard the front door slam. He was off.

Not a kiss, not a goodbye. He's so grown up, so independent, she thought, feeling a bit offended. Antonieta sat down at her desk and began going through the mound of mail. The Women's Committees had been active. She would talk to them tomorrow. Nothing from her lawyer about the Supreme Court. Nothing! Diego had called, and there were several messages from Manuel. She felt restless, eager to share the success of the campaign and hear news of the *Contemporaneos* and her students. She telephoned Manuel.

"Manuel, I'm back. May I come up to the studio for a visit?"

"Of course. I have missed you." There was warmth in his voice. "I will be here all afternoon."

Diego invited her to meet him at the Opera Bar at seven. He would wait at the ladies' entrance.

Although the campaign had been arduous and exhausting, the euphoria that had carried it forward remained. And something more.... Antonieta closed her eyes and let the memory of warm salt water wash over her as she lay with José on the beach.

She bathed and changed and was ready when Ignacio returned.

The climb up the familiar stairs to Manuel's studio shifted her mood. He was standing at his easel. Even wearing the blue shirt covered with paint stains and the sleeves rolled up, he was handsome, elegant. He kissed her on the cheek, leaned back against the drawing table while she arranged the flowers from her garden in the Chinese vase with the crack. She looked around with an appraising eye at the large sketches tacked to the wall, then sat on the high stool near his easel surrounded by Manuel's strong, stark Mexicans. She pushed the campaign back, dulling the feeling of the waves.

"You have really progressed, Manuel. The mural will be a gigantic success."

"I want to talk about you." Sensuous eyes searched hers. "How do you like politics? What was it like? Tell me." He picked up his paint brush again.

She sketched experiences, highlights, described the countryside but she could not talk about José.

Manuel let her talk.

"Tampico was our crowning success. It was as though he were riding in his triumphal parade. Thousands of people jostled and pushed just to see him!"

"Are you in love with him?" Manuel asked abruptly.

"I don't know," she lied.

Silently Manuel daubed color on a tortured face. "I missed you more than I thought possible, and recognized what a true friend you've been, Antonieta. I'm worried about you."

Antonieta could not meet his eyes.

"You know, when I was at the military academy, Vasconcelos taught at the University. Once I went over there just to hear him talk. His brilliance shone on a whole generation, made us envision a live nation, one to be challenged by intelligent, capable minds. Vasconcelos name blew up on campus like a whirlwind, gathering young students around him. It was his dream that made them call Calles' bluff and propose Vasconcelos for President. And it's that same dream that has forged new students into his vanguard, as you call it."

Manuel stepped back and studied his painting.

"Mexico has changed in ten years. Calles and the Revolutionary Family are entrenched, just like those bootleggers in New York. He is not about to let go, even if it means killing Vasconcelos, like he has the others."

Manuel put down his paint brush and forced Antonieta to meet his eyes. "You'll be hurt. I know the military, and I know what politics can do to you. It's a ruthless game. He's using you. Get out, Antonieta. He can't win."

"He will win!" she said defiantly. "The people are with him. If it's a clean election, he will carry the country by a landslide!"

"My dear idealist lady of letters, if it were in my power I would persuade you to recant before you are tied and burned at the stake." Manuel shrugged and picked up his paint brush.

Antonieta's step was light as she entered through the ladies' door at the Opera Bar. Diego had his foot on the brass rail, talking to an attractive woman. He was dressed in a new suit and wore a conservative tie. He saw her, waved, and left the woman standing at the bar.

"Antonieta!"

Diego escorted her to a booth and squeezed in. "You have come up from the sea, my dear, like Venus. I want to know all about it. They say you are lovers and you write all his speeches. Is it true? What will you have?"

"A vermouth. I don't write his speeches. They are his words. I only help organize them." She smiled engagingly. "And what have you been doing?"

"I have been working with the Party."

"You mean the Communist Party, of course," Antonieta said facetiously.

Diego threw a handful of peanuts into his mouth. "Your friend could be more cooperative. We offered an alliance, strength in numbers, you know." A waiter came up. "A vermouth and a tequila," Diego said. "Maybe you could persuade him to join forces. It's to his advantage."

"The licenciado discarded Communism while he was still in Europe," Antonieta said.

"So it's the licenciado." Diego cocked his head, eyes at half mast.

"All right, I call him José. Here, I'll read you his views on Communism. She took a pamphlet out of her portfolio. These are his words:

'Lenin has proved in Russia that Communism does not work. State capitalism is not as productive as private capitalism. I will respect existing *ejidos,* but I will give the campesino every resource to buy his own parcel, and capital to work it with modern methods.'" Antonieta smiled smugly.

"You are sure you don't write that speech?" Diego pushed the dish toward her. Peanuts?"

"Why don't you talk to him yourself? Maybe you know a magic formula that will make democracy and Communism blend. You are such a sorcerer, Diego. Seriously, I will arrange a meeting if you want to talk to him."

Diego laughed, his huge body shaking, eyes bulging wide. "Did you see my picture of him on the second floor of the Education building?"

"No."

"Vasconcelos is riding a white elephant and handing out his classics. I don't think he wants to talk to me."

"Diego!" A white elephant was the vulgar term for a toilet. "Why did you insult him?"

"Because Vasconcelos caters to the gente decente and doesn't know a damned thing about art."

"He gave you your walls to paint on. Why have you held him up to public ridicule? I accuse you of bad taste. And I don't think you are a legitimate Communist. I can't smell the sweat anymore."

"I do have to eat, you know. In fact, I am about to reap a bountiful harvest. Your friend Morrow has commissioned me to paint a mural in Cortés' palace in Cuernavaca. His gift to the town." Diego threw a peanut in the air and caught it in his mouth.

"Hmm. What will you paint?"

"The Conquest according to the Aztecs, and the Revolution according to Zapata."

Antonieta laughed. "My father used to say that you like to create waves. "I am sure it will be stunning." She patted Diego's hand. "You are looking exceedingly well. Bachelorhood becomes you."

"It may not for long," Diego whispered. "That man standing at the bar who has been staring at us is a gossip columnist. He may marry us off in the press. Another drink"

"I can't," Antonieta said. "I have to go to work now."

Diego accompanied her to the Cadillac, prominently parked in a no-parking zone in front of the popular bar. She kissed Diego on the cheek.

"You are still the most elegant lady in Mexico, with the brightest mind," Diego said fondly. "A classic, like your father."

At headquarters, an avid corps of workers surrounded Antonieta, eager for a firsthand account of the campaign. Their welcome indicated full acceptance of the wealthy aristocrat who had become the leader of the women's movement.

Fighting the desire to sleep late, Antonieta was in her study early and set about the primary task of organizing her calendar. It was August twenty-second. Mario was playing in a golf tournament, Toñito had left for school, and she could hear Memela talking with Sabina in the breakfast room. Suddenly she was hungry.

"Hola, your friend is all over the papers," Amelia greeted her. "Seems he stirred up a lot of trouble in Tampico. Not the great successful scene you talked about at all."

"What paper is that in?"

"Excelsior."

"Controlled by Calles. There's not a free newspaper left."

Amelia rested her elbows on the table. "Antonieta, don't you think you have done enough for this campaign? The house is full of women and refugees. I don't like it."

"Listen, my sweet, if you had a burning desire to do something, something important, something you believed in, would you just give it up and let it go? There are only nine weeks until the election. I have to double my efforts."

"Mario thinks it's dangerous."

She cuffed her sister affectionately on the chin. "Columbus would never have discovered America if he hadn't believed in himself and been willing to take a risk. Here, let me see that article."

Amelia handed her the paper and sat looking at her sister. "You've got circles under your eyes and you're skinny."

"Diego Rivera said I looked like Venus."

"Are you in love with him?"

"Who? Diego!"

"Don't pretend. You know who I mean."

Antonieta looked up from the paper. Memela always saw through her to the

truth. "Yes, I am."

"Have you gone to bed with him?"

"Memela! That's none of your affair."

"You have. Antonieta, he's married."

"So am I," Antonieta said.

Amelia got up and put her arms around her sister. "I don't want you to get hurt. Love is the worst pain there is." She said. "Eat something decent. You are going to need your strength." She kissed her on the cheek. "I am going to the Club. Be back for supper."

A society column caught Antonieta's eye and she read down the page: "Seen with Diego Rivera at the Opera Bar last night: an extraordinary patroness of the arts and exponent of the feminist movement. Might she be shifting her interest from politics to murals?" The item annoyed her. She picked up "El Universal." There was only a brief mention of José, but on an inside page a picture of Diego and Frido Kahlo riveted her attention. "Diego and Frida Kahlo will be married in a private civil ceremony this afternoon." He was getting married! And hadn't breathed a word. It was a farewell to bachelorhood they had celebrated. Well, the tomboyish hoyden of the prepa had finally reeled in her big fish.

At noon, Antonieta drove down to headquarters. José was received like a hero. He arrived refreshed and fired with zeal for the grueling weeks ahead. With barely an acknowledgment of her presence, he plunged into work with his staff. When most workers had left for lunch, she approached him.

"When can we go over these proofs, licenciado?"

His eyes were cold. "Now, if you still have the energy."

The office was empty now. "What's the matter?"

"Let's go. I haven't much time."

Bewildered, Antonieta followed him down the wide marble stairway and along the street to his hotel.

With the bundle of proofs under his arm, they went up to his suite. Other members of the staff now occupied rooms on the same floor. Most of the time, José left the door ajar when they were working. Today, he closed it.

Angrily, he stepped away when Antonieta tried to kiss him.

"What's the matter?" There was hurt in her voice.

"You have been alone in the city one day and already you're a subject for the gossip columns," José said acidly. "Did you see Rivera last night?"

"Yes. You know he is an old friend."

"He has no integrity or gratitude," José said, his voice grating. "If I had known what Rivera was going to plaster on those walls, I would never have given him an opportunity to paint. The man is vain and outrageous. Damn him!"

"Look at me, José. I admit Diego's vanity, his outrageous behavior and conception of himself, but I appreciate him as a person. He is an artist in every fiber of his being. If he achieves anything enduring, it will be because he gives every bit of himself to his work. Nothing else matters to Diego."

José looked out the window.

"I have pledged myself totally to this campaign," she continued, "to your cause, José, because I believe in it and I believe in you. Does that matter to you?"

He did not answer.

"There is room for many men in a woman's life, but she can love only one. Can you accept that?"

Suddenly José caught her around the waist and kissed her mouth, her neck. "Yes," he whispered. "I can accept it in you. But I don't want to share you. Can you accept that?"

Antonieta awakened before dawn. She looked at the man sleeping beside her and gently pulled the blanket up over his naked chest. With lithe movement, she slipped out of bed and dressed. José needed to rest.

She tiptoed down the narrow inside stairway and walked quickly past the dozing night clerk, then hurried around the Alameda Park, shaking off the lethargy of heavy slumber. At headquarters she let herself in with her key. A new day had begun.

Antonieta took her typewriter out of the case and picked up José's schedule of speeches and meetings. With total concentration, she worked, going through her notes and extracting key phrases for his speeches.

The sun was pouring in the long French windows that faced the park when the first campaign workers began to arrive. Antonieta put away her typewriter and gave up her desk to a young secretary. She laid her outlines on José's desk and left for home, for a bath and breakfast.

Before nine o'clock there was a knock on her study door. It was Lucha, Mario's fiancee.

"Oh, Antonieta, I couldn't wait to tell you. Mother has given us permission to be married!"

Proper, impeccable, impatient, Lucha Rule kissed her on the cheek. Antonieta rose and hugged the girl affectionately.

"You will make a beautiful bride." An old Cornish miner and a young Mexican *mestiza* had produced this perfect beauty. A spirited beauty, thank God, who would know how to handle Mario.

"I want Toñito to be the ring bearer and Amelia a bridesmaid. Do they have your permission?"

"Of course, *querida*, of course! Have you set a date?"

"October tenth," Lucha said with a smile. "Ten-ten. I want to make it easy for Mario to remember."

At midday Mario burst into the study like a tornado.

"How could you sell my property! By what right did you take it upon yourself to sell my lot!"

Exhaustion had caused a headache and guilt now dredged up a taste of bile. She did not get up.

"I had to. For the campaign. I will buy you another lot, a bigger one. Oh, Mario, forgive me."

"I don't want another lot. Lucha and I have a house planned for that lot, the one you sold. Get it back! This damned campaign is making you lose all sense of reason. I am not staying for lunch."

He stormed out.

Vasconcelistas became experts at street battles. The young orators were constantly harassed and beaten, their meetings broken up, the houses of supporters pelted with stones and garbage thrown by hired gangs. Stickers claiming "Victory with Vasconcelos" were ripped off streetcars, walls, display windows, the doors of private homes, the jagged remnants covered with big posters of Ortiz Rubio. It became almost automatic for the vanguard to spend a night in jail, unless they escaped to the house on Monterrey Street.

By mid-September, alarming telegrams began to arrive from the clubs in the provinces. Calles had dropped his disguises. Defying the guns of the police, leaders in Oaxaca and Veracruz had fought back, only to mysteriously disappear a few days later. The Independence celebration on September sixteenth was an excuse to flood the city with police and paid gangs who left dead vasconcelistas in their wake.

"I have told the boys not to go running to your house and I want the women's committees to meet here at the office," José said. "Listen to me, Antonieta, you must in no way be exposed to the slightest danger."

Antonieta made no promise. José never stayed in the Capital for more than a few days, alternating his time with trips to outlying towns. Guarded by a tight cordon, the candidate walked through the working-class neighborhoods shaking hands with carpenters, mechanics, shop keepers, housewives. "Victory With Vasconcelos" stickers went up again and enthusiastic supporters slapped stickers on canine rumps. "Even the dogs are with him," a bold reporter stated.

Police began to watch the house on Monterrey Street. With satisfying cunning, Antonieta took her overnight refugees out in the Cadillac, lying flat on the floor of the car, her own legs covered by the black fur lap robe. So far, her automobile had not been stopped.

September 20th. Antonieta made a thick black circle around the date on her calendar.

"A big man I had never seen before was waiting by the gate at school when the children came out," Ignacio reported. "He was dressed in a suit, and I thought he was someone's father. I was parked right in front of the school gate, standing by the car, as usual, when Toñito came out. He waved, and I began to walk toward him to take his books, when the man grabbed him by the wrist and started running."

Antonieta gasped.

"Toñito screamed my name and two other chauffeurs helped me chase after him. The man turned and fired a gun but the bullet hit a tree. It slowed him down, and we tripped him around the corner, where a car was waiting with the door open and the motor running. Toñito broke loose and we almost got the canalla, but the man jumped in the car and they took off, tires screeching."

Toñito was shaking. "Where did they want to take me, Mamá?" Was he a robber?"

Antonieta held her son in her arms while Sabina rushed to the kitchen to brew sedative herbs. She comforted and kissed the trembling boy, while her mind churned. Calles or Albert? She would have to confine Toñito to the house. Damn Calles! Damn Albert! Damn the Supreme Court! Tears of anger and remorse streamed down her face.

"They have torn off their masks and shown their faces as kidnappers and rapists!" José declared to his staff. "We are witnesses to the rape of all moral values, launched against innocent people. To win, we can only count on the will of the people. Now go out there and tell them to vote!"

"If you profess democracy, you must vote at any cost. Demand that the voting stations be guarded. If you condone fraud, you are guaranteeing that your children, too, will be victimized. Your only weapon is your vote," Antonieta typed. Printed on handbills, this message would be spread through the city and country.

The Ericsson rang in the vestibule.
"Antonieta?"
"Malu. Hello."

"Amelia told me about Toñito. If I can help..."

"Ask your father to light a fire in the Supreme Court. I must have my divorce."

"I know. He says your case is up for revision soon."

Antonieta felt the uncomfortable pause.

"What do you think about this Diego affair?" Malu asked brightly, changing the subject.

"What do you mean, 'affair?' He married Frida."

"Not that. Your friend Diego has been expelled from the Communist Party!" Malu informed her.

"I don't believe it!" Antonieta said. "There was nothing in the paper."

"You know there are no secrets in this city. They say he was accused of 'heresy' for associating with wealthy people and certain government officials. While he has been painting the hammer and sickle on walls, Portes Gil broke relations with the Russians."

"What does it matter," Antonieta fumed, angry at a party which did not comprehend its debt to Diego. "While Calles kowtows to the United States, he grants asylum to Augusto Sandino to protest the presence of American marines in Nicaragua. Sandino is in every newsreel, but do you hear Morrow protest?"

"I called to invite you to Salvador's new play."

"I can't, Malu. Sorry."

Sabina placed an ice cold towel soaked in arnica on Antoineta's head. "You must rest. You are driving yourself to the grave."

"I can't." Antonieta took her old nana's hand and kissed it. "Thank you, *querida*."

She was obsessed with doubts and fears. Food had lost its appeal, and sleep eluded her. As she turned the page of her calendar to October, a new fear began its insidious path, a fear she did not want to face.

The government net began to close. Telegrams from the provinces were frightening: the leader in Tampico had been killed, another shot in Sonora, others beaten, their families threatened, rallies broken up with machine guns. A new handbill declared: "'Tyranny has degraded Latin America to a class of brutes. The habit of blind obedience has stupefied her spirit.' SIMON BOLIVAR. 1814. 'Are we going to continue to be a nation of goats?' JOSE VASCONCELOS. 1929."

Hundreds of clubs had been formed to sign up voters for the Antireelection Party. Now hired agitators started street fights, and it was normal for members to spend the night in jail. Anger flared in the Capital. The PNR headquarters was attacked by a yelling mob, hurling bricks and shattering windows.

"We couldn't get past the American Embassy," Amelia said, arriving late for lunch. "There was a mob of protestors shouting 'Down with Calles'. It was frightening. I wish this damned election was over!"

"It will be over when the licenciado is President," Toñito piped up.

Antonieta didn't say anything.

"I got tickets for Chavez' concert tonight. He's playing Beethoven and Stravinsky on the same program. Malu is going with us. Now, no excuses, Antonieta. You're coming with us."

"All right."

Driving to the concert along the Alameda Park, Antonieta noticed a long cordon of people crossing through the garden paths carrying placards and singing a new popular song: "I don't give a damn if Calles' doesn't like it..."

"Ignacio, stop the car," Antonieta ordered. "I see Andrés and Mauricio. That's our vanguard leading those people. Look, girls, Ignacio will take you home. Sorry, I am not in the mood for Chavez. I want to join the boys and go on to the big rally."

Before Amelia could argue, Antonieta was out of the car and the Cadillac was forced forward by the traffic.

Maybe José would be there, Antonieta thought, running to catch up with her friends. Euphoria carried her forward, swept up with the enthusiasm and momentum of the giant snake. At a little plaza near the old house on Héroes Street, the scheduled speaker had just finished and German De Campo, Vasconcelos' most fiery and eloquent speaker, jumped up on the fountain and faced the huge crowd. The flashing lights of a movie house across the street showered his hair with confetti-like flecks, and his eyes shone with an inner flame.

The clear voice of the young orator rang out: "Citizens, I am going to quote a Mexican President. He said, 'I firmly believe that Mexico is ready to enter an institutional era. I shall therefore step down so that Mexicans, with absolute freedom, can elect the citizen they consider best suited to govern Mexico.' That was said by Plutarco Elias Calles in his address to Congress on September first, 1928. Now, I ask, has he kept his promise?"

"No! Death to Calles! Death to the traitors of democracy!"

No one had noticed the long automobiles with official license plates parked in front of the movie house.

De Campo continued to speak, his eyes rivaling the lights of the marquee. A hush fell over the crowd as he pounded grievances against the Government and lit patriotic passions.

Suddenly the hush was pierced by the rapid fire of a machine gun. The doors of the parked vehicles swung open and other guns began to fire, causing panic, driving people against the walls of buildings, the walls of the old church. De Campo fell in front of Antonieta and Andrés, confetti lights flickering across the stream of blood which ran down his face and gushed over the paving stones around the fountain. Antonieta fell to her knees to help him and was yanked to her feet by Andrés.

"He's dead. Come on!"

They stumbled over the body of a workman as the crowd pressed around. Andrés hustled her into a dark alley, mildew flowering like mushrooms in the damp brick. She could hear machine guns still firing. Andrés held her arm; others flanked her as they moved along the wall. Someone shot at them, dislodging plaster that rained down on their heads. A ray of light slanted from a single light bulb swaying over an entrance. They ran toward the door, ducked inside. Now fewer footsteps ran down the alley. They joined a fleeing group and ran on. As they emerged from the alley, a stranger turned and shot at two policemen who had begun to chase them. One policeman fell. They raced along the bright, wide street to a taxi stand. Hardly speaking, they rode across the city to the house on Monterrey Street.

Antonieta's nerves were shattered. Emotionally drained, she was unable to raise her head from the pillow. One thought recurred over and over, like the lights on the marquee of the movie house. The policeman who abandoned his dead companion to chase them had seen her clearly. A terrifying perspective filled her vision: jail!

Images of Tina Modotti's drawn, drained face, looking out at her through bars, haunted her. How long would it be before the police came around? There would be no escaping arrest.

Another new fear tore at her as well. She hadn't been feeling right, and had to know why. Anxiety gnawed at the pit of her stomach, her head was throbbing. Antonieta forced herself to get up and dress, her mind jolted by a thought that demanded attention: She must leave Mexico. Flee. Today. Tonight. Mario and Lucha would be back from their honeymoon tomorrow. Memela would not be alone. But Toñito? She must hide him. Alicia's, of course. Pepe might hate her, but he could not refuse to take her son. Albert could see him there, but Alicia would protect him, keep him until she got back. And José? He would be hurt, hurt that she didn't call him, see him. But she was a hindrance to him now. "Hold him up, cover him with your wings, Father," she prayed. "Don't let him falter."

Amelia wasn't up yet. Quietly, Antonieta descended to her study and closed the door. She must leave, not listen to arguments, to lawyers. Good, understanding doctor Lee, her brother-in-law in Chicago, would help her. No. She would go to New York. Yes, New York was the place to go, where she had friends. There was a train for Monterrey at nine. She would pack, take Toñito to Alicia's. No, Ignacio should take him, ruling out any argument Alicia might offer not to accept him.

Feverishly, Antonieta wrote a note to Alicia. The nightmare persisted as she wrote to José: "I did not know the depth of my own fear. Andrés and Mauricio will tell you about last night. Machine guns. I cry for German, his body lay in a pool of blood. Your victory will avenge him! Someone killed a policeman, not one of our boys. Even in the face of murder, they would not sully your name. Not one carries a gun. But Calles will accuse us. They saw us run. I cannot face the thought of jail. I am a coward, José, but there is something more. If they put me in jail it will compromise you. I know you. Every moment I will carry a prayer in my heart that God will protect you in these coming weeks. When you are President-elect, I shall return to Mexico to celebrate your triumph. Will wire my address as soon as I settle in New York. If I could but speak all the words that are in my heart. A."

She heard Toñito call to Sabina from the dining room. His best friends, Sabina and Ignacio. Gathering her strength, she walked in and sat beside her son.

"I am going away, Toñito?"

"Oh." Accustomed to his mother's sudden absences, he heaped sugar on his oatmeal. "When, Mamá?"

"Today." Her voice trembled. "I am not well, my darling, and I must get to a hospital in the United States."

The boy had only to look at his mother to know that something was terribly wrong. "But you will miss the election!"

"I will come back when licenciado Vasconcelos wins. Meanwhile, you will stay at Tía Alicia's."

"Can I take my electric train? Luis never lets me run his."

Toñito fully understood that this was a measure to prevent kidnapping, and that his mother would come home as soon as she was well.

He kissed his mother goodbye without letting a tear gather in his eye.

CHAPTER XXXIII

1929

An icy December wind blew down the canyon streets of New York, penetrating the camel's hair coat with the big red fox collar. Antonieta pulled the collar closer around her neck and walked faster toward the residential hotel for women near Times Square. She had tried to eat a peach cobbler in the Automat, but after two bites she gave up. Her only nourishment all day had been three cups of tea. It would be quiet in the hotel during the dinner hour. She would be able to write without hearing a door slam or the elevator screech. It was urgent to get the truth published. Walking rapidly, she tried to dismiss the new fear. Soon she would have to see a doctor.

In her room, Antonieta pulled off her hat, tossed her coat on the bed and forced herself to sit at the typewriter. The crumpled telegram from José still lay on the table. She smoothed it out and looked once again at the terse message. "It is over. Will write from California." A door banged and she jumped. It had been two weeks since the election. Not a word from Andrés or anybody at campaign headquarters. Only the report in The New York Times: "ELECTION RETURNS IN MEXICO. Ortiz Rubio, PNR candidate garners 2,000,000 votes. Triana, Communist Party, 40,000 votes. Vasconcelos, Anti-Reelection Party, 12,000 votes." Not one tear was left, only anger at Mexico, which now blocked out all other feelings. She crumpled the telegram into a tight ball and threw it the waste basket. She had to work!

Antonieta picked up copies of the two articles she had written for Latin America Speaks, not a well-known magazine, but the first one to buy her articles. They had published "Street Performers of Mexico" and "The Submissive Latin Woman." Now they had commissioned her to write a political piece, specifically on the recent election.

She shoved her articles to one side and fed a clean sheet of paper into the typewriter. She tried to clear her mind, but "Vasconcelos, 12,000 Votes" screamed at her.

Muddled thoughts chased each other as she tried to find an opening sentence. "Washington must recognize the truth. The Mexican election was the most fraudulent in its history. FRAUD!" Thousands of faces looking up at José in the plazas swam before her eyes. She stared at the blank page, then feverishly began to type: "In this great democracy, where the United States can be sued by its citizens, in this country governed by constitutional law and in which the opposition openly speaks in Congress and the press, how can a vicious, fraudulent election be understood? If the popular vote had been honestly counted, José Vasconcelos would be President-elect of Mexico today, and that nation would be headed along the path to real justice and progress."

Her fingers faltered. She wrote and crossed out words, phrases. Words could not win battles, but she must find words: "For supporting the strong man, Calles, for interfering with its powerful influence, for placing protection of its commercial interests above the ideals for which this nation stands, for failing to understand the real needs of Mexico, I blame the United States..."

Tears blinded her and she was unable to finish the accusation. It was too painful to write.

Vasconcelistas had ripped off their stickers of "Victory with Vasconcelos" from their stores and houses as soon as the police began to threaten. Those who raised their voices in protest were manhandled, kicked, some shot. The "San Antonio Light" had run incriminating pictures. She dug her finger tips into her temples. The truth? The real truth was that Mexicans had knuckled under again.

In the Shadow of the Angel

Slowly, Antonieta reeled the paper from the typewriter and crumpled it up. Her head was shooting darts and the pain in her stomach was excruciating. The world was collapsing and there was nothing she could do. No one to listen. No one.

With every nerve-end screaming, she willed her mind to think of Toñito. Toñito, hidden with Lucha's mother, Mrs. Rule. Pepe had refused to take him into his house. "No one gets past Mrs. Rule," Amelia had wired. "He is safely hidden." The legal battle was over too. After all the agony and anxiety, Albert had won.

Antonieta forced herself to walk over to the dresser. There it was, the telegram from her lawyer. "I have not lost!" she said aloud. She must sneak back into Mexico like a thief and take her son away. Someplace. Somewhere...

All her energy drained from her body. Her legs were heavy. Shivering, Antonieta moved over to the narrow bed and flopped down, giving in to the familiar void that pulled her down into a black hole.

In the morning a maid, entering to clean the room, found the Mexican lady lying on the bed, feverish, fully dressed, her skin clammy.

A uniformed nurse was hovering over Antonieta when her eyes focused, at last, on the white room. The smell told her it was a hospital room. Saint Luke's Hospital in New York City, the nurse informed her, smiling as she took her blood pressure.

"You have been very ill."

"Did I..." Antonieta began, her dry mouth unable to form the question. She ran her tongue over her lips and tried again. "Did I have a miscarriage?" she asked.

"No, my dear, nothing like that," the heavyset nurse said. "You are not pregnant. The doctor diagnosed a nervous crisis." She wrote on her chart. "You'll recover rapidly now." Smiling, she patted her wan patient and left the room.

In a week, Antonieta was propped up on a daybed in the apartment of her friends, Clemente and Margarita Orozco. She had been in the hospital four weeks; a nervous breakdown, they had called it. Friends had found out her whereabouts, and gone out of their way to let her know she was in the land of the living. Even Alma Reed and the tight little knot of Mexican fans she had haughtily accused of promoting Mexican "folklore" in New York had come to see her. Clemente's fame as a painter was growing in New York, thanks to Alma. And, thanks to Federico Garcia Lorca, she had a project to work on. Her new friend, the brilliant, baby-faced Spanish poet and playwright, had suggested they produce a play together in Spanish, giving her a goal, a reason to recover. She felt the healing touch of kindness and learned to lean on friends. José had written, letters filled with bitterness. He had gone north to try and fan an incipient revolt. Caught by Calles' men, he had agreed to exile instead of jail, and had returned to his family in California. Manuel and Mario had written their versions of the election. "Stop playing Mary Magdalene and the Virgin Mary to your crucified Christ," Mario had written, "and come home." Home? It was a dead issue. She wrote in her diary: "I see Mexico revolving in a circle, and I am gyrating in the center, a captive in its infernal torment. A handful of rebels who rose in arms in support of Vasconcelos were executed in Nogales. Now the game is over. For a year, the government tolerated the farce of democracy. Now it's time to return to 'normal.'"

At the beginning of February she returned to the residential hotel. Her body was growing stronger, but there was a void where her spirit once dwelled. She was a spectator, watching herself go through the motion of living. She wrote to Manuel: "Thanks for your letter. It was an anchor in that white tomb where I existed for weeks, lost, without memory. Now I only want peace, to work, to be, to become a universal citizen. I don't know whether I'll ever return to Mexico. Meanwhile, I live in a cloister, of which I am the abbess."

To mask her emptiness, Antonieta filled her nights with diversion. A circle of Spanish writers, actors, poets, headed by Federico Garcia Lorca, was an oasis from the Mexican group. She felt safe with these men, like her *Contemporaneos*. She could let herself go, feel the pulse of the cabarets, the magnificent Harlem Negro reviews, bawdy cabarets in Greenwich Village, movies, theater, dinners that lasted until three in the morning, or nights at Federico's, when he would play the piano and mimic every accent in Spain. Then home on the subway, exhausted, to sleep at last.

Antonieta covered the typewriter and took the elevator down to the lobby. The afternoon mail had arrived. She tore open a letter from Mario. After affectionate salutations and inquiry about her health, a sentence underlined with a red marker stood out:

"Sit down because this news will shock you. First, I must tell you that I closed the house on Monterrey Street and went over the inventory with Boari's administrator. Countless antiques were missing, small pieces. Did you take them to the pawn shop in your frenzy, or were they stolen? Of course I had to pay for them, as well as the last two months rent. Lucha and I moved into a small house Mrs. Rule bought for us in that new development called Colonia del Valle. Having little furniture, I of course thought of our things gathering dust in that storeroom at San Jerónimo. Amelia found the key to the lock in the jewelry case you entrusted her with. We went together, Amelia, Lucha and I. The storeroom was empty. Cleaned out!! Not a single piece, large or small, left. Not even one of Papá's drawings. The locks were sawed through. Of course, no one knows anything; the watchmen heard nothing and your dear administrator, Manuel's father, denies ever knowing about the storeroom. Did you ever tell him? Where is the inventory? The devil with it now. Everything has been stolen."

Stunned, Antonieta took the letter up to her room and read it again. Her treasures, their treasures, Mario's and Amelia's. Toñito's treasures. They would be dispersed through the thieves' market and appear in the homes of the *nouveau riche*, who would never know that RM, interwoven with a gold edge, stood for Rivas Mercado. Slowly the shock gave way to reality. The jewelry was safe, and a few mortgaged buildings remained.

The letter ended with a request for money, cash Mario needed urgently. The airline in Acapulco would soon prosper. "We are flying payrolls and freight up and down the coast. I enclose some pictures of the natives when they see us land. The laugh might do you good."

Antonieta's laughter was acrid. "It pains me to tell you that I have no money to give you, mi amor. You seem to think that I have piles of dollars in the banks here. Surely you saw pictures of bankers bodies splattered on Wall Street this past October." Her broker had spelled out the truth: the last twenty thousand dollars were lost. Enough was salvaged to pay her expenses in the hospital and her lawyers in Mexico. If she lived frugally, she could pay her expenses in New York until her writing could sustain her.

Antonieta lay back against the pillows and let Mario's letter slip through her fingers. A wall had cracked deep inside her and she knew she was in danger of collapsing again. Short, painful notes from José had forced her to be strong so that she could lend strength to him. From letters received during the lonely, confused weeks in the hospital, she had pieced together José's path after the election. "The weight of a nation I let down is on my shoulders," he had written. "Why didn't they kill me?"

The murder of his staunch friend and ally de Campo had stained the purity of his beautiful national ardor. People had shown their teeth and began to answer fire with fire. Twelve thousand soldiers were in the barracks in Mexico City. The day of the election had been a nightmare of rifles blocking voting stalls; voting stalls moved to evade the Anti-Reelectionist inspectors; polls closed early, leaving voters standing; thousands arrested all over the country. Ten thousand protested to the Attorney General because they were not permitted to vote. All protests fell on deaf ears. Only an armed uprising could possibly have any effect. A letter from Andrés had ripped at her heart: "We waited at headquarters a week, but there was no call to arms, and the police were after us. Twenty vasconcelistas were shot on the outskirts of the city. A dog sniffed out their bodies, where they had been piled up in a common grave."

She thought back to the day when José was nominated at the party convention. Telegrams had flooded the office from intellectuals all over Latin America, Europe, and the United States, people who knew him and felt he was fighting for a just cause, running for an honorable office. Again, Andrés' words burned her mind: "We had inherited Tolstoy and our heads were above the clouds. Today it has all vanished. It was a puff of smoke. How does one live with a dream that has been destroyed?"

Andrés, Mauricio, Alfonso. Germán.

As she grew stronger, despondency had given way to anger against Mexico. She would go back for Toñito, then erase Mexico from her life forever!

A telegram from José forced Antonieta to take stock of her situation. "I am desolate. Only your loyalty has sustained me. Come to California. Must discuss publication of a magazine which will keep alive a small flame of truth. Details follow by mail. José."

That night, alone in the hotel, Antonieta battled with her conscience. She could not deny that the campaign had given birth to ambition, and to a beautiful fantasy: She would be the First Lady of the land, the wife of the President of Mexico. Not just his wife, but a woman who would make a mark in history, a woman who defended human rights and the rights of women who had been denied them for centuries. She had dreamed of being the wife of the incorruptible President who set an example of justice for the poor, for the aged, for the homeless, for all those victims of corruption who were denied their rights. For Indians brutalized by alcohol because life was too painful to bear. Mexicans knew how to die. She wanted to help José teach them how to live.

She lay still, letting conscious thoughts take shape. It was as if her whole childhood and youth had been spent preparing for this role. Not the role of President's wife, but of a woman whose life had meaning. Life had to mean something!

The glow of the dream seemed to light the dark room. But when she held her dream up to the hard metal of reality, she saw it melt, like a wax casting, slowly collapsing like the wall inside her. It was over. Vasconcelos was defeated. The pain was too acute for tears.

Antonieta stared at a speck on the ceiling.

What about him? How much did she love José? José, stripped of the presidency, stripped of his followers, of adulation and expectation? What could she offer a defeated José? What could he offer her? Did loving a man mean sharing pain, joy, and depression, or was it just sharing a bed? She wanted total possession and total commitment. She stripped him down to his naked body and looked.

"I love you, José," she whispered, and a new emotion began to fill the void.

He needed her. Now she let the tears flow. Poor proud defeated José. He needed her love.

The trip to California by air was long and tedious, waiting in chilly airports, changing airplanes. But she arrived in two days. He was standing by the ramp, an aged José who kissed her and led her to his outmoded Ford. They stayed in a rented bungalow in Hollywood for a week, talking, talking, talking. Bitterness and disillusionment had changed his face. Hatred haunted his eyes when he talked of those last few weeks, guarded by Calles' men, when he recounted his futile attempt to gather a military force. Then his heartbreaking decision to leave Mexico. Bitter words enveloped them like a suffocating mantle. Only in each other's arms did they find respite and refuge. A temporary refuge, until the oppressive mantle would enfold them again.

Venom poured out while he damned "the orgy of cannibals they called the Revolution!" He was like Nietzsche, the tragic Superman who had only ascetic sarcasm and hatred left in the end. But pure hatred purified. Finally the sac of venom was empty and José could talk of the magazine he wanted to publish in Paris. It would speak to all Latin America, to all countries plagued by the same ills that bedeviled Mexico.

"I have friends in Colombia who will contribute, and friends in Venezuela and Argentina. It won't take too much capital. Our magazine will circulate throughout the Spanish-speaking world, and your educated, magic pen, *querida*, will give it life."

Paris. The City of Light. Yes, light! They would meet in Paris, live like all the other exiles from Latin America. The magazine would reveal truths. One could tell the truth in Paris.

José's eyes were glazed by an inner vision. "My mother once said that we are each born with a few drops of God's grace to keep us humble. Perhaps, by God's grace, I can rebuild my life into something useful."

And I? Where do I fit into your life? Antonieta did not ask the question. José's wife and children were living in Los Angeles; he had to support them, he had told her. But said no more than that.

"Let me just put my affairs in order and I will meet you in Paris. It is better for you to go ahead over there and get settled." He took her in his arms. "I cannot publish the magazine without you." His tone was intense, but the light had gone from his eyes.

"I dread going back to Mexico," Antonieta said. "But I must. I must enter without anyone knowing and take Toñito. Amelia says Albert has hired the best detective to track him down."

"I'll write Jorge. You and Toñito can hide on his finca in Tampico until you can take a ship or freighter for Europe."

Antonieta and Toñito stood across the street from Héroes 45 and looked at the old house, half hidden in shadows. Black clouds rolled through the clear May sky like approaching monsters, the impetuous wind beating the branches of the old trees, dislodging dead leaves and blowing them down the street. In minutes, the sprinkle of raindrops was over and little puffs of dark clouds, like vanquished soldiers, drifted quickly away to hide in the mountains.

"Why did you want to say goodbye to the old house?" Toñito asked.

"Because that is where I started," Antonieta replied softly.

Sunlight now heightened the bougainvillea spilling over the wall, a brilliant burst of purple that awakened a comforting response in Antonieta. No matter who lived there, it was her house, the place from whence she came. She let her eyes wander over the premises, aware of the muted voices of children playing somewhere. She wondered if Huitzilopochtli watched them from his cave.

Like casual strollers who pause to admire a garden, she took Toñito by the hand and crossed the street. They peered through the high wrought iron gates. Shifting shadows played along the gallery, and children began to emerge from the foyer. Noisily they started down the twin stairways. Antonieta stepped back against the wall, out of sight, hiding from that other self she so desperately needed to touch.

"Isn't it time to go, Mamá?" Toñito asked. He tugged at her hand impatiently.

"Yes, it is time to go. You will love the airplane ride to Tampico. Your uncle Mario said you could sit up with the pilot."

She turned her back on the house and walked away.

CHAPTER XXXIV
BORDEAUX FEBRUARY 9, 1931

It was still dark outside. Not a sound in the boarding house. Antonieta opened her eyes, fully awake now. She lifted her head from the pillow and looked across the shabby room at Toñito, asleep, curled up on the sofa that served as an extra bed. She had slept fitfully, plagued by a cold, numb ache in her elbows, her knees, her feet, her hands. The temperature had hovered below freezing since Christmas. She tucked the quilt around her neck and rolled over to look at the clock. Just six. An hour before she would pull back the faded velvet draperies and wake Toñito for school. Three hours before she would take the train to Paris.

He had arrived. After continual postponements and six months of making her wait while she struggled to stay alive, he was in Paris. Their conversation had been strained. She recognized a twinge of jealousy when he mentioned his long lecture tour through Central and South America. Surely banquets and champagne had helped alleviate the defeat!

Hugging her legs close to her body, Antonieta tucked the flannel nightgown around her feet, huddling under the down quilt. The thought of José brought on a wave of homesickness, nostalgia for the sounds and smells of Mexico, the warmth of sunshine and glory of

555

blue skies.

She squeezed her eyes shut to prevent the tears from escaping. "Toñito," she whispered to the sleeping boy, "it's all empty here. I have brought you to an empty place." She lay still, feeling the warm tears trickle down her cheeks. Tears were so close to the surface these days.

Antonieta forced herself to get up. She slipped her feet into satin mules, ignoring the shock of cold. She pulled a wool bathrobe tight to her body and wrapped the belt twice around her small waist. On tip-toes she went to the bureau and turned on the lamp. The bureau was piled high with books and folders; she sorted them, clinging to the dull reality of this place.

Their "suite" in the boarding house consisted of a bedroom, closet, wash basin and sitting alcove. The bath, down the hall, was shared with Madame Lavigne, her daughter, Irene, and two gentlemen boarders.

Antonieta unrolled a sheet from her typewriter, the last page of a letter to Manuel. She had offered to arrange an exhibition for him, a ruse to bring him to Paris. Manuel would alleviate the desperation that was gnawing at her life. Manuel, who dreamed of recognition as a great painter, who had abandoned her because he had no more to give, no more he could give. Antonieta moved her chair to the bureau and diverted the light to the sheets in her hand:

Manuel, friend and painter extraordinaire:
Your letter arrived at last. Don't be caught in the whirlwind which is still sweeping Mexico. I was spun in the middle and it cast me out. You must finish your work for the exhibition. Come to Paris! Your creations will return home triumphant.

Manuel, in you I see myself. Your dreams and torment for perfection is my torment for the same, and when your eyes fall upon a bare horizon, think of mine, which daily sweep across an internal desolation, a loneliness which, ironically, constitutes my strength.

I repeat, it was necessary for me to leave Mexico, to burn my ships behind me. I could no longer justify a life of self-deceit. So I plunged alone into the unknown, like a thief who has stolen a jewel. Not knowing its value, it takes all his courage to open his fingers and look at what he has taken. He risks finding a common piece of glass instead of an eternal diamond. I am now living this trial by fire.

Antonieta began to shiver. Thoughts of her reunion with José had broken through her concentration. She forced her eyes back to the letter.

Exciting news! I am writing a novel, studying and working ten hours a day, even taking on two hours of Latin so I can understand the most insignificant footnote. The novel is a constant struggle, toward goals so high that the highest star seems low, and a yardstick of 'those who count' piled on my bureau. I am obsessed by my work. The passion lasts while there are still paragraphs to polish and pages to conquer. But when I review yesterday's achievement, I feel nauseated. .

Bear with me for a few notes: The heroine rebels against reality, but consigns to silence every one of her former illusions. She sees through newborn eyes the civilization of her country, without the veil of humanitarianism, without vapors of democracy, without justice, without mercy, without love. She sees only the beauty that comes from centuries of struggle and pagan mystery, an ancient beauty—hard but with soul, submissive but strong, like an emerging mountain. It is not a story of defeat, but an attempt to make a vital evaluation.

My heroes are not heroes in the ordinary sense. I hope to develop 'types,' our types. Of course it's Mexico. Newborn, yet ancient. I want to link that crater of the volcano, which is our land, with the rest of the world. I want to dive into something purely Mexican, without it ever occurring to the reader to speak of 'local color.' I hope to create something human, humble, penetrating. I feel Mexico so deeply, so very deeply.

Tomorrow I go to Paris. José has arrived, finally. It is ironic—no, bitter--that he should come here as an exile. He is determined to publish his magazine here. He has called it "La Antorcha", a light which will bare the truth, not only about Mexico but all Latin America. Tomorrow we are going to talk about the format and a starting date. I have reams of articles already written. Only to you, Manuel, will I say that I approach this meeting with certain trepidation.

You will come to Europe. You need Paris!
Toñito grows like a noble plant in healthy soil. And I survive.
My love, A.

The letter dispelled her earlier mood. She addressed it and sealed the envelope, the very act injecting a note of optimism.

The alarm rang. Toñito began to stir. Antonieta put away her typewriter and cleared the bureau. She began to set up the family pictures. She liked to leave Toñito in the company of familiar faces in her absence. She looked at them: her father, Tío Beto, her mother, Mario and Lucha, Alicia and the cousins, Amelia and Sabina. She opened the bottom drawer and took out another picture—Albert. It was inscribed "to my son, Donald" as though "Toñito" would tarnish his British heritage. Finally she took out the family album.

"Mamá," Toñito called out. It's cold. Can't you turn up the radiator?"

Antonieta pulled back the draperies behind his bed and bent to kiss her son.

"Bon jour, mon amour. You will feel warmer when you get up and let the blood begin to circulate. Get ready," she warned, "time to crawl out of the cocoon." She threw back the covers. "I'll see if the bathroom is free."

"Have you been working in the dark again?"

"No, my little worrier, I just got up. Here, put on your bathrobe."

"Do I have to take my boxing lesson today?"

"Of course! How else will you develop enough muscle to defend yourself against those brutes at your school?"

"I hate school."

"You won't when your French improves. I'm not much help. Every day I say I will not speak to you in Spanish, but then I do."

While Toñito was packing his books in his satchel, Antonieta casually mentioned that she was going to Paris.

"Again, Mamá? Why must you go?"

"The licenciado called me yesterday. He's arrived."

"Oh."

"It will be so good to work, I mean professionally. We will be rich again, Toñito. You'll see."

"And then can we go back to Mexico? Even if the licenciado is not President?"

"You want to go back very much, don't you?"

Tears flooded Antonieta's eyes and the little boy flung his arms around his mother's neck.

She gestured toward the bureau. "I set up the family to keep you company."

"Why did you put my father there?"

"Because he is your father and someday you will have British and American relatives to add to your family collection.

"I don't want them! I'm Mexican!"

"Your father is not a bad man, Toñito."

"Then why did you hide me from him? Why does he make you so angry?"

"Look, I took out the family album too. Maybe you would like to show it to Mrs. Lavigne's grandson. He's coming over tonight, and if it's a nice day tomorrow Irene said she would take you boys ice-skating."

Carefully, Toñito took the big velvet book down from the dresser and opened it. On the first page was a photograph of the Angel Monument with a picture of the architect superimposed.

Antonieta embraced her son. "Do you remember your grandfather?"

"Mamá, I was seven when he died. You remember everything when you're seven."

"Will you remember everything when you were eleven? Choose a dress for me, so you will remember which dress I wore today."

Toñito took his mandate seriously and riffled through the dresses in the closet. He put a soft beige shift on the bed.

"I like you in this better than the black or mauve. Madame Lavigne says that you are very elegant for being so poor. When we get rich again, can I change schools?" he asked solemnly.

"Of course, mi amor." Antonieta laughed. "Anything you want."

"How many days will you be gone?"

"Three, or four at most. I will telephone tomorrow when you get home from school. Now let me inspect you." Antonieta put her hands on her hips. "Knee socks pulled up, proper short pants, tie, blue blazer. Here, put on your overcoat and I'll strap your satchel on. There. You are a fully French school boy," she said, attempting to tease.

"Except for this." Toñito held up his sleeve for inspection. "See, there's a button missing. Shall I ask Irene to sew one on?"

"Indeed not! I will buy an exact brass button in Paris and sew it on when I get back. Now hurry. You barely have time for some milk and a croissant."

Antonieta cleared a patch of moisture from the window and waved goodbye to her son as he passed by, head bent against the wind. There was something sad in Toñito. She must control her emotions in his presence. He was so sensitive. He felt her insecurities.

One more letter and then she would dress. Antonieta took out her typewriter and began to write:

Memela, my precious little sister:

The mail is so slow and I am desperate for money. I shall send you a telegram from the station in Paris. José has arrived and I am about to leave Bordeaux. No answer to my last letter. I remembered only last night that there may be a balance in my account at the Banco de Londres. Please find that bank book and send me every cent you can.

Tell Mamá that I have been to confession, if she is still concerned. I can't think of why she is suddenly worried about me, but if it assuages her conscience you may give her that message.

Am I a pauper? Surely there are some properties left. Mario will not give me a true accounting, so forgive me, my darling, if I throw this burden on your shoulders. You both have your own money now. My money is almost gone. I had to borrow enough to buy Toñito an electric train for Christmas, with barely enough left over for dinner at a decent restaurant.

Oh Memelita, I don't really care whether I have money or not. I don't mind austerity. We are comfortable and I can earn money, but every day I grow weaker. My vitality is drained, the cork crumbling. How I long to see you. Will you come to Europe? I will pay your way if there is a building left that can be rescued from the hands of the mortgage company.

I long to drink sun, water, sky, silence - to wrap myself up in peaceful existence like an Indian in his sarape. To let go, to let go.

I have cut my hair short again. I look modish. You would approve. I would like to be like those carefree flappers in the night clubs in New York; I am thin enough, but short skirts are not my style. Both of the boarders are in love with me. One is a wheezy old bird who still considers himself a bon vivant and tries to ply me with dreadful pâtés and cheap wines. Shall I tell him that pâté makes me nauseous, that Papá wrapped the last of the fois gras in a moldy tortilla to celebrate my fifteenth birthday? Do you remember? You were seven. And do you remember Jeanne Bucher? Her gallery is among the most select in Paris. She has Picasso, Lipchitz, Lurcat, Jean Hugo, Miro, all old friends who Manuel taught me to appreciate. Wouldn't Papá die again if he knew my tastes, and that Diego's 'ugly monkeys' have quite captured the critics in Europe? Has Diego finished the murals in the Palace?

Forgive me if my thoughts jump around. Some days I wonder who I am. Did you know that matter cannot be destroyed? It can only be transformed, like water. Whether liquid, ice, or steam, it is water. I am the sum of dozens upon dozens of ancestors none of whom can be destroyed. How I would like to get inside their skin, like the Aztec Eagle Knights, and feel all those ancestors in me. When I used to play the piano for them, I felt their presence.

I shall post this letter in Paris. Come to us, Memela! If only you had wings to fly. Your gaiety and mere presence would be that sun and sky and water I long to drink.

Hurry, my precious baby sister. Every day I must gather energy drop by drop just to stay alive.

My love always,
Antonieta

The compartment on the train was stuffy. Antonieta's eyes became fixed on a spreading crack in the window pane, oblivious to the changing landscape. She had prepared so long for this meeting, and now she felt unprepared. Lulled by the monotonous click-clack, finally she dozed.

"Next station, Paris," the conductor called out. He opened the door to the compartment and shouted. "Par-ee ... Par-ee."

Antonieta scanned the faces on the platform as the train pulled into Austerlitz station. He wasn't there. She had told him it was better to meet at the hotel. She had even set the hour, seven o'clock. She pulled down her valise and blended in with the crowd. It was only five-thirty. She would walk to the hotel. The air would do her good.

The Paris drizzle wove an icy curtain of desolation. She crossed the river to the left bank and wound down familiar alleys in the Latin Quarter, remembering her big bear of a father who had held a little girl by the hand, a little girl whose eyes drank in every image, whose vision of the future was limitless. "I shall mold my future as I desire," she told herself, "free and hard and solitary. The truth is that he needs me more than I need him."

Walking down familiar streets, she found the small, commercial hotel. An indifferent clerk handed her a room key. José had reserved her a room down the hall from his. The rug was threadbare and the room smelled of stale tobacco, but it had an armoire and a wash basin. A toilet and tub were down the hall. An electric sign flashed outside her window. Antonieta pulled down the shade. She washed, combed her hair and changed into the beige dress, which fell from her hips in soft folds. Finally she picked up the portfolio and closed the door behind her. It was seven-twenty. Dropping the key in her small black purse, Antonieta approached José's room. Her heart was pounding.

José threw open the door and embraced her. His strength flowed through her body and she raised her face for his kiss. There was someone else in the room. Carlos Deambrosis, of course.

"I have waited and waited for this day, Antonieta, and for the first time you're late," José chided.

"I have waited six months without complaining," she said with a wan smile. "Hello, Carlos. How is the family? Toñito asks about your little boy." Carlos was a journalist, an avid follower of Vasconcelos, and her link between France and America. "Did I interrupt something?"

"Of course not!" José said. "Carlos met me and we rode up on the train together. I have just convinced him to act as our editor, without salary, of course. And, to celebrate this historic encounter, I am inviting you both to dinner. There's a little bistro by the Tour Eiffel which serves a superb table wine."

"Don't you want to look at these?" Antonieta asked, holding out the portfolio.

José laid the portfolio on his dresser. "Tomorrow we work. Come on, I'm starved."

José tried to sustain an animated conversation during dinner, but the light in his eyes was gone. His cuffs were frayed. The subject of money began to dominate. Carlos' irreverence for people whose money had not been made by the sweat of their brow had been obvious to her when they first met. She listened to the pragmatic questions uncomfortably.

"How did the South American tour go?" Carlos asked.

"South Americans are stingy, I discovered. I came back with only eight thousand dollars."

He did not mention the banquets and the champagne. There was a parsimonious side to José she had never noticed before.

"I must be frank. I can't sustain a loss. Without the support of Hispanic America, our 'Antorcha' will die an early death."

Carlos got off the elevator at his floor and José walked with Antonieta to her door. He embraced her and buried his face in her neck, breathing in the perfume of her skin, kissing her neck, her lips ardently.

"Shall we stay here tonight or in my room?" he whispered.

She pushed him back. "Not tonight. I… I haven't felt well, and we have so much work to do tomorrow."

"All right." Hurt in his eyes. He kissed her on the cheek. "Will I see you at breakfast?"

"After lunch. You and Carlos are going to look for an office in the morning and I have things to do. I'll put a note in your box if I get back before you do. Good night, licenciado." She kissed her finger and placed it on his lips.

A gray haze covered Paris in the morning. Antonieta strolled along the Seine, idly thumbing a few books in the book stalls. He was grasping at straws. His suit looked worn, misshapen, and he was locked inside himself, unable to see out. He had not really seen her and had not even bothered to open the portfolio. They were playing a part. He was broken. She was broken.

Antonieta stared down at the water. The reflection of these buildings had been there for centuries, as though between Paris and the Seine a harmony existed that could never be broken. The harsh silhouette of Notre Dame appeared, giving stability to the suddenly clear water. Nebulous images of gargoyles trembled on the surface; a mirage, gone as a boat violated their form. The forms realigned and the towers of Notre Dame reappeared in the living water.

A biting gust of wind threw a few grains of dust in her eyes; reality was a gritty, vexing blur. Antonieta stopped in a nearly empty cafe and had some hot soup. Arturo Pani, the Mexican Consul, should be in his office by now. He would lend her money again, and she wanted to talk to him about a passport for Toñito. Just in case. She stood up and took a deep breath. She felt dizzy.

Arturo Pani got up from his desk and greeted Antonieta with a kiss on the cheek.

"Antonieta, what a surprise and what a pleasure. If you had called me from Bordeaux I would have invited you to dinner. Unfortunately, we're going to some silly concert. But please sit down. How is your son? How is the writing?" He looked at her paternally. "You are thin, too thin."

The consul led her to a deep sofa in his office.

"Tell me about yourself?"

"Vasconcelos is here. I am meeting him later."

"So he has finally arrived. What kept him?"

"A trip through South America. And trying to raise money in Spain for the magazine," Antonieta replied. "I came to help him put together the first issue,"

"Then you still plan to collaborate with him." The consul puckered his lips.

"Yes."

"Do you think that's wise?"

"Why do you ask?"

"Well, I have been thinking about your situation. With Ortiz Rubio in, there have been changes in the Supreme Court. I think you can obtain a reversal of their decision."

"You want me to go back to Mexico. Is that what you are advising?"

"Yes."

"Because you don't think I should work with José, isn't that it? You know, Arturo, for such a decent person as I know you really are, I can't understand how you bear working with Calles and his assassins."

Arturo let the remark pass. "Vasconcelos is a bitter man," he said. "I don't think you are good for each other." He took her hand. "You can remake your life in Mexico."

Antonieta laughed. "Remake my life in jail?"

"That's an aberration. No one will put you in jail."

"They have put Tina in jail again. She's there for the attempted assassination of Ortiz Rubio, although I have it on good authority she was nowhere near him!" Antonieta took off her hat and ran her fingers through her bobbed hair. "Anyway, if Calles didn't put me in jail, Albert would. And he would take Toñito." She paused, pensive. "What does it matter? I will never go back to Mexico!"

"Well, you should have a Mexican passport, anyway," the consul said gently, noticing the tremor in her voice. "Keep your British passport, but let me issue you a Mexican passport too. Your son can be included."

She leaned her head against the sofa. "No one can go back, can they?"

"Antonieta, are you all right?" the consul asked, aware that she seemed strangely distant.

"I feel a bit dizzy, that's all. Thanks for your concern." She fluffed out the short, black tendrils and put her hat back on. "Arturo, if anything happens to me, I want you to pick up Toñito."

565

"What could happen?"

She stood up. "Oh, I might be run over. Or drop dead from fatigue. Or commit suicide." She breathed deeply and smiled.

"Don't say such a thing, even in jest. Look, promise me you'll attend to your passport tomorrow. No, how about today.? Now. I'll cancel this damned concert. You can get your picture taken around the corner, then we'll drive out to the house. A fire and a nice dinner with the family will cheer you up."

"I can't." Antonieta shivered slightly. "I'm so tired, Arturo. So tired." With a sudden change, she looked at her watch. "My God, it's four o'clock. José will be frantic."

"Where are you meeting him?"

"At the Hotel Lombardy."

It was four-thirty when Antonieta arrived at the hotel. Her box was stuffed with messages from José. He had been waiting since two o'clock.

In her room, she quickly took off the damp black wool dress and let the soft beige folds fall over her hips. As an afterthought, she picked up her white Spanish mantilla and draped it over her shoulders.

José threw open the door. "Where have you been? You said after lunch."

"I knew you had a lot to discuss with Deambrosis, so I didn't hurry. Forgive me."

Antonieta removed the mantilla and draped it over the high brass bed, fringes spilling over the edge, hiding the dust beneath.

José watched as she sat down in one of the small chairs by the window and crossed her legs, the toe of her patent leather pump gracefully pointed downward.

"Antonieta enters the drab room and it is transformed into a place of elegance," José said. "You are beautiful, but so thin. Are you well, Antonieta?"

"Yes, of course." She smiled.

"Can I kiss you now? I sent Carlos away for the evening."

"I think we should talk business first," Antonieta said. "How are you, José? His eyes looked tired.

"I guess all right. It's been rough. So many criticize me...no, accuse me, for leaving Mexico. They prefer a dead martyr." His laugh was mirthless. "I want to talk about your articles. They're brilliant! Compelling, riveting, just what we need to get started."

Antonieta reached for the portfolio on the low table between them. "I think the chronicle of the campaign should be published in our first issue. Then this one, where I trace militarism in Latin AmericaAnd the analysis of Primo de Rivera's debacle in Spain? Did you like the long piece on Ghandi? That one should wait. We can run it with the biography of Trotsky I'm working on, to compare two contemporary revolutionaries."

"Whoa! Look at all these pages. You have worked hard, *querida*." José stood with his back to the window. "I was trying to figure out how much I owe you."

"José, I wasn't working for the money."

"You need money to live. I understand you've been borrowing."

"Deambrosis told you."

"He said he had loaned you money from his savings, and that you bought Toñito an electric train. I told him I would repay him as soon as the magazine makes money."

"José, that is not your debt!"

José flung his arms in the air. "I can't even pay you for all the work you've already done."

"Then let us share our poverty," Antonieta said with a rueful smile.

José sat down and pulled his chair close to hers. "Antonieta, listen. Mexicans are noted for making passionate decisions, decisions based on emotion. Well, I have to make intelligent decisions now, for us both. I can't ask you to work for nothing. For a magazine to succeed it must be a business, everyone has to receive a salary."

"Let me translate, then, for my meals. We can share them in a garret. I don't care."

"The bohemian life doesn't exist anymore! Can you understand that? There is only poverty, and you don´t have the slightest idea of what poverty is." José took her hand and caressed it. "You have been on my mind every minute. Don't you know that my heart has been chipped away in bits and pieces by the knowledge that I have caused you such pain and anxiety?"

Antonieta looked into moist eyes, eyes in mourning for a dream destroyed. Tired eyes. Everything about him seemed tired.

"You must put your affairs in order, *querida*. You must go back to Mexico, at least for a month or two months. Sell your jewelry and pay off mortgages. You say you still have some properties. And fight for custody of your son. There are some new judges on the Supreme Court. You'll get custody. By the time you get back to Paris, I'll have the magazine off the ground. Antonieta…"

She was silent, wrapped in herself, short gold earrings moving imperceptibly against the delicate neck. She did not seem to be listening, but when he called her name, she looked up.

"Maybe you're right. Yes, you are right, José. I should leave here." Each word weighed on her lips. Then she looked at him and said brightly, "I can get free passage home. The Captain of that freighter was a beautiful *macho*, preening in his gold braid. Toñito was impressed." She laughed. "I slept with him. He has been writing to me. We go could home on his boat. It wouldn't cost a cent."

José looked at her, his eyes scolding a recalcitrant child, not lit with the anger a man feels when he is jealous.

"Do you expect me to believe that?" he asked.

"It's true."

"True or not true, it doesn't alter our situation."

"Doesn't it?"

"No."

José pulled her to her feet and carried her over to the bed, moving aside the mantilla as he laid her down. Carefully he folded the beautiful shawl and placed it on the night stand. Then he undressed her, laying each garment on the shawl as though they might be soiled any other place. In the narrow bed their bodies entwined, drinking his passion from her lips like great gulps of oxygen after long asphyxiation. He bit her neck, bore down hard as though possessed by a dark urge. Finally, Antonieta was carried off in space until her head burst into a thousand sparks.

Passion spent, they slept.

Near midnight, Antonieta carefully extricated herself from José's arms and began to dress. She was fastening the last button when he spoke.

"You're deserting me. Why?"

"You'll be more comfortable," she whispered. "Go back to sleep."

"But I didn't take you to dinner."

"I'll see you at breakfast," she continued to whisper. "Shh. Go back to sleep."

"No. We haven't toasted the 'Antorcha'. My bathrobe is on a hook in there by the wash stand. Just toss it to me."

"José, you have been driving yourself. You need the rest."

"I want to have a drink with you, to toast your work. And we didn't finish talking. There's some Hennessy in the Gladstone in the closet. Please."

Antonieta found the familiar bag in the closet and opened it. Down among the books and papers her hand encountered metal. His pistol, tucked away where it always was. She took out the bottle of brandy and handed him his wool robe.

Sitting with their knees touching, they toasted each other and joked, recalling intimate details they had shared. Then José returned to the hard facts of her situation and talked of Mexico again. That was the unfinished conversation, she thought. He walked over to the window.

"I am bringing Serafina and José over from Spain once I get settled. José wants to finish university here." He flung his arms in the air and faced her. "What else could I do?"

"Of course, he's your son," Antonieta said flatly. "And Serafina is your wife."

"You know my situation. We don't have to discuss it. It's you I worry about. You must put your affairs in order." José came over and knelt beside her, caressing her hands. "What argument can I use to persuade you, *querida*? Go to Mexico, put your affairs in order, then return to Paris renewed. You are not looking well. The sunshine will do you good."

So he didn't want her here now, she reflected. She was in the way.

"Fine," she said. "Perhaps you're right."

"After breakfast, we'll go and have your passport pictures made. Then you can keep your appointment with Pani at eleven. While you wait for your passport, I'll meet with Carlos. The three of us will have lunch together; then I'll take you to the steamship office. Agreed?" José lifted her chin with his hand. "No argument, please. I have enough money for tickets on a steamer, not a freighter. It's settled. then?"

"Yes," she said softly.

"You may not be able to book passage for a week or two. Time to close up your affairs in Bordeaux." He settled back in his chair. "Antonieta, do you understand how difficult this is for me, letting you go? The magazine will have to live on your literary genius in these articles until you get back. Among the many things I deeply admire in you is your literary genius. Did you know you are a genius?"

"Genius," she said with a shrug. "I have accomplished so little. I set myself a three-year plan when I arrived. I want to master Latin, Greek, German. Play the piano again. I even began a Spanish translation of Rabelais. You should see my outlines of unfinished plays." Her laughter was brittle. "Xavier Villaurrutia once said that I live in the high realm of transcendence, implying that I can't keep my feet on the ground." She pointed to her head. "It's all here in the archives of my mind.... Do you suppose mortality confines it all or will my unwritten works drift over to the life of the spirit?"

"Only God knows," José said, relaxing. He poured another brandy in the little silver tumblers. "I hope the first sailing is booked. I need your help. I want you to polish the format. Carlos is a pedestrian in comparison to you."

Antonieta got up and walked to the window, watching the blurred lights in the street. A fog had rolled in.

"And I need you to schedule all these articles, position them right," he went on.

"José," she said abruptly.

"What is it?"

Antonieta turned and looked at him. "Do you really need me? I mean, in all truth, do you really need me?"

José sipped his brandy, reflecting upon the question. He rubbed the little silver cup with his finger. "Nobody really needs anybody else," he replied quietly. "All we need is God. The ultimate destiny of each of us is linked to God. We need only Him." He paused and looked at her. "What made you ask?"

She didn't move for a moment. "To affirm my faith." She came over to him and smiled. "Your faith is so strong." She kissed her finger and placed it tenderly on his lips. "Good night, licenciado. Breakfast at eight?"

"Make it seven-thirty," he replied.

After she left him, she returned to her room and sat in the darkness, on the little chair near the window, and let nostalgia flood her, nostalgia for something gone, perhaps for something never possessed. Can you miss something you have never known? She thought of her mother. What was Cristina doing at that very instant, her mother who was always so beautiful? Mamá. So beautiful. Why was it important to be beautiful? Most of the people on earth were ordinary creatures, ugly even. She thought of Sabina, whose beauty was all on the inside. She sighed, thinking now of her father and Tío Beto. They had loved her. Yes, they had loved her. Suddenly, she wanted to feel their love. She wanted to feel herself cradled in their arms. Papá.... Chela. "Chela." She spoke her name softly. Then she spoke it again silently. More dear to me than my sisters. We made a blood pact. We chose to be sisters. She could almost feel Chela's presence. Or was it just sentimentality? She was tired of reality, tired of everything around her, tired of everything in her. This pain in her stomach, this sharp pounding in her head. Was it pain or hate she felt? She wanted to feel love. She wanted to be cradled in love's arms.

She stood up, trying to drive away the pain and the old fears, flinging out her arms as though to scatter them. But invisible hands closed around her throat, blurring her vision with tears.

The gun was in his bag, in the closet. She would wait until he had gone down to breakfast. If he knocked, she would tell him to order breakfast for her. She would say she hadn't slept well. The chamber maid started to clean at his end of the floor early.

Suddenly she cried out, "Toñito's button! My God what am I thinking!" She turned on the light and paced, searching for the sample in her bag, her coat pocket, wrestling with tortuous thoughts. How could she return to Mexico? Mexico had stabbed her. Alicia had rejected her child. Albert would take him. There was no escape.

She would give her coat to one of those poor women who sat for hours in Notre Dame just to stay out of the cold. She would wear her black wool dress. She would buy a veil in that store near the Cathedral.. Yes, a veil, in case anyone was there who might recognize her. Inside those high vaults, the spirit lived. This shell that encased her would shrivel and turn to ashes. In just a little while, she would face Jesus, the crucified Christ. She knew the very bench.

The decision was made. Freedom flooded her now. Freedom, and blessed peace. Even the headache pounded less. José would not be alone; he would be with Deambrosis when Arturo informed him. Arturo must have talked to him, or why would he have brought up the business about the passport?

They would tell Toñito that she was ill, in a sanatorium, too ill to be seen. He would soon forget. He loved ships. He would be a manly little figure, crossing the ocean alone.... Perhaps Albert would take him to visit the cousins in Chicago. Lee would take him sailing...dear Lee, and Grace. Albert. She remembered how she had once loved him, once longed for him, when she was little more than a child. A lifetime ago. How is it possible for love to turn to such hate? No, no, it was not hate. Albert. Her arms reached out, invisible arms reached out to embrace him.

She must write to Mario. Yes, she would write to Mario for all the family. And Manuel? No, she would not write Manuel. He would brood. It was José, José who would grieve.

Antonieta's eyes clouded. In the depths of his being, José will feel relieved, she thought, one burden less in his gigantic load. Only much later will he understand that it was better for my son and better for him. He will be moved and touched, and he will never be able to forget me. I shall be encased in his heart until the day he dies.

Dawn was breaking through the gray sky when Antonieta put down her pen. There would be hot water now.

She bathed leisurely and dressed with great care. Her short black hair was washed and shining, her brown skin unblemished. She had always been the ugly one, but now she felt beautiful. Beautiful, melancholy eyes looked back at her in the mirror.

She heard a knock at the door. José was knocking at the door.

"Antonieta. His voice was a hoarse whisper. "Antonieta!" This time more assertively.

She spoke through the door. "Forgive me, José. I'm not quite ready, but I am starved. Please order me a sliced orange and an omelet and a heap of croissants. Oh yes, cafe au lait right away. I'll be right down."

"All right. But hurry. My poor stomach is crying for attention."

She heard the elevator descend and stepped into the hall. The chambermaid was already pushing her cart up to his door.

"Pardon," she said, jostling past the old woman. "He forgot something. I am his sister."

The chambermaid shrugged.

Antonieta went straight to the closet. The Gladstone bag was never locked. She took the pistol in her hand, checking the chamber as he had taught her to do. It was loaded. She dropped the small black weapon into her purse.

Antonieta hurried to the elevator and rang for the lift. She could hear the creaky cage on the floor below. Impatiently she rang again. They were loading something.

"Where is the stairway," she asked a chambermaid.

"Are you in such a hurry, Madame? The elevator will be here in a moment."

Antonieta flashed a smile at the woman. "I'll take the stairs. You see, I have an appointment I must keep."

EPILOGUE
BORDEAUX FEBRUARY 12, 1931

It is freezing cold in the boarding house. About 2:00 A.M., Toñito awakened, crying. "Mamá" he sobbed, and turned on the light. But no one was there, although he felt her presence.

Deep in his heart, he knew his mother was dead.

ACKNOWLEDGEMENTS

My profound gratitude to the following people, who opened their hearts to me and shared their anecdotes and experiences, including long-locked memories and letters from Antonieta:

Donald Blair Rivas Mercado
Albert Blair
Alicia Rivas Mercado de Gargollo
Amelia Rivas Mercado de Goeters
Lucha Rule de Rivas Mercado
General Raúl Madero
Luis Gargollo Rivas Mercado
Grace Blair Gatewood
Andrés Henestrosa
Mauricio Magdaleno
Lupe Marin Rivera
Juan O'Gorman
Judith Martinez de Van Beuren
Malu Cabrera de Bloch

I also want to express my gratitude to the dozens of people I interviewed who lived during the late 1920s. Albert Blair's stories of the Revolution are true. About Antonieta, he would only say, "That's a closed chapter," and declines to talk about her.

The following books were invaluable: *Ulises Criollo* (1935) and *El Proconsulado* (1939) by José Vasconcelos; the latter contains Antonieta's chronicles of the presidential campaign of 1929. *87 Cartas de Amor,* letters from Antonieta to Manuel Rodriguez Lozano, published by Isaac Rojas Rosillo (1975). *Ayer* by Arturo Pani (1954), which includes Antonieta's Bordeaux Diary. *Las Obras Completas de María Antonieta Rivas Mercado* (1981) by Luis Mario Schneider. *A Wall to Paint On* by Ione Robinson (1929). *Las Palabras Perdidas* by Mauricio Magdaleno (1956). *Germán de Campo* (1930) and *Vientos de los Veinte* (1973) by Juan Bustillo Oro. *The Fabulous Life of Diego Rivera* by Bertram Wolfe (1968).

The letter in English from Antonieta to her sister-in-law, Grace Gatewood, when her son was born, is quoted verbatim; her letter to Manuel Rodriguez Lozano from Bordeaux is my translation and compilation of her letters to him in Spanish.

ABOUT THE AUTHOR

Kathryn Skidmore Blair was born in Cuba in 1920 and moved to Mexico with her American parents when she was three. Mexico has been her home base ever since. Her father was the Manager of an international graphic arts firm and she says she grew up with two unmistakable aromas: ink and tacos Being bilingual and bicultural has opened doors all her life. At fifteen she was sent to school in California - a real cultural shock. To Americans, Mexico was border towns, half-naked children and tequila. Kathryn's Mexico was a city of volcanoes and pyramids, a castle, an Opera house, beautiful gardens and school mates from all over the world.

A recent graduate of UCLA when Pearl Harbor was attacked, Kathryn remained in Los Angeles during the war. She worked at NBC Hollywood for Nelson Rockefeller's Office of Inter-American Affairs creating radio programs in Spanish aired in the US and across Latin America. Later, she had a radio program of her own. Divorced with one child, Kathryn embarked on a new, successful career, Interior Design. In 1959, she returned to Mexico and, with a partner, established her own Interior Design firm.

Stating she would never marry again, Kathryn met Donald Antonio Blair Rivas Mercado and they were married in six months. The Blairs formed a family of four children, two dogs and a score of new Mexican, American and English relatives. Today they have 10 grandchildren and 12 great grandchildren. In 2011 they will celebrate their 50th wedding anniversary.

To write a book about Mexico had always been Kathryn's dream. She was intrigued with stories about Don's grandfather, the architect of Mexico's Independent Monument, known by all as the "Angel". When she discovered that her husband's mother, Antonieta Rivas Mercado, had committed suicide in Notre Dame Cathedral, Paris, a scandal hushed by the family, her husband included, for thirty years, she found her heroine. This led to twenty years of tracing Antonieta's footsteps. A defender of women's rights, brilliant and independent, heiress of a fortune, Antonieta was the center of a postrevolutionary group of young writers, painters, poets, musicians and playwrights eager to join the modern world. Today, Kathryn's book has triggered official recognition of Antonieta as the prime promoter of Mexico's modern culture. Felipe Calderón, the President of Mexico, called her "our national Angel".

Kathryn says that life began again at 75. And adds: Never stop dreaming.

"In the Shadow of the Angel" is Kathryn Blair's first book. Published in Spanish in 1995, it is now considered a classic. It and "Forged by Fire", a brief history of Mexico, are both available at:

Amazon.com

San Miguel Historical Press, Mexico City, Mexico

San Miguel Historical Press USA, 4600 West Guadalupe St., Suite B-210, Austin, TX 78751.

Shadowoftheangel.com

GLOSSARY

- a sus ordenes - at your service
- abrazo - hug, embrace
- adios - goodbye (lit., go with God)
- aficionado - fan, follower
- agapandas -   agapanthus
- aguardiente – liquor, spirits
- ahuehuete - type of cypress tree
- alamo - poplar tree
- almuerzo - lunch
- amigo - friend
- amorcita - darling, lovey
- amparo - writ of habeas corpus.
- Anda, huevón, levanta la chingada caja! Hijo de tu puta madre, muévela tu! - C'mon! Lift the fucking box! Lazy son of a bitch, move it yourself!
- ándale - get going!
- angelita - little angel
- antorcha - torch
- arquitecto –architect
- atención - attencion
- Atila - Attila
- atole - drink made from corn flour or rice

- Ay, Diós! - Oh my God! For God's sake!
- Banco de Londres - Bank of London
- bienvenida – welcome
- bonita, bonito – pretty; good; beautiful
- brasero - brazier, outdoor cookstove
- brinco mortal - fatal leap
- Buenas días – Good morning; Good day
- Buenas noches- Good evening
- buñuelo – large, flat, crispy sweet cookie
- caballero – gentleman; lit., man on horseback
- caballito - statue of Charles IV on horseback in Mexico City
- cabrón, pl., cabrones - bastard
- cacique - local political boss, chief
- Cálmate!– calm down!
- campesino - peasant
- canalla - dog, swine, rotten person
- cantina - low-class bar, saloon
- caña - small cylindrical glass made from hollow cane for tequila or mescal
- capitán - captain
- caro, caro mía – dear, my dear one
- carrancistas - followers loyal to Venustiano Carranza
- casa chica - home for a mistress or kept woman
- cena - supper
- centavo - Mexican penny, one-hundredth of a peso.
- charro - cowboy; horseman in traditional costume
- chile, pl., chiles -chili peppers
- chile relleno -stuffed chili pepper
- chingadera – total mess
- Chucho - nickname for Jesús
- Científicos – political group that believed in science and industrialization as guarantees of progress. influential during last term of Porfirio Díaz
- chingona – tough lady
- coco - noggin, head; lit., coconut

- Colón - Columbus
- Contemporaneos, Los - group of post-revolution contemporary writers, poets, musicians, etc.
- copita - a drink, a shot glass of liquor
- coronel - colonel
- corrida, bullfight; improvised story-telling song
- Cortés – Cortez, conqueror of Mexico
- criollo - Creole
- Cristeros - group fighting the anti-religion restrictions imposed by President Calles in 1928
- danzón, pl., danzones – traditional ballroom dance form
- democracia - democracy
- desgraciado - wretch, disgraced person
- División del Norte – Pancho Villa's tough northern army division
- Doña - lady; Mrs.
- dorados - Pancho Villa's elite horsemen (lit., gilded)
- ejército -army
- ejido –small tract of land granted to peasants after the revolution
- El Imparcial – principal newspaper during the rule of Porfirio Díaz; lit., impartial
- el pa-ja-ri-to can-tó y el ga-ti-to brin-có - the little bird sang and the little cat jumped
- Estás loca! - You are crazy!
- excusado- flush toilet
- estudiantinas - roving student troubadour groups that originated in Spain.
- fado – mournful Portugese song and dance form
- faranduleros - good-for-nothings, playboys
- federales - government troops
- feria - local fair that travels from town to town.
- finca - country residence
- frac - formal dress coat, tails
- frijoles - beans

- fuego - fire
- general - general
- gente decente - people who are accepted in a strata of society higher than that of their origin.
- gordita - small, fat tortilla
- Gracias a Diós! - Thank God!
- gringo – slang term for person from the United States
- grito, El Grito – shout; the rallying cry of independence
- guayule - native mexican rubber plant
- habanero - a type of hot pepper; a lively dance form
- hacendado - hacienda owner
- hija - daughter
- hijo - son
- Hijos de la chingada! - Sons of bitches!
- Hijos de puta! - Sons of whores!
- historia - history
- huaraches - sandals
- Huitzilipochtli - Aztec god of war who demanded sacrifice
- inglés - English; Englishman
- inocente- innocent, unsophisticated
- Ixtlacihuatl - volcano known as "The Sleeping Lady"
- Jarabe –a Mexican dance; lit., syrup
- jefe máximo - chief of chiefs; name given to President Calles after he left office, but continued to control his appointed successors.
- jota aragonesa – Spanish dance accompanied by castanets
- Las mañanitas - traditional birthday song (lit., the mornings)
- ley de fuga - the "law of escape," which permits shooting an escaping prisoner
- licenciado - lawyer, attorney
- linda- pretty
- loco, loca - crazy, loco
- macho - tough guy; lit., masculine
- maderistas - loyalists of Francisco Madero
- maestro - teacher, professor

- Maestro de las Américas   Educator of the Américas, honorific given to José Vasconcelos
- maguey - agave
- mamá- mama, mom
- mantilla - elaborate embroidered Spanish shawl
- manzanilla - camomile
- máquinas locas - locomotives turned loose on the tracks to crash into oncoming trains
- mariachis – group of musicians, in charro dress, hired for serenades and celebrations.
- merienda –light supper; afternoon tea
- mestizo - person of mixed blood
- Moctezuma – Montezuma, the Aztec emperor
- mi amor - my love, my beloved
- Mierda! -Shit!
- mole - any of a variety of spicy sauces known for their regional ingredients
- moreno- dark-skinned person
- mosca - fly
- muchacho, muchacha - boy, girl
- Noche Triste (lit, Sad Night) night when many of Hernando Cortez' men were captured and sacrificed as they fled the Aztec capital, Tenochitlán
- nopal, pl., nopales- tender, nutritious spiny cactus plant
- Oiga! – listen, pay attention
- Oye! - listen
- oratorio -chapel, oratory
- oso - bear
- papá-dad, papa
- papel picada- colorful decorative cut-out tissue paper, usually hung as banners
- partido - political party
- Partido Anti-Reelecionista - Anti-Re-election Party established by Francisco Madero

- Partido Nacional Revolucionario - National Revolutionary Party, founded by Plutarcho Elías Calles in 1929
- Pase! - Enter! Come in!
- paso doble- Spanish ballroom dance
- patrón - boss
- patrona – boss's wife, female boss
- pendejo   asshole, jerk
- peon; pl. peones - unskilled laborer, peasant
- perfumado -a dandy; effete
- peso – coin; Mexican coin equivalent to 100 centavos.
- petite singe, ma petite singe - Fr., my little monkey
- pinche chingada - a messy affair; creep
- pirata - pirate
- plata - silver
- Popocatepetl – volcano near Mexico City
- Por Diós ! - For God's sake!
- porfiriato - period of Porfirio Diaz' regime (1878-1910)
- porfiristas - loyalists of Porfirio Diaz
- posada – inn; Christmas Nativity celebration
- preciosa - precious one
- prepa - preparatory school, high school
- princesa- princess
- profesor – professor; teacher
- pulque - drink made from fermented maguey juice
- Puta madre! - Whore mother! Fuck you!
- Que mueran los gringos! - Kill the gringos!
- querido, querida -beloved
- quesadilla - folded cheese-filled tortilla
- Quetzalcoatl – sun god of indigenous tribes, also called "The plumed serpent."
- Quien vive? Who goes there?
- rápido - fast
- rebozo - traditional peasant shawl
- regeneración - regeneration, rebirth
- reina , mi reina queen, my queen

- revolucionarios - revolutionaries
- rurales - country people .
- sabino - willow tree
- sala - living room, salon
- Santiago de Tlaltelolco - area in Mexico City where Cortez won his last battle. Church named for St. James built on site.
- sarape - serape : heavy cloak that often doubles as a blanket
- sargento – sergeant
- señorita – unmarried woman, young woman
- señor- Mr., Sir
- señora – Mrs., Madame, married woman
- Sobre las Olas– "Over the Waves:, " a popular 19th c. waltz
- Somos gente pacífica - We are peaceful people
- taco - any food rolled in a tortilla
- tamale –food made with lard and corn, wrapped in corn husks or banana leaves.
- tapas – Spanish-style snack dishes, mostly offered in bars
- teatro - theater
- Tengo mucho gusto en conocerles - I am pleased to meet you
- teniente - lieutenant
- Tenochtitlán - capital city of the Aztec empire
- tepetate – a type of sandstone
- tercera llamada - last call (before a performance; lit., last call)
- terremoto earthquake
- tía - aunt
- tierra - land, earth
- tigre -tiger
- tío - uncle
- Tlaloc - the rain god
- tuerto – person who is blind in one eye
- Ulises - Ulysses
- Usté disculpe – excuse me
- Vámanos! - Let's go!
- vasconcelistas -loyalists of José Vasconcelos
- velorio - wake

- viejo, - old; old one, often an endearing term
- villistas - loyalists of Pancho Villa
- Virgen Santisima - Sainted Virgin
- Virgencita, Sálvanos! - Save us, dear Virgin!
- Viva! - Hooray! Long live…!
- Viva Cristo Rey! - Long live Christ the King!
- voladores - lit., flyers. Participants in indigenous ceremony who climb a 30' high pole and descend by spinning in slow circles upside down from a rope attached to one foot, to the tune of a flute player, who remains atop the pole
- Ya llegan los revolucionaries! – Here come the revolutionaries!
- yanquí – Yankee; Mexican term used to indicate anyone from the United States
- zapatistas - loyalists of Emiliano Zapata
- zócalo -town square, main square

FAMILY PHOTOS

Front entrance to house
Alicia and Antonieta on balcony
For more photos: shadowoftheangel.com

Antonieta´s mother Cristina, Antonieta, Alicia and baby Mario, 1905
For more photos: shadowoftheangel.com

Antonieta on terrace entrance, 1917
For more photos: shadowoftheangel.com

Cap. ALBERTO E. BLAIR (inglés)   Corl. FRANCISCO VILLA
y Cap. JULIO MADERO.
Cd. Juárez Chih. Mayo 10-1911 después del asalto y toma
de esta plaza por fuerzas del Ejercito Libertador organizado
por el caudillo de la Revolucion Presidente Provisional
Don FRANCISCO I. MADERO

Albert Blair, Pancho Villa and Julio Madero
For more photos: shadowoftheangel.com

Albert Blair, Antonieta and baby Donald, 1919
For more photos: shadowoftheangel.com

Antonieta, Antonio Rivas Mercado, Amelia, Alicia and Mario, 1920
For more photos: shadowoftheangel.com

José Vasconcelos and Antonieta in Los Angeles, 1928
For more photos: shadowoftheangel.com

CPSIA information can be obtained at www.ICGtesting.com
Printed in the USA
LVOW13s0234120514

385378LV00001B/155/P

9 781467 932561